PREVENTING SUDDEN DEATH
in Sport and Physical Activity

Edited by

DOUGLAS J. CASA, PHD, ATC, FACSM, FNATA

Professor, Department of Kinesiology
Chief Operating Officer, Korey Stringer Institute
Director, Athletic Training Education
Neag School of Education
University of Connecticut

JONES & BARTLETT
LEARNING

World Headquarters
Jones & Bartlett Learning
40 Tall Pine Drive
Sudbury, MA 01776
978-443-5000
info@jblearning.com
www.jblearning.com

Jones & Bartlett Learning
Canada
6339 Ormindale Way
Mississauga, Ontario
L5V 1J2
Canada

Jones & Bartlett Learning
International
Barb House, Barb Mews
London W6 7PA
United Kingdom

Jones & Bartlett Learning books and products are available through most bookstores and online booksellers. To contact Jones & Bartlett Learning directly, call 800-832-0034, fax 978-443-8000, or visit our website, www.jblearning.com.

Substantial discounts on bulk quantities of Jones & Bartlett Learning publications are available to corporations, professional associations, and other qualified organizations. For details and specific discount information, contact the special sales department at Jones & Bartlett Learning via the above contact information or send an email to specialsales@jblearning.com.

Production Credits
Publisher, Higher Education: Cathleen Sether
Senior Acquisitions Editor: Shoshanna Goldberg
Senior Associate Editor: Amy L. Bloom

V.P., Manufacturing and Inventory Control: Therese Connell
Composition: Glyph International
Cover Design: Kate Ternullo
Rights and Permissions Manager: Katherine Crighton
Photo Researcher: Sarah Cebulski
Cover Image: © Cal Sport Media/Landov
Printing and Binding: Malloy, Inc.
Cover Printing: Malloy, Inc.

Tennessee Titans for the use of the cover photo.

a

y / edited by Douglas J. Casa.

s. I. Casa, Douglas J.

2011011966

DEDICATION

This book is dedicated to numerous people:

To my parents for giving me life (and being the best parents any kid could ever want) and to my brothers (Mike and Chris) for making it fun.

To Kent Scriber for saving my life.

To my wife (Tutita Casa) and kids (Montana, Navia, and Alessio) for enriching my life.

To Kelci Stringer and James Gould for giving my life's work greater purpose.

To Carl Maresh and Lawrence Armstrong for being great mentors.

To all my former and current students for constantly challenging the status quo and for assisting me in the pursuit of preventing sudden death in sport and physical activity. We have come to realize that the pursuit of "the right thing" is often an enormous fight, and worth it every time.

To Rebecca (Becca) Stearns, MA, ATC—without her assistance this book would have never come to fruition. I am indebted to her time and dedication to this project.

To the parents, grandparents, spouses, children, brothers, sisters, friends, coaches, and medical providers who have lost someone due to sudden death in sport—this book is for the memory of those loved ones and the hope that with our efforts together we can prevent future tragedies.

To Leo W. Anglin, PhD (1946–1998), the former dean of the School of Education and Human Sciences at Berry College in Rome, Georgia. When attempting to land my first professorial job in 1997, I applied to 54 positions. I received only one job offer—from Dean Anglin. I will never forget the chance Dean Anglin took on an unproven (yet hypermotivated) young grad. I hope my efforts with this book and my career would have made him proud.

BRIEF CONTENTS

CONTENTS

CHAPTER 1

Fatal and Catastrophic Injuries in Athletics: Epidemiologic Data and Challenging Circumstances 1
Frederick O. Mueller, PhD, FACSM
Douglas J. Casa, PhD, ATC, FACSM, FNATA

CHAPTER 2

Prevention of Sudden Cardiac Death in Young Athletes 15
Jonathan A. Drezner, MD

CHAPTER **15** **Strategies to Reduce the Risk of Sudden Death in Mass Participation Sporting Events**

Kevin R. Ronneberg, MD
William O. Roberts, MD, MS, FACSM

CHAPTER **16** **Educational Considerations for the Prevention of Sudden Death in Sport and Physical Activity**

Stephanie M. Mazerolle, PhD, ATC
Rebecca M. Lopez, PhD, ATC, CSCS
Tutita M. Casa, PhD

APPENDIX A

APPENDIX B

Compiled by Julie DeMartini, MA, ATC
Written by the following:
Kristin Applegate, MA, ATC
Douglas J. Casa, PhD, ATC, FACSM, FNATA
Julie DeMartini, MA, ATC
Holly Emmanuel, MA, ATC
Kerri Gavin, MA, ATC
Katherine Jensen, MA, ATC
Rachel Karslo, MA, ATC
Jessica Martschinske, MA, ATC
Lindsey McDowell, MA, ATC
Kelly Pagnotta, MA, ATC, PES
Danielle Pinkus, MA, ATC
Roberto Ruiz, MA, ATC
Rebecca (Becca) Stearns, MA, ATC
Megan VanSumeren, MA, ATC

The Confluence of Conspiring Factors

Kent Scriber, EdD, ATC, PT

Professor, Department of Exercise and Sport Sciences
Ithaca College

Almost every year since the early 1980s, I have served as a volunteer athletic trainer for the New York State Empire State Games (ESG). These annual games, generally held in late July, serve as a statewide Olympic-type event for several thousand amateur athletes. I was assigned as the head athletic trainer for Athletics (track and field) during the 1985 Empire State Games that were held in Buffalo, New York. Although this was quite some time ago, I vividly recall a frightening life-threatening scenario that has had a tremendous impact on me in many ways.

The scholastic boys' 10,000-meter run started in the late morning. Although I'm not certain of the exact temperature and humidity readings, it was definitely a hot and humid morning. I was positioned with a physician outside the track around the 250-meter mark, or somewhere between the third and fourth turns. On the final lap, we noticed the third-place runner staggering. He collapsed just as he was coming into the turn. He stood up, took a few more strides, and then collapsed again. He was lying unconscious not more than a hundred meters from the finish line. His coaches quickly warned the physician and me not to touch this young athlete because he would be disqualified and lose his chance at a medal.

Ignoring the coaches' request, we were quickly able to get the athlete to the ambulance area, which was stationed very near where he happened to collapse. He was initially placed in the shade of the ambulance, and ice bags and wet towels were placed on his neck, forehead, axilla, and groin areas while the emergency medical technicians (EMTs) called the emergency room (ER) where he was to be transported. Initially, the Empire State Games physician at the site ordered the administration of IV fluids. However, the EMTs would not administer it without approval from the ER physicians. Instead, the athlete was placed in the back of the ambulance, which also was warm since it had been sitting in direct sunlight. Precious minutes passed before the ambulance left the venue. Although I do not recall the patient's core temperature at the time, I later heard it was above 106°F (rectal) when he arrived at the ER.

After several hours of concern about this young man's health status, I was greatly relieved to learn later that afternoon that our young runner's core temperature had quickly returned to normal and that he was conscious and alert. If memory serves me correctly, he returned to the track in two days to cheer on his teammates.

The Empire State Games sports medicine staff wanted to ensure that this type of heat-related episode would never again occur (a road cyclist also had a serious heat illness on the same day). The night of the emergency, the staff met to determine what precautionary measures could be implemented. They determined that athletes could have water during their races, longer endurance events would take place in the earlier part of the day, and several events would take mandatory breaks during their competitions (e.g., soccer played periods instead of halves and took rest and hydration breaks between each). Later, certain policies and procedures for the care of athletes were also changed to better care for future emergency situations. In particular, a clearer chain of command was established to avoid confusion and discussions relating to who was responsible for whom at the time of an emergency. The 1985 Empire State Games ended with no further serious heat-related incidents.

In the years since this near-catastrophic event, I have discussed this scenario with my athletic training students for a number of reasons. Obviously, a major teaching point is the need to be knowledgeable and prepared ahead of time for heat-related problems and other emergencies. In addition to the administration of the most appropriate treatment plan, of great importance is the establishment of a clearly communicated emergency action plan that can facilitate emergency care quickly when there is a potentially life-threatening situation.

For many years I was somewhat curious about the young man from Long Island who had collapsed on that fateful day and wondered what had happened to him. Through an interesting set of circumstances at the 2001 NATA Clinical Meeting and Symposium in Los Angeles, I found out that the young man who had collapsed from exertional heat stroke that day was Douglas Casa. We have since spent time together as professional colleagues. We have been able to visit each other's campuses, speak to each other's students and faculty members, serve on national committees together, and collaborate on a publication. Most important, we have developed a wonderful friendship. I was impressed with Dr. Casa's research long before I realized our paths had crossed years earlier. I still remain in awe of Dr. Casa's passion for the work he does, and I am proud to know that my actions many years ago have been a catalyst for the work that he has done since then.

Douglas Casa, PhD, ATC, FACSM, FNATA

Chief Operating Officer, Korey Stringer Institute
Department of Kinesiology, University of Connecticut

The story that Kent recounts was the seminal moment of my life. I have nearly no memory of approximately 6 hours of my life, while I was in a coma due to severe exertional heat stroke. A few lingering snapshots from those 6 hours dangle inside my mind, which I occasionally see at the oddest of moments. For instance, I remember saying my dad's work phone number, the only comprehensible item to leave my mouth in the 6-hour span. Why I could recite that number over my home number is still a mystery to me. I still wonder if a call to my dad about my demise would have been better than the news being delivered to my mother. It's amazing how the mind functions at such stressful times. I also remember chaos and worry and desperation surrounding me at one point in the emergency room and the calming sound of a person in charge (who I came to realize later during my hospital stay was the physician in charge of my care). I also oddly remember ice-water towels on me during the ambulance ride and a peculiar combination of oppressive, crushing heat and wonderfully cold water dripping on my chest.

The most important part of my story stems from the night of my collapse. After being released from intensive care to a regular hospital room, I watched the local late-night news at 11:00 P.M. and watched them tell the story of my exertional heat stroke. It was powerful to lay alone (Buffalo was 10 hours from my house on Long Island) in a hospital room—utterly exhausted yet peacefully thankful—and watch a news account about myself. On August 8, 1985, somewhere between 11:00 and 11:10 P.M. EST, the path of my life unfurled in front of me. For all the years since then, I have been on a quest to try to prevent and treat exertional heat stroke. My story is not overly complicated. My survival penance has been to save as many lives as posssible from heat stroke and to prepare others who can do the same. The following story from Benjamin Arthur is one such example of the lives I have been able to touch.

While exertional heat stroke is one of the most common fatalities related to sports, it certainly is not the only one. This book is the culmination of the efforts of more than 30 of the most respected sports medicine professionals and scientists in the world related to preventing sudden death in sports. It is another chance for me to recognize my gift of survival and pay it forward with information about the top 10 causes of death in sport that can assist in creating more survival stories. I have experienced a wide array of emotions in my life, but no feeling is greater than playing a role in saving a life. When you see a person like Ben, whom you helped save, it stops you in your tracks and you realize your life has purpose.

Benjamin Arthur, MD
United States Army
Fort Benning, Georgia

At the time of the Marine Corps Marathon in 2008, I was beginning my third year of medical school. I was a student at the Uniformed Services University of Health Sciences, the military's medical school. I had been married for 4 years to my wife, Sara, and we recently had our first child, Mariella Rae.

I'm not sure what I dreamed about the night before the marathon, what I had for breakfast, or what was on my mind as I rode the Metro-rail into DC from my home. Maybe I thought about where I was going to meet everyone after the race or the chili that was going to be on the menu for dinner that night. I do know that the possibility of never seeing my wife and 6-month-old daughter again was not in those pre-race thoughts. No matter what I was thinking about, it took a lot of preparation by the Marine Corps Marathon Medical Staff and the "heat deck" team, and a heroic effort by Dr. Casa and his team, to save me from dying.

Beginning the marathon, I decided that I was going to try to beat my only other marathon time by roughly 20 minutes. I had trained for the previous 3 months and thought I was ready to run my goal time the morning of the marathon. Several high-ranking Marine Corps officers generated a lot of excitement from the crowd at the start of the race. There were thousands of runners, and there was an excitement in the air that only a huge race could cause.

I started the race fast. I was running under my pace each mile, but I felt good. The temperature was in the upper 50s and I was trained; I thought I could handle it. It wasn't until mile 16 that I felt like I had hit a wall. I thought mile 16 was too early to hit that wall, so I pushed harder. I maintained my pace through mile 20, then 22, then 24. During those miles, I started getting tunnel vision and becoming angry. All I could think about was finishing and how it was almost over. I thought if I finished strong and made my time, it would all be over soon. I didn't know how right I was. I made it from mile 24 to 26 with my tunnel vision increasing and my general attitude worsening as well. I hit the final 0.2 miles and tried to sprint to the end. That is where everything went downhill in a hurry. I fell twice on the final hill and was helped across the line by my running partner as well as a race official. Looking down as my feet crossed the finish line was the last thing I remembered until the middle of my treatment for exertional heat stroke.

Next, cue Dr. Casa and his team. Twenty to thirty of the most important minutes of my life passed without me knowing how hard perfect strangers were working to keep me alive. The next thing I remember after seeing the finish line was looking up at the top of a blue tent as I was lying in the ice bath with people all around me cooling me off as fast as they could. I answered a few questions to prove that I was conscious, and continued to be cooled. From that moment, it was a whirlwind of activity, a short trip to the ER, and I was still home with time enough to eat that chili I probably thought about on the Metro-rail.

Dr. Casa and I have exchanged several emails, but I have had only one opportunity to meet him. It was a year later, when he and his team were gearing up for the next Marine Corps Marathon at a local restaurant. Over the course of the meal, he shared his perspective on my treatment as well as some new projects he was working on. It was evident that he has a passion for preventing deadly sports injuries and is one of the best in the world at what he does. He and I are connected forever because we both had heat strokes during a sporting event, and, through our profession, we have the opportunity to help others in similar situations.

Now, having just graduated from medical school, I am blessed with a unique opportunity. I will start my family medicine residency in Ft. Benning, Georgia—where, coincidentally, the most heat injuries in the Army occur due to the high temperatures and intense training programs. While in Georgia, I will have the opportunity to treat heat injuries at various training events, both immediately on site and after the initial incident away from the event.

It is a great honor to provide care for soldiers. One day I will be the senior medical provider treating heat injuries and will have lives depend on my training and care. Over the past several years, I have gained a new-found respect and professional interest in heat injuries and will hopefully provide excellent care—the same kind of care I received in my hour of need.

PREFACE

Published in cooperation with the American College of Sports Medicine, *Preventing Sudden Death in Sport and Physical Activity* is an important contribution to the sports medicine profession. It is the first book of its type that has individual topic chapters written by content area experts. The book was carefully designed to offer a blend of clinical, scientific, and research expertise regarding each medical condition that could cause sudden death during sport and physical activity. The chapter authors actively work in clinical settings to prevent and treat the conditions described and perform research to further our understanding of the condition.

This book presents several unique and significant offerings that bolster a reader's clinical competence and educational opportunities. These include, but are not limited to, the following:

- Cardiac conditions (the leading cause of death in sport) are separated into three chapters to give greater attention to the multiple potential etiologies related to cardiac causes: heart disease (more common to older populations), genetic conditions (more common to younger populations), and commotio cordis.
- Exertional sickling is offered as a stand-alone chapter, which may be a first in a sports medicine textbook. We feel that the stand-alone chapter will give exertional sickling the recognition it deserves, as the condition was the leading cause of death in Division I college football during the decade spanning 2000 to 2009, and many medical providers were not educated regarding this condition while in school.
- Eleven of the top causes of death in sport are covered in individual chapters: heart disease, congenital cardiac conditions, commotio cordis, exertional heat stroke, exertional hyponatremia, head injuries, cervical spine injuries, lightning, asthma, exertional sickling, and traumatic injuries. Additionally, another chapter covers anaphylaxis, hypothermia, diabetes, and issues in wilderness medicine.
- Supporting chapters focus on issues that can influence the infrastructure for preventing sudden death during sport and physical activity. These include chapters on epidemiology, emergency action plans, educational programs, and issues related to mass medical coverage.
- Instructors who use the text have access to PowerPoint lecture outlines and 11 problem-based learning scenarios (PBLs), complete with staged instructional implementation, questions, and grading. They cover the range of topics in the book. Additionally, more PBLs will be added on a regular basis as they are developed.

Ultimately, the greatest asset readers of this book gain is an in-depth understanding of the conditions and issues being discussed as imparted by content area experts who have been on the front lines. This connection with cutting-edge information will, it is hoped, afford medical providers with the best opportunity to prevent sudden death during sport and physical activity.

In December 2010, I had the opportunity to speak with numerous parents and spouses who had either lost a loved one or had a loved one experience a near-death episode (some with long-term complications that will last into the foreseeable future), and I was struck with a powerful thought: nearly every death in sport (or event with a long-term medical consequence) is preventable. Imagine the crushing grip of sadness when a parent or spouse comes to realize that the tragedy could have been averted, often with minimal effort and cost. Although not all deaths or serious medical outcomes in sport are preventable, a close examination of them makes us realize that most are. My mantra has always been, "Do whatever you can *before* they die." Changes that are made after a death (as they usually are) leave us wondering "What if?" That is a burden none of us wants to bear.

ACKNOWLEDGMENTS

I have numerous people to thank. The people at Jones & Bartlett Learning have made a challenging project relatively painless: Shoshanna Goldberg, Prima Bartlett, and Julie Bolduc. Thanks also to Cindy Kogut for her excellent copyediting skills. Becca Stearns, MA, ATC gave an enormous assist to make sure the editorial process went smoothly. A huge thank you is offered to the world-class authors who were willing to give so much of their time to contribute the chapters in this book. I am very grateful to have had such incredible-caliber authors come together for such an important cause. I also thank Julie DeMartini, MA, ATC, and Kelly Pagnotta, MA, ATC, for compiling the appendices and problem-based learning scenarios (respectively) that accompany the text.

I'd also like to thank the American College of Sports Medicine (ACSM) for the thorough reviews they conducted on all of the chapters, and for the feedback they provided along the way. It is a great honor to have ACSM on board with the book.

Finally, thanks to the following external reviewers, who gave valuable insights and suggestions to enhance the final product: Steve Blivin, MD, United States Navy; Fred Brennan, MD, University of New Hampshire, Durham, New Hampshire; Tutita Casa, PhD, University of Connecticut, Storrs, Connecticut; John Cianca, MD, FACSM, Baylor College of Medicine, Houston, Texas; Gianluca Del Rossi, PhD, ATC, University of South Florida, Tampa, Florida; Craig Denegar, PhD, ATC, PT, FNATA, University of Connecticut, Storrs, Connecticut; Michael Ferrara, PhD, ATC, FNATA, University of Georgia, Athens, Georgia; Robin Grenier, PhD, University of Connecticut, Storrs, Connecticut; Kim Harmon, MD, University of Washington, Seattle, Washington; Jolene Henning, PhD, ATC, University of North Carolina at Greensboro, Greensboro, North Carolina; Thomas Howard, MD, Fairfax Family Practice, Fairfax, Virginia; Shawn Kane, MD, United States Army; Shishir Mathur, MD, Hartford Hospital, Hartford, Connecticut; Brendon McDermott, PhD, ATC, University of Tennessee at Chattanooga, Chattanooga, Tennessee; James Moriarty, MD, Notre Dame University, South Bend, Indiana; Scott Pyne, MD, United States Navy; and Chris Troyanos, ATC, Boston Marathon.

Douglas J. Casa earned his bachelor's degree in biology from Allegheny College in 1990, his master's degree in athletic training from the University of Florida in 1993, and his doctorate in exercise physiology from the University of Connecticut in 1997. For the past 11 years, Dr. Casa has worked toward his goal of preventing sudden death in sport at the Department of Kinesiology, Neag School of Education, University of Connecticut. During this time he has published more than 110 peer-reviewed publications and presented more than 300 times on subjects related to exertional heat stroke, heat-related illnesses, preventing sudden death in sport, and hydration. Dr. Casa has successfully treated more than 130 cases of exertional heat stroke (with 0 fatalities).

In April 2010, Kelci Stringer (Korey Stringer's widow) and James Gould (Korey's agent) asked Dr. Casa to develop and run the Korey Stringer Institute (KSI) at the University of Connecticut. Korey was an All-Pro offensive tackle for the Minnesota Vikings of the NFL. He died from exertional heat stroke in August 2001. The KSI (ksi.uconn.edu) serves the public to work toward preventing sudden death in sport by means of education, advocacy, public policy, research, media outreach, and publications.

Dr. Casa was named full professor at the University of Connecticut in August 2010. In 2008 he was the recipient of the Medal for Distinguished Athletic Training Research from the National Athletic Trainers' Association. He was named a fellow of the National Athletic Trainers' Association in 2008. He received the Sayers "Bud" Miller Distinguished Educator Award from the National Athletic Trainers' Association in 2007 and has been a fellow of the American College of Sports Medicine since 2001. He has been a lead author or coauthor on numerous sports medicine (ACSM, NATA) position statements related to heat illness and hydration. He is an associate editor of the *Journal of Athletic Training* and on the editorial board of *Current Sports Medicine Reports, Journal of Sport Rehabilitation,* and the *Journal of Strength and Conditioning Research.* Dr. Casa has worked with numerous media outlets across the country in discussing his research, including NBC's *Today Show, Good Morning America,* ESPN, CNN, PBS, *Sports Illustrated, USA Today, Runners' World,* National Geographic, the *Wall Street Journal,* and the *New York Times.*

Dr. Casa has been happily married to his wife, Tutita Casa, PhD, for 15 years; they have three children.

CONTRIBUTORS

Jeffrey M. Anderson, MD, FACSM
Team Physician
University of Connecticut
Storrs, CT

Scott Anderson, ATC
Head Athletic Trainer
University of Oklahoma
Norman, OK

Lawrence E. Armstrong, PhD, FACSM
Human Performance Laboratory
Professor, Department of Kinesiology
University of Connecticut
Storrs, CT
Member, Korey Stringer Institute Medical
    and Science Advisory Board

Robert J. Baker, MD, PhD, ATC, FACSM,
FAAFP
Program Director, Primary Care Sports Medicine
    Fellowship
Michigan State University
East Lansing, MI

Douglas J. Casa, PhD, ATC, FACSM, FNATA
Professor, Department of Kinesiology
Chief Operating Officer, Korey Stringer Institute
Director, Athletic Training Education
Neag School of Education
University of Connecticut
Storrs, CT

Tutita M. Casa, PhD
Assistant Professor, Department of Educational
    Psychology
Neag School of Education
University of Connecticut
Storrs, CT

Mary Ann Cooper, MD
Professor Emerita, Department of Emergency
    Medicine
University of Illinois at Chicago
Chicago, IL

Ron Courson, ATC, PT, NREMT-I, CSCS
Director of Sports Medicine
University of Georgia
Athens, GA
Member, Korey Stringer Institute Medical
    and Science Advisory Board

Julie DeMartini, MA, ATC
Director of Research, Korey Stringer Institute
Department of Kinesiology
Neag School of Education
University of Connecticut
Storrs, CT

Jonathan A. Drezner, MD
Associate Professor, Department of Family
    Medicine
Team Physician, Division of Athletics
University of Washington
Team Physician, Seattle Seahawks
Seattle, WA

E. Randy Eichner, MD, FACSM
Emeritus Professor of Medicine
University of Oklahoma Health Sciences Center
Oklahoma City, OK

Kevin M. Guskiewicz, PhD, ATC, FACSM,
FNATA
Professor and Chair, Department of Exercise
    and Sport Science
University of North Carolina at Chapel Hill
Chapel Hill, NC

John A. Kalin, MD
The Cardiac Arrhythmia Center
Tufts Medical Center
Boston, MA

Fawad A. Kazi, MD
Cardiology Fellow
Hartford Hospital
Hartford, CT

Glen P. Kenny, PhD
Professor, School of Human Kinetics
Human and Environmental Physiology
    Research Unit
University of Ottawa
Ottawa, Ontario, Canada
Member, Korey Stringer Institute Medical
    and Science Advisory Board

Mark S. Link, MD, FACC
The Cardiac Arrhythmia Center
Tufts Medical Center
Boston, MA

Rebecca M. Lopez, PhD, ATC, CSCS
Assistant Professor, Department of Orthopaedics
    and Sports Medicine
University of South Florida
Tampa, FL
Member, Korey Stringer Institute Medical and
    Science Advisory Board

Christopher Madias, MD
The Cardiac Arrhythmia Center
Tufts Medical Center
Boston, MA

Shishir Mathur, MD
Preventive Cardiology Fellow
Hartford Hospital
Hartford, CT

Stephanie M. Mazerolle, PhD, ATC
Assistant Professor, Department of Kinesiology
Neag School of Education
University of Connecticut
Storrs, CT

Brendon P. McDermott, PhD, ATC
Graduate Athletic Training Education Program
Department of Health and Human Performance
University of Tennessee at Chattanooga
Chattanooga, TN
Member, Korey Stringer Institute Medical and
    Science Advisory Board

Jason P. Mihalik, PhD, CAT(C), ATC
Assistant Professor, Department of Exercise and
    Sport Science
University of North Carolina at Chapel Hill
Chapel Hill, NC

Michael G. Miller, PhD, EdD, ATC, CSCS
Director of Graduate Athletic Training Education
Professor, Department of Health, Physical
    Education, and Recreation
Western Michigan University
Kalamazoo, MI

Frederick O. Mueller, PhD, FACSM
Professor, Department of Exercise and Sport
    Science
University of North Carolina at Chapel Hill
Chapel Hill, NC

Francis G. O'Connor, MD, MPH, FACSM
Professor, Uniformed Services University for the
    Health Sciences (USUHS)
Bethesda, MD
Member, Korey Stringer Institute Medical and
    Science Advisory Board

Kelly Pagnotta, MA, ATC, PES
Chief Information Officer, Korey Stringer
    Institute
Department of Kinesiology
Neag School of Education
University of Connecticut
Storrs, CT

Margot Putukian, MD, FACSM
Director of Athletic Medicine, Princeton
    University
Associate Clinical Professor, Robert Wood
    Johnson Medical School
University of Medicine and Dentistry of
    New Jersey
Princeton, NJ
Member, Korey Stringer Institute Medical
    and Science Advisory Board

William O. Roberts, MD, MS, FACSM
Professor, Family Medicine and Community
    Health
Director, St. John's Hospital Family Medicine
    Residency Sports Medicine Fellowship
University of Minnesota
Minneapolis, MN

Kevin R. Ronneberg, MD
Medical Director
Fairview Sports and Orthopedic Care
Minneapolis, MN

Rebecca L. Stearns, MA, ATC
Vice President of Operations and Director of
    Education, Korey Stringer Institute
Department of Kinesiology
Neag School of Education
University of Connecticut
Storrs, CT

Erik E. Swartz, PhD, ATC, FNATA
Associate Professor, Department of Kinesiology
University of New Hampshire
Durham, NH

Charlie Thompson, MS, ATC
Head Athletic Trainer
Princeton University
Princeton, NJ

Paul D. Thompson, MD, FACC, FACSM
Director of Cardiology
Hartford Hospital
Hartford, CT

Katie M. Walsh, EdD, ATC
Director of Sports Medicine and Athletic Training
Associate Professor, Department of Health
    Education and Promotion

East Carolina University
Greenville, NC

Kevin N. Waninger, MD, MS, FACSM
Director, Primary Care Sports Medicine
    Fellowship Program
St. Luke's Hospital and Health Network
Bethlehem, PA

Brad E. Yeargin, MEd, ATC, CES
Assistant Athletic Trainer
Indiana State University
Terre Haute, IN

Susan W. Yeargin, PhD, ATC
Assistant Professor, Department of
    Athletic Training
Indiana State University
Terre Haute, IN
Member, Korey Stringer Institute Medical
    and Science Advisory Board

Appendices

Compiled by Julie DeMartini, MA, ATC

Written by the following:

Kristin Applegate, MA, ATC
Douglas J. Casa, PhD, ATC, FACSM, FNATA
Julie DeMartini, MA, ATC
Holly Emmanuel, MA, ATC
Kerri Gavin, MA, ATC

Katherine Jensen, MA, ATC
Rachel Karslo, MA, ATC
Jessica Martschinske, MA, ATC
Lindsey McDowell, MA, ATC
Kelly Pagnotta, MA, ATC, PES
Danielle Pinkus, MA, ATC
Roberto Ruiz, MA, ATC
Rebecca (Becca) Stearns, MA, ATC
Megan VanSumeren, MA, ATC

Problem-Based Learning Scenarios

Compiled by Kelly D. Pagnotta, MA, ATC, PES

A team at the University of Connecticut
created all problem based learning scenarios:

William Adams, ATC
Kristin Applegate, MA, ATC
Danielle Carlough, ATC

Douglas J. Casa, PhD, ATC, FACSM, FNATA
Stephanie (Stevie) Clines, ATC
Patrick Curry, ATC
Julie DeMartini, MA, ATC, PES
Holly Emmanuel, MA, ATC
Megan Fenton, ATC
Kerri Gavin, MA, ATC
Jeanelle Guerrero, ATC

Joseph Ingriselli, ATC
Katherine Jensen, MA, ATC
Rachel Karslo, MA, ATC
Jessica Martchinske, MA, ATC
Lindsey McDowell, MA, ATC
Emily Miller, ATC
Kelly Pagnotta, MA, ATC, PES

Danielle Pinkus, MA, ATC
Hannah Rosemont, ATC
Roberto Ruiz, MA, ATC
Erica Simone, ATC
Rebecca (Becca) Stearns, MA, ATC
Megan VanSumeren, MA, ATC

AMERICAN COLLEGE OF SPORTS MEDICINE REVIEWERS

Review Panel Chair
Erik S. Adams, MD, PhD, FACSM

Reviewers
Steve J. Blivin, MD, FACSM

Dennis A. Cardone, DO

Aashish Contractor, MD

Pierre A. d'Hemecourt, MD, FACSM

Anastasia Fischer, MD

Peter G. Gerbino II, MD, FACSM

Heather M. Gillespie, MD

John Hatzenbuehler, MD

Sandra J. Hoffmann, MD, FACSM

Balu Natarajan, MD SC

Elizabeth Rothe, MD

Aaron L. Rubin, MD, FACSM

Founding of the Korey Stringer Institute

In August 2001, Korey Stringer, a Minnesota Vikings offensive lineman who had earned Pro Bowl honors during his five-year tenure with the team, died from exertional heat stroke. Since the time of Korey's death, Korey's wife, Kelci Stringer, and his agent, James Gould, have worked tirelessly to develop a heat stroke prevention institute to honor her husband's legacy. To that end, in 2009, they joined forces with exertional heat stroke expert Douglas J. Casa, PhD, ATC, from the Neag School of Education at the University of Connecticut to make this dream a reality. The Korey Stringer Institute (KSI) officially opened on April 23, 2010.

Background

Exertional heat stroke is one of the leading causes of sudden death in sport. During certain times of the year, it is likely the leading cause of death. Many cases of exertional heat stroke could be prevented if strategies to enhance the health and safety of athletes were improved, such as focusing on hydration, phasing in programs for heat acclimatization, and ensuring access to on-site medical care. When an exertional heat stroke does occur—since not all cases can be prevented, given the situation of athletes performing intense exercise in the heat—proper recognition, treatment, and emergency action plans need to be in place to ensure athlete survival.

The crux of the problem is that current policies for decreasing the incidence of exertional heat illness are extremely ineffective, and the potential for inappropriate care continues to be a large threat. The Korey Stringer Institute strives to help resolve these problems.

Korey Stringer Institute's Mission Statement and Goals

The mission of the Korey Stringer Institute is to provide first-rate information, research, resources, assistance, and advocacy for the prevention of sudden death in sport, especially as it relates to exertional heat stroke.

The Korey Stringer Institute is housed in the Department of Kinesiology and Neag School of Education at the University of Connecticut. The University of Connecticut has a strong tradition and reputation as one of the leading institutions studying heat and hydration issues related to athletes and the physically active. In 2010, the university's Department of Kinesiology was ranked the number one doctoral program in the country by the National Academy of Kinesiology and number one for research productivity by the National Research Council. KSI is partnered with Gatorade, the National Football League (NFL), the National Football League Players Association (NFLPA), and Timex to further advance its efforts and goals.

KSI serves the needs of active people and athletes at all levels—youth, high school, college, and professional and recreational athletes—and those who supervise and care for these individuals. Components of these services include consultations, advocacy, education, research, and mass-market outreach.

Accomplishments of the Korey Stringer Institute

Since the inception of the KSI, it has been hard at work assisting numerous organizations and individuals with education, policies, advocacy, research, and information. A sampling of these include the U.S. Army, American Football Coaches Association (AFCA), National Collegiate Athletic Association (NCAA), National Athletic Trainers' Association (NATA), National Strength and Conditioning Association (NSCA), American College of Sports Medicine (ACSM), Centers for Disease Control and Prevention (CDC), Safe Kids, Advocates for Injured Athletes, International Tennis Federation, NFL, NFLPA, PBS, NBC, ABC, *USA Today*, the *Washington Post*, the *New York Times*, Youth Sports Safety Alliance, the National Air and Space Administration (NASA), United States Tennis Association (USTA), Women's Tennis Association (WTA), USA Cycling, *Runners' World*, Marine Corps Marathon, Falmouth Road Race, the Boston Marathon, numerous state organizations, and 50 elite triathletes, among many others.

The KSI is very proud that 12 individuals involved with this book are affiliated with the KSI.

For more information, visit the Korey Stringer Institute website: http://ksi.uconn.edu.

The KSI logo is used courtesy of University of Connecticut's Neag School of Education.

Fatal and Catastrophic Injuries in Athletics: Epidemiologic Data and Challenging Circumstances

Frederick O. Mueller, PhD, FACSM

Douglas J. Casa, PhD, ATC, FACSM, FNATA

In 1931 the American Football Coaches Association (AFCA) initiated the first annual survey of football fatalities. In 1982, this research was expanded to all sports for both males and females. The expansion was made possible by a grant from the National Collegiate Athletic Association (NCAA) and was the beginning of the National Center for Catastrophic Sports Injury Research at the University of North Carolina at Chapel Hill. The decision to expand the research was based on the following factors:

1. Research based on reliable data is essential if progress is to be made in sports safety.
2. There was a paucity of injury data for sports other than football.
3. Women's sports were undergoing rapid expansion, and there was a lack of information regarding injuries in these sports.

Data Collection and Definitions

Data were drawn from high school and college sports that were associated with a catastrophic injury. Non-school sports, club sports, and intramural sports were not included. Youth football catastrophic injuries were included, as were injuries in professional (National Football League) and semiprofessional football. Other than football, youth and professional sports were not included.

Data were compiled with the assistance of coaches, athletic trainers, athletic directors, team physicians, executive officers of state and national organizations, online news reports, and professional associates of the researchers. Data collection would have been impossible without the support of the AFCA, the NCAA, and the National Federation of State High School Associations (NFHS). Information collected included athlete demographic data, accident information, immediate and postaccident medical care, type of injury, and equipment involved. To enhance the collection of medical data, a joint endeavor was initiated with the Section on Sports Medicine of the American Association of Neurological Surgeons. Robert C. Cantu was selected as the medical director of the center. Autopsy reports were used when available.

Athletic fatalities were considered **direct** when the injury resulted directly from participation in the fundamental skills of the sport and were considered **indirect** when caused by systemic failure as a result of exertion while participating in a sport activity or by a complication that was secondary to a nonfatal injury. Examples of indirect fatalities are cardiac failure or an asthma attack.

Football

The AFCA initiated the annual survey of football fatalities in 1931 because of the great number of football fatalities and catastrophic injuries. From 1931 through the 2009 football season, there have been 1016 fatalities: 674 in high school football, 178 in recreational play, 86 at the college level, and 78 in professional football.[1,2] Prior to 1931, football had been in a state of crisis, and President Theodore Roosevelt seriously considered eliminating the game.[3] Football recovered from that crisis, but in 1968 there was a second crisis when 36 football head and neck fatalities occurred: 26 high school, 5 college, 4 recreational, and 1 professional. This period of time was associated with initial head contact while tackling and blocking and resulted in major litigation cases against coaches, schools, and helmet manufacturers.

Several factors in the late 1970s resulted in a dramatic decrease in the number of fatalities, such as a major rule change in 1976 eliminating initial head contact while tackling and blocking, improved medical care of athletes, better teaching of the fundamentals by coaches, and a National Operating Committee on Standards in Athletic Equipment (NOCSAE) helmet standard that went into effect in 1978. In 1990 there were no direct football fatalities at any level for the first time ever. Since 1990, direct football fatalities have been in the single digits, with a high of nine in 2001.[2]

Table 1.1 illustrates the history of direct football fatalities at all levels of play by decades, starting in 1931–1940 and ending in 2001–2009. Direct football fatalities declined steadily through the decade from 1951 to 1960, but dramatically increased in the decade from 1961 to 1970. Every decade following this dramatic increase shows a steady decline. Approximately half of the injuries were caused by tackling and being tackled, followed by blocking, being blocked, collisions, and kick-off and punt activity. It is

TABLE 1.1	Direct Football Fatalities by Decade				
Decade	Sandlot	Pro	High School	College	Total
1931–1940	54	35	100	25	214
1941–1950	32	23	84	5	144
1951–1960	30	11	89	12	142
1961–1970	37	5	178	24	244
1971–1980	12	1	105	9	127
1981–1990	7	0	50	5	62
1991–2000	1	0	36	5	42
2000–2009	5	3	32	1	41
Total	178	78	674	86	1016

TABLE 1.2 Indirect Football Fatalities by Decade

Decade	Sandlot	Pro	High School	College	Total
1931–1940	43	3	70	19	135
1941–1950	16	6	13	3	38
1951–1960	13	3	31	8	55
1961–1970	18	4	83	20	125
1971–1980	6	1	63	16	86
1981–1990	2	0	55	16	73
1991–2000	6	1	73	10	90
2001–2009	10	5	73	20	108
Total	114	23	461	112	710

important to mention that one third of the activities involved in direct football deaths were unknown due to the early data collection methods. A majority of the football deaths occurred during games. The data also show that it is much more dangerous playing defensive football as opposed to being on the offensive side of the ball.[2]

In addition to the direct fatalities, there were 710 indirect fatal injuries, as shown in **Table 1.2**. Indirect injuries included exertional heat stroke (EHS) deaths, heart attacks, asthma attacks, and other medical problems that were not the direct result of a football-related activity. In the early years direct fatalities outnumbered indirect fatalities, but Table 1.2 illustrates how that trend has been reversed.[1]

A major concern in football has been the number of heat stroke deaths associated with the sport. The first recorded exertional heat stroke death took place in 1955; why there were none prior to that time is a question that has not been answered. Since 1955 there have been an additional 127 exertional heat stroke deaths. The greatest number was 8 in 1970.

Fall Sports

High school fall sports have been associated with 118 direct fatal injuries during the past 27 years (academic years 1982/83 through 2008/09), with 111 being in football and 7 in soccer (**Table 1.3**). All of the direct deaths involved male athletes. The data related to football were discussed in the previous section. Of the seven soccer fatalities, six happened in games and one in a practice session. Three of the fatal injuries were brain trauma, one a fractured cervical vertebra, two internal injuries, and one was due to a lacerated heart. Three of the seven fatalities were goalies, and four were related to collisions in the field of play.

The number of fatalities more than doubled when looking at indirect fatal injuries in high school fall sports. Football was associated with the greatest number (184 males), followed by soccer (28 males and 6 females), cross-country running (16 males and 9 females), water polo (3 males and 1 female), and field hockey (1 female). Thirteen of the cross-country fatalities took place in meets and 12 in practice. Twenty-four of these **indirect fatalities** were heart related, and one was associated with a seizure. All of the soccer indirect fatalities and the one field hockey indirect fatality were also heart related. Three of the water polo deaths were heart related, and one was related to a seizure. Seventy percent of the football indirect deaths were heart and heat related. Other and unknown causes accounted for the remainder. An interesting fact is that exertional heat stroke deaths were almost 100% associated with the sport of football.

indirect fatality A fatality caused by systemic failure as a result of exertion while participating in a sport activity or by a complication that was secondary to a nonfatal injury; examples include cardiac failure and an asthma attack.

TABLE 1.3	High School Fall Sports Fatalities, Academic Years 1982/83 Through 2008/09			

	Direct		Indirect	
Sport	Male	Female	Male	Female
Cross-country	0	0	16	9
Football	111	0	184	0
Soccer	7	0	28	6
Field hockey	0	0	0	1
Water polo	0	0	3	1
Total	118	0	231	17

As illustrated in **Table 1.4**, direct fatalities in college fall sports were all associated with football and followed the same pattern as the high school injuries. Indirect fatalities for the same period of time far outnumbered the direct fatalities (51 to 9). Football again led the list, with 44 fatalities (all male), followed by soccer (2 male and 3 female athletes), cross-country running (1 male), and water polo (1 male). The three male soccer indirect deaths were heart related; the female soccer deaths included one heart-related death, one heat stroke–related fatality, and one athlete struck by lightning. The cross-country and water polo deaths were both heart related.

Winter Sports

High school winter sports were associated with seven direct fatal injuries during the past 27 years (academic years 1982/83 through 2008/09), with two in basketball, one in gymnastics, two in ice hockey, and two in wrestling **(Table 1.5)**. All of the fatalities involved male participants. The basketball fatalities both occurred during games, with one involving a brain injury and the second being a fractured skull. The brain injury was associated with a fall (head to floor), whereas the fractured skull occurred when the player was hit in the head by the elbow of an opponent. The gymnastics injury took place in a practice session when the athlete fell from the parallel bars and suffered a severe brain injury. The two ice hockey injuries both took place during games, both involved males, and both were caused by commotio cordis. One player was checked to the chest by an opponent, and the second player was hit in the chest by the puck. The wrestling deaths both happened in a match, and both involved takedowns from a standing position. One of the athletes suffered a fractured cervical vertebra; the second athlete suffered a severe brain injury.

As shown in Table 1.5, indirect fatalities outnumbered direct fatalities (155 to 7), with basketball leading the list with 123 indirect fatalities (108 males and 15 females). Sixty of the basketball deaths occurred in practice, 57 in games, and 6 at other times from unknown causes. All of these deaths, with the exception of the 6 unknowns, were heart related. Males accounted for all four ice hockey indirect deaths, with three taking place in games and one in practice. All four of these deaths were heart related. As shown in Table 1.5, swimming was the only sport in which there were more indirect deaths of females than males. Four of the deaths happened in practice, three in meets, and one at an unspecified time. With the exception of two

TABLE 1.4	College Fall Sports Fatalities, Academic Years 1982/83 Through 2008/09			

	Direct		Indirect	
Sport	Male	Female	Male	Female
Cross-country	0	0	1	0
Football	9	0	44	0
Soccer	0	0	2	3
Water polo	0	0	1	0
Total	9	0	48	3

unknowns, all of these deaths were heart related. Wrestling was associated with 19 indirect deaths, with 14 taking place in matches and 5 in practice sessions. Seventeen of the deaths were heart related, and the cause of 2 was unknown. Volleyball accounted for one indirect death, which took place in practice and was heart related. Of the 155 indirect deaths for high school winter sports, males accounted for 132 and females for 23. With very few exceptions all of the deaths were related to the heart.

College winter sports were associated with 2 direct fatalities and 47 indirect fatal injuries for the same span of years as discussed previously (Table 1.6). The direct injuries occured to one male in basketball and one female in skiing. The basketball injury took place in practice while running sprints: the athlete hit the wall at the end of the court, fractured his cervical vertebra, and died. The female athlete was participating in skiing practice and ran off the course into a tree, suffering a massive brain injury.

College athletes also accounted for 47 indirect fatalities, with 38 involving males and 9 involving females. As shown in Table 1.6, basketball led the list of indirect fatalities with 27 male fatalities and 4 female ones. Nineteen took place in practice, nine in games, and three at unknown times. Twenty-nine were heart-related deaths, one was due to a brain aneurysm, and the cause of one was unknown. Gymnastics had one indirect death: a lung embolism in a female athlete. Ice hockey also had one indirect heart-related death, of a male participating in a practice session. Swimming was associated with eight indirect deaths (six males and two females). Six of the swimming deaths occurred in practice and two in meets. Seven of the eight indirect fatalities were heart related, and the cause of the other was an asthma attack. Wrestling had three indirect deaths, all of which were exertional heat stroke deaths that happened while athletes were trying to make weight for a match. All three athletes were wearing sweat clothes or rubber sweats and working in a hot environment with a coach present. These were the only known exertional heat stroke deaths related to wrestlers trying to make weight. Skiing had one indirect male death; the circumstance was unknown. Volleyball was associated with two female indirect deaths, of which one took place in a game and both were heart related.

TABLE 1.5 High School Winter Sports Fatalities, Academic Years 1982/83 Through 2008/09

	Direct		Indirect	
Sport	Male	Female	Male	Female
Basketball	2	0	108	15
Gymnastics	1	0	0	0
Ice hockey	2	0	4	0
Swimming	0	0	1	7
Wrestling	2	0	19	0
Volleyball	0	0	0	1
Total	7	0	132	23

TABLE 1.6 College Winter Sports Fatalities, Academic Years 1982/83 Through 2008/09

	Direct		Indirect	
Sport	Male	Female	Male	Female
Basketball	1	0	27	4
Gymnastics	0	0	0	1
Ice hockey	0	0	1	0
Swimming	0	0	6	2
Wrestling	0	0	3	0
Skiing	0	1	1	0
Volleyball	0	0	0	2
Total	1	1	38	9

Spring Sports

High school spring sports from 1982/83 through 2008/09 were associated with 36 direct fatal injuries, with 11 in baseball, 2 in lacrosse, 21 in track (20 males and 1 female), and 2 in softball (1 male and 1 female) (Table 1.7).

TABLE 1.7	High School Spring Sports Fatalities, Academic Years 1982/83 Through 2008/09			

	Direct		Indirect	
Sport	Male	Female	Male	Female
Baseball	11	0	15	0
Lacrosse	2	0	7	0
Track	20	1	31	6
Tennis	0	0	3	0
Softball	1	1	0	0
Golf	0	0	1	0
Total	34	2	57	6

The baseball injuries constituted four athletes hit by a batted ball, one hit by a ball from a pitching machine, two hit by a thrown ball, two involved in a collision, one injured diving for a ball, and one hit by a pitch. Six of the injuries took place in games and five in practice. Four of the injuries were to the brain, three commotio cordis, one a ruptured carotid artery, two internal injuries, and one a crushed larynx. There were two male deaths in lacrosse games. One was a result of a fractured cervical vertebra from head-down contact, and one was due to commotio cordis after being hit in the chest by a shot. The two deaths in softball involved a male who died after being hit in the chest with a pitched ball during a game and a female who was struck in the head by accident while pitching a baseball to a male baseball player. The cause of death for the male athlete was not available at this time, but it was most likely commotio cordis.

Track was involved with 21 fatal accidents during this time period. Seventeen of the deaths involved pole vaulting accidents, three involved being hit by a thrown discus (two male athletes and one female), and one involved an athlete who ran into an unpadded goal post during a freak accident. All of the pole vaulting accidents involved the athlete bouncing out of the landing pit, missing the pit and landing on a hard surface, or falling into the pole plant area. All were head or neck injuries.

High school spring sports were also associated with 63 indirect deaths during the time period illustrated in Table 1.7. Baseball was associated with 15, of which 9 happened in practice, 3 in games, and 3 at unknown times. Thirteen of the deaths were heart related, and the causes of 2 were unknown. The lacrosse indirect deaths all involved males, with two occurring in practice and five in games. Four of these deaths were heart related, two were caused by aneurysms, and the cause of one was unknown. The three tennis deaths all involved males and were all heart related; two occurred in practice and one in a match. The golf fatality involved the heart; additional information was unknown. Track was associated with the greatest number of indirect deaths, with 37 (31 males and 6 females). Nineteen took place in practice, 12 in games, and 2 at unknown times. Thirty of the deaths were heart related, 1 was due to unknown causes, and 5 involved other causes.

As illustrated in Table 1.8, college spring sports were associated with 11 direct fatalities (10 males and 1 female). Lacrosse had four direct fatalities, baseball three, track three, and equestrian sports one (the female athlete). Two of the lacrosse fatalities occurred in practice and two in games. All four of the injuries were the result of being hit by the ball. Three of these four cases involved balls to the chest (two of which were shots and one a thrown ball), and in all three the cause of death was commotio cordis. The fourth injury was caused by a thrown ball to the neck that ruptured the carotid artery.

The three college baseball direct fatalities comprised two in practice and one in a game. One involved being hit in the chest with a ball, resulting in commotio cordis; one involved two outfielders colliding, resulting in a brain injury; and one involved a pitcher being hit in the head with a batted ball, causing a subdural hematoma. All three of the track direct fatalities involved the pole vault, and all three were brain injuries. One of the participants bounced out of the landing pit onto a hard surface, one missed the mat completely and landed on a hard surface, and one landed head first onto the pole plant area. The one death in equestrian involved a horse falling on a female rider during a practice ride.

TABLE 1.8 College Spring Sports Fatalities, Academic Years 1982/83 Through 2008/09

Sport	Direct		Indirect	
	Male	Female	Male	Female
Baseball	3	0	2	0
Lacrosse	4	0	2	0
Track	3	0	1	0
Softball	0	0	0	0
Equestrian	0	1	0	0
Tennis	0	0	1	1
Rowing	0	0	3	0
Total	10	1	9	1

College spring sports were also involved in 10 indirect deaths, as illustrated in Table 1.8. Rowing accounted for three indirect deaths, baseball two, lacrosse two, tennis two (one male and one female), and track one. Nine of the 10 indirect deaths involved male athletes, with one in tennis. Two of the rowing deaths happened in practice and one in a meet, with two being associated with the heart and one with heat stroke. Baseball was associated with two heart-related deaths, as was lacrosse. The one death in track was also associated with the heart. One tennis death was related to a cerebral hemorrhage and one to a brain aneurysm.

Summary of Epidemiologic Data

From the fall of 1982 through the spring of 2009, there were a total of 183 direct sport-related deaths in high school and college, 161 of which involved high school athletes (159 males and 2 females) **(Table 1.9)**. In college sports, direct deaths numbered 22, with 20 involving males and 2 involving females. For this 27-year-period of time high schools averaged 5.9 direct deaths each year and colleges averaged 0.8 a year. High school participation for the same years for the sports with catastrophic injuries numbered 161,885,409 (104,926,117 males and 56,959,292 females). High school sports had a **direct fatality** rate of 0.09 per 100,000 participants. The male rate was 0.15, and the female rate was 0.01 per 100,000 participants. The indirect rate for high school sports was 0.28 per 100,000 participants, with the male rate being 0.40 and the female rate 0.08.

direct fatality A fatality resulting directly from participation in the fundamental skills of a sport.

College participation for the sports that had a catastrophic injury numbered 8,887,421 (5,753,902 males and 3,133,519 females). The college direct fatality rate was 0.24 per 100,000 participants, with the male rate being 0.34 and the female rate being 0.06. The college indirect fatality rate per 100,000 participants was 1.21, with the male rate being 1.65 and the female rate 0.41.

It should be noted that in addition to the fatalities in high school and college sports there were a number of catastrophic injuries that resulted in permanent disability and an additional number of catastrophic injuries that eventually led to recovery. High school sports for the dates under discussion were associated with 425 permanent disability injuries and 398 catastrophic injuries with full recovery (all head and neck injuries). College sports for this same time period were associated with 65 permanent disability injuries and 133 catastrophic injuries with full recovery.

TABLE 1.9 — Summary of High School and College Sports Fatalities, Academic Years 1982/83 Through 2008/09

Year	High School			Collegiate			Total
	Direct	Indirect	Total	Direct	Indirect	Total	
1982/83	10	17	27	0	5	5	32
1983/84	8	14	22	0	6	6	28
1984/85	5	12	17	1	0	1	18
1985/86	4	6	10	2	1	3	13
1986/87	12	14	26	1	3	4	30
1987/88	5	12	17	0	8	8	25
1988/89	8	15	23	0	3	3	26
1989/90	5	18	23	2	3	5	28
1990/91	4	18	22	0	4	4	26
1991/92	4	10	14	1	3	4	18
1992/93	4	19	23	1	4	5	28
1993/94	5	23	28	1	2	3	31
1994/95	2	11	13	1	4	5	18
1995/96	4	15	19	0	4	4	23
1996/97	10	18	28	0	2	2	30
1997/98	9	16	25	1	7	8	33
1998/99	8	22	30	2	1	3	33
1999/2000	10	26	36	2	0	2	38
2000/01	3	21	24	2	4	6	30
2001/02	10	23	33	1	8	9	42
2002/03	3	18	21	1	7	8	29
2003/04	3	15	18	2	5	7	25
2004/05	5	27	32	1	5	6	38
2005/06	4	18	22	0	5	5	27
2006/07	2	24	26	0	5	5	31
2007/08	4	18	22	0	4	4	26
2008/09	9	15	24	0	6	6	30
Total	160	465	625	22	109	131	756
Five-Year Breakdowns							
1983–1988	34	58	92	4	18	22	114
1988–1994	30	103	133	5	19	24	157

(continued)

TABLE 1.9	Summary of High School and College Sports Fatalities, Academic Years 1982/83 Through 2008/09 *(Continued)*							
	High School			**Collegiate**			
Year	Direct	Indirect	Total	Direct	Indirect	Total	Total
1994–1999	33	82	115	4	18	22	137
1999–2004	29	103	132	8	24	32	164
2004–2009	24	102	126	1	25	26	152

Data were obtained from the website of the University of North Carolina at Chapel Hill's National Center for Catastrophic Injury Research (NCCIR). This center is run by Dr. Frederick Mueller and Dr. Robert Cantu. The table was compiled by Kelly Pagnotta, MA, ATC, Chief Information Officer, Korey Stringer Institute, University of Connecticut.

Challenging Circumstances

The causes of death described in the first part of this chapter indicate that numerous medical conditions must be addressed.[4–6] The data indicate that the most common causes of death in organized sport are the following (numeric order does not necessarily reflect incidence rate):

1. Cardiac
2. Head injuries
3. Heat stroke
4. Exertional sickling
5. Asthma
6. Trauma (not to head/neck)
7. Neck injuries
8. Other (lightning, diabetes, etc.)

The benefit of being aware of the different potential causes of death is that appropriate emergency action plans can be developed to specify prevention, recognition, treatment, and return-to-play guidelines for each of the individual medical conditions.[4–6]

In many organized sports situations (e.g., in approximately 50% of high schools), medical staff is not present on site to implement the policies related to the conditions noted previously. In these circumstances the sport coach, athletic director, or strength and conditioning coach is the person responsible for implementing the policies (if the school even has them). For example, in the case of exertional heat stroke, the coach would be responsible for developing and implementing polices related to prevention (heat acclimatization, hydration, work-to-rest ratios, environmental condition policies for practices, policies for athletes with acute illnesses or medication issues, etc.), recognition (central nervous system function, cardiac function, accurate core body temperature via rectal temperature), treatment (cold water immersion), and return-to-play considerations (lost acclimatization and fitness, cause of original problem, lingering problems). These are some of the considerations for just one medical condition.

The matter is complicated by the fact that many of the life-threatening conditions in question manifest similar signs and symptoms **(Table 1.10** and **Table 1.11)**, and any delay in appropriate care is very likely to increase the odds of an adverse outcome. Nearly all of the life-threatening medical conditions in sport need to be properly dealt with in the first few minutes. In nearly all circumstances, it is what happens before the ambulance arrives that will dictate whether the outcome is life or death. It is clear that no parent would want a coach to be responsible for the life-saving recognition of the problem and the treatment of their child. Nor, in defense of coaches, would coaches want to have the pressure of this responsibility on their shoulders. It is the strong recommendation of the authors of this book that coaches be trained in first aid, cardiopulmonary resuscitation (CPR), and the use of an automated external defibrillator (AED) so that they can provide immediate care, but that every high school have an on-site athletic trainer who can assume responsibility within a minute or two following the time of the incident. (Colleges and professional teams already typically have athletic trainers present.) An athletic trainer is a licensed medical professional specifically trained to prevent, recognize, and treat emergencies related to physically active individuals. Additionally, they work in concert with a supervising physician to develop and implement emergency action plans and to implement the physician-directed guidelines for return to play following an incident.

TABLE 1.10	How to Prevent, Recognize, and Treat Sudden Death in Sport		
Condition	**Prevention[a]**	**Recognition[b]**	**Treatment**
Exertional heat stroke	Heat acclimatization[c] Proper hydration Adequate work-to-rest ratios Practice modifications for WBGT over 28°C Phasing in of practice and equipment[c] Proper hydration	CNS dysfunction Core body temperature above 105°F when taken rectally	Aggressive cooling via cold water immersion or whole-body cold water dousing Cool first, transport second if AT is on site (cool down to 102°F before transport)
Heat exhaustion[d]	Same as EHS	Core body temperature below 105°F when taken rectally Paleness, fatigue, headache, and dizziness	Remove from the heat Rest with feet elevation Cooling via cold/wet towels Monitoring of vitals and core body temperature
Exertional sickling	Testing for sickle cell trait Conditioning modification for sickle cell trait–positive athletes	Collapse without intense cramping or pain Complaints of cramping/tightness/ pain feeling in the legs (without muscle contraction)	Immediate removal from activity Activate EMS Supplemental O_2
Heat cramps[d]	Proper hydration Nutritional considerations (i.e., adequate salt in the diet)	Intense painful cramping, typically in lower legs Muscles in obvious contracture when felt	Cessation of activity Rehydration with electrolyte beverage Mild stretching
Cardiac arrest	Proper PPE AED on site CPR and AED training for all coaches	Collapse Lack of breathing Loss of pulse	Activate EMS Initiate CPR and AED

(continued)

TABLE 1.10

How to Prevent, Recognize, and Treat Sudden Death in Sport (*Continued*)

Condition	Prevention[a]	Recognition[b]	Treatment
Head injury	Proper technique	CNS dysfunction	Removal from play
	Proper equipment (properly fit and maintained)	Cognitive examination	Monitoring of symptoms and vitals
	Baseline testing (cognitive and balance)	Balance assessment	Referral if symptoms worsen or cranial nerves are disrupted
		Signs and symptoms questionnaire	
		Cranial nerve assessment	
Asthma	Patient education	Wheezing after activity	Activate EAP
	Adherence to treatment plan	Chest tightness	Administer rescuer inhaler
	Warm-up and cool-down	Shortness of breath and coughing	Reassure the athlete
		Dizziness or light-headedness	

Abbreviations: AED, automated external defibrillator; AT, athletic trainer; CNS, central nervous system; CPR, cardiopulmonary resuscitation; EAP, emergency action plan; EHS, exertional heat stroke; EMS, emergency medical services; PPE, preparticipation examination; WBGT, wet bulb globe temperature.

[a] Preexisting conditions and/or previous history of condition should be known.

[b] Not all signs or symptoms will be present in all cases.

[c] For an in-depth discussion of the appropriate measures for acclimatization, see the National Athletic Trainers' Association statement on preseason heat acclimatization guidelines for secondary school athletics.

[d] Heat cramps and heat exhaustion are included because they are often confused for exertional sickling and EHS, respectively. Casa DJ, Csillan D, Armstrong LE, et al. Pre-season heat-acclimatization guidelines for secondary school athletics. *J Athl Train.* 2009;44(3):332–333.

Source: Pagnotta KD, Mazerolle SM, Casa DJ. Exertional heat stroke and emergency issues in high school sport. *J Strength Conditioning Res.* 2010;24(7):1707–1709. Reprinted with permission from National Strength and Conditioning Association, Colorado Springs, CO.

Furthermore, numerous youth sporting events outside the confines of organized high school sport should seriously consider having an athletic trainer present to deal with potential emergencies should they arise.[4–6] Examples include summer sports camps, youth sports festivals (e.g., weekend soccer tournaments), competitive travel team events, and so on.

The bottom line is that every organized sports program needs to develop an emergency action plan that specifically addresses the following areas:

- The education, training, and expectations of the sport coaches, strength and conditioning coaches, athletics director, and athletes
- The medical staff that will be covering the practices and games and that will be overseeing the general implementation of the polices and procedures related to medical care
- The specific prevention strategies for each of the most common causes of death in sport (at a minimum the eight noted earlier in this chapter)
- The specific recognition strategies for each of the most common causes of death in sport (at a minimum the eight noted earlier)
- The specific treatment strategies for each of the most common causes of death in sport (at a minimum the eight noted earlier)
- The specific return-to-play strategies for each of the most common causes of death in sport (at a minimum the eight noted earlier)

These items (discussed in more detail in Chapter 14) should be supervised by the on-site athletic trainer or sports medicine physician.

TABLE 1.11 Preventing Sudden Death in Sport: A Potentially Complex Overlap of Signs and Symptoms of Common Causes of Death[a]

	Exertional Heat Stroke	Heat Cramp[b]	Heat Syncope[b]	Exercise Heat Exhaustion[b]	Exertional Hyponatremia	Exertional Sickling	Head Injury	Cardiac[c]	Respiratory[d]	Shock
CNS dysfunction[e]	X		X	X	X	X	X	X	X	X
Dizziness	X		X	X	X		X	X	X	X
Drowsiness	X	X			X		X			X
Fatigue	X		X	X	X	X	X	X	X	X
Headache	X			X	X		X			
Light-headedness			X	X	X	X	X	X		X
Staggering	X			X	X		X	X	X	
Syncope	X		X	X				X	X	
Tunnel vision			X					X		
Personality changes[f]	X			X	X		X			
Lethargy		X	X	X	X	X	X	X	X	X
Core body temperature usually < 40°C		X			X		X	X	X	
Core body temperature > 40°C	X									
Cool, clammy skin				X	X			X		X
Hot and wet or dry skin	X	X	X	X		X				
Pale skin			X	X				X		X
Cerebral edema					X		X			
Chills			X	X						
Decreased pulse								X	X	X

(continued)

Condition/Symptom					
Decresed urine output	X		X		X
Dehydration	X	X	X	X	
Diarrhea	X		X		
Hyperventilation	X		X		X
Hypotension	X		X		X
Low blood-sodium levels (<130 mEqNa⁺L⁻¹)			X		
Nausea/vomiting	X		X	X	X
Muscle cramps/pain		X		X	
Pulmonary edema			X	X	X
Seizures	X		X		
Swelling of hands and feet			X		
Tachycardia (100–120 bpm)	X		X	X	X

CNS, central nervous system.

[a] This table is not meant to be inclusive of all signs and symptoms of the conditions listed or of all conditions that could cause sudden death in sport. Nor is the table implying that all the signs and symptoms indicated for a particular condition would be present on each occasion.

[b] Heat cramps, heat syncope, and heat exhaustion are not life threatening, but are included due to similarity of these conditions with other conditions that could cause sudden death and the potential for confusion with acute recognition.

[c] Cardiac coditions could be commotio cordis, heart attack, hyperthrophic cardiomyopathy, etc.

[d] Respiratory could be asthma, pneumothorax, pulmonary edema, etc.

[e] CNS dysfunction could include altered consciousness, coma, confusion, disorientation, collapse, etc.

[f] Personality changes could include hysteria, irrational behavior, combativeness, aggressiveness, irritability, apathy, decreased mental acuity, etc.

Source: Casa DJ, Pagnotta KD, Pinkus DE, Mazerolle SM. Should coaches be in charge of medical care for emergencies in high school sport? *Athl Train Sports Health Care.* 2009; 1(4):144–146.

A sports organization that does not have medical supervision present at practices and games and involved with the medical infrastructure runs the risk of legal liability. Those participating in an organized sport situation have a reasonable expectation of receiving appropriate emergency care, and if they do not, the sports organization will have to explain why participant safety was not properly addressed. We are hopeful that the information contained within this book will serve to assist the relevant staff with the appropriate planning and implementation of a successful health care plan so that emergencies can be avoided whenever possible, or properly dealt with when they do arise.

Key Terms

direct fatality

indirect fatality

References

1. Mueller FO, Colgate B. *Annual Survey of Football Injury Research: 1931–2009.* Chapel Hill, NC: National Center for Catastrophic Sport Injury Research; February 2010. http://www.unc.edu/depts/nccsi/2009AnnualFootball.pdf.
2. Mueller FO, Cantu RC. *Catastrophic Sports Injury Research: Twenty-Seventh Annual Report, Fall 1982–Spring 2009.* Chapel Hill, NC: National Center for Catastrophic Sport Injury Research; June 2010. http://www.unc.edu/depts/nccsi/2009ALLSPORT .pdf.
3. Hawes K. The NCAA century series. Part 1: 1900–39. *NCAA News.* November 8, 1999.
4. Pagnotta KD, Mazerolle SM, Casa DJ. Exertional heat stroke and emergency issues in high school sport. *J Strength Conditioning Res.* 2010;24(7):1707–1709.
5. Casa DJ, Pagnotta KD, Pinkus DE, Mazerolle SM. Should coaches be in charge of medical care for emergencies in high school sport? *Athl Train Sports Health Care.* 2009;1(4):144–146.
6. Casa DJ, Guskiewicz KM, Anderson SA, et al. National Athletic Trainers' Association position statement: preventing sudden death during sport and physical activity. *J Athl Train.* 2011; in press.

Prevention of Sudden Cardiac Death in Young Athletes

Jonathan A. Drezner, MD

Definition of Condition

Sudden cardiac death (SCD) is the leading cause of death in young athletes on the playing field and is typically the result of undiagnosed structural or electrical cardiovascular disease. SCD is defined as the sudden death of an individual during or within 1 hour after exercise due to a cardiovascular disorder.[1]

Epidemiology

Incidence of Sudden Cardiac Death

SCD is the leading cause of death in young athletes during exercise.[2,3] However, the exact frequency of SCD in athletes is unknown, and it is difficult to compare incidence studies with highly variable methodology and from widely different geographic regions **(Table 2.1)**. Reports in the United States have relied heavily on case identification through searches of public media reports, catastrophic insurance claims, and other electronic databases, with estimates ranging from 1 in 160,000 to 1 in 300,000 deaths per year in young competitive athletes (ages 12–35).[2,4,5] These studies risk underestimating the incidence of SCD due to the lack of a mandatory reporting system and the potential for incomplete identification of all cases.

Accurate calculation of the incidence of SCD in athletes requires a reliable reporting system with precise reflection of the number of cases per year (numerator) and a universal definition of "athlete"

TABLE 2.1 — Incidence of Sudden Cardiac Death in Young Athletes

Study	Population	Methods and Reporting System	Incidence
Van Camp[5] (1995)	High school and college athletes aged 13–24 (U.S.)	Public media reports and other reported cases	1:300,000
Maron[4] (1998)	High school athletes in Minnesota aged 13–19 (U.S.)	Catastrophic insurance claims	1:200,000
Eckart[7] (2004)	Military recruits aged 18–35 (U.S.)	Mandatory, autopsy based	1:9,000
Drezner[8] (2005)	College athletes aged 18–23 (U.S.)	Retrospective survey	1:67,000
Corrado[6] (2006)	Competitive athletes aged 12–35 (Italy)	Mandatory registry for sudden cardiac death	1:25,000
Maron[2] (2009)	Competitive athletes aged 12–35 (U.S.)	Public media reports and other electronic databases	1:166,000
Drezner[11] (2009)	High school athletes aged 14–17 (U.S)	Cross-sectional survey	1:23,000
Asif[3] (2010)	College athletes aged 17–23 (U.S.)	NCAA Resolutions Database, public media reports, and catastrophic insurance claims	1:45,000

with an exact count of athlete participants per year (denominator). A 5-year review was conducted on the etiology and incidence of sudden death in National Collegiate Athletic Association (NCAA) athletes from 2004 to 2008.[3] Cases were identified primarily through the NCAA Resolutions Database, a recommended reporting system for institutions to the NCAA Director of Health and Safety on the death of any NCAA athlete. Forty-four cardiovascular-related sudden deaths were identified during this period, with an average of 400,000 individual athlete participants per year. Cardiovascular-related sudden death represented 72% of fatalities during exertion, with an SCD incidence of 1 in 45,000 NCAA athletes per year.[3]

Other studies have also reported a higher incidence of SCD than initial estimates in the United States.[6–11] The Veneto region of Italy utilizes a regional registry for juvenile sudden death and reported an SCD incidence of 1 in 28,000 for young competitive athletes (ages 12–35 years) prior to implementing a national screening program.[6] In U.S. military recruits (ages 18–35 years), the incidence of nontraumatic exercise-related sudden cardiac arrest (SCA) was 1 in 9000.[7] A prospective population-based study conducted in 11 U.S. and Canadian cities and utilizing rigorous methodology, with all cases of SCA collected through the emergency medical services system, reported an incidence of SCA from cardiovascular disease of 1 in 27,000 in children and young adults (ages 14–24 years).[9] Another U.S. population-based study found the incidence of SCA in children aged 10 to 14 to be 1 in 58,000.[10]

Distribution and Key Populations

SCD in athletes occurs more commonly in males, with male-to-female gender differences ranging from 5:1 to 9:1.[2,12,13] Although SCD can occur in any sport, these deaths occur most frequently in basketball and football in the United States (sports that have the highest levels of participation). A disproportionate amount (>40%) of SCD in U.S. athletes occurs in African American athletes, greater than the proportion of African Americans in athletics.

Incidence studies raise the question as to whether SCA/SCD is more common in competitive athletes than in an age-matched general population, and whether this risk justifies a separate cardiovascular screening program for competitive athletes. It is generally accepted that exercise and intense physical exertion through athletic participation increase the likelihood of sudden death for many disorders predisposing to SCA. Corrado et al.[14] identified a 2.5 times relative risk for SCD due to sports activity in athletes versus an age-matched nonathletic population. Exercise is considered the exposure (risk factor) for SCA in individuals with an underlying cardiovascular disorder, and athletes may be at elevated risk of SCD compared with nonathletes due to the frequency of their exercise, perhaps justifying a more intensive screening program.

On the other hand, not all children are competitive athletes but most children are active and exercise in some way. According to statistics from the Centers for Disease Control, cardiovascular disease is second only to malignancy as the leading medical cause of death in individuals younger than 24 years, accounting for over 2400 fatalities per year in the United States.[15] Thus, if specific preventive measures are valuable for the minority of children and young adults who participate in organized sports, should these tests also be available for all children?[16]

Pathophysiology

Vigorous exercise appears to be a trigger for lethal arrhythmias in athletes with underlying heart disease.[13] The precise mechanism leading to a ventricular arrhythmia will vary depending on the underlying heart condition. In cardiomyopathy, myocardial disarray can be an arrhythmogenic focus, and myocardial hypertrophy can outgrow its blood supply, leading to local ischemia. An anomalous coronary artery may be pinched during exercise between the great vessels or within the myocardium, also leading to ischemia and a subsequent arrhythmia. In ion channel disorders, exercise increases catecholamines that can produce a primary electrical disorder, and in commotio cordis **ventricular fibrillation** (VF) is triggered by blunt trauma.

> **ventricular fibrillation (VF)**
> A lethal ventricular arrhythmia characterized by rapid ventricular depolarization leading to disorganized and asynchronous contraction of the ventricular muscle and inability to pump blood effectively.

About 40% of out-of-hospital cardiac arrest victims in the United States demonstrate VF on first rhythm analysis.[17] However, the rate of VF in young athletes with SCA is much higher. In a study reporting outcomes of high school student athletes with a witnessed SCA who received prompt defibrillation, 93% had a shockable rhythm, presumed VF or rapid ventricular tachycardia (VT), on first rhythm analysis.[11]

Ventricular fibrillation is characterized by chaotic, rapid ventricular depolarization that leads to the disorganized and asynchronous contraction of ventricular muscle. As a result, the heart muscle loses its ability to pump blood effectively. It is likely that a larger percentage of victims in the United States have VF or rapid VT at the time of collapse but that the rhythm has already deteriorated to asystole before the first rhythm analysis. The probability of successful defibrillation for SCA involving VF diminishes rapidly over time, with survival rates declining 7% to 10% per minute for every minute that defibrillation is delayed.[18,19] Defibrillation through deployment of electric energy terminates VF and allows the normal cardiac pacemakers to resume firing and produce an effective rhythm if the heart tissue is still viable. Survival after SCA is unlikely once VF has deteriorated to asystole.

Cardiopulmonary resuscitation (CPR) is important both before and after defibrillation; it provides a small but critical amount of blood flow to the heart and brain and increases the likelihood that defibrillation will restore a normal rhythm in time to prevent neurologic damage. Chest compressions create blood flow by increasing intrathoracic pressure and directly compressing the heart. Bystander CPR increases the window in which defibrillation will be effective and can greatly improve survival from witnessed SCA for any given time interval to defibrillation.[18,20] Resuming CPR immediately after shock delivery is also critical. Many victims have pulseless electric activity or asystole for several minutes after defibrillation, and CPR is needed to provide perfusion.[21–23] Unfortunately, bystander CPR is initiated in less than one third of cases of witnessed SCA,[24,25] and, if initiated, more than 40% of chest compressions are of insufficient quality.[26] These deficiencies illustrate the tremendous need for increased public education and training in CPR.

Automated external defibrillators (AEDs) are computerized devices that analyze a victim's rhythm, determine whether a shock is needed, charge to an appropriate shock dose, and use audio and visual instructions to guide the rescuer. These devices are easy to use and extremely accurate in recommending a shock only when VF or rapid VT is present.[27] In one study, AEDs were safely and successfully operated by untrained sixth graders almost as quickly as trained paramedics in a simulated resuscitation, with only a 23-second difference in mean time to defibrillation.[28]

Prevention and Predisposing Factors

Extrinsic Factors

Although most SCD in athletes is caused by intrinsic heart disease, SCA can also occur secondary to blunt trauma. **Commotio cordis**, also called cardiac concussion, discussed in Chapter 4, involves a blunt, nonpenetrating blow to the chest during a vulnerable phase of ventricular repolarization, leading to a ventricular arrhythmia with no structural damage or cardiac contusion present. Commotio cordis occurs most commonly in young male adolescents (mean age 13.6 years) with compliant chest walls.[29] Approximately 80% of cases involve blunt chest impact by a firm projectile, such as a baseball, softball, hockey puck, or lacrosse ball, and 20% of cases are due to chest contact with another person.[29] To date, commercially available chest protectors have not been shown to prevent commotio cordis.[30]

Survival after commotio cordis closely depends on the time to defibrillation.[31] Overall survival as reported from the U.S. Commotio Cordis Registry was only 16%, but for those victims still in VF who were reached in time to receive defibrillation, the survival rate was 46%.[29] Young athletes who collapse shortly after being struck in the chest should be suspected of having commotio cordis until the athlete is clearly responsive. Rescuers can improve survival by promptly recognizing SCA due to commotio cordis, activating the emergency medical services (EMS) system, immediately initiating CPR, and using an AED as soon as possible.

Intrinsic Factors

SCD in young athletes is primarily caused by a heterogeneous group of structural cardiovascular abnormalities and primary electrical diseases that typically go undetected in otherwise healthy-appearing athletes **(Table 2.2)**.[13,32–39] In the United States, **hypertrophic cardiomyopathy (HCM)** and congenital coronary artery anomalies are the most common etiologies of SCD.[2] The combined prevalence of all cardiovascular disorders known to cause SCD in the young athletic population is estimated to be 3 per 1000.[33]

Hypertrophic Cardiomyopathy

HCM accounts for about one third of SCD deaths in U.S. athletes under age 30.[13,32,33] The characteristic morphologic features of HCM include asymmetric left ventricular (LV) hypertrophy (usually involving the ventricular septum), LV wall thickness of 16 mm or more (normal, <12 mm; borderline, 13–15 mm), a ratio between the septum and free wall thickness of more than 1.3, and a nondilated LV with impaired diastolic function.[40] Histologic analysis shows a disorganized cellular architecture with cardiac myocyte disarray and intramural tunneling (myocardial bridging) in which a segment of coronary artery is completely surrounded by myocardium in about one third of cases.

The prevalence of HCM is 1 in 500 in the general population and approximately 1 in 1000 to 1 in 1500 in competitive athletes.[41–43] It is inherited as an autosomal dominant disorder with variable expression in over half of cases.[44] Morphologic expression of HCM may appear in childhood, but typically develops in early adolescence to young adulthood and is characteristically

TABLE 2.2

Causes of Sudden Cardiac Death in Young Athletes

Structural/Functional	Electrical	Other
Hypertrophic cardiomyopathy (HCM)[a]	Long QT syndrome (LQTS)[a]	Drugs and stimulants
Coronary artery anomalies	Wolff-Parkinson-White syndrome (WPW)	Commotio cordis
Aortic rupture/Marfan syndrome[a]	Brugada syndrome[a]	Primary pulmonary hypertension (PPH)[a]
Dilated cardiomyopathy (DCM)[a]	Catecholaminergic polymorphic ventricular tachycardia (CPVT)[a]	
Myocarditis		
Left ventricular outflow tract obstruction	Short QT syndrome[a]	
Mitral valve prolapse (MVP)	Complete heart block (CHB)	
Coronary artery atherosclerotic disease[a]		
Arrhythmogenic right ventricular cardiomyopathy (ARVC)[a]		
Postoperative congenital heart disease		

[a] Familial/genetic.

present by the end of physical maturity in most individuals who are genetically predisposed to the disorder. The phenotypic expression of HCM in adolescence is the primary rationale supporting the recommendation that preparticipation cardiovascular screening begin in middle school and be performed every other year while in high school and upon matriculation to college.[33,34]

An electrocardiogram (ECG) will be abnormal in up to 95% of patients with HCM,[45,46] with prominent Q waves, deep negative T waves, or dramatic increases in QRS voltage associated with ST depression or T-wave inversion. Echocardiography remains the standard to confirm the diagnosis of HCM by identifying pathologic LV wall thickness (>16 mm) and a nondilated LV with impaired diastolic function. In cases in which the diagnosis of HCM is uncertain (e.g., borderline LV wall thickness of 13 to 15 mm), magnetic resonance imaging (MRI) with gadolinium or repeat echocardiography after 4 to 6 weeks of deconditioning may help in distinguishing HCM from athletic heart syndrome.

Coronary Artery Anomalies

Coronary artery anomalies are the second leading cause of SCD in athletes and account for approximately 17% of cases.[13,33] The most common coronary anomaly is an abnormal origin of the left coronary artery arising from the right sinus of Valsalva. Impingement of the anomalous artery as it traverses between the expanding great vessels during exercise may lead to ischemia and a subsequent arrhythmia. Other features that may contribute to ischemia during exercise include an acute angled take-off, a hypoplastic ostium, or an intramyocardial course of the anomalous artery.

If an anomaly is suspected, transthoracic echocardiography can identify the coronary artery origins in about 80% to 97% of patients.[47] Advanced cardiac imaging such as computed tomographic (CT) angiography, cardiac MRI, or coronary angiography may be needed to detect coronary anomalies in some cases.

Myocarditis

Myocarditis accounts for 6% of cases of SCD in U.S. athletes.[33] Acute inflammation of the myocardium may lead to an arrhythmogenic focus and sudden death. Coxsackie B virus is implicated in more than 50% of cases, but echovirus, adenovirus, influenza, and *Chlamydia pneumoniae* have also been associated with myocarditis. The acute phase of myocarditis presents with a flulike illness that may lead to dilated cardiomyopathy and signs and symptoms of congested heart failure. Histologic analysis shows a lymphocytic infiltrate of the myocardium with necrosis or degeneration of adjacent myocytes. Myocardial scarring or fibrosis can also develop, which can act as an arrhythmogenic focus.

Characteristic symptoms of myocarditis include a prodromal viral illness followed by progressive exercise intolerance and congestive symptoms of dyspnea, cough, and orthopnea. If suspected, ECG may show diffuse low voltage, ST-T wave changes, heart block, or ventricular arrhythmias. Serologic testing may show leukocytosis, eosinophilia, an elevated sedimentation rate or C-reactive protein, and increased myocardial enzymes. Echocardiography will confirm the diagnosis within the right clinical context, showing a dilated LV, global hypokinesis or segmental wall abnormalities, and decreased LV ejection fraction.

Arrhythmogenic Right Ventricular Cardiomyopathy

arrhythmogenic right ventricular cardiomyopathy (ARVC) Progressive fibro-fatty replacement of the right ventricular myocardium, causing wall thinning and right ventricular dilatation.

Arrhythmogenic right ventricular cardiomyopathy (ARVC) represents 4% of cases of SCD in the United States,[33] but was reported as the leading cause of SCD (22%) in the Veneto region of northeastern Italy.[41] ARVC is characterized by a progressive fibro-fatty replacement of the right ventricular myocardium, causing wall thinning and right ventricular dilatation. The estimated prevalence is 1 in 5000 in the general population and results from mutations in genes encoding for desmosomal (cell adhesion) proteins.[48]

ARVC can present with myocardial electrical instability leading to ventricular arrhythmias that precipitate cardiac arrest, especially during physical activity. ECG may show right precordial T-wave inversion (beyond V_1), an epsilon wave (small terminal notch seen just beyond the QRS in V_1 or V_2), prolongation of QRS duration more than 110 ms, or right bundle-branch block pattern. Echocardiogram, cardiac MRI, or CT may demonstrate right ventricular dilatation and wall thinning, reduced right ventricular ejection fraction, focal right ventricular wall motion abnormalities, or right ventricular aneurysms. Fibro-fatty infiltration of the right ventricle is best seen on cardiac MRI or by histologic analysis in selected cases.

Aortic Rupture in Marfan Syndrome

Marfan syndrome Inherited disorder of connective tissue that affects multiple organ systems, causing a progressive dilatation and weakness (cystic medial necrosis) of the proximal aorta that can lead to rupture and sudden death.

Marfan syndrome is the most common inherited disorder of connective tissue that affects multiple organ systems, with a reported incidence of 2 to 3 in 10,000 individuals.[49] Marfan syndrome causes a progressive dilatation and weakness (cystic medial necrosis) of the proximal aorta that can lead to rupture and sudden death. Myxomatous degeneration of the mitral and aortic valves may also lead to valvular dysfunction. Marfan syndrome is caused by mutations in the fibrillin-1 gene, with 75% of cases inherited through autosomal dominant transmission with variable expression and 25% of cases from de novo mutations.[49]

Cardiovascular complications are the major cause of morbidity and mortality in patients with Marfan syndrome. The risk of aortic rupture or dissection increases during adolescence, and 50% of undiagnosed patients with Marfan syndrome die by 40 years of age.[49] Symptoms of aortic dissection typically include sudden, excruciating chest or thoracic pain, often described as tearing or ripping. Physical exam findings are highly variable, including kyphoscoliosis, high-arched palate, pectus excavatum, arachnodactyly, arm span greater than height, hyperlaxity, myopia, mitral valve prolapse, and aortic insufficiency. Diagnosis of Marfan syndrome is primarily based on the Ghent criteria.[50]

Ion Channel Disorders

ion channel disorder A primary electrical disease of the heart predisposing to lethal ventricular arrhythmias and characterized by mutations in ion channel proteins that lead to dysfunctional sodium, potassium, calcium, and other ion transport across cell membranes.

Ion channel disorders are primary electrical diseases of the heart predisposing to potentially lethal ventricular arrhythmias and are characterized by mutations in ion channel proteins that lead to dysfunctional sodium, potassium, calcium, and other ion transport across cell membranes. Confirmed channelopathies account for approximately 3% of cases of SCD in U.S. athletes.[33] In an additional 3% of cases of SCD in athletes, routine postmortem examination fails to identify a structural cardiac cause of death,[13,33] which may be due to inherited arrhythmia syndromes and ion channel disorders such as long QT syndrome, short QT syndrome, Brugada syndrome, or familial catecholaminergic polymorphic ventricular tachycardia.[13]

The prevalence of ion channel disorders as a cause of SCD in U.S. athletes may be underestimated because autopsy-negative sudden unexplained death (SUD) represents a substantially larger proportion of SCD in the young than in other study populations, and the accurate diagnosis of ion channelopathies postmortem is still limited. In Australia, autopsy-negative SUD represents approximately 30% of cases of SCD in individuals younger than 35 years,[38,39] and in U.S. military recruits autopsy-negative SUD accounts for 35% of nontraumatic sudden deaths.[7,51]

Long QT syndrome (LQTS) is the most common ion channelopathy and is characterized by prolongation of ventricular repolarization as measured by the QT interval corrected for heart rate (QTc). There are 10 recognized gene abnormalities for LQTS, involving potassium and sodium ion channels important in cardiac repolarization.[52] Most arrhythmias from LQTS are triggered by emotional or physical stress and manifest by syncope or near-syncope, seizures, or sudden death. Syncope is usually due to torsade de pointes, a specific form of polymorphic ventricular tachycardia. Up to 20% of patients who have LQTS and present with syncope (but are not diagnosed and treated) will experience SCD in the first year after their syncope, and 50% will experience SCD by 5 years.[53]

Catecholaminergic polymorphic ventricular tachycardia (CPVT) is a familial disorder characterized by stress-induced ventricular arrhythmias that result in SCD in children and young adults and most commonly involves a cardiac ryanodine receptor/calcium release channel mutation. CPVT can present with syncope, drowning or near-drowning, seizure, or sudden death triggered by vigorous physical exertion or acute emotion. Syncope is the presenting symptom in most patients with CPVT, with the first syncopal event occurring around 8 years of age.[54] A family history of syncope or sudden death is also present in 30% of cases.[54]

The diagnosis of an ion channel disorder is often delayed due to the misdiagnosis of epilepsy or vasovagal events in the evaluation of syncope in the young.

All children and young athletes presenting with a history of syncope or unexplained seizure-like activity deserve at minimum an ECG to evaluate for the presence of an ion channel disorder. Recurrent episodes of syncope or unexplained seizure-like activity require additional testing, such as an exercise-ECG and ambulatory monitoring, and should initiate evaluation by a cardiologist.

Early Identification and Screening

Cardiovascular screening in athletes is routinely practiced and is endorsed by most major sporting and medical associations, including the American Heart Association (AHA), European Society of Cardiology (ESC), and the International Olympic Committee (IOC).[33,55,56] However, universal agreement on a single screening strategy to identify athletes at risk for SCD remains elusive and a topic of tremendous debate. The screening controversy is centered on the inclusion (or not) of a resting 12-lead ECG in addition to a history and physical examination during the preparticipation evaluation.

The goal of screening is to identify young athletes with cardiovascular conditions at risk for SCD. The American College of Cardiology contends that the "ultimate objective of pre-participation screening of athletes is the detection of 'silent' cardiovascular abnormalities that can lead to SCD."[57] Many of the conditions that may predispose to SCD can be effectively managed through activity modification and medical intervention (pharmacotherapy, radiofrequency ablation, implantable cardioverter defibrillator, or even surgery) to reduce the risk of sudden death. The AHA estimates that the combined disease prevalence of all cardiovascular disorders that potentially predispose young athletes to SCD is 0.3%.[33] In contrast to the wide range of estimates for SCD incidence, the prevalence of potentially lethal cardiovascular diseases in athletes has consistently ranged between 0.2% to 0.7% in studies using noninvasive cardiovascular testing.[6,58–62] In other words, approximately 1 in 500 athletes or more may harbor an occult cardiovascular condition that places them at risk for SCD.

History and Physical Examination

In 1996, the AHA first provided consensus guidelines on preparticipation cardiovascular screening in athletes with specific recommendations for a detailed personal and family history and physical examination.[34] More than a decade later, little is known about the sensitivity and specificity of such a protocol, and no study to date using history and physical examination alone has demonstrated any significant detection of underlying cardiovascular disease in athletes. A substantial challenge to screening is that most apparently healthy athletes with unsuspected cardiovascular disease are asymptomatic. Sudden death is the first clinical manifestation of cardiac disease in up to 60% to 80% of athletes with SCD.[32,63,64] The lack of sensitivity of a screening model based only on history and physical examination is demonstrated in a report of 115 cases of SCD in young athletes, in which screening led to the correct diagnosis in only 1 athlete (0.9%).[32]

Successful detection of athletes with symptoms of cardiovascular disease requires that physicians ask the appropriate questions. Warning symptoms or a significant family history may be present in an important but limited proportion of athletes at risk for SCD. Unfortunately, standardized questionnaire forms developed to assist health care providers in performing a comprehensive preparticipation evaluation have been grossly underutilized in the primary care and scholastic communities.[65,66]

Electrocardiographic Screening

The value of adding noninvasive cardiovascular tests such as ECG to the screening process in athletes is widely debated.[67,68] In 2007, the AHA reaffirmed its recommendations against universal ECG screening in athletes, citing a low prevalence of disease, poor sensitivity, high false-positive rate, poor cost-effectiveness, and a lack of clinicians to interpret the results.[33] In contrast, the ESC,[55] IOC,[56,69] and the governing associations of several U.S. and international professional sports leagues endorse the use of ECG in the preparticipation screening of athletes. These recommendations are supported by studies showing that ECG is more sensitive than history and physical examination alone in identifying athletes with underlying cardiovascular disease.

In 2006, Corrado et al.[6] reported data from a national preparticipation screening program in Italy in 42,386 athletes over 25 years. The Italian model consists of an integrated screening protocol using a standardized history, physical examination, and ECG. Disqualification and subsequent medical care of athletes found to have cardiovascular disorders produced a 10-fold reduction in the incidence of SCD in young competitive athletes, and an 89% reduction of SCD as a result of cardiomyopathy.[6] This is the only study to date with long-term outcome-based data on survival after screening and disqualification of athletes found to be at increased risk of SCD. Although only 0.2% of athletes were disqualified for potentially lethal cardiovascular conditions, the study reported a 7% false-positive rate and a 2% overall disqualification rate, raising concerns that adopting such a program in the United States would lead to an unacceptable number of disqualifications in athletes with a low risk of SCD.[70]

Concern regarding a high number of false-positive results leading to unnecessary diagnostic testing and restriction from athletic participation is the primary objection to adopting ECG screening in the United States. An initial screening study performed in the United States over two decades ago reported a false-positive rate of 15%.[71] However, more recent studies applying modern, strict ECG criteria to screen athletes have resulted in substantially lower false-positive rates. Pelliccia et al.[72] reported on 32,652 ECGs in mostly young amateur athletes (median age 17, range 8–78 years); distinct ECG abnormalities suggesting cardiac disease were found in only 4.8% of athletes. In a study of 2720 competitive athletes and physically active school children in the United Kingdom, Wilson et al.[59] reported a false-positive rate of 3.7% using history, physical examination, and ECG, with only 1.9% of false positives determined by ECG alone. In this study nine athletes (0.3% of those screened) were found to have a cardiovascular condition known to cause SCD in the young; all of these athletes were detected by ECG and not by history or physical examination.[59] Nora et al.[73] reported preliminary findings of ECG screening in 9125 young adults (ages 14–18) from the Midwest region of the United States and found only 2% of ECGs to be abnormal using modern ECG criteria. A study by Baggish et al.[61] screened 510 college athletes with history, physical examination, ECG, and echocardiography. Three athletes were identified with a potentially lethal cardiovascular disease: two detected by ECG (HCM and myocarditis) and one by physical examination (moderate pulmonic stenosis). All three athletes were asymptomatic, and inclusion of the ECG improved sensitivity for detecting important cardiac abnormalities from 45.5% to 90.9%.

It is critical to recognize that the total-positive and false-positive rates for any ECG screening study are immensely affected by the criteria chosen to define "abnormal." There is an urgent need for uniform terminology when describing ECG findings in athletes.[74] Many ECG changes once referred to as "abnormal" are now recognized as physiologic and part of benign cardiac adaptation in athletes (so-called athlete's heart). Physicians interpreting ECGs in athletes should be familiar with common training-related ECG alterations that are normal variants. In contrast, training-unrelated ECG changes suggest the possibility of underlying pathology, require further diagnostic workup, and should be considered abnormal. The ESC Section on Sports Cardiology published an international position statement in 2010 summarizing modern recommendations to distinguish pathologic ECG abnormalities from physiologic ECG alterations in athletes.[75]

Recognition of Sudden Cardiac Arrest

Identifying Factors

Immediately Precollapse

Most athletes who suffer from SCA are asymptomatic, and sudden death is often the first clinical event of their disease.[32,63,64] Collapse from SCA is typically rapid once a ventricular arrhythmia has occurred, with no significant period of prodromal symptoms such as chest pain, light-headedness, or palpitations. However, cardiovascular warning symptoms in athletes, if present, should be evaluated appropriately to rule out conditions that predispose to SCA.

Immediately Postcollapse

Prompt recognition of SCA is the first step to an efficient emergency response. Sports medicine professionals and other potential first responders to SCA in an athlete must maintain a high index of suspicion for SCA in any collapsed and unresponsive athlete. Delayed recognition of SCA by first responders can lead to critical delays or even failure to activate the EMS system, initiate CPR, and provide early defibrillation. Resuscitation can be delayed because the victim is reported to have signs of life, and SCA is commonly mistaken for a seizure.[76] Brief seizurelike activity or involuntary myoclonic jerks have been reported in approximately 50% of young athletes with SCA.[77,78]

Another challenge to recognizing SCA in athletes is inaccurate rescuer assessment of pulse or respirations. Occasional or agonal gasping can occur in the first minutes after SCA and is often misinterpreted as normal breathing, especially by lay responders.[79] Occasional gasping does not represent adequate breathing and if present should not prevent rescuers from initiating CPR. Lay rescuers and even health care professionals can be inaccurate in assessing signs of circulation and the presence of a pulse. Rescuers with basic CPR training failed to recognize the absence of a pulse in 10% of pulseless victims, failed to correctly identify a pulse in 45% of victims with a pulse, and accurately identified pulselessness in only 2% of pulseless victims within 10 seconds.[80,81] In high school and college athletes with SCA, ongoing respirations or a pulse after collapse were reported in approximately half the cases.[77,78]

To avoid potentially fatal delays in resuscitation, a collapsed and unresponsive athlete should be treated as having had a cardiac arrest until a noncardiac cause of collapse can be clearly determined or the athlete becomes responsive. Brief seizurelike activity in a collapsed athlete should be assumed to be due to SCA. A high suspicion of SCA must be maintained for any collapsed and unresponsive athlete and an AED applied as soon as possible for rhythm analysis and defibrillation if indicated.[82]

Key Differential Diagnosis

The differential diagnosis of nontraumatic exercise-related syncope includes but is not limited to SCA, exertional heat stroke, heat exhaustion, hyponatremia, hypoglycemia, exercise-associated collapse, neurocardiogenic syncope, seizures, pulmonary embolus, cardiac arrhythmias, valvular disorders, coronary artery disease, cardiomyopathies, ion channel disorders, and other structural cardiac diseases. A collapsed athlete who is also unresponsive should be treated as a potential cardiac arrest until spontaneous breathing and a pulse are documented and the cardiac rhythm analyzed or the victim becomes responsive. If cardiovascular-related collapse is ruled out but the athlete remains unresponsive, further immediate evaluation to determine the cause of collapse is needed, because other emergent medical interventions may still be required.

Treatment and Actions

Comprehensive and thoughtful emergency response planning is essential to prepare for and effectively manage an SCA in the athletic setting.[37] Public access to defibrillators and first-responder AED programs improve survival from SCA by increasing the likelihood that SCA victims will receive bystander CPR and early defibrillation. These programs require an organized and practiced response plan with rescuers trained and equipped to recognize SCA, activate the EMS system, provide CPR, and use an AED.[83] The American Heart Association emphasizes the time-sensitive interventions for victims of SCA and has outlined four critical steps in a "chain of survival" to save lives in the event of a cardiovascular emergency:[19]

1. Early recognition of the emergency and activation of the local emergency response system (call 9-1-1)
2. Early cardiopulmonary resuscitation (CPR)
3. Early defibrillation (AED)
4. Early advanced life support and cardiovascular care (hospital)

Emergency response planning is required to ensure an efficient and structured response to SCA. Every school, club, and organization that sponsors athletic activities should have an emergency response plan for SCA with written policies and procedures.[37,84] Essential elements of emergency planning include training of anticipated responders in CPR and AED use, establishing an effective communication system, ensuring access to early defibrillation, integrating on-site responder and AED programs with the local EMS system, and practicing and reviewing the response plan **(Table 2.3)**.[37] Consensus guidelines and several public access defibrillation studies uniformly support access to early defibrillation, targeting a time interval of less than 3 to 5 minutes from collapse to first shock.[37,84–86] The plan also should identify the individual(s) responsible for documentation of personnel training, equipment maintenance, actions taken during an emergency, and the postevent evaluation of the emergency response.[37,84]

Goals or Objectives Within the First 10 to 15 Minutes of Onset

- Prompt recognition of SCA. (*Note:* Brief seizurelike activity after collapse is common in athletes with SCA.)
- Early activation of the EMS system and call for additional rescuer assistance.
- Early CPR.

TABLE 2.3 Core Elements of a Comprehensive Emergency Response Plan for Sudden Cardiac Arrest

Develop a written emergency response plan.

Establish an effective and efficient communication system.

Identify and train likely responders in CPR and AED use.

Ensure access to early defibrillation through on-site AED(s).

Integrate and register the AED with the local EMS system.

Practice and review the response plan with potential first responders at least annually.

Abbreviations: AED, automated external defibrillator; CPR, cardiopulmonary resuscitation; EMS, emergency medical services; SCA, sudden cardiac arrest.

- Immediate retrieval of the AED.
- Application of the AED as soon as possible for rhythm analysis and shock delivery if indicated. (*Note:* If no shock is recommended, a nonshockable SCA [i.e., asystole or pulseless electrical activity] is still possible, and CPR and life support measures should be continued until the patient becomes responsive or a noncardiac etiology can be clearly established.)
- Advanced airway and ventilation equipment, including bag-valve masks, oxygen delivery systems, oral and nasopharyngeal airways, and advanced airways (i.e., endotracheal tube, Combitube [Tyco Healthcare Nellcor, Pleasanton, CA], or laryngeal mask airway), and emergency cardiac medications should be considered if available and physicians or advanced cardiac life support (ACLS)–certified responders are on site.

Goals or Objectives Within 1 Hour of Onset

- Transport of the SCA victim to a hospital facility capable of advanced cardiac life support.

Goals or Objectives Within 24 Hours of Onset

- Management of resuscitated SCA is ideally guided by subspecialty care in the intensive care unit setting.
- Rapid cooling and induced hypothermia (24 hours) for SCA victims with VF arrest has been shown to improve survival and decrease neurologic complications.[87]

Goals or Objectives After 24 Hours of Onset

- Proper diagnosis of the etiology of SCA in young athletes requires a careful cardiac evaluation for both structural and primary electrical disorders known to cause SCA in the young.
- Proper management will depend on the specific etiology found and should be guided by subspecialty cardiovascular care.
- Family members should be screened for hereditary causes of SCA.
- In cases of SCD with a negative autopsy (no structural heart disease), postmortem genetic testing (so-called molecular autopsy) for ion channel disorders should be considered.

Recovery

Factors Contributing to Mortality and Morbidity

The single greatest factor affecting survival from SCA is the time interval from cardiac arrest to defibrillation.[19] In the United States, historical survival rates from out-of-hospital cardiac arrest are less than 5%.[88–90] Drezner et al.[12] reported a 7-year analysis of survival trends in the United States following exercise-related SCA in youth. During the 7-year period from 2000 to 2006, 486 total cases of exercise-related SCA were identified in individuals aged 5 to 22, with an overall survival rate of 11% (range 4–21%) per year.[12] Survival following SCA has been greatly improved by lay rescuer and public access defibrillation programs designed to shorten the time interval from SCA to shock delivery.[8,83,91–97] These programs train lay rescuers and nontraditional first responders in CPR and AED use and place AEDs in public locations where risk for SCA is high. Rapid defibrillation in public settings such as casinos, airlines, and airports has led to survival rates ranging from 41% to 74% if bystander CPR was provided and defibrillation occurred within 3 to 5 minutes of collapse.[8,83,91–97]

Limited research is available regarding early defibrillation programs in the athletic setting. Questions also exist as to whether early defibrillation in young athletes who suffer SCA from a diverse etiology of structural and electrical cardiac diseases can provide the same survival benefit as demonstrated in the older general population with a predominance of coronary artery disease as the cause of SCA. Initial research on AED utilization at college athletic venues found an overall immediate resuscitation rate of 54% in older nonstudents but did not identify a survival benefit in a small number of intercollegiate athletes with SCA.[8,78,98]

Recent research suggests for the first time an improved survival rate for young athletes with SCA if early defibrillation is achieved. Drezner et al.[77] reported on a cohort of 1710 U.S. high schools with an on-site AED program. Thirty-six cases of SCA were described, including 14 cases in high school student-athletes (mean age 16; range 14–17) and 22 cases in older nonstudents (mean age 57; range 42–71) such as employees and spectators. All but one case of SCA were witnessed, 94% received bystander CPR, and an AED deployed a shock in 30 of 36 (83%) cases. Twenty-three of the 36 SCA victims (64%) survived to hospital discharge, including 9 of 14 student-athletes (64%) and 14 of 22 older nonstudents (64%). Although this was a retrospective cohort study, the consistent reported use of on-site school-based AEDs makes this the largest study of early defibrillation to treat SCA in the school or athletic setting, and the first study to suggest a survival benefit for early defibrillation in young athletes with SCA.

Expected Time Course

Recovery after SCA depends on the amount of cardiac, neurologic, or other end-organ damage caused by the event. For young athletes who survive SCA, this is a life-changing event not only for them but also for their families, team, and community. Every effort must be made to educate athletes and families about their cardiac disorder. The psychological and emotional well-being of the athlete also must be attended to as he or she transitions out of competitive athletics and into new lifestyle modifications.

Return-to-Play Issues

Careful activity recommendations involving temporary or permanent sports disqualification for athletes with identified cardiovascular disease should be made in consultation with a cardiologist. Withdrawal from athletic training and competition in athletes with disorders predisposing to SCA can reduce the occurrence of SCD.[6] The 36th Bethesda Conference sponsored by the American College of Cardiology led to eligibility recommendations for competitive athletes with cardiovascular abnormalities.[57] These expert consensus recommendations provide a framework on which to base clearance decisions once a cardiovascular abnormality is identified. The 36th Bethesda recommendations take into account the severity of disease, potential for sudden death or disease progression, and the type and intensity of exercise involved in a particular sport.[57] The majority of athletes with a history of malignant ventricular arrhythmias, SCA, or conditions placing them at significant risk of these arrhythmias should be restricted from participation in moderate- and high-intensity sports.[99] Early detection of clinically significant cardiovascular disease through preparticipation screening will, in some cases, permit timely therapeutic interventions that may alter clinical course and allow for future athletic participation. If an individual is disqualified from competitive athletics, careful consideration should be made to develop exercise limitations and recommendations for the patient based on national guidelines.[100]

Summary

SCD is the leading fatality in sport, with compelling justification to implement effective preventive strategies. A comprehensive personal and family history and physical examination are recommended components of cardiovascular screening in athletes but offer little sensitivity in identifying athletes at risk for SCD. Integrated programs utilizing ECG offer the only model shown to reliably identify athletes at risk for SCD, and the only evidence that such a program can reduce the rate of SCD in athletes. Concern about excessively high false-positive results does not reflect more contemporary standards of ECG interpretation. ECG screening must be conducted using modern criteria to distinguish physiologic cardiac adaptations from underlying pathology and limit unnecessary diagnostic evaluations. Feasibility and practical concerns still exist regarding large-scale implementation of ECG screening in the United States, and advances in physician education are needed to improve our health system infrastructure in order to be prepared and trained in ECG screening.

Emergency response planning can greatly improve survival from SCA. The most important factors influencing such survival are the presence of a trained rescuer to initiate CPR and access to early defibrillation through on-site AEDs. The athletic community is in a unique position to have trained rescuers such as coaches, athletic trainers, and sports medicine clinicians respond immediately to SCA at organized practices and competitions. SCA in the athletic setting can be effectively treated through prompt recognition of SCA, a coordinated emergency response, early CPR, and defibrillation. Myoclonic activity is common after SCA in young athletes and should not be mistaken for a seizure. High suspicion of SCA should be maintained in any collapsed and unresponsive athlete, with application of an AED as soon as possible for rhythm analysis and defibrillation if indicated.

Clinical Case Scenarios

1. A 17-year-old male high school basketball player complained of chest pain and light-headedness during practice. The light-headedness was severe enough that he thought he might pass out. He has no known medical conditions, and this is the first time he has complained of these symptoms. He was removed from practice and allowed to rest, and his symptoms resolved. The player is asking to return for the end of practice.
    1. Should the player be allowed to return to practice?
    2. What are some underlying heart conditions that may be responsible for his symptoms and need to be ruled out before he can return to play?
2. A 13-year-old boy is playing lacrosse and is struck in the chest by the lacrosse ball. He takes a few steps after being hit in the chest and then collapses to the ground and is not moving. Rescuers respond to his side and find him to be unresponsive and not breathing.
    1. What condition has likely occurred from the chest impact of the ball?
    2. Name three things the first responder should do as part of the emergency response to this athlete.
    3. The rescuers call for an AED. What should be provided while waiting for the AED?
3. A 20-year-old male college soccer player is playing in a game and collapses. After he is on the ground for a few seconds, his arms and legs begin to move in an uncontrolled manner and it appears as if he is having a seizure. He has no history of a seizure disorder, and there was no head trauma prior to his collapse.
    1. As the first responder, what condition do you think is most likely?
    2. Should cardiopulmonary resuscitation be started?
    3. When should the AED be applied?
    4. Describe the ideal emergency response to this athlete.

Key Terms

arrhythmogenic right ventricular cardiomyopathy (ARVC)

automated external defibrillator (AED)

commotio cordis

hypertrophic cardiomyopathy (HCM)

ion channel disorder

Marfan syndrome

sudden cardiac death (SCD)

ventricular fibrillation (VF)

References

1. Rai M, Thompson PD. The definition of exertion-related cardiac events [published online ahead of print April 19, 2010]. *Br J Sports Med.* doi:10.1136/bjsm.2009.057653.
2. Maron BJ, Doerer JJ, Haas TS, Tierney DM, Mueller FO. Sudden deaths in young competitive athletes: analysis of 1866 deaths in the United States, 1980–2006. *Circulation.* 2009;119(8):1085–1092.
3. Asif I, Harmon K, Drezner J, Klossner D. Incidence and etiology of sudden death in NCAA athletes. *Clin J Sport Med.* 2010;20(2):136.

4. Maron BJ, Gohman TE, Aeppli D. Prevalence of sudden cardiac death during competitive sports activities in Minnesota high school athletes. *J Am Coll Cardiol.* 1998;32(7):1881–1884.

5. Van Camp SP, Bloor CM, Mueller FO, Cantu RC, Olson HG. Nontraumatic sports death in high school and college athletes. *Med Sci Sports Exerc.* 1995;27(5):641–647.

6. Corrado D, Basso C, Pavei A, et al. Trends in sudden cardiovascular death in young competitive athletes after implementation of a preparticipation screening program. *JAMA.* 2006;296(13):1593–1601.

7. Eckart RE, Scoville SL, Campbell CL, et al. Sudden death in young adults: a 25-year review of autopsies in military recruits. *Ann Intern Med.* 2004;141(11):829–834.

8. Drezner JA, Rogers KJ, Zimmer RR, Sennett BJ. Use of automated external defibrillators at NCAA Division I universities. *Med Sci Sports Exerc.* 2005;37(9):1487–1492.

9. Atkins DL, Everson-Stewart S, Sears GK, et al. Epidemiology and outcomes from out-of-hospital cardiac arrest in children: the Resuscitation Outcomes Consortium Epistry–Cardiac Arrest. *Circulation.* 2009;119(11):1484–1491.

10. Chugh SS, Reinier K, Balaji S, et al. Population-based analysis of sudden death in children: the Oregon Sudden Unexpected Death Study. *Heart Rhythm.* 2009;6(11):1618–1622.

11. Drezner JA, Rao AL, Heistand J, Bloomingdale MK, Harmon KG. Effectiveness of emergency response planning for sudden cardiac arrest in United States high schools with automated external defibrillators. *Circulation.* 2009;120(6):518–525.

12. Drezner JA, Chun JS, Harmon KG, Derminer L. Survival trends in the United States following exercise-related sudden cardiac arrest in the youth: 2000–2006. *Heart Rhythm.* 2008;5(6):794–799.

13. Maron BJ. Sudden death in young athletes. *N Engl J Med.* 2003;349(11):1064–1075.

14. Corrado D, Basso C, Rizzoli G, Schiavon M, Thiene G. Does sports activity enhance the risk of sudden death in adolescents and young adults? *J Am Coll Cardiol.* 2003;42(11):1959–1963.

15. Heron M, Hoyert D, Murphy S, et al. Deaths: final data for 2006. *National Vital Statistics Reports.* 2009;57(14):1–136.

16. Drezner J, Berger S, Campbell R. Current controversies in the cardiovascular screening of athletes. *Curr Sports Med Rep.* 2010;9(2):86–92.

17. Rea TD, Eisenberg MS, Sinibaldi G, White RD. Incidence of EMS-treated out-of-hospital cardiac arrest in the United States. *Resuscitation.* 2004;63(1):17–24.

18. Larsen MP, Eisenberg MS, Cummins RO, Hallstrom AP. Predicting survival from out-of-hospital cardiac arrest: a graphic model. *Ann Emerg Med.* 1993;22(11):1652–1658.

19. The American Heart Association in collaboration with the International Liaison Committee on Resuscitation. Guidelines 2000 for cardiopulmonary resuscitation and emergency cardiovascular care. Part 4. The automated external defibrillator: key link in the chain of survival. *Circulation.* 2000;102(8 suppl):I60–I76.

20. Valenzuela TD, Roe DJ, Cretin S, Spaite DW, Larsen MP. Estimating effectiveness of cardiac arrest interventions: a logistic regression survival model. *Circulation.* 1997;96(10):3308–3313.

21. White RD, Russell JK. Refibrillation, resuscitation and survival in out-of-hospital sudden cardiac arrest victims treated with biphasic automated external defibrillators. *Resuscitation.* 2002;55(1):17–23.

22. Berg MD, Clark LL, Valenzuela TD, Kern KB, Berg RA. Post-shock chest compression delays with automated external defibrillator use. *Resuscitation.* 2005;64(3):287–291.

23. Carpenter J, Rea TD, Murray JA, Kudenchuk PJ, Eisenberg MS. Defibrillation waveform and post-shock rhythm in out-of-hospital ventricular fibrillation cardiac arrest. *Resuscitation.* 2003;59(2):189–196.

24. Herlitz J, Ekstrom L, Wennerblom B, et al. Effect of bystander initiated cardiopulmonary resuscitation on ventricular fibrillation and survival after witnessed cardiac arrest outside hospital. *Br Heart J.* 1994;72(5):408–412.

25. Stiell I, Nichol G, Wells G, et al. Health-related quality of life is better for cardiac arrest survivors who received citizen cardiopulmonary resuscitation. *Circulation.* 2003;108(16):1939–1944.

26. Wik L, Kramer-Johansen J, Myklebust H, et al. Quality of cardiopulmonary resuscitation during out-of-hospital cardiac arrest. *JAMA.* 2005;293(3):299–304.

27. Kerber RE, Becker LB, Bourland JD, et al. Automatic external defibrillators for public access defibrillation: recommendations for specifying and reporting arrhythmia analysis algorithm performance, incorporating new waveforms, and enhancing safety. A statement for health professionals from the American Heart Association Task Force on Automatic External Defibrillation, Subcommittee on AED Safety and Efficacy. *Circulation.* 1997;95(6):1677–1682.

28. Gundry JW, Comess KA, DeRook FA, Jorgenson D, Bardy GH. Comparison of naive sixth-grade children with trained professionals in the use of an automated external defibrillator. *Circulation.* 1999;100(16):1703–1707.

29. Maron BJ, Gohman TE, Kyle SB, Estes NA 3rd, Link MS. Clinical profile and spectrum of commotio cordis. *JAMA.* 2002;287(9):1142–1146.

30. Weinstock J, Maron BJ, Song C, et al. Failure of commercially available chest wall protectors to prevent sudden cardiac death induced by chest wall blows in an experimental model of commotio cordis. *Pediatrics.* 2006;117(4):e656–662.

31. Link MS, Maron BJ, Stickney RE, et al. Automated external defibrillator arrhythmia detection in a model of cardiac arrest due to commotio cordis. *J Cardiovasc Electrophysiol.* 2003;14(1):83–87.

32. Maron BJ, Shirani J, Poliac LC, et al. Sudden death in young competitive athletes. Clinical, demographic, and pathological profiles. *JAMA.* 1996;276(3):199–204.

33. Maron BJ, Thompson PD, Ackerman MJ, et al. Recommendations and considerations related to preparticipation screening for cardiovascular abnormalities in competitive athletes: 2007 update—a scientific statement from the American Heart Association Council on Nutrition, Physical Activity, and Metabolism, endorsed by the American College of Cardiology Foundation. *Circulation.* 2007;115(12):1643–1655.

34. Maron BJ, Thompson PD, Puffer JC, et al. Cardiovascular preparticipation screening of competitive athletes. A statement for health professionals from the Sudden Death Committee (clinical cardiology) and Congenital Cardiac Defects Committee (cardiovascular disease in the young), American Heart Association. *Circulation.* 1996;94(4):850–856.

35. Maron BJ, Carney KP, Lever HM, et al. Relationship of race to sudden cardiac death in competitive athletes with hypertrophic cardiomyopathy. *J Am Coll Cardiol.* 2003;41(6):974–980.

36. Corrado D, Basso C, Thiene G, et al. Spectrum of clinicopathologic manifestations of arrhythmogenic right ventricular cardiomyopathy/dysplasia: a multicenter study. *J Am Coll Cardiol.* 1997;30(6):1512–1520.

37. Drezner JA, Courson RW, Roberts WO, et al. Inter-association task force recommendations on emergency preparedness and management of sudden cardiac arrest in high school and college athletic programs: a consensus statement. *Heart Rhythm.* 2007;4(4):549–565.

38. Doolan A, Langlois N, Semsarian C. Causes of sudden cardiac death in young Australians. *Med J Aust.* 2004;180(3): 110–112.

39. Puranik R, Chow CK, Duflou JA, Kilborn MJ, McGuire MA. Sudden death in the young. *Heart Rhythm.* 2005;2(12): 1277–1282.

40. Maron BJ, Pelliccia A, Spirito P. Cardiac disease in young trained athletes. Insights into methods for distinguishing athlete's heart from structural heart disease, with particular emphasis on hypertrophic cardiomyopathy. *Circulation.* 1995;91(5): 1596–1601.

41. Corrado D, Basso C, Schiavon M, Thiene G. Screening for hypertrophic cardiomyopathy in young athletes. *N Engl J Med.* 1998;339(6):364–369.

42. Stefani L, Galanti G, Toncelli L, et al. Bicuspid aortic valve in competitive athletes. *Br J Sports Med.* 2008;42(1):31–35; discussion 35.

43. Basavarajaiah S, Wilson M, Whyte G, et al. Prevalence of hypertrophic cardiomyopathy in highly trained athletes: relevance to pre-participation screening. *J Am Coll Cardiol.* 2008;51(10):1033–1039.

44. Maron BJ. Hypertrophic cardiomyopathy. *Lancet.* 1997;350(9071):127–133.

45. Maron BJ, Roberts WC, Epstein SE. Sudden death in hypertrophic cardiomyopathy: a profile of 78 patients. *Circulation.* 1982;65(7):1388–1394.

46. Melacini P, Cianfrocca C, Calore C, et al. Abstract 3390. Marginal overlap between electrocardiographic abnormalities in patients with hypertrophic cardiomyopathy and trained athletes: implications for preparticipation screening. *Circulation.* 2007;116(II):765.

47. Pelliccia A, Spataro A, Maron BJ. Prospective echocardiographic screening for coronary artery anomalies in 1,360 elite competitive athletes. *Am J Cardiol.* 1993;72(12):978–979.

48. Basso C, Corrado D, Thiene G. Arrhythmogenic right ventricular cardiomyopathy in athletes: diagnosis, management, and recommendations for sport activity. *Cardiol Clin.* 2007;25(3):415–422.

49. Ammash NM, Sundt TM, Connolly HM. Marfan syndrome: diagnosis and management. *Curr Probl Cardiol.* 2008;33(1):7–39.

50. De Paepe A, Devereux RB, Dietz HC, Hennekam RC, Pyeritz RE. Revised diagnostic criteria for the Marfan syndrome. *Am J Med Genet.* 1996;62(4):417–426.

51. Eckart RE, Scoville SL, Shry EA, Potter RN, Tedrow U. Causes of sudden death in young female military recruits. *Am J Cardiol.* 2006;97(12):1756–1758.

52. Lehnart SE, Ackerman MJ, Benson DW, et al. Inherited arrhythmias: a National Heart, Lung, and Blood Institute and Office of Rare Diseases workshop consensus report about the diagnosis, phenotyping, molecular mechanisms, and therapeutic approaches for primary cardiomyopathies of gene mutations affecting ion channel function. *Circulation.* 2007;116(20): 2325–2345.

53. Hobbs JB, Peterson DR, Moss AJ, et al. Risk of aborted cardiac arrest or sudden cardiac death during adolescence in the long-QT syndrome. *JAMA.* 2006;296(10):1249–1254.

54. Leenhardt A, Lucet V, Denjoy I, et al. Catecholaminergic polymorphic ventricular tachycardia in children. A 7-year follow-up of 21 patients. *Circulation.* 1995;91(5):1512–1519.

55. Corrado D, Pelliccia A, Bjornstad HH, et al. Cardiovascular pre-participation screening of young competitive athletes for prevention of sudden death: proposal for a common European protocol. Consensus Statement of the Study Group of Sport Cardiology of the Working Group of Cardiac Rehabilitation and Exercise Physiology and the Working Group of Myocardial and Pericardial Diseases of the European Society of Cardiology. *Eur Heart J.* 2005;26(5):516–524.

56. Ljungqvist A, Jenoure P, Engebretsen L, et al. The International Olympic Committee (IOC) consensus statement on periodic health evaluation of elite athletes March 2009. *Br J Sports Med.* 2009;43(9):631–643.

57. Maron BJ, Zipes DP. 36th Bethesda Conference: eligibility recommendations for competitive athletes with cardiovascular abnormalities. *J Am Coll Cardiol.* 2005;45(8):1312–1377.

58. Fuller CM, McNulty CM, Spring DA, et al. Prospective screening of 5,615 high school athletes for risk of sudden cardiac death. *Med Sci Sports Exerc*. 1997;29(9):1131–1138.

59. Wilson MG, Basavarajaiah S, Whyte GP, et al. Efficacy of personal symptom and family history questionnaires when screening for inherited cardiac pathologies: the role of electrocardiography. *Br J Sports Med*. 2008;42(3):207–211.

60. Bessem B, Groot FP, Nieuwland W. The Lausanne recommendations: a Dutch experience. *Br J Sports Med*. 2009;43(9):708–715.

61. Baggish AL, Hutter AM Jr, Wang F, et al. Cardiovascular screening in college athletes with and without electrocardiography: a cross-sectional study. *Ann Intern Med*. 2;152(5):269–275.

62. Hevia AC, Fernandez MM, Palacio JM, et al. ECG as a part of the preparticipation screening programme: an old and still present international dilemma [published online ahead of print July 15, 2010]. *Br J Sports Med*. doi:10.1136/bjsm.2009.063958.

63. de Noronha SV, Sharma S, Papadakis M, et al. Aetiology of sudden cardiac death in athletes in the United Kingdom: a pathological study. *Heart*. 2009;95(17):1409–1414.

64. Basso C, Maron BJ, Corrado D, Thiene G. Clinical profile of congenital coronary artery anomalies with origin from the wrong aortic sinus leading to sudden death in young competitive athletes. *J Am Coll Cardiol*. 2000;35(6):1493–1501.

65. Gomez JE, Lantry BR, Saathoff KN. Current use of adequate preparticipation history forms for heart disease screening of high school athletes. *Arch Pediatr Adolesc Med*. 1999;153(7):723–726.

66. Glover DW, Glover DW, Maron BJ. Evolution in the process of screening United States high school student-athletes for cardiovascular disease. *Am J Cardiol*. 2007;100(11):1709–1712.

67. Chaitman BR. An electrocardiogram should not be included in routine preparticipation screening of young athletes. *Circulation*. 2007;116(22):2610–2614; discussion 2615.

68. Myerburg RJ, Vetter VL. Electrocardiograms should be included in preparticipation screening of athletes. *Circulation*. 2007;116(22):2616–2626; discussion 2626.

69. International Olympic Committee Medical Commission. *Sudden Cardiovascular Death in Sport: Lausanne Recommendations on Preparticipation Cardiovascular Screening*. December 10, 2004. http://multimedia.olympic.org/pdf/en_report_886.pdf.

70. Thompson PD, Levine BD. Protecting athletes from sudden cardiac death. *JAMA*. 2006;296(13):1648–1650.

71. Maron BJ, Bodison SA, Wesley YE, Tucker E, Green KJ. Results of screening a large group of intercollegiate competitive athletes for cardiovascular disease. *J Am Coll Cardiol*. 1987;10(6):1214–1221.

72. Pelliccia A, Culasso F, Di Paolo FM, et al. Prevalence of abnormal electrocardiograms in a large, unselected population undergoing pre-participation cardiovascular screening. *Eur Heart J*. 2007;28(16):2006–2010.

73. Nora M, Zimmerman F, Ow P, Fenner P, Marek J. Abstract 3718. Preliminary findings of ECG screening in 9,125 young adults. *Circulation*. 2007;116(II):845.

74. Drezner J, Pluim B, Engebretsen L. Prevention of sudden cardiac death in athletes: new data and modern perspectives confront challenges in the 21st century. *Br J Sports Med*. 2009;43(9):625–626.

75. Corrado D, Pelliccia A, Heidbuchel H, et al. Recommendations for interpretation of 12-lead electrocardiogram in the athlete. *Eur Heart J*. 2010;31(2):243–259.

76. Hauff SR, Rea TD, Culley LL, et al. Factors impeding dispatcher-assisted telephone cardiopulmonary resuscitation. *Ann Emerg Med*. 2003;42(6):731–737.

77. Drezner J, Harmon K, Heistand J, Cramer M, Rao A. Effectiveness of emergency response planning for sudden cardiac arrest in United States high schools with automated external defibrillators. *Br J Sports Med*. 2008;42:515.

78. Drezner JA, Rogers KJ. Sudden cardiac arrest in intercollegiate athletes: detailed analysis and outcomes of resuscitation in nine cases. *Heart Rhythm*. 2006;3(7):755–759.

79. Ruppert M, Reith MW, Widmann JH, et al. Checking for breathing: evaluation of the diagnostic capability of emergency medical services personnel, physicians, medical students, and medical laypersons. *Ann Emerg Med*. 1999;34(6):720–729.

80. ECC Committee, Subcommittees and Task Forces of the American Heart Association. 2005 American Heart Association guidelines for cardiopulmonary resuscitation and emergency cardiovascular care. Part 4. Adult basic life support. *Circulation*. 2005;112(24 suppl):IV19–34.

81. Eberle B, Dick WF, Schneider T, et al. Checking the carotid pulse check: diagnostic accuracy of first responders in patients with and without a pulse. *Resuscitation*. 1996;33(2):107–116.

82. Drezner JA, Courson RW, Roberts WO, et al. Inter-association task force recommendations on emergency preparedness and management of sudden cardiac arrest in high school and college athletic programs: a consensus statement. *Clin J Sport Med*. 2007;17(2):87–103.

83. Hallstrom AP, Ornato JP, Weisfeldt M, et al. Public-access defibrillation and survival after out-of-hospital cardiac arrest. *N Engl J Med*. 2004;351(7):637–646.

84. Andersen J, Courson RW, Kleiner DM, McLoda TA. National Athletic Trainers' Association position statement: emergency planning in athletics. *J Athl Train*. 2002;37(1):99–104.

85. Hazinski MF, Markenson D, Neish S, et al. Response to cardiac arrest and selected life-threatening medical emergencies: the medical emergency response plan for schools: a statement for healthcare providers, policymakers, school administrators, and community leaders. *Circulation*. 2004;109(2):278–291.

86. Myerburg RJ, Estes NA 3rd, Fontaine JM, Link MS, Zipes DP. Task Force 10: automated external defibrillators. *J Am Coll Cardiol*. 2005;45(8):1369–1371.

87. Kim F, Carlbom D. Therapeutic hypothermia for cardiac arrest: yes, we can. *Rev Esp Cardiol*. 2009;62(7):726–728.

88. Becker LB, Ostrander MP, Barrett J, Kondos GT. Outcome of CPR in a large metropolitan area—where are the survivors? *Ann Emerg Med.* 1991;20(4):355–361.
89. Gallagher EJ, Lombardi G, Gennis P. Effectiveness of bystander cardiopulmonary resuscitation and survival following out-of-hospital cardiac arrest. *JAMA.* 1995;274(24):1922–1925.
90. Bobrow BJ, Clark LL, Ewy GA, et al. Minimally interrupted cardiac resuscitation by emergency medical services for out-of-hospital cardiac arrest. *JAMA.* 2008;299(10):1158–1165.
91. Caffrey SL, Willoughby PJ, Pepe PE, Becker LB. Public use of automated external defibrillators. *N Engl J Med.* 2002;347(16): 1242–1247.
92. Page RL, Joglar JA, Kowal RC, et al. Use of automated external defibrillators by a U.S. airline. *N Engl J Med.* 2000;343(17): 1210–1216.
93. Valenzuela TD, Roe DJ, Nichol G, et al. Outcomes of rapid defibrillation by security officers after cardiac arrest in casinos. *N Engl J Med.* 2000;343(17):1206–1209.
94. Weaver WD, Hill D, Fahrenbruch CE, et al. Use of the automatic external defibrillator in the management of out-of-hospital cardiac arrest. *N Engl J Med.* 1988;319(11):661–666.
95. White RD, Asplin BR, Bugliosi TF, Hankins DG. High discharge survival rate after out-of-hospital ventricular fibrillation with rapid defibrillation by police and paramedics. *Ann Emerg Med.* 1996;28(5):480–485.
96. Myerburg RJ, Fenster J, Velez M, et al. Impact of community-wide police car deployment of automated external defibrillators on survival from out-of-hospital cardiac arrest. *Circulation.* 2002;106(9):1058–1064.
97. White RD, Bunch TJ, Hankins DG. Evolution of a community-wide early defibrillation programme experience over 13 years using police/fire personnel and paramedics as responders. *Resuscitation.* 2005;65(3):279–283.
98. Coris EE, Miller E, Sahebzamani F. Sudden cardiac death in Division I collegiate athletics: analysis of automated external defibrillator utilization in National Collegiate Athletic Association Division I athletic programs. *Clin J Sport Med.* 2005;15(2):87–91.
99. Link MS. Prevention of sudden cardiac death: return to sport considerations in athletes with identified cardiovascular abnormalities. *Br J Sports Med.* 2009;43(9):685–689.
100. Maron BJ, Chaitman BR, Ackerman MJ, et al. Recommendations for physical activity and recreational sports participation for young patients with genetic cardiovascular diseases. *Circulation.* 2004;109(22):2807–2816.

Prevention of Sudden Cardiac Death in Older Athletes

Shishir Mathur, MD

Fawad Kazi, MD

Paul D. Thompson, MD, FACC, FACSM

Studies of exercise-related **sudden cardiac death** (**SCD**) in adults have defined "adults" as individuals older than 35 to 40 years.[1,2] This age distinction is based on the observation that the causes of exercise-related SCD are different in young and older individuals. **Coronary artery disease** (**CAD**) is the most frequent cause of exercise-related SCD in adults, whereas congenital or inherited cardiac conditions are the most frequent causes of exercise-related SCD in the young.[1,2] Sudden death in young athletes is discussed in Chapter 2, so the present chapter addresses exercise-related SCD in adult athletes.

A competitive athlete has been described as "one who participates in an organized team or individual sport requiring systematic training and regular competition against others while placing a high premium on athletic excellence and achievement."[3] Compared with young individuals, fewer adults participate in such organized training and competition. In addition, although exercise-related SCD is more frequent in adults, it is still relatively rare. The combination of fewer athletes and fewer events necessitates that any discussion of SCD in adult athletes be based on exercise-related cardiac events in the general adult population and not be restricted to individuals meeting the definition of an athlete.

Exercise-related cardiac events are defined as those occurring during or within 1 hour after vigorous physical exertion.[4,5] Vigorous exercise is usually defined as an absolute exercise work rate of 6 **metabolic equivalents** (**METs**) or an oxygen uptake of approximately 21 mL/kg/min.[5] This level of exertion is usually elicited by activities such as jogging. This definition of vigorous exercise facilitates studying exercise-related events, but the intensity and cardiovascular stress of any exercise task for an individual vary inversely with that individual's

sudden cardiac death (SCD)
Sudden death occurring during or within 1 hour after exercise due to a cardiovascular disorder.

coronary artery disease (CAD)
Condition in which plaque builds up inside the coronary arteries.

metabolic equivalent (MET)
Ratio comparing a person's metabolic rate while seated and resting to his or her metabolic rate while performing some task.

exercise capacity. Consequently, a specific exercise work rate for a less fit individual elicits a higher heart rate, systolic blood pressure, and myocardial oxygen demand than it does for a more fit subject, and levels of exercise (<6 METs) may represent maximal or near-maximal exercise for individuals with poor maximal exercise capacity.

Epidemiology

The incidence of exercise-related SCD is higher in adults than in young athletes because of the increasing prevalence of occult CAD with advancing age. There are few studies providing incidence figures for exercise-related SCD in adults, but among the most cited are the Rhode Island[6] and Seattle[7] studies. Both studies suffer from being over 25 years old and from including only 10 and 9 sudden cardiac deaths, respectively. Nevertheless, both report a similar incidence of SCD among previously healthy individuals.

The Rhode Island study collected data on all individuals dying during jogging, using the state's medical examiner's office and the fact that sudden unexplained deaths in the state require a medical examiner's evaluation.[6] The prevalence of jogging was estimated using state population statistics and a random-digit telephone survey that inquired about exercise habits. There were 10 cardiac deaths during jogging, but half of these victims had a history or prior electrocardiographic evidence of coronary artery disease. If these individuals were eliminated, the exercise-related SCD rate for healthy men over age 30 was only 1 death per year for every 15,240 men, or an hourly death rate of 1 death per 792,000 hours of jogging.[6] There were no jogging deaths in women.

The Seattle study utilized that city's highly developed emergency medical system to collect reports of cardiac arrests during vigorous physical activity in previously healthy men. The prevalence of vigorous activity was estimated by surveying a community sample of healthy men. The incidence of SCD during vigorous exertion was 1 death per year for every 18,000 physically active men, or an hourly death rate of 1 death per 4.76 million person hours.

There are few reported exercise-related SCDs in adult women. In the Nurses' Health Study, which followed the cardiovascular health of 84,888 women for 1.93 million person years, there were only 9 SCDs during moderate to vigorous physical exercise (defined as physical activity greater than 5 METs on a scale of 1 to 8 METs), yielding an incidence of 1 death per 36.5 million hours of moderate to vigorous exertion.[8] This difference between men[7] and women[8] can be explained in part by the lower CAD prevalence in women compared with men of similar age and the probability that older adult women, who are more likely to have CAD and therefore be at risk, are less likely to participate in vigorous exercise compared with younger women. Nevertheless, there is also evidence that nonathletic women have a lower risk of CAD-related SCD than men, suggesting that female gender protects against SCD.[9,10]

Both the Rhode Island and Seattle studies demonstrated that exercise increases the risk of SCD. This appears somewhat paradoxical because overall regular physical exertion reduces CAD events,[11] but the risk of SCD is transiently increased during the exercise period. Exercise also transiently increases the risk of myocardial infarction (MI) by the mechanisms discussed later in this chapter.[12–14]

The CAD event rates reported in these studies, obtained from healthy individuals in the general population, are likely lower in athletes because regular exercise not only decreases the incidence of acute cardiac events but also decreases the risk that such events will occur during exercise. In the Seattle study the risk of a cardiac arrest during vigorous exercise relative to less strenuous activities was 56-fold higher in habitually sedentary men, but only 5-fold higher in active men.[7] Similarly, the relative risk of an MI during exercise compared with rest is highest in the most physically inactive men and lowest in those who are most physically active.[12,13,15]

Some more direct estimates of the frequency of exercise-related SCDs in adult athletes exist. The risk of SCD during a marathon is approximately 1 death per 125,000 participants, or 1 death per 500,000 hours of participation.[16]

Because CAD is the primary cause of exercise-related SCD, it should be apparent that the risk of such events increases with the risk of occult CAD or the prevalence of diagnosed disease. Among Dutch athletes aged 13 to 68 years who suffered an exercise-related acute cardiac event, the most powerful predictor of the event was a prior history of cardiovascular disease.[17]

Pathophysiology

CAD accounts for approximately 80% of sudden deaths during physical exertion in exercising adults and in adult athletes.[1] The remaining deaths are due to a variety of noncoronary causes, such as hypertrophic cardiomyopathy, mitral valve prolapse, or acquired mitral or aortic valve disease.[1]

Plaque disruption or rupture leading to acute coronary thrombosis is the most common pathophysiologic mechanism of acute myocardial infarction (AMI) and subsequent sudden cardiac death in previously asymptomatic adults during exertion.[18,19] How exercise initiates plaque disruption is not clear, but increased coronary artery wall stress from increases in heart rate and blood pressure, exercise-induced coronary artery vasomotion in diseased artery segments, and increased flexing and bending of the epicardial coronary arteries are all possible contributors to plaque rupture during exercise.[18,19]

Alternatively, the increased wall stress and coronary flexing just mentioned could deepen existing coronary plaque fissures, leading to thrombosis. The increase in circulating catecholamines during exercise could also increase platelet aggregation and contribute to thrombosis.[20,21] It is likely that all or combinations of these processes participate in causing SCD and AMI in adults during exercise. Consequently, plaque disruption producing acute cardiac ischemia and MI or SCD is responsible for most SCD in previously healthy adult exercisers and athletes. The common final pathway for SCD is usually ventricular fibrillation produced by the acute ischemia and myocardial injury.

In contrast, patients with prior CAD and MI could have plaque disruption and the processes just discussed, but they can also develop ventricular fibrillation arising from scarred myocardium.

Prevention of Sudden Cardiac Death in Adult Athletes

There are no proven strategies to reduce acute cardiovascular events during vigorous physical exercise in adult athletes. The strategies described in this section appear to be potentially beneficial, although none has been evaluated in randomized controlled trials.

Preparticipation Screening

A medical history and physical examination seeking increased CAD risk factors and evidence of valvular heart disease are routinely recommended prior to vigorous physical exertion. Even low CAD risk factors and a normal physical examination do not guarantee against sudden cardiovascular events during physical exertion and should not provide a false sense of security.

Exercise stress testing is frequently recommended as a screening procedure prior to vigorous exercise. A "positive" exercise test with or without imaging indicates a flow-limiting coronary lesion and therefore cannot detect individuals with a nonobstructive, but vulnerable, atherosclerotic plaque, the likely cause of most exercise-related cardiac events in adult athletes. Consequently, a negative exercise test does not rule out the presence of vulnerable plaques and the risk of an exercise-related cardiac event. On the other hand, exercise testing is prudent in individuals with known CAD to ensure that they do not have exercise-induced ischemia.

Although there are no controlled clinical trials evaluating the utility of exercise stress testing in asymptomatic healthy adults before vigorous physical exercise, there are consensus recommendations from the American College of Cardiology (ACC)/American Heart Association (AHA), the American College of Sports Medicine (ACSM), and the United States Preventive Services Task Force (USPSTF) (Table 3.1). Both the ACC/AHA and ACSM recommend routine exercise testing prior to vigorous exercise training in individuals at increased risk of having underlying CAD, including those with diabetes, asymptomatic men older than 45 years and women older than 55 years, and those with two or more risk factors (other than age and gender) for CAD (Table 3.2). In contrast, the USPSTF recommends against routine exercise stress testing in healthy individuals due to insufficient evidence for any benefits of exercise stress testing prior to starting an exercise training program.[22] Furthermore, a 2009 decision analysis recommended against exercise testing in asymptomatic individuals at all levels of risk because the exercise deaths prevented by exercise testing were fewer than the deaths produced by medical intervention.[23] There is general consensus that patients with known CAD should undergo assessment of left ventricular function and maximal exercise treadmill testing for risk stratification before participation in athletic activities **(Table 3.3)**.[24–26]

Education and Awareness

Educating athletes, exercise attendants, physicians, and other health care providers about warning symptoms for CAD events may lead to early recognition of subjects at high risk for cardiac events. Between 50% and 80% of adult athletes who suffered SCD during an athletic event had probable cardiac symptoms before death **(Table 3.4)**.[27] Because these symptoms were often atypical and assumed to be gastrointestinal in origin, subjects either did not seek medical attention or received inappropriate medical advice. Nonspecific symptoms such as fatigue and flulike symptoms are associated with a 12% greater likelihood of exercise-related acute cardiac events.[17] The specificity of such complaints is poor, but advising athletes to seek medical advice if they develop new symptoms, especially if these are associated with exercise, seems prudent.

TABLE 3.1	Recommendations for Exercise Testing Before Exercise Training in Subjects with No Known Coronary Artery Disease	
ACC/AHA	**ACSM**	**USPSTF**
Recommended for symptomatic persons with diabetes mellitus who plan to start vigorous exercise (class IIa[a])	Recommended for symptomatic persons with diabetes mellitus (or other metabolic disease) who plan to start moderate (40% to 50% Vo_2 reserve) to vigorous (>60% Vo_2 reserve) exercise	Recommends against routine exercise testing of low-risk adults in general and finds insufficient evidence for exercise testing before exercise training
Recommended for symptomatic men >45 years and women >55 years who plan to start vigorous exercise (class IIb[a])	Recommended for asymptomatic men >45 years and women >55 years or those who meet the threshold for more than two risk factors who plan to start vigorous exercise	

Abbreviations: ACC, American College of Cardiology; AHA, American Heart Association; ACSM, American College of Sports Medicine; USPSTF, United States Preventive Services Task Force; Vo_2, maximal exercise oxygen uptake capacity (maximum capacity of an individual's body to transport and utilize oxygen during incremental exercise, which reflects the physical fitness of the individual).

[a] ACC/AHA class IIa indicates that the weight of evidence or opinion is in favor of usefulness or efficacy; class IIb indicates that the usefulness or efficacy is less well established by evidence or opinion.

Source: From Thompson PD, Franklin BA, Balady GJ, et al. Exercise and acute cardiovascular events placing the risks into perspective: a scientific statement from the American Heart Association Council on Nutrition, Physical Activity, and Metabolism and the Council on Clinical Cardiology. *Circulation*. 2007;115:2358–2368. Reprinted with permission. Copyright © 2007, American Heart Association, Inc.

<table>
<tr><td colspan="2">TABLE 3.2   Atherosclerotic Cardiovascular Disease (CVD) Risk Factor Thresholds For Use with ACSM Risk Stratification</td></tr>
</table>

Positive Risk Factors	Defining Criteria
Age	Men $\geq$45 yr; Women $\geq$55 yr
Family history	Myocardial infarction, coronary revascularization or sudden death before 55 yr of age in father or other male first-degree relative, or before 65 yr in mother or other female first-degree relative
Cigarette smoking	Current cigarette smoker or those who quit within previous 6 months or exposure to environmental tobacco smoke
Sedentary lifestyle	Not participating in at least 30 min of moderate intensity (40%–60%VO_2R) physical activity on at least three days of week for at least 3 months
Obesity	BMI $\geq$30 kg/m$_2$ or waist girth >102 cm (>40 inches) for men and >88 cm (35 inches) for women
Hypertension	Systolic Blood Pressure $\geq$140 mmHg and/or Diastolic Blood Pressure $\geq$90 mmHg, confirmed by measurements on at least two separate occasions or on anti-hypertensive medication
Dyslipidemia	Low Density Lipoprotein cholesterol (LDL-C) $\geq$130 mg/dl (3.37 mmol/L) or High Density Lipoprotein cholesterol (HDL-C) <40 mg/dl (1.04 mmol/L) or on lipid-lowering medication. If total serum cholesterol is all that is available use $\geq$200 mg/dl (5.18 mmol/L)
Pre-diabetes	Impaired fasting glucose (IFG) = fasting plasma glucose $\geq$100 mg/dl (5.50 mmol/L) but <126 mg/dl (6.93 mmol/L) or impaired glucose tolerance = 2-hour values in oral glucose tolerance test (OGTT) $\geq$140 mg/dl (7.70 mmol/L) but < 200 mg/dl (11.00 mmol/L) confirmed by measurements on at least two separate occasions
Negative Risk Factor	**Defining Criteria**
HDL-C	$\geq$60 mg/dl (1.55 mmol/L)

Source: *American College of Sports Medicine's Guidelines for Exercise Testing and Prescription; Eighth Edition.* Lippincott Williams & Wilkins; 2009. Reprinted with permission.

Preparing Athletic Facilities for Handling Cardiac Emergencies

The AHA and ACSM have recommended that fitness facility staff be trained in cardiopulmonary resuscitation, that fitness facilities have automatic external defibrillators available, and that fitness facilities screen participants using the questionnaire developed by AHA/ACSM to identify individuals at risk from exercise.[28,29] AHA/ACSM also recommend that fitness centers establish protocols and a hotline to summon emergency medical services. These protocols and skills should be practiced during regularly scheduled emergency drills. These recommendations are reasonable, although there is no evidence that questionnaires are effective in preventing exercise-related cardiac events. Emergency medical services should be available during sporting events where a large number of people are participating. These services should include on-site paramedical staff trained in performing cardiopulmonary resuscitation and fully equipped ambulances for prompt transfer of patients to hospitals.

TABLE 3.3	Risk Stratification and Recommendations for Subjects with Known Coronary Artery Disease[a] Prior to Exercise Training, Based on a 36th Bethesda Conference Task Force

Low Risk	High Risk
• Normal LV function (EF > 50%)	• Abnormal LV function (EF < 50%)
• Normal exercise tolerance for age[b]	• Evidence of exercise-induced myocardial ischemia or complex ventricular arrhythmias
• No exercise-induced ischemia or complex ventricular arrhythmias	• Hemodynamically significant coronary artery stenosis (>50%) (if angiography performed)
• Absence of hemodynamically significant coronary stenosis (>50%) in any major coronary artery (if angiogram performed)	
• Successful myocardial revascularization (if performed)	

Exercise Recommendations

• Participate in low-intensity dynamic and low- to moderate-intensity static competitive sports	• Participate in low-intensity competitive sports only
• Avoid intensely competitive situations	• Restricted from moderate- and high-intensity sports
• Aggressive treatment of atherosclerotic risk factors	• Aggressive treatment of atherosclerotic risk factors

Abbreviations: EF, ejection fraction; LV, left ventricle.

[a] Known coronary artery disease is identified as any one of the following: (1) history of myocardial infarction; (2) history suggestive of angina pectoris with objective evidence of inducible ischemia; (3) coronary atherosclerosis of any degree demonstrated by coronary imaging studies, including catheter-based angiography, coronary computed tomography, or magnetic resonance angiography.

[b] Metabolic equivalents (METs) > 10 or maximal exercise oxygen uptake capacity (Vo$_2$max) > 35 mL O$_2$/kg-min for age < 50 years; METs > 9 or Vo$_2$max > 31 mL O$_2$/kg-min for ages 50–59 years; METs > 8 or Vo$_2$max > 28 mL O$_2$/kg-min for ages 60–69 years; METs > 7 or Vo$_2$max > 24 mL O$_2$/kg-min for age > 70 years.

Source: Data from Thompson PD, Balady GJ, Chaitman BR, et al. Task Force 6: coronary artery disease. *J Am Coll Cardiol.* 2005;45(8):1348–1353.

Exercise Recommendations

Because the highest rate of cardiac events occurs in individuals unaccustomed to physical exercise,[7,12–15] it is possible that a gradually progressive exercise training program will reduce the likelihood of exercise-related cardiac events. Also, some healthy adults initiate an exercise program because they are concerned that new symptoms may be CAD. Consequently, ostensibly healthy adults seeking advice on initiating an exercise program should be queried about new symptoms, and those experiencing symptoms suggestive of cardiac ischemia should undergo appropriate evaluation prior to exercise training.

Patients with known CAD should undergo risk stratification using left ventricular function assessment and maximal exercise treadmill testing based on recommendations from the 36th Bethesda Conference (Table 3.3). Athletes who have mildly increased risk can participate in low-intensity dynamic and low- to moderate-intensity static competitive sports but should avoid intensely competitive situations. Athletes with known CAD who are high risk should generally be restricted to low-intensity competitive sports.[26,30] These recommendations are not rigid, however, and some athletes can be allowed to return to more vigorous and even very competitive activities depending on their risk profile. All athletes with atherosclerotic

TABLE 3.4 Prodromal Symptoms Reported by Forty-Five Subjects Within One Week of Their Sudden Death

Symptom	Number of Reports
Chest pain/angina	15
Increasing fatigue	12
Indigestion, heartburn, or gastrointestinal symptoms	10
Excessive breathlessness	6
Ear or neck pain	5
Vague malaise	5
Upper respiratory tract infection	4
Dizziness/palpitations	3
Severe headache	2

Source: From Thompson PD, Franklin BA, Balady GJ, et al. Exercise and acute cardiovascular events placing the risks into perspective: a scientific statement from the American Heart Association Council on Nutrition, Physical Activity, and Metabolism and the Council on Clinical Cardiology. *Circulation*. 2007;115:2358–2368. Reprinted with permission. Copyright © 2007, American Heart Association, Inc.

CAD should receive aggressive treatment for atherosclerotic risk factors. Patients with known advanced CAD should be advised to perform at least 5 minutes of warm-up and cool-down before and after exercise training sessions. A warm-up will reduce the likelihood of cardiac ischemia with sudden intense physical effort, and a cool-down will prevent the sudden decrease in central blood volume that can occur with sudden cessation of physical activity.[31,32]

Environmental factors such as extreme cold conditions have been associated with acute cardiovascular events.[33–36] Physically inactive subjects and patients with known CAD should therefore avoid unaccustomed strenuous physical exercise under extreme environmental conditions. Increased altitude increases the hemodynamic response to a given submaximal work rate due to decreased oxygen concentration in inhaled air. Individuals exercising at altitudes higher than 1500 m should gradually increase their exercise training to allow acclimatization.[25,37]

Summary

The benefits of physical exercise outweigh the risk of exercise-related cardiac events. Nevertheless, exercise acutely and transiently increases the risk of cardiac events, especially in those performing unaccustomed physical exercise and those with underlying CAD. This chapter summarizes prevention strategies that seem prudent **(Table 3.5)** while recognizing that none has been tested by randomized controlled clinical trials.

Clinical Case Scenarios

1. A 40-year-old man wants to start intensive training for running a marathon. He does not report any symptoms of cardiac ischemia during mild to moderate exercise. He does not have any cardiovascular risk factors by history, and physical examination is completely normal.
   1. What screening recommendations would you perform in this scenario?
   2. What exercise recommendations would you provide in this scenario?
   3. What main factors should you take into consideration when making these decisions?

TABLE 3.5	Strategies to Prevent Sudden Cardiac Death in Adult Athletes

1. Perform preparticipation screening history and physical examination (or AHA/ACSM screening questionnaires at fitness facilities).
2. Perform exercise stress testing and other appropriate cardiac investigations in selected healthy subjects based on risk factors and physical exam findings.
3. Risk-stratify using left ventricular function assessment and exercise stress testing in patients with known CAD and recommend appropriate exercise restrictions based on risk assessment in these subjects.
4. Educate athletes and trainers on reporting possible prodromal symptoms suggestive of CAD.
5. Prepare fitness centers with external cardiac defibrillators and staff trained in cardiopulmonary resuscitation.
6. Gradually increase the physical training program for individuals who are relatively physically inactive, rather than using a sudden or strenuous onset.
7. Avoid unaccustomed physical activity, especially in extreme environmental conditions such as heat, cold, and high altitude.

Abbreviations: ACSM, American College of Sports Medicine; AHA, American Heart Association; CAD, coronary artery disease.

2. A 56-year-old man wants to start an intensive aerobic exercise program and wants to run a marathon in 6 to 12 months' time. He has been physically active doing mild to moderate aerobic exercise for at least 2 years. He has a past history of myocardial infarction approximately 3 years ago. His other risk factors for CAD are hypercholesterolemia and family history of CAD in his father at age 48.
   1. What kind of screening should this athlete undergo to determine exercise recommendations?
   2. What restrictions should you probably place on his exercise habits?
   3. What type of exercise is best for this athlete?

Key Terms

coronary artery disease (CAD)

metabolic equivalent (MET)

sudden cardiac death (SCD)

References

1. Maron BJ, Epstein SE, Roberts WC. Causes of sudden death in competitive athletes. *J Am Coll Cardiol.* 1986;7:204–214.
2. Maron BJ, Thompson PD, Ackerman MJ, et al. Recommendations and considerations related to preparticipation screening for cardiovascular abnormalities in competitive athletes—2007 update: a scientific statement from the American Heart Association Council on Nutrition, Physical Activity, and Metabolism. *Circulation.* 2007;115(12):1643–1645.
3. Maron BJ, Mitchell JH. Revised eligibility recommendations for competitive athletes with cardiovascular abnormalities. *J Am Coll Cardiol.* 1994;24(4):848–850.
4. Rai M, Thompson PD. The definition of exertion-related cardiac events [published online ahead of print April 19, 2010]. *Br J Sports Med.* doi:10.1136/bjsm.2009.057653.
5. Thompson PD, Franklin BA, Balady GJ, et al. Exercise and acute cardiovascular events: placing the risks into perspective: a scientific statement from the American Heart Association Council on Nutrition, Physical Activity, and Metabolism and the Council on Clinical Cardiology. *Circulation.* 2007;115:2358–2368.
6. Thompson PD, Funk EJ, Carleton RA, Sturner WQ. Incidence of death during jogging in Rhode Island from 1975 through 1980. *JAMA.* 1982;247(18):2535–2538.
7. Siscovick DS, Weiss NS, Fletcher RH, Lasky T. The incidence of primary cardiac arrest during vigorous exercise. *N Engl J Med.* 1984;311(14):874–877.

8. Whang W, Manson JE, Hu FB, et al. Physical exertion, exercise, and sudden cardiac death in women. *JAMA*. 2006;295:1399–1403.

9. Kaikkonen KS, Kortelainen ML, Huikuri HV. Comparison of risk profiles between survivors and victims of sudden cardiac death from an acute coronary event. *Ann Med*. 2009;41(2):120–127.

10. Ni H, Coady S, Rosamond W, et al. Trends from 1987 to 2004 in sudden death due to coronary heart disease: the Atherosclerosis Risk in Communities (ARIC) study. *Am Heart J*. 2009;157(1):46–52.

11. Thompson PD, Buchner D, Pina IL, et al. Exercise and physical activity in the prevention and treatment of atherosclerotic cardiovascular disease: a statement from the Council on Clinical Cardiology (Subcommittee on Exercise, Rehabilitation, and Prevention) and the Council on Nutrition, Physical Activity, and Metabolism (Subcommittee on Physical Activity). *Circulation*. 2003;107(24):3109–3116.

12. Mittleman MA, Maclure M, Tofler GH, et al. Triggering of acute myocardial infarction by heavy physical exertion. Protection against triggering by regular exertion. Determinants of Myocardial Infarction Onset Study Investigators. *N Engl J Med*. 1993;329:1677–1683.

13. Hallqvist J, Möller J, Ahlbom A, et al. Does heavy physical exertion trigger myocardial infarction? A case-crossover analysis nested in a population-based case-referent study. *Am J Epidemiol*. 2000;151(5):459–467.

14. Giri S, Thompson PD, Kiernan FJ, et al. Clinical and angiographic characteristics of exertion-related acute myocardial infarction. *JAMA*.1999;282:1731–1736.

15. Willich SN, Lewis M, Löwel H, et al. Physical exertion as a trigger of acute myocardial infarction. Triggers and Mechanisms of Myocardial Infarction Study Group. *N Engl J Med*. 1993;329(23):1684–1690.

16. Redelmeier DA, Greenwald JA. Competing risks of mortality with marathons: retrospective analysis. *BMJ*. 2007;335(7633):1275–1277.

17. van Teeffelen WM, de Beus MF, Mosterd A, et al. Risk factors for exercise-related acute cardiac events. A case-control study. *Br J Sports Med*. 2009;43(9):722–725.

18. Burke AP, Farb A, Malcom GT, et al. Plaque rupture and sudden death related to exertion in men with coronary artery disease. *JAMA* 1999;281(10):921–926.

19. Black A, Black MM, Gensini G. Exertion and acute coronary artery injury. *Angiology*. 1975;26(11):759–783.

20. Ikarugi H, Taka T, Nakajima S, et al. Norepinephrine, but not epinephrine, enhances platelet reactivity and coagulation after exercise in humans. *J Appl Physiol*. 1999;86(1):133–138.

21. Ikarugi H, Shibata M, Shibata S, et al. High intensity exercise enhances platelet reactivity to shear stress and coagulation during and after exercise. *Pathophysiol Haemost Thromb*. 2003;33(3):127–133.

22. U.S. Preventive Services Task Force. Screening for coronary heart disease: recommendation statement. *Ann Intern Med*. 2004;140:569–572.

23. Lahav D, Leshno M, Brezis M. Is an exercise tolerance test indicated before beginning regular exercise? A decision analysis. *J Gen Intern Med*. 2009;24(8):934–938.

24. Gibbons RJ, Balady GJ, Bricker JT, et al. ACC/AHA 2002 guideline update for exercise testing: a report of the American College of Cardiology/American Heart Association Task Force on Practice Guidelines. *Circulation*. 2002;106:1883–1892.

25. American College of Sports Medicine. *Guidelines for Exercise Testing and Prescription*. 7th ed. Baltimore, MD: Lippincott Williams & Wilkins; 2005.

26. Thompson PD, Balady GJ, Chaitman BR, et al. Task Force 6: coronary artery disease. *J Am Coll Cardiol*. 2005;45(8):1348–1353.

27. Northcote RJ, Flannigan C, Ballantyne D. Sudden death and vigorous exercise—a study of 60 deaths associated with squash. *Br Heart J*. 1986;55:198–203.

28. Balady GJ, Chaitman B, Foster C, et al. Automated external defibrillators in health/fitness facilities: supplement to the AHA/ACSM recommendations for cardiovascular screening, staffing, and emergency policies at health/fitness facilities. *Circulation*. 2002;105(9):1147–1150.

29. Balady GJ, Chaitman B, Driscoll D, et al. Recommendations for cardiovascular screening, staffing, and emergency policies at health/fitness facilities. *Circulation*. 1998;97(22):2283–2293.

30. Maron BJ, Zipes DJ. Eligibility recommendations for competitive athletes with cardiovascular abnormalities—general considerations. *J Am Coll Cardiol*. 2005;45(8):1318–1321.

31. Barnard RJ, MacAlpin R, Kattus AA, Buckberg GD. Ischemic response to sudden strenuous exercise in healthy men. *Circulation*. 1973;48(5):936–942.

32. Barnard RJ, Gardner GW, Diaco NV, MacAlpin RN, Kattus AA. Cardiovascular responses to sudden strenuous exercise—heart rate, blood pressure, and ECG. *J Appl Physiol*. 1973;34(6):833–837.

33. Faich G, Rose R. Blizzard morbidity and mortality: Rhode Island, 1978. *Am J Public Health*. 1979;69:1050–1052.

34. Hammoudeh AJ, Haft JI. Coronary-plaque rupture in acute coronary syndromes triggered by snow shoveling. *N Engl J Med*. 1996;335:2001.

35. Glass RI, Zack MM Jr. Increase in deaths from ischaemic heart disease after blizzards. *Lancet*. 1979;1:485–487.

36. Pandolf KB, Cafarelli E, Noble BJ, Metz KF. Hyperthermia: effect on exercise prescription. *Arch Phys Med Rehabil*. 1975;56:524–526.

37. Levine BD, Zuckerman JH, deFilippi CR. Effect of high-altitude exposure in the elderly: the Tenth Mountain Division study. *Circulation*. 1997;96:1224–1232.

Prevention of Sudden Cardiac Death: Commotio Cordis

John A. Kalin, MD

Christopher Madias, MD

Mark S. Link, MD, FACC

Sudden death in the athlete is an uncommon event.[1,2] Although many high-profile deaths in competitive sport have been associated with underlying structural heart disease, a number of deaths have resulted from chest wall impacts in individuals with normal hearts.[2–4] The phenomenon of sudden arrhythmic death from low-energy chest wall impact has been termed **commotio cordis**. Commotio cordis is uncommon, occurring with a reported incidence of 5 to 20 events per year in the United States.[5,6] These events most commonly have been reported in young athletes between 8 and 18 years of age.[5–7] Victims are most often struck by projectiles that are regarded as standard implements of the sport, such as baseballs or hockey pucks. Sudden death is instantaneous and carries a grim prognosis without institution of early resuscitation and defibrillation.[8]

> **commotio cordis** Sudden death as a result of a seemingly innocent chest wall impact that occurs in the absence of any significant thoracic or cardiac history, usually occurring in athletes between 8 and 18 years of age. Although an uncommon event, sudden death is instantaneous and carries a grim prognosis without early resuscitation and defibrillation.

Definition

The term *commotio cordis* is derived from the Latin for disturbance or concussion of the heart. More specifically, commotio cordis refers to sudden death as a result of a seemingly innocent chest wall impact that occurs in the absence of any significant thoracic or cardiac trauma.[3,9,10–19] Commotio cordis is distinct from contusio cordis, in which high-energy chest wall impacts result in direct pathologic injury to the heart and the thoracic cage. Contusio cordis is most commonly seen in motor vehicle accidents and can result in myocardial hemorrhage, coronary artery disruptions, and rib fractures.[20–22]

History

Reports in the medical literature describe sudden death after chest wall impacts as early as 1763.[23] In the 19th century, sudden death after falls or industrial accidents prompted experimental work with rabbits in an attempt to explain the pathophysiology.[21] A 2010 review of deaths occurring in the United States during baseball games in the early 20th century revealed 18 deaths likely attributable to commotio cordis.[24] In the 1930s, Georg Schlomka at Bonn University was the first to describe a number of arrhythmic events induced by chest impacts in small animals.[25,26] Over the subsequent decades, commotio cordis was largely forgotten, represented in medical literature only by sporadic case reports. The first fully documented case of commotio cordis in the United States occurred in 1978 during a T-ball game.[10] In 1995, a series of 25 cases of sudden death from blunt chest impact in children and young adults engaged in competitive sport was reported.[3] Through the identification of these cases, a clinical profile of commotio cordis began to be defined, resulting in the creation of a national registry.[5,8,18,27,28] Development of a contemporary animal model has led to further insight into the underlying pathophysiology of commotio cordis.

Clinical Profile

A 2003 review of sudden deaths in young athletes reveals commotio cordis to be the second leading cause of death, behind only hypertrophic cardiomyopathy.[2] Since the creation of the National Commotio Cordis Registry in 1996, more than 220 cases of sudden death from chest impact have now been accrued **(Figure 4.1)**.[8,18,27,28] Approximately 75% of these cases occurred in the setting of sport: 50% during competitive sporting events and 25% during recreational sport.[29] In most cases victims were struck by projectiles normally implemented in the game, such as balls and pucks **(Figure 4.2)**. The majority of cases occured in sports that involve a small projectile with a dense core that tends to be propelled at a high velocity, such as baseball, lacrosse, and hockey.[8] All impacts were sustained over the left precordium, directly over the cardiac silhouette.[3] Half of the subjects in the registry collapsed instantaneously, whereas others experienced brief light-headedness before losing consciousness.[3] The initial rhythm seen in the majority of patients with attempted resuscitation was **ventricular fibrillation (VF)**, but in those victims undergoing prolonged resuscitation, asystole has also been reported.[8]

Commotio cordis is not exclusive to sport, with approximately 25% of cases in the National Commotio Cordis Registry occurring during nonsporting activities, such as playful fighting

ventricular fibrillation (VF)
An arrhythmia that occurs when the heart's electrical activity becomes disordered or irregular, causing unsynchronized pumping of the heart's chambers. This condition results in little to no ejection of blood.

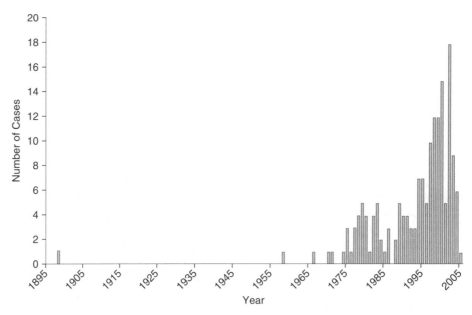

Figure 4.1   Case reports of commotio cordis since 1895, with most cases falling after 1978 in the United States and accelerating markedly after 1995.

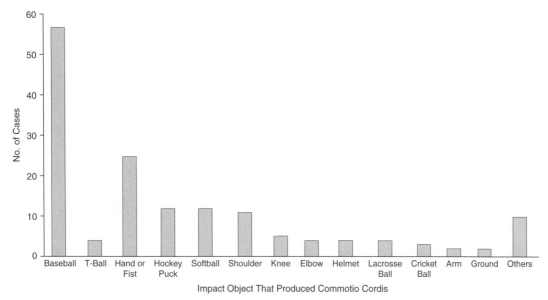

Impact Object That Produced Commotio Cordis

Figure 4.2 Distribution of projectiles implicated in commotio cordis, including a number of common balls and projectiles seen in youth sports.
Source: Adapted from Link MS, Estes III NAM, Maron BJ. Sudden death caused by chest wall trauma (commotio cordis). In Kohl P, Sachs F, Franz MR, eds. *Cardiac Mechano-Electric Feedback and Arrhythmias: From Pipette to Patient*. Philadelphia: Elsevier Saunders; 2005:270–276.

between individuals or child discipline (Figure 4.2).[8] Some of these cases of fist or hand strikes have resulted in criminal charges.[30,31] Notable cases in the registry have included a young boy who died after being hit in the chest by a sled and a young girl who died suddenly after the head of her family dog struck her in the chest.[8]

A review of the spectrum of cases within the national registry reveals that commotio cordis is most commonly but not exclusively seen in the young, with a peak incidence between the ages of 13 and 19 years (median age 14 years; **Figure 4.3**). Males account for 95% of cases for unclear reasons, but theories have included disproportionate participation in implicated sports and possibly increased chest wall compliance.[8,29] The predominance of young subjects in the registry likely relates to the high level of participation in youth sports in American culture. Furthermore, young individuals might also be at higher risk for commotio cordis due to an increased compliance of the chest wall as compared with adults.[32]

Experimental Model

In 1998 a reliable, contemporary experimental model of commotio cordis was first described. In this model, anesthetized juvenile swine are placed prone in a sling. Projectiles impact the precordium, gated to the cardiac cycle by a cardiac stimulator that triggers off the surface electrocardiogram of the swine. Intracardiac pressures are monitored during all chest impacts. Projectile speed is adjustable from 20 to 70 mph, and impacts are aimed directly over the cardiac silhouette by transthoracic echocardiographic guidance. Using this model, VF is consistently and reproducibly induced by chest wall impact if a confluence of several factors is achieved.[33]

Initial experiments revealed that timing of impact is among the most crucial of variables for VF induction.[33] Impacts that were timed to strike during a narrow window of vulnerability during cardiac repolarization (10 to 30 milliseconds prior to the peak of the T wave; **Figure 4.4**) consistently resulted in VF. This phenomenon appeared analogous to the "shock-on-T" maneuver used to induce VF during defibrillator threshold testing in the electrophysiology laboratory. Impacts at other time periods of the cardiac cycle, such as during the QRS complex or ST segment, did not result in VF, but were noted to

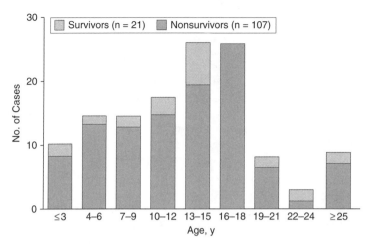

Figure 4.3 Age distribution at the time of impact of cases in the commotio cordis registry, showing a similar distribution of survivors and nonsurvivors. Median age is 14 years, with 80% of cases occurring in individuals 18 years or younger.
Source: Adapted from Link MS, Estes III NAM. Mechanically induced ventricular fibrillation (commotio cordis). *Heart Rhythm*. 2007;4(4):529–532.

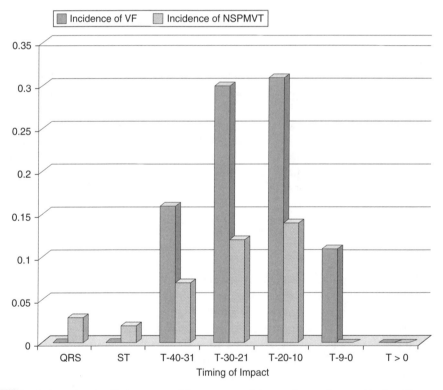

Figure 4.4 Timing of projectile impact at different parts of the cardiac cycle, specifically with respect to the timing of the peak of the T wave. The highest incidence of ventricular fibrillation occurs between 10 and 30 msec before the T-wave peak. VF indicates ventricular fibrillation; NSPMVT, nonsustained polymorphic ventricular tachycardia.
Source: Adapted from Link MS, Wang PJ, Pandian NG, et al. An experimental model of sudden death due to low-energy chest-wall impact (commotio cordis). *N Engl J Med.* 1998;338(25):1805–1811.

cause other arrhythmic events, such as premature ventricular contractions, heart block, ST elevation, and bundle-branch block.[33]

Impact velocity has also proven to be an important variable for induction of commotio cordis. In the swine model, faster, higher-energy impacts more consistently resulted in VF as compared with low-velocity impacts. In animals weighing between 10 and 25 kilograms, chest impacts induced VF over 50% of the time at speeds between 40 and 50 mph. These data are of particular relevance for youth baseball, in which ball velocity is typically between 30 and 50 mph.[32] At impacts faster than 50 mph, an increased incidence of direct thoracic and myocardial damage was observed.

Consistent with the clinical profile of commotio cordis in humans, impact location directly over the heart is necessary for VF induction in the swine model. Examination of impact location from base to apex using echocardiography revealed that impacts over the center of the left ventricle most frequently induced VF. Impacts at the base or apex of the heart were less likely to result in VF.[33–35] Impacts that occurred outside the borders of the cardiac silhouette never resulted in VF induction.

Object hardness and shape proved to be other important variables for VF induction. Softer projectiles were associated with a lower incidence of VF.[33] In a series of experiments, a dense wooden object, similar in size but harder than a regulation baseball, was noted to result in the highest incidence of VF. The lowest incidence of VF was seen with a safety baseball commonly known as a "T-ball."[4,8,34,36] Smaller, more compact objects, such as those shaped like a golf ball, produced VF more frequently than objects with a larger surface that distributed the energy of impact over a wider area.

The variables of velocity, hardness, shape, and location all likely relate to the creation of a critical threshold pressure in the heart that is necessary for VF induction (**Figure 4.5**). It is theorized that the clinical manifestations of commotio cordis are a result of the instantaneous rise in peak left ventricular

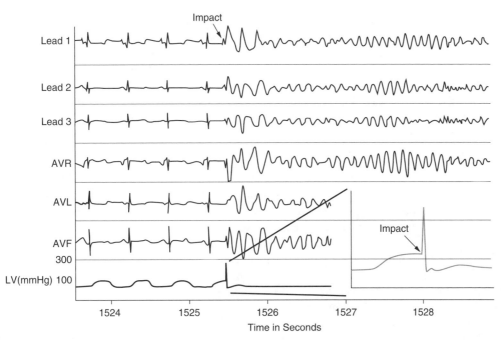

Figure 4.5 Six-lead electrocardiogram showing the electrophysiologic and hemodynamic consequences of chest wall impact at 30 miles per hour, timed to occur 16 milliseconds before the peak of the T wave in a 9-kilogram pig. Ventricular fibrillation begins immediately (within one cardiac cycle) after the chest impact, which was associated with instant loss of effective left ventricular (LV) pressure.
Source: Adapted from Link MS, Maron BJ, VanderBrink BA, et al. Impact directly over the cardiac silhouette is necessary to produce ventricular fibrillation in an experimental model of commotio cordis. *J Am Coll Cardiol.* 2001;37(2):649–654.

pressure seen with chest wall impact. In the experimental swine model, impact velocity correlated with the peak left ventricular pressure created by chest impacts. Similarly, higher peak left ventricular pressures were more likely to result in VF induction.[7,34,35]

Mechanisms of Commotio Cordis

Early theories relating to the pathophysiology of commotio cordis focused on coronary ischemia, vasospasm, and changes in autonomic tone.[26] Experiments in the contemporary swine model of commotio cordis have largely disproved these early theories while shedding substantial light on the underlying pathophysiology.[33] Physical stimulation of the heart with the production of electrical consequences (such as intracardiac catheters stimulating premature ventricular contractions) has been termed **mechanoelectric coupling**. This phenomenon has been attributed to the presence of stretch-sensitive ion channels within cardiac myocytes.[37–39] The stretch-sensitive K^+_{ATP} channel that is responsible for the phenomenon of ST-segment elevation and VF in acute myocardial ischemia has also been implicated in commotio cordis.[40] In the swine model of commotio cordis, K^+_{ATP} blockade prior to chest wall impact resulted in significantly less VF induction.[34,38,41,42] The potential role of other ion channels remains a target of ongoing and future research.

Despite the achievement of appropriate conditions for VF induction (timing, location, velocity, and appropriate rise in left ventricular pressure), not all chest wall impacts in the swine model produce VF. Of these impacts that do not result in VF, 70% result in premature ventricular contractions, suggesting activation of mechanosensitive ion channels without lethal arrhythmia induction. This has raised the theory that VF induction in commotio cordis is dependent not only on a mechanoelectric trigger but also on the presence of an appropriate substrate myocardium that is necessary to sustain VF. Studies of VF induction by inflation of a balloon in Langendorff-perfused rabbit hearts revealed that VF could only be induced during a vulnerable time window that corresponded to a period of increased dispersion of myocardial repolarization. In addition, compared with baseline action potentials, pressure pulses that induced VF further increased repolarization dispersion across the myocardium.[42–44] Thus, it appears that chest impacts not only provide the trigger for lethal arrhythmia but also might themselves contribute to the creation of a suitable substrate for VF induction. Ongoing studies in the swine model of commotio cordis also suggest that repolarization abnormalities manifested by QT prolongation might underlie individual animal susceptibility to VF induction by chest wall impacts.

Prevention of Commotio Cordis

Of the 125 events that occurred during competitive sport noted in the National Commotio Cordis Registry, 32% involved individuals who were wearing some sort of chest protection at the time of impact.[3,4,8,27,29,33] Despite the use of chest protectors, sudden death was not prevented in these individuals. In some cases, it appears the chest protector moved during play and was not overlying the cardiac silhouette at the time of impact. In other cases, however, impact occurred directly over the chest protector, but commotio cordis was not prevented.[3] Standard chest protectors are not currently designed to prevent commotio cordis. In fact, in experiments using the swine model of commotio cordis, seven commercially available lacrosse chest protectors and nine baseball chest protectors proved ineffective at preventing VF induction.[45,46] These findings support the need for further research in the development of adequate chest protectors designed for the prevention of commotio cordis in youth sports.

The use of safety baseballs might also decrease the risk of commotio cordis. In the swine model, safety baseballs significantly reduced the incidence of VF induction by chest impacts.[33] Data from this model and other clinical data from the United States Consumer Protection Agency have led to calls for the utilization of age-appropriate safety baseballs in sports. Safety baseballs are similar in weight and feel during competitive play and represent an inexpensive and effective preventive measure.

Age-appropriate coaching and rules changes might also be instrumental in preventing commotio cordis. Although recent rules changes in youth baseball have prohibited the use of the chest in stopping the ball while in play, attention by coaches and parents to the playing technique and style of the participant is critical. Although unpredictable motion of the projectile cannot be prevented, coaching can provide a measure of preparedness and understanding that might allow participants to avoid unnecessary chest wall impact.

	Lacrosse	Baseball	Hockey and Other Sports
Avoidance of chest wall impact	Coaching, rules changes	Coaching, rules changes	Coaching
Chest protectors	Modification of current lacrosse chest protectors	Appropriately sized and age appropriate	Appropriately sized and age appropriate
Safety equipment	Automated external defibrillators (AEDs)	AEDs, safety baseballs	AEDs
Projectile/ball	Possible safety lacrosse ball	Safety baseballs	

Treatment

Outcomes of commotio cordis events are usually quite grim, with an overall survival of only 25% in the national registry.[4,8,27,29] Given that the registry is derived largely from case reports, episodes in which VF might have terminated spontaneously are obviously not documented, and this bias likely influences the overall survival data. Nevertheless, it is clear that early resuscitation from commotio cordis is the key to survival. The poor survival rates have been in part attributed to delayed recognition and therapy despite the typical presence of bystanders.[8]

With broader visibility and understanding, commotio cordis is now recognized with increasing frequency. This improved awareness, along with the recent increased distribution of automatic external defibrillators (AEDs) at many sport facilities, has correlated with an improved survival rate of approximately 35% over the last decade in the registry.[29,47–50] The importance of readily available AEDs on the field of play cannot be stressed enough. AEDs provide a potentially highly effective life-saving therapy for commotio cordis and other arrhythmic death events.[47,51–54] Survival of commotio cordis is most likely to occur with institution of early defibrillation. Coaches, strength coaches, and athletic trainers involved in youth athletics should be made aware of the risk of commotio cordis and become familiar with the use of AEDs. Commotio cordis should be suspected if an athlete collapses suddenly (or after several seconds) following a chest impact and remains unarousable. Emergency medical services should be contacted immediately, and an AED should be placed on the victim as soon as possible. Cardiopulmonary resuscitation should be performed as guided by standard out-of-hospital cardiac arrest algorithms.[55]

Survivors of commotio cordis in the absence of structural heart disease might consider a return to competitive sports. There are limited data to guide clinical decision making in this regard. The guidelines issued by the 36th Bethesda Conference recommend decisions based on individual cases and clinical judgment.[56] There have been no recurrences of commotio cordis events reported from survivors in the national registry. However, recent data from the swine model of commotio cordis suggest that individual susceptibility to commotio cordis might play a role in this phenomenon. Survivors should have a thorough cardiac evaluation. After review of clinical data and careful weighing of the risks and benefits of sports participation, a return to play should be an individual decision between the survivor, his or her family, and his or her clinician.[56]

Conclusion

Commotio cordis is a rare but tragic event that typically occurs in young men and boys in the setting of organized sport. Through the development of a comprehensive registry and the creation of a reliable animal model, our understanding of the clinical profile and the underlying pathophysiology has evolved considerably over the last 10 to 15 years. Whereas the earliest experimental and observational findings pointed to the basic physiologic requirements for VF induction by chest impact, more recent work has been directed at more specific scenarios and parameters, such as the possibility of individual susceptibility to commotio cordis. Research in the areas of chest wall protection and the use of safety baseballs is directed at prevention. The safety of young athletes would be further advanced by increased awareness of commotio cordis and by more widespread access to AEDs at youth sporting events.

Clinical Case Scenario

1. A 13-year-old boy participating in youth baseball is struck in the chest by a pitch. He is not wearing a chest protector, which is typical for the sport. He collapses several seconds after recoiling from the pain of impact. The umpire finds him unarousable and quickly determines that he is pulseless and is not breathing.
   1. What potential life-saving steps should be performed immediately?
   2. What are the most important factors in surviving a commotio cordis event?
   3. If the boy survives, should he be allowed to return to the field of play?

Key Terms

commotio cordis

mechanoelectric coupling

ventricular fibrillation

References

1. Link MS, Mark Estes NA. Athletes and arrhythmias. *J Cardiovasc Electrophysiol.* 2010;21(10):1184–1189.
2. Maron BJ. Sudden death in young athletes. *N Engl J Med.* 2003;349(11):1064–1075.
3. Maron BJ, Poliac LC, Kaplan JA, Mueller FO. Blunt impact to the chest leading to sudden death from cardiac arrest during sports activities. *N Engl J Med.* 1995;333(6):337–342.
4. Maron BJ, Link MS, Wang PJ, Estes NA 3rd. Clinical profile of commotio cordis: an under appreciated cause of sudden death in the young during sports and other activities. *J Cardiovasc Electrophysiol.* 1999;10(1):114–120.
5. Link MS. Commotio cordis, sudden death due to chest wall impact in sports. *Heart.* 1999;81:109–110.
6. Haq CL. Sudden death due to low-energy chest-wall impact (commotio cordis). *N Engl J Med.* 1998;339:1399.
7. Madias C, Maron BJ, Weinstock J, Estes NA 3rd, Link MS. Commotio cordis—sudden cardiac death with chest wall impact. *J Cardiovasc Electrophysiol.* 2007;18(1):115–122.
8. Maron BJ, Gohman TE, Kyle SB, Estes NA 3rd, Link MS. Clinical profile and spectrum of commotio cordis. *JAMA.* 2002;287(9):1142–1146.
9. Link MS, Ginsburg SH, Wang PJ, et al. Commotio cordis: cardiovascular manifestations of a rare survivor. *Chest.* 1998;114(1):326–328.
10. Dickman GL, Hassan A, Luckstead EF. Ventricular fibrillation following baseball injury. *Phys Sport Med.* 1978;6:85–86.
11. Froede RC, Lindsey D, Steinbronn K. Sudden unexpected death from cardiac concussion (commotio cordis) with unusual legal complications. *J Forensic Sci.* 1979;24:752–756.
12. Green ED, Simson LR, Kellerman HH, Horowitz RN. Cardiac concussion following softball blow to the chest. *Ann Emerg Med.* 1980;9:155–157.
13. Frazer M, Mirchandani H. Commotio cordis, revisited. *Am J Forensic Med Path.* 1984;5(3):249–251.
14. Rutherford GW, Kennedy J, McGhee L. *Baseball and Softball Related Injuries to Children 5–14 Years of Age.* Washington, DC: United States Consumer Product Safety Commission; 1984.
15. Edlich RF, Mayer NE, Fariss BL, et al. Commotio cordis in a lacrosse goalie. *J Emerg Med.* 1987;5:181–184.
16. Abrunzo TJ. Commotio cordis, the single, most common cause of traumatic death in youth baseball. *Am J Dis Child.* 1991;145:1279–1282.
17. Kaplan JA, Karofsky PS, Volturo GA. Commotio cordis in two amateur ice hockey players despite the use of commercial chest protectors: case reports. *J Trauma.* 1993;34(1):151–153.
18. Maron BJ, Strasburger JF, Kugler JD, et al. Survival following blunt chest impact induced cardiac arrest during sports activities in young athletes. *Am J Cardiol.* 1997;79:840–841.
19. Riedinger F, Kummell H. Die verletzungen und erkrankungen des thoraz und seines inhaltes. In: von Bergman E, von Bruns P, eds. *Handbuch der Praktischen Chirurgie.* 2nd ed. Stuttgart: Ferd. Enke; 1903:373–456.
20. Nelaton A. *Elements de pathologie chirurgicale.* 2nd ed. Paris: Librairie Germer Bateliere; 1876.
21. Meola F. La commozione toracica. *Gior Internaz Sci Med.* 1879;1:923–937.
22. Nesbitt AD, Cooper PJ, Kohl P. Rediscovering commotio cordis. *Lancet.* 2001;357:1195–1197.

23. Akenside M. An account of a blow upon the heart and of its effects. *Phil Trans.* 1763;53:353–355.
24. Maron BJ, Boren S, Estes NAM III. Early descriptions of sudden cardiac death due to commotio cordis occurring in baseball. *Heart Rhythm.* 2010;7(7):992–993.
25. Schlomka G, Schmitz M. Experimentelle untersuchungen uber den einfluss stumpfer brustkorbtraumen auf das electrokardiogramm. *S Ges Exp Med.* 1932;83:779–791.
26. Schlomka G. Commotio cordis und ihre folgen. Die einwirkung stumpfer brustwandtraumen auf das herz. *Ergebn Inn Med Kinderheilk.* 1934;47:1–91.
27. Maron BJ, Poliac LC, Kyle SB. Clinical profile of commotio cordis: an under-appreciated cause of sudden cardiac death in the young during sporting activities [abstract]. *Circulation.* 1997;96:I755.
28. Maron BJ, Shirani J, Poliac LC, et al. Sudden death in young competitive athletes: clinical, demographic, and pathologic profiles. *JAMA.* 1996;276:199–204.
29. Maron BJ, Estes NA 3rd. Commotio cordis. *N Engl J Med.* 2010;362(10):917–927.
30. Maron BJ, Mitten MJ, Burnett CG. Criminal consequences of commotio cordis. *Am J Cardiol.* 2002;89:210–213.
31. Swift EM. A cruel blow; a seemingly harmless slash to the chest resulted in the death of a hockey player in Italy. Now, Jimmy Boni will go on trial for manslaughter. *Sports Illustrated.* 1993(Dec 6):66–79.
32. Link MS, Maron BJ, Wang PJ, et al. Upper and lower limits of vulnerability to sudden arrhythmic death with chest-wall impact (commotio cordis). *J Am Coll Cardiol.* 2003;41(1):99–104.
33. Link MS, Wang PJ, Pandian NG, et al. An experimental model of sudden death due to low-energy chest-wall impact (commotio cordis). *N Engl J Med.* 1998;338(25):1805–1811.
34. Link MS. Mechanically induced sudden death in chest wall impact. *Prog Biophys Molecular Biol.* 2003;82:175–186.
35. Link MS, Maron BJ, VanderBrink BA, et al. Impact directly over the cardiac silhouette is necessary to produce ventricular fibrillation in an experimental model of commotio cordis. *J Am Coll Cardiol.* 2001;37(2):649–654.
36. Link MS, Maron BJ, Wang PJ, et al. Reduced risk of sudden death from chest wall blows (commotio cordis) with safety baseballs. *Pediatrics.* 2002;109(5):873–877.
37. Kohl P, Hunter P, Noble D. Stretch-induced changes in heart rate and rhythm: clinical observations, experiments and mathematical models. *Prog Biophys Molecular Biol.* 1999;71:91–138.
38. Kohl P, Nesbitt AD, Cooper PJ, Lei M. Sudden cardiac death by commotio cordis: role of mechanico-electrical feedback. *Cardiovasc Res.* 2001;50:280–289.
39. Kohl P, Ravens U. Cardiac mechano-electric feedback: past, present, and prospect. *Prog Biophys Mol Biol.* 2003;82(1–3):3–9.
40. Van Wagoner DR. Mechanosensitive gating of atrial ATP-sensitive potassium channels. *Circ Res.* 1993;72(5):973–983.
41. Madias C, Maron BJ, Supron S, Estes NA 3rd, Link MS. Cell membrane stretch and chest blow-induced ventricular fibrillation: commotio cordis. *J Cardiovasc Electrophysiol.* 2008;19(12):1304–1309.
42. Link MS, Wang PJ, VanderBrink BA, et al. Selective activation of the K(+)(ATP) channel is a mechanism by which sudden death is produced by low-energy chest-wall impact (commotio cordis). *Circulation.* 1999;100(4):413–418.
43. Bode F, Franz MR, Wilke I, et al. Ventricular fibrillation induced by stretch pulse: implications for sudden death due to commotio cordis. *J Cardiovasc Electrophysiol.* 2006;17(9):1011–1017.
44. Fabritz CL, Kirchhof PF, Behrens S, Zabel M, Franz MR. Myocardial vulnerability to T wave shocks: relation to shock strength, shock coupling interval, and dispersion of ventricular repolarization. *J Cardiovasc Electrophysiol.* 1996;7:231–242.
45. Weinstock J, Maron BJ, Song C, et al. Failure of commercially available chest wall protectors to prevent sudden cardiac death induced by chest wall blows in an experimental model of commotio cordis. *Pediatrics.* 2006;117(4):e656–662.
46. Viano DC, Bir CA, Cheney AK, Janda DH. Prevention of commotio cordis in baseball: an evaluation of chest wall protectors. *J Trauma.* 2000;49:1023–1028.
47. Salib EA, Cyran SE, Cilley RE, Maron BJ, Thomas NJ. Efficacy of bystander cardiopulmonary resuscitation and out-of-hospital automated external defibrillation as life-saving therapy in commotio cordis. *J Pediatr.* 2005;147(6):863–866.
48. Myerburg RJ, Estes NA 3rd, Fontaine JM, Link MS, Zipes DP. Task Force 10: automated external defibrillators. 36th Bethesda Conference: eligibility recommendations for competitive athletes with cardiovascular abnormalities. *J Am Coll Cardiol.* 2005;45(8):1369–1371.
49. England H, Hoffman C, Hodgman T, et al. Effectiveness of automated external defibrillators in high schools in greater Boston. *Am J Cardiol.* 2005;95(12):1484–1486.
50. Drezner JA, Rogers KJ, Zimmer RR, Sennett BJ. Use of automated external defibrillators at NCAA Division I universities. *Med Sci Sports Exerc.* 2005;37(9):1487–1492.
51. Marenco JP, Wang PJ, Link MS, Homoud MK, Estes NA 3rd. Improving survival from sudden cardiac arrest: the role of the automated external defibrillator. *JAMA.* 2001;285(9):1193–1200.
52. Drezner JA, Rogers KJ. Sudden cardiac arrest in intercollegiate athletes: detailed analysis and outcomes of resuscitation in nine cases. *Heart Rhythm.* 2006;3(7):755–759.
53. Friedman FD, Dowler K, Link MS. A public access defibrillation programme in non-inpatient hospital areas. *Resuscitation.* 2006;69(3):407–411.
54. Link MS, Maron BJ, Stickney RE, et al. Automated external defibrillator arrhythmia detection in a model of cardiac arrest due to commotio cordis. *J Cardiovasc Electrophysiol.* 2003;14(1):83–87.
55. American Heart Association. *Advanced Cardiovascular Life Support Provider Manual.* Dallas, TX: American Heart Association; 2006.
56. Maron BJ, Estes NA 3rd, Link MS. Task Force 11: commotio cordis. *J Am Coll Cardiol.* 2005;45:1371–1373.

Exertional Heat Stroke

Rebecca L. Stearns, MA, ATC

Francis G. O'Connor, MD, MPH, FACSM

Douglas J. Casa, PhD, ATC, FACSM, FNATA

Glen P. Kenny, PhD

Any participation in sports or physical activity is associated with inherent risks. Among those of greatest concern are conditions that present risks associated with long-term morbidity and the possibility of death, such as exertional heat stroke (EHS). Surprisingly, this potentially deadly condition has received relatively little attention considering it is the second leading cause of death in sport, after cardiac conditions.[1] Although there have been many advances in knowledge and research in the area of heat illnesses, the incidence of heat stroke deaths continues to rise. According to the University of North Carolina's National Center for Catastrophic Injury Research, if the last 35 years are broken down into 5-year blocks, the last 5 years (2005 to 2009) are the worst in terms of deaths in football due to EHS since the 1970s **(Table 5.1)**.[1] Unlike some other potentially fatal conditions, however, death from EHS can be prevented if the condition is promptly diagnosed in combination with swift and effective treatment.

Definition of Condition

Exertional heat stroke (EHS) occurs when core body temperature is elevated to a dangerous level (usually ≥40.5°C [105°F]), with concomitant signs of organ system failure due to hyperthermia.[2,3] This condition occurs when the temperature regulation system is overwhelmed due to excessive heat production or inhibited heat loss and can progress to thermoregulatory system failure. The first marker of EHS is often central nervous system dysfunction or alterations. If not treated immediately and effectively, EHS can lead to death.[2,3]

exertional heat stroke (EHS) a medical emergency involving life-threatening hyperthermia (rectal temperature > 40.5°C [105°F]) with concomitant central nervous system dysfunction; treatment involves cooling the body.

TABLE 5.1	Number of Football Deaths from Exertional Heat Stroke in the Last Thirty-Five Years	
Years	**Number of Deaths**	
1975–1979	8	
1980–1984	9	
1985–1989	5	
1990–1994	2	
1995–1999	13	
2000–2004	11	
2005–2009	18	
5-year average	9	

Source: Mueller F, Cantu R. *Twenty Sixth Annual Report of the National Center for Catastrophic Sports Injury Research: Catastrophic Football Injuries*. Chapel Hill, NC: National Center for Catastrophic Sports Injury Research; 2009.

Epidemiology

Exertional heat stroke is the second leading cause of sudden death in athletes and can rise to the number one cause of sudden death in athletes during the summer months.[1] The incidence of fatal EHS in American football players was about 1 in 350,000 participants from 1995 to 2002.[1] Popular road races have reported as many as 1 to 2 EHS cases per 1000 entrants.[4]

Pathophysiology

EHS occurs when thermoregulatory mechanisms are unable to dissipate the heat being gained and produced by the body during exercise. There are multiple mechanisms by which a body may gain heat during exercise, either internal (e.g., working muscles producing heat) or external (e.g., high ambient temperature). There are also many mechanisms by which cooling (heat loss) may occur (e.g., conduction or evaporation). The **heat balance equation**[5] describes this fragile balance:

$$S = M - (\pm \text{Work}) - E \pm R \pm C \pm K$$

heat balance equation
Describes the net rate at which a person generates and exchanges heat with his or her environment. It is composed of body heat content (S), metabolic rate (M), work rate (W), evaporative heat transfer (E), convective heat transfer (C), conductive heat transfer (K), and radiant heat exchange (R): $S = M - (\pm W) - E \pm R \pm C \pm K$.

S represents overall heat storage, M represents metabolic heat production, E represents evaporation, R represents radiation, C represents convection, and K represents conduction. Heat gain is indicated by a positive value, whereas heat loss is indicated by a negative value. Options for heat loss include the E, R, C, and K pathways, whereas options for heat gain include the M, E, R, C, and K pathways. Note that for an exercising individual, M will always be positive and contribute to heat gain.

Radiation

Radiation is heat gained or lost due to the energy transferred in the infrared electromagnetic energy spectrum independent of air temperature. Radiation, such as that from the sun, depends on the gradient that exists between the surfaces receiving and producing the heat.[6]

Convection

Convection is heat loss or gain through a transfer layer of either air or water. Wind chill is based on this principle. High winds increase the heat loss and the perceived feeling of "cold" in the air. Water has an even greater ability to transfer heat. It is approximately 40 times more effective than air at removing or releasing heat to or from the body.[6] This is an extremely important consideration when determining course of treatment for an EHS victim.

Evaporation

Evaporation occurs as the result of the latent heat of vaporization of water from the skin. The evaporation of water requires energy in the form of heat, which is called the latent heat of vaporization.[6] Given this input, the heat from the body is transferred to sweat. When this liquid is evaporated and converted to a gaseous state, the heat is transferred and removed. This is the main method of cooling that the body relies on in high ambient temperatures. However, high humidity hinders the ability of the body to cool itself in this fashion. Humidity becomes a large factor because once ambient temperature rises above skin temperature, cooling by radiation and convection is lost and now contributes to heat gain as opposed to loss. This leaves only evaporation as a means of cooling. Unfortunately, the rate at which the body can cool through this last method decreases as humidity rises. Sweat that cannot evaporate will drip off the body. Without evaporating, sweat does not contribute to cooling the body and only leads to further **dehydration** via fluid loss.[6]

> **dehydration** The process of water loss leading to hypohydration. Usually measured by body mass loss, urine color, urine osmolality, urine specific gravity, or serum osmolality (the gold standard).

Conduction

Conduction is the transfer of heat from one object to another that is in direct contact with it—for example, the heat lost when transferred from the body to clothes. This type of cooling makes up a small amount of the total heat exchange (approximately 1%) and does not contribute greatly to cooling of the body.[6]

Temperature Regulation and the Brain

Temperature regulation in the body occurs primarily in the preoptic area of the anterior hypothalamus (POAH). The normal set temperature the POAH maintains is around 37°C (98.6°F). Other factors, such as menstrual cycle, infections or fever, and circadian rhythms, can cause fluctuations in body temperature.[6,7]

Fever Versus Exercise-Induced Temperature Changes

The mechanism by which a fever causes an increase in **core body temperature** is quite different from what occurs during exercise. When a virus or bacteria attacks the body, the initial response is to release pyrogens,[6] which are chemical substances that cause the POAH to "reset" to a higher temperature than normal. Pathways are then put in place to reduce heat loss and maintain or increase heat gain. This response is believed to help the body fight the attack, but will also result in the symptom of chills until the body reaches the new set temperature.[6]

> **core body temperature** Temperature of the internal organs or thermal core as measured by a valid device (i.e., rectal thermometer, gastrointestinal thermistor).

During exercise, the rise in core body temperature is a result of the heat produced by the exercising or contracting muscle. Heat is a product of the oxidation of carbohydrates, fats, and proteins in the process of energy consumption by the muscle. During high-intensity exercise or exercise that incorporates a large amount of muscle mass, a high demand for energy is created; consequently, the body produces a large amount of heat. It is important to differentiate between these two mechanisms (febrile vs. exercise-induced hyperthermia) for the purpose of treating the hyperthermic state. In a febrile individual, aspirin-like drugs will block the chemical response to the illness and prevent the individual's body temperature from increasing. Because the increase in temperature during exercise is due to muscular activation and not a chemical response, providing an athlete with aspirin-like drugs will not have the same effect on temperature regulation. This point is particularly important to remember when treating EHS.

Heat Gain

The body's muscles are constantly producing heat during exercise. This heat production may be exacerbated by hot and humid environments, eventually leading to an accumulation of heat within the body at a rate at which the body is unable to dissipate. During maximal exercise, heat production can be increased by a factor of 10 or more.[8]

To cope with these stressors, the body will increase cardiac output, causing increased blood flow to the muscles and skin, which in turn causes a decreased venous return to the heart. This cycle ultimately fuels competing demands for blood flow between the cardiovascular system, splanchnic organs, muscles, and skin.[7] The body is perfusing the skin with blood in order to aid in cooling via sweat and evaporation; however, the working muscles also demand blood for oxygen and nutrient requirements. Muscle blood flow eventually takes precedence over skin blood flow, and the current rate of cooling cannot be maintained. Ultimately, the body defends arterial pressure above all else; muscle blood flow is prioritized second.

Signs of this stress on the body are seen as increases in heart rate (and ultimately cardiovascular strain) due to the lack of venous return; performance decreases, heat storage increases, and eventually hyperthermia occurs, resulting in a likely increase for a potential EHS.

Heat Loss

Combining all the heat balance factors previously mentioned, there are numerous methods by which the body can gain heat. Ironically, as the contributing environmental risks for heat illness increase, the options for cooling the body decrease. The three main cooling methods that the body uses are radiation, convection, and evaporation. Radiation and convection work as methods of heat loss when ambient temperature is low, or at least lower than skin temperature. However, when ambient temperature is greater than skin temperature, these forms of heat transfer become factors of heat gain rather than heat loss. Similarly, evaporation is the most effective and heavily relied upon form of heat loss in the body. However, in conditions of high humidity this method of heat loss is severely limited, leaving the body with few cooling options, if any. It is at this point that the core body temperature starts to rise; without a cessation of exercise or the application of external cooling methods, it will continue to do so.

Physiologic Factors Affecting Heat Stress Response

Although the body has methods of heat gain and loss as well as intrinsic and extrinsic factors influencing how intense heat stress exposure is, understanding the underlying physiologic changes that occur may also help one understand the occurrence of EHS in the athletic population. A "critical core temperature" has been proposed as the defining limit at which humans will volitionally stop exercising at a particular core body temperature.[9–11] This core body temperature is coincidentally also similar to the limit used to diagnose heat stroke (i.e., 40.5°C [105°F]). Other similar models state that the body recognizes feedback in the form of a steadily or rapidly increasing core body temperature as a signal to slow or lower intensity. By these means the body compensates for the heat stress and is able to work longer before reaching the critical temperature and therefore exhaustion.[12–14] This theory, however, does not take into account the mechanism by which athletes are able to override this signal and continue to exercise past the 40.5°C/105°F mark (most times with no ill effects).

An alternative theory suggests that the mechanism behind these observations is in actuality a combination of cardiovascular strain as a result of high skin blood flow. The maintenance of skin blood flow causes a decrease in the central blood volume, causing greater cardiovascular strain. More recent studies have demonstrated that subjects will volitionally cease exercise when skin blood flow is high in combination with high core temperature, creating a high cardiovascular demand.[15] Overall, this leads us to conclude that the physiologic explanation for cessation of exercise in the heat is multifaceted but largely based on the perceived stress on the individual, core body temperature, and skin temperature.

Although exercising individuals are limited by physiologic factors, there are other factors that may be trained or adjusted to help expand exercise capacity and heat tolerance. The factors that likely influence an individual's exercise heat tolerance are extensive, but five of the most important are environmental conditions as measured by the **wet bulb globe temperature (WBGT)**; heat acclimatization status; hydration status; the amount or type of equipment or clothing; and last, but also most important, intensity of exercise in relation to fitness status. It has been known since the 1940s that heat acclimation plays a large part in the body's physiologic responses, adaptations, and overall ability to cope with heat exposure.[16] Heat **acclimation** is a broad term and can be loosely defined as a complex series of adaptations that occur in a controlled environment over the course of 7 to 14 days that leads to reductions in heart rate, decreased core and skin temperature responses, decreased perceived exertion, increased **sweat rate**, hastened sweat onset, increased stroke volume, and an overall enhanced ability to perform in the heat.[17,18] Other physiologic changes include increased plasma volume and

wet bulb globe temperature (WBGT) The most widely used heat stress index in industry and sports; may be used to assess the severity of hot environments. It is derived from a formula that incorporates the dry bulb, wet bulb, and black globe temperature.

acclimation Adaptive changes that occur in response to experimentally induced changes in particular climatic factors. Used most often in research studies to refer to the artificial process of acclimatization that is induced via climate-controlled chambers.

decreased sodium chloride losses in sweat and urine.[17] Heat **acclimatization** results in the same physiologic changes; however, it occurs in the natural environment.

It has been shown that factors affecting these changes determine the extent to which adaptations occur. For example, acclimation in hot and dry environments has been shown to be different from that in hot and humid environments (a greater sweat rate increase has been seen in the latter case).[17] It is also highly important for the athlete to train in the heat at an intensity great enough to induce these changes. This intensity is needed for the core temperature to elevate, the main stimulus behind heat acclimation. Although the evidence specifying the ideal intensity at which to train for acclimation is diverse, acclimation is known to depend on volume, intensity, and maintenance of an elevated core body temperature during exercise.[17,19]

When attempting to acclimatize to the heat, athletes should gain a base level of fitness in a cool environment prior to heat exposure. Highly fit individuals already have some of the physical advantages that are gained with acclimation—for example, an increased sweat rate. Additionally, athletes should exercise at intensities greater than 50% of their maximal oxygen consumption (Vo_2max), with intensity increasing throughout training to maximize adaptation.[17] After an athlete is acclimatized to the heat, he or she will lose less sodium and potassium during exercise, thereby retaining more water. The athlete will increase his or her sweat rate, which aids in cooling but at the same time increases the demand for water consumption during exercise. This last point is extremely important to note because as athletes gain fitness and become acclimatized to the heat, their water needs increase. Guidelines have been introduced for the high school population for the purpose of gradual heat acclimatization during the preseason.[20] The main recommendations can be seen in **Table 5.2**, starting with the first day of preseason practice.

> **acclimatization** A complex of adaptive responses that demonstrate improved homeostatic balance in multiple organs; usually requires 10 to 14 days for responses to develop adequately. The body can acclimatize (to varying degrees) to hot, cold, high altitude, and underwater environments.

TABLE 5.2 Preseason Heat Acclimatization Guidelines

Day(s)	Recommendations
General	Total practice time should not exceed 3 hours in any 1 day. Warm-up, stretching, cool-down, walk-throughs, conditioning, and weight room activities are included as practice time.
1–5	No more than one practice per day. A 1-hour maximum walk-through is permitted; however, it cannot occur immediately prior to or following the general 3-hour practice session.
1–2	If the sport requires protective equipment (helmets/shoulder pads), a helmet is the only protective equipment permitted. Goalies (i.e., field hockey) should *not* wear full protective equipment.
3–5	Only helmets and shoulder pads should be worn for protective equipment.
6	All protective equipment may be worn. Full contact may begin.
6–14	Double-practice-session days may begin, but must be followed by a single-practice day and separated within practice by at least 3 hours of continuous rest in a cool environment.
Double practices	On these days neither practice should exceed 3 hours in duration. Athletes should not participate in more than 5 total hours of practice.

Source: Adapted from Casa DJ, Csillan D, et al. Preseason heat-acclimatization guidelines for secondary school athletics. *J Athl Train.* 2009;44(3):332–333.

Hydration status is another important factor in heat tolerance. It is widely known that water is essential for life; however, in terms of daily functioning, it also has a large impact on heat tolerance and exercise performance.[2,21] Although the term *dehydration* is used here to indicate water deficit, it should be clarified that dehydration by definition is the process of water loss, whereas *hypohydration* is a steady state of fluid deficit.[22] The term *dehydration* will be used for the purpose of this chapter.

Although hydration status may receive the most attention in the public eye, it should be clearly noted that EHS results from multiple factors and from a combination of factors. Therefore, an athlete may have a normal hydration status, but with high-intensity exercise he or she can still succumb to EHS. However, dehydration alone can place such a large stress on the body that it can negate the positive effects of heat acclimatization. Dehydration has been proven to decrease sweating sensitivity[23] and increase core temperature to a greater extent than that seen in an unacclimatized and euhydrated individual.[24] Research studies have found about a 0.4 to 0.5° F body temperature increase for every additional 1% body mass loss during intense exercise in the heat. Therefore, while dehydration can place athletes at greater risk, the alternative of an optimal hydration status can be protective in high risk scenarios. It is recommended that athletes take routine water breaks during which they may replace fluids as needed.

Once an athlete is acclimatized, he or she will require even more fluid during exercise due to the increase in sweat rate.[21] It is recommended that athletes attempt to consume fluids at the same rate as their individual sweat rate, but not to consume a greater amount than their sweat rate.[25] Consuming enough fluid can be challenging because high intensity of exercise, the rules/structure of the particular sport, equipment, high humidity, and other factors can cause sweat rate to increase more than normal.[21]

WBGT is also a large factor in the body's response to the environment. WBGT is a widely used indicator of heat stress that incorporates the dry bulb temperature, wet bulb temperature, and black globe (solar) temperature. It is calculated by the following formula: WBGT = 0.7(Wet Bulb Temperature) + 0.2(Black Globe Temperature) + 0.1(Dry Bulb Temperature). When indoors, the globe temperature cannot be incorporated and the new WBGT = 0.7(Wet Bulb Temperature) + 0.3(Dry Bulb Temperature). This highlights the large impact (and relative contribution) a change in the wet bulb temperature (reflecting humidity in the air) plays on heat stress. This consequently also mirrors the risk for exertional heat illness as WBGT increases, due to the reduced ability to utilize evaporation to dissipate heat as discussed earlier.

Clothing or equipment is another factor that can alter exercise capacity in the heat. Extra clothing in warm environments creates a barrier to sweat evaporation and consequently to cooling. This causes a greater physiologic strain, increases sweat rate, and increases the potential for a greater level of dehydration (the athlete must now work harder to replace the amount of fluid being lost). The added stress is the main reason why acclimatization guidelines are put into place for preseason practices as discussed earlier.

Finally, intensity of exercise, which is based on individual physical fitness, has been demonstrated to be the greatest influence on rate of core body temperature increase.[26–28] When risk factors that are outside the control of the athlete are not present, intensity of exercise will largely determine the extent of core body temperature rise. This factor is most evident when pressure to succeed or perform is high, such as new football players trying to make the team, or marathon runners trying to obtain a qualifying time. Therefore, it is important during high-risk scenarios to modify rest-to-work ratios, among other modifiable factors (if possible), to allow recovery and to minimize rises in core body temperature.

Prevention and Predisposing Factors

Certain precautions may be taken to help avoid EHS. Recognizing and understanding predisposing risk factors can aid in prevention strategies for EHS. Although extrinsic factors are outside the control of the exercising individual, there are also intrinsic factors, which the exercising individual can (in most cases) control **(Table 5.3)**. Efforts can also work to minimize extrinsic factors, such as exercise at a cooler time of day.

A study by Rav-Acha et al.[29] examined the prevalence of predisposing factors for EHS in six fatal cases. The authors looked at 134 cases of exertional heat stroke (6 fatal, 128 nonfatal) and attempted to

TABLE 5.3	Extrinsic and Intrinsic Risk Factors for Exertional Heat Stroke

Extrinsic Risk Factors	Intrinsic Risk Factors
High ambient temperature, solar radiation, and humidity	High intensity of exercise and/or poor physical conditioning
Athletic gear or uniforms	Sleep loss
Peer or organizational pressure	Dehydration or inadequate water intake
Inappropriate work-to-rest ratios based on intensity, wet bulb globe temperature, clothing, equipment, fitness, and athlete's medical condition	Use of diuretics or certain medications (e.g., antihistamines, diuretics, antihypertensives, attention deficit hyperactivity disorder drugs)
Predisposing medical conditions (e.g., malignant hyperthermia, cystic fibrosis)	Overzealousness or reluctance to report problems, issues, or illness
Lack of education and awareness of heat illnesses among coaches, athletes, and medical staff	Inadequate heat acclimation
No emergency plan to identify and treat exertional heat illnesses	High muscle mass to body fat ratio
Minimal access to fluids before and during practice and rest breaks	Presence of a fever
Delay in recognition of early warning signs	Skin disorder (e.g., miliaria rubra or sunburn)

Source: Adapted from Binkley HM, Beckett J, Casa DJ, Kleiner DM, Plummer PE. National Athletic Trainers' Association position statement: exertional heat illnesses. *J Athl Train.* 2002;37(3):329–343.

isolate the factors that initiated the exertional heat stroke and determined which items were more likely to cause death. Many of these fatal cases had variables that could be mitigated or controlled to lower the risk of EHS, and certainly of death from EHS **(Figure 5.1)**. Low physical fitness, sleep deprivation, a high heat load (WBGT $\geq$ 27°C [80.6°F]), high solar radiation, and training during the hottest hours of the day were each present in 83% of the cases. Physical effort unmatched to physical fitness and absence of proper medical triage were present in 100% of the fatal cases.[29] Because these last two factors were present in 100% of these fatal cases, it is important to examine them closer.

Effort unmatched to physical fitness is a common scenario in sporting venues, where athletes are pressured to perform well or possess internal pressure to perform well. In many distance running and cycling events, athletes are motivated by others vying for position. This causes many to push beyond the normal limits at which they would volitionally cease exercise. Working at this intensity only drives the athlete's core body temperature higher.

The absence of proper medical triage is a large problem, which, in most cases of organized sport, can be prevented. Although almost all college and professional teams hire physicians or athletic trainers, high schools represent the largest athletic population that still lacks proper medical personnel. About half of America's high schools have an employed athletic trainer.

Efforts should be made to control factors to help lower the risk of EHS. In respect to extrinsic factors, adjustments can be made such as exercising in the cooler times of the day, practicing without the use of protective equipment, having proper medical care on site, and preparing and planning ahead of time (e.g., having appropriate equipment and protocols in place) in the event that there is an instance of EHS.

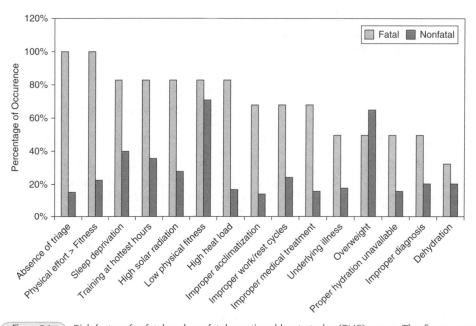

Figure 5.1 Risk factors for fatal and nonfatal exertional heat stroke (EHS) cases. The figure represents data in which there were 6 fatal and 128 nonfatal EHS cases.
Source: McDermott BP, Casa DJ, Yeargin SW, et al. Recovery and return to activity following exertional heat stroke: considerations for the sports medicine staff. *J Sport Rehabil.* 2007;16:163–181. Reprinted with permission.

Preventive steps can be categorized into setting-specific and athlete-specific measures.

Setting Specific

- Employ on-site medical personnel (i.e., athletic trainers or sports medicine physicians) who have the authority to restrict the athlete from participating because of any associated risk factors (medical, environmental, or other).[2]
- Ensure that appropriate medical treatment equipment (e.g., immersion tub, accurate temperature measurement device, water/ice) is available and ready for use in the event that an athlete has EHS.[2]
- When possible, adjust starting times and practice times to avoid the hottest part of the day (usually between 10 AM and 5 PM).[2] If unable to do so, adjust work-to-rest ratios.
- Implement heat acclimatization guidelines.[2,3] Updated guidelines were introduced in 2009 specifically for secondary school athletes (see Table 5.2).[20] These guidelines help the athlete to adjust to physical stressors in combination with the environment without overwhelming the body's system.

Athlete Specific

- Educate athletes and coaches regarding the prevention, recognition, and treatment of heat illnesses and the risks associated with exercising in hot, humid environmental conditions.[30] Every year there should be a coach's meeting at which the medical staff can address these concerns along with other pertinent medical topics.
- Ensure that the preparticipation physical exam includes medical history questions specific to heat illnesses.[30] The following questions should be included:
  - Have you ever had a heat illness? If so, when? What was your final diagnosis?
  - Do you find it hard or have you ever had trouble exercising in the heat?

- How much sleep do you get per night on average? In the last week?
- Do you sleep in an air-conditioned room?
- In the last 2 weeks have you been exercising in the heat? On average, how long each day did you perform aerobic conditioning?
- In the past 3 months, on average, how many days per week did you perform some sort of aerobic workout?
- For how many years have you been participating in sports? Do you participate year-round? If not, how many months of the year are you active?

These questions will help one to gain insight into whether an athlete is fit, has a history that might indicate a predisposition to a heat illness, and is acclimatized to exercising in the heat.

- Ensure that athletes have access to water and are allowed water breaks throughout practice.[2,3] Athletes should be encouraged to drink fluids throughout practice, and at no point should an athlete be refused fluids. Water should be accessible, bountiful, and chilled, and athletes should have plenty of time to consume fluids. If athletes become dehydrated this can completely negate the advantages gained with heat acclimatization.[24]
- Monitor body weight changes during multiple practice days or at the end of practice to ensure proper rehydration.[2] Although weight is not a good indicator of hydration status globally, it can reflect and account for water loss during a practice session. This means that while the precise level of dehydration is not known, the amount lost during a session can be calculated and replenished at the end of practice. An important caveat, however, is that if an athlete starts exercise in fluid deficit, his or her body weight change will not reflect this. If the athlete replaces only the fluids lost during that session, but started the session dehydrated, the athlete will only return to his/her pre-practice level of dehydration.
- On hot days, limit the use of protective equipment and athletic equipment that act as a barrier to evaporation.[2,3] A sudden increase in environmental temperature can increase the physical strain on the body, even in an individual who is acclimatized.
- Ensure that athletes have proper fitness leading into preseason/practice and get proper sleep every night.[2,26] Research has found that sleep deprivation is a common factor reported in multiple EHS cases.[29]

Recognition

EHS may or may not arise slowly, but in most cases athletes are not aware of how close they are to this serious condition. EHS is more common in bouts of intense exercise lasting in the range of 30–90 minutes, such as the Falmouth road race. As exercise duration increases, relative intensity of the exercise must decrease, which is why EHS in the marathon occurs, but is not as prevalent as shorter duration races. On the other side of this, EHS in running events such as a 5k is rare because the athletes usually are not running long enough to obtain a dangerous core body temperature. Precollapse symptoms may include fatigue, irritability, dizziness, inability to run or continue on, and irrational thought. Collapse will soon follow and in most cases is the first indication to medical personnel that something is wrong.

Immediate postcollapse symptoms include the following:

- Core body temperature usually higher than 40.5°C (105°F) taken via a rectal thermometer within a few minutes after collapse or suspicion of EHS
- Central nervous system (CNS) dysfunction (disorientation, confusion, dizziness, irrational or unusual behavior, inappropriate comments, irritability, headache, inability to walk, loss of balance or muscle function, vomiting, diarrhea, loss of consciousness)

These symptoms are the main two criteria for diagnosing EHS.[2,3,30,31] It is important to note that the athlete may have a lucid interval prior to experiencing rapidly deteriorating symptoms. This is

TABLE
5.4

Signs and Symptoms of EHS

EHS Diagnostic Criteria Signs and Symptoms	Other Potential Signs and Symptoms
1. Rectal temperature ≥40.5°C or 105°F	Hot, wet skin
2. Central nervous system dysfunction such as:	Dehydration
Dizziness	Tachycardia
Collapse	Hyperventilation
Confusion	Hypotension
Irrational behavior	Vomiting
Hysteria	Diarrhea
Aggressiveness	
Disorientation	
Seizures	
Coma	

Sources: Binkley H, Beckett J, Casa D, Kleiner D, Plummer P. National Athletic Trainers' position statement: exertional heat illnesses. *J Athl Train*. 2002;37:329–343; Armstrong L, Casa D, Millard-Strafford D, et al. American College of Sports Medicine position stand. Exertional heat illnesses during training and competition. *Med Sci Sports Exerc*. 2007;39(3):556–572.

commonly misleading and delays proper treatment. EHS should be considered in any collapsed athlete who is exercising intensely in a warm environment until it is ruled out.

The differential diagnosis includes the following:

- Heat exhaustion
- Exertional hyponatremia
- Exertional sickling
- Diabetic emergency
- Concussion
- Heat syncope

rectal temperature Body temperature taken rectally. In most medical situations this involves a rectal probe inserted 10 cm past the anal sphincter. This has been validated as an accurate tool for temperature assessment in exercising individuals and is the most common form used in heat stroke cases.

If an athlete is both hyperthermic (≥40.5°C [105°F]) and exhibiting CNS dysfunction, he or she should be treated immediately as an EHS victim. Hyperthermia should be determined only via a rectal thermometer because all other temperature measurement devices or methods have been found to be invalid in exercising individuals.[3,32–35] The exception to this rule is ingestible thermistors; however, these are only useful if the athlete has ingested the pill approximately 5 hours prior to the event, and they are not widely used in training or race scenarios. Simply obtaining a **rectal temperature** soon after collapse can rule out a concussion or head injury, heat exhaustion, cardiac events, heat syncope, postural hypotension, and shock.

Treatment

Within the first 5 minutes of collapse or onset, the athlete should have his or her rectal temperature assessed and should be immersed in ice water **(Figure 5.2)**. Ice water immersion is the gold standard of treatment for EHS. Of the 252 cases of EHS that occurred between 1975 and 1990 that were treated by immersion in cold water, no deaths occurred.[36] Such a statement cannot be made about any other method.[36]

It is extremely important to minimize the length of time at which a person's temperature remains above 40.5°C (105°F). The heat stress incurred by either the magnitude by which a person's temperature

Figure 5.2   An example of cold water immersion set up and treatment, including the use of a rectal thermometer, towels for the head and to hold the athlete above water.

exceeds 40.5°C (105°F), the length of time that it remains over this temperature, or a combination of both factors determines the extent of multisystem tissue injury and long-term sequelae.[36–39] The goal in any EHS case should be to cool the athlete down to 39°C (102°F) within the first 30 minutes after collapse.

Cold Water Immersion: A Powerful Cooling Modality

Effective treatment of EHS must include a rectal temperature cooling rate exceeding 0.1° to 0.2°C/min (0.18–0.36°F/min) when cooling begins immediately and should be no less than 0.15°C/min (0.27°F/min) if cooling is delayed.[40] **Cold water immersion (CWI)** (<10°C) is considered the most effective strategy for the rapid treatment of EHS, with circulated ice-water immersion (2°C) providing some of the highest core temperature cooling rates (0.35°C/min), especially for the second-degree drop in core temperature (0.50°C/min).[41] These rates are approximately 2- to 17-fold greater than other cooling modalities such as regional or whole-body application of wet towels and ice or cold packs, evaporative cooling (i.e., spraying water over the patient and facilitating evaporation and convection with use of fans), and temperate or tap water immersion (≥15°C or 59°F).[40,42]

The superior cooling rate of CWI provides an important advantage in reducing the likelihood of morbidity and mortality associated with the condition **(Figure 5.3 and Figure 5.4)**. Evidence of the powerful influence of cold water on cooling of actual EHS patients has been well documented in the athletic field, mass medical tents, and military training centers. For example, in the over three-decade-long history of the Falmouth Road Race in Falmouth, Massachusetts, CWI treatment provided 100% survival for the more than 400 EHS victims.[43] Similar evidence of success has been reported when using ice water at numerous athletic events, such as the Marine Corps Marathon, and at military bases such as Fort Benning, Quantico, Parris Island, and others. While the authors agree that CWI is the most powerful treatment for EHS, it is also recognized that in some scenarios it may not always be practical or available (e.g., in remote hiking areas). In these cases it is recommended that the medical staff try to aggressively douse the patient continuously with cold water. This is the best option, without being able to fully immerse the athlete. Other options include rotation of wet ice towels. While these are options in the absence of CWI availability, it does not omit medical staff from the responsibility of planning for such an event and having the best treatment materials (e.g., immersion tub) at athletic venues.

Physical Properties of Water and Cooling Capacity

Whole-body heat loss can be severely compromised in individuals suffering from EHS. Under these conditions, cooling treatments that enhance heat dissipation by increasing conductive heat transfer or evaporative heat loss or both are critical for the survival of the EHS victim **(Figure 5.5)**. Immersion in a circulated cold water bath enhances heat dissipation by dramatically increasing nonevaporative (conductive/convective) heat transfer.

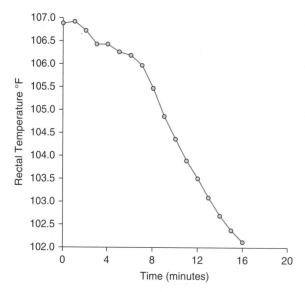

Figure 5.3 Hypothetical cooling curve via cold water dousing. Note: cooling rate = 0.29°F/min or 0.16°C/min.

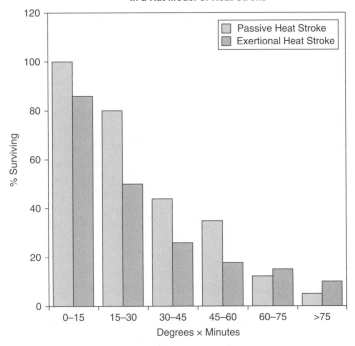

Survival as it Relates to Severity and Duration of Hyperthermia in a Rat Model of Heat Stroke

Passive Heat Stroke
Exertional Heat Stroke

% Surviving

Degrees × Minutes

Figure 5.4   Relationship between severity of hyperthermia measured in degree-minutes and rate of survivability. Thermal area (degrees × minutes) = ∑ Time interval (min) × ½[°C above 40.4°C at start of interval + °C above 40.4°C at end of interval].
Source: Casa DJ, Kenny GP, Taylor NA. Immersion treatment for exertional hyperthermia: cold or temperate water? *Med Sci Sports Exerc*. 2010;42(7):1246–1252. Reprinted with permission.

Figure 5.5   A 150-gallon tub for cold water immersion treatment.

Water has many physical characteristics that differentiate it from air, helping to explain the powerful cooling that occurs when an individual with EHS is treated with CWI. The advantages of using water cooling over air cooling include water's higher specific heat capacity (i.e., the amount of heat that is required to change a body's temperature by a given amount: air 1.007 vs. water 4.18 $J \cdot g^{-1} \cdot K^{-1}$), density (air 0.0012 vs. water 0.9922 $g \cdot cm^{-3}$), and thermal conductivity (the property of a material that indicates its ability to conduct heat: air 26.2 vs. water 630.5 $mW \cdot m^{-1} \cdot K^{-1}$). The high volume-specific heat capacity of water, defined as the product of specific heat capacity and density (i.e., 3500 times that of air), combined with the high thermal conductivity of water (~24 times greater than air), translates into a much greater potential for heat transfer. Sitting in a tub of cool water, for example, can remove a significantly greater amount of heat in a relatively shorter period of time than sitting in air that is 11°C cooler.[44]

The rate of heat loss is proportional to the thermal gradient between the surface of the object and the layer of water adjacent to that surface. As such, cooling efficiency will improve as the heat sink gets colder (i.e., temperature of the water bath vs. temperature of body core) or water circulation is increased (circulating or stirring the water bath enhances convective heat transfer), or both. Moreover, increasing the body surface area (i.e., full-body versus partial-body immersion) that is in direct contact with the water will significantly enhance the rate of heat dissipation, resulting in a greater core cooling rate.[42]

Biophysical Considerations

Irrespective of the cooling modality employed in the treatment of EHS, variations in physical characteristics among individuals, such as differences in body size, shape, and composition, can influence the rate of whole-body cooling. For example, high levels of tissue insulation (i.e., subcutaneous fat) and a small body surface area to mass ratio are associated with a reduced core cooling rate in normothermic individuals exposed to a cold stress.[45] Evidence shows that immersion of hyperthermic individuals (rectal temperature ≥40.5°C [105°F]) in cold water (<10°C [50°F]) can minimize variations in cooling rate caused by large differences in physical characteristics. For example, it has been shown that greater levels of adipose tissue insulation in females—in particular, subcutaneous fat—have little effect in reducing the rate of heat transfer during CWI (8°C [46.4°F]).[46] Similarly, differences in body adiposity within a range of 8% to 30% had no significant effect on the overall core cooling rate (2°C [35.6°F] circulated water bath) in previously hyperthermic males.[47] Although some advocate use of warmer immersion temperatures, arguing that they provide a result equivalent to that of ice-water or cold water immersion,[48] the principles of thermodynamics ultimately dictate that a colder water bath is required to increase heat transfer in larger individuals.

Despite the growing evidence in support of CWI as a gold standard treatment for EHS, misconceptions have arisen about its use within the medical and scientific literature. Some experts suggest that aggressive skin cooling will induce peripheral vasoconstriction (preventing heat transfer to the skin) and induce shivering (cause an increase in the heat production), thereby reducing cooling efficiency.[48,49] This misguided belief stems largely from responses derived from normothermic individuals subjected to cold water immersion.[44] However, the physiologic responses to cold water immersion differ between a normothermic and hyperthermic individual. The notion that the suppression of skin blood flow during ice-water or cold water immersion will dramatically decrease heat loss is unsupported. Proulx et al.[50] showed that the temperature gradient between the skin and the ice water is so great (7.7°C [46°F]) that an elevated skin perfusion is not essential for the body to cool. Moreover, the short duration of exposure during ice-water immersion also minimizes the effect of increased heat production via shivering thermogenesis.[46,47,50]

Keeping It Safe: Managing the Power of Cold Water Immersion

Although cold water immersion is a safe and powerful cooling modality for the treatment of EHS, extreme care should be taken when considering when to remove individuals from a water bath. One potential danger associated with this treatment is the risk of causing hypothermia as a result of too much cooling. It has been suggested that for water temperatures below 10°C, 100% of the heat gained during exercise in the heat is removed when rectal temperature reaches 38.6°C or 101.5°F (an equivalent immersion time of 9 minutes).[41] From a clinical standpoint, the dangers associated with hyperthermia far outweigh those associated with overcooling. Therefore, cooling of the hyperthermic individual should be undertaken as quickly as possible even if a measurement of core temperature is not readily available. Immersion time in water temperatures below 10°C (50°F) should be restricted to approximately 9 minutes (i.e., exit rectal temperature of approximately 38.6°C [101.5°F]) to reduce any potential risk of overcooling.[51] Medical providers should also place a towel or other device under the athlete's arms to ensure that the athlete's head remains above water during treatment, especially in obtunded or comatose patients who are unable to protect their own airway.

Common Misconceptions

A multitude of misconceptions exist regarding all facets of EHS. The following list addresses these misconceptions.

- *Heat stroke has to occur in the heat.* Because of the name of the condition, many fail to recognize EHS if the athlete is not participating in hot conditions. However, as mentioned previously, environmental conditions are not the only factor that can contribute to EHS, and many times they are not the primary factor. There have been reports of EHS in temperatures of 9.4°C (49°F) and 62% humidity.[52]
- *Nutritional supplements contribute to EHS deaths.* Many supplements have been implicated in the deaths occurring from EHS. Among these are creatine and ephedra. The evidence supporting creatine as a drug that decreases heat tolerance is lacking or demonstrates no change.[53,54] Ephedra has been implicated as decreasing heat tolerance, but much less research has been done in this area. However, even with a decrease in exercise heat tolerance that may arise from supplement use or any other cause, an individual with EHS should survive if given immediate and effective treatment.
- *Axillary, oral, tympanic, aural canal, and temporal artery thermometers and temperature stickers are all valid methods of temperature assessment for EHS.* The only temperature assessment method that has been validated for use in EHS victims is rectal and gastrointestinal thermometry.[3,32–35] It is recommended that rectal temperatures be used in EHS scenarios because they provide an immediate and accurate body temperature. It is *not* recommended that an inaccurate temperature device be used in the absence of an accurate device, since this can mislead the medical diagnosis. In this circumstance it is much better to base the diagnosis on history and presenting signs and symptoms.
- *Rectal temperature must be over 40.5°C (105°F).* Although this temperature is the defining temperature for EHS, it is quite possible that temperature assessment may be delayed and may not accurately reflect the heat stress incurred. In this case it is safer to err on the side of caution and cool the athlete, because it is rare that cooling would ever cause another potential medical condition to worsen.
- *The athlete must be severely dehydrated to experience EHS.* Although core temperature does increase with dehydration,[24,55,56] intensity of exercise and environmental temperature are also important factors that can contribute to an increase in core body temperature. It is certainly possible, and evident in past cases, that EHS can occur without severe dehydration.
- *The athlete with EHS will become unconscious.* Although an athlete with EHS *may* become unconscious, this may not occur and CNS dysfunction may present in other fashions, often as irritability or confusion. It is also very important to note that the athlete may have a lucid interval in which CNS function may appear normal, followed by quickly deteriorating symptoms.[31]
- *Cooling an athlete with EHS via cold water immersion will cause peripheral vasoconstriction and inhibit cooling or can cause cardiovascular shock.* No other cooling modality has ever proved faster than cold water immersion.[31,40,57] It is believed that in a normal, healthy, individual the risk of cardiovascular shock is extremely low, and without proper treatment for EHS the risk for death is very high; therefore, treatment should commence with cold water immersion. If a cardiovascular event occurs, the athlete should be removed from the water and treated accordingly.[31]

Recovery

One hour after collapse, the athlete should have been cooled and have been monitored for approximately 15 minutes to observe for hypothermia. (This is in the absence of other emergency medical issues that could potentially arise.) At this point the athlete should be transported to the hospital for follow-up blood work. The athlete should *not* be transported to the hospital until a safe core temperature has been attained. Only in the event that there is no effective cooling modality and a lack of appropriate on-site medical care should an EHS victim be immediately transported to the hospital.

Long-term prognosis and recovery from EHS is improved if the initial treatment includes rapid whole-body cooling. Therefore, a person with a core body temperature of 41°C (106°F) for an hour could be at much greater risk for mortality and morbidity than one who has a core body temperature of 42.8°C (109°F) and is cooled within 15 minutes. The majority of EHS cases that are not cooled immediately but survive have an extended recovery time (many lasting up to 1 year after the event) with likely organ function complications. Individuals treated immediately on site are usually released and return home the same day.

Return-to-Play Considerations

The primary skill that a medical provider contributes to the sports medicine team is the diagnosis and management of athletic injuries or illness. At the 2000 American College of Sports Medicine's (ACSM) Team Physician conference, the core concepts of athlete medical management were described and published as a consensus statement.[58] The return-to-play (RTP) process, defined as deciding when an injured or ill athlete may safely return to practice or competition, is arguably the most challenging component of athlete injury management. The final decision for safe and timely return to practice or competition is the desired result of an integrated process of evaluation, treatment, and rehabilitation.[59]

RTP decision-making can be a complex and demanding process. Although the final decision is most commonly left in the hands of the providing physician, the assessments frequently require the incorporation of information from and execution by the athletic trainer, physical therapist, coach, and family members, as well as the athlete. An ACSM guideline on RTP identified several key considerations to assist in safely returning athletes to activity:[59]

- Status of anatomic and functional healing
- Status of recovery from acute illness and associated sequelae
- Status of chronic injury or illness
- Whether the athlete poses an undue risk to the safety of other participants
- Restoration of sport-specific skills
- Psychosocial readiness
- Ability to perform safely with equipment modification, bracing, and orthoses
- Compliance with applicable federal, state, local, school, and governing body regulations

The cornerstone assessment in the RTP decision requires a fundamental understanding of the anatomic, as well as the functional, healing of the particular disorder that affects the athlete. Exertional heat illness RTP is especially challenging because we have an incomplete understanding of the pathophysiologic processes involved in the development of and recovery from this disorder.[31,60]

Despite the frequency of EHI, current civilian and military RTP guidelines are largely based on anecdotal observation and caution.[60,61] At this time, no evidence-based guidelines or recommendations exist for returning athletes or warfighters to play or duty. Most guidelines are commonsense recommendations that require an asymptomatic state and normal laboratory parameters, coupled with a cautious reintroduction of activity and gradual heat acclimatization. Current suggestions for a return of EHS victims to full activity range from 7 days to 15 months.[62] This lack of consistency and clinical agreement can negatively affect athletes and soldiers and force medical providers to guess about the best solution for each individual; the inconsistencies also can directly affect military force readiness. Additionally, whereas current guidance states that EHS casualties may return to practice and competition when they have reestablished heat tolerance, no evidence-based tools are available to assess when the body's thermoregulatory system has returned to normal.[60]

The lack of clear evidence-based guidance has allowed some sports medicine professionals to clear athletes for return to participation following EHS without considering exercise heat tolerance deficits, neuropsychological impairments, or the altered fitness status or acclimatization status from not being actively engaged in training during recovery.[38,63,64] Return to play after EHS should, however, like return from any other injury, involve a carefully planned and incrementally increased physical challenge that is closely supervised by an athletic trainer and physician, as previously identified in the ACSM conference statement. Current research indicates that most individuals will eventually recover fully from EHS; indeed, this occurs in the vast majority of cases when the athlete is treated promptly with aggressive cooling strategies (i.e., ice-water immersion).[31,38,65] Although definitive, evidence-based guidelines regarding RTP do not presently exist, the current recommendations are summarized in the following sections.

Current Civilian Recommendations

In the authors' opinion, the consensus RTP guidelines set forth by the ACSM are clear, succinct, and provide a rational process for guiding athletes who have experienced an exertional heat illness. Current recommendations from the ACSM for returning an athlete to training and competition are as follows:[62]

1. Refrain from exercise for at least 7 days following release from medical care.
2. Follow up about 1 week postincident for a physical examination and lab testing or diagnostic imaging of the affected organs, based on the clinical course of the heat stroke incident.
3. When cleared for return to activity, begin exercise in a cool environment and gradually increase the duration, intensity, and heat exposure over 2 weeks to demonstrate heat tolerance and to initiate acclimatization.
4. If return to vigorous activity is not accomplished over 4 weeks, a laboratory exercise-heat tolerance test should be considered.
5. Clear the athlete for full competition if heat tolerant between 2 and 4 weeks of full training.

Current Army Recommendations

The military services do not share consensus recommendations on returning warfighters to duty after experiencing an exertional heat illness (EHI).[61] In fact, the individual service recommendations are more diverse and varied than those in the civilian sector. An ACSM roundtable was convened at the Uniformed Services University of the Health Sciences (Bethesda, MD) on October 22 and 23, 2008, to address this issue of variability with both military and civilian experts. Specifically, the conference sought to (1) discuss the issue of returning victims (athletes and soldiers) of EHI to either play or duty and (2) develop consensus-based recommendations. The conference convened over 20 recognized EHI experts from both civilian and Department of Defense sports medicine communities. The conference comprised seven 1-hour EHI topic blocks, including definitions and basic epidemiology; pathophysiology; recognition and treatment; the role of thermal tolerance testing in recovery and return to play/duty; the role of genetic and biomarkers in recovery and return to play/duty; prevention of an ensuing incident of EHS; and current civilian and military guidelines for return to play/duty.[66]

Conference agenda and presentations are available at http://www.usuhs.mil/mem/champ.html; a publication is pending detailing these proceedings. The conference results were used as a foundation to develop new guidance that is presently used by the Army medical department (**Appendix 5.1**), and are further elaborated upon at http://champ.usuhs.mil/chclinicaltools.html.

Summary

Exertional heat stroke is a medical emergency that, if not promptly recognized and treated immediately, can result in death. Many factors either independently or in combination, such as exercise intensity, hydration status, environmental conditions, and use of protective equipment, can cause an overwhelming of the thermoregulatory system. This accumulation of heat within the body causes a dangerously high temperature, with concomitant central nervous system dysfunction. Although there are preventive steps that should be taken, there is no method to fully protect athletes from exertional heat stroke. Although EHS is unfortunately not always preventable, death from heat stroke is. Cooling an athlete via cold water immersion is the only treatment, if performed immediately, that has a 100% survival rate. If prevention strategies are followed and emergency action plans incorporate accurate temperature measurement (via rectal thermometry) and cold water immersion is utilized for treatment of exertional heat stroke, the incidence of and death from this condition can be dramatically reduced.

Clinical Case Scenarios

1. James is a 6′0″, 240-pound lineman. He had just graduated from high school and was trying to make the starting line for a Division I college in the northeast. It was preseason and the first day of practice in full pads. James had struggled the day before with an intense conditioning bout the team had performed, but was set on proving his ability to be a starter. The past few days the air temperature had been much higher than usual. The second practice for the day started at 3:00 PM and ended at 5:00 PM with more conditioning. James collapsed during the end of some sprinting drills. He tried to get up and was able to stagger across the line. His coaches came to his side and noted that he was unable to talk coherently or answer simple questions. James's skin was hot and sweaty, and there were salt stains all over his clothes. The coaches quickly called the athletic trainer, who took his core temperature, which read 42.8°C (109°F). The athletic trainer was able to douse James with cold water and lower his body temperature to 39.4°C (103°F) before transporting him to the hospital. Because of the prompt recognition and care James received, he was able to recover and return to football the next week.
   1. What other medical conditions could present with similar signs and symptoms?
   2. What materials would you need to treat an athlete with exertional heat stroke?
   3. What is your ideal cooling modality for this situation?
2. Ann is a 23-year-old former Division I collegiate runner. She has been a runner since high school, and in her postcollegiate years she was working on her goal of qualifying for the Boston marathon. She trained all summer and entered her first marathon in the fall. She had a friend who ran the last 10 miles with her to help pace her and push her to finish. Toward the end of the race, the air temperature had reached 15.6°C (60°F). With the help of her friend, Ann made it to the finish and barely made the qualifying time. However, directly after she crossed the finish line, she collapsed and could not regain her ability to walk. She was immediately carried to a nearby medical tent while her friend screamed orders at the medical staff. As the medical staff began to diagnose her, they decided to obtain a rectal body temperature. At this point she became combative and tried to refuse treatment. Her initial rectal temperature was 42°C (107.5°F). She was immediately moved to the immersion tub; however, she started to shout obscenities and thrash violently. The medical team restrained her during her cooling treatment. Over the course of the next 15 minutes her temperature lowered under 40.6°C (105°F), at which point she quickly became lucid and returned to a compliant state. She was removed from cooling once her temperature reached 39.4°C (103°F) and transferred to the hospital for follow-up care.
   1. How would you organize a mass medical tent to accommodate this scenario?
   2. What other conditions would you want to rule out that might present with symptoms similar to this athlete's central nervous system disorder?
   3. What steps or considerations should you take before this athlete returns to play?

Key Terms

acclimation

acclimatization

cold water immersion (CWI)

core body temperature

dehydration

exertional heat stroke (EHS)

heat balance equation

rectal temperature

wet bulb globe temperature (WBGT)

References

1. Mueller F, Cantu R. *Twenty Sixth Annual Report of the National Center for Catastrophic Sports Injury Research: Catastrophic Football Injuries.* Chapel Hill, NC: National Center for Catastrophic Sports Injury Research; 2009.
2. Binkley H, Beckett J, Casa D, Kleiner D, Plummer P. National Athletic Trainers' position statement: exertional heat illnesses. *J Athl Train.* 2002;37:329–343.
3. Casa D, Armstrong L. Exertional heatstroke: a medical emergency. In: Armstrong LE, ed. *Exertional Heat Illnesses.* Champaign, IL: Human Kinetics; 2003:29–56.
4. Armstrong L, Casa D, Millard-Strafford D, et al. American College of Sports Medicine position stand. Exertional heat illnesses during training and competition. *Med Sci Sports Exerc.* 2007;39(3):556–572.
5. Santee W, Gonzalez R. Characteristics of the thermal environment. In: Pandolf KB, Sawka MN, Gonzalez RR, eds. *Human Performance Physiology and Environmental Medicine at Terrestrial Extremes.* Indianapolis, IL: Benchmark Press; 1988:1–44.
6. Stitt J. Central regulation of body temperature. In: Gisolfi CV, Lamb DR, Nadel ER, eds. *Exercise, Heat and Thermoregulation.* Traverse City, MI: Cooper Publishing Group; 2001.
7. Castellani J. Physiology of heat stress. In: Armstrong LE, ed. *Exertional Heat Illnesses.* Champaign, IL: Human Kinetics; 2003.
8. Neilsen M. Die regulation der korper temperatur bei muskelarbiet. *Skan Arch Physiol.* 1938;79:193–230.
9. Booth J, Marino F, Ward J. Improved running performance in hot humid conditions following whole body precooling. *Med Sci Sports Exerc.* 1997;29:943–949.
10. Cheung S, Sleivert G. Multiple triggers for hyperthermic fatigue and exhaustion. *Exerc Sport Sci Rev.* 2004;32(3):100–106.
11. Marino F. Anticipatory regulation and avoidance of catastrophe during exercise-induced hyperthermia. *Comp Biochem Physiol B Biochem Mol Biol.* 2004;139:561–569.
12. Tucker R, Marle T, Lambert EV, Noakes T. The rate of heat storage mediates an anticipatory reduction in exercise intensity during cycling at a fixed rating of perceived exertion. *J Physiol.* 2006;574(3):905–915.
13. Tucker R, Rauch L, Harley Y, Noakes T. Impaired exercise performance in the heat is associated with an anticipatory reduction in skeletal muscle recruitment. *Pflügers Archiv.* 2004;448:422–430.
14. Cheung S. Hyperthermia and voluntary exhaustion: integrating models and future challenges. *Appl Physiol Nutr Metab.* 2007;32(4):808–817.
15. Ely B, Cheuvront S, Kenefick R, Sawka M. Aerobic performance is degraded, despite modest hyperthermia, in hot environments. *Med Sci Sports Exerc.* 2010;42(1):135–141.
16. Pandolf K. Time course of heat acclimation and its decay. *Int J Sports Med.* 1998;19:S157–S160.
17. Armstrong L, Maresh C. The induction and decay of heat acclimatisation in trained athletes. *Sports Med.* 1991;12(5):302–312.
18. Pawelczyk J. Neural control of skin and muscle blood flow during exercise and thermal stress. In: Gisolfi CV, Lamb DR, Nadel ER, eds. *Exercise, Heat and Thermoregulation.* Traverse City, MI: Cooper Publishing Group; 2001.
19. Pandolf K. Effects of physical training and cardiorespiratory physical fitness on exercise-heat tolerance: recent observations. *Med Sci Sports Exerc.* 1979;11:60–65.
20. Casa D, Csillan D. Preseason heat-acclimatization guidelines for secondary school athletics. *J Athl Train.* 2009;44(3):332–333.
21. Casa D, Armstrong L, Hillman S, et al. National Athletic Trainers' Association position statement: fluid replacement for athletes. *J Athl Train.* 2000;35(2):212–224.
22. Sawka M, Pandolf K. Effects of body water loss on physiological function and exercise performance. In: Gisolfi CV, Lamb DR, eds. *Fluid Homeostasis During Exercise.* Traverse MI: Cooper Publishing Group; 2001.
23. Armstrong L, Maresh C, Gabaree C, et al. Thermal and circulatory responses during exercise: effects of hypohydration, dehydration, and water intake. *J Appl Physiol.* 1997;82:2028–2035.
24. Sawka M, Latzka W, Matott R, Montain S. Hydration effects on temperature regulation. *Int J Sports Med.* 1998;19:S108–S110.

25. Ganio M, Casa D, Armstrong L, Maresh C. Evidence-based approach to lingering hydration questions. *Clinics Sports Med.* 2007;26:1–16.

26. Saltin B, Hermansen L. Esophageal, rectal and muscle temperature during exercise. *J Appl Physiol.* 1966;21(6):1757–1762.

27. Noakes TD, Myburgh KH, du Plessis J, et al. Metabolic rate, not percent dehydration, predicts rectal temperature in marathon runners. *Med Sci Sports Exerc.* 1991;23(4):443–449.

28. Davies CT. Influence of skin temperature on sweating and aerobic performance during severe work. *J Appl Physiol.* 1979;47(4):770–777.

29. Rav-Acha M, Hadad E, Epstein Y, Heled Y, Moran D. Fatal exertional heat stroke: a case series. *Am J Med Sci.* 2004;328:84–87.

30. Casa D, Almquist J, Anderson SEA. Inter-Association Task Force on Exertional Heat Illnesses consensus statement. *NATA News.* June 2003:24–29.

31. Casa D, Armstrong L, Ganio M, Yeargin S. Exertional heat stroke in competitive athletes. *Curr Sports Med Rep.* 2005;4:309–317.

32. Low D, Vu A, Brown M, et al. Temporal thermometry fails to track body core temperature during heat stress. *Med Sci Sports Exerc.* 2007;39(7):1029–1035.

33. Casa D, Becker S, Ganio M, et al. Validity of devices that assess body temperature during outdoor exercise in the heat. *J Athl Train.* 2007;42(3):333–342.

34. Ganio MS, Brown CM, Casa DJ, et al. Validity and reliability of devices that assess body temperature during indoor exercise in the heat. *J Athl Train.* 2009;44(2):124-35.

35. Moran D, Mendal L. Core temperature measurement methods and current insights. *Sports Med.* 2002;32:879–885.

36. Costrini A. Emergency treatment of exertional heatstroke and comparison of whole body cooling techniques. *Med Sci Sports Exerc.* 1990;22(1):15–18.

37. Casa DJ, Kenny GP, Taylor NA. Immersion treatment for exertional hyperthermia: cold or temperate water? *Med Sci Sports Exerc.* 2010;42(7):1246-52.

38. Armstrong L, Maresh C. Can humans avoid and recover from exertional heat stroke? In: Pandolf KB, Takeda N, Singal PK, eds. *Adaptation Biology and Medicine.* Vol. 2. New Delhi, India: Narosa Publishing; 1999:344–351.

39. Shibolet S, Lancaster M, Danon Y. Heatstroke: a review. *Aviation Space Environ Med.* 1976;47:280–301.

40. Casa D, McDermott B, Lee E, et al. Cold water immersion: the gold standard for exertional heatstroke treatment. *Exerc Sport Sci Rev.* 2007;35(3):141–149.

41. Proulx C, Ducharme M, Kenny G. Safe cooling limits from exercise-induced hyperthermia. *Eur J Appl Physiol.* 2006;96:434–445.

42. McDermott BP, Casa DJ, Ganio MS, et al. Acute whole-body cooling for exercise-induced hyperthermia: a systematic review. *J Athl Train.* 2009;44:84–93.

43. O'Malley D. Hyperthermia on a short race course: the Falmouth road race experience. Paper presented at: American Medical Athletic Association's 37th Annual Sport Medicine Symposium at the Boston Marathon; April 19, 2008; Boston, MA.

44. Golden F, Tipton M. *Essentials of Sea Survival.* Champaign, IL: Human Kinetics; 2002.

45. Sloan RE, Keatinge WR. Cooling rates of young people swimming in cold water. *J Appl Physiol.* 1973;35(3):371–375.

46. Lemire BB, Gagnon D, Jay O, Kenny GP. Differences between sexes in rectal cooling rates after exercise-induced hyperthermia. *Med Sci Sports Exerc.* 2009;41(8):1633–1639.

47. Lemire B, Gagnon D, Jay O, et al. Influence of adiposity on cooling efficiency in hyperthermic individuals. *Eur J Appl Physiol.* 2008;104(1):67–74.

48. Taylor NA, Caldwell JN, Van den Heuvel AM, Patterson MJ. To cool, but not too cool: that is the question—immersion cooling for hyperthermia. *Med Sci Sports Exerc.* 2008;40(11):1962–1969.

49. Wyndham CH, Strydom NB, Cooke HM, et al. Methods of cooling in subjects with hyperpyrexia. *J Appl Physiol.* 1959;14:771–776.

50. Proulx CI, Ducharme MB, Kenny GP. Effect of water temperature on cooling efficiency during hyperthermia in humans. *J Appl Physiol.* 2003;94(4):1317–1323.

51. Gagnon D, Lemire B, Casa DJ, Kenny GP. Cold-water immersion and the treatment of hyperthermia: using 38.6°C as a safe rectal temperature cooling limit. *J Athl Train.* 2010;45(5):439–444.

52. Roberts W. Exertional heat stroke during a cool weather marathon: a case study. *Med Sci Sports Exerc.* 2006;38(7):1197–1203.

53. Kilduff L, Georgiades E, James N, et al. Effects of creatine supplementation on cardiovascular, metabolic and thermoregulatory responses during exercise in the heat in endurance trained humans. *Int J Sport Nutr Exerc Metab.* 2004;14(4):443–460.

54. Watson G, Casa D, Fiala K, et al. Creatine use and exercise heat tolerance in dehydrated men. *J Athl Train.* 2006;41(1):18–29.

55. Montain S, Coyle E. Influence of graded dehydration on hyperthermia and cardiovascular drift during exercise. *J Appl Physiol.* 1992;73:1340–1350.

56. Adolph E. *Physiology of Man in the Desert: Survival in an Arid Land.* New York: Interscience Publishers; 1947:172–196, 208–221.

57. McDermott B, Casa D, O'Connor F, et al. Cold-water dousing with ice massage to treat exertional heat stroke: a case series. *Aviation Space Environ Med.* 2009;80(8):720–722.

58. American College of Sports Medicine. Team physician consensus statement. *Med Sci Sports Exerc.* 2000;32(4):877–878.

59. American College of Sports Medicine. The team physician and return-to-play issues: a consensus statement. *Med Sci Sports Exerc.* 2002;34(7):1212–1214.

60. McDermott BP, Casa DJ, Yeargin SW, et al. Recovery and return to activity following exertional heat stroke: considerations for the sports medicine staff. *J Sport Rehabil.* 2007;16:163–181.

61. O'Connor FG, Williams AD, Blivin S, et al. Guidelines for return to duty (play) after heat illness: a military perspective. *J Sport Rehabil.* 2007(16):227–237.

62. Armstrong LE, Casa DJ, Millard-Stafford M, et al. Exertional heat illness during training and competition. *Med Sci Sports Exerc.* 2007:39(3):556–572.

63. Mehta AC, Baker RN. Persistent neurological deficits in heat stroke. *Neurology.* 1970;20:336–340.

64. Royburt M, Epstein Y, Solomon Z, Shemer J. Long term psychosocial and physiological effects of heat stroke. *Physiol Behav.* 1993;54:265–267.

65. Roberts WO. Death in the heat: can football heat stroke be prevented? *Curr Sports Med Rep.* 2004;3(1):1–3.

66. O'Connor FG, Casa DJ, Bergeron MF, et al. American College of Sports Medicine Roundtable on Exertional Heat Stroke— Return to duty/return to play: Conference proceedings. *Current Sports Medicine Reports.* 2010;9(5):314–321.

U.S. Army Medical Department Policy on Managing and Profiling Exertional Heat Illness

Heat stroke should be the working diagnosis for any Soldier with altered mental status and collapse or debilitation in the setting of heat stress. Rectal core temperature assessment is imperative, with the final diagnosis delayed until the entire clinical picture is evident. Heat exhaustion, heat injury and/or heat stroke are potential causes for referral to a medical evaluation board (MEB), with careful attention to complications and contributing factors.

a. Heat Exhaustion

(1) Heat exhaustion (HE) is defined as a syndrome of hyperthermia (core temperature at time of event usually ≤40°C or 104°F) with collapse or debilitation occurring during or immediately following exertion in the heat, with no more than minor central nervous system (CNS) dysfunction (headache, dizziness), which resolves rapidly with intervention.

(2) Profile Disposition of Soldiers with HE.
    a) Soldiers diagnosed with HE will be individually profiled as determined by the treating provider.
    b) Soldiers with HE pending MEB will be profiled as per Table 1.

(3) MEB Disposition of Soldiers with HE.
    a) Individual episodes of HE are not cause for MEB referral. However, Soldiers who experience three episodes of HE in less than 24 months require referral to a MEB.

Source: This appendix is from U.S. Army. Heat illness Medical Evaluation Board (MEB) and Profile Policy. Washington, DC: Headquarters, U.S. Army Medical Command; 2009. Policy Memo 09-039.

TABLE 1	Profile Progression Recommendations for the Soldier with Heat Stroke (HS), or Heat Exhaustion (HE), Heat Injury (HI), Pending Medical Evaluation Board (MEB)				

Profile Code*	Restrictions**	HS Without Sequelae	HS with Sequelae	Complex HS or HE/HI Pending MEB
T-4 (P)	Complete duty restrictions.	2 weeks	2 week minimum; advance when clinically resolved.	2 week minimum; advance when clinically resolved.
T-3 (P)	Physical Training and running/ walking/swimming/bicycling at own pace and distance not to exceed 60 min per day. No maximal effort; no APFT; no wear of IBA; no MOPP gear; no ruck marching. No airborne operations (AO).	1 month minimum	2 months minimum	Pending MEB
T-3 (P)	Gradual acclimatization (TB Med 507). No maximal effort; no APFT; no MOPP IV gear. IBA limited to static range participation. May ruck march at own pace/distance with no more than 30 lbs. Non-tactical AO permitted.	1 month Minimum	2 months Minimum***	N/A
T-2 (P)	Continue gradual acclimatization. May participate in unit PT; CBRN training with MOPP gear for up to 30 min; IBA on static and dynamic ranges for up to 45 min; no record APFT. Ruck march at own pace/distance with no more than 30 lbs up to 2 hrs. Non-tactical AO permitted.	N/A	Pending completion of 30 day heat exposure requirement, if not accomplished during prior profile***	N/A

*Temporary Profile; Physical Category P(PULHES).

**Soldiers manifesting no heat illness symptomatology or work intolerance after completion of profile restrictions can advance and return to duty without a MEB. Any evidence/manifestation of heat illness symptomatology during the period of the profile requires a MEB referral.

***HS with Sequelae return to full duty requires a minimum period of heat exposure during environmental stress (Heat Category 2 during the majority of included days).

b. Heat Injury

(1) Heat Injury (HI) is defined as heat exhaustion with clinical evidence of organ (e.g. liver, renal, gut) and/or muscle (e.g. rhabdomyolysis) damage without sufficient neurological symptoms to be diagnosed as heat stroke.

(2) Profile disposition of Soldiers with HI.
   a) All Soldiers diagnosed with HI will be placed on a temporary profile, level 4, PULHES category P [T4 (P)] for a period of one week, at which time they will be re-evaluated. Soldiers will subsequently be individually profiled as determined by the treating provider.
   b) Soldiers with HI pending MEB will be profiled as per Table 1.
(3) MEB disposition for Soldiers with HI.
   a) Individual episodes of HI are not cause for an immediate MEB referral. However, Soldiers who experience three episodes of HI in less than 24 months or a single episode with either severe complications (e.g. compartment syndrome), or of such a nature that sequelae interfere with successful performance of duty, require referral to a MEB.
   b) Soldiers demonstrating any of the following criteria, despite two weeks of rest should be referred to an appropriate specialist for consideration of MEB:
      i. persistent residual kidney injury;
      ii. persistent elevation of CK above five times the upper limit of the lab normal range;
      iii. persistent elevation of transaminases above three times the upper limit of the lab normal range.

c. Heat Stroke

(1) Heat stroke (HS) is defined as a syndrome of hyperthermia (core temperature at time of event usually ≥ 40°C or 104°F), collapse or debilitation, and encephalopathy (delirium, stupor, coma) occurring during or immediately following exertion or significant heat exposure. HS can be complicated by organ and/or tissue injury, systemic inflammatory activation, and disseminated intravascular coagulation.
(2) Following an episode of HS the affected Soldier(s) will be placed on a [T4 (P)] profile for a period of two weeks. For the purpose of further profile and MEB determination, the Soldier will be reassessed weekly for the presence or absence of both complications and contributing risk factor(s). The Soldier will then be classified into one of the following three categories:
   a) HS without sequelae: all clinical signs and symptoms resolved by two weeks following the event;
   b) HS with sequelae: any evidence of cognitive or behavioral dysfunction, renal impairment, hepatic dysfunction, rhabdomyolysis, or other related pathology that does not completely resolve by two weeks following the event;
   c) Complex HS: recurrent, or occurring in the presence of a non-modifiable risk factor, either known (e.g. chronic skin condition such as eczema or burn skin graft) or suspected (e.g. sickle cell trait, malignant hyperthermia susceptibility).
(3) Profile Disposition of Soldiers with HS. See Table 1.
(4) MEB Disposition for Soldiers with HS.
   a) Individual episodes of HS with or without sequelae are not cause for an immediate MEB referral. However, any evidence/manifestation of repeat or new heat illness symptomatology during the period of the profile requires a MEB referral.
   b) Soldiers demonstrating any of the following criteria, despite two weeks of rest, should be referred to an appropriate specialist for consideration of MEB:
      i. persistent residual kidney injury;
      ii. persistent elevation of CK above five times the upper limit of the lab normal range;
      iii. persistent elevation of transaminases above three times the upper limit of the lab normal range;
      iv. persistent signs of cognitive/behavioral dysfunction.
   c) Initial Entry Training Soldiers will not be separated based upon the diagnosis of HS with or without sequelae, but will be placed into a Warrior Training and Rehabilitation Program (WTRP) for the duration of their profile.
   d) Soldiers with complex HS require a MEB referral. Consideration should be given for referral to a center with clinical expertise in heat illness for further evaluation.

Brain Injuries

Jason P. Mihalik, PhD, CAT(C), ATC

Kevin M. Guskiewicz, PhD, ATC, FACSM, FNATA

No other sports injury has generated as much public interest in recent years as brain injuries. Brain injuries vary by name, type, and severity in the athletic setting. It should be noted, however, that these injuries do not only occur in the athletic arena. Brain injuries also occur in recreational and workplace/industrial settings, and are common following motor vehicle accidents.

It has been estimated that between 1.6 and 3.8 million traumatic brain injuries (TBI) result from sports each year in the United States.[1] These injuries cost the American health care system approximately $56.3 billion in direct and indirect costs,[2] and make TBI among the most expensive conditions to treat in children.[3] Further, there has been a recent surge in the number of publications pertaining to sport-related mild TBI. For example, a 2010 PubMed search identified that more than half the publications related to "sport mild traumatic brain injury" were published in the past 5 years alone. The lay media has also highlighted several high-profile professional athletes forced into early retirement as a result of recurrent cerebral concussion. Thus, the media have served to elevate the general public's awareness of this type of injury.

The Centers for Disease Control and Prevention (CDC) has stated that the study of TBI, and more specifically its prevention, must continue to be a national priority. This chapter serves to define the various types of brain injury common in sport; describe their epidemiology, pathophysiology, recognition, treatment, and recovery; and provide some return-to-play considerations for the brain-injured athlete.

Definitions

The mildest type of brain injury is a **cerebral concussion**. Although there is no universally accepted definition of concussion, it has more recently been defined as a "complex pathophysiological process affecting the brain, induced by traumatic biomechanical forces."[4] As discussed later in this chapter, cerebral concussions may be caused by direct impacts to the head or by

cerebral concussion
A complex pathophysiologic process affecting the brain, induced by traumatic biomechanical forces that result in a rapid but transient onset of neurologic dysfunction; typically does not result in any structural brain injury that can be identified using traditional imaging techniques, including computed tomography scans and magnetic resonance imaging.

diffuse brain injury Brain injuries that result in widespread or global disruption of neurologic function and are not usually associated with macroscopically visible brain lesions except in the most severe cases. Structural diffuse brain injury (diffuse axonal injury) is the most severe type of diffuse injury because when axonal disruption occurs, it often results in disturbance of cognitive functions, such as concentration and memory.

second impact syndrome A brain injury that occurs when an athlete sustains a second injury to the brain before the symptoms associated with an initial brain injury have fully cleared; may cause delayed catastrophic deterioration resulting in death or persistent vegetative state after a brain injury, caused by transtentorial brainstem herniation.

subdural hematoma A brain injury characterized by accumulation of blood between the outermost (dura mater) and middle (arachnoid mater) meningeal layers.

epidural hematoma A brain injury characterized by pooling of blood between the dura mater (outermost meningeal layer) and the skull.

impulsive forces transmitted to the head through indirect impacts. Cerebral concussions result in a rapid but transient onset of neurologic dysfunction, and typically do not result in any structural brain injury that can be identified using traditional imaging techniques, including computed tomography (CT) scans or magnetic resonance imaging (MRI).[4]

Diffuse brain injuries result in widespread or global disruption of neurologic function and are not usually associated with macroscopically visible brain lesions except in the most severe cases. Structural **diffuse brain injury** (diffuse axonal injury) is the most severe type of diffuse injury because axonal disruption occurs. In its most severe form, diffuse axonal injury can disrupt the brainstem centers responsible for breathing, heart rate, and wakefulness.[5,6] Cerebral concussion, the most common sport-related TBI, can best be classified as a mild diffuse axonal injury and is often referred to as mild TBI. The injury usually results in one or more of the following symptoms: headache, nausea, vomiting, dizziness, balance problems, feeling "slowed down," fatigue, trouble sleeping, drowsiness, sensitivity to light or noise, loss of consciousness, blurred vision, difficulty remembering, or difficulty concentrating.[7,8]

Sudden death rarely occurs in athletes who suffer a cerebral concussion. However, cerebral concussions may catalyze a neurometabolic cascade during which time the brain is believed to be extremely sensitive to head trauma. It is during this neurometabolic cascade that a large majority of **second impact syndrome** cases have been identified. Sudden death in sport due to brain injuries typically results from cases of subdural or epidural hematomas. In a **subdural hematoma**, blood accumulates between the outermost meningeal layer—the dura mater—and the arachnoid mater. With **epidural hematoma**, blood pools between the dura mater and the skull. In either case, the risk for death is high if the condition is unnoticed or mismanaged. **Table 6.1** identifies and describes a number of conditions that may result in sudden death in athletes and for which immediate transport to an emergency facility is needed for successful recovery.

Epidemiology

Since 1945, over 510 fatalities have resulted from brain injuries in football alone.[9] **Table 6.2** presents these data over the past six decades. The sharp reduction in the number of football fatalities due to brain injuries beginning in the mid-1970s can likely be attributed to improvements in helmet and equipment design introduced to the game at that time. Also important are the playing regulation changes implemented since then that prohibit spearing and other mechanisms of injury associated with brain injury in football.

Although the number of fatalities has seen a drastic reduction over the past 25 years compared with their frequency between 1945 and 1974, the number of nonfatal brain injuries has seen a gradual increase over time. In a report on TBI sponsored by the CDC in the United States for the period of 1995 to 2001, information reported from emergency departments suggested that at least 1.4 million people sustain a TBI from all causes annually. Of these injuries, 1.1 million are treated and released in emergency rooms and as many as 235,000 result in hospitalization. As many as 50,000 people die every year in the United States as a result of all forms of TBI. Subdural hematoma, to be discussed later, is in fact the leading cause of brain-related deaths among participating athletes in the United States, according to the National Center for Catastrophic Sport Injury Research at the University of North Carolina at Chapel Hill.

Children younger than 15 years represent the majority of all cases of TBI; during the period of time under discussion, they represented as many as 475,000 cases each year. A more interesting, and perhaps speculative, statistic suggests that many more TBIs are sustained annually in the United States for which care is either not sought in emergency departments or not sought at all. Adolescents are at an increased risk for second impact syndrome, in which a catastrophic injury results from returning to activity or full sport participation while still experiencing symptoms from a prior injury. Further, in almost every

TABLE 6.1 Traumatic Intracranial Lesions

Type	Mechanism	Injured Structures	Signs and Symptoms	Care/Other
Cerebral contusion	Object impacts skull Skull impacts object	Injured vessels bleed internally Progressive swelling may injure brain tissue not originally harmed	LOC, partial paralysis, hemiplegia, unilateral pupil dilation, altered vital signs	Adequate ventilation, CPR if necessary, proper transport, expert evaluation May not require surgery
Cerebral hematoma				
Epidural	Severe blow to head Skull fracture	Middle meningeal artery	Neurologic status deteriorates in 10 minutes to 2 hours	Transport and expert evaluation Immediate surgery may be required
Subdural	Force of blow thrusts brain against point of impact	Subdural vessels tear and result in venous bleeding	Neurologic status deteriorates in hours, days, or even weeks	Prolonged observation/monitoring Surgical intervention may be required
Intracerebral	Depressed skull fracture, penetrating wound, acceleration-deceleration injury	Ruptured artery bleeds within brain substance	Rapid deterioration of neurologic status	Immediate transport to emergency room Death may occur before athlete can be transported
Second impact syndrome (SIS)	Sustains second brain injury before symptoms from first injury fully resolve	Brain loses autoregulation of blood supply; brain rapidly swells and brainstem herniates	Typically occurs in athletes <18 years of age within 1 week of previous concussion; pupils rapidly dilate, loss of eye movement, respiratory failure, eventual coma	Rapid intubation; 50% mortality rate; 100% morbidity rate

Abbreviations: CPR, cardiopulmonary resuscitation; LOC, loss of consciousness.

age group, the rate of TBI in the United States is higher for males than for their female counterparts for reasons that remain unclear to researchers at this time.[2]

Pathophysiology

Cerebral concussions, a form of mild TBI, occur when an athlete sustains a direct blow to the head or when an indirect blow to the body causes the transmission of impulsive forces to the brain. There are multiple mechanisms by which an athlete may sustain a mild TBI. This section describes the intrinsic protective

TABLE 6.2 Number of Football Brain Injury Fatalities in the Last Sixty-Five Years

Years	Number of Fatalities
1945–1954	87
1955–1964	115
1965–1974	162
1975–1984	69
1985–1994	33
1995–2004	44
Totals	510

Source: Data from Mueller FO, Colgate B. *Annual Survey of Football Injury Research: 1931–2009*. Chapel Hill, NC: National Center for Catastrophic Sport Injury Research; 2010.

mechanisms of the brain, the biomechanics related to brain injury, and the metabolic cascade associated with mild TBI.

Intrinsic Protective Mechanisms of the Brain

As a result of its intricate design, function, and significance, the brain has several structures that help protect it from external trauma. The eight cranial bones enclose and protect the brain, the meninges are membranous connective tissue coverings that surround the brain and spinal cord, and the cerebrospinal fluid (CSF) provides a buoyant cushion around the brain and its structures. The eight cranial bones consist of the frontal, two parietal, two temporal, and the occipital, sphenoid, and ethmoid bones. The frontal bone forms the anterior roof of the cranium—the forehead—and the roof of the nasal cavity; it also contains the frontal sinuses, which are connected to the nasal cavity. These sinuses act with others to lessen the weight of the skull. The spinal cord attaches to the brainstem through the foramen magnum located at the base of the skull.

In addition to the eight cranial bones, three membranous connective tissue coverings called the meninges protect the brain. From outermost to innermost, they are the dura mater, the arachnoid mater, and the pia mater. The separation of the three meninges allows for spaces between the meningeal layers. The dura mater is the outermost and toughest of the membranes covering the central nervous system (CNS). Of special interest is the fact that the attachment of the dura mater to the bones in the floor of the cranial fossae is firmer than its other points of attachment. Thus, a blow to the head at other points of attachment can detach the dura mater without fracturing the bones, whereas a basal fracture usually tears the dura mater and results in leakage of CSF into the soft tissues of the neck, nose, ear, and nasopharynx. The arachnoid mater is a delicate, transparent membrane and, as its name suggests, is composed of a weblike tissue. Although the pia mater is very thin, it is thicker than the arachnoid. The pia is the innermost of the three layers of meninges and is a highly vascularized, loose connective tissue membrane that adheres closely to the surface of the brain.

The CSF is also a protective barrier, assisting the meningeal layers in sheltering the brain from mechanical injury. The CSF acts as a buoy for the CNS, reducing the damaging effects of brain trauma by spreading the force over a larger area. The CSF reduces the effective mass of the brain by 97%. Although up to 800 mL of CSF is produced daily, only 140 to 200 mL is present at any time.[10] Leakage of the CSF at the level of the spine or into the middle ear in acute settings should trigger appropriate emergency transport to a medical facility. It has been reported that headaches caused by decreases in intracranial pressure are often due to spontaneous leaks of CSF.[11] Furthermore, a case study was presented in which computed tomography revealed leakage of CSF in the epidural space, causing postural headaches in a 33-year-old woman.[12]

In addition to the skeletal protection afforded by the cranial bones, the brain's autoregulatory system also provides some form of internal protection. Existing data suggest that an increase in norepinephrine release following cerebral contusion may act to stabilize the blood–brain barrier in areas surrounding the injury site.[13] However, this protective mechanism does not come without a price. One study also revealed a blockade of norepinephrine function during the first few hours after TBI, suggesting that a return to play in this time period may predispose the brain to further insult.[13] Furthermore, animal studies suggest that these alterations and elevations in norepinephrine and other hormones can be prolonged and may, in some cases, impair catecholaminergic function following brain trauma.[14]

Biomechanics of Traumatic Brain Injury

The biomechanics of traumatic brain injury remains an area elusive to many researchers. Investigators in this area are faced with a number of issues pertaining to understanding brain injury impact mechanics. Current ethics standards have made the use of primate and other mammalian animal models very difficult to pursue; animal basic research in this area has been limited to the rat and small mammals in recent years. Second, the use of postmortem cadavers does not allow researchers the ability to study impact mechanics in the context of everyday activities, including sports participation and work. The lack of muscle tonus and decreased volumes of CSF further make it difficult to replicate an in vivo sample in the context of this area of study. The degree of complexity in quantifying the biomechanics of sport-related brain injury has led some people to question whether a comprehensive understanding of the dynamics of brain injury could ever be achieved.[15]

The diversity of brain injury mechanisms all involve a near-instant transfer of kinetic energy that requires either an absorption (acceleration) or release (deceleration). Although force is the product of mass and acceleration, little trade-off occurs between the two. For example, a high-velocity bullet may penetrate the skull and brain but not cause a concussion because the mass of the bullet is too small to impart the necessary kinetic energy to the head and brain.[16] In an alternative scenario more realistic to athletics, a larger projectile (e.g., soccer ball, lacrosse stick) traveling at a lower speed and striking the head may more easily cause concussion.

The brain may also be injured by acceleration or deceleration mechanisms. In either case, the end result is either caused by impact or impulse. An **impact injury** occurs when a direct blow is made to or with the head. An **impulse injury** causes an acceleration or deceleration force, setting the head—and therefore the brain—in motion, without directly contacting the head. Impulse injuries are best suited for biomechanical reconstructions of acceleration or deceleration TBI because there is no contamination by impact mechanics.[17]

impact injury A brain injury resulting from a direct blow to the head.

impulse injury A brain injury resulting from an acceleration or deceleration force, setting the head—and therefore the brain—in motion, without directly contacting the head (e.g., whiplash injuries).

Regardless of whether the injury occurs via impact or impulse forces, the severity of the TBI is often related to the acceleration forces exerted on the brain. These forces are identified as linear (or translational) acceleration or deceleration, and angular (or rotational) acceleration or deceleration. The contribution of the translational and rotational acceleration forces to the concussive insult remains a topic of debate. In terms of sport-related concussion, it is accepted that a combination of the two acceleration forces plays a role in the concussive injury.[15] Although both acceleration forces are passed onto the brain when imparted on the head, studies on primates have shown that it is primarily the rotational forces that invoke a loss of consciousness, whereas translational forces are more likely to result in contusion or hemorrhage.[17]

As discussed later in this chapter, loss of consciousness is not the only indicator of concussion, and therefore earlier work in this area has been questioned in this regard. This suggests that significant brain injuries may occur without an accompanying loss of consciousness. Regardless of the role linear or rotational forces play in the outcome of the TBI, it is important that we recognize that the forces imparted on the head cause the brain to be set in motion. Methods of determining the extent of such forces have been developed. Several groups have published accelerometer-based research in a number of sports, including college football,[18-24] high school football,[23,25] and youth ice hockey.[26-28]

Neurometabolic Cascade

Animal studies have described an acute neurometabolic cascade (Figure 6.1) involving accelerated glycolysis and increased lactate production immediately following concussion.[29-31] The increased lactate is believed to leave neurons more vulnerable to secondary ischemic injury, and has been considered a possible predisposition to repeat injury. Later steps in this physiologic cascade involve increased intracellular calcium, mitochondrial dysfunction, impaired oxidative metabolism, decreased glycolysis, axonal disconnection, neurotransmitter disturbances, and delayed cell death.[29] Contrary to this proposed

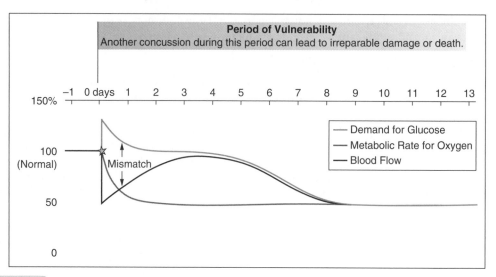

Figure 6.1   The neurometabolic cascade.
Source: Courtesy of *Journal of Athletic Training.*

deleterious effect of lactate production following concussion, a 2006 animal study suggests that lactate produces a dose-dependent response possibly enabling the mitochondria to meet the increasing metabolic demands of the brain following fluid percussion injury in rats.[32] Future research should attempt to gain a better understanding of the role lactate plays throughout the acute neurometabolic cascade following concussion.

Decreased cerebral blood flow has been reported to last approximately 10 days following concussive injuries in animal models,[29] which is consistent with the finding of an apparent 7- to 10-day period of increased susceptibility to recurrent injury. Additional analyses of cases involving players with recurrent concussive injury will be necessary to better understand the role the neurometabolic cascade plays in clinical recovery. Most important, these studies support the notion that the brain is still in a vulnerable state during the initial 7 to 10 days following sport-related concussion. It is during this period following an initial head trauma that the younger athlete is at greatest risk for sudden death as a result of second impact syndrome, a condition described later in this chapter.

Prevention and Predisposing Factors

A number of preventive measures and predisposing factors have been discussed in the context of athletic cerebral concussions. The obvious method of minimizing impacts transmitted to the brain is to wear properly fitted playing equipment, practice proper techniques, and respect playing rules at all times during athletic participation. A number of organizations have established standards for commercially available playing equipment. These organizations include the National Operating Committee for Standards on Athletic Equipment (NOCSAE), the Hockey Equipment Certification Council (HECC), and the Canadian Standards Association (CSA). Because all equipment has a limited lifespan of effective protection, sports medicine professionals, coaches, and school or league officials should ensure that the athletes they are supervising are using adequate equipment.

Cervical Muscle Strength

Different forms of energy are associated with cerebral concussions, as discussed earlier. If an athlete's head is not mobile, the kinetic forces imparted on the head and brain are thought to travel through the cranial cavity and be transmitted elsewhere, often leaving brain function intact. In football, an athlete may tense his neck muscles prior to collision to decrease the mobility of the head and therefore allow for the kinetic energy to be dispersed throughout the rest of the body.[33] This has catalyzed the belief among health care professionals that cervical muscle strength may lead to further reduction of brain injury, and indeed cervical muscle strength has to some extent been shown to mitigate the severity of head impacts among youth athletes.[26]

The basic tenet of the neck muscle theory for reducing brain injury is that athletes who anticipate an oncoming collision will be better able to control head movement by contracting (i.e., tensing) their cervical musculature. Using a Newtonian approach, acceleration is the result of force divided by mass. When the cervical musculature is contracted, it is thought to significantly increase the effective mass of the head-neck-trunk segment, resulting in a lower acceleration of the head. When an impact is unanticipated and the cervical musculature is not tensed and prepared for a collision, the effective mass is reduced to that of the head. Given an equal force from a body collision, the head would experience a substantially greater acceleration and therefore would be more likely to sustain an injury. In theory, this seems rather intuitive; however, there remains a general lack of research to support these claims. Notwithstanding, there is still strong anecdotal support for the role neck musculature may play in reducing the risk of mild TBI, which is worthy of investigation in a young, at-risk sample.

The question remains, Why do humans sustain mild TBI at relatively low loads and other animals (e.g., woodpeckers, rams, buffalo) appear to be unaffected by repetitive high-magnitude loading? The woodpecker, for example, decelerates at a rate of approximately 1000 g each time its beak strikes a tree.[34] It is believed the powerful muscles of the head and neck act not only to control the rapid head movement of the woodpecker, but also to concurrently absorb the energy generated by the collision of its bill with the wood.[35] Further investigation into this area reveals that the woodpecker typically strikes the tree with its bill in a linear fashion. As mentioned earlier in this chapter, Ommaya and Genarelli[17] reported that concussion almost always occurred following angular acceleration, but that very few of their primate subjects experienced concussion following a linear mechanism.

Player Behaviors and Respect for Playing Regulations

Although the purpose of this chapter is not to speculate about the influence of coaches' and players' aggressive behaviors, it is difficult to ignore this aspect of athletics, and a brief discussion of this subject is warranted in the context of the current topic. Although many amateur athletic associations (e.g., USA Hockey and Hockey Canada) extensively promote sportsmanlike conduct, the culture of sport among participants often predicates a mentality among players to ignore injury and to play recklessly. This behavior encourages unsportsmanlike conduct that may include disrespecting opponents and infracting upon playing regulations.

In one study exploring young ice hockey players in the United States, it was reported that fighting broke out in approximately 17 of 52 games observed; players considered fighting a natural consequence of the game and experienced a certain resignation about fighting.[36] Another interesting finding reported by these researchers is that whereas 100% of coaches responded that sportsmanship was "real important," only 59% of players shared this attitude.[37] Parents and coaches, in this sample, viewed the enforcement of rules as being the most important factor in reducing all injuries, including cerebral concussions.

In some of our own work, we have identified that head contact, high sticking, and elbowing body collisions in youth ice hockey result in more severe head impacts than those resulting from otherwise legal collisions within the regulatory framework of youth ice hockey.[27] These findings have some very natural extensions to other collision sports since the underlying message of "play within the rules" applies to all levels of competitive and recreational sport. Although the assumption could be made that rule changes occurring at the professional levels (e.g., an elimination of fighting in the National Hockey League) will have a direct effect on playing behavior in younger amateur ice hockey players, there are very little data to support the truth of this prediction.

Previous Injury

The previous number of concussions is believed to be a predisposing factor for subsequent brain injuries. Why are athletes with a history of cerebral concussion more likely to sustain a subsequent brain injury? The neuromechanics behind this phenomenon are not yet clearly understood by researchers.

Some theories exist in this regard, which include mismanaged previous injuries, a lowering of the brain structure's injury threshold, and an increased likelihood that a previously injured athlete will recognize and report a subsequent brain injury to medical professionals.

Earlier work in this area identified that previous history of concussion may be a predisposing factor associated with subsequent concussive injury in collegiate football players.[8] We observed that collegiate football players reporting one, two, or more than three prior concussions were 1.5, 2.8, and 3.4 times more likely, respectively, to sustain a concussion than athletes with no history of concussion.

As medical professionals, we should be concerned with performing comprehensive preseason physical screenings for all potentially fatal conditions. This should include identifying athletes with a history of concussion or other forms of TBI. Although fatality may occur as a result of head trauma, the likelihood of suffering from long-term cognitive problems as a result of multiple brain injuries is much higher. Therefore, the importance of recognizing these injuries on the field, and promptly removing from participation those athletes suspected of sustaining a concussive injury for more extensive evaluation, can have a direct impact on minimizing the extent of secondary brain injury that can have catastrophic outcomes.

Recognition

The recognition of a cerebral concussion is usually not straightforward with the exception of the athlete who has an observed bout of loss of consciousness following a collision. We recognize that in many instances, athletic trainers may not be present at the time of injury (e.g., they may be covering another field or event). Loss of consciousness or altered central nervous system could occur with other conditions described in this text, making the blanket diagnosis of concussion with all cases of loss of consciousness incorrect. The large majority of concussions (approximately 90–95%) involve no loss of consciousness. The athlete will likely appear dazed, dizzy, and disoriented. In more obvious injurious collisions, the sideline medical professional may observe an athlete struggling to stand on his or her own, may observe the athlete not conforming to plays, or, in a more obvious scenario, not moving from the field following injury. Often, concussions are not identified at the time of injury unless an athlete approaches medical personnel and reports symptoms following a head injury. That said, the first step to recognizing a brain injury begins in the preseason with educational interventions with players, coaches, and parents to teach the signs and symptoms of concussion, the importance of reporting them to medical professionals, and the injury management policies employed by the team.

retrograde amnesia Difficulty remembering events immediately preceding (or leading up to) the injury.

anterograde amnesia Sometimes referred to as posttraumatic amnesia, it is characterized by difficulty remembering events immediately following the injury.

Graded Symptom Checklist Sometimes referred to as a Postconcussion Symptom Scale, it is a Likert symptom inventory scale used to evaluate both the number and severity of symptoms commonly associated with cerebral concussion and other forms of traumatic brain injury.

The *signs* of cerebral concussion are those observed by medical personnel. These signs may include any of the following: disorientation and momentary confusion, **retrograde amnesia**, **anterograde** (or posttraumatic) **amnesia**, loss of consciousness (even for seconds), automatism, unequal pupil size, combativeness, slowness to answer questions, loss of balance, and a change in typical behavior or personality.[38–40] *Symptoms* of cerebral concussion are those reported by the athlete. These usually include headache, nausea, balance problems or dizziness, tinnitus ("ringing in the ears"), diplopia (double vision) or blurred vision, changes in sleep patterns, problems with concentration or memory, irritability, sadness, and sensitivity to light or noise.[39]

Sharing a **Graded Symptom Checklist** with players, coaches, and parents may help them identify that a concussion has been sustained in a player when they otherwise would have dismissed those signs and symptoms as a natural consequence of athletic participation. **Table 6.3** provides a sample 18-symptom Graded Symptom Checklist. Different versions of this assessment tool exist, including 12-, 16-, and 22-item lists, and it is sometimes referred to as the Postconcussion Symptom Scale. It should be noted that the Graded Symptom Checklist is used not only for the initial evaluation but for each subsequent follow-up assessment, which should be periodically repeated until all postconcussion signs and symptoms have cleared at rest and during physical exertion.

There is currently no gold standard imaging technique capable of identifying concussion in athletes who otherwise do not report any symptoms. As was noted earlier in this chapter,

TABLE 6.3   Graded Symptom Checklist

	None		Mild		Moderate		Severe	
Headache	0	1	2	3	4	5	6
Nausea	0	1	2	3	4	5	6
Vomiting	0	1	2	3	4	5	6
Dizziness	0	1	2	3	4	5	6
Poor balance	0	1	2	3	4	5	6
Sensitivity to noise	0	1	2	3	4	5	6
Ringing in the ear	0	1	2	3	4	5	6
Sensitivity to light	0	1	2	3	4	5	6
Blurred vision	0	1	2	3	4	5	6
Difficulty concentrating	0	1	2	3	4	5	6
Feeling mentally "foggy"	0	1	2	3	4	5	6
Difficulty remembering	0	1	2	3	4	5	6
Trouble falling asleep	0	1	2	3	4	5	6
Drowsiness	0	1	2	3	4	5	6
Fatigue	0	1	2	3	4	5	6
Sadness	0	1	2	3	4	5	6
Irritability	0	1	2	3	4	5	6
Neck pain	0	1	2	3	4	5	6

Circle appropriate number for each symptom experienced.

concussion is a functional injury, and standard structural imaging techniques are not sensitive to this condition. In these cases, the sports medicine professional's use of the Graded Symptom Checklist will often be the only manner in which the injury is recognized on the field.

Evaluation

In the past, the field and clinical assessments for brain injuries were often conducted independent of each other. This disjointed approach to managing the injury has been eliminated because the clinician requires information from the initial assessment conducted by the emergency care provider such as the athletic trainer, emergency medical technician, or other medical personnel on site at the time of the injury. Information from the on-field assessment is quintessential in understanding the natural course of recovery that the sports medicine professional may expect to observe in a controlled clinical setting.

There are three primary objectives for the clinician dealing with a brain-injured athlete: (1) recognition of the injury and its severity, (2) determining whether the athlete requires additional attention or assessment, and (3) deciding when the athlete may return to sports activity. Performing a thorough initial evaluation can easily address the first of these objectives. As with the other catastrophic injuries presented throughout this text, a well-prepared protocol is the key to the successful initial evaluation of an athlete suspected of sustaining a brain injury or any other type of trauma.

On-Field Assessment

Assessment of the concussed athlete on the field presents a number of concerns to medical personnel. First, one must be able to recognize the signs that may be presented by an unconscious athlete. Unconscious athletes must always be managed by first dealing with life-threatening conditions such as obstructed airways, lack of breathing, hemorrhage, and the possibility of spinal injuries. Second, physical signs of concussion and skull fracture, such as a red or pale face color, cool or moist skin, deep or shallow breathing, dilated and unequal pupils, and signs of deformity over the injured area, must be assessed.[41] This would represent an *athlete-down* scenario, signified by the athletic trainer or team physician responding to the athlete directly on the playing surface (i.e., field, court, or rink). Conversely, *ambulatory* scenarios involve those in which the brain-injured athlete is evaluated by team medical personnel at some point following the injury, whether this is on the sideline, in the locker room, or even in the ensuing days in the athletic training room. Regardless of the scenario, brain trauma in an athletic situation requires immediate assessment for appropriate emergency action; if at all possible, the athletic trainer or team physician should perform the initial evaluation of the athlete at the time of injury.

A primary survey involving basic life support should be performed first. This is easily done and usually takes only a matter of 10 to 15 seconds to assess respiration and cardiac status to rule out a life-threatening condition. In any case involving loss of consciousness, controlling the athlete's cervical spine for the remainder of the evaluation is paramount. All members of the sports medicine team should rehearse basic life support procedures on a regular basis and remain current in their respective certifications in this area of emergency care. In settings where immediate access to the athletic trainer may be limited or may not exist, these potentially life-saving procedures should be shared with all supervising personnel of student-athletes, including coaches, athletic directors, student volunteers, and school nurses, at a minimum.

Once the airway has been secured, breathing has been evaluated, and there are no obvious bleeds and circulation is determined to be otherwise intact, the secondary survey may begin. An important step of the secondary survey is to perform a comprehensive history—to help narrow down the assessment. The clinician should attempt to gain as much information as possible about any (1) mental confusion, (2) loss of consciousness, and (3) amnesia. Confusion can be determined rather quickly by noting facial expression (dazed, stunned, glassy-eyed) and any inappropriate behavior such as running the wrong play or returning to the wrong huddle.

If the athlete is unconscious or is regaining consciousness—but is still disoriented and confused—the management of this injury should be likened to that of a cervical spine injury because the clinician may not be able to rule out the latter. Therefore, the unconscious athlete should be transported from the field or court on a spine board with the head and neck immobilized. Vital signs should be monitored at regular intervals every 1 to 2 minutes, and the clinician should continue to awaken the unconscious athlete. If the athlete remains in a state of lethargy or stupor or otherwise appears to be unconscious, the athlete should not be physically shaken in an attempt to arouse him or her. Shaking the athlete is contraindicated when a cervical spine injury is suspected. If loss of consciousness is brief, lasting less than 1 minute, and the remainder of the primary on-field assessment presents the clinician with a non-life-threatening situation, the athlete may be removed from the playing surface, observed on the sideline, and referred to a physician at a later time. Prolonged unconsciousness, lasting 1 minute or longer, requires inline immobilization and immediate transfer to an emergency facility where the athlete will undergo a thorough neurologic examination.

The clinician can perform amnesia testing by first asking the athlete simple questions directed toward recent memory and progressing to more involved questions. Asking the athlete what the first thing was that he or she remembered after the injury will test for length of anterograde amnesia. Asking what the play was before the injury or who the opponent was last week are some questions the clinician may use to evaluate the extent of retrograde amnesia. Retrograde amnesia is generally associated with a more serious brain injury. Questions of orientation (name, date, time, and place) may be asked; however, research suggests that orientation questions are not good discriminators between injured and noninjured athletes.[42]

Because of the immediate proximity of the eyes to the brain, injuries to the brain can result in disturbances of vision and pupillary reflexes. These functional discrepancies may provide important information. This section of the secondary assessment should investigate the reflex of the pupils to light exposure, onset of blurred vision or diplopia, inability of the pupils to rapidly accommodate to light, and the inability of the eyes to track smoothly. Involuntary movement of the eyeball is referred to as *nystagmus*, and may indicate possible cerebral involvement.[40] At this time, the athlete should also be asked if he or she is experiencing any tinnitus, blurred vision, or nausea. The clinician should use a concussion symptom checklist similar to that found in Table 6.3 to facilitate the follow-up assessment of signs and symptoms.

Portions of the observation and examination should take place during the initial on-field evaluation. The clinician should observe for any deformities as well as abnormal facial expressions (potentially indicative of injury to cranial nerve VII) speech patterns, quality of respirations, and movement of the extremities, all of which can be done while asking the athlete questions. Additionally, gentle palpation of the skull and cervical spine should be performed to rule out any obvious fractures. In sports with helmets, careful removal of the helmet in a conscious athlete may be permitted after a suspected cervical spine injury has been ruled out. The sports medicine professional should also look for any signs indicating a potential basilar skull fracture, including posterior auricular hematoma (Battle sign), otorrhea (CSF draining from the ear canal), cerebrospinal fluid rhinorrhea (CSF draining from the nose), and periorbital ecchymosis ("raccoon eyes") secondary to blood leaking from the anterior fossa of the skull.

The conscious athlete or one who was momentarily rendered unconscious should be transported to the sidelines or locker room for further evaluation after the initial on-field evaluation. Again, if the athlete is unconscious, any patient movement or positioning should be carefully performed, and all precautions related to potential cervical spine injury should be assumed. A helmet does not have to be removed at this time unless it compromises maintenance of adequate ventilation. The procedures related to helmet and equipment removal are more thoroughly described in Chapter 7. An adequate airway can often be maintained simply by removing the face mask without any concomitant equipment removal. Any unconscious player must be moved with care, avoiding motion of the cervical spine by gentle, firm support, and transported while secured on a spine board. **Table 6.4** highlights the components of the primary and secondary survey involved with the on-field assessment of a brain-injured athlete.

TABLE 6.4 On-Field Assessment

Primary Survey	Secondary Survey	
Establish level of consciousness	History	Mental confusion
Ensure open airway		Loss of consciousness
Check respirations (breathing)		Amnesia
Check cardiac status	Observation	Monitor eyes
Control significant hemorrhaging		Graded Symptom Checklist
Rule out life-threatening condition		Abnormal facial expressions, speech patterns, respirations, extremity movement, palpable deformities
	Palpation	Skull and cervical spine deformities
		Pulse and blood pressures (especially if deteriorating)

Sideline Assessment

Once an athlete has been safely removed from play, a more detailed examination can be conducted on the sideline or in the training room. At this time, the clinician should proceed with the remainder of the observation and palpation. A quick cranial nerve assessment should test the integrity of cranial nerve II (optic nerve; visual acuity) by asking the athlete to read or identify selected objects at near and far ranges. Cranial nerves III (oculomotor nerve) and IV (trochlear nerve)—both of which control eye movement—can be evaluated by determining visual coordination and asking the athlete to track a moving object. The pupils should again be observed to determine whether they are equal in size and equally reactive to light; the pupils should constrict when light is shined into the eyes. Observation of the pupils also assesses the oculomotor nerve (cranial nerve III). Abnormal movement of the eyes, irregular changes in pupil size, or atypical reaction to light often indicate increased intracranial pressure.

If the athlete's condition appears to be worsening, the pulse and blood pressure should be taken. The development of an unusually slow heart rate or an increased pulse pressure—characterized by increased systolic and decreased diastolic pressures—after the athlete has calmed down may be a sign of increasing intracranial involvement.

The overwhelming majority of cerebral concussions will not reveal positive results for these tests; however, they are important considerations for detecting a more serious injury such as an epidural or subdural hematoma. In both cases, deterioration of signs and symptoms—including changing levels of consciousness—will indicate an emergent medical situation requiring immediate transportation to an emergency or neurosurgical department. In most cases, a CT scan to locate the exact pathology will be conducted, followed by neurosurgical evacuation of the developing hematoma.

For these procedures to occur in a timely and efficient manner, it is essential for the sports medicine staff's emergency action plan to include procedures for managing the injury. The presence of trained emergency care providers capable of intubating or medicating a rapidly deteriorating athlete prior to or during transport is essential. Careful and thorough planning with local emergency medical personnel is critical. The sports medicine professional is ultimately responsible for identifying deteriorating conditions that would warrant immediate physician referral or transfer to the emergency department. **Table 6.5** presents a physician referral checklist. Athletes should never be returned to play on the same day as a suspected cerebral concussion.

Objective Measures of Balance

Balance testing should be done if the athlete is able to stand. The amount of unsteadiness should be noted. The inclusion of objective balance testing in the assessment of concussion has been recommended. The **Balance Error Scoring System (BESS)** is currently recommended over the standard Romberg test, which for years had been used as a subjective tool for the assessment of balance. The BESS was developed to provide sports medicine professionals with a rapid and cost-effective method of objectively assessing postural stability in athletes on the sideline or athletic training room following a suspected concussion.[43]

Balance Error Scoring System (BESS) A clinical sideline measure of postural stability.

The BESS consists of three different stances (double leg, single leg, and tandem) performed on two different surfaces (firm and foam), for a total of six conditions (**Figure 6.2**). The BESS trials require athletes to balance for 20 seconds with their eyes closed and hands on their iliac crests. During the single-leg balance tasks, athletes should balance on their nondominant leg, with their contralateral leg in 20° hip flexion and 30° knee flexion. The athlete's dominant leg is determined by asking which leg he or she would prefer to use to kick a ball. Athletes should be instructed to stand quietly and motionless in the stance position, keeping their hands on their iliac crests with their eyes closed. In the event they lose their balance during one of the trials, they are to make any necessary adjustments and return to the initial testing position as quickly as possible.

Participants are scored by adding one error point for each error committed during each of the six balance tasks (with a maximum of 10 errors allotted for any single trial). Errors include lifting their hands off their iliac crest; opening their eyes; stepping, stumbling, or falling; moving their non-stance hip into more

TABLE 6.5	Physician Referral Checklist

Day-of-Injury Referral
- Loss of consciousness on the field
- Amnesia lasting longer than 15 minutes
- Deterioration of neurologic function[a]
- Decreasing level of consciousness[a]
- Decrease or irregularity in respirations[a]
- Decrease or irregularity in pulse[a]
- Increase in blood pressure
- Unequal, dilated, or unreactive pupils[a]
- Cranial nerve deficits
- Any signs or symptoms of associated injuries, spine or skull fracture, or bleeding[a]
- Mental status changes: lethargy, difficulty maintaining arousal, confusion, agitation[a]
- Seizure activity[a]
- Vomiting
- Motor deficits subsequent to initial on-field assessment
- Sensory deficits subsequent to initial on-field assessment
- Balance deficits subsequent to initial on-field assessment
- Cranial nerve deficits subsequent to initial on-field assessment
- Postconcussion symptoms that worsen
- Additional postconcussion symptoms as compared with those on the field
- Athlete still symptomatic at the end of the game (especially at high school level)

Delayed Referral (After the Day of Injury)
- Any of the findings in the day-of-injury referral category
- Postconcussion symptoms worsen or do not improve over time
- Increase in the number of postconcussion symptoms reported
- Postconcussion symptoms begin to interfere with the athlete's daily activities (e.g., sleep disturbances, cognitive difficulties)

[a] Requires the athlete be transported immediately to the nearest emergency department.

than 30° abduction; lifting their forefoot or heel; and remaining out of the test position for more than 5 seconds **(Table 6.6)**.

Balance test results during injury recovery are best used when compared with baseline measurements, and sports medicine professionals working with athletes or patients on a regular basis should attempt to obtain baseline measurements when possible. Although modified BESS protocols (such as those included in the Sport Concussion Assessment

TABLE 6.6	Balance Error Scoring System Errors

Hands lifted off iliac crest

Opening eyes

Step, stumble, or fall

Moving hip into more than 30° of flexion or abduction

Lifting forefoot or heel

Remaining out of testing position for more than 5 seconds

The BESS score is calculated by adding one error point for each error or any combination of errors occurring during a movement.

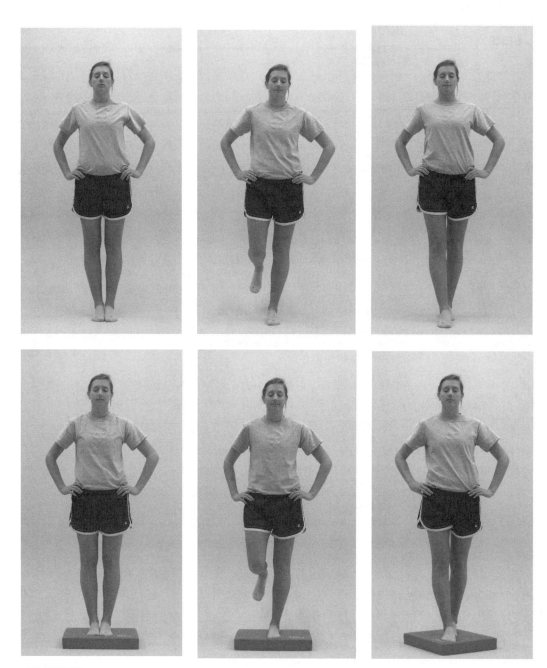

Figure 6.2   Balance Error Scoring System conditions.

Tool 2) have been proposed, research has found the traditional six-condition protocol to be a reliable and valid assessment tool for the management of sport-related concussion.[43–45]

Objective Measures of Cognition

Standardized Assessment of Concussion (SAC) A clinical measure of mental status commonly used in the management of concussion.

The cognitive evaluation should begin shortly following the primary survey by giving the athlete three words to remember (e.g., *bear*, *red*, *hat*); he or she will be asked to recall the words at the conclusion of the sideline assessment. A brief mental status examination should be conducted using the **Standardized Assessment of Concussion** (SAC). The SAC is a brief screening instrument designed for the mental status assessment of cerebral concussion by a medical professional with no prior expertise in neuropsychological testing.[46] Studies have demonstrated the psychometric properties and clinical sensitivity of the SAC in assessing concussion and tracking postinjury recovery.[47–50] The SAC requires approximately 6 to 7 minutes to administer and assesses four domains of cognition: orientation, immediate memory, concentration, and delayed recall. A composite total score of 30 possible points is summed to provide an overall index of cognitive impairment and injury severity. The SAC also contains a brief neurologic screening and documentation of injury-related factors (e.g., loss of consciousness, anterograde amnesia, retrograde amnesia).[51] To minimize practice effects from serial testing following injury, equivalent alternate forms of the SAC are available to clinicians. The SAC is capable of identifying significant differences between concussed athletes and noninjured controls, and is also capable of distinguishing between preseason baselines and postinjury scores.[48,49]

More recently, the **Sport Concussion Assessment Tool 2 (SCAT2)** has been developed. This tool incorporates the SAC and firm-surfaced BESS conditions in their entirety within its construct **(Appendix 6.1)**. This test takes approximately 12 to 14 minutes to complete.

A number of computerized neuropsychological testing platforms have been used to evaluate athletes following concussion. The Automated Neuropsychological Assessment Metrics (ANAM), CNS Vital Signs, CogSport, HeadMinder Concussion Resolution Index, and the Immediate Postconcussion Assessment and Cognitive Test (ImPACT) are all currently available and have shown promise for reliable and valid concussion assessment.[52–61] The primary advantages to computerized testing include the ability to assess reaction time, to administer baseline testing to large groups of athletes in a short period of time, and the existence of multiple forms within the testing paradigm to reduce practice effects. Although the primary purpose of this book chapter precludes a lengthy discussion of the psychometric properties of computerized neurocognitive testing, the advantages and disadvantages of computerized neuropsychological testing versus traditional paper-and-pencil testing have been previously summarized.[58] **Table 6.7** provides an overview of the commercially available computerized neuropsychological test platforms.

Sport Concussion Assessment Tool 2 (SCAT2) A clinical evaluation tool that combines measures of orientation, mental status, postural stability, and symptoms.

There remain some limitations to neuropsychological testing in athletes with suspected concussion, particularly regarding the best course of action for optimal follow-up testing and how results should be interpreted. Further, computerized test platforms are often costly, which make their implementation in the high school setting difficult. Regardless, once a decision has been made to institute a testing program, preseason baseline measures should be recorded so that in the event of a concussive injury postinjury measures can be compared with preseason measures. These comparisons are most useful in making return-to-play decisions if the athlete is assessed after the athlete has been rendered asymptomatic.[51,62] The development and implementation of a neuropsychological testing program should be performed in consultation with a medical professional. Neuropsychological tests should be used in the context of the overall concussion evaluation when making informed return-to-play decisions.

Medications

At this time, no evidence-based pharmacologic treatment options for an athlete with a concussion exist for the sports medicine professional.[63] The majority of pharmacologic studies have been performed in severely brain-injured patients, which represent a very small portion of the number of concussions sports medicine professionals are likely to observe in their athletes. Typically, athletes with concussion should avoid medications containing acetylsalicylic acid (i.e., aspirin) or nonsteroidal anti-inflammatory agents, which may decrease platelet function and potentially increase intracranial bleeding, masking the severity and duration of symptoms and possibly leading to a more severe injury. It is also recommended that acetaminophen (e.g., Tylenol) be used sparingly in the treatment of headache-like symptoms in the athlete with a brain injury after all other structural brain injuries have been ruled out. Other medications to avoid during the acute postconcussion period include those that adversely affect CNS function, in particular alcohol and narcotics.

In emergent situations, when a risk of rapid brain swelling and brainstem herniation is suspected, it has been suggested that drugs such as mannitol (an osmotic diuretic) may be indicated to reduce intracranial pressure and brain mass in pediatric and adult patients following brain injury. Although mannitol is often used, a number of studies[64–66] supporting its use in treating severe cases of TBI have

TABLE 6.7	Computerized Neuropsychological Test Platforms	
Neuropsychological Test	**Developer/Contact Information**	**Cognitive Tests/Outcomes**
Automated Neuropsychological Assessment Matrix (ANAM)	Center for the Study of Human Operator Performance (C-SHOP) University of Oklahoma Norman, OK *cshop.ou.edu*	Simple reaction metrics Sternberg memory Math processing Continuous performance Matching to sample Spatial processing Code substitution
CNS Vital Signs	CNS Vital Signs, LLC Morrisville, NC *www.cnsvs.com*	Verbal memory Visual memory Psychomotor speed Reaction time Complex attention Cognitive flexibility Processing speed Executive functioning Reasoning
CogSport	CogState Ltd Victoria, Australia New Haven, CT (U.S. office) *www.cogstate.com*	Simple reaction time Complex reaction time One-back Continuous learning
Concussion Resolution Index	HeadMinder, Inc. New York, NY *www.headminder.com*	Reaction time Cued reaction time Visual recognition 1 Visual recognition 2 Animal decoding Symbol scanning
ImPACT	ImPACT Applications, Inc. Pittsburgh, PA *www.impacttest.com*	Verbal memory Visual memory Information processing speed Reaction time Impulse control

been the recent focus of reevaluation, and the Cochrane review[67] recommending high-dose mannitol has been withdrawn because there is some evidence that this drug may actually worsen cerebral edema. Mannitol was found to reduce the likelihood of death compared with the use of barbiturates such as pentobarbital;[68] however, a concentrated saline solution—hypertonic saline—yielded better mortality outcomes than mannitol.[69] To date, there is little evidence to support the prehospital administration of mannitol to treat patients with severe brain injuries.[70]

Recovery

The majority of concussions sustained in athletics typically resolve in 5 to 7 days for collegiate athletes,[8,71] but on average take longer in high school athletes.[72] It is important to clinically evaluate the athlete on a regular basis throughout the course of recovery by employing the use of graded symptom checklists and objective measures of postural stability and cognition. Clinicians must recognize that approximately 10% of all concussions resolve along a prolonged recovery course, and in some cases it may take weeks or months for symptoms to resolve. Ensuring full recovery is paramount in protecting the athlete from adverse and potentially catastrophic outcomes such as second impact syndrome.

Second Impact Syndrome

Second impact syndrome occurs when an athlete sustains a second injury to the brain before the symptoms associated with the first have fully cleared.[73] Although rare, it is a well-documented cause of delayed catastrophic deterioration resulting in death or persistent vegetative state after a brain injury, caused by transtentorial brainstem herniation.[74] Although this condition is poorly understood, it is thought to be a disruption of the brain's blood autoregulatory system that results in brain swelling and rapidly increasing intracranial pressure, leading to cerebral herniation.[75] The time from second impact syndrome to brainstem failure, and ultimately death, is usually 2 to 5 minutes.[73] Brainstem failure causes rapidly dilating pupils, loss of eye movement, respiratory failure, and eventually coma. On-field management of second impact syndrome should include rapid intubation. Unfortunately, the mortality rate of second impact syndrome is 50%, and the morbidity rate is 100%.

Although the involved structures associated with second impact syndrome may vary depending on the mechanisms of injury, the presentation of signs and symptoms and recommended care is rather standard (Table 6.1). Because cases of second impact syndrome are relatively rare, case-control studies provide us with the only feasible means to establish risk factors.[74] There have been 17 published cases of second impact syndrome in athletes under the age of 19 years.[76] The U.S. National Center for Catastrophic Sport Injury Research has further identified 35 possible cases of second impact syndrome, but lacks the corroborating details to publish them as such.[73,77] Although the number of reported cases is relatively low, the potential for second impact syndrome to occur in mildly head-injured athletes should be a major consideration when making return-to-play decisions.[78]

Return-to-Play Considerations

Over the last 20 years a number of concussion severity and return-to-play guidelines have been proposed.[7,73,79–83] Return-to-play guidelines have been based in large part on concussion grading scales. Although grading systems have encouraged the use of uniform terminology and increased awareness of concussion signs and symptoms, no prospective, randomized clinical trial has established any one system as superior.[39,84] The blanket use of return-to-play guidelines is difficult because head injuries should be managed on a case-by-case basis. Ultimately, the resolution of concussive symptoms does not necessarily mean that the underlying pathology has resolved; there may be prolonged neurocognitive dysfunction in the absence of any self-reported symptoms.[85] Should the sports medicine team elect to use a concussion grading scale, which many clinicians are moving away from, they should only grade the injury after the athlete is declared symptom free because duration of symptoms is the most important factor in grading the injury. No athlete should return to participation while still symptomatic.

It has been suggested that athletes should undergo a stepwise return-to-play process once they are deemed to be asymptomatic and free of any postural stability or neurocognitive problems (Table 6.8). Each step should typically take 24 hours, which will allow the sports medicine team ample time to determine whether a particular stage results in exacerbation of symptoms experienced by the athlete. Ultimately, the return-to-play process should take approximately 5 to 7 days from the time at which the athlete first presents symptom free to the medical team.

A number of factors should also be considered when making decisions regarding an athlete's readiness to return following head injury. These include the athlete's previous history of concussion, the nature of

TABLE 6.8 Graduated Return-to-Play Protocol

Rehabilitation Stage	Functional Exercise at Each Stage of Rehabilitation	Objective of Each Stage
1. No activity	Complete physical and cognitive rest	Recovery
2. Light aerobic exercise	Walking, swimming, or stationary cycling keeping intensity <70% MPHR; no resistance training	Increase HR
3. Sport-specific exercise	Skating drills in ice hockey, running drills in soccer; no head impact activities	Add movement
4. Noncontact training drills	Progression to more complex training drills (e.g., passing drills in football and ice hockey); may start progressive resistance training	Exercise, coordination, cognitive load
5. Full-contact practice	Following medical clearance, participate in normal training activities	Restoration of confidence and assessment of functional skills by coaching staff
6. Return to play	Normal game play	

Abbreviations: HR, heart rate; MPHR, maximum predicted heart rate.
Source: From McCrory P, Meeuwisse W, Johnston K, et al. Consensus statement on concussion in sport: the Third International Conference on Concussion in Sport held in Zurich, November 2008. *Clin J Sport Med.* 2009;19(3):185–200. Reprinted with permission.

the sport (contact vs. noncontact), and whether there are signs the athlete's condition is deteriorating. In the event of a more serious brain injury (i.e., epidural or subdural hematoma), proper management should be supervised by a neurosurgeon, and full clearance to begin a graduated return-to-play protocol should be authorized by the attending neurosurgeon. These cases are often more complicated than concussions, and decisions as to whether to disqualify athletes from further competition or return them to play safely should be carried out on an individual basis.

Summary

The management of sport-related TBI has evolved considerably over the last 15 years. This evolution has brought technology and objective testing methods to the forefront of concussion management aimed at identifying neurologic deficits and preventing catastrophic outcomes. The increased emphasis on education and awareness has likewise played a major part in helping to prevent these injuries, but there is still a lot of needed work if we are to progress in this area of patient care (Appendix 6.2). The greatest influence that clinicians can have on preventing catastrophic brain injuries is to educate athletes, coaches, and parents about the recognition of concussion and the dangers of playing while symptomatic following a concussion and how to better protect the brain while participating in contact sports. Instituting a preseason baseline testing program for concussion is important, and a graduated exertional testing program should be included as part of every return-to-play protocol to ensure the athlete can handle the added physical stresses of his or her respective sport. Clinicians must recognize that recovery and return-to-play considerations involve many factors and that relying solely on self-report of symptoms can be dangerous. Clearly written documentation of serial evaluations conducted on the athlete is important for managing the injury as well as for minimizing the risk of legal action in the event that an apparent mild TBI turns into something more serious.

Beyond improving the assessment and management of concussions, clinicians must also recognize that catastrophic brain injuries such as subdural and epidural hematomas occasionally occur in sport, and they must be prepared to properly manage these potentially fatal injuries. In both cases, deterioration of signs and symptoms—including changing levels of consciousness—will indicate an emergent medical situation requiring immediate transportation to an emergency or neurosurgical department. In most cases, a CT scan to locate the exact pathology will be conducted, followed by neurosurgical evacuation of the developing hematoma. For these procedures to occur in a timely and efficient manner, it is essential for the sports medicine staff's emergency action plan to include procedures for managing the injury. The presence of trained emergency care providers capable of intubating or medicating a rapidly deteriorating athlete prior to or during transport is essential. Careful and thorough planning with local emergency medical personnel is critical.

Finally, athletic trainers, team physicians, emergency medical personnel, neurosurgeons, neurologists, and neuropsychologists must work together as a team to establish both an emergency action plan and a sound concussion assessment protocol to prevent brain-related sudden death.

Clinical Case Scenarios

1. Terry is a 16-year-old high school quarterback. In the middle of the second quarter, his offensive line breaks coverage and he is blindsided by the opposing linebacker during a first-and-ten play. He seems stunned on the field, but rises to his feet under his own power a few seconds later and assembles the huddle as usual. The offensive coordinator observes that Terry proceeds to make the same play call for the ensuing two plays, and the star quarterback returns to the sideline as the punt team is sent on the field to complete the fourth-down play. One of the offensive linemen approaches the athletic trainer and mentions that something "just isn't right" with the quarterback. Upon further evaluation on the sideline, the athletic trainer identifies that Terry may have a concussion and informs the coach that his quarterback will not be returning to play on that day and not until he can follow up with the team physician. Because of this decision by the athletic trainer, Terry was able to recover and return to football after missing only one game.

    1. What could the athletic trainer or other sports medicine professionals present at the game have done differently to have better identified this head injury?
    2. If the athlete only complained of a headache and slight confusion, what other medical conditions could be present with these similar signs and symptoms?

2. Josie is a 15-year-old ice hockey player. She has been playing for the past 8 years and has ambitions to work toward a Division I collegiate scholarship. Last week she was involved in a minor motor vehicle accident, after which she complained of a headache, had difficulty remembering the events leading up to the accident, and was confused. Standard diagnostic CT scans and MRI did not reveal any brain structure abnormalities, and she was promptly released from the emergency department with no real follow-up instructions. You are aware of the accident, but think nothing of it since the emergency department discharged her. She returns to the ice 4 days later, where she loses her footing during a tournament and crashes into the end boards. She does not appear to be moving, and lays motionless on the playing ice surface. The play is stopped and the on-ice official assists you safely over to her location on the playing surface.

    1. What would be the first things you seek to accomplish in managing this scenario?
    2. After performing the primary survey, you evaluate her vitals at regular intervals (1 to 2 minutes). She is still unresponsive, and her vitals show signs of rapid deterioration. What condition(s) do you suspect, and what are your immediate actions?
    3. How might this scenario have been prevented, and what prevention programs might you implement to limit the chances of these brain injuries occurring?

Key Terms

anterograde amnesia

Balance Error Scoring System (BESS)

cerebral concussion

diffuse brain injury

epidural hematoma

Graded Symptom Checklist

impact injury

impulse injury

retrograde amnesia

second impact syndrome

Sport Concussion Assessment Tool 2

Standardized Assessment of Concussion (SAC)

subdural hematoma

References

1. Langlois JA, Rutland-Brown W, Wald MM. The epidemiology and impact of traumatic brain injury: a brief overview. *J Head Trauma Rehabil.* 2006;21(5):375–378.
2. Langlois JA, Rutland-Brown W, Thomas KE. *Traumatic Brain Injury in the United States: Emergency Department Visits, Hospitalizations, and Deaths.* Atlanta, GA: Centers for Disease Control and Prevention, National Center for Injury Prevention and Control; 2004.
3. Schneier AJ, Shields BJ, Hostetler SG, Xiang H, Smith GA. Incidence of pediatric traumatic brain injury and associated hospital resource utilization in the United States. *Pediatrics.* 2006;118(2):483–492.
4. McCrory P, Meeuwisse W, Johnston K, et al. Consensus statement on concussion in sport: the Third International Conference on Concussion in Sport held in Zurich, November 2008. *Clin J Sport Med.* 2009;19(3):185–200.
5. Gennarelli TA. Mechanisms of brain injury. *J Emerg Med.* 1993;11(suppl 1):5–11.
6. Schneider RC. *Head and Neck Injuries in Football.* Baltimore: Williams & Wilkins; 1973.
7. American Academy of Neurology. Practice parameter: the management of concussion in sports (summary statement). Report of the Quality Standards Subcommittee. *Neurology.* 1997;48(3):581–585.
8. Guskiewicz KM, McCrea M, Marshall SW, et al. Cumulative effects associated with recurrent concussion in collegiate football players: the NCAA Concussion Study. *JAMA.* 2003;290(19):2549–2555.
9. Mueller FO, Colgate B. *Annual Survey of Football Injury Research: 1931–2009.* Chapel Hill, NC: National Center for Catastrophic Sport Injury Research; 2010.
10. Van De Graaff KM, Fox SI. *Concepts of Human Anatomy and Physiology.* 5th ed. Boston: WCB/McGraw-Hill; 1999.
11. Mokri B. Headaches caused by decreased intracranial pressure: diagnosis and management. *Curr Opin Neurol.* 2003;16:319–326.
12. Goadsby P, Jager HR. Postural headache and cerebrospinal fluid leak: believing is seeing. *Headache.* 2003;43(6):681.
13. Dunn-Meynell AA, Hassanain M, Levin BE. Norepinephrine and traumatic brain injury: a possible role in post-traumatic edema. *Brain Res.* 1998;800(2):245–252.
14. Prasad MR, Tzigaret C, Smith DH, Soares H, McIntosh TK. Decreased alpha-adrenergic receptors after experimental brain injury. *J Neurotrauma.* 1993;9:269–279.
15. Shetter AG, Demakas JJ. The pathophysiology of concussion: a review. *Adv Neurol.* 1979;22:5–14.
16. Gurdjian ES, Lissner HR, Webster JE, Latimer FR, Haddad BF. Studies on experimental concussion: relation of physiologic effect to time duration of intracranial pressure increase at impact. *Neurology.* 1954;4:674–681.
17. Ommaya AK, Gennarelli TA. Cerebral concussion and traumatic unconsciousness. Correlation of experimental and clinical observations of blunt head injuries. *Brain.* 1974;97(4):633–654.
18. Brolinson PG, Manoogian S, McNeely D, et al. Analysis of linear head accelerations from collegiate football impacts. *Curr Sports Med Rep.* 2006;5(1):23–28.
19. Duma SM, Manoogian SJ, Bussone WR, et al. Analysis of real-time head accelerations in collegiate football players. *Clin J Sport Med.* 2005;15(1):3–8.
20. Guskiewicz KM, Mihalik JP, Shankar V, et al. Measurement of head impacts in collegiate football players: relationship between head impact biomechanics and acute clinical outcome after concussion. *Neurosurgery.* 2007;61(6):1244–1252.
21. McCaffrey MA, Mihalik JP, Crowell DH, Shields EW, Guskiewicz KM. Measurement of head impacts in collegiate football players: clinical measures of concussion after high- and low-magnitude impacts. *Neurosurgery.* 2007;61(6):1236–1243; discussion 1243.

22. Mihalik JP, Bell DR, Marshall SW, Guskiewicz KM. Measurement of head impacts in collegiate football players: an investigation of positional and event-type differences. *Neurosurgery.* 2007;61(6):1229–1235.

23. Schnebel B, Gwin JT, Anderson S, Gatlin R. In vivo study of head impacts in football: a comparison of National Collegiate Athletic Association Division I versus high school impacts. *Neurosurgery.* 2007;60(3):490–495; discussion 495–496.

24. Rowson S, Brolinson G, Goforth M, Dietter D, Duma S. Linear and angular head acceleration measurements in collegiate football. *J Biomech Eng.* 2009;131(6):061016.

25. Broglio SP, Sosnoff JJ, Shin S, et al. Head impacts during high school football: a biomechanical assessment. *J Athl Train.* 2009;44(4):342–349.

26. Mihalik JP, Blackburn JT, Greenwald RM, et al. Collision type and player anticipation affect head impact severity among youth ice hockey players. *Pediatrics.* 2010;125(6):e1394–1401.

27. Mihalik JP, Greenwald RM, Blackburn JT, et al. The effect of infraction type on head impact severity in youth ice hockey. *Med Sci Sports Exerc.* 2010;42(8):1431–1438.

28. Mihalik JP, Guskiewicz KM, Jeffries JA, Greenwald RM, Marshall SW. Characteristics of head impacts sustained by youth ice hockey players. *Proc Institution Mech Engineers P J Sports Eng Tech.* 2008;222(1):45–52.

29. Giza CC, Hovda DA. The neurometabolic cascade of concussion. *J Athl Train.* 2001;36(3):228–235.

30. Meyer JS, Kondo A, Nomura F, Sakamoto K, Teraura T. Cerebral hemodynamics and metabolism following experimental head injury. *J Neurosurg.* 1970;32(3):304–319.

31. Nilsson B, Nordstrom CH. Rate of cerebral energy consumption in concussive head injury in the rat. *J Neurosurg.* 1977;47(2):274–281.

32. Levasseur JE, Alessandri B, Reinert M, et al. Lactate, not glucose, up-regulates mitochondrial oxygen consumption both in sham and lateral fluid percussed rat brains. *Neurosurgery.* 2006;59(5):1122–1130; discussion 1130–1131.

33. Cantu RC. Cerebral concussion in sport. Management and prevention. *Sports Med.* 1992;14(1):64–74.

34. May PR, Fuster JM, Haber J, Hirschman A. Woodpecker drilling behavior. An endorsement of the rotational theory of impact brain injury. *Arch Neurol.* 1979;36(6):370–373.

35. May PR, Fuster JM, Newman P, Hirschman A. Woodpeckers and head injury. *Lancet.* 1976;1(7957):454–455.

36. Gerberich SG, Finke R, Madden M, et al. An epidemiological study of high school ice hockey injuries. *Childs Nerv Syst.* 1987;3(2):59–64.

37. Brust JD, Leonard BJ, Pheley A, Roberts WO. Children's ice hockey injuries. *Am J Dis Child.* 1992;146(6):741–747.

38. Hafen BQ, Karren KJ, Mistovich JJ. *Prehospital Emergency Care.* 5th ed. Upper Saddle River, NJ: Prentice-Hall; 1996.

39. Collins MW, Lovell MR, McKeag DB. Current issues in managing sports-related concussion. *J Am Med Assoc.* 1999;282(24):2283–2285.

40. Arnheim DD, Prentice WE. *Principles of Athletic Training.* 9th ed. Boston: WCB McGraw-Hill; 1997.

41. Torg JS, Shephard RJ, eds. *Current Therapy in Sports Medicine.* St. Louis, MO: Mosby; 1995.

42. Maddocks DL, Dicker GD, Saling MM. The assessment of orientation following concussion in athletes. *Clin J Sport Med.* 1995;5(1):32–35.

43. Riemann BL, Guskiewicz KM. Effects of mild head injury on postural stability as measured through clinical balance testing. *J Athl Train.* 2000;35(1):19–25.

44. Guskiewicz KM, Ross SE, Marshall SW. Postural stability and neuropsychological deficits after concussion in collegiate athletes. *J Athl Train.* 2001;36(3):263–273.

45. Riemann BL, Guskiewicz KM, Shields EW. Relationship between clinical and forceplate measures of postural stability. *J Sport Rehabil.* 1999;8:71–82.

46. McCrea M, Kelly JP, Randolph C, et al. Standardized assessment of concussion (SAC): on-site mental status evaluation of the athlete. *J Head Trauma Rehabil.* 1998;13(2):27–35.

47. McCrea M. Standardized mental status assessment of sports concussion. *Clin J Sport Med.* 2001;11(3):176–181.

48. McCrea M. Standardized mental status testing on the sideline after sport-related concussion. *J Athl Train.* 2001;36(3):274–279.

49. McCrea M, Kelly JP, Kluge J, Ackley B, Randolph C. Standardized assessment of concussion in football players. *Neurology.* 1997;48(3):586–588.

50. McCrea M, Kelly JP, Randolph C, Cisler R, Berger L. Immediate neurocognitive effects of concussion. *Neurosurgery.* 2002;50(5):1032–1040; discussion 1040–1042.

51. Guskiewicz KM, Bruce SL, Cantu RC, et al. National Athletic Trainers' Association position statement: management of sport-related concussion. *J Athl Train.* 2004;39(3):280–297.

52. Bleiberg J, Cernich AN, Cameron K, et al. Duration of cognitive impairment after sports concussion. *Neurosurgery.* 2004;54(5):1073–1078.

53. Bleiberg J, Garmoe WS, Halpern EL, Reeves DL, Nadler JD. Consistency of within-day and across-day performance after mild brain injury. *Neuropsychiatry Neuropsychol Behav Neurol.* 1997;10(4):247–253.

54. Bleiberg J, Halpern EL, Reeves D, Daniel JC. Future directions for the neuropsychological assessment of sports concussion. *J Head Trauma Rehabil.* 1998;13(2):36–44.

55. Erlanger D, Saliba E, Barth J, et al. Monitoring resolution of postconcussion symptoms in athletes: preliminary results of a web-based neuropsychological test protocol. *J Athl Train.* 2001;36(3):280–287.

56. Lovell MR, Collins MW, Iverson GL, et al. Recovery from mild concussion in high school athletes. *J Neurosurg.* 2003;98(2):296–301.

57. Bleiberg J, Kane RL, Reeves DL, Garmoe WS, Halpern E. Factor analysis of computerized and traditional tests used in mild brain injury research. *Clin Neuropsychol.* 2000;14(3):287–294.

58. Collie A, Darby D, Maruff P. Computerised cognitive assessment of athletes with sports related head injury. *Br J Sports Med.* 2001;35(5):297–302.

59. Collie A, Maruff P, Makdissi M, et al. CogSport: reliability and correlation with conventional cognitive tests used in postconcussion medical evaluations. *Clin J Sport Med.* 2003;13(1):28–32.

60. Daniel JC, Olesniewicz MH, Reeves DL, et al. Repeated measures of cognitive processing efficiency in adolescent athletes: implications for monitoring recovery from concussion. *Neuropsychiatry Neuropsychol Behav Neurol.* 1999;12(3):167–169.

61. Makdissi M, Collie A, Maruff P, et al. Computerised cognitive assessment of concussed Australian Rules footballers. *Br J Sports Med.* 2001;35(5):354–360.

62. McCrea M, Barr WB, Guskiewicz K, et al. Standard regression-based methods for measuring recovery after sport-related concussion. *J Int Neuropsychol Soc.* 2005;11(1):58–69.

63. McCrory P. New treatments for concussion: the next millennium beckons. *Clin J Sport Med.* 2001;11(3):190–193.

64. Cruz J, Minoja G, Okuchi K. Improving clinical outcomes from acute subdural hematomas with the emergency preoperative administration of high doses of mannitol: a randomized trial. *Neurosurgery.* 2001;49(4):864–871.

65. Cruz J, Minoja G, Okuchi K, Facco E. Successful use of the new high-dose mannitol treatment in patients with Glasgow Coma Scale scores of 3 and bilateral abnormal pupillary widening: a randomized trial. *J Neurosurg.* 2004;100(3):376–383.

66. Cruz J, Minoja G, Okuchi K. Major clinical and physiological benefits of early high doses of mannitol for intraparenchymal temporal lobe hemorrhages with abnormal pupillary widening: a randomized trial. *Neurosurgery.* 2002;51(3):628–637; discussion 637–638.

67. Kaufmann AM, Cardoso ER. Aggravation of vasogenic cerebral edema by multiple-dose mannitol. *J Neurosurg.* 1992;77(4):584–589.

68. Schwartz ML, Tator CH, Rowed DW, et al. The University of Toronto head injury treatment study: a prospective, randomized comparison of pentobarbital and mannitol. *Can J Neurol Sci.* 1984;11(4):434–440.

69. Vialet R, Albanèse J, Thomachot L, et al. Isovolume hypertonic solutes (sodium chloride or mannitol) in the treatment of refractory posttraumatic intracranial hypertension: 2 mL/kg 7.5% saline is more effective than 2 mL/kg 20% mannitol. *Crit Care Med.* 2003;31(6):1683–1687.

70. Sayre MR, Daily SW, Stern SA, et al. Out-of-hospital administration of mannitol does not change systolic blood pressure. *Acad Emerg Med.* 1996;3(9):840–848.

71. McCrea M, Guskiewicz KM, Marshall SW, et al. Acute effects and recovery time following concussion in collegiate football players: the NCAA Concussion Study. *JAMA.* 2003;290(19):2556–2563.

72. Field M, Collins MW, Lovell MR, Maroon J. Does age play a role in recovery from sports-related concussion? A comparison of high school and collegiate athletes. *J Pediatr.* 2003;142(5):546–553.

73. Cantu RC, Voy R. Second impact syndrome: a risk in any contact sport. *Physician Sportsmed.* 1995;23(6):27–28.

74. McCrory P. Does second impact syndrome exist? *Clin J Sports Med.* 2001;11(3):144–149.

75. Bruce DA, Alavi A, Bilaniuk L, et al. Diffuse cerebral swelling following head injuries in children: the syndrome of "malignant brain edema." *J Neurosurg.* 1981;54(2):170–178.

76. McCrory P, Berkovic SF. Second impact syndrome. *Neurology.* 1998;50(3):677–683.

77. Mueller FO, Cantu RC, Van Camp SP. *Catastrophic Injuries in High School and College Sports.* Champaign, IL: Human Kinetics; 1996.

78. Cantu RC. Guidelines for return to contact sports after a cerebral concussion. *Physician Sportsmed.* 1986;14:75–83.

79. Collins MW, Field M, Lovell MR, et al. Relationship between postconcussion headache and neuropsychological test performance in high school athletes. *Am J Sports Med.* 2003;31(2):168–173.

80. Cantu RC. Posttraumatic retrograde and anterograde amnesia: pathophysiology and implications in grading and safe return to play. *J Athl Train.* 2001;36(3):244–248.

81. Colorado Medical Society. *Reports of the Sports Medicine Committee: Guidelines for the Management of Concussion in Sports.* Denver, CO: Colorado Medical Society; 1991.

82. Roberts WO. Who plays? Who sits? Managing concussions on the sidelines. *Physician Sportsmed.* 1992;20(8):66–72.

83. Torg JS. *Athletic Injuries to the Head, Neck, and Face.* 2nd ed. St. Louis, MO: Mosby-Year Book; 1991.

84. Bailes JE, Hudson V. Classification of sport-related head trauma: a spectrum of mild to severe injury. *J Athl Train.* 2001;36(3):236–243.

85. Lovell MR, Collins MW, Iverson GL, et al. Recovery from mild concussion in high school athletes. *J Neurosurg.* 2003;98(2):296–301.

Sport Concussion Assessment Tool 2 (SCAT2)

SCAT2

Sport Concussion Assessment Tool 2

Name _____

Sport/team _____

Date/time of injury _____

Date/time of assessment _____

Age _____ Gender ▢ M ▢ F

Years of education completed _____

Examiner _____

What is the SCAT2?[1]

This tool represents a standardized method of evaluating injured athletes for concussion and can be used in athletes aged from 10 years and older. It supersedes the original SCAT published in 2005[2]. This tool also enables the calculation of the Standardized Assessment of Concussion (SAC)[3,4] score and the Maddocks questions[5] for sideline concussion assessment.

Instructions for using the SCAT2

The SCAT2 is designed for the use of medical and health professionals. Preseason baseline testing with the SCAT2 can be helpful for interpreting post-injury test scores. Words in Italics throughout the SCAT2 are the instructions given to the athlete by the tester.

This tool may be freely copied for distribution to individuals, teams, groups and organizations.

What is a concussion?

A concussion is a disturbance in brain function caused by a direct or indirect force to the head. It results in a variety of non-specific symptoms (like those listed below) and often does not involve loss of consciousness. Concussion should be suspected in the presence of **any one or more** of the following:

- Symptoms (such as headache), or
- Physical signs (such as unsteadiness), or
- Impaired brain function (e.g. confusion) or
- Abnormal behaviour.

Any athlete with a suspected concussion should be REMOVED FROM PLAY, medically assessed, monitored for deterioration (i.e., should not be left alone) and should not drive a motor vehicle.

Symptom Evaluation

How do you feel?

You should score yourself on the following symptoms, based on how you feel now.

	none	mild		moderate		severe	
Headache	0	1	2	3	4	5	6
"Pressure in head"	0	1	2	3	4	5	6
Neck Pain	0	1	2	3	4	5	6
Nausea or vomiting	0	1	2	3	4	5	6
Dizziness	0	1	2	3	4	5	6
Blurred vision	0	1	2	3	4	5	6
Balance problems	0	1	2	3	4	5	6
Sensitivity to light	0	1	2	3	4	5	6
Sensitivity to noise	0	1	2	3	4	5	6
Feeling slowed down	0	1	2	3	4	5	6
Feeling like "in a fog"	0	1	2	3	4	5	6
"Don't feel right"	0	1	2	3	4	5	6
Difficulty concentrating	0	1	2	3	4	5	6
Difficulty remembering	0	1	2	3	4	5	6
Fatigue or low energy	0	1	2	3	4	5	6
Confusion	0	1	2	3	4	5	6
Drowsiness	0	1	2	3	4	5	6
Trouble falling asleep (if applicable)	0	1	2	3	4	5	6
More emotional	0	1	2	3	4	5	6
Irritability	0	1	2	3	4	5	6
Sadness	0	1	2	3	4	5	6
Nervous or Anxious	0	1	2	3	4	5	6

Total number of symptoms (Maximum possible 22) ▢▢

Symptom severity score ▢▢
(Add all scores in table, maximum possible: 22 x 6 = 132)

Do the symptoms get worse with physical activity? ▢ Y ▢ N
Do the symptoms get worse with mental activity? ▢ Y ▢ N

Overall rating

If you know the athlete well prior to the injury, how different is the athlete acting compared to his / her usual self? Please circle one response.

no different	very different	unsure

Cognitive & Physical Evaluation

1 **Symptom score** (from page 1)

22 **minus** number of symptoms [of 22]

2 **Physical signs score**

Was there loss of consciousness or unresponsiveness? ☐ Y ☐ N

If yes, how long? [_____] minutes

Was there a balance problem/unsteadiness? ☐ Y ☐ N

Physical signs score (1 point for each negative response) [of 2]

3 **Glasgow coma scale (GCS)**

Best eye response (E)

No eye opening	1
Eye opening in response to pain	2
Eye opening to speech	3
Eyes opening spontaneously	4

Best verbal response (V)

No verbal response	1
Incomprehensible sounds	2
Inappropriate words	3
Confused	4
Oriented	5

Best motor response (M)

No motor response	1
Extension to pain	2
Abnormal flexion to pain	3
Flexion/Withdrawal to pain	4
Localizes to pain	5
Obeys commands	6

Glasgow Coma score (E + V + M) [of 15]

GCS should be recorded for all athletes in case of subsequent deterioration.

4 **Sideline Assessment – Maddocks Score**

"I am going to ask you a few questions, please listen carefully and give your best effort."

Modified Maddocks questions (1 point for each correct answer)

At what venue are we at today?	0	1
Which half is it now?	0	1
Who scored last in this match?	0	1
What team did you play last week/game?	0	1
Did your team win the last game?	0	1

Maddocks score [of 5]

Maddocks score is validated for sideline diagnosis of concussion only and is not included in SCAT 2 summary score for serial testing.

5 **Cognitive assessment**

Standardized Assessment of Concussion (SAC)

Orientation (1 point for each correct answer)

What month is it?	0	1
What is the date today?	0	1
What is the day of the week?	0	1
What year is it?	0	1
What time is it right now? (within 1 hour)	0	1

Orientation score [of 5]

Immediate memory

"I am going to test your memory. I will read you a list of words and when I am done, repeat back as many words as you can remember, in any order."

Trials 2 & 3:

"I am going to repeat the same list again. Repeat back as many words as you can remember in any order, even if you said the word before."

Complete all 3 trials regardless of score on trial 1 & 2. Read the words at a rate of one per second. Score 1 pt. for each correct response. Total score equals sum across all 3 trials. Do not inform the athlete that delayed recall will be tested.

List	Trial 1	Trial 2	Trial 3	Alternative word list		
elbow	0 1	0 1	0 1	candle	baby	finger
apple	0 1	0 1	0 1	paper	monkey	penny
carpet	0 1	0 1	0 1	sugar	perfume	blanket
saddle	0 1	0 1	0 1	sandwich	sunset	lemon
bubble	0 1	0 1	0 1	wagon	iron	insect
Total						

Immediate memory score [of 15]

Concentration

Digits Backward:

"I am going to read you a string of numbers and when I am done, you repeat them back to me backwards, in reverse order of how I read them to you. For example, if I say 7-1-9, you would say 9-1-7."

If correct, go to next string length. If incorrect, read trial 2. One point possible for each string length. Stop after incorrect on both trials. The digits should be read at the rate of one per second.

Alternative digit lists

4-9-3	0 1	6-2-9	5-2-6	4-1-5
3-8-1-4	0 1	3-2-7-9	1-7-9-5	4-9-6-8
6-2-9-7-1	0 1	1-5-2-8-6	3-8-5-2-7	6-1-8-4-3
7-1-8-4-6-2	0 1	5-3-9-1-4-8	8-3-1-9-6-4	7-2-4-8-5-6

Months in Reverse Order:

"Now tell me the months of the year in reverse order. Start with the last month and go backward. So you'll say December, November ... Go ahead"

1 pt. for entire sequence correct

Dec-Nov-Oct-Sept-Aug-Jul-Jun-May-Apr-Mar-Feb-Jan [0 1]

Concentration score [of 5]

---

[1] This tool has been developed by a group of international experts at the 3rd International Consensus meeting on Concussion in Sport held in Zurich, Switzerland in November 2008. The full details of the conference outcomes and the authors of the tool are published in British Journal of Sports Medicine, 2009, volume 43, supplement 1.
The outcome paper will also be simultaneously co-published in the May 2009 issues of Clinical Journal of Sports Medicine, Physical Medicine & Rehabilitation, Journal of Athletic Training, Journal of Clinical Neuroscience, Journal of Science & Medicine in Sport, Neurosurgery, Scandinavian Journal of Science & Medicine in Sport and the Journal of Clinical Sports Medicine.

[2] McCrory P et al. Summary and agreement statement of the 2nd International Conference on Concussion in Sport, Prague 2004. British Journal of Sports Medicine. 2005; 39: 196-204

[3] McCrea M. Standardized mental status testing of acute concussion. Clinical Journal of Sports Medicine. 2001; 11: 176-181

[4] McCrea M, Randolph C, Kelly J. Standardized Assessment of Concussion: Manual for administration, scoring and interpretation. Waukesha, Wisconsin, USA.

[5] Maddocks, DL; Dicker, GD; Saling, MM. The assessment of orientation following concussion in athletes. Clin J Sport Med. 1995;5(1):32–3

[6] Guskiewicz KM. Assessment of postural stability following sport-related concussion. Current Sports Medicine Reports. 2003; 2: 24-30

6 Balance examination

This balance testing is based on a modified version of the Balance Error Scoring System (BESS)⁶. A stopwatch or watch with a second hand is required for this testing.

Balance testing

"I am now going to test your balance. Please take your shoes off, roll up your pant legs above ankle (if applicable), and remove any ankle taping (if applicable). This test will consist of three twenty second tests with different stances."

(a) Double leg stance:
"The first stance is standing with your feet together with your hands on your hips and with your eyes closed. You should try to maintain stability in that position for 20 seconds. I will be counting the number of times you move out of this position. I will start timing when you are set and have closed your eyes."

(b) Single leg stance:
"If you were to kick a ball, which foot would you use? [This will be the dominant foot] Now stand on your non-dominant foot. The dominant leg should be held in approximately 30 degrees of hip flexion and 45 degrees of knee flexion. Again, you should try to maintain stability for 20 seconds with your hands on your hips and your eyes closed. I will be counting the number of times you move out of this position. If you stumble out of this position, open your eyes and return to the start position and continue balancing. I will start timing when you are set and have closed your eyes."

(c) Tandem stance:
*"Now stand heel-to-toe with your **non-dominant foot** in back. Your weight should be evenly distributed across both feet. Again, you should try to maintain stability for 20 seconds with your hands on your hips and your eyes closed. I will be counting the number of times you move out of this position. If you stumble out of this position, open your eyes and return to the start position and continue balancing. I will start timing when you are set and have closed your eyes."*

Balance testing – types of errors
1. Hands lifted off iliac crest
2. Opening eyes
3. Step, stumble, or fall
4. Moving hip into > 30 degrees abduction
5. Lifting forefoot or heel
6. Remaining out of test position > 5 sec

Each of the 20-second trials is scored by counting the errors, or deviations from the proper stance, accumulated by the athlete. The examiner will begin counting errors only after the individual has assumed the proper start position. **The modified BESS is calculated by adding one error point for each error during the three 20-second tests. The maximum total number of errors for any single condition is 10.** If a athlete commits multiple errors simultaneously, only one error is recorded but the athlete should quickly return to the testing position, and counting should resume once subject is set. Subjects that are unable to maintain the testing procedure for a minimum of **five seconds** at the start are assigned the highest possible score, ten, for that testing condition.

Which foot was tested: ☐ Left ☐ Right
(i.e. which is the **non-dominant** foot)

Condition	Total errors
Double Leg Stance (feet together)	of 10
Single leg stance (non-dominant foot)	of 10
Tandem stance (non-dominant foot at back)	of 10
Balance examination score (30 **minus** total errors)	of 30

7 Coordination examination

Upper limb coordination
Finger-to-nose (FTN) task: *"I am going to test your coordination now. Please sit comfortably on the chair with your eyes open and your arm (either right or left) outstretched (shoulder flexed to 90 degrees and elbow and fingers extended). When I give a start signal, I would like you to perform five successive finger to nose repetitions using your index finger to touch the tip of the nose as quickly and as accurately as possible."*

Which arm was tested: ☐ Left ☐ Right

Scoring: 5 correct repetitions in < 4 seconds = 1

Note for testers: Athletes fail the test if they do not touch their nose, do not fully extend their elbow or do not perform five repetitions. Failure should be scored as 0.

Coordination score	of 1

8 Cognitive assessment
Standardized Assessment of Concussion (SAC)
Delayed recall
"Do you remember that list of words I read a few times earlier? Tell me as many words from the list as you can remember in any order."

Circle each word correctly recalled. Total score equals number of words recalled.

List	Alternative word list		
elbow	candle	baby	finger
apple	paper	monkey	penny
carpet	sugar	perfume	blanket
saddle	sandwich	sunset	lemon
bubble	wagon	iron	insect

Delayed recall score	of 5

Overall score

Test domain	Score
Symptom score	of 22
Physical signs score	of 2
Glasgow Coma score (E + V + M)	of 15
Balance examination score	of 30
Coordination score	of 1
Subtotal	**of 70**
Orientation score	of 5
Immediate memory score	of 15
Concentration score	of 5
Delayed recall score	of 5
SAC subtotal	**of 30**
SCAT2 total	**of 100**
Maddocks Score	**of 5**

Definitive normative data for a SCAT2 "cut-off" score is not available at this time and will be developed in prospective studies. Embedded within the SCAT2 is the SAC score that can be utilized separately in concussion management. The scoring system also takes on particular clinical significance during serial assessment where it can be used to document either a decline or an improvement in neurological functioning.

Scoring data from the SCAT2 or SAC should not be used as a stand alone method to diagnose concussion, measure recovery or make decisions about an athlete's readiness to return to competition after concussion.

Athlete Information

Any athlete suspected of having a concussion should be removed from play, and then seek medical evaluation.

Signs to watch for

Problems could arise over the first 24-48 hours. You should not be left alone and must go to a hospital at once if you:

- Have a headache that gets worse
- Are very drowsy or can't be awakened (woken up)
- Can't recognize people or places
- Have repeated vomiting
- Behave unusually or seem confused; are very irritable
- Have seizures (arms and legs jerk uncontrollably)
- Have weak or numb arms or legs
- Are unsteady on your feet; have slurred speech

Remember, it is better to be safe.
Consult your doctor after a suspected concussion.

Return to play

Athletes should not be returned to play the same day of injury. When returning athletes to play, they should follow a stepwise symptom-limited program, with stages of progression. For example:
1. rest until asymptomatic (physical and mental rest)
2. light aerobic exercise (e.g. stationary cycle)
3. sport-specific exercise
4. non-contact training drills (start light resistance training)
5. full contact training after medical clearance
6. return to competition (game play)

There should be approximately 24 hours (or longer) for each stage and the athlete should drop back to the previous asymptomatic level if any post-concussive symptoms recur. Resistance training should only be added in the later stages.
Medical clearance should be given before return to play.

Tool	Test domain	Time	Score			
		Date tested				
		Days post injury				
SCAT2	Symptom score					
	Physical signs score					
	Glasgow Coma score (E + V + M)					
	Balance examination score					
	Coordination score					
SAC	Orientation score					
	Immediate memory score					
	Concentration score					
	Delayed recall score					
	SAC Score					
Total	SCAT2					
Symptom severity score (max possible 132)						
Return to play			☐ Y ☐ N	☐ Y ☐ N	☐ Y ☐ N	☐ Y ☐ N

Additional comments

Concussion injury advice (To be given to concussed athlete)

This patient has received an injury to the head. A careful medical examination has been carried out and no sign of any serious complications has been found. It is expected that recovery will be rapid, but the patient will need monitoring for a further period by a responsible adult. Your treating physician will provide guidance as to this timeframe.

If you notice any change in behaviour, vomiting, dizziness, worsening headache, double vision or excessive drowsiness, please telephone the clinic or the nearest hospital emergency department immediately.

Other important points:
- **Rest and avoid strenuous activity for at least 24 hours**
- **No alcohol**
- **No sleeping tablets**
- **Use paracetamol or codeine for headache. Do not use aspirin or anti-inflammatory medication**
- **Do not drive until medically cleared**
- **Do not train or play sport until medically cleared**

Clinic phone number

Patient's name

Date/time of injury

Date/time of medical review

Treating physician

Contact details or stamp

Pocket SCAT2

Concussion should be suspected in the presence of **any one or more** of the following: symptoms (such as headache), or physical signs (such as unsteadiness), or impaired brain function (e.g confusion) or abnormal behaviour.

1. Symptoms

Presence of any of the following signs & symptoms may suggest a concussion.

- Loss of conciousness
- Seizure of convulsion
- Amnesia
- Headache
- "Pressure in head"
- Neck Pain
- Nausea or vomiting
- Dizziness
- Blurred vision
- Balance problems
- Sensitivity to light
- Sensitivity to noise
- Feeling slowed down
- Feeling like "in a fog"
- "Don't feel right"
- Difficulty concentrating
- Difficulty remembering
- Fatigue or low energy
- Confusion
- Drowsiness
- More emotional
- Irritability
- Sadness
- Nervous or anxious

2. Memory function

Failure to answer all questions correctly may suggest a concussion.
"At what venue are we at today?"
"Which half is it now?"
"Who scored last in this game?"
"What team did you play last week I game?"
"Did your team win the last game?"

3. Balance testing
Instructions for tandem stance

*"Now stand heel-to-toe with your **non-dominant** foot in back. Your weight should be evenly distributed across both feet. You should try to maintain stability for 20 seconds with your hands on your hips and your eyes closed. I will be counting the number of times you move out of this position. If you stumble out of this position, open your eyes and return to the start position and continue balancing. I will start timing when you are set and have closed your eyes."*

Observe the athlete for 20 seconds. If they make more than 5 errors (such as lift their hands off their hips; open their eyes; lift their forefoot or heel; step, stumble, or fall; or remain out of the start position for more that 5 seconds) then this may suggest a concussion.

Any athlete with a suspected concussion should be IMMEDIATELY REMOVED FROM PLAY, urgently assessed medically, should not be left alone and should not drive a motor vehicle.

Reprinted from McCrory P, Meeuwisse W, Johnston K, et al. Consensus statement on concussion in sport: the Third International Conference on Concussion in Sport held in Zurich, November 2008. *Clin J Sport Med.* 2009;19(3):185–200.

Concussion State Legislation Matrix as of May 20, 2010

	Donahue's Suggested "Three Principles"	Colorado	Washington (Zackery Lystedt Law, 7/26/09)	Oregon (Max's Law, 2009)	Texas (Will's Law, 10/1/07)	Virginia (SB 652, gov signed 4/11/10)	Missouri (pending)	Oklahoma (pending)	Connecticut (pending gov signature 5/4/10)	Idaho (pending gov signature)
Educational Programs	Educate and verify CDC's Heads Up education guidelines (3/10)	New CHSAA by-law (4/10)	Annual education and information sheet & sign-off by youth athlete and parents (public and private schools)	Annual coach training on concussion, public education system, 12,000 Heads Up	Requires coaches, sponsors, & directors to undergo safety training	Multiagency development of education of coaches, players, & parents	Athletes and families need to be provided information	Annual education sheet & sign-off by coaches, athletes, and parents	Initial coaches' training, then refresher every 5 years	Bd of Ed and IHSAA to develop education programs for coaches, parents, & athletes
Verification/ Compliance	Leave up to the states		School District WIAA develops guidelines for educational 30-min video	6,000 youth coaches plus online training funded by grant ACTIVE $25	Texas UIL for high school	Annual education—Bd of Ed and school divisions	?	Districts to work with OSSAA on guidelines and ed sheets	CIAC to develop training courses	
Pre–High School Youth	?		If they use public property	?	?	?	Considering	?		
Concussion Equals Removal from Play	Identify and protect: when in doubt, sit them out	New CHSAA by-law (2/10)	Youth athlete "suspected of" concussion shall be removed from play at that time	If exhibits signs following blow or diagnosis may be removed from play	Unconscious = remove from play	"Suspected of" = remove from play	Concussion = remove from play	"Suspected of" = removal from play at that time	"Signs, symptoms, behavior" or diagnosis	No; stripped from bill by coaches lobby
Return to Play Requirements/ Guidelines	Written clearance by licensed provider trained in eval & mgmt	Written clearance required	Written clearance by licensed provider trained in eval & mgmt per WIAA	Medical release form from a health care professional	Requires written clearance	Written clearance by licensed provider trained in eval & mgmt	Written clearance by licensed provider trained in eval & mgmt	Written clearance by licensed health care provider, who may be a volunteer	Written clearance by physician	No; stripped from bill by coaches lobby
Baseline Testing		Voluntary (unknown no. of schools)			Voluntary (60 schools)					
Disciplines "Licensed"	Leave up to the states	CHSAA: MD, DO, ND, PA	MD, NP, DO, ATC, PA						MD only	

Abbreviations: ATC, Athletic Trainer, Certified; CDC, Centers for Disease Control and Prevention; CHSAA, Colorado High School Activities Association; CIAC, Connecticut Interscholastic Athletic Conference; DO, Doctor of Osteopathic Medicine; eval & mgmt, evaluation and management; gov, governor; IHSAA, Idaho High School Activities Association; MD, Doctor of Medicine; ND, Doctor of Naturopathic Medicine; NP, Nurse Practitioner; OSSAA, Oklahoma Secondary Schools Activities Association; PA, Physician Assistant; UIL, University Interscholastic League; WIAA, Washington Interscholastic Activities Association.

Source: Table used with permission from Parsons JT, Valovich McLeod TC (AT Still University, Meza, AZ); Unpublished data.

Cervical Spine Injury

Erik E. Swartz, PhD, ATC, FNATA

Kevin N. Waninger, MD, MS, FACSM

Sudden death in sport and athletics may occur from a serious, or catastrophic, cervical spinal cord injury. The incidence of catastrophic cervical spine injuries in the exercising individual is low,[1,2] yet when these injuries occur they are troubling due to high morbidity and the potential for permanent loss of neural function (i.e., **tetraplegia**). Cervical spine injuries have been reported in most contact sports, as well as in several noncontact sports, such as skiing, track and field, cheerleading, diving, surfing, power lifting, and equestrian events. The recognition and management of cervical spine injuries represents one of the most challenging roles for those who care for the exercising individual. Proper, timely management and accurate diagnosis of acute spinal cord injuries is paramount because of the recognized risk of sudden death and neurologic deterioration during or after the **emergency management** process.[3,4]

Definition of Condition

A **catastrophic cervical spinal cord injury** (SCI) is one in which a structural distortion of the cervical spinal column has occurred and is associated with actual or potential damage to the spinal cord.[5] The National Center for Catastrophic Sports Injury Research classifies catastrophic injuries as **direct injuries** (resulting from participation in the skills of a sport) or indirect injuries (resulting from systemic failure secondary to exertion while participating in a sport) and subdivides each classification into three categories: fatal (the injury causes the death of the athlete), nonfatal (the injury causes a permanent neurologic functional disability), and serious (a severe injury, but the athlete has no permanent functional disability; for example, a fractured cervical vertebra that does not cause paralysis). [2]

tetraplegia Paralysis caused by illness or injury to a human that results in the partial or total loss of use of all of the individual's limbs and torso.

emergency management Treatment of an acute injury or condition that poses a risk of sudden death.

catastrophic cervical spinal cord injury An injury in which a structural distortion of the cervical spinal column has occurred and is associated with actual or potential damage to the spinal cord.

direct injury An injury resulting from participation in the skills of a sport.

A catastrophic cervical SCI infrequently results in sudden death, but the risk of death in the athlete increases in cases when the injury involves the C5 level and above, which can inhibit central nervous system control of ventilation. Further complicating this condition is the risk of complications due to the complex biochemical cascade of events that occurs in the injured spinal cord during the 24 to 72 hours following the initial injury.[6,7] Therefore, immediate recognition and timely treatment in the prehospital setting, with close and careful emergency department management focusing on decompression of the spinal cord and controlling the secondary injury process, are critical.

Epidemiology

An accurate incidence of sudden death due to SCI in the United States is challenging to report. The National Spinal Cord Injury Statistical Center (NSCISC) collects and reports data regarding SCI in the United States, but it only collects data on those patients who are transported to one of the system's hospitals, and therefore does not include those who die on the scene.[8,9] According to the NSCISC, there are an estimated 12,000 new cases of SCI in the United States each year.[9] Vehicle crashes constitute the most frequent cause for SCI, at 42%.[8] Sport participation constitutes the fourth most common cause (approximately 7.9%) of spinal injuries,[8] and for those younger than 30 years, it is the second most common cause after motor vehicle crashes.[10] Approximately 80% of SCIs occur in males.

Historically, American football is associated with the highest rates of sudden death due to catastrophic spinal injuries among all sports.[2] In 1968, 36 documented deaths occurred directly due to participation in American football alone.[2] Death due to SCI from participation in American football has been dramatically reduced due to rules changes enacted in 1976 to prevent head-first contact,[11] and a documented case of sudden death due to SCI in American football has not occurred in several years.[2] During the 2009 football season, there were 9 cervical spinal cord injuries with incomplete neurologic recovery, with an additional 16 spinal injuries with complete neurologic recovery.[2] Of concern is that between 1999 and 2008 there was an average of 9.4 cervical cord injuries with incomplete neurologic recovery, compared with the 10 years prior, during which the average was 7.9 annual cervical cord injuries with incomplete recovery.[12] Clearly, the risk of serious SCI, and thus sudden death, associated with participation in American football persists.

It is important to recognize that epidemiologic data have established the risk of catastrophic SCI in other sports as well. Sports such as ice hockey,[13] skiing,[14] rugby,[15] gymnastics,[2] swimming and diving,[11] track and field (e.g., pole vaulting),[2,16] cheerleading,[2,17] and baseball[18] all involve activities that place participants at risk for SCI and sudden death. In fact, the incidence of nonfatal, direct catastrophic injuries in the sports of lacrosse, gymnastics, and men's ice hockey is higher than that in American football **(Table 7.1)**.[2]

Pathophysiology

axial load A situation in which the head and neck is flexed between 20° and 30° and the head serves as a point of contact.

The most common mechanism of injury in sport leading to a cervical SCI is an **axial load**,[19–22] in which the neck is flexed and the head serves as a point of contact, such as when diving into a pool or leading with the head during blocking or tackling. Large compressive forces are transferred to the cervical spine because contact at the top of the head has stopped its forward motion, but the weight of the torso continues to move in the same direction and creates a buckling effect in the cervical segment. This buckling produces large angulations within the cervical spine as a means of releasing the additional strain energy that has been produced due to the vertical loading, and is the causative factor of injury **(Figure 7.1)**.[23,24] The resultant injury may be a cervical fracture, dislocation, disc herniation, torn ligaments, or a combination of these, which invades the space naturally surrounding the spinal cord and physically comes into contact with it, causing acute tissue trauma. The most common level of SCI in sport is at the C4 to C5 level.[25]

The initial mechanism of injury to the cord may be laceration, compression, distraction, shear, or transient impact, in many instances being a combination of more than one of these. These mechanisms

TABLE 7.1 Combined High School and College Catastrophic Injury Data in Select Sports

Sport and Setting	Direct Catastrophic Injuries	Direct Injury Incidence Rates (Nonfatal[a]) per 100,000
American football (M)		
High school	699	0.83
College	147	1.74
Gymnastics		
High school	13	1.98 (M), 0.91(F)
College	6	19.19 (M), 4.97 (F)
Ice hockey		
High school	21	1.18 (M), 2.47 (F)
College	12	3.85 (M), 0.00 (F)
Track and field		
High school	65	0.11 (M), 0.01 (F)
College	10	0.34 (M), 0.12 (F)
Lacrosse		
High school	13	0.42 (M), 0.00 (F)
College	11	1.86 (M), 1.76 (F)
Wrestling (M)		
High school	58	0.55
College	1	0.54
Cheerleading		
High school	46	NA
College	23	NA

Abbreviations: F, female; M, male.
[a] Nonfatal is defined as permanent severe functional disability.
Source: Data adapted and reprinted with permission from the National Center for Catastrophic Sport Injury Research, fall 1982 through spring 2009.

result in one of four types of injury to the spinal cord: (1) cord maceration, in which the cord is crushed; (2) cord laceration, usually from a knife or gun shot wound; (3) cord contusion, which involves necrosis of the central gray matter of the spinal cord; and (4) solid cord injury, in which injury is distributed throughout both the gray and white matter.[6] Of these injury types, cord contusion injury represents 25% to 40% of cases and is the most common type in sports and recreation.[6] Even though in most cases the spinal cord will not be torn completely, permanent neurologic dysfunction, paralysis, and even death can still occur.

Acute trauma to the spinal cord results in a primary and secondary injury response.[6,26] Further changes in the spinal cord, generally involving necrosis of more central nervous system tissue, can take place during the chronic phase, which can last for months, but are not discussed in more detail here. The primary phase of injury is due directly to the initial mechanical impact placed on the spinal cord.

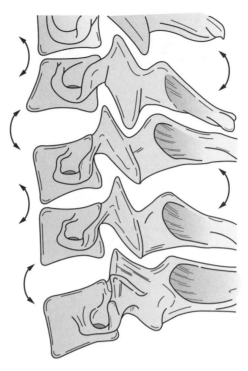

Figure 7.1 Buckling effect in the cervical column under axial load.
Source: Reprinted with permission from Swartz EE, Floyd RT, Cendoma M. Cervical spine functional anatomy and the biomechanics of injury due to compressive loading. *J Athl Train*. 2005;40(3):152–158.

Subsequent compression may result from penetrating bone fragments or disc material that invade the spinal canal space or pressure that develops from edema and inflammation. The secondary phase of injury involves a cascade of events that are a direct result of the primary phase but contribute to continuing necrosis and increasing the zone of injury.[6,26]

This has been shown in animal models, which are similar to human spinal cord injury (SCI), in relation to the cell loss that continues radially in all directions, causing the lesion to expand over time. By 60 days post-SCI, there remains only a thin rim of white matter. Massive cell death occurs immediately over the initial impact in the central core region. These cells are not rescuable. However, cell death continues to occur over several days and weeks and offers an opportunity for therapeutic intervention to rescue the neural cell populations that are at risk of dying after the first few hours.[6]

Primary Phase of Injury

The pathophysiologic processes of the primary phase start at the moment of injury and can last up to several days.[6] The mechanical damage the tissue experiences from the initial insult not only involves neural tissue, but also other soft tissues such as the protective meningeal layers of the cord and endothelial cells of blood vessels. Death is immediate in those cells that are destroyed at impact, but cell death is also attributed to the initial hemorrhage and resultant ischemia from torn blood vessels. Necrosis of these cells launches a complex biochemical cascade that will begin within minutes and continue into the secondary phase of injury.[27] There is an acute vasospasm in the spinal cord's capillary network at the site of injury. This, along with the hemorrhage from the damaged blood vessels, a loss of autoregulation of the vasculature, and thrombosis, contributes to localized ischemia. In response to the injury, the nerve cells experience an increased flow of action potentials that induce a shift in electrolyte concentrations. Intracellular concentrations of Na^+ and Ca^+ increase while K^+ decreases.

Normal neural function stops and is characterized as spinal shock, which can last up to 24 hours.[6] Neural injury is also aggravated by compression that will increase proportionately to the amount of inflammation and edema that builds over time. The more extensive the injury, the more pronounced this response will be, leading to a greater degree of compression on the spinal cord. This cycle leads to further cellular necrosis.

Secondary Phase of Injury

The secondary response in spinal cord injury begins within the first few minutes following trauma and can last for several weeks.[6] The primary and secondary phases overlap each other, so many of the responses in the primary phase carry over into the secondary phase. These include edema formation, electrolyte imbalances, and decreased oxygen perfusion. By the first 15 minutes following the initial trauma, there is an increased presence of neurotransmitters (such as glutamate) and amino acids outside the cells. Free radical production as a by-product of phagocytic activity causes lipid peroxidation, or the oxidation of lipids, which removes electrons from the cell walls, causing further damage. The lymphocytes and neutrophils from the phagocytic activity invade the area and produce cytokines and chemokines,[6,26] which trigger a programmable cell death response referred to as **apoptosis**. Cellular death from apoptosis and decreased ATP production limits the nervous cell's ability to carry signals coming from the brain.[6,26,27] Further loss of spinal cord perfusion persists due to clotting and neurogenic shock (bradycardia, hypotension, and decreased cardiac output), extending the zone of injury in all directions. Again, the greater the initial injury, the greater the response will be, leading to more inflammation, edema, and compression. This will augment the secondary response, leading to further cellular necrosis.

> **apoptosis** Process of programmed cell death.

Prevention and Predisposing Factors

Certain precautions may be taken to help avoid catastrophic cervical spine injury. These precautions include attempting to control or avoid certain extrinsic and intrinsic predisposing factors of acute cervical spine injury, examples of which can be seen in **Table 7.2**. Extrinsic factors are generally outside the control of the exercising individual, especially in respect to accidental contact to the crown of the head due to a fall or unintentional contact with another object (e.g., the ground), participant, or piece of equipment (e.g., goal post). Intrinsic factors (in most cases) can be controlled, and every effort should be made to control these intrinsic factors to help prevent catastrophic cervical spine injury in athletes. Preventive steps can be categorized into setting-specific and athlete-specific measures.[1,2,28,29]

Setting Specific

- Individuals responsible for coordinating the use of facilities for the participants of sports and exercise should ensure the conditions, set-up, physical environment, and implementation of the activity are safe in respect to minimizing the risk of cervical spine injury.
- Individuals responsible for coordinating athletic events and the use of facilities for the participants of sports and exercise that carry a risk of cervical spine injury should ensure that such events are covered by physicians, certified athletic trainers, or emergency service personnel.
- Individuals responsible for coordinating and administering organized sports and activities should arrange to have a sports medicine professional, such as an athletic trainer, physician, or other qualified emergency medical personnel, present in order to respond to potential SCIs in a timely manner.
- Individuals responsible for teaching, coaching, or training, as well as those responsible for the emergency care of athletes, should be familiar with safety rules enacted for the prevention of cervical spine injuries and should take actions to ensure that such rules are followed.
- Individuals responsible for teaching, coaching, or training, as well as those responsible for the emergency care of athletes, should be familiar with sport-specific causes of catastrophic cervical spine injury and understand the acute physiologic response of the spinal cord to injury.
- Spotters should be used in activities such as cheerleading and gymnastics.

TABLE 7.2	Examples of Risk Factors for Cervical Spine Injury

Extrinsic Risk Factors	Intrinsic Risk Factors
No emergency plan to identify and treat cervical spine injury	Improper technique, such as leading with the head into contact
Lack of education and awareness of causes of cervical spine injury among coaches when instructing and training athletes	Poor physical conditioning
	Lack of adherence to rules enacted to protect the participant from cervical spine injury
Faulty athletic gear	Performing skills or stunts without receiving proper training, such as in cheerleading or gymnastics
Improperly placed or secured sporting equipment (e.g., goal posts or gymnastics beams) or lack of signs indicating risk (e.g., poolside indications of depth of water)	Lack of awareness of the athletic environment where unsecured equipment such as goal posts pose a threat of spine injury
Failure to restrict exposure to areas that pose danger, such as throwing areas for javelin and discus or athletic fields with equipment, when no supervision is present	Lack of confirmation of the presence or readiness of spotters in gymnastics or cheerleading prior to performing activities that pose a threat of spine injury
Faulty emergency equipment	
Not fitting protective equipment properly, altering protective equipment against recommendations, or neglecting to maintain or recertify equipment	Not wearing protective equipment properly or altering protective equipment against recommendations
Officials not calling penalties for illegal play known to cause cervical spine injury, such as helmet contact or checking from behind in hockey	Predisposing medical conditions, such as cervical stenosis, spina bifida, or Klippel-Feil syndrome

- Individuals responsible for the emergency care of athletes, athletes themselves, coaches, and parents should be familiar with pertinent protective equipment manufacturers' recommendations and specifications relative to fit and maintenance. Maintaining the integrity of protective equipment helps to minimize the risk of injury.
- Individuals responsible for the emergency care of athletes should educate coaches and athletes about the mechanisms of catastrophic spine injuries, the dangers of head-down contact, and pertinent safety rules enacted for the prevention of cervical spine injuries.
  - Planning in advance of events carrying a risk of cervical spine injury should include preparation of a venue-specific emergency action plan. Components of the emergency action plan include appointing a team leader and acquiring appropriate equipment to facilitate stabilization **(Table 7.3)**, **immobilization**, and removal of treatment barriers (i.e., sporting equipment). The emergency action plan should also incorporate communication with local emergency medical services (EMS) and identification of the most appropriate emergency care facility to receive the injured athlete. These groups should be involved in creating the emergency action plan.
  - All individuals responsible for the care of athletes should be involved in regular (at least annual) rehearsals of the emergency action plan, as well as training and practice in the special skills inherent to managing a cervical spine injury. Skills requiring training and regular practice may include manual head and neck stabilization techniques, the multiple methods of transferring injured athletes (e.g., log-rolling, lift-and-slide techniques),

immobilization The use of external stabilization devices such as extrication collars and a spine board with straps to secure an injured patient's body so that it will not move during transport or emergency treatment.

equipment management (e.g., gaining access to the airway or chest), and immobilization methods (e.g., long spine board, cervical collar application).

Athlete Specific

- Participants in sports and exercise should be conditioned and trained to the level necessary to safely participate in the desired sport or activity.
- Participants in sports and exercise should be familiar with sport-specific causes of catastrophic cervical spine injury and avoid behaviors that increase the risk of sustaining acute spinal cord injury.
- Participants in sports or activities known to carry risk for SCI should have complete medical examinations that include identifying factors that increase the risk or severity of an SCI (e.g., cervical stenosis) prior to participating.
- Participants in sports and exercise should be familiar with the specific safety rules enacted for the prevention of cervical spine injuries and should take actions to ensure they follow such rules (e.g., regarding helmet-to-helmet contact or checking from behind) for their own safety and the safety of others.
- Participants in sports and exercise should be familiar with pertinent protective equipment manufacturers' recommendations and specifications relative to fit and maintenance. Maintaining the integrity of protective equipment helps to minimize the risk of injury and enhances treatment by emergency responders in the event of an injury.

TABLE 7.3	Equipment List for Items That May Be Needed in the Emergency Treatment of a Catastrophic Cervical Spinal Cord Injury

Pocket mask

Advanced airway equipment for intubation

Cervical collar

Spine board

Straps to secure the athlete to the spine board

Tape to secure head

Head-immobilization device

Wrist straps or tape to secure the patient's hands together on spine board

Various sizes of padding or toweling to fill gaps during immobilization

EMT shears or scissors to cut jerseys, pads, or straps

Air-pump needle or small-gauge needle to deflate air pads

Reflex hammer with flat handle to detach cheek pads

Cordless, powered screwdriver and face mask removal cutting tools

Automatic external defibrillator

Abbreviation: EMT, emergency medical technician.

Recognition

Recognition of a potential catastrophic cervical spine injury occurs in two phases. An initial recognition, or awareness, phase for a potential acute cervical spine injury occurs when a common injury mechanism is witnessed, such as being checked into the boards in ice hockey from behind or striking a player with the top of the helmet in football. The injury mechanism itself is not always witnessed, so the initial recognition may come about by observing that an athlete has remained down, or inactive, following a play. However it comes about, this initial recognition should heighten the awareness of coaches or emergency responders that the potential for SCI exists.

The assessment phase, discussed in more detail in the next section, involves determining the presence of injury and extent of disability. During the initial assessment of an injured athlete suspected of having a potential catastrophic cervical SCI, the presence of any or all of the following four clinical indicators warrants the activation of the spine injury management protocol: unconsciousness or altered level of consciousness, bilateral neurologic findings or complaints, significant cervical spine pain with or without palpation, and obvious spinal column deformity.[28,30–32] Although unilateral neurologic findings or complaints are more suggestive of spinal nerve root or plexus injury, conservative treatment is recommended in the event that there is an underlying cervical spine or spinal cord injury.

Treatment

Primary Survey

Once emergency responders have become aware of a potential cervical SCI, they should approach the situation as in any emergency and perform a primary survey, because at this time little to nothing is known about the extent of the injury. These steps focus on assessing the ABCDEs of standard trauma management: airway, breathing, circulation, disability, and exposure. However, two important steps must first be taken during the primary survey: surveying the scene and applying manual cervical stabilization.

Survey of the Scene

An abbreviated survey of the scene within the immediate area of the injured athlete must be performed to determine whether the scene is safe for patient management. A survey of the scene in the athletic environment ensures that the athlete(s) involved, and those responsible for their treatment, are under no further threat or danger by remaining at the initial area of the injury. For example, the rescue scene may be at a gymnastics event where a large piece of equipment was not properly secured and now presents a danger in remaining in the immediate area to continue the treatment. This step should be initiated simultaneously while approaching the injured athlete(s) and in most cases can be completed even before arriving at the athlete's side, wasting no time in continuing with the primary survey.

Manual Cervical Spine Stabilization

When a potential spine injury is suspected, rescuers should immediately apply manual cervical spine stabilization.[31,33–38] The rescuer should position his or her hands so the thumbs are pointed toward the face of the injured athlete. This technique ensures that hand placement does not have to be changed with repositioning of the injured person, unless rolling from a prone to a supine position, for which the rescuer's arms should be crossed before rolling. Rescuers should not apply traction to the cervical spine, because this may cause distraction at the site of injury.[31,39] If the rescuer is alone, it may be appropriate to use the knees to maintain spine stabilization, thus freeing the rescuer's hands to assist with ventilation or conduct further tests.

neutral alignment A situation in which the head and neck rest in an aligned position, as in the anatomic position. The cervical spine will present in a slight lordotic curve and the space around the cord will be maximized.

space available for the cord (SAC) The natural space surrounding the spinal cord, where cerebral spinal fluid will freely circulate.

Neutral Alignment

If the spine is not in a neutral position, rescuers should realign the cervical spine back to neutral if possible,[28,31] for this is the optimal position for immobilization of an injured cervical spine.[35,40] **Neutral alignment** of the spine is recommended for airway management procedures and facilitates the application of cervical immobilization devices. More important, the space within the spinal canal, or **space available for the cord (SAC)**, must be maintained for proper functioning of the spinal cord and optimal tissue perfusion, thus reducing spinal cord morbidity.[31,41,42]

However, the presence or development of any of the following, alone or in combination, while moving the head back to neutral represents a contraindication for this action:[34,36] the movement causes increased pain, neurologic symptoms, muscle spasm, or airway compromise; it is physically difficult to reposition the spine; resistance is encountered during the attempt at realignment; or the patient expresses apprehension.[28,31]

Realignment of the head and neck is achieved by moving the head in the appropriate direction such that it returns the spine to a neutral position, as in the anatomic position, and can be performed by the person who is already maintaining manual stabilization of the head. When and how this action is performed is dictated by the individual scenario. If the patient is lying supine, the realignment maneuver can be performed after the assessment is complete and prior to the application of an external cervical immobilization device. The head is carefully laterally flexed and/or rotated back toward the neutral position. Repeatedly ask the patient whether any changes in neurologic symptoms or increases in pain are associated with the movement. During this maneuver, the emergency responder should also feel for any resistance to motion, as could happen with a bony block or dislocated vertebral facet joints. If the athlete complains of worsening symptoms or increased pain, or the motion is resisted, then return slightly to resolve the symptom and stabilize the head in that position and continue with the transfer and full-body immobilization steps.

Keep in mind that if the airway becomes compromised at any time thereafter the head and neck will need to be aligned to facilitate airway support. Anecdotally, a log-roll maneuver may automatically realign a head and neck to neutral, but should any of the contraindications to realignment noted earlier be discovered during the actual execution of a prone log roll, it will be extremely difficult to coordinate all responders performing the log roll to stop in a synchronous fashion. For that reason, if the patient is lying prone, realignment should take place after the individual has been log-rolled onto a full-body immobilization device.

Once the determination has been made that the potential exists for a catastrophic cervical SCI, rescuers should immediately attempt to expose the airway by removing any existing barriers. The airway should be kept open and clear of any obstructions. Potential instability in the cervical spine due to an injury necessitates careful airway management procedures should rescue breathing or introduction of an artificial airway be necessary. If rescue breathing becomes necessary, the individual with the most training and experience should establish an airway and commence rescue breathing using the safest technique.[28,31,43] During airway management, rescuers should cause as little motion as possible.[31] The jaw-thrust maneuver is recommended over the head-tilt technique, which produces unnecessary motion at the head and in the cervical spine. Advanced airway management techniques (e.g., laryngoscope, endotracheal tube) are recommended in the presence of appropriately trained and certified rescuers; these methods have been shown to cause less motion and therefore are less likely to worsen neurologic status.[31,44]

Primary Assessment

The injured patient's ventilatory (breathing) and circulatory status should also be assessed. This is performed through visual observation of the nose, mouth, and chest and listening (through auscultation if possible) and feeling for normal breathing and pulse. Normal breathing is verified by counting the number of breaths per minute (BPM) and should be between 10 and 30 BPM. Recognize that the exercising individual has likely just been participating in a sporting event that may yield breathing rates closer to 30 BPM. The patient's circulation, and an impression of the patient's blood pressure, is determined through assessing the carotid, femoral, and radial pulses. The patient's pulse should be evaluated for its quality (strong, weak), rate (tachycardia, bradycardia), and rhythm (normal, abnormal, or asynchronous). Any signs of airway blockage, absence of or irregular breathing, or absence of or diminished circulation should be addressed before any other action is taken.

If it has been concluded that the injured patient's airway, breathing, and circulation are all viable, then an abbreviated assessment of the patient's neurologic status must be performed to determine the extent of disability. The patient's level of consciousness (LOC) is established by determining his or her ability to respond to verbal or painful stimuli. If there is no response, pinching the skin or firmly rubbing a knuckle into the patient's sternum should elicit a pain response. If the patient is completely unresponsive, even though he or she may be breathing normally, no further evaluation is necessary and the sports medicine team or emergency rescuers should immediately prepare the athlete for immobilization and transport. If the patient is alert and responsive, then a general upper and lower extremity sensory test should be performed. Lightly brush the patient's skin bilaterally on both the upper and lower extremities and ask the patient if the sensation can be felt. It is not necessary at this time to perform a detailed assessment for each dermatome. While still maintaining stabilization of the head and neck, ask the patient to move his or her fingers and toes. Again, a detailed myotome assessment is reserved for a later time. A lack of sensation or inability to move a distal extremity alerts the emergency responder to impending neurologic involvement.

The final step of the primary survey is determining the degree to which one should expose the patient's body for examination. If certain signs (breathing, LOC) indicate a more serious situation, exposure of vital areas for impending treatment should be established. For example, exposure of the chest by removing equipment or jerseys for the application of an automated external defibrillator or removing the face mask to have access to the airway may be necessary. If the rescue occurs outdoors or on a cold surface indoors (e.g., figure skating, ice hockey), rescuers should attempt to limit the amount or time of exposure to protect the athlete from becoming hypothermic.

Transfer and Immobilization

Manual stabilization of the head should be converted to immobilization using a combination of external devices (e.g., cervical collars, foam blocks). The capacity of various collars to restrict range of motion in healthy participants and in cadaver models has been assessed, with no clear superiority of any single device.[45–48] Interestingly, two studies have reported that not only did cervical collars provide no support to the injured cervical spines of cadavers, but also that in some cases they actually increased motion[49] or increased traction[50] at the site of injury. Furthermore, application of a cervical collar in an equipment-intensive sport may be difficult or impossible. Regardless, a combination of padding (e.g., foam blocks, towels), rigid collar application, and taping to a backboard or full-body splint is recommended,[34] as this approach has demonstrated the greatest degree of motion limitation at the head during active range of motion in healthy volunteers.[49,51]

Studies report that manual cervical spine immobilization is superior to the use of external devices in reducing cervical motion during airway intubation,[52,53] which suggests that manual stabilization should be continued whether or not external stabilization devices are applied. Finally, sports medicine professionals must recognize that the application of a cervical collar may interfere with the ability to open the patient's mouth adequately for certain airway management techniques.[54]

After application of an external cervical immobilization device, the injured individual must be transferred to a full-body immobilization device. To achieve full spinal immobilization during on-field management of an injury, patients are typically transferred to and secured on a long spine board. The task of moving a patient to a spine board can prove challenging, as the head and trunk must be moved as a unit. Spine boarding athletes may present additional challenges, such as the size of the patient, the implications of equipment being worn, and sporting venue barriers or obstacles, such as spine boarding a patient from a swimming pool, a pole vault pit, or a gymnastics foam pit. A variety of techniques exist to move and immobilize the injured patient. Rescuers should use the technique that they have rehearsed and are most comfortable with and, most important, that produces the least amount of spinal movement for the given situation.[28]

Currently, certified athletic trainers or emergency personnel typically perform a log roll onto a traditional spine board to stabilize and prepare a patient for transport.[34,55] The log-roll maneuver is versatile in that it can be used for a patient who is in a face-down or face-up position. For the patient lying in a face-down position, a prone log-roll transfer onto a full-body immobilization device may be performed. A standard prone log-roll maneuver has the rescuers positioned on the side toward which the injured patient will be rolled. An alternative prone log-roll technique, referred to as the prone log-roll push, has the rescuers positioned on the side opposite to that of the immobilization device, performing a "push" maneuver to position the patient onto the immobilization device.[28] For patients who are lying face up, a supine log roll can be performed. Typically, log rolls are performed in two steps: the first step rolls the patient onto his or her side, either from prone or supine, at which point the immobilization device is positioned; the next step lowers the patient onto the immobilization device. Careful attention should be focused on the patient's position once lowered onto the board. Often the patient may not be squarely placed onto the board and an adjustment is required. The person at the head remains in charge and should direct the others in their preferred method for realignment. The number of rescuers required to perform a log roll can range between two and seven. Specific protocols for performing log rolls may differ slightly, and step-by-step procedures can be found in many resources.[28]

lift and slide A transfer technique to a spine board for a potential spine-injured victim who is lying supine.

An alternative to the log roll is a lift-and-slide transfer technique, which includes the six-plus-person lift and the straddle **lift and slide**. In contrast to the log roll, in which the patient is rolled to his or her side and the spine board is positioned beneath him or her, with the lift and slide the patient is simply lifted off the ground to allow for the spine board to be slid underneath. The premise behind the lift-and-slide technique is that the patient is lifted by four to eight rescuers in a linear fashion **(Figure 7.2)**, in contrast to a curvilinear path during a log roll; the former has been reported to create less motion in injured cervical spine cadaveric research studies.[56,57] In addition, this technique avoids the difficulty in synchronously rolling the injured patient's head and torso as one unit, as well as rolling the patient over the arm or bulky protective equipment, minimizing lateral malalignment due to proportional differences between the upper torso and lower body **(Figure 7.3)**.[56–58] A limitation is that the lift-and-slide technique may only be used for supine patients, whereas a prone patient must be log-rolled for transfer to a spine board. It has also been proposed that the lift-and-slide technique provides for an advantageous maneuver to remove protective equipment.

Regardless of the transfer technique used, individuals responsible for the emergency care of patients with cervical spine injuries should immobilize these patients with a long spine board or other full-body immobilization device. Although the traditional spine board represents the most common device used for full-body immobilization, devices such as the full-body vacuum splint are more comfortable for patients, reduce superficial irritation and sores over bony prominences, and may be used in appropriate situations.[59]

The Equipment-Intensive Patient

The treatment described in the previous section for the patient with a potential cervical SCI did not address the fact that many exercising individuals wear protective equipment, such as helmets and shoulder

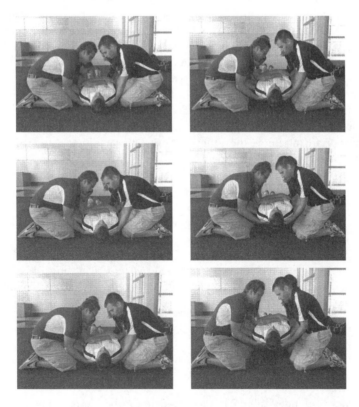

Figure 7.2   A lift-and-slide transfer technique. The rescuers are performing a lift maneuver on a supine athlete. Observe the path the head travels during the execution of the lift, starting from the upper left image and ending at the lower right. The rescuer normally positioned at the head is removed for illustrative purposes. Source: From Swartz EE, Del Rossi G. Cervical spine alignment during on-field management of potential catastrophic cervical spine injuries. *Sports Health*. 2009;1:247–252. Reprinted with permission.

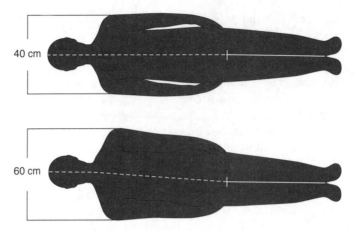

Figure 7.3 Lateral displacement in the log-rolled individual due to proportional differences in the upper torso compared with the lower body. This effect may be exacerbated in an equipment-laden patient. Source: From Swartz EE, Del Rossi G. Cervical spine alignment during on-field management of potential catastrophic cervical spine injuries. *Sports Health*. 2009;1:247–252. Reprinted with permission.

pads, during participation. Exercising individuals wear helmets, face guards, mouth guards, and a variety of padding to shield their head, face, and other body parts from impacts sustained from sporting equipment (i.e., balls, pucks, bats, sticks) and playing surfaces (i.e., court, turf, walls) or from collisions with other participants; this equipment has been used in a variety of sports for decades. Although the benefit of wearing protective equipment in reducing the number and severity of impact injuries is obvious, sometimes the equipment itself can act as a barrier to full access to the head, face, and chest for emergency life support measures, and in other cases the equipment may not allow for neutral alignment of the spine or adequate stabilization of the head when immobilized to a spine board. The challenge rescuers are faced with is making the decision as to whether it is appropriate to remove these pieces of protective equipment to facilitate treatment and immobilization in neutral alignment.

equipment removal Skills executed in an emergency injury situation to remove protective equipment that interferes with the ability to effectively treat or immobilize a victim.

equipment intensive Sports or activities that require the user to wear protective equipment such as helmets and shoulder pads.

In an effort to address the issue of **equipment removal**, a recommendation has been published that proposes an alternative perspective for the sports medicine team responsible for care of a cervical spine–injured patient in an **equipment-intensive** activity.[28] The National Athletic Trainers' Association (NATA) position statement on the acute care of the cervical spine injured athlete states that

regardless of the sport or the equipment being used, two underlying principles should guide management of the equipment laden athlete with a potential cervical spine injury:

1) Exposure and access to vital life functions (airway, chest for cardiopulmonary resuscitation or use of an automated external defibrillator) must be established or easily achieved in a reasonable and acceptable manner.
2) Neutral alignment of the cervical spine should be maintained while allowing as little motion at the head and neck as possible.[28]

When emergency responders adhere to these guidelines when responding to a cervical SCI in an equipment-intensive activity, their actions regarding what to do with any type of protective equipment will be dictated accordingly. It must be stressed that staying up to date on current evidence-based management recommendations and changes in equipment use or design should remain a priority so that the treatment applied in any given situation can be as effective as possible.

Keeping in mind the two underlying principles, the following sections review the evidence from current research pertaining to recommendations that can be made for specific sports or types of equipment. It should be emphasized that equipment-specific and sport-specific recommendations can quickly become outdated as changes in design and technology continue to occur.

Football

In the sport of American football, the protective face mask of the football helmet impedes **airway access** during management of a potentially catastrophic head or neck injury and must be removed should the injured patient need airway support. However, removal of a football helmet creates alterations in the position of adjacent cervical vertebrae,[60,61] and removal of a football helmet without simultaneous removal of the shoulder pads places the cervical spine in a malaligned, hyperextended position.[62,63] At least one study has reported no change in disc height, cervical vertebrae translation, or SAC when removing the helmet in healthy subjects.[64] However, because of the concerns that exist relative to the motion created when removing a football helmet and because the helmet and shoulder pads in football players maintain neutral alignment of the cervical spine, current recommendations state that the helmet and shoulder pads should remain in place and that the face mask be removed in order to access the airway.[28]

There has been some research devoted to investigating the best method of face mask removal.[65–67] A cordless screwdriver has been reported to be faster[66,68,69] and easier to use[66] and to create less motion[66] at the head than many cutting tools used to remove the face mask. **Table 7.4** shows the results for time, motion, and difficulty for the cordless screwdriver compared with other cutting tools on one style of a football helmet face mask and loop strap.[66] Because of this research, the cordless screwdriver has been recommended for removal of the face mask.[66,70] However, relying solely on a screwdriver carries risk because screws can fail

> airway access Ability to expose and maintain breathing through an injured patient's airway.

| TABLE 7.4 | Means, Standard Deviations (SD), and Effect Sizes for Time to Complete Task, Rate of Perceived Exertion, and Movement Variables for Tools with the Schutt Helmet and ArmourGuard Loop Strap Configuration |

Dependent Variables	Screwdriver Mean ± SD ($N = 15$)	FM Extractor Mean ± SD ($N = 7$)	Trainer's Angel Mean ± SD ($N = 9$)	Effect Size
Time (s)	47 ± 7.8[a, b]	160.6 ± 62.6	131 ± 28.9	0.71
RPE	2.1 ± 2.1[a]	5.9 ± 2.9	3.9 ± 1.1	0.362
Lateral flexion movement (°)	3.4 ± 1.4[a, b]	9.9 ± 4.5	7.8 ± 2.7	0.542
Flexion/extension movement (°)	7.6 ± 2[a, b]	14.6 ± 4.7	13.6 ± 6.1	0.398
Rotation movement (°)	3.2 ± .8[a, c]	7.7 ± 2.1[b]	4.7 ± .089	0.688

Abbreviation: RPE, rate of perceived exertion.
[a] Significantly different from FM Extractor ($P < 0.01$)
[b] Significantly different from Trainer's Angel ($P < 0.01$)
[c] Significantly different from Trainer's Angel ($P < 0.05$)
Source: Data are from Swartz EE, Norkus S, Cappaert T, Decoster LC. Football equipment design affects face mask removal efficiency. *Am J Sports Med.* 2005;33(8):1210–1219.

to be removed due to problems with the helmet hardware (e.g., screws, T-nuts) such as corrosion and rust, which can cause the screw face to shred or the T-nut to spin with the screw while turning.[71] Studies have reported a failure rate of up to 16% in removing face mask screws with a cordless screwdriver.[71,72]

Because screw failure is a possibility, a combined-tool technique has been recommended.[71] This technique takes advantage of the efficiency found in using a cordless screwdriver, but in the event a screw fails to be removed, provides the rescuer the added security of a backup cutting tool. This backup cutting tool must be appropriately matched to the helmet and loop strap type being used. Research investigating the success rates of this combined-tool technique found it to be an extremely reliable approach with a high rate of success (97–100%).[70,73]

Helmet, face mask, loop strap fasteners, and tool designs continually evolve. For example, recent changes in the design of some manufacturers' football helmets include a quick-release attachment system for the face mask. Researchers have reported that such a device allows for quick and easy face mask removal that minimizes head motion when compared with traditional screw and T-nut–secured loop strap removal with a cordless screwdriver.[74]

There may be cases in which the face mask does not come off or times when immediate rescue breathing is necessary and time does not allow for removal of the face mask. In this situation, it has been suggested that a pocket mask could be inserted through or under the face mask and attached to a bag-valve mask, allowing rescuers to ventilate the patient while others continue with attempting to remove the face mask or prepare for full equipment removal.[74] Although placement of the pocket mask over the airway may be established, it has yet to be determined whether the technique creates a definitive airway that can be supported or can protect the airway from aspiration, as endotracheal intubation could. Therefore, in a breathing emergency, rescuers may appropriately elect to remove the face mask or remove the helmet entirely until pocket mask insertion has been demonstrated to effectively support an airway.

This brings us to the reality that there may be situations in which exposure of the head, chest, or body is necessary, and removal of the football helmet and shoulder pads may be required. As stated earlier, any time either the helmet or shoulder pads must be removed, rescuers should remove both the helmet and shoulder pads, because removal of both the helmet and shoulder pads leaves the cervical spine in neutral alignment.[63,75] It is also much easier to remove the shoulder pads if the helmet has already been removed. Removal of the helmet and shoulder pads using four health care providers has been shown to be effective in limiting motion in the cervical spine of a healthy volunteer,[64] although other reports have provided conflicting results.[60,61] Different helmets may require different steps to prepare them for removal, such as deflating air cells within the helmet or removing cheek pads or the chin strap. Familiarity with current available equipment used in football, and in any activity for that matter, is extremely important.

Ice Hockey

In ice hockey, players lying supine with the helmet and shoulder pads left in place have neutral cervical spine alignment, and removing the helmet may alter that alignment.[76,77] Ice hockey helmets were reported to adequately immobilize the head of an athlete when secured on a spine board, provided the helmets were fitted correctly and securely.[78] These findings suggest that when an ice hockey player may have a cervical spine injury, the helmet should be left in place. However, Mihalik et al.[79] investigated head motion created during a prone log roll in hockey players wearing properly fitted helmets, improperly fitted helmets, and no helmets. The smallest amount of head motion occurred when the volunteers wore no helmet at all. With the improperly fitted helmets, the volunteers' heads moved independently within the helmet, suggesting that the rescuers would be unable to obtain appropriate head immobilization during transfer or transport if the helmet were left on. It is also important to note that the face guards used in ice hockey may vary depending on level of play (e.g., full cage, plastic visor).

Lacrosse

For supine lacrosse players, equipment may not create the same neutral positioning of the cervical spine as that created for football and ice hockey players.[80,81] Whether this malalignment actually affects the critical SAC has been questioned.[80] Lacrosse helmets were previously reported to provide head immobilization when an athlete was immobilized on a spine board, provided the helmet was applied correctly and fitted securely.[78] However, more recent research found that the best immobilization of healthy collegiate lacrosse athletes was in a no-equipment condition compared with conditions in which helmets were both improperly and properly fit.[82] These findings suggest that leaving the equipment in place precludes neutral alignment of the cervical spine and may not provide adequate stabilization of the head. Anecdotally, in many lacrosse helmets the face masks are not easily removed. Based on these factors, and even though no research has reported on motion created in the cervical spine during lacrosse helmet removal, the lacrosse helmet may need to be removed on the field in an athlete with a suspected SCI.[28]

Other Equipment-Intensive Activities

Additional data for the many other equipment-laden sports and recreational activities, such as horseback riding, downhill skiing, baseball, softball, field hockey (goalies), and mountain biking, are not available. When dealing with a suspected catastrophic cervical SCI in patients in these sports, adhering to the two underlying principles of managing the equipment-laden athlete dictates the necessary steps in making decisions about equipment removal during the management process.[28] For example, participants in several of the sports just listed wear only a helmet. This would likely take the spine out of neutral alignment, therefore requiring the rescuer to remove the helmet to establish neutral alignment.

In summary, for the equipment-intensive athlete, the rescuer should perform whatever tasks are necessary to comply with the underlying principles for the acute management of the equipment-intensive SCI athlete. If an athlete who is wearing a helmet and shoulder pads has a potential cervical spine injury and the helmet does not provide adequate immobilization or cervical spine alignment, or if face mask removal is not possible, the rescuer may need to remove the helmet. If time and personnel allow, the shoulder pads should also be removed. If time or resources do not allow simultaneous removal of the helmet and shoulder pads, then foam padding or a similar article (e.g., folded towel) should be placed under the head of the patient to maintain neutral alignment in the cervical spine.[28]

Other Treatment Considerations

In the early 1990s, the use of high-dose methylprednisolone for the treatment of acute spinal cord injury became the standard of care. Bracken et al.[83] found that patients with acute SCI who were treated with high-dose methylprednisolone within the first 8 hours of injury had significant neurologic improvement at the 6-month follow-up compared with a placebo group. The recommended dose of methylprednisolone is an intravenous bolus of 30 mg/kg body weight over 1 hour, followed by infusion at 5.4 mg/kg per hour for 23 hours. One evidence-based review of the published literature on methylprednisolone revealed serious flaws in data analysis and conclusions, with no clear support for the use of methylprednisolone in patients with acute SCI.[84] In fact, several studies showed a higher incidence of respiratory and infectious complications with methylprednisolone.[84] Until further reliable data are available, the use of high-dose methylprednisolone for acute spinal cord injury remains controversial. When possible, the patient or family should be consulted on the risks and benefits of the medication prior to use.[28]

Clinical data on the practice of inducing hypothermia as treatment for brain injury and myocardial infarction are abundant, but few clinical reports have addressed hypothermia for SCI.[85] Laboratory experiments have shown inconsistent effects, and clinical studies have been limited by small sample sizes and a lack of controls.[86–92] The exact mechanism of action is unclear, but hypothermia may slow metabolism, decrease the demand for oxygen, and inhibit a cascade of deleterious chemicals, such as inflammatory agents and excitatory amino acids.[93,94] Clinical hypothermia has shown promise as a treatment for patients with myocardial infarction, yet potentially deleterious effects (such as sepsis, bleeding, and cardiac arrhythmias) have been demonstrated in patients with brain injury.[93,94] In addition, rewarming may lead to dangerous drops in blood pressure.[93] At this time, hypothermia should be considered an experimental treatment that requires further research before being recommended as a standard component of the on-field spinal cord injury management protocol.[28]

Transportation and the Emergency Department

The athletic trainer or team physician should accompany the injured patient to the hospital. This practice provides continuity of care, allows for accurate delivery of clinical information to the emergency department staff, and allows the sports medicine professionals to assist emergency department personnel during equipment removal. Unfortunately, this may be difficult or impossible in some settings.[28] Communication between sports medicine and emergency department staffs during the emergency planning phase is important. Hospital personnel may be unfamiliar with athletic equipment, including helmets, face masks, visors, shoulder pads, and chest protectors. At a minimum, hospital personnel should understand standards of on-field care for the athlete with a potential SCI and should receive training regarding the proper approach to equipment removal. Sports medicine professionals can be a resource for such information, simultaneously increasing communication and improving collegiality. Improved communication between the sports medicine team and hospital personnel can only enhance the care delivered.[28]

Equipment Removal and Imaging

Protective equipment should be removed by appropriately trained professionals in a controlled environment. Previous recommendations call for clearance plain radiographs to be taken before equipment removal.[95] Although removal of athletic equipment can cause motion in the cervical spine during the process,[61,96] one group concluded that it was possible to remove a football helmet and shoulder pads from healthy volunteers without creating significant motion.[64] Two reports documented that obtaining adequate radiographs in healthy, helmeted football players was difficult.[97,98] In fact, it is difficult to attain adequate radiographs of the full cervical spine even in patients without equipment.[99–102] Missed diagnoses with negative consequences in nonhelmeted cervical spine–injured patients have been reported, often due to delayed diagnoses related to improper radiographic choices or interpretations.[102,103] Based on this evidence, the timing of equipment removal in the evaluation of the helmeted athlete remains at the discretion of the practitioner caring for the athlete.[28]

The advent of readily available multidetector computed tomography (CT) has replaced the use of plain radiography at many trauma centers, and initial CT evaluation has been recommended in acute cervical spine trauma.[104–107] Not only is CT more sensitive than radiography, but it also carries lower rates of missed primary and secondary injuries.[108] The use of CT in the initial evaluation of the helmeted athlete has been well established.[28]

Management protocols in the emergency room for the athlete with a potential cervical spine injury should not deviate from other trauma protocols, with the exception of dealing with the additional issues of equipment management and removal. Three main issues complicate management of the trauma patient with suspected cervical spine injury: inability to give an adequate history (e.g., other injuries); inability to complete a comprehensive examination (e.g., intoxication); and poor bone health (e.g., osteoporosis). Although these issues may complicate the initial evaluation of cervical spine–injured trauma patients, most athletic injuries do not fall into these categories. Most injured athletes can give an adequate history, can undergo a comprehensive physical and neurologic examination, and are usually young, with adequate bone health. Most injuries in athletes are low-velocity injuries with an axial loading mechanism that may put these athletes at risk. If the patient has a concomitant head injury, that may complicate management, but most cervical spine injuries in athletes are not associated with a concomitant head injury or concussion.

After initial evaluation, the treating physician may attempt to risk-stratify the patient according to the history and clinical findings (Table 7.5). Those athletes who present with neurologic findings on examination (paralysis, motor weakness) may improve with aggressive management, but prognosis for complete recovery is low. Despite aggressive surgical and pharmacologic management, most of these patients may have some permanent neurologic functional disability. Likewise, many athletes will arrive at the hospital with or without neck pain but no neurologic findings or symptoms on examination. These athletes will have their cervical spine cleared by examination or radiographic testing or both, but most will have no underlying disease.

TABLE 7.5	Risk Stratification for a Patient with Cervical Spinal Cord Injury
1	++ Neurologic finding on examination
2	Neck pain, neurologic symptoms, no clinical deficits on examination
3	Neck pain, no neurologic symptoms or clinical deficits on examination
4	No neck pain, no symptoms, no clinical findings on examination

The one group for whom prudent on-field and prehospital management may make a difference is athletes with neck pain and neurologic symptoms on arrival, but no neurologic deficit on physical examination. This is a high-risk group for having underlying pathology due to mechanism and symptoms, and these patients will require a full radiographic evaluation and physical examination to clear their cervical spine. Theoretically, improper management of this group of athletes may lead to iatrogenic neurologic injury, but to date there are no reported cases of helmeted athletes with suspected cervical spine injury and clinical neurologic symptoms with a normal examination who experienced iatrogenic clinical worsening after adequate on-field and prehospital evaluation and management.

Treatment Summary

As can likely be appreciated from this section on treatment, the acute care of a potentially catastrophic cervical spine–injured athlete can be complicated. It is important to remember that each situation will be unique and that blanket recommendations to follow for all spine-injured patients may not be appropriate. Given that caveat, **Figure 7.4** represents a flow chart that illustrates the process of the acute treatment of a cervical SCI from emergency planning through transport to serve merely as a guide for approaching these injuries.

Recovery

Animal model research has suggested that recovery from and long-term prognosis after catastrophic cervical spine injury are directly related to the severity, or magnitude, of the initial tissue trauma and the duration of compression to the spinal cord.[42] The less tissue involved and the shorter the duration of compression to the cord, the more favorable the outcome. In addition, retrospective studies have reported that outcomes for spinal cord injury become more favorable as the SAC surrounding the level of injury in the spinal canal increases.[109] A systematic review that examined the outcomes of actual SCI patients based on the time of decompression surgery indicates that more favorable outcomes will come with urgent decompression surgery performed in under 72 or even 24 hours.[110]

An individual's recovery from SCI is difficult to predict, considering that the extent of his or her permanent disability, or final degree of injury, may not be determined for up to 72 hours or more following the injury itself. Whenever the extent of injury is determined, the factors that then determine the SCI individual's recovery will include the extent of the primary and secondary injury response, surgical invasiveness and extent of repair, age, previous level of conditioning, current health, and quality of continuing care and rehabilitation support.

Recovery from cervical SCI may be complete, that is, no permanent neurologic impairment within 1 year following the injury. The level of recovery for an SCI individual may also be incomplete, that is, there is an absence of complete resolution of the neurologic sequelae beyond 1 year following the injury. Incomplete recovery may mean that there is either partial neurologic recovery that has resulted

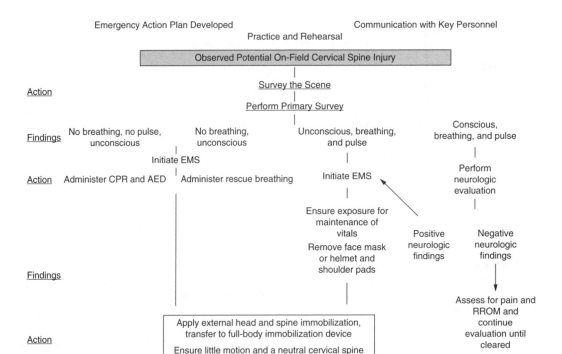

Figure 7.4 Flow chart for the acute treatment of an athlete who has a potential cervical spine injury. AED, automated external defibrillator; CPR, cardiopulmonary resuscitation; EMS, emergency medical services; RROM, resistive range of motion.

in a paraplegic, or tetraplegic, state or that the injury has had no neurologic recovery and has left the individual quadriplegic.[2]

Return-to-Play Issues

Athletes should be returned to play only when they are asymptomatic, with full, pain-free range of motion of the cervical spine and a normal neurologic examination, and the athlete does not have a congenital or developmental contraindication to a return to contact or collision sports.[111] The decision to return an athlete to play after a cervical spine injury should be individualized based on the type of injury, persistence of symptoms, recurrence of injury, sports played, and the amount of risk of future injuries with each sport played. Rule changes in sport and emphasis on proper technique should be addressed when appropriate.

Summary

Although sudden deaths due to catastrophic cervical spine injuries are relatively rare, the nature of collision sports and the unpredictability of accidental injury in any sport demand that steps be taken to prevent and prepare for them. Time is critical, and the effective execution of the skills necessary to manage a suspected catastrophic cervical spine injury could mean the difference between saving a life or preventing permanent neurologic outcome and death or permanent neurologic damage for the athlete.

Clinical Case Scenario

1. Jay is a 6-foot, 220-pound defenseman for the local semiprofessional ice hockey team. During the second period an opposing player checks Jay from behind as he approaches his own defensive corner of the ice in pursuit of a loose puck. Jay falls forward and collides into the boards head first. The officials immediately call the penalty, and play is stopped. It is apparent that Jay is lying face down in the corner of the ice against the boards and is not moving. The athletic trainer has seen the entire play and immediately suspects that Jay may have suffered a serious head or neck injury.

1. What are the initial steps that should be taken during the assessment phase?
2. What challenges is the athletic trainer faced with?
3. What steps must be taken if the assessment reveals that the athlete is not breathing?

Key Terms

airway access

apoptosis

axial load

catastrophic cervical spinal cord injury

direct injury

emergency management

equipment intensive

equipment removal

immobilization

lift and slide

neutral alignment

space available for the cord (SAC)

tetraplegic

References

1. Mueller FO, Cantu RC. *Annual Survey of Catastrophic Football Injuries 1977–2009*. Chapel Hill, NC: University of North Carolina; 2010.
2. Mueller FO, Cantu RC. *Twenty-Seventh Annual Report, Fall 1982–Spring 2009*. Chapel Hill, NC: National Center for Catastrophic Sport Injury Research, University of North Carolina; 2010.
3. Masini M, Alencar MR, Neves EG, Alves CF. Spinal cord injury: patients who had an accident, walked but became spinal paralysed. *Paraplegia*. 1994;32:93–97.
4. Toscano J. Prevention of neurological deterioration before admission to a spinal cord injury unit. *Paraplegia*. 1988;26:143–150.
5. Banerjee R, Palumbo MA, Fadale PD. Catastrophic cervical spine injuries in the collision sport athlete, part 1: epidemiology, functional anatomy, and diagnosis. *Am J Sports Med*. 2004;32:1077–1087.
6. Hulsebosch CE. Recent advances in pathophysiology and treatment of spinal cord injury. *Adv Physiol Educ*. 2002;26:238–255.
7. Tator CH. Experimental and clinical studies of the pathophysiology and management of acute spinal cord injury. *J Spinal Cord Med*. 1996;19:206–214.
8. National Spinal Cord Injury Statistical Center. *The 2007 Annual Statistical Report for the Spinal Cord Injury Model Systems*. Birmingham, AL: National Spinal Cord Injury Statistical Center, University of Alabama–Birmingham; 2008.
9. National Spinal Cord Injury Statistical Center. *Spinal Cord Injury: Facts and Figures at a Glance*. Birmingham, AL: National Spinal Cord Injury Statistical Center, University of Alabama–Birmingham; 2008:2.
10. Nobunaga A, Go B, Karunas R. Recent demographic and injury trends in people served by the model spine cord injury case systems. *Arch Phys Med Rehabil*. 1999;80:1372–1382.
11. Torg JS. Epidemiology, pathomechanics, and prevention of athletic injuries to the cervical spine. *Med Sci Sports Exerc*. 1985;17:295–303.

12. Mueller F, Cantu R. *Twenty-Fourth Annual Report, Fall 1982–Spring 2006.* Chapel Hill, NC: National Center for Catastrophic Sport Injury Research, University of North Carolina; 2008.

13. Tator CH, Carson JD, Edmonds VE. Spinal injuries in ice hockey. *Clin Sports Med.* 1998;17:183–194.

14. Hagel BE, Pless B, Platt RW. Trends in emergency department reported head and neck injuries among skiers and snowboarders. *Can J Public Health.* 2003;94:458–462.

15. Scher AT. Rugby injuries to the cervical spine and spinal cord: a 10-year review. *Clin Sports Med.* 1998;17:195–206.

16. Boden BP, Pasquina P, Johnson J, Mueller FO. Catastrophic injuries in pole-vaulters. *Am J Sports Med.* 2001;29:50–54.

17. Boden BP, Tacchetti R, Mueller FO. Catastrophic cheerleading injuries. *Am J Sports Med.* 2003;31:881–888.

18. Boden BP, Tacchetti R, Mueller FO. Catastrophic injuries in high school and college baseball players. *Am J Sports Med.* 2004;32:1189–1196.

19. Boden BP. Direct catastrophic injury in sports. *J Am Acad Orthop Surg.* 2005;13:445–454.

20. Cantu RC. Cervical spine injuries in the athlete. *Semin Neurol.* 2000;20:173–178.

21. Cantu RC, Mueller FO. Catastrophic football injuries: 1977–1998. *Neurosurgery.* 2000;47:673–675; discussion 675–677.

22. Torg JS. Epidemiology, pathomechanics, and prevention of football-induced cervical spinal cord trauma. *Exerc Sport Sci Rev.* 1992;20:321–338.

23. Nightingale RW, McElhaney JH, Richardson WJ, Best TM, Myers BS. Experimental impact injury to the cervical spine: relating motion of the head and the mechanism of injury. *J Bone Joint Surg Am.* 1996;78:412–421.

24. Nightingale RW, McElhaney JH, Richardson WJ, Myers BS. Dynamic responses of the head and cervical spine to axial impact loading. *J Biomech.* 1996;29:307–318.

25. Torg JS. Epidemiology, biomechanics, and prevention of cervical spine trauma resulting from athletics and recreational activities. *Operative Tech Sports Med.* 1993;1(3):159–168.

26. Tator CH, Fehlings MG. Review of the secondary injury theory of acute spinal cord trauma with emphasis on vascular mechanisms. *J Neurosurg.* 1991;75:15–26.

27. Sekhon LH, Fehlings MG. Epidemiology, demographics, and pathophysiology of acute spinal cord injury. *Spine (Philadelphia PA).* 2001;26:S2–S12.

28. Swartz EE, Boden BP, Courson RW, et al. National Athletic Trainers' Association position statement: acute management of the cervical spine-injured athlete. *J Athl Train.* 2009;44:306–331.

29. Andersen J, Courson RW, Kleiner DM, McLoda TA. National Athletic Trainers' Association position statement: emergency planning in athletics. *J Athl Train.* 2002;37:99–104.

30. Banerjee R, Palumbo MA, Fadale PD. Catastrophic cervical spine injuries in the collision sport athlete, part 2: principles of emergency care. *Am J Sports Med.* 2004;32:1760–1764.

31. Crosby ET. Airway management in adults after cervical spine trauma. *Anesthesiology.* 2006;104:1293–1318.

32. Sanchez AR 2nd, Sugalski MT, LaPrade RF. Field-side and prehospital management of the spine-injured athlete. *Curr Sports Med Rep.* 2005;4:50–55.

33. Cantu RC. The cervical spinal stenosis controversy. *Clin Sports Med.* 1998;17:121–126.

34. De Lorenzo RA. A review of spinal immobilization techniques. *J Emerg Med.* 1996;14:603–613.

35. De Lorenzo RA, Olson JE, Boska M, et al. Optimal positioning for cervical immobilization. *Ann Emerg Med.* 1996;28:301–308.

36. Gabbott DA, Baskett PJ. Management of the airway and ventilation during resuscitation. *Br J Anaesth.* 1997;79:159–171.

37. Lennarson PJ, Smith D, Todd MM, et al. Segmental cervical spine motion during orotracheal intubation of the intact and injured spine with and without external stabilization. *J Neurosurg.* 2000;92:201–206.

38. Lennarson PJ, Smith DW, Sawin PD, et al. Cervical spinal motion during intubation: efficacy of stabilization maneuvers in the setting of complete segmental instability. *J Neurosurg.* 2001;94:265–270.

39. Kaufman HH, Harris JH Jr, Spencer JA, Kopanisky DR. Danger of traction during radiography for cervical trauma. *JAMA.* 1982;247:2369.

40. Tierney RT, Maldjian C, Mattacola CG, Straub SJ, Sitler MR. Cervical spine stenosis measures in normal subjects. *J Athl Train.* 2002;37:190–193.

41. Delamarter RB, Sherman J, Carr JB. Pathophysiology of spinal cord injury. Recovery after immediate and delayed decompression. *J Bone Joint Surg Am.* 1995;77:1042–1049.

42. Carlson GD, Gorden CD, Oliff HS, Pillai JJ, LaManna JC. Sustained spinal cord compression, part I: time-dependent effect on long-term pathophysiology. *J Bone Joint Surg Am.* 2003;85A:86–94.

43. Aprahamian C, Thompson BM, Finger WA, Darin JC. Experimental cervical spine injury model: evaluation of airway management and splinting techniques. *Ann Emerg Med.* 1984;13:584–587.

44. Burkey SM, Jeanmonod R, Fedor P, Stromski C, Waninger K. Evaluation of standard endotracheal intubation, assisted laryngoscopy (AirTraq), and laryngeal mask airway in the airway management of the helmeted football player. *Clin J Sport Med.* 2010;20(2):136–137.

45. Askins V, Eismont FJ. Efficacy of five cervical orthoses in restricting cervical motion. A comparison study. *Spine.* 1997;22:1193–1198.

46. James CY, Riemann BL, Munkasy BA, Joyner AB. Comparison of cervical spine motion during application among 4 rigid immobilization collars. *J Athl Train.* 2004;39:138–145.

47. McCabe JB, Nolan DJ. Comparison of the effectiveness of different cervical immobilization collars. *Ann Emerg Med.* 1986;15:50–53.

48. Podolsky S, Baraff LJ, Simon RR, et al. Efficacy of cervical spine immobilization methods. *J Trauma*. 1983;23:461–465.
49. Bednar DA. Efficacy of orthotic immobilization of the unstable subaxial cervical spine of the elderly patient: investigation in a cadaver model. *Can J Surg*. 2004;47:251–256.
50. Ben-Galim P, Dreiangel N, Mattox KL, et al. Extrication collars can result in abnormal separation between vertebrae in the presence of a dissociative injury. *J Trauma*. 2010;69:447–450.
51. Hamilton RS, Pons PT. The efficacy and comfort of full-body vacuum splints for cervical-spine immobilization. *J Emerg Med*. 1996;14:553–559.
52. Gerling MC, Davis DP, Hamilton RS, et al. Effects of cervical spine immobilization technique and laryngoscope blade selection on an unstable cervical spine in a cadaver model of intubation. *Ann Emerg Med*. 2000;36:293–300.
53. Majernick TG, Bieniek R, Houston JB, Hughes HG. Cervical spine movement during orotracheal intubation. *Ann Emerg Med*. 1986;15:417–420.
54. Goutcher CM, Lochhead V. Reduction in mouth opening with semi-rigid cervical collars. *Br J Anaesth*. 2005;95:344–348.
55. Dasen KR. On-field management for the injured football player. *Clin J Sport Med*. 2000;10:82–83.
56. Del Rossi G, Horodyski M, Heffernan TP, et al. Spine-board transfer techniques and the unstable cervical spine. *Spine*. 2004;29:E134–E138.
57. Del Rossi G, Horodyski MH, Conrad BP, et al. The 6-plus-person lift transfer technique compared with other methods of spine boarding. *J Athl Train*. 2008;43:6–13.
58. Swartz EE, Del Rossi G. Cervical spine alignment during the acute management of potential catastrophic cervical spine injuries in sport. *Health*. 2009;1:242–257.
59. Luscombe MD, Williams JL. Comparison of a long spinal board and vacuum mattress for spinal immobilisation. *Emerg Med J*. 2003;20:476–478.
60. Aprahamian C, Thompson BM, Darin JC. Recommended helmet removal techniques in a cervical spine injured patient. *J Trauma*. 1984;24:841–842.
61. Prinsen RK, Syrotuik DG, Reid DC. Position of the cervical vertebrae during helmet removal and cervical collar application in football and hockey. *Clin J Sport Med*. 1995;5:155–161.
62. Gastel JA, Palumbo MA, Hulstyn MJ, Fadale PD, Lucas P. Emergency removal of football equipment: a cadaveric cervical spine injury model. *Ann Emerg Med*. 1998;32:411–417.
63. Swenson TM, Lauerman WC, Blanc RO, Donaldson WF 3rd, Fu FH. Cervical spine alignment in the immobilized football player. Radiographic analysis before and after helmet removal. *Am J Sports Med*. 1997;25:226–230.
64. Peris MD, Donaldson WW 3rd, Towers J, Blanc R, Muzzonigro TS. Helmet and shoulder pad removal in suspected cervical spine injury: human control model. *Spine*. 2002;27:995–998; discussion 998–999.
65. Swartz EE, Norkus SA, Armstrong CW, Kleiner DM. Face-mask removal: movement and time associated with cutting of the loop straps. *J Athl Train*. 2003;38:120–125.
66. Swartz EE, Norkus SA, Cappaert T, Decoster L. Football equipment design affects face mask removal efficiency. *Am J Sports Med*. 2005;33:1210–1219.
67. Waninger KN. On-field management of potential cervical spine injury in helmeted football players: leave the helmet on! *Clin J Sport Med*. 1998;8:124–129.
68. Jenkins HL, Valovich TC, Arnold BL, Gansneder BM. Removal tools are faster and produce less force and torque on the helmet than cutting tools during face-mask retraction. *J Athl Train*. 2002;37:246–251.
69. Ray R, Luchies C, Bazuin D, Farrell RN. Airway preparation techniques for the cervical spine-injured football player. *J Athl Train*. 1995;30:217–221.
70. Copeland AJ, Decoster LC, Swartz EE, Gattie ER, Gale SD. Combined tool approach is 100% successful for emergency football face mask removal. *Clin J Sport Med*. 2007;17:452–457.
71. Swartz EE, Decoster LC, Norkus SA, Cappaert TA. The influence of various factors on high school football helmet face mask removal: a retrospective, cross-sectional analysis. *J Athl Train*. 2007;42:11–19; discussion 20.
72. Decoster LC, Shirley CP, Swartz EE. Football face-mask removal with a cordless screwdriver on helmets used for at least one season of play. *J Athl Train*. 2005;40:169–173.
73. Gale SD, Decoster LC, Swartz EE. The combined tool approach for face mask removal during on-field conditions. *J Athl Train*. 2008;43:14–20.
74. Toler JD, Petschauer MA, Mihalik JP, et al. Comparison of 3 airway access techniques during suspected spine injury management in American football. *Clin J Sport Med*. 2010;20:92–97.
75. Palumbo MA, Hulstyn MJ, Fadale PD, O'Brien T, Shall L. The effect of protective football equipment on alignment of the injured cervical spine. Radiographic analysis in a cadaveric model. *Am J Sports Med*. 1996;24:446–453.
76. Laprade RF, Schnetzler KA, Broxterman RJ, Wentorf F, Gilbert TJ. Cervical spine alignment in the immobilized ice hockey player. A computed tomographic analysis of the effects of helmet removal. *Am J Sports Med*. 2000;28:800–803.
77. Metz CM, Kuhn JE, Greenfield ML. Cervical spine alignment in immobilized hockey players: radiographic analysis with and without helmets and shoulder pads. *Clin J Sport Med*. 1998;8:92–95.
78. Waninger KN, Richards JG, Pan WT, Shay AR, Shindle MK. An evaluation of head movement in backboard-immobilized helmeted football, lacrosse, and ice hockey players. *Clin J Sport Med*. 2001;11:82–86.
79. Mihalik JP, Beard JR, Petschauer MA, Prentice WE, Guskiewicz KM. Effect of ice hockey helmet fit on cervical spine motion during an emergency log roll procedure. *Clin J Sport Med*. 2008;18:394–398.

80. Higgins M, Tierney RT, Driban JB, Edell S, Watkins R. Lacrosse equipment and cervical spinal cord space during immobilization: preliminary analysis. *J Athl Train*. 2010;45:39–43.

81. Sherbondy PS, Hertel JN, Sebastianelli WJ. The effect of protective equipment on cervical spine alignment in collegiate lacrosse players. *Am J Sports Med*. 2006:1675–1679.

82. Petschauer MA, Schmitz R, Gill DL. Helmet fit and cervical spine motion in collegiate men's lacrosse athletes secured to a spine board. *J Athl Train*. 2010;45:215–221.

83. Bracken MB, Shepard MJ, Collins WF, et al. A randomized, controlled trial of methylprednisolone or naloxone in the treatment of acute spinal-cord injury. Results of the Second National Acute Spinal Cord Injury Study. *N Engl J Med*. 1990;322:1405–1411.

84. Hurlbert RJ. The role of steroids in acute spinal cord injury: an evidence-based analysis. *Spine*. 2001;26:S39–46.

85. Cappuccino A, Bisson LJ, Carpenter B, et al. The use of systemic hypothermia for the treatment of an acute cervical spinal cord injury in a professional football player. *Spine (Philadelphia PA)*. 2010;35:E57–E62.

86. Guest JD, Vanni S, Silbert L. Mild hypothermia, blood loss and complications in elective spinal surgery. *Spine J*. 2004;4:130–137.

87. Martinez-Arizala A, Green BA. Hypothermia in spinal cord injury. *J Neurotrauma*. 1992;9(suppl 2):S497–S505.

88. Yu CG, Jimenez O, Marcillo AE, et al. Beneficial effects of modest systemic hypothermia on locomotor function and histopathological damage following contusion-induced spinal cord injury in rats. *J Neurosurg*. 2000;93:85–93.

89. Chatzipanteli K, Yanagawa Y, Marcillo AE, et al. Posttraumatic hypothermia reduces polymorphonuclear leukocyte accumulation following spinal cord injury in rats. *J Neurotrauma*. 2000;17:321–332.

90. Green BA, Khan T, Raimondi AJ. Local hypothermia as treatment of experimentally induced spinal cord contusion: quantitative analysis of beneficent effect. *Surg Forum*. 1973;24:436–438.

91. Busto R, Dietrich WD, Globus MY, Ginsberg MD. Postischemic moderate hypothermia inhibits CA1 hippocampal ischemic neuronal injury. *Neurosci Lett*. 1989;101:299–304.

92. Green EJ, Pazos AJ, Dietrich WD, et al. Combined postischemic hypothermia and delayed MK-801 treatment attenuates neurobehavioral deficits associated with transient global ischemia in rats. *Brain Res*. 1995;702:145–152.

93. Couzin J. The big chill. *Science*. 2007;317:743–745.

94. Guest JD, Dietrich WD. Spinal cord ischemia and trauma. In: Tisherman SA, Sterz F, eds. *Therapeutic Hypothermia*. New York: Springer; 2005:101–118.

95. Kleiner DM, Almquist JL, Bailes J, et al. *Prehospital Care of the Spine-Injured Athlete: A Document from the Inter-Association Task Force for Appropriate Care of the Spine-Injured Athlete*. Dallas, TX: National Athletic Trainers' Association; 2001.

96. Donaldson WF 3rd, Lauerman WC, Heil B, Blanc R, Swenson T. Helmet and shoulder pad removal from a player with suspected cervical spine injury. A cadaveric model. *Spine*. 1998;23:1729–1732; discussion 1732–1733.

97. Davidson RM, Burton JH, Snowise M, Owens WB. Football protective gear and cervical spine imaging. *Ann Emerg Med*. 2001;38:26–30.

98. Veenema K, Greenwald R, Kamali M, Freedman A, Spillane L. The initial lateral cervical spine film for the athlete with a suspected neck injury: helmet and shoulder pads on or off? *Clin J Sport Med*. 2002;12:123–126.

99. Woodring JH, Lee C. Limitations of cervical radiography in the evaluation of acute cervical trauma. *J Trauma*. 1993;34:32–39.

100. Spain DA, Trooskin SZ, Flancbaum L, Boyarsky AH, Nosher JL. The adequacy and cost effectiveness of routine resuscitation-area cervical-spine radiographs. *Ann Emerg Med*. 1990;19:276–278.

101. Gerrelts BD, Petersen EU, Mabry J, Petersen SR. Delayed diagnosis of cervical spine injuries. *J Trauma*. 1991;31:1622–1626.

102. Davis JW, Phreaner DL, Hoyt DB, Mackersie RC. The etiology of missed cervical spine injuries. *J Trauma*. 1993;34:342–346.

103. Poonnoose PM, Ravichandran G, McClelland MR. Missed and mismanaged injuries of the spinal cord. *J Trauma*. 2002;53:314–320.

104. Quencer RM, Nunez D, Green BA. Controversies in imaging acute cervical spine trauma. *AJNR Am J Neuroradiol*. 1997;18:1866–1868.

105. Schleehauf K, Ross SE, Civil ID, Schwab CW. Computed tomography in the initial evaluation of the cervical spine. *Ann Emerg Med*. 1989;18:815–817.

106. Li AE, Fishman EK. Cervical spine trauma: evaluation by multidetector CT and three-dimensional volume rendering. *Emerg Radiol*. 2003;10:34–39.

107. Hanson JA, Blackmore CC, Mann FA, Wilson AJ. Cervical spine injury: a clinical decision rule to identify high-risk patients for helical CT screening. *AJR Am J Roentgenol*. 2000;174:713–717.

108. Griffen MM, Frykberg ER, Kerwin AJ, et al. Radiographic clearance of blunt cervical spine injury: plain radiograph or computed tomography scan? *J Trauma*. 2003;55:222–226; discussion 226–227.

109. Eismont FJ, Clifford S, Goldberg M, Green B. Cervical sagittal spinal canal size in spine injury. *Spine*. 1984;9:663–666.

110. Fehlings MG, Perrin RG. The timing of surgical intervention in the treatment of spinal cord injury: a systematic review of recent clinical evidence. *Spine (Philadelphia PA)*. 2006;31:S28–S35; discussion S36.

111. Ellis JL, Gottlieb JE. Return-to-play decisions after cervical spine injuries. *Curr Sports Med Rep*. 2007;6:56–61.

Exertional Sickling

E. Randy Eichner, MD, FACSM

Scott Anderson, ATC

In everyday life, **sickle cell trait (SCT)** is considered generally benign and consistent with top athleticism and a long, healthy life. More than 3 million Americans carry SCT, and almost all live normal lives, no different from Americans without SCT. In other words, SCT is not sickle cell disease. Unlike sickle cell disease, SCT causes no anemia and few clinical problems. In sports medicine, by and large, SCT poses only four clinical concerns. Three of these—occasional bouts of gross hematuria, defects in urine-concentrating ability, and splenic infarction at altitude—are not life threatening, and are covered elsewhere.[1,2] The fourth clinical concern, **exertional sickling** collapse, is the focus of this chapter because it can pose a grave risk for some athletes.

Evidence suggests that, in SCT, sickling can begin within a few minutes of any sustained, intense exertion or successive bouts of maximal exertion with little or no interval of rest. Research in physiology and hematology suggests how and why sickle red blood cells can accumulate in the bloodstream during intense exercise, and how they can "logjam" blood vessels to cause **fulminant ischemic rhabdomyolysis**. The clinical and metabolic consequences of this "explosive" rhabdomyolysis can threaten life. Over the past decade in National Collegiate Athletic Association (NCAA) Division I football, exertional sickling has accounted for 10 (63%) of the 16 deaths from conditioning drills. Exertional sickling also causes deaths in other sports and has been reported in female athletes and in athletes as young as 12 years.[3] These deaths are potentially preventable.

Definition of Condition

SCT is a condition, not a disease. It comes from inheriting one gene for normal hemoglobin (A) and one gene for sickle hemoglobin (S). It is useful to think of SCT as "malarial," not racial. The sickle gene is common in people who come from where malaria is common, like parts

sickle cell trait (SCT)
A condition resulting from inheriting one gene for normal hemoglobin (A) and one gene for sickle hemoglobin (S). Strenuous exertion in SCT can cause red blood cells to sickle when they release their oxygen. This may then cause these cells to "logjam" in small blood vessels, which, as the athlete tries to continue exercising, may result in fulminant rhabdomyolysis.

exertional sickling Medical emergency occurring when an athlete with sickle cell trait experiences the sickling of red blood cells.

fulminant ischemic rhabdomyolysis Rapid breakdown of muscle tissue due to decreased blood flow.

of Africa. Over the millennia, carrying one sickle gene—SCT—helped prevent early death from malaria, making it more likely that SCT individuals would survive to procreate. As a result, SCT is common in African Americans; it occurs in about 8%. But because SCT is "malarial," skin phenotype does not predict hemoglobin genotype. SCT occurs in about 0.5% of Hispanics,[4] and because malaria was also common in the Mediterranean, the Middle East, and parts of India, SCT occurs in about 0.2% of whites.[4]

Each red blood cell in SCT typically has about 40% hemoglobin S and nearly 60% hemoglobin A, with trace amounts of minor hemoglobins such as hemoglobin F or A_2. The co-inheritance of alpha-thalassemia trait, which occurs in up to 30% of African Americans, lowers the amount of hemoglobin S in each red blood cell and thus mitigates the risk of exertional sickling in SCT.[5]

Epidemiology

The epidemiologic evidence can be grouped into three categories: (1) field studies of athletes in Africa that suggest a pattern regarding SCT and performance; (2) U.S. Army studies of SCT and sudden death in recruits in military basic training, along with accumulating case reports of career military men and women who collapsed during intense physical exertion—usually timed runs—and died from exertional sickling; and (3) the steady accumulation of reports and case studies of college and high school athletes—and even younger athletes—who collapsed in sports training and died from exertional sickling.

Field Studies in Africa

Field studies in Africa suggest that elite SCT runners are limited not in single sprints but in middle-distance, semi-marathon, and altitude racing. A study of all 145 students at a school for elite young athletes in Cameroon found SCT at the same rate as the general population, suggesting that SCT is no barrier to general sports excellence. In Ivory Coast, 13 SCT runners won 33 titles, but only 1 at 800 m or more. SCT racers were underrepresented among top finishers in a semi-marathon in Ivory Coast and underperformed in high-altitude stretches of a distance race in Cameroon. In contrast, a study of 16 French West Indian elite sprinters found that the 3 sprinters with SCT were winners.[6] Taken together, however, these African field studies suggest that SCT runners may be disadvantaged at altitude or at races of 800 m and beyond.[6] This pattern seems to hold in training for American college football, where successive sprints that total about 800 m or beyond seem to pose a sickling hazard.

Army Studies of SCT and Sudden Death in Basic Training

The U.S. military was the first to link SCT to sudden death during the physical training of recruits. In a comprehensive study of all deaths that occurred among 2 million recruits in military basic training in the U.S. Armed Forces from 1977 to 1981, the risk of unexplained sudden death in black recruits with SCT was 28 times higher than in black recruits without SCT, and 40 times higher than in all other recruits. The numerator, however, was small: there were only 13 sudden deaths among the SCT recruits.[7] In a later analysis, the relative risk of exercise-related death for black recruits with SCT, compared with black recruits without SCT, was 30.[5]

The risk fell sharply for career military people after basic training. This led to speculation that the risk of death in SCT is mainly during intense conditioning (to novel exercise) or during sustained exertion for which the recruit is unprepared. Deaths continue to be reported in military basic training, and case reports are accumulating of career military men (or police academy men) with SCT who suffer fatal or near-fatal collapse from exertional sickling, typically when trying to finish a 1.5- to 2-mile fitness run or a longer run.[8–10] It seems that the risk of fatal sickling can apply across a physically demanding career.

Analysis clarified the type of death in SCT military recruits.[5] Most collapses occurred as recruits ran 1 to 3 miles. Of 40 deaths or near-deaths from exertional sickling collapse, some had features of heat illness (but not exertional heat stroke) and others were sudden cardiac arrhythmias. Most deaths, however, were delayed for hours to a day or two and were from metabolic complications of fulminant rhabdomyolysis and myoglobinuric renal failure. Indeed, it is likely that the sudden, fatal arrhythmias came from hyperkalemia, lactic acidosis, and hypocalcemia, all a result of the fulminant rhabdomyolysis.

Thus, the main cause of death in exertional sickling is **explosive rhabdomyolysis**. In the Army studies, the risk of fatal rhabdomyolysis in SCT recruits in basic training was increased about 200-fold.[5]

Sickling Collapse in Athletes

The increasing reports of athletes collapsing or dying from exertional sickling are troubling. Most sickling deaths have been in football players, but at least two deaths have been in basketball players, one in a boxer, and one in a runner during a track tryout. For every death reported, there are several nonfatal collapses. These have resulted in compartment syndromes, lumbar paraspinal myonecrosis, or acute renal failure requiring dialysis. An adolescent runner was hospitalized twice for collapse from exertional sickling in two cross-country races a year apart; he survived.[11]

The first well-known exertional sickling collapse tied to SCT in college football was a player at the University of Colorado, new to altitude. He collapsed sprinting on the first day of practice in 1973, and survived. He collapsed again in 1974 on the first day of practice, after sprinting for only 2 minutes or 650 m. This time, he died from complications of sickling.[12] At least 18 college football players have died from exertional sickling (Table 8.1). Most have not been reported in the medical literature. One who was reported sprinted for only 3 minutes or 800 m on the first day of practice before he collapsed and soon died from sickling.[13] Another collapsed in the fall, after running 16 successive sprints of 100 yards each. He died about 15 hours later from hyperkalemic cardiac arrhythmia (pulseless electrical activity), a metabolic consequence of fulminant rhabdomyolysis and acute myoglobinuric renal failure.[14]

The recent spate of exertional sickling deaths in NCAA Division I football is alarming. In the decade from 2000 to 2010, no death occurred in the play of the game or in the practice of the game. However, 16 deaths occurred in conditioning for the game: 15 in sprinting or high-speed agility drills, and 1 in weight-lifting. Of the 16 deaths, 4 were caused by sudden cardiac arrest, 1 was secondary to asthma, and 1 was due to exertional heat stroke. Ten (63%) of the 16 deaths were tied to complications of sickling. Thus, SCT, carried by an estimated 3% to 4% of all these players, accounts for 63% of the deaths, an excess of 16- to 21-fold. The high intensity of football conditioning seems to play a pivotal role in many of these deaths.

Pathophysiology

Exercise physiology research helps explain why strenuous exertion in SCT can cause fulminant rhabdomyolysis. In SCT, in which typically about 40% of the hemoglobin in each red blood cell

TABLE 8.1 Exertional Sickling Deaths in College Football

Year	State	Setting
1974	CO	Ran 650 m, new at altitude
1985	AK	Ran ¾ mile
1986	MS	Ran 1 mile
1987	IN	Ran 1200 m, first day of practice
1987	UT	Ran ¾ mile, new at altitude
1990	NM	Ran 800 m, first day of practice
1992	GA	Ran 1000 m, first day of off-season practice
1995	AZ	Ran 900 m, first day of practice
2000	TN	Ran 800 m, first day of practice
2001	FL	One-hour mat drill
2004	OH	Sprinting, 10 min, day 1 of practice
2004	TX	Ran gassers for about 30 min
2005	MO	One-hour multistation field drill
2006	TX	Ran 16 sprints, 100 yards each
2008	FL	Station drills, running, just back from break
2008	NC	Ran 15 short uphill sprints
2009	NC	Ran 700 yards, new at modest altitude
2010	MS	Station drills, first day of team conditioning

is hemoglobin S, maximal exertion evokes four forces that lead to sickling (i.e., change in red-cell shape, when the cell releases its oxygen, from round to quarter moon or "sickle"). These four forces are hypoxemia, lactic acidosis, hyperthermia of muscles, and dehydration of red cells coursing through muscles. In concert, these forces foster sickling. Sickle cells are "stiff" and "sticky" and so tend to "logjam" the small blood vessels supplying working muscles. This causes fulminant ischemic rhabdomyolysis as the athlete tries to keep going on muscles that are getting no blood. It seems likely that the harder and faster SCT athletes try to go, the earlier and more severe the sickling and its consequences.

In fact, sickling-promoting perturbations in athletes going all-out can be rapid and profound. In one study, when young men (without SCT) cycled to exhaustion in 5 minutes at sea level, femoral vein oxygen saturation fell to 19% and blood pH fell to 7.15.[15] In another study, when young athletes without SCT ran on a treadmill to exhaustion in 1 minute, the pH in femoral artery blood fell below 7.1, while lactate rose to 17 mM.[16] In a third study, of young men, also without SCT, doing maximal cycling to exhaustion in 2 minutes or intermittent maximal running or cycling to exhaustion in less than 1 minute—or running races of 100 m, 200 m, 400 m, 800 m, 1500 m, or 5000 m—the pH in arterialized capillary blood from the finger fell as low as 6.8, lactate spiked as high as 32 mM, and bicarbonate fell to less than 3 mEq/L.[17] Thus maximal exertion can evoke profound lactic acidosis and hypoxemia in only 1 to 5 minutes. Hyperthermia of working muscles and dehydration of red cells coursing through the hyperosmotic (high-lactate) milieu of those muscles—which concentrates the amount of hemoglobin S in each red cell—complete the sickling foursome.

Just as these adverse forces develop within minutes, so too sickling occurs within minutes. Research on SCT military recruits in El Paso found sickling in venous blood from exercising muscles. Young men did two brief, maximal arm-cranking exercise tests, one at 1270 m, the other at a simulated altitude of 4000 m. Sickle cells were counted in venous blood draining the arms. At 1270 m, exercise evoked a mean of 2.3% sickle cells; at 4000 m, this increased to a mean of 8.5%, and to 25% in one recruit. It is vital to note that sickling was seen within 2 to 5 minutes of starting this strenuous exercise.[18] In a follow-up study published only as an abstract, when SCT recruits exercised to near exhaustion via *leg* cycling, sickle cells were seen in venous blood draining the *arm*.[19] This suggests the possibility that as exercise stress increases, sickle cells accumulate in the arterial circulation. Note that here too the exercise was done mainly with the legs but the sickling was seen in venous blood from the arms, implying that sickle cells may be pumped bodywide.

Research shows that dehydration can increase exertional sickling. Two men with SCT walked briskly for 45 minutes in the heat, once with fluids to offset sweat loss and once without fluids. Without fluids to offset dehydration, core temperature rose slightly higher and sickling (in forearm venous blood) increased steadily to peaks of 3.5% and 5.5%.

The timing of the pathophysiology fits the timing of the clinical collapse. In the face of maximal exertion, the four sickling forces develop in 2 to 5 minutes. Sickle cells are seen in the blood in 2 to 5 minutes, and some football players with SCT have collapsed from exertional sickling after only 2 to 5 minutes of sustained sprinting. The explosive rhabdomyolysis from major exertional sickling can cause death in less than an hour from metabolic arrhythmia of a normal heart (e.g., pulseless electrical activity), or can cause death over the next several hours from metabolic complications of acute myoglobinuric renal failure.

Recognition

Settings and Patterns of Collapse

It seems likely that the harder and faster SCT athletes go, the earlier and greater the sickling. That may be why sickling collapse occurs sooner, or at a shorter distance, in top college football players sprinting than in military recruits running. Many college football collapses have occurred after sustained or successive sprinting, totaling between 600 and 1200 m, often on the first day of conditioning or early in the season (Table 8.1). In contrast, most sickling collapses in military recruits have occurred while running 1 to 3 miles.[5]

The patterns of collapse teach other lessons. For example, sickling collapse in college football players is not typically triggered by an exertional heat illness (EHI). Army researchers concluded that EHI was a culprit in deaths in SCT recruits,[5] but most cases they gave as examples of EHI and sickling had no temperature recorded or the core temperature on collapse was only 38.9°C (102°F) or lower. It seems that many of these recruits did not have an EHI but only the expected physiologic hyperthermia of strenuous exercise.[14] The same applies to most of the football players who collapsed sickling. Some had been on-field only briefly, from an air-conditioned locker room, sprinting as briefly as 2 to 5 minutes before they collapsed. How could this be an EHI? Others collapsed on a cool day or had only mildly elevated core body temperature, or both.[14] And even one in whom the medical examiner diagnosed exertional heat stroke as well as sickling had a core temperature of only 39°C (102.4°F) soon after collapse. Odds are he had only the expected physiologic hyperthermia of the brief uphill successive sprinting he did before his exertional sickling collapse.

In other words, at least in college football, heat is no more a trigger for exertional sickling than is unaccustomed altitude, uncontrolled asthma, a heedless fervor on the part of the athlete, or a reckless intensity on the part of the coach. As one editorialist has said, problematic drills in football seem to have a common theme: too much, too fast, too soon, and too long.[20] The sickling trigger is maximal intensity, sustained for at least a few minutes, that pushes the athlete beyond his or her limits. Exertional sickling collapse is an *intensity* syndrome.

Differential Diagnosis of Collapse

Bear in mind that when an athlete takes the field healthy—and barring trauma—most ominous collapses on-field are caused by one of four major problems: heart disease, heat stroke, severe asthma, or exertional sickling. In general, the features of these four causes of sudden on-field collapse differ, and telltale clues can help observers differentiate among these medical emergencies.

Asthma tends to be unique and stark in its features. In general, asthma attacks severe enough to cause collapse occur in athletes with known asthma and prior problems with exercise-induced asthma, including frequent or urgent use of inhalers and a tendency for uneven control of their asthma. Thus, a grave asthma attack is usually easy to recognize.[21,22]

Heart disease comes in many forms, but among the most common causes of sudden cardiac death in athletes are cardiomyopathies, coronary artery anomalies, myocarditis, and ion channelopathies.[23] It seems that, too often in the past two decades, sickling deaths have been misdiagnosed as "cardiomyopathy" deaths in athletes who had only athlete's heart.[24] Cardiac collapses typically differ from sickling collapses in that the former are not merely sudden but nearly instantaneous. The athlete hits the ground, does not speak, and is unresponsive and pulseless because of a grave arrhythmia. The only way to save the athlete is by immediate cardiopulmonary resuscitation (CPR) and the use of an automated external defibrillator (AED).

Exertional heat stroke (EHS) is the syndrome that can most closely mimic sickling collapse. Here too the setting and pattern of collapse can help. If it is the first hot day of summer training and a huge lineman collapses after 2 to 3 hours in the heat, it is likely EHS. However, if a small wide receiver fresh out of the locker room collapses after sprinting only 2 to 3 minutes, it is likely sickling. It also goes without saying that it pays to know your athletes—for example, who has asthma, who tends to struggle in the heat, and who has sickle cell trait.

Exertional heat stroke is covered in Chapter 5, so will not be detailed here. Suffice it to say that the **prodrome** to collapse usually evolves more slowly in EHS than sickling, but the early features of pending EHS—confusion, bizarre behavior, and physical decline—may be subtle, especially in the heat of competition or hard training. Mental clouding prevents athletes from realizing they are overheating, so unless someone who knows them well is watching them closely, their EHS collapse may catch everyone unaware. Exertional heat stroke is defined as central nervous system dysfunction and a core temperature greater than 40.5 C (105°F) at time of collapse. Usually, in EHS in football, core body temperature is higher than this—often 41°C to 43.3°C (106–110°F). An immediate, accurate, core body temperature taken rectally can help differentiate EHS from sickling **(Table 8.2)**, but when in doubt, treat for both.

prodrome An early indication or symptom of impending disease or illness.

TABLE 8.2	Differentiating Features Among Common Causes of On-Field Collapse		
Sickling	**Heat Cramping**	**Cardiac**	**Heat Stroke**
Weakness > pain	Pain > weakness	No cramping	Fuzzy thinking
Slumps to ground	Hobbles to a halt	Falls like a rock	Bizarre behavior
Can talk at first	Yelling from pain	Unconscious	Incoherent
Muscles "normal"	Muscles locked up	Limp or seizing	Can be in coma
Temp < 103°F	Temp < 103°F	Temp irrelevant	Temp usually > 105°F
Can occur early	Usually occurs late	No warning	Usually occurs late

Heat cramping is not life threatening, but sometimes, in the face of a sickling collapse, precious time is lost with sideline treatment for presumed heat cramping. Football players who have suffered both heat cramping and sickling can differentiate the two:

- Heat cramping often has a prodrome. Hours or minutes before the cramping, the athlete may see or feel twitches or twinges in tired muscles, those destined to cramp. Sickling has no prodrome.
- The pain is different. Heat-cramping pain is excruciating, from a sustained contraction of muscles, a "lock-up." Sickling pain tends to be milder; it is an ischemic pain from muscles starved of blood supply.
- What stops the athlete is different. With heat cramping, athletes "hobble to a halt" or grab a cramping leg muscle and fall down. With sickling, athletes "slump to a stop," as their legs become weak and wobbly and no longer hold them up.
- The physical findings are different. In major heat cramping, one can see and feel large, rock-hard muscles in full tonic contraction, and the athlete often is writhing and yelling in pain. With sickling, the exhausted athlete lies fairly still and complains little, except to say that he feels bad and his legs hurt and are weak. The muscles look and feel normal to the medical staff (Table 8.2).

Also vital to know is that exertional sickling collapse can occur at any season and in any setting. It can occur on a hot day or a cold day. It can occur on a misty day in the mountains, when the athlete is unaccustomed to a jump in altitude of as little as 2000 feet or so. It can occur early on-field, within the first few minutes of successive sprinting, as on the first day of summer camp, or at the end of an hour-long, fast-tempo, multistation, "agility-drill" workout. It can occur at the end of a mat drill that starts at dawn. It can occur when a high school player returns to football after a year off and joins the team in sprinting drills. It can occur when a college football player returns after an injury and joins the team for the first fast-tempo, multistation drill of winter conditioning, or when the football players are just back from a 1½-week holiday. It can occur when a basketball player new to altitude sprints up and down the court only 10 times. It can occur when a coach (or drill instructor) joins the struggling athlete in running to urge them on to finish a planned series of uphill sprints or a timed 2-mile fitness run. It can occur when an athlete, a star sprinter in high school, walks on for college football and is told to sprint for 10 minutes: too much, too fast, too soon.

The common denominator is a perfect storm of irrational or undue intensity, sustained for at least a few minutes—an intensity beyond the fitness level or physical limits, or both, of that particular SCT athlete on that day in that setting. Sickling collapse is an intensity syndrome, and this fact shapes our precautions. In our experience in college football, it seems that some or many SCT players may occasionally have at least mild—and sometimes disabling—symptoms from what seems to be exertional sickling. Admittedly, no test exists to prove on-field, immediately, that a given event *is* exertional sickling. The risk may vary not only with the amount of hemoglobin S in each red cell, and with other inherited or acquired conditions, but also with the sport, setting, drill, or fitness of the athlete. We have seen an SCT player collapse writhing in severe back pain after a grueling conditioning drill that included pushing a weighted sled in a bear-crawl posture. He developed paraspinal myonecrosis. We and others have reported other SCT football players with the same syndrome, some disabled for weeks or months. We do not argue that paraspinal myonecrosis is specific to SCT athletes, but that it seems more common in them.[25]

Not all sickling collapses are the same, and not all football players describe them in the same way. However, they are unique enough that they can be differentiated from the other three common nontrauma causes of collapse on-field. Some SCT players say it begins with leg and/or low back pain or "cramps" that "spread up my body." Some complain of leg weakness more than pain, saying that their legs "got wobbly, like jello." Some say even their chest muscles are "tight" and "I can't catch my breath," or "I just don't feel right." By this point, they can be on their hands and knees, very anxious, with rapid breathing (up to 50 to 60 times a minute). This rapid breathing is not asthma, but hyperventilation to blow off carbon dioxide to try to offset a rapidly progressing, profound lactic acidosis, which comes from running hard on ischemic muscles. Some stoic players with exertional sickling will just stop, for example, after 700 yards of a planned 800-yard wind sprint, and sit or lie down, saying "I can't go on" or "my legs won't go." This self-limiting feature—the wisdom to read their body even in the heat of battle or with coaches yelling at them—has likely saved the lives of SCT athletes. They stop, refuse to go on, rest, "unsickle," walk home that day in good health, and return to their sport the next day.

Prevention

In our opinion, prevention hinges on knowing who has SCT so the SCT athletes and the staff can be educated on the early sickling symptoms and signs to heed, and so precautions can be taken. Some argue that these precautions could just be taken for the entire team, without the need to know who has SCT. But in college football, at least, this seems unrealistic. Also, the medical staff and coaches are better able to respond quickly and properly if they know who has SCT. Athletes with SCT should never be disqualified, because education and simple precautions seem to work and to enable SCT athletes to thrive in their sport.

These precautions are outlined in the 2007 National Athletic Trainers' Association (NATA) "Consensus Statement on Sickle Cell Trait and the Athlete"[26] and in the 2010 *NCAA Sports Medicine Handbook.*[27] All athletes with SCT should know these precautions, as well as the early signs and symptoms of exertional sickling, and institutions should establish an environment in which these precautions will be activated. These precautions include the following:

- SCT athletes should be allowed to set their own pace. This simple precaution is the heart of the matter. If followed, odds are *no* athlete would ever die from exertional sickling.
- SCT athletes should build up slowly in training, with paced progressions and longer periods of rest and recovery between repetitions, especially during "gassers" and intense station or "mat" drills.
- Extreme performance tests are especially risky and often unphysiologic for the sport. SCT athletes should not be urged to perform all-out exertion of any kind beyond 2 to 3 minutes without a breather. Serial sprinting, timed mile runs, and fast-tempo multistation drills with little or no rest between stations are especially risky for SCT athletes and are not advised.
- SCT athletes should stop activity immediately upon struggling, or upon any unusual muscle pain or weakness, "cramping," breathlessness, discomfort, or undue fatigue. They should seek and get immediate aid from medical staff.
- Predisposing factors include heat, altitude, dehydration, asthma, and other illness, because they make any workout harder. Adjust work/rest cycles for ambient heat stress and for a jump of even 2000 feet in altitude. Emphasize hydration. Control asthma. Have supplemental oxygen ready at altitude. An SCT athlete who feels ill should not begin a workout.

Table 8.3 provides a terse list of our SCT precautions in football at the University of Oklahoma.

<table>
<tr><td>

TABLE 8.3

</td><td>

Sickle Cell Trait Training Precautions at University of Oklahoma

</td></tr>
</table>

1. Stop at onset of symptoms (pain, cramping, weakness, breathlessness, fatigue).
2. Report any symptoms immediately to certified athletic trainer and coach.
3. Avoid "preseason conditioning tests."
4. Acclimate to onset of conditioning or lifting program.
5. Modify conditioning drills (no timed sprints, no sustained running without breaks).
6. Take part in a conditioning program each season before return to sport activity.
7. Hydrate before, during, and after all activity.
8. Decrease activity in hot and/or humid conditions.
9. Monitor if new to altitude, even a jump of 2000 feet. Cut effort; have an oxygen tank ready.
10. Decrease activity after any illness, especially with vomiting or diarrhea.
11. Control asthma to cut risk of exertional sickling.
12. Decrease activity after nights of poor sleep.

Treatment

An exertional sickling collapse is a medical emergency. The collapsed athlete can usually still talk or respond to you, but in some cases can deteriorate rapidly and become unresponsive within minutes. Practice an emergency action plan. Check vital signs; watch especially for shock, decreased levels of arousal and responsiveness, or a tachycardia that begins to evolve into a bradycardia. Give supplemental oxygen at 15 L/min by face mask, even at sea level, in case there is hypoxemia from rapid breathing (and consequent pulmonary ventilation/perfusion imbalance) or sickle red cells in the lungs, or both. Cool the athlete if necessary. Failing immediate improvement, call 911, attach an AED, start an intravenous line with normal saline, and be ready to start CPR if needed. Get the athlete to the hospital quickly. Tell the doctors to anticipate explosive rhabdomyolysis and its grave metabolic complications.

Return to Play

Return to play must be individualized. First, it is key to know that the mortality rate is high for athletes who collapse from exertional sickling and deteriorate to shock and coma on site. They can die within an hour or so, from cardiac arrhythmias caused by the metabolic complications of the explosive rhabdomyolysis: hyperkalemia, hypocalcemia, and profound lactic acidosis. The terminal rhythm may be an ever-slower bradycardia with widening of the QRS complex, then pulseless electrical activity (PEA), then asystole. That may be why, when the AED is activated, it says: "Do not shock. Continue CPR." Their best chance of survival is a very rapid trip to the emergency room, where experienced physicians, including a cardiologist and a nephrologist, are ready to treat the dire metabolic emergencies.

Some athletes survive the sickling collapse but spend a long time in the hospital with major, debilitating rhabdomyolysis, compartment syndromes, renal failure, and other complications. They may not return to play, either. One college football player in Texas survived the collapse but lost 55 pounds of muscle in the hospital, was too weak at first even to feed himself, spent 2 weeks on renal dialysis and 2 months in hospitals, and then was not cleared to return to play because he had lost about half of his renal function. He did, however, come back in all other ways and after college played some semiprofessional football. At the other extreme—the happy extreme—are the informed SCT athletes who stop at the first sign of sickling trouble and are attended to immediately with rest, supplemental oxygen, fluids, and, if needed, cooling. In our experience in football, these athletes can rebound quickly. Likely many or most of their sickle red cells revert to normal shape as they traverse the lungs and pick up oxygen, having done little damage to the tissues before the athlete stopped. These athletes can return to play the next day, with careful watching by staff.

Some SCT athletes fall between these two extremes. This has been the case for football players who develop moderate rhabdomyolysis, especially if associated with some lumbar paraspinal myonecrosis or a leg compartment syndrome. We have seen sharp rises in serum creatine kinase levels, sometimes to the range of 10,000 to 50,000 IU/L, in these cases without renal failure. We and others have seen occasional SCT football players who had two to four similar sickling bouts of disabling rhabdomyolysis, either because a new college coach intensified a conditioning drill or because the athlete had trouble elsewhere, such as in training for arena football or playing in an intense recreational basketball game. These athletes in the middle of the sickling spectrum tend to have limiting muscle pain and weakness for at least a week or two and need frequent assessment to ensure prudent, gradual return to play.

Summary

SCT, generally benign in everyday life, can pose a grave risk for some athletes. U.S. Army research first tied SCT to risk of sudden death in military recruits in basic training. The risk of fatal rhabdomyolysis in SCT recruits was increased 200-fold. Similar deaths have occurred for decades in young athletes, and in the past decade an alarming spate of exertional sickling death has occurred in NCAA Division I college football conditioning. SCT occurs in 3% to 4% of all these football players, but is tied to 10 (63%) of 16 conditioning deaths, an excess of up to 21-fold.[24]

Exercise physiology research explains how and why sickle cells can accumulate during intense exercise bouts and "logjam" blood vessels, causing explosive rhabdomyolysis. Several lines of research suggest that sickling can begin in only 2 to 5 minutes of all-out exertion, and can reach grave levels soon thereafter if the athlete struggles on or is urged on by coaches despite warning signs. The sickling collapse is an *intensity* syndrome that can be differentiated from the other three common causes of nontrauma collapse on-field. It is a medical emergency that calls for fast action to save lives. We believe that screening and tailored precautions[26, 27] can prevent these tragic collapses and deaths and enable all SCT athletes to thrive in their sports.

Clinical Case Scenario

1. A 19-year-old African American football player in Kentucky collapsed during an outdoor training session. He is a freshman on a Division I football team. His medical history included seasonal allergies and possible asthma when he was a young child. He has no history of exertional heat illnesses or use of tobacco, drugs, or alcohol. He is not aware whether he has sickle cell trait. When he collapsed it was 75°F on a partly cloudy day with 80% humidity and partly overcast skies.

   1. What would your differential diagnosis include?
   2. Consider that the workout leading up to this athlete's collapse was at the end of a long training day and consisted of twelve 100-meter sprints with 1 minute of rest between each sprint and 2 minutes after the fourth and eighth sprints. The athlete seemed to be struggling but was able to complete the sprints. What would your suspected diagnosis be at this point?
   3. The athletic trainer examines the athlete. The athlete complains of shortness of breath and lower extremity discomfort. As he is being questioned he becomes lethargic and his legs are too weak to support him. At this point the athletic trainer calls emergency medical services and suspects exertional sickling. What are the primary objectives and what actions should be taken at this point?
   4. What are the main actions you can take to prevent an exertional sickling case from occurring?
   5. What are the factors determining survival *after* an athlete with SCT begins an exertional sickling episode?

Key Terms

exertional sickling

explosive rhabdomyolysis

fulminant ischemic rhabdomyolysis

prodrome

sickle cell trait (SCT)

References

1. Eichner ER. Sickle cell trait and athletes: three clinical concerns. *Curr Sports Med Rep.* 2007;6:134–135.
2. Eichner ER. Exertional sickling. *Curr Sports Med Rep.* 2010;9:3–4.
3. Pretzlaff RK. Death of an adolescent athlete with sickle cell trait caused by exertional heat stroke. *Pediatr Crit Care Med.* 2002;3:308–310.
4. Bonham VL, Dover GJ, Brody LC. Screening student athletes for sickle cell trait—a social and clinical experiment. *N Engl J Med.* 2010;363:997–999.
5. Kark JA, Ward FT. Exercise and hemoglobin S. *Semin Hematol.* 1994;31:181–225.
6. Eichner ER. Sickle cell trait. *J Sport Rehabil.* 2007;16:197–203.
7. Kark JA, Posey DM, Schumacher HR, Reuhle CJ. Sickle-cell trait as a risk factor for sudden death in physical training. *N Engl J Med.* 1987;317:781–787.
8. Sanchez CE, Jordan KM. Exertional sickness. *Am J Med.* 2010;123:27–30.
9. Dincer HE, Raza T. Compartment syndrome and fatal rhabdomyolysis in sickle cell trait. *Wisc Med J.* 2005;104:67–71.
10. Makaryus JN, Catanzaro JN, Katona KC. Exertional rhabdomyolysis and renal failure in patients with sickle cell trait: is it time to change our approach? *Hematology.* 2007;12:349–352.
11. Helzlsouer KJ, Hayden FG, Rogol AD. Severe metabolic complications in a cross-country runner with sickle cell trait. *J Am Med Assoc.* 1983;249:777–779.
12. Eichner ER. Sickle cell trait, heroic exercise, and fatal collapse. *Physician Sportsmed.* 1993;21:51–64.
13. Rosenthal MA, Parker DJ. Collapse of a young athlete. *Ann Emerg Med.* 1992;21:1493–1498.
14. Anzalone ML, Green VS, Buja M, et al. Sickle cell trait and fatal rhabdomyolysis in football training: a case study. *Med Sci Sports Exerc.* 2010;42:3–7.
15. Hartley LH, Vogel JA, Landowne M. Central, femoral, and brachial circulation during exercise in hypoxia. *J Appl Physiol.* 1973;34:87–90.
16. Medbo JI, Sejersted OM. Acid-base and electrolyte balance after exhausting exercise in endurance-trained and sprint-trained subjects. *Acta Physiol Scand.* 1985;125:97–109.
17. Osnes J-B, Hermansen L. Acid-base balance after maximal exercise of short duration. *J Appl Physiol.* 1972;32:59–63.
18. Martin TW, Weisman IM, Zeballos J, Stephenson SR. Exercise and hypoxia increase sickling in venous blood from exercising limb in individuals with sickle cell trait. *Am J Med.* 1989;87:48–56.
19. Bergeron MF, Cannon JG, Hall EL, Kutlar A. Erythrocyte sickling during exercise and thermal stress. *Clin J Sport Med.* 2004;14:354–356.
20. McGrew CA. NCAA football and conditioning drills. *Curr Sports Med Rep.* 2010;9:185–186.
21. Becker JM, Rogers J, Rossini G, Mirchandani, D'Alonzo GE Jr. Asthma deaths during sports: report of a 7-year experience. *J Allergy Clin Immunol.* 2004;113:264–267.
22. Eichner ER. Asthma in athletes: scopes, risks, mimics, trends. *Curr Sports Med Rep.* 2008;7:118–119.
23. Maron BJ, Doerer JJ, Haas TS, Tierney DM, Mueller FO. Sudden deaths in young competitive athletes. Analysis of 1866 deaths in the United States, 1980–2006. *Circulation.* 2009;119:1085–1092.
24. Eichner ER. Sickle cell trait in sports. *Curr Sports Med Rep.* 2010;9:347–351.
25. Schnebel B, Eichner ER, Anderson S, Watson C. Sickle cell trait and lumbar myonecrosis as a cause of low back pain in athletes [abstract]. *Med Sci Sports Exerc.* 2008;40(5 suppl):537.
26. National Athletic Trainers' Association. Consensus statement: sickle cell trait and the athlete. Paper presented at: Annual Meeting of the National Athletic Trainers' Association; June 27, 2007; Anaheim, CA.
27. National Collegiate Athletic Association. Section 3c: the student-athlete with sickle cell trait. In: *2009–2010 NCAA Sports Medicine Handbook.* Indianapolis, IN: NCAA; 2009:86–88. Available at: http://www.nata.org/sites/default/files/SickleCellTraitAndTheAthlete.pdf.

Traumatic Injuries

Margot Putukian, MD, FACSM

Charlie Thompson, MS, ATC

Catastrophic injury in sport is uncommon, and most commonly the injuries that do occur are to the head, spine, or heart. In children, trauma is a leading cause of morbidity and mortality, resulting in over 1.5 million injuries, 500,000 hospital admissions, and 20,000 deaths per year.[1] In 80% of these injuries, the mechanism of injury is blunt force trauma.[2] In children, the risk of catastrophic injury in sport has been reported to be 0.6 per 100,000 participants annually.[3] This compares favorably with the risk level of 10- to 15-year-olds in automobile accidents, where the risk of catastrophic injury is reported to be 5.0 per 1,000,000 participants annually.[4] Whereas most catastrophic injuries in sport are head and spinal cord injuries, as well as cardiac injuries, less common causes of sudden death also occur in sport and warrant consideration. These include injuries to joints and major vessels[5] as well as injuries to the thorax and abdomen.

Injuries to the thorax and abdomen are often associated with sudden deceleration impact injuries and are therefore more common in sports such as football, ice hockey, lacrosse, skiing, and snowboarding. Injuries that occur in the thorax and abdomen include injuries to the mediastinum, lung, or heart or their pleura, as well as injuries to the aorta and other major vessels. Injuries that occur in the abdomen are often associated with high-velocity impact injuries that then cause injury to the intra-abdominal organs, most notably the spleen, kidney, and liver.[6] These types of injuries often occur if an individual is tackled and falls onto an object (e.g., a football), or falls and lands on a solid object (e.g., bicycle handlebars). Other mechanisms in sport include a solid structure penetrating or "almost penetrating" the body, which can occur when a hockey or lacrosse stick goes into the abdomen.

The literature regarding traumatic injuries to the chest and abdomen is dominated by mechanisms outside of sport.[7,8] In a series of 1696 patients with blunt chest trauma, only 70 cases (4%) were related to outdoor falls or sports injuries.[9] The most commonly reported injuries in sport that relate to chest wall trauma appear to be related to commotio cordis,[10] which is covered in greater detail in Chapter 4. Penetrating injuries from composite hockey sticks have been reported,[11] but these remain uncommon.

"Almost penetrating" injuries can occur with a handlebar in cycling or a stick in ice hockey, lacrosse, or other sports involving sticks or similar equipment.

Anatomically, the thorax and abdomen are often split into three regions, with the structures at risk grouped together based on these locations. The left region includes the spleen, left kidney, left adrenal gland, and left hemidiaphragm. The right region includes the liver, right kidney, right adrenal gland, and right hemidiaphragm. Injuries to the left and right region include lung contusions, pneumothorax, hemothorax, pneumomediastinum, and rib fractures, as well as injuries to the spleen, liver, kidneys, and adrenal glands. Rarely, rupture of the aorta, tracheobronchial tree, or diaphragm may occur. Finally, the midline region contains the left lobe of the liver, pancreas, duodenum, transverse colon, small bowel and mesentery, aorta, inferior vena cava, sternum, lower ribs, and heart. Understanding these anatomic regions is useful in considering injury to each location and the organs at risk.

Children's abdominal organs are lower and more anterior in position, their musculature is less developed, and their ribs and costochondral structures are more pliable, all potentially increasing the risk for thoracic and abdominal injury. In addition, because of the increased pliability, it takes more force for fractures to occur, and therefore the index of suspicion must be high in evaluating the youth athlete with traumatic injury.

This chapter focuses on injuries to the mediastinum and lungs, the intra-abdominal organs, joints, and great vessels. Injuries to the spinal cord, congenital issues, and cardiac injury are addressed in other chapters.

Specific Thoracic Injuries

Pulmonary Contusion

There is a paucity of information regarding pulmonary contusion in sport, because most of the literature relates to high-speed motor vehicle accidents and falls or suicide attempts, in which pulmonary contusion is often the most minor of multiple injuries that occur. Several case reports of pulmonary contusion in sport demonstrate that the most common mechanism is blunt trauma to the chest, most often during contact sports.[12–14] Pulmonary contusion often manifests as dyspnea and hypoxemia, which can occur acutely or be delayed for several hours. Other common symptoms include hemoptysis, tachypnea, chest pain, and wheezing.[15] Hemoptysis can be an unsettling symptom that is infrequently present for more than a day or two. The majority of pulmonary contusions that occur in sport are mild, and rarely are these life threatening. When fatal, they are often seen in conjunction with other injuries that are more serious[16–20] and often unrelated to sport.

The initial assessment should include airway management, assessing oxygenation using pulse oximetry, and auscultation to determine the need for emergent versus nonemergent transfer if additional diagnostic testing is necessary. Auscultation of the lungs may reveal decreased breath sounds or crackles, but if the injury is small, auscultation may be normal. Radiographs are often normal or take several hours to show abnormalities, whereas computed tomography (CT) can be very useful in identifying and determining the extent of injury immediately, as well as excluding other diagnoses such as pneumothorax, pneumomediastinum, hemothorax,[21] ruptured diaphragm,[22] and fracture.[23] It is important to consider more serious conditions such as bronchial vessel disruption if persistent abnormalities or hemoptysis occurs; in these situations, bronchoscopy may be necessary.[24] The majority of pulmonary contusions are treated with relative rest, and return to play is often rapid—within 1 to 2 weeks based on the reported literature.[12–14]

Sternal Fracture

Sternal fracture is uncommon in sport, although it can occur as a result of blunt trauma and, more important, is often associated with other intrathoracic injury. The chest wall in children is more compliant, and therefore these intrathoracic injuries may be more common in children and can be missed without a high index of suspicion. The presentation is often chest pain, made worse with direct palpation, along with shortness of breath and pleuritic pain. Associated injuries to consider include pneumothorax, pneumomediastinum, pulmonary contusion, and injury to the heart or aorta. In addition, if the injury is at the level of the sternoclavicular (SC) joint, SC dislocation, particularly posterior dislocation, must be considered. Posterior SC dislocation should be referred emergently because there is a significant concern for underlying vessel injury. These injuries should be reduced in a monitored setting. In children and young adults, the SC joint is often a growth plate, further complicating management decisions.

Pneumothorax and Pneumomediastinum

Pneumothorax (PTX) and pneumomediastinum (PM) can both occur as a result of sports participation, although the literature reviewing their occurrence as well as management and return-to-play issues is sparse.[25–27] PTX is defined as air that has leaked into the pleural space, either spontaneously or as a result of traumatic tears in the pleura following chest injury or iatrogenic/surgical procedures. Treatment of PTX entails removing air from the pleural space, reexpanding the underlying lung, and preventing recurrence.[28]

pneumothorax (PTX) Air that has leaked into the pleural space, either spontaneously or as a result of traumatic tears in the pleura following chest injury or iatrogenic/surgical procedures.

PTX can occur spontaneously or secondary to trauma. Primary spontaneous PTX often occurs in tall, thin, young men, and there may be a history of substance use or smoking.[29,30] Secondary spontaneous PTX occurs in individuals with underlying pulmonary disease, commonly chronic obstructive pulmonary disease, although it has been reported in individuals with subpleural blebs as well as Marfan syndrome.[31–33] There are approximately 20,000 cases of spontaneous PTX each year, but fewer than 10% of these are associated with exercise.[29,34] Spontaneous PTX can occur with Valsalva-type maneuvers and has been reported with weightlifters[32,35] as well as divers holding their breath.[36]

The incidence of spontaneous pulmonary air leaks does not seem to be increased at high altitude, but the same may not be true during scuba or other compressed air diving activities,[37,38] where the barotraumas are felt to occur when the individual holds his or her breath during the ascent. A PTX that occurs underwater during an ascent may rapidly progress to a tension PTX, more so than one on land, and thus a history of spontaneous air leak is considered an absolute contraindication to scuba diving.[37,38]

Traumatic PTX can occur as a result of penetrating or nonpenetrating trauma. In sport, it is most common in contact or collision sports[26,39–41] and may be associated with fractures of the ribs, scapula, or clavicle. Rib fractures are common, and certain segments are more likely to be associated with complications. These include fractures of the first four ribs, the last two ribs, fracture of multiple ribs, and flail segments.[42] In children, given their more pliable chest wall and rib structures, more impact is necessary for fracture to occur, and thus a greater morbidity and mortality is associated with these injuries.[43] Sixteen percent to 38% of scapular fractures are associated with PTX, although one study reported pneumothorax in over 50%.[44–46] Therefore, in the setting of scapular fracture, a high index of suspicion is necessary for associated PTX.

Tension PTX is an uncommon, yet life-threatening, complication of pneumothorax and is defined as a progressive collection of air in the pleural space.[47] Tension PTX can develop slowly or quickly, depending on the degree of lung injury and the underlying health of the patient. The deterioration that occurs in tension PTX is a multifactorial process that includes hypoxemia, compensatory mechanisms, and mechanical obstruction. Hypotension occurs late, just before cardiorespiratory collapse. Additional symptoms include progressive hypoxemia, tachycardia, and respiratory distress. Tension PTX is a life-threatening emergency that must be considered in the athlete who presents with respiratory distress.

The presentation of PTX is classically dyspnea and pleuritic chest pain, which is present in 80% to 90% of patients, although 10% will be asymptomatic.[30] The pain is generally ipsilateral to the side of injury and can radiate to the shoulder, neck, and back. It worsens with inspiration and with exertion, and can be associated with both dyspnea and a dry cough.[26] On physical examination, tachypnea, tachycardia, hyperresonance to percussion, and diminished breath and voice sounds (the Laennec sign), as well as asymmetry of chest wall expansion on inspiration, may be evident. Tension pneumothorax should be considered if there is any tracheal deviation away from the pneumothorax, distended neck veins, hypotension, respiratory distress, or cyanosis. In the stable athlete with pneumothorax, an electrocardiogram will often show a right axis, decreased amplitude of the QRS complex, and precordial T-wave inversion.

The presentation of pneumomediastinum is slightly different in that the pleuritic chest pain is often accompanied by subcutaneous emphysema over the anterior neck and supraclavicular area. In addition, complaints of dysphagia or dysphonia or both are not uncommon.[26] On auscultation over the pericardium there may be a "crunching sound" (the Hamman crunch) that is synchronous with the heartbeat.

If an athlete is evaluated and pneumothorax or pneumomediastinum is considered, then evaluation that includes an assessment of vital signs, oxygenation, and breathing should occur. The evaluation should occur in an environment that is appropriate; transporting an athlete to a location where breath sounds can be heard is essential. Observation of breathing and looking for asymmetry or splinting and confirming that the trachea is midline is important. Ensure that an adequate airway and oxygenation is present; if there is any concern, then emergent transportation to an emergency facility should be performed. In the athlete who appears stable, it is also important to perform serial assessments, because some injuries may not be apparent immediately and may present over time. The classic signs of tension pneumothorax, tracheal deviation, decreased lung expansion, decreased breath sounds, and distended neck veins, are not always evident, and thus a high suspicion should be maintained. If the athlete is hemodynamically unstable, and these classic signs are evident, then immediate needle aspiration with an 16–18 G needle between the second and third rib on the side of the tension (the side that the trachea is deviating away from) should be performed. Although this procedure is not without risk or complications, it can be life saving. Oxygen should be supplied and an intravenous line placed, with transportation to an emergency facility arranged.

Confirmation of PTX most often occurs with posteroanterior chest radiographs, which will show a pleural line with the absence of lung markings outside of it. Expiratory films in a lateral decubitus position

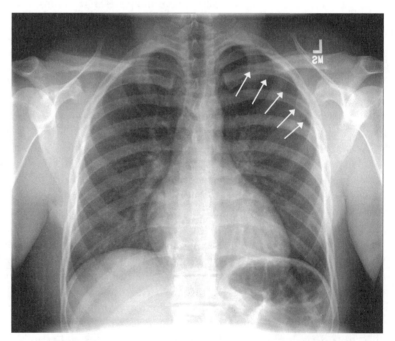

Figure 9.1   Computed Tomography (CT) image of a pulmonary contusion from a coronal view.

can optimize visualization.[31] A lateral neck soft tissue series can sometimes demonstrate pneumomediastinum, but CT is often indicated for diagnosing PM because the injury can be subtle.

During the evaluation for PTX and PM, other injuries, such as tracheobronchial disruption, aortic injury, hemopericardium, cardiac contusion, and diaphragmatic injuries, should also be considered. These injuries all present with chest symptoms, with a variable degree of hemodynamic compromise. If there is significant hypotension, decreased mental status, cardiac arrhythmia, or respiratory distress, then emergent stabilization and transportation to an emergency facility will be necessary. The evaluation in the emergency room will include emergent radiographs and ultrasound, as well as additional imaging, most often CT scanning.

For children with thoracic injuries, a clinical prediction protocol exists that helps to identify those with increased likelihood for injury. Holmes et al.[48] evaluated 986 children prospectively in the emergency department who underwent chest radiography after blunt chest trauma. There were 80 patients with thoracic injuries, including pulmonary contusion (71%), hemothorax (35%), PTX (25%), PM (8%), tracheobronchial disruption (3%), and aortic injury (3%), along with hemopericardium, cardiac contusion, rib fracture, sternal fracture, and diaphragm injury. The predictors of thoracic injury included low systolic blood pressure, elevated age-adjusted respiratory rate, abnormal thorax exam, abnormal chest auscultation, femur fracture, and a Glasgow Coma Scale score of less than 15. In this series, 98% of patients with thoracic injury had at least one of these predictive factors. It is important to recognize that this series was not specific to athletes, and that most injuries were not those seen in sport but rather were motor vehicle, auto–pedestrian, auto–bicycle, and bicycle accidents; assaults; crush injuries; and abuse injuries. However, these factors may be associated with significant injury and should be evaluated.

The treatment of PTX depends on the clinical stability of the athlete as well as the size of the PTX. For spontaneous PTX in clinically stable patients with PTX less than 15% to 20%, the American College of Chest Physicians[49] believes that close observation in the emergency department for 3 to 6 hours with appropriate monitoring is adequate as long as a repeat radiograph is performed prior to discharge and again after 12 to 48 hours. If the patient is clinically stable and the PTX is greater than 15% to 20%, then a small-bore chest tube should be inserted and the patient admitted to the hospital. Thoracoscopy should be considered, more so than pleurodesis, if persistent air leak occurs in these patients. Thoracoscopy should also be considered for recurrent PTX. Air will be reabsorbed from the pleural space at a rate of 1.25% per day,[50] although this can be increased threefold by adding supplemental oxygen.[33]

PM also presents as a result of trauma, although it has been reported in noncontact settings as well. Many of these cases are seen in conjunction with pneumothorax and are often not considered life threatening because they will resolve on their own without intervention. PM may be associated with significant esophageal or tracheal compromise, and therefore further evaluation with bronchoscopy or endoscopy is essential to exclude any associated injuries. With blunt trauma, other associated injuries can include pneumopericardium, which has been reported in a 15-year-old football player as a result of blunt trauma.[51] Cardiac injuries are considered in a separate chapter. Most cardiothoracic injuries can be treated successfully, and return to play is often uncomplicated. Tension PTX, hemothorax, and diaphragmatic injury, as well as pulmonary contusion with persistent hemorrhage, are issues that require emergent care because they are life threatening.[52]

Abdominal Injuries

Splenic Injury

Splenic injuries are the most common intra-abdominal organ injuries in sport; the spectrum of injury includes contusion, intrasplenic hematoma, laceration, and rupture.[53,54] Although splenic rupture can occur spontaneously, it often occurs as a result of direct or indirect trauma.[54–56] Complicating factors include concomitant rib fracture and splenomegaly, with the latter commonly due to infectious mononucleosis. Splenic rupture in infectious mononucleosis is not common, although because of the risk of splenic rupture athletic participation is restricted for 3 to 4 weeks after the onset of symptoms.[57] It is also not uncommon to see splenic injury in combination with other intra-abdominal organ injury, such as liver or kidney injury.

The symptoms and signs of splenic injury include hypotension; abdominal pain with or without referral to the left shoulder; abdominal distension, tenderness, and rebound along with guarding; and syncope or presyncope. If there is concern regarding possible intra-abdominal injury and the athlete has hypotension, orthostatic changes, or significant abdominal findings, referral to an emergency facility should be arranged. It is not uncommon to obtain a blood count as well as urinalysis to exclude renal injury, as well as obtaining radiographs.[58] Although ultrasound, and specifically a focused assessment with sonography in trauma (FAST) scan, can be used to identify traumatic injury,[59,60] CT scanning remains the study of choice to best evaluate the severity of trauma as well as exclude other injuries, such as bony fracture of the ribs, pelvis, and spine or other abdominal organ injury.[2,61–63] CT can determine the extent of intraperitoneal bleeding as well as detect and quantify the extent of injury to both solid and hollow organs. The sensitivity of CT with double contrast IV in detecting splenic injury is close to 100%.[61] Ultrasonography, on the other hand, has been found to miss between one fourth and one third of injuries to solid viscous organs.[64,65]

Splenic injury is often graded from 0 to 5, with 0 being no injury, grade 1 being a single laceration of the spleen, grade 2 being multiple fractures or contusions of the spleen involving less than 25% of the spleen, grade 3 involving 25% to 50%, grade 4 involving 50% to 75%, and grade 5 being a "shattered spleen."[66] There does appear to be a correlation between evidence of radiographic healing on CT and the grading of these injuries, where grade 1 injuries require 3.1 weeks; grade 2, 8.2 weeks; grade 3, 12.1 weeks; and grade 4, 201 weeks.[67] Treatment of splenic injury varies, although if the athlete is clinically stable, nonoperative treatment is preferred. With splenectomy, case reports describe a return to play in 3 weeks in contact sports,[54] although the majority of reports describe a more lengthy return-to-play time, especially if nonoperative treatment is considered.[55,56,67–70]

Other intra-abdominal injuries that can occur are injuries to the liver, kidney, pancreas, or gastrointestinal (GI) tract. These are not common in sport, and most reports in the literature describe motor vehicle accidents or pedestrian–motor vehicle accidents. Both renal and liver laceration can be graded, and evaluation and treatment of these injuries is important, although they are rarely life threatening. These injuries generally present similarly, with abdominal pain or hypotension or both. Less commonly they may present with GI bleeding. The presentation may be delayed, and a high index of suspicion should be present if there is a history of abdominal trauma. Hematuria is a common presentation,[71] although not always indicative of renal injury.[72,73]

Evidence-based guidelines exist for children with isolated liver and spleen injury,[74] as well as evidence-based guidelines for resource utilization in children with isolated spleen or liver injury.[62,74,75] The 2000 and 2005 guidelines from the American Pediatric Surgical Association provide some recommendations for the emergent treatment of these injuries.[62,74] These authors use CT grading to determine the appropriate utilization of resources. For grade I through III injuries, the guidelines do not recommend intensive care unit (ICU) stay, predischarge imaging, or postdischarge imaging. For grade IV injuries, they do recommend an ICU stay of 1 day, although they do not recommend pre- or postdischarge imaging. For grades I, II, III, and IV injuries, they recommend a hospital stay of 2, 3, 4, and 5 days, respectively, as well as activity restriction from "age-appropriate activities" of 3, 4, 5, and 6 weeks, respectively. The authors do note that for return to full-contact competitive sports, the decision must be an individualized one made by the pediatric trauma surgeon.[62,74]

Prediction rules for the identification of both children and adults with intra-abdominal injuries after blunt trauma to the torso also exist that are useful in determining which athletes may need emergent treatment.[76,77] For children with blunt torso trauma, a prediction rule using the six variables of low age-adjusted systolic blood pressure, abdominal tenderness, femur fracture, increased liver enzyme levels (serum aspartate aminotransferase concentration > 200 U/L or serum alanine aminotransferase concentration > 125 U/L), microscopic hematuria (urinalysis > 5 red blood cells per high-powered field), and an initial hematocrit level of less than 30% demonstrated a sensitivity of 94.9% and a specificity of 37.1%.[75] Deciding on the sideline which athletes may require emergent transportation and evaluation after blunt trauma to the abdomen is difficult. The athlete's blood pressure and pulse can be measured to look for orthostatic changes consistent with intravascular volume loss, abdominal tenderness, significant costovertebral angle tenderness, or hematuria can all be assessed on the sideline and may be indicative of more serious intra-abdominal injury. There are no clear guidelines for sideline assessment and what findings merit emergent transportation and evaluation.

For adults with blunt torso trauma, a prediction rule using a Glasgow Coma Scale score less than 14, costal margin tenderness, abdominal tenderness, femur fracture, hematuria level greater than or equal to 25 red blood cells per high-powered field, hematocrit level less than 30%, and abnormal chest radiograph result (PTX or rib fracture) was found to have a sensitivity of 95.8%, a specificity of 29.9%, and a negative predictive value of 98.6%.[76] It is important to remember that in both of these studies, sport-related trauma was infrequent, and therefore the application of these rules to athletes may be limited.

Vascular Injuries and Conditions

Although sport-related orthopedic injuries are seldom considered "catastrophic" in the true definition of the word, they can often be season ending and even career ending, which in the eyes of athletes and possibly their family and coaches could be considered catastrophic. In the worst-case scenarios, these injuries are associated with neurovascular injuries secondary to the major injury that run the risk of being missed because of the severe nature of the original injury. It is imperative for the clinician to be cognizant of the possibility of these neurovascular injuries.

Knee Dislocations

Knee dislocations typically occur with high-velocity forces (car accidents) but also occur with low-velocity forces (sports). They were once thought to be relatively uncommon. One study put the rate between 0.001% and 0.013%.[78] Another reported 26 knee dislocations in a 27-year period.[79] Twaddle et al.[80] reported 63 knee dislocations in 66 patients, with 38% related to sports. Many authors believe that knee dislocations are underdiagnosed because they most often spontaneously reduce.[81] Patients with multiple-ligament knee injuries should be treated as having a reduced knee dislocation and must be monitored for neurovascular injury.[82] One study demonstrated vascular injuries in 38% of the patients presenting with multiple-ligament injuries of the knee.[83] It is imperative that the clinician pay close attention to the potential for vascular and nerve damage when evaluating multiple-ligament injuries in the knee. All multiple-ligament injuries to the knee should be treated as a medical emergency, regardless of the findings during the on-field evaluation.[84]

Popliteal Artery Injuries

Popliteal artery (PA) injuries can result in amputation of the lower leg. In fact, amputation was at one time the treatment of choice for PA injuries.[85] Because the popliteal artery is tethered proximally at its origin as it emerges from the adductor hiatus and also tethered distally at the tendinous arch of the soleus, it is at risk with both anterior and posterior shear. Anterior shearing causes stretching and small intimal tears, whereas posterior shearing is associated with complete disruption of the artery. As a side note, the clinician should be aware that isolated posterior cruciate ligament injuries resulting from a hyperextension mechanism could be enough to cause PA damage.[86] Johnson et al.[82] reported an 86% amputation rate if the integrity of the popliteal artery is not restored within 6 to 8 hours; they also reported an 89% salvage rate when the integrity is restored within 8 hours, making this issue critical for the clinician.[82]

Peroneal Nerve Injuries

Although not considered life or limb threatening, peroneal nerve injuries can be another significant cause of morbidity following knee dislocations.[82] The incidence of nerve damage following a knee dislocation varies from 25%[87] to 40%.[88] The peroneal nerve is considered to be superficial and relatively immobile, causing it to be susceptible to injury. The mechanism of injury is usually a varus stress that causes a traction-type injury, as seen in posterolateral corner injuries[89] and avulsion fractures of the fibular head.[90] The degree of stretching will determine the extent of the injury, ranging from a mild stretch to a complete transection. Prognosis is usually poor, with a slow and often incomplete recovery. Foot drop is considered a common manifestation of peroneal nerve damage.[82]

Vascular Exam

The incidence of PA injury associated with knee dislocation ranges from 23% to 32%.[83] It is important to note that vascular injury may not be readily apparent because vascular compromise may not be completely evident at the time of the dislocation.[84] For those dislocations that do not spontaneously reduce, it is important to measure distal pulses (dorsalis pedis and posterior tibial) before and after reduction.[80] All suspected knee dislocations or actual reduced dislocations should have serial evaluations performed every 4 to 6 hours for 48 hours, noting abnormalities with the pulses, expanding hematoma, pulsatile hemorrhaging, and obvious ischemia.[82]

There are disagreements in the literature regarding the procedure for evaluating for vascular damage following a knee dislocation. Some authors report that pulse examination is sufficient to evaluate for vascular damage.[91] Others argue that the risk of potential devastating consequences requires evaluation techniques beyond that of merely monitoring pulses.[92] That being said, the following is a synopsis of those additional diagnostic tests that are used in determining the possibility and extent of vascular injuries following knee dislocations.

arterial pressure index (API)
A measure of arterial flow determined by dividing the systolic pressure of the lower extremity (cuff just above the ankle) by the systolic pressure of the upper extremity (brachial artery); acceptable level is greater than 0.90.

In addition to monitoring as mentioned previously, the use of the **arterial pressure index (API)** has been recommended by several authors.[82] The API is determined by dividing the systolic pressure of the lower extremity (cuff just above the ankle) by the systolic pressure of the upper extremity (brachial artery) **(Table 9.1)**. In one study, 11 of 38 patients had an API of less than 0.90, and all required vascular restoration. The remaining 27 had an API of more than 0.90 and did not require vascular restoration.[93] This fact is often cited by authors advocating for noninvasive examination in these cases.[91]

Other studies used include duplex ultrasonography and arteriography, which is considered the gold standard. Duplex ultrasonography is a noninvasive and safe technique to evaluate

TABLE 9.1	Arterial Pressure Index Information
	Arterial Pressure Index (API)
Description	An effective diagnostic tool using the systolic pressure of the lower extremity (dorsalis pedis or posterior tibial artery, whichever is higher from both legs) divided by the highest systolic pressure of the upper extremity (brachial artery from both arms)
Implications	API < 0.90 vascular restoration (arteriography) most likely needed	API > 0.90 vascular restoration unlikely needed
	Provides a noninvasive and safe method for diagnosing vascular injury from traumatic injuries (e.g., knee dislocations)
Sensitivity (API < 0.90)	95%
Specificity (API < 0.90)	97%

Sources: Adapted from Mills WJ, Barei DP, McNair P. The value of the ankle-brachial index for diagnosing arterial injury after knee dislocation: a prospective study. *J Trauma.* 2004;24:403–407; Bravman JT, Ipaktchi K, Biffl WL, Stahel PF. Vascular injuries after minor blunt upper extremity trauma: pitfalls in the recognition and diagnosis of potential "new miss" injuries. *Scand J Trauma, Resuscitation and Emerg Med.* 2008;16:16.

vascular damage. Byone[94] found it to be 95% sensitive and 99% specific, with an overall accuracy rate of 98%. The downside is that it is reliant on the skill of the technician and radiologist.[95]

Johnson et al.[82] reported on several studies that advocate for selective arteriography. Their recommendation is to obtain an arteriogram only when noninvasive modalities such as pulse examination and API suggest the possibility of vascular compromise. The significant downside to arteriography is typically the delay of 2 to 3 hours to arrange the testing, which may not allow for vascular restoration in a timely manner.[96,97] McDonough[91] and others have also reported the possibility of false-positive results, with ensuing unnecessary surgery. Additional concerns include thrombosis, bleeding, reaction to contrast material, and, as with many medical procedures, cost.

Neurologic Exam

A thorough neurologic evaluation should be performed, checking both the sensory and motor functions of the superficial and deep branches of the peroneal nerve. An incomplete nerve injury could be indicated by loss of sensation with motor function intact or by a partial motor function loss. The Tinel sign can be utilized by percussing the nerve as it traces over the fibular head. Electromyography and nerve conduction velocity are used to determine whether further treatment is needed and to predict prognosis.[98]

Deep Vein Thrombosis and Pulmonary Embolism

The U.S. Department of Health and Human Services reported in a September 15, 2000, news release that between 350,000 to 600,000 people are affected by **deep vein thrombosis (DVT)** or **pulmonary embolism (PE)**, or both, per year, resulting in over 100,000 deaths per year.[99] It has been postulated that improved care of trauma patients has resulted in a decrease in morbidity from the actual trauma but may be the cause of an increase in the number of deaths related to PE in this same group of patients.[100] With trauma patients living longer after the trauma, the risk of DVT increases, and therefore the risk of PE increases.[101]

deep vein thrombosis (DVT) A blood clot that forms in a vein deep in the body, most typically in the lower extremity but possibly in the upper extremity.

pulmonary embolism (PE) Complication of a venous thromboembolism; a clot (embolus) breaks off and travels through the blood to the lung, impeding blood flow.

The majority of the research on DVT and PE has been done with major trauma patients, and much of the data includes elderly patients, who are frequently affected by either or both of the maladies. Although there is a lack of research regarding athletic injuries and DVT/PE, many athletes are faced with the prospect of suffering a significant injury and possibly major surgery, making them susceptible to these problems as a result of the actual trauma or the treatment that occurs subsequent to the trauma, thus forcing clinicians to be aware of the possibility of their occurrence.

In simplest terms, a deep vein thrombosis is a blood clot that forms in a vein deep in the body; most occur in the leg.[102] The three most common causes of clotting are local venous damage as the result of trauma or possibly surgery; venous stasis as the result of immobilization and pressure; and the effect of being in a hypercoagulable state.[100]

Pulmonary embolism is not a disease in its own right, but is a complication of venous thromboembolism.[103] Prandoni et al.[102] described a PE as a clot in a deep vein that breaks off (becoming an embolus) and travels through the bloodstream to the lungs, blocking blood flow to the lungs. The evidence that PE is predominantly a complication of venous thrombosis, typically occurring in the veins of the legs, is compelling.[103]

Typical signs and symptoms of DVT include swelling, pain and tenderness, warmth, and red or discolored skin. However, it is thought that DVT can occur without any of the common symptoms being present, and that only objective testing can confirm its absence or presence.[101] Clinicians need to be aware of this and must monitor patients who have suffered significant injury, have had major surgery, or need to be immobilized for any length of time.

Treatment of lower extremity DVT includes the use of anticoagulant medicines as well as mechanical devices such as graded elastic compression stockings, intermittent compression, and electrical stimulation. The mechanical devices are considered effective in low- to medium-risk patients.[104] The discussion of specific pharmacologic treatment for DVT is beyond the scope of this chapter.

DVT is more common in the lower extremity, but it does occur in the upper extremity and is typically referred to as an "effort thrombosis," occurring in the dominant arm of overhead athletes. This is known as **Paget-Schroetter syndrome (PSS)**, and generally refers to axillosubclavian deep vein thrombosis without secondary cause (trauma, surgery, catheter placement, etc.).[105] Although PSS normally occurs in the dominant arm, there is at least one report in the literature of a non-dominant-arm PSS related to repetitive bilateral arm activity.[106] It has been reported that 80% of all PSS cases are associated with thoracic outlet syndrome, whereas only 1% to 12% of all thoracic outlet cases have complaints related to PSS.[107] The signs and symptoms of PSS are typical of any DVT. They can improve with rest and can present with normal pulses.[105]

Diagnosis includes the use of the **Adson test** (humeral abduction to 90°; external rotation; elbow flexed to 90°; and the head turned to the side being tested) and the Wright test (same as the Adson test but with the head rotated to the opposite side). Diminished radial pulses indicate a positive test. The results of these tests are more important if they are negative when performed on the opposite extremity. Doppler ultrasound is also utilized; however, as with lower extremity Doppler ultrasound, there is some controversy over its use. Venography is considered the gold standard for diagnosis.

Treatment for PSS includes the use of thrombolytics and anticoagulants followed by surgical intervention.[108] Controversy remains regarding the indications for surgery, the timing of the surgery, and the technical approaches of surgery.[109]

Summary

The catastrophic nature of the conditions described in this section **(Table 9.2)** do not have to cause devastating outcomes. The ability of the clinician to recognize secondary injuries in a timely manner when evaluating sport-related orthopedic injuries can be crucial to the outcome of the overall injury. Focusing only on the obvious and apparent damage can be devastating in some cases. Not ignoring warning signs of possible life- or limb-threatening conditions is critical in the overall care of the athlete.

Clinical Case Scenarios

1. A 22-year-old male football player (offensive lineman, 288 pounds) suffered a right ankle sprain on October 19, 2009. He had no time loss due to this injury. He did, however, see the team physician and was prescribed diclofenac (Voltaren).

   On December 18, 2009, he went to a movie; after the movie, he felt like he had strained his calf. He tried stretching the calf, with no improvement. He was scheduled to fly home on December 20, but his flight was cancelled because of snow. He mentioned to his parents that his calf was sore and swollen, and they insisted he go to the local hospital emergency room. There, he had a Doppler ultrasound exam, which revealed a popliteal vein DVT. He was administered a shot of enoxaparin (Lovenox) and allowed to fly home the next day.

   Evaluation by a physician at home was arranged. Blood work was obtained that indicated he was heterozygous for factor V Leiden deficiency. On exam, he denied any chest pain, shortness of breath, cough, or hemoptysis. He only reported swelling in the calf and an occasional cramp. It was revealed that a family history of DVT existed.

   He was prescribed warfarin (Coumadin) and enoxaparin. On January 18, 2010, he was allowed to commence biking and restricted weight lifting. He did not participate in winter or spring football drills or practice. On August 24, he was cleared to play football during his senior season, which he did without incident.

   1. What do you believe were the main factors contributing to this athlete's condition?
   2. What other conditions could present similarly that you would need to rule out? What would your differential diagnosis be initially?

TABLE 9.2 Sampling of Traumatic Conditions, Standard RTP Implications Relative to Severity, and Common Signs and Symptoms

Injury	Severity	RTP Implications	Most Common Signs and Symptoms
Pulmonary contusion	NA	Rest, RTP within 1–2 weeks	Dyspnea, hypoxemia (possibly delayed for several hours), hemoptysis
Sternal fracture	If occurring at the SC level requires emergency response	Dependent upon severity, age (growth plate implications), and location of injury	Chest pain worsening with palpation, shortness of breath
Pneumothorax	NA	Variable	Dyspnea, pleuritic chest pain, hypoxemia, tachycardia, respiratory distress, diminished breath sounds
Pneumomediastinum	NA	Variable	Pleuritic chest pain with subcutaneous emphysema, dysphagia, dysphonia, "crunching" sound in sync with the heartbeat
Splenic rupture	Grade	Timeline (full contact sports decision should be individualized)	Hypotension, abdominal pain with or without referral to the left shoulder, abdominal tenderness/guarding and positive rebound sign
	1	3 weeks (hospital stay of 2 days)	
	2	4 weeks (hospital stay of 3 days)	
	3	5 weeks (hospital stay of 4 days)	
	4	6 weeks (ICU stay of 1 day, hospital stay of 5 days)	
	5	Probable splenectomy - variable	
Deep Vein Thrombosis (DVT)	NA	Dependent upon if surgical intervention is required	Pain and tenderness, swelling, warmth, red or discolored skin, highly susceptible athletes with a history of recent injury or immobilization

3. Looking back, is there anything this athlete could have done to help prevent this incident?
4. If you were this athlete's health care provider, what preventive steps would you take when this athlete begins to participate in sports again?

2. A 20-year-old female college gymnast was diagnosed with a torn anterior cruciate ligament. She was evaluated by the institution's consulting orthopedist. She was placed in a compression bandage and a straight leg immobilizer. She later developed calf pain on the involved side and returned to see the medical staff. Her calf pain was addressed with ice, elevation, and gentle massage. She later returned

to the facility because she wasn't feeling well and had flulike symptoms. She was instructed to report to the institution's Health Service unit, which she refused to do because her parents were visiting.

1. At this point, what is your differential diagnosis?
2. If this were your athlete, would you follow the same actions? What would your course of care be if she were under your care?
3. Later that day, the athlete was rushed to the hospital, where she died as a result of a pulmonary embolism. Knowing this, is there anything regarding the care this athlete was given that you would change? What could have realistically been changed to alter the outcome of this scenario?
4. What was the largest factor that resulted in this fatal outcome? What would you do to prevent this from occurring again?

Key Terms

Adson test

arterial pressure index (API)

deep vein thrombosis (DVT)

Paget-Schroetter syndrome (PSS)

pneumothorax (PTX)

pulmonary embolism (PE)

References

1. Wegner S, Colletti JE, Van Wie D. Pediatric blunt abdominal trauma. *Pediatr Clin North Am.* 2006;53:243–256.
2. Sivit CJ. Abdominal trauma imaging: imaging choices and appropriateness. *Pediatr Radiol.* 2009;39(suppl 2):S158–S160.
3. Zemper ED. Catastrophic injuries among young athletes. *Br J Sports Med.* 2010;44:12–20.
4. The Disaster Center. Motor vehicle occupant fatality and injury rates per 100,000 population by age group, 1975–1997, per year. http://www.disastercenter.com/traffic/AgeGroup.html. Accessed March 2010.
5. Heller G, Immer FF, Savolainen H, et al. Aortic rupture in high-speed skiing crashes. *J Trauma.* 2006;61(4):979–980.
6. Ryan JM. Abdominal injuries and sport. *Br J Sports Med.* 1999;33:155–160.
7. Keel M, Meier C. Chest injuries—what is new? *Curr Opin Crit Care.* 2007;13(6):674–679.
8. McGillicuddy D, Rosen P. Diagnostic dilemmas and current controversies in blunt chest trauma. *Emerg Med Clin North Am.* 2007;25(3):695–711.
9. Galan G, Penalver JC, Paris F, et al. Blunt chest injuries in 1696 patients. *Eur J Cardiothorac Surg.* 1992;6:284–287.
10. Maron BJ, Pollac DC, Kaplan JA, Mueller FO. Blunt impact to the chest leading to sudden death from cardiac arrest during sports activities. *N Engl J Med.* 1995:333;337–342.
11. Kennedy J, Green RS, Henteleff H. Penetrating chest trauma secondary to a composite hockey stick injury. *Can J Emerg Med.* 2006;8(6):437–440.
12. Steinlight S, Putukian M. Hemoptysis in a varsity collegiate football athlete. *Med Sci Sports Exerc.* 2010;42(5):183.
13. Lively MW, Stone D. Pulmonary contusion in football players. *Clin J Sport Med.* 2006;16:177–178.
14. Meese MA, Sebastianelli WJ. Pulmonary contusion secondary to blunt trauma in a collegiate football player. *Clin J Sport Med.* 1997;7(4):309–310.
15. Cohn SM. Pulmonary contusion: review of the clinical entity. *J Trauma.* 1997;42:973–979.
16. Lotfipour S, Kaku SK, Vaca F, et al. Factors associated with complications in older adults with isolated blunt chest trauma. *West J Emerg Med.* 2009;10:79–84.
17. Balci AE, Kazez A, Eren S, et al. Blunt thoracic trauma in children: review of 137 cases. *Eur J Cardiothoracic Surg.* 2004;26:387–392.
18. Freixinet J, Beltran J, Rodriguez PM, et al. Indicators of severity in chest trauma [in Spanish]. *Arch Bronconeumol.* 2008;44(5):257–262.
19. Jones NS. An audit of the management of 250 patients with chest trauma in a regional thoracic surgical centre. *Arch Emerg Med.* 1989;6:97–106.
20. Perna V, Morera R. Prognostic factors in chest traumas: a prospective study of 500 patients [in Spanish]. *Cir Esp.* 2010;87(3):165–170.
21. Hayes D. Chest pain. *Clin Pediatr.* 2007;46(8):746–747.
22. Halil O, Gokhan G, Turkay K. A case of diaphragmatic rupture after strenuous exercise (swimming) and jump into the sea. *Turk J Trauma Emerg Surg.* 2009;15(2):188–190.
23. Trupka A, Waydas C, Hallfeldt KKJ, et al. Value of thoracic computed tomography in the first assessment of severely injured patients with blunt chest trauma: results of a prospective study. *J Trauma.* 1997;43:405–412.

24. Song JK, Beaty CD. Diagnosis of pulmonary contusions and a bronchial laceration after a fall. *AJR Am J Roentgenol.* 1996;167:1510.

25. Putukian M. Pneumothorax and pneumomediastinum. *Clin Sports Med.* 2004;23(3):443–454.

26. Curtin SM, Tucker AM, Gens DR. Pneumothorax in sports: issues in recognition and follow-up care. *Phys Sportsmed.* 2000;28(8):23–32.

27. Currie GP, Alluri R, Christie GL, Legge JS. Pneumothorax: an update. *Postgrad Med J.* 2007;83(981):461–465.

28. Jenkinson SG. Pneumothorax. *Clin Chest Med.* 1985;6(1):153–161.

29. Erickson SM, Rich BSE. Pulmonary chest wall emergencies: on-site treatment of potentially fatal conditions. *Phys Sportsmed.* 1995;23(11):95–104.

30. Volk CP, McFarland EG, Horsmon G. Pneumothorax: on field recognition. *Phys Sportsmed.* 1995;23(10):43–46.

31. Jantz MA, Pierson DJ. Pneumothorax and barotraumas. *Clin Chest Med.* 1994;15(1):75–91.

32. Marnejon T, Sarac S, Cropp AJ. Spontaneous pneumothorax in weightlifters. *J Sports Med Phys Fitness.* 1995;35(2):124–126.

33. Simons S. Pneumothorax and exercise. *Sports Med Consult.* 2000;1(6):1–6.

34. Voge VM, Anthracite R. Spontaneous pneumothorax in the USAF aircrew population: a retrospective study. *Aviat Space Environ Med.* 1986;57:939–949.

35. Simoneaux SF, Murphy BJ, Tehranzadeh J. Spontaneous pneumothorax in a weightlifter. *Am J Sports Med.* 1990;18:647–648.

36. Harker CP, Neuman TS, Olson LK, et al. The roentgenographic findings associated with air embolism in sport scuba divers. *J Emerg Med.* 1993;11:443–449.

37. Bove AA, Dabis JC. *Bove and Davis' Diving Medicine.* 3rd ed. Philadelphia: WB Saunders; 1997:176–183, 270–277, 336–337.

38. Kizer KW. Dysbaric cerebral air embolism in Hawaii. *Ann Emerg Med.* 1987;16:535–541.

39. Partridge RA, Coley A, Bowie R, Woolard RH. Sports-related pneumothorax. *Ann Emerg Med.* 1997;30(4):539–541.

40. Fink DA, McGanity PL, Hagemeier KF 3rd, Schenck RC Jr. Pneumothorax in high school football. *Tex Med.* 1998;94(5):72–74.

41. Sadat-Ali M, Al-Arfaj AL, Mohanna J. Pneumothorax due to soccer injury. *Br J Sports Med.* 1986;20(2):91.

42. Miles JW, Barrett GR. Rib fractures in athletes. *Sports Med.* 1991;12(1):66–69.

43. Garcia VF, Gotschall CS, Eichelberger MR, et al. Rib fractures in children: a marker of severe trauma. *J Trauma.* 1990;30:695–700.

44. Armstrong CP, Vanderspuy J. The fractured scapula: importance in management based on series of 62 patients. *Injury.* 1984;15:324–329.

45. Ferro RT, McKeag DB. Neck pain and dyspnea in a swimmer: spontaneous pneumomediastinum presentation and return-to-play considerations. *Phys Sportsmed.* 1999;27(10):67–71.

46. Neer CS II. Fractures about the shoulder. In: Rockwood CA Jr, Green DP, eds. *Fractures.* Philadelphia: JB Lippincott; 1984:713–721.

47. Barton ED. Tension pneumothorax. *Curr Opin Pulm Med.* 1999;5(4):259–274.

48. Holmes JF, Sokolove PE, Brant WE, Kuppermann N. A clinical decision rule for identifying children with thoracic injuries after blunt torso trauma. *Ann Emerg Med.* 2002;39(5):492–499.

49. Baumann MH, Strange C, Heffner JE, et al. Management of spontaneous pneumothorax. An American College of Chest Physicians Delphi Consensus Statement. *Chest.* 1999;112:789–804.

50. Kirby TJ, Ginsberg RJ. Management of the pneumothorax and barotraumas. *Clin Chest Med.* 1992;13(1):97–112.

51. Franklin WJ, Arora G, Ayres NA. Pneumopericardium and pneumomediastinum after blunt chest trauma. *Tex Heart Inst J.* 2003;30(4):338–339.

52. Shanmuganathan K, Killeen K, Mirvis SE, White CS. Imaging of diaphragmatic injuries. *J Thorac Imaging.* 2000;15(2):104–111.

53. Rifat SF, Gilvydis RP. Blunt abdominal trauma in sports. *Curr Sports Med Rep.* 2003;2:93–97.

54. Terrell T, Lundquist B. Management of splenic injury and return-to-play decisions in a college football player. *Clin J Sports Med.* 2002;12:400–402.

55. Flik K, Callahan LR. Delayed splenic rupture in an amateur hockey player. *Clin J Sport Med.* 1998;8:309–310.

56. Gangei JJ, Binns OA, Young JS. Splenic injury after athletic trauma: a case report of splenic rupture induced by a lacrosse ball. *J Trauma.* 1999;46:736–737.

57. Putukian M, O'Connor FG, Stricker PR, et al. Mononucleosis and athletic participation: an evidence based subject review. *Clin J Sports Med.* 2008;18:309–315.

58. Walter KD. Radiographic evaluation of the patient with sport-related abdominal trauma. *Curr Sports Med Rep.* 2007;6:115–119.

59. Lee BC, Ormsby EL, McGahan JP, et al. The utility of sonography for the triage of blunt abdominal trauma patients to exploratory laparotomy. *AJR Am J Roentgenol.* 2007;188:415–421.

60. Noble VE, Blaivas M, Benkenship R, et al. Decision rule for imaging utilization in blunt abdominal trauma—where is ultrasound? *Ann Emerg Med.* 2010;55(5):487–489.

61. Emery KH. Splenic emergencies. *Radiol Clin North Am.* 1997;35:831–843.

62. Stylianos S, APSA Trauma Committee. Evidence based guidelines for resource utilization in children with isolated spleen or liver injury. *J Pediatr Surg.* 2000;35:164–169.

63. Poletti PA, Mirvis SE, Shanmuganathan K. CT criteria for management of blunt liver trauma: correlation with angiographic and surgical findings. *Radiology*. 2000;216(2):418–427.

64. Poletti PA, Kinkel K, Vermeulen B, et al. Blunt abdominal trauma: should US be used to detect both free fluid and organ injuries? *Radiology*. 2003;227:97–103.

65. Richards JR, Knopf NA, Wong L, et al. Blunt abdominal trauma in children: evaluation at emergency US. *Radiology*. 2002;222:749–754.

66. Pranikoff T, Hirschl R, Schlesinger QE, et al. Resolution of splenic injury after nonoperative management. *J Pediatr Surg*. 1994;29:1366–1369.

67. Brown RL, Irish MS, McCabe AJ, et al. Observation of splenic trauma: when is a little too much? *J Pediatr Surg*. 1999;34:1124–1126.

68. Wasvary H, Howells G, Villala M, et al. Nonoperative management of adult blunt splenic trauma: a 15 year experience. *Am Surg*. 1997;63:73–76.

69. Pearl RH, Wesson DE, Spence LJ, et al. Splenic injury: a 5 year update with improved results and changing criteria for conservative management. *J Pediatr Surg*. 1989;24:428–431.

70. Croce MA, Fabian TC, Menke PG, et al. Nonoperative management of blunt hepatic trauma is the treatment of choice in hemodynamically stable patients; results of a prospective trial. *Ann Surg*. 1995;221:744–753.

71. Taylor GA, O'Donnell BA, Sivit CJ, et al. Abdominal injury score: a clinical score for the assignment of risk in children after blunt trauma. *Radiology*. 1994;190:689–694.

72. Taylor GA, Eichelberger MR, Potter BM. Hematuria: a marker of abdominal injury in children after blunt trauma. *Ann Surg*. 1988;208:688–693.

73. Stalker HP, Kaufman RA, Stedje K. The significance of hematuria in children after blunt abdominal trauma. *AJR Am J Roentgenol*. 1990;154:569–571.

74. Stylianos S. Outcomes from pediatric solid organ injury: role of standardized care guidelines. *Curr Opin Pediatr*. 2005;17:402–406.

75. Mcleod RS, Webber E. Evidence-based guidelines for children with isolated spleen or liver injury. *Can J Surg*. 2004;44:458–460.

76. Holmes JF, Mao A, Awasthi S, et al. Validation of a prediction rule for the identification of children with intra-abdominal injuries after blunt torso trauma. *Ann Emerg Med*. 2009;54:528–533.

77. Holmes JF, Wisner DH, McGahan JP, Mower WR, Kuppermann N. Clinical prediction rules for identifying adults at very low risk for intra-abdominal injuries after blunt trauma. *Ann Emerg Med*. 2009;54:575–584.

78. Hegyes MS, Richardson MW, Miller MD. Knee dislocation: complications of non-operative and operative management. *Clin Sports Med*. 2000;19(3):519–543.

79. Shields L, Mital M, Cave EF. Complete dislocation of the knee: experience at the Massachusetts General Hospital. *J Trauma*. 1969;9(3):192–215.

80. Twaddle BC, Bidwell TA, Chapman JR, Simonia PT, Escobedo EM. MRI in complete knee dislocation: a prospective study of clinical, MRI, and surgical findings. *J Bone Joint Surgery Br*. 1996;18(4):573–579.

81. Schenck RC, Stannard JP, Wascher DC. Dislocations and fracture: dislocations of the knee. In: Bucholz RW, et al., eds. *Rockwood and Green's Fractures in Adults*. 6th ed. Philadelphia: Lippincott Williams & Wilkins; 2006:2031.

82. Johnson ME, Foster L, DeLee J. Neurologic and vascular injuries associated with knee ligament injuries. *Am J Sports Med*. 2008;36:2448–2462.

83. Green NE, Allen BL. Vascular injuries associated with dislocation of the knee. *J Bone Joint Surgery Am*. 1977;59(2):236–239.

84. Nicandri G, Chamberlain A, Wahl C. Practical management of knee dislocations. *Clin J Sports Med*. 2009;19:125–129.

85. DeBakey ME, Simeone FA. Battle injuries in the arteries in World War II; an analysis of 2471 cases. *Ann Surg*. 1946;123(4):534–579.

86. Kennedy JC. Complete dislocation of the knee joint. *J Bone Joint Surg Am*. 1963;45:889–904.

87. Niall DM, Nutton RW, Keating JF. Palsy of the common peroneal nerve after traumatic dislocation of the knee. *J Bone Joint Surg Br*. 2005;87:664–667.

88. Sisto DJ, Warren RF. Complete knee dislocation: a follow-up study of operative treatment. *Clin Orthop Relat Res*. 1985;198:94–101.

89. LaPrade RF, Terry GC. Injuries to the posterolateral aspect of the knee: association of anatomic injury patterns with clinical instability. *Am J Sports Med*. 1997;25(4):433–438.

90. Bottomley N, Williams A, Birch R, et al. Displacement of the common peroneal nerve in posterolateral corner injuries of the knee. *J Bone Joint Surg Br*. 2005;87(9):1225–1226.

91. McDonough B, Wojyts E. Multiligamentous injuries of the knee and associated vascular injuries. *Am J Sports Med*. 2009;37(1):156–159.

92. Barnes CJ, Pietrobon R, Higgins LD. Does the pulse examination in patients with traumatic knee dislocation predict a surgical arterial injury? *J Trauma*. 2002;53(6):1109–1114.

93. Mills WJ, Barei DP, McNair P. The value of the ankle-brachial index for diagnosing arterial injury after knee dislocation: a prospective study. *J Trauma*. 2004;24:403–407.

94. Byone RP, Miles WS, Bell RM, et al. Noninvasive diagnosis of vascular trauma by duplex ultrasonography. *J Vasc Surg*. 1991;14:346–352.

95. Levy BA, Zlowodzki MP, Graves M, Cole PA. Screening for extremity arterial injury with arterial pressure index. *Am J Emerg Med*. 2005;23:689–695.

96. Johansen K, Lynch K, Paun M, Copass M. Noninvasive vascular tests reliably exclude occult arterial trauma in injured extremities. *J Trauma*. 1991;31(4):515–519.

97. Treiman GS, Yellin AE, Weaver FA, et al. Examination of the patient with knee dislocation: the case for selective arteriography. *Arch Surg*. 1992;127:1056–1063.

98. Frykman GK, Wolf A, Coyle T. An algorithm for management of peripheral nerve injuries. *Orthop Clin North Am*. 1981;12(2):239–244.

99. U.S. Department of Health and Human Services, National Heart Lung and Blood Institute. Deep vein thrombosis. http://www.nhlbi.nih.gov/health/dci/Diseases/Dvt/DVT_WhatIs.html.

100. Verstraete M. Prevention and treatment of venous thromboembolism after major surgery. *Trauma*. 1991;1:39–51.

101. Shackford S, Moser K. Deep vein thrombosis and pulmonary embolism in trauma patients. *J Intensive Care Med*. 1988;3:87–98.

102. Prandoni P, Polistena P, Bernardi E, et al. Upper-extremity deep vein thrombosis: risk factors, diagnosis, and complications. *Arch Intern Med*. 1997;157(1):57–62.

103. Seed WA. Pulmonary embolism: part 1. *Vasc Med*. 1991;2:71–83.

104. Knudson MT, Dawson R. Prevention of venous thromboembolism in trauma patients. *J Trauma*. 1994;37:480–487.

105. Treat SD, Smith PA, Wen DY, Kinderknecht JJ. Deep vein thrombosis of the subclavian vein in a college volleyball player. *Am J Sports Med*. 2004;32:529–532.

106. Snead D, Marberry KM, Rowdon G. Unique treatment regimen for effort thrombosis in the non-dominant extremity of an overhead athlete: a case report. *J Athl Train*. 2009;44(1):94–97.

107. Adelman MA, Stone DH, Riles TS, et al. Multidisciplinary approach to the treatment of Paget-Schroetter syndrome. *Ann Vasc Surg*. 1997;11:149–154.

108. Rutherford RB, Hurlbert SN. Primary subclavian-axillary vein thrombosis: consensus and commentary. *Cardiovasc Surg*. 1996:4:420–423.

109. Nemmers DW, Thorpe PE, Knibbe MA, Beard DW. Upper extremity venous thrombosis: case report and literature review. *Orthop Rev*. 1990;19:164–172.

Lightning

Katie M. Walsh, EdD, ATC

Mary Ann Cooper, MD

Lightning has intrigued people long before Ben Franklin flew a kite in a thunderstorm. The phenomenon has been viewed with both awe and fear throughout history. Death by lightning is the second-highest storm-related fatality; only flooding kills more people annually.[1,2] Lightning kills approximately 50 people and injures hundreds more each year.[3–7] The overwhelming majority of fatalities are attributed to being outdoors during a thunderstorm. According to the National Lightning Safety Institute (NLSI), during the years 2000 to 2006, lightning in the United States caused 12,000 wildfires and burned an average of 5.2 million acres annually.[8] Property damages exceed $32 million dollars annually.[8] There are about 25 million cloud-to-ground lightning strikes annually in the United States.[9] Although more and more people know how to prevent lightning injury, there are always some who refuse to acknowledge lightning's danger. This chapter addresses the properties of lightning, the medical consequences of being injured by lightning, and prevention strategies to lower one's risk of being injured or killed by lightning.

Pathomechanics of Lightning and Thunder

Although there have been reports of lightning striking "out of the blue,"[10] the typical approach of a thunderstorm is quite noticeable. Lightning is an extremely high current (tens of kiloamperes) electrical discharge most often resulting from interaction within or between clouds, and between clouds and the ground.[11] Most lightning is cloud to cloud. Because cloud-to-cloud lightning does not cause harm on the earth, this chapter focuses on cloud-to-ground lightning.

As clouds form over the earth, heavier ice and water gather in the lower portions of the cloud, creating a negative charge. It is the ice in the clouds that is critical to the development of lightning.[9] An electric charge is generated between the cloud (typically negative) and the earth (positive) as the thunderstorm passes over, until a path of ionized air begins to form. Leader strokes leave the cloud, creating an ionized channel toward the earth. Each subsequent stroke (stepped leader) follows the established path downward in an intermittent progression (hence the term *stepped* leader). A leader stroke channels through virgin air, whereas the stepped leader follows the channel created by the leader stroke.[11] This intermittent drive toward the earth occurs in milliseconds, yielding a flickering aspect to lightning. In reality, each leader stroke is moving closer to completing the channel with the earth. When lightning gets within a few tens of meters from the ground, upward streamers are induced in any objects that project above ground level. Attachment occurs when one or more downward leaders joins with one or more upward streamers. Upward return strokes fill the channel[11,12] and create a wave that rapidly heats the lightning channel to temperatures of up to 50K (five times hotter than the surface of the sun) and generates a channel pressure upward of 10 atm (the earth is 1 atm).[11–13] The pressure wave results in channel expansion, intense optical radiation, and an outward-propagating shock wave that produces the associated thunder.[11]

The shock wave produced by lightning has caused property damage in addition to casualties. The repercussions of thunder have caused glass windows to be broken, and drywall to be torn away from the nails securing it.[8,13] Thunder noise is expressed in decibels (dB) and registers about 120 dB close to the ground stroke.[13] That noise level is comparable to sitting in front of the speakers at a rock concert. One of the more common consequences of lightning injury is a ruptured tympanic membrane. Given the noise level and concussive pressure of lightning, this is understandable.

The lightning channel has been reported to travel up to 10 miles away from the main thunderstorm body.[14] People have been killed from a distant storm, while the sky overhead is relatively clear of clouds.[10] Lightning does occur in the winter during snowstorms.[15] In recent years, there have been reports of snow-related lightning deaths.[13] Lightning can also form due to volcanic eruptions, as a result of the dust created in forest fires, and near fireballs created by nuclear explosions and is very common with tornadoes.[11,13]

Signs of impending thunderstorms are very noticeable. Clouds thicken and darken, the wind shifts or becomes faster, and the humidity changes. Paying attention to the weather in the local and surrounding vicinity can make the difference between life and death, particularly with fast-moving violent weather. The National Weather Service (NWS) broadcasts severe storm warnings to the public. A *watch* indicates that conditions are favorable for severe weather, whereas a *warning* is indicative that severe weather has been detected in the area. Neither a watch nor a warning is definitive to a particular storm cell, nor to lightning in general.

The warning sign of thunder must not be ignored, because lightning causes thunder. As the NWS advises, "When thunder roars, go indoors." On occasion, thunder may be muffled by snow, mountainous terrain, or local noise. As loud as thunder is near the ground strike, it is rarely heard over a distance of 10 miles.[16] One must be observant of the weather patterns and forecasts prior to participating in outdoor events in the summer.

How Lightning Relates to Electrical Injury

Lightning and generated electricity are the same physical phenomenon. However, that is about where any similarity, including in the immediate injuries they cause, ends (Table 10.1). The physics (and the mathematics to describe them) of the two common types of electrical phenomena with which we are familiar are as dissimilar as the physics of Newton and of Einstein. The rise and fall of lightning energy levels is quite different from more familiar household AC or DC current. Extrapolation of knowledge of electrical injuries to the effects of lightning will almost always be wrong, because lightning injury is not "scalable" to electrical injury. It is far better to learn what lightning does than to try to predict its effects using "common sense."

For instance, most people assume that given the incredibly high amperage and voltage of lightning, the primary cause of death from lightning must be burns. In reality, burns occur in fewer than one third of lightning survivors and, in the vast majority of cases, are quite superficial when they do occur.[17] Lightning does not last long enough to cause significant burns. In addition, most lightning injuries are indirect, so that not all of the energy is delivered to the victim.[18,19] It is unlikely that lightning burns in developed countries will require even rudimentary treatment and even more rare for them to require grafting, in contrast to high-energy electrical injuries, which often result in deep muscle damage, extensive time in the intensive care unit and burn care unit, and major amputations. The vast majority of lightning survivors, on the other hand, can be safely discharged from the emergency department. In fact, a significant number of lightning survivors do not present to an emergency department or seek medical care for several days after the injury.

Technically produced electricity is a voltage phenomenon.

TABLE 10.1	A Comparison of the Properties of Lightning and Electricity	
	Lightning	Power Line/Electricity
Voltage	10 million to 2 billion V	110 to 70,000 V
Amperage	20,000 to 200,000 A	<1000 A
Duration	1/1000 to 1/10 second	Seconds
Pathway	Flashover	Internal
Burns	Uncommon and superficial	Deep

Source: Reprinted from Muehlberger T, Vogt PM, Munster AM. The long-term consequences of lightning injuries. *Burns*. 2001;27:829–833. Copyright © (2001) with permission from Elsevier.

Lightning, on the other hand, is a current phenomenon, and when attachment of lightning from a cloud to an object on the ground occurs, all voltage disappears. The classic six Kouwenhoven factors often discussed in electrical injury have little application to lightning injury. To be fair, there are two similarities: (1) in some circumstances, both types of injury may have significant barotrauma with blunt injuries in addition to any burn or electrical injury; and (2) both may cause significant neurologic damage that may manifest after the acute phase as chronic pain, brain injury, cognitive deficits, and other neurologically based disability. The critical difference is the amount of time during which victims receive the electrical charge.

In electrical injuries, a victim remains in contact with current (albeit a lower voltage and amperage than lightning) until the power source is terminated. This could take several seconds. Providing care to a victim of an electrical shock injury is not safe until the current is shut off. Otherwise, the first responder would join the connection between the victim and the circuit and become prey to the same charge as the victim. In lightning injuries, contact with current is literally milliseconds. The current tends to "flash over" a person. Because lightning victims are not connected to a power source, they are safe to touch and treat as long as the rescuer does not endanger himself or herself by entering the storm before the lightning danger has passed. Both injuries require prompt, aggressive resuscitative efforts.[20,21]

More than 99% of the body's resistance to electric current is at the skin.[22] Once a current has breached the skin, it can cause great damage internally, largely due to the aqueous nature of the internal tissues. Because lightning flashes over the skin, the deep internal injuries typical of electrical shock victims are not common in the lightning victim. The rapid heating of the lightning channel has been demonstrated to cause sweat to evaporate with such force and speed that victims' clothing and shoes are literally blown off.[16,23] In flashover injuries, this energy rarely exceeds the normal resistance of the skin.[24] In both electrical shock and lightning injuries, cardiovascular consequences are likely.

Casualty Demographics

The National Oceanic and Atmospheric Administration (NOAA) maintains casualty demographics on lightning through its publication *Storm Data*. Consistently, lightning has been confirmed to occur most frequently in the summer months (May through September) and between the hours of 10:00 AM and 7:00 PM.[9] This time frame coincides with athletic and outdoor activity, which makes awareness even more critical. As with most weather-related casualties, July is the month with the most fatalities. The southeastern and midwestern United States are the areas with the greatest casualties. Florida has led national lightning fatality statistics for decades.[9,25] It also leads the country in the number of lightning flashes, with nearly 1.5 million cloud-to-ground flashes annually.[26] In the last decade, the top ten states with the highest fatalities due to lightning were (in descending order) Florida, Colorado, Texas, Georgia, North Carolina, Alabama, South Carolina, Ohio, Pennsylvania, and Louisiana.[25] The data for 2007 to 2009 also demonstrate that 95% of lightning fatalities involved people who were outdoors when they were injured.[27]

Military and occupational data are consistent with NOAA records. Lightning strikes injured 350 military personnel in a 3-year period between 1998 and 2001.[28] In a 10-year period, lightning was identified as being among the top ten mechanisms of injury by external causes in relation to years of life lost.[29] The occupations with the greatest propensity for fatal lightning injury were agriculture, forestry, fishing, construction, and manufacturing.[30,31] The average lightning victim lost 41 years of life.[29] All of the occupations had a common denominator: they were outdoor professions. The military report also illuminated the danger of multiple people being affected at once, as 87% of the strikes involved more than one person. One strike injured 44 persons.[28] Other reports have also documented multiple casualties from lightning, which underlines the importance of vacating to a safe place prior to lightning danger becoming imminent.[32–35]

The activities in which people were engaged at the time of being injured by lightning also show a trend. Eighteen percent of recent deaths involved people in or around the water.[27] They were swimming, fishing, boating, jet skiing, or scuba diving. Swimming pools, regardless of whether they are indoor or out, are not safe from the effects of lightning.[36,37] Eight percent of victims were headed to a safe place to wait out the storm when they were fatally injured. These data do not include survivors, who tend to constitute 10 times the number of fatalities.[38]

Being indoors is not entirely safe from harm by lightning. Lightning can enter a building via the plumbing or electrical system. Therefore, using water (e.g., washing dishes, showering) or electrical devices or appliances (e.g., computers) is not safe during a thunderstorm. Neither is using a land-line telephone. The electrical charge from the strike has traveled through telephone lines into buildings and injured people.[39] Other unsafe areas in buildings are open doors and windows—this is a result of the static charges induced in these structures, not because lightning is going through them to ground. Because current has an affinity for the path of least resistance, it tends to follow electrical, telephone, and plumbing lines. Staying indoors and away from these channels increases your chance of protection from lightning.

Some places that people sought for refuge from a storm have contributed to their demise. Nearly all fatalities occurred while the victim was outdoors,[27] with the majority occurring to those sheltering under trees. Many also happened to people who sought protection from the storm under "shelters" that provided no safety from lightning. **Table 10.2** lists places that do not provide adequate protection from lightning.

TABLE 10.2 Places That Are *Not* Safe for Waiting Out a Lightning Storm	
Tent	Convertible car
Screened-in porch	Golf cart
Picnic shelter	In garage with open garage door
Rain shelter	Storage shed (garden/tools/athletic equipment)
Beach pavilion	Under a tall tree
Bus stop shelter	Under an awning
Dug-out	Under bleachers

Mechanisms of Injury

To fully appreciate the type of damage people suffer as a consequence of lightning, one must understand the basic mechanisms of how lightning can create injury. There are six mechanisms by which lightning strikes can injure people:

- A **direct injury** occurs when lightning hits the person with no intermediary object taking the impact. These are typically strikes to the head, because that is often the highest point between the ground and the cloud.
- A **contact injury** is sustained when a person is in contact with the object struck by the lightning. Examples include leaning against a tree or tent pole, holding an umbrella, sitting on bleachers, holding hard-wired telephones, and being in contact with plumbing or another object that transmits the charge to the person.
- A **side flash** is the mechanism that causes injury to those seeking shelter under trees, in a dugout or picnic shelter, and so on (see Table 10.2). People mistakenly believe that if they are out of the rain, they are safe from lightning. In a side flash, lightning strikes an object (a tree, for example) and a portion side-steps to a nearby person.
- The mechanism most disconcerting for participants in athletics and outdoor recreation is when a single bolt hits the ground and creates a **step voltage** (also known as a **ground current**). In this situation, there is danger of suffering the effects of lightning energy for a considerable distance from where the lightning hit the ground. The step voltage can radiate outward from the strike and cause multiple casualties, and is the mechanism responsible for the majority of lightning injuries.[18]
- An **upward leader** is an incomplete lightning channel arising from the ground through a person.[40] It does not complete the lightning channel, but nevertheless the person suffers the effects of the energy generated by the upward leader.
- **Blunt injury**. The energy created by the lightning channel acts similarly to an explosion, creating a shock wave. A person can sustain violent muscular contractions, be thrown a distance, or suffer internal damage due to the concussive nature of the strike. Injuries sustained via blunt injury include ruptured tympanic membranes, fractures, dislocations, and contusions.

direct injury A mechanism of lightning injury by which the lightning strikes the person or object directly.

contact injury A mechanism of lightning injury by which the lightning strikes an object to which the victim is connected.

side flash A mechanism of lightning injury by which the lightning strikes a nearby object, then a portion of the strike side-steps to a nearby person.

step voltage A mechanism of lightning injury by which the lightning strikes the ground and radiates outward from the strike to affect those within the radiating current. Also known as *ground current*.

upward leader A mechanism of lightning injury by which the victim becomes a weak, incomplete part of an electrical channel attempting to complete the lightning channel to earth.

blunt injury A mechanism of lightning injury by which the lightning strike causes a concussive force creating blunt injuries such as ruptured tympanic membranes or violent muscular contractions that cause dislocations or fractures.

Prevention Strategies

Because thunderstorms can arise and dissipate precipitously, the National Weather Service will never be able to warn of each dangerous situation like it does for weather hazards such as tornadoes, hurricanes, and floods. The majority of lightning deaths occur to individuals who are alone, not in large groups.[27] Avoiding becoming a casualty of lightning thus requires personal responsibility for one's own safety. Being aware of the weather conditions, especially in the summer months, is very important. **Table 10.3** includes federal weather-monitoring websites (NOAA and NWS) that can assist with the gross estimation of current weather. There is often a significant time lag between detection and broadcast of the data, so caution should be used in relying on these sites for real-time warning. No place outside is safe when thunderstorms are in the area. Modifying, postponing, or canceling outdoor activities and events may prevent injury and loss of life. The vast majority of deaths since 2005 have been to people who were within a few feet of safety but chose to continue their outdoor activity or left a good shelter prior to the storm passing.

Prevention begins with education and appreciation of the danger of lightning. It is absolutely critical that adults who supervise or are responsible for children (e.g., teachers, lifeguards, coaches, scout leaders, camp directors) know and execute lightning safety guidelines.[41–44] Further, teaching children simple lightning safety guidelines is strongly recommended. The NOAA's Lightning Safety website

TABLE 10.3	Related Websites
Lightning Safety	http://www.lightningsafety.noaa.gov/
Lightning Strike and Electric Shock Survivors, International (LSESSI)	http://www.lightning-strike.org
National Athletic Trainers' Association	http://www.nata.org
National Collegiate Athletic Association	http://www.ncaa.org
National Lightning Safety Institute	http://www.lightningsafety.com
National Oceanic and Atmospheric Administration (NOAA)	http://www.noaa.gov
National Weather Service (NWS)	http://www.nws.noaa.gov

(see Table 10.3) has outstanding educational materials suitable for youth, as well as catchy phrases to teach children to remember what to do (Table 10.4). In other situations, adults may be under the direction of others, such as in collegiate athletics, where young adults are led by coaches. The National Collegiate Athletic Association (NCAA) declares that an identified individual must have "unchallengeable authority" to modify or cancel workout sessions or events if lightning is a threat.[43]

Strategies to employ for prevention include adhering to published lightning safety guidelines. The NCAA, the National Athletic Trainers' Association (NATA), and the American Meteorological Society have all published documents addressing lightning safety. All of these guidelines stress the importance of knowledge of weather in the region, clear directions regarding when to vacate and return to the outdoors, and knowledge and use of buildings or areas deemed safer from lightning consequences.[41–44]

Keeping on top of developing weather can include using the NWS website and weather radios. Subscribing to a professional lightning detection service that has been externally verified may be worth the cost when working with large groups of people. It requires considerably more time to evacuate masses at large events to safe buildings than it does to clear a swimming pool. Hand-held personal lightning detectors have not been sufficiently reviewed to determine their effectiveness.[44,45]

Identifying and knowing the properties of a safe place to go to prevent a lightning injury is also a part of lightning safety strategy. Substantial buildings where people live and work are a good place to wait out storms.[4] Too often, people resort to a *shelter* instead of a building. A shelter typically will not prevent lightning from striking the person via a side flash.[46,47] Most people identify shelters with a place of refuge from the rain. Current lightning protection codes establish that a building is safe from total destruction by lightning, but these codes do not address the safety of the occupants within these dwellings. Whereas structures and safe buildings all have a roof, certain structures often do not have the other properties required for safety from lightning hazard—namely, four solid walls, a roof, plumbing, and wiring, all of which are common to places

TABLE 10.4	Lightning Safety Catch Phrases and Educational Tools

No Place Outside Is Safe When Thunderstorms Are in the Area!

When Lightning Roars, Go Indoors

When You Hear It [thunder], Clear It; When You See It [lightning], Flee It

Half an Hour Since Thunder Roars, Now It's Safe to Go Outdoors!

Leon the Lion's Safety Game (http://www.lightningsafety.noaa.gov/multimedia/Lightning_Game.swf)

Source: Modified from National Weather Service. Lightning Safety. Available at: http://www.lightningsafety.noaa.gov/. Accessed April 15, 2011.

people live or work. Lightning protection and grounding of a building is different from what is needed to protect individuals in a shelter. Certain structures are safer than others. Substantial buildings that have wiring, plumbing, and telephone service have consistently been determined to be safe places, as long as one avoids the indoor hazards discussed previously (e.g., land-line telephones and game boxes, water use, computer use, etc.).[3,11–13,44,48–50] Another safe place is a fully enclosed metal car with all the windows fully rolled up.[2,6,13,44,48–50]

When a large group of children were injured by lightning while sleeping in a tent, a contributory factor may have been their body positions on the ground.[33] Because they were unprotected by not being in a substantial building, and lightning travels along the ground, laying flat afforded more opportunity for the lightning strike to traverse through the children. This mass casualty situation might not have occurred had the children been in a building deemed safe from lightning.

In addition to the unsafe shelters listed in Table 10.2, people often have sought protection from lightning hazard in other places. Flagpoles; open fields; near or on elevated coaching stands, deer stands, or bleachers; metal fences; and beaches, swimming pools, lakes, and the ocean are not safe. Golf carts, bicycles, motorcycles, and open farm equipment offer no protection from lightning injury.[51,52] When outdoors in an unfamiliar area, be certain to inquire about the nature of weather systems indigenous to the regions. For example, in some mountainous areas, lightning occurs much earlier in the day than in the Southeast. Tracking storms that suddenly appear through valleys is challenging, so a clear appreciation of the characteristics of thunderstorms specific to the locale is paramount.[53]

It is important to note that nothing "attracts" lightning including metal. Mobile phones and iPods do not cause one to be injured by their presence. Instead, it is likely that victims using such devices were distracted by them and not paying attention to the weather surrounding them.[54–58]

Recognition

Sometimes it is difficult to unravel the cause of injury when a lightning incident to an individual is unwitnessed or when an entire group is affected and remembers only that they encountered inclement weather at the time of their disaster. In contrast, team sporting and mass participation events disrupted by lightning often have many witnesses, although they may have differing accounts. Immediate response to injured individuals by athletic trainers, coaches, and emergency personnel shifts the focus to a multi-casualty incident (MCI) response. Because it is unlikely that the lightning is an isolated event, the main concern becomes to secure the scene and move everyone to safety until all lightning danger has passed.

Treatment

Death by lightning is due to cardiac arrest at the time of the injury.[59,60] A lightning strike can cause fibrillation or asystole. Cardiac physiology allows for automaticity, in which the heart spontaneously restarts itself. In the absence of respiration, cardiac function may cease a second time, and without intervention, a person will die.

Victims often present in asystole, pulseless, and with fixed and dilated pupils. It is absolutely essential for rescuers to violate the basic principle of triage (that is, "treat the living first") and provide cardiopulmonary resuscitation to those who appear to be dead. People injured by lightning and found with asystole and fixed and dilated pupils, even with a Glasgow Coma Scale (GCS) score as low as 5, have survived following aggressive resuscitation.[61–64] Those who receive delayed care often suffer hypoxia and do not usually fully recover. The current literature notes two victims in asystole with GCS scores of 3; it was not documented how long each was without cardiopulmonary ventilation, but both succumbed.[65,66]

Survivors of lightning strikes suffer a number of physical and psychological symptoms. Neurologic symptoms are the most common, but ocular, tympanic, and dermatologic systems often sustain damage as well. There are a few unique physical manifestations of lightning injury. **Keraunoparalysis** designates a transient paralysis, extreme vasoconstriction, and sensory disturbance caused by a lightning strike.[67]

keraunoparalysis
A transient paralysis, extreme vasoconstriction, and sensory disturbance caused by a lightning strike.

Cherington noticed that the majority of damage involved the central nervous system rather than the peripheral nervous system,[68] and established four levels of neurologic complications subsequent to lightning strikes.[69] Category I includes transient symptoms of numbness, weakness, loss of consciousness, and headaches. These rarely require long-term intervention or rehabilitation.[59,69] Category II involves protracted or permanent symptoms. Most serious is posthypoxic encephalopathy resulting from delayed resuscitation. This condition, if not fatal, can be extremely debilitating and is irreversible.[68] Intracranial hemorrhages and persistent and progressive neuropsychological dysfunction are also in category II.

Category III patients have delayed neurologic syndromes, often displaying new neurologic signs or symptoms long after the initial damage has occurred. The link between the lightning strike and the subsequent damage is not always established. Syndromes in this category include movement disorders, seizures, and amyotrophic lateral sclerosis (ALS). All have been rarely reported in lightning strike survivors, and a definite relationship has not been established.[68,70]

The final category of neurologic complications of lightning strikes is category IV: lightning-linked complications resulting from the barotrauma from lightning. Blunt trauma injuries, including intracranial hemorrhages caused by trauma and spinal injuries, fall into this category. Ocular and tympanic injuries are common in lightning strike survivors. The intense optical radiation can create a number of eye injuries. Cataracts have been reported to occur fairly early, within the first few weeks to months of the injury.[71] Anisocoria, hyphema, retinal detachment, photophobia, and transient blindness have also been reported.[16,46,72] Ruptured tympanic membranes are reported in 30% to 50% of survivors,[16,39,60] and a few suffer fractured ossicles. Follow-up studies indicate that the majority of hearing deficits have been restored to preinjury levels.[47] Conductive hearing loss has been infrequently documented in association with eardrum rupture.[57] Injuries to the eighth cranial nerve cause vertigo, persistent tinnitus, dizziness, and ataxia. Facial palsies may also occur.[16,39]

Fewer than one third of survivors have burns or skin markings. This is most likely because of the frequently indirect nature of lightning injury and the very short time of exposure. Lightning flashes over the dermis, preventing the deep penetrating burns that are common with electric shock injuries. Burns are found, however, along the sweat patterns in the skin. They tend to congregate in the midaxillary region, below the breasts, and down the midchest and are first- or second-degree burns. Other burns are due to contact with metal (e.g., jewelry, belt buckles, underwire in bras, body piercings, cleats on shoes). Keraunographic markings **(Figure 10.1)**, also referred to as Lichtenberg figures, are a pathognomonic sign of a lightning strike but rarely occur. These markings are transient and may be attributed to vascular and dermatologic reactions to lightning; they are not true burns.[16,60,73]

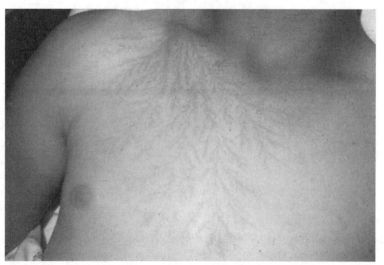

Figure 10.1   Keraunographic markings on a lightning strike patient.

Long-Term Sequelae of Lightning Strikes

The majority of lightning strike victims survive, but many may have significant disability. Their symptoms may be debilitating, persistent, and have little chance of improvement over time. Neurologic sequelae are found in 70% of lightning survivors.[24,74] **Table 10.5** summarizes the common chronic symptoms reported by lightning strike survivors. The symptoms are similar to those of a traumatic brain injury and are difficult to quantify via traditional medical testing.[69] Electroencephalograms (EEG), computed tomography (CT), radiography, and magnetic resonance imaging (MRI) typically yield results within normal ranges.[23,69]

TABLE 10.5	Long-Term Sequelae of Lightning Survivors

Headache

Dizziness

Personality changes

Concentration issues

Depression

Self-isolation

Chronic pain

Sleep disturbances

Behavioral changes

Absence-type seizure activity

Palpitations

Sources: Adapted from Cooper MA. Disability, not death, is the main problem with lightning injury. *Natl Weather Digest.* 2001;25(1,2):43–47; and Muehlberger T, Vogt PM, Munster AM. The long-term consequences of lightning injuries. *Burns.* 2001;27:829–833.

Life skills may be altered in the lightning survivor. Despite the fact that nearly one third of lightning injuries are work-related and survivors may qualify for disability benefits, it is often difficult for them to be awarded disability benefits.[2] Frequently, short-term memory is impaired, and survivors returning to work may be unable to learn new skills, organize thoughts, or multitask, resulting in unemployment.[23] Survivors may suffer unrelenting headaches that do not respond to traditional relief pharmaceuticals. Personality changes, depression, loss of cognitive reasoning, and self-isolation are common.[23]

Neuropsychological testing has recently been strongly suggested for those affected by lightning.[39,60,69] Cognitive therapy and counseling has also been shown to be beneficial.[39] An international support group for survivors and loved ones has been successful in addressing issues and concerns germane to survivors.[75] Within the group organization, support can be found for both survivors and family members who seek to better understand the effects of lightning injury. There is solidarity and comfort in knowing that others (both survivors and family) are experiencing and coping with the life changes associated with the trauma.

Return-to-Play Considerations

Most of the time, it is not a question of whether an individual can return to the same game, as it is likely that the entire event has been disrupted. Whether someone was injured by direct strike, contact, ground current, or upward streamer makes little difference. The individual injuries are what will direct the individual's care.

The vast majority of victims will not need hospitalization, although some may be too confused or shaken up to resume play. It is safe for an individual to return to play in a later game if he or she is clear minded enough to follow commands, is physically coordinated, has good balance, has overcome most of the musculoskeletal pain, and can pass the SCAT2. For the individual who only experienced tingling, hair standing on end, or similar static electrical feeling with no other symptoms, there is no danger in immediately returning to play.

Summary

Death from lightning is a largely preventable occurrence. There is no place outdoors that is safe from the effects of this phenomenon, and most so-called shelters under which people seek refuge from the rain are not proper protection from lightning. The best practice is to identify a substantial building in which to wait out the storm. Everyone should be inside the building by 30 seconds from the time lightning is seen to when thunder is heard. Waiting a full 30 minutes after the last lightning or thunder is critical before resuming outdoor activity.

Those injured by lightning are safe to touch and treat, as long as the rescuer is not also in danger of being struck. Because lightning victims may appear to be dead (pulseless, with fixed and dilated pupils), it is paramount to begin aggressive cardiopulmonary resuscitation and not adhere to normal triage protocol.

With education, most lightning injuries and deaths can be averted. It is imperative that the message gets out that there is no place outdoors that is safe during a thunderstorm. It is critical that everyone be responsible for his or her own safety, but also to be a vocal spokesperson promoting lightning safety.

Clinical Case Scenarios

1. An adult male was working on his riding lawn mower in his open garage during a lightning storm. He was using an electric drill on the lawn mower when lightning struck the power transformer on the power line outside of his home. The resulting surge traveled through the electrical wires to the drill and threw him across the garage floor. He suffered no reported permanent damage.
   1. How could he have prevented this injury?
2. An 18-year-old woman and her grandmother were in a park in Omaha, Nebraska, on a July afternoon, waiting for fireworks. They had decided to pass the time during a storm by sitting on the lawn under a tarp. The grandmother reported that the victim screamed and was lifted off the ground 6 inches when she was struck by lightning. She remained conscious, but was confused and disoriented. She was combative in the ambulance, but discharged from the hospital 3.5 hours after she arrived. Her resulting injuries included temporary right-sided paralysis/weakness, chronic fatigue syndrome, migraines, and lethargy.
   1. How could they have prevented this injury?
   2. How many different things can you identify that these two women did wrong in terms of their personal safety?
   3. What other long-term effects could lightning cause?
3. A North Carolina mother was home with her teenage daughter during a thunderstorm when she decided to call her husband, who was putting in a swimming pool, and warn him of the impending storm. The mother was using the land-line telephone when lightning struck and thunder resounded over the house. Because she was conscious and functional, she did not seek medical attention. A few weeks after the incident, she began to suffer petit mal seizures due to the traumatic brain injury caused by the lightning strike.
   1. How did this injury occur?
   2. How could it have been prevented?
   3. If lightning hit the house, how was it that the daughter was not affected?

Key Terms

blunt injury

contact injury

direct strike

ground current

keraunoparalysis

side flash

step voltage

upward leader

References

1. Curran EB, Holle RL, López RE. *Lightning Fatalities, Injuries, and Damage Reports in the United States: 1959–1994.* Washington, DC: National Oceanic and Atmospheric Administration; 1997. Technical Memorandum NWS SR-193.
2. López RE, Holle RL, Heitkamp TA, et al. The underreporting of lightning injuries and deaths in Colorado. *Bull Am Meteorol Soc.* 1993;74:2171–2178.
3. Duclos PJ, Sanderson LM. An epidemiological description of lightning-related deaths in the United States. *Int J Epidemiol.* 1990;19:673–679.
4. Craig SR. When lightning strikes: pathophysiology and treatment of lightning injuries. *Postgrad Med.* 1986;79:109–112, 121–123.
5. Zegel FH. Lightning deaths in the United States: a seven-year survey from 1959 to 1965. *Weatherwise.* 1967;20:169.
6. López RE, Holle RL. Demographics of lightning casualties. *Semin Neurol.* 1995;15:286–295.
7. National Weather Service. Lightning safety. Available at: http://www.lightningsafety.noaa.gov. Accessed June 2010.
8. National Lightning Safety Institute. Annual USA lightning costs and losses. Available at: http://www.lightningsafety.com/nlsi_lls/nlsi_annual_usa_losses.htm. Accessed June 2010.
9. National Weather Service. Lightning science. Available at: http://www.lightningsafety.noaa.gov/science.htm. Accessed June 2010.
10. Dwyer JR. A bolt out of the blue. *Sci Am.* 2005;292(5):64–71.
11. Rakov VA, Uman MA. *Lightning: Physics and Effects.* Cambridge, England: Cambridge University Press; 2003.
12. Uman MA. *All About Lightning.* New York: Dover Publications; 1986.
13. Vavrek JR, Holle RL, López RE. Updated lightning safety recommendations. In: *Preprints of the American Meteorological Society 8th Symposium on Education; January 10–15, 1999; Dallas, TX.* 1993;22(pt 2):378–387.
14. Holle RL, López RE, Howard KW, Vavrek J, Allsopp J. Safety in the presence of lightning. *Semin Neurol.* 1995;15:375–380.
15. Cherington M, Breed DW, Yarnell PR, Smith WE. Lightning injuries during snowy conditions. *Br J Sports Med.* 1998;32(4): 333–335.
16. Gatewood MO, Zane RD. Lightning injuries. *Emerg Med Clin North Am.* 2003;22(2):369–403.
17. Cooper MA, Andrews CJ, Holle RL. Lightning injuries. In: Auerbach PS, ed. *Wilderness Medicine.* 5th ed. St. Louis, MO: Mosby/Elsevier; 2007.
18. Cooper MA, Holle RL, Andrews C. Distribution of lightning injury mechanism. Presented at 20th International Lightning Detection Conference, Tucson, AZ. Available at: http://www.vaisala.co.jp/files/Short_notice_outdoor_lightning_risk_reduction_-_evaluating_its_performance_and_discussion_on_why_it_should_not_be_taught.pdf
19. Cooper MA, Holle RL. How to use public education to change lightning safety standards (and save lives and injuries). Paper presented at: American Meteorological Society 14th Symposium on Education; January 2005; San Diego, CA.
20. Fontanarosa PB. Electrical shock and lightning strike. *Ann Emerg Med.* 1993;22(pt 2):378–387.
21. Adukauskiene D, Vizgirdaite V, Mazeikiene S. Electrical injuries [in Lithuanian]. *Medicina (Kaunas).* 2007;43(3):259–266.
22. Fish RM, Geddes LA. Conduction of electrical current to and through the human body: a review. *Eplasty.* 2009;9:e44.
23. Cooper MA. Disability, not death, is the main problem with lightning injury. *Natl Weather Digest.* 2001;25(1,2):43–47.
24. Muehlberger T, Vogt PM, Munster AM. The long-term consequences of lightning injuries. *Burns.* 2001;27:829–833.
25. Holle RL. Number of lightning deaths by state from 2000–2009. Available at: http://www.nws.noaa.gov/om/hazstats.shtml. Accessed May 2010.
26. Holle RL. Number of cloud-to-ground flashes by state from 1996–2008. National Lightning Detection Network. May 2009.
27. Holle RL. Summary of 2007–2009 US lightning fatalities. National Lightning Detection Network. November 2009.
28. Lightning-associated injuries and deaths among military personnel—United States, 1998–2001. *MMWR.* 2002;51(38): 859–862.
29. Bailer AJ, Bena JF, Stayner LT, Halperin WE, Parks RM. External cause-specific summaries of occupational fatal injuries. Part II: an analysis of years of potential life lost. *Am J Ind Med.* 2003;43:251–261.
30. Robinson CF, Halperin WE, Alterman T, et al. Mortality patterns among construction workers in the United States. *Occup Med.* 1995;10(2):269–283.
31. Adekoya N, Nolte KB. Struck-by-lightning deaths in the United States. *J Environ Health.* 2005;67(9):45–50, 58.
32. Cherington M, Martorano FJ, Siebuhr LV, Stieg RL, Yarnell PR. Childhood lightning injuries on the playing field. *J Emerg Med.* 1994;12(1):39–41.
33. Carte AE, Anderson RB, Cooper MA. A large group of children struck by lightning. *Ann Emerg Med.* 2002;39(6):665–670.
34. Duppel H, Lobermann M, Reisinger EC. Hit by lightning out of the blue. *Dtsch Med Wochenschr.* 2009;134(23):1214–1217.
35. Delaney JS, Drummond R. Mass casualties and triage at a sporting event—review. *Br J Sport Med.* 2002;36:85–88.

36. Wiley S. Shocking news about lightning and pools. *USA Swimming Safety Q.* 1998;4:1–2.

37. Cherington M. Lightning injuries in sports—situations to avoid. *Sports Med.* 2001;31(4):301–308.

38. Cherington M, Walker M, Boyson R, et al. Closing the gap on actual numbers of lightning casualties and deaths. Paper presented at: American Meteorological Society's 11th Conference on Applied Climatology; January 10–15, 1999; Dallas, TX.

39. Gluncic I, Roje Z, Gluncic V, Poljak K. Ear injuries caused by lightning: report of 18 cases. *J Laryngol Otol.* 2001;115:4–8.

40. Cooper MA. A fifth mechanism of lightning injury. *Acad Emerg Med.* 2002;9(2):172–174.

41. Walsh KM, Bennett B, Cooper MA, et al. National Athletic Trainers' Association Position Statement: lightning safety for athletics and recreation. *J Athl Train.* 2000;35(4):471–477.

42. Zimmermann C, Cooper MA, Holle RL. Lightning safety guidelines. *Ann Emerg Med* 2002;39(6):660–665.

43. Bennett BL, Holle RL, López RE. Lightning safety guideline 1D. In Klossner D, ed. *2009–2010 National Collegiate Athletic Association Sports Medicine Handbook.* Overland Park, KS: National Collegiate Athletic Association; 2009.

44. Roeder WP, Vavrek RJ. Lightning safety for schools—an update. Available at: http://www.weather.gov/os/lightning/resources/ASSE-Schools.pdf. Accessed May 2010.

45. Roeder WP. Last minute outdoor lightning risk reduction—a method to estimate its effectiveness and comments on its utility in public education. Paper presented at: The American Meteorological Society's Fourth Conference on the Meteorological Applications of Lightning Data; January 11–15, 2009; Phoenix, AZ.

46. Cooper MA. Emergent care of lightning and electrical injuries. *Semin Neurol.* 1995;15(3):268–278.

47. Soni UK, Mistry B, Mallya SV, Grewal DS, Varadkar S. Acoustic effects of lightning. *Auris Nausus Larynx.* 1993;20(4):285–289.

48. Holle RL, Lopez RE, Vavrek J, Howard KW. Educating individuals about lightning. Paper presented at: American Meteorological Society 7th Symposium on Education; January 11–16, 1998; Phoenix, AZ.

49. Holle RL, López RE. Lightning: impacts and safety. *World Meterol Bull.* 1998;47:148–155.

50. Holle R. Lightning-caused deaths and injuries in and near dwellings and other buildings. Available at: www.lightningsafety.com/nlsi_lls/lightning-caused-deaths.pdf. Accessed June 2010.

51. American Meteorological Society. Lightning safety awareness statement. *Bull Am Met Soc.* 2002;83. Available at: http://www.ametsoc.org/policy/lightningpolicy_2002.html. Accessed June 2010.

52. Cherington M. Hazards of bicycling: from handlebars to lightning. *Semin Neurol.* 2000;20(2):247–254.

53. Zafren K, Durrer B, Herry JP, Brugger H. Lightning injuries: prevention and on-site treatment in mountains and remote areas. Official guidelines of the International Commission for Mountain Emergency Medicine and the Medical Commission of the International Mountaineering and Climbing Federation (ICAR and UIAA MEDCOM). *Resuscitation.* 2005;65:369–372.

54. Faragher RM. Injury from lightning strike while using mobile phone. Statistics and physics do not suggest a link. *BMJ.* 2006;332(7556):1513.

55. Esprit S, Kothari P, Dhillon R. Injury from lightning strike while using a mobile phone. *BMJ.* 2006;332(7556):1513.

56. Althaus CW. Injury from lightning strike while using mobile phone—mobile phones are not lightning strike risk. *Br J Med.* 2006;333:96.

57. Cooper MA. More on thunderstorms and iPods. *NEJM.* 2007;357(14):1447–1448.

58. Andrews CJ, Darveniza M. Telephone-mediated lightning injury: an Australian survey. *J Trauma.* 1989;29:665–671.

59. Cooper MA. Lightning: prognostic signs for death. *Ann Emerg Med.* 1980;9:134–138.

60. Cooper MA. Lightning injuries. eMedicine. Available at: http://emedicine.medscape.com/article/770642. Accessed June 2010.

61. Steinbaum S, Harviel JD, Haffin JH, Jordan MH. Lightning strike to the head: case report. *J Trauma.* 1994;36(1):113–115.

62. Slesinger TL, Bank M, Drumheller BC, et al. Immediate cardiac arrest and subsequent development of cardiogenic shock caused by lightning strike. *J Trauma.* 2010;68(1):E5–E7.

63. Dronacharya L, Poudel R. Lightning induced atrial fibrillation. *Kathmandu Univ Med J.* 2008;6(24):514–515.

64. Dhawan S, Sultan-Ali IA. Lightning-induced ECG changes and hydrostatic pulmonary edema. *Clin Cardiol.* 2009;32(8):E71.

65. Rash W. Cardiac injury and death by lightning strike. *J Emerg Nurs.* 2008;34(5):470–471.

66. Saglam H, Yavuz Y, Yurumez Y, Ozkececi G, Kilit C. Lightning strike at St. Albans game kills Bethesda student, injures 10. *Washington Post.* May 18, 1991:A1.

67. Ten Duis HJ, Klasen HJ, Reenalda PE. Keraunoparalysis, a 'specific' lightning injury. *Burns Incl Therm Inj.* 1985;12(1):54–57.

68. Cherington M. Central nervous system complications of lightning and electrical injuries. *Semin Neurol.* 1995;15:233–239.

69. Cherington M. Neurologic manifestations of lightning strikes. *Neurology.* 2003;60(2):182–185.

70. Jafari H, Courztier P, Camu W. Motor neuron disease after electric injury. *J Neurol Neurosurg Psychiatry.* 2001;71:265–267.

71. Cooray V, Cooray C, Andrews CJ. Lightning caused injuries in humans. *J Electrostatics.* 2007;65:386–394.

72. Zane RD. Lightning injuries. *Emerg Med Clin North Am.* 2004;22:369–403.

73. Andrews CJ, Cooper MA, Darveniza M. *Lightning Injuries: Electrical, Medical, and Legal Aspects.* Boca Raton, FL: CRC Press; 1992.

74. Lewis AM. Understanding the principles of lightning injuries. *J Emerg Nurs.* 1997;23:535–541.

75. Cooper MA, Marshburn S. Lightning Strike and Electrical Shock Survivors, International. *Neuro Rehabil.* 2005;20:43–47.

Michael G. Miller, PhD, EdD, ATC, CSCS

Robert J. Baker, MD, PhD, ATC, FACSM, FAAFP

CHAPTER

11

Asthma

Asthma is a chronic inflammatory disease affecting millions of individuals throughout the United States and the world. Albeit controllable, asthma **exacerbations** can lead to fatality or to near sudden death. Death from asthma, although rare, appears to be linked to triggers, including **anaphylaxis**, allergens, and exercise, or to a delay in medical treatment when a severe asthma exacerbation occurs. Of note, asthma and sudden death asthma are difficult to delineate, and both topics are intermixed within this chapter. Although asthma deaths are unfortunate, proper recognition and immediate management of asthma exacerbations can decrease the likelihood of a fatality. This chapter discusses sudden death asthma and near sudden death asthma, concentrating on the physiologic reactions that cause airway inflammation and on medical management to prevent severe asthma exacerbations or asthma death.

> **exacerbation** Worsening of a disease or condition.

> **anaphylaxis** A life-threatening allergic reaction with symptoms that develop rapidly.

Definition

Asthma

According to the National Heart Lung and Blood Institute and the Global Initiative for Asthma, asthma is defined as a lung disease in which the airways become inflamed and restricted to airflow.[1,2] Asthma involves two physiologic components: inflammation (with concomitant airway constriction) and **bronchoconstriction**. Inflammation directly limits air flow in small airways in the lungs and may lead to airway hyperresponsiveness and narrowing in response to a trigger. Clinical signs of airway constriction include chest tightness, shortness of breath, and coughing or wheezing. Together, inflammation and bronchoconstriction reduce the amount of oxygen available during respiration. Asthma episodes can be variable and symptoms may resolve spontaneously; however, early identification and management of signs and symptoms can decrease exacerbations and prevent loss of life.

> **bronchoconstriction** Constriction of the airways.

Sudden Death Asthma

Sudden death asthma usually results from a severe exacerbation or multiple exacerbations.[3] Sur et al.[3] reported that individuals who died within 1 hour of onset of asthma symptoms had more neutrophils and less eosinophils compared with those who died 2.5 hours or more from onset, suggesting that death may be caused by two distinct pathologic processes. The risk factors for sudden death asthma include a previous severe or life-threatening attack, previous hospital admission for asthma, and failure to control asthma symptoms.[4,5] Exacerbations that cause **near-fatal asthma** are often classified as "sudden-onset asthma exacerbations" that severely obstruct the airway within 1.5 to 3 hours from the first sign of symptoms.[6–9] According to Martinez,[10] death from asthma is rare in sports, and the benefits of sport participation, both physiologic and psychological, outweigh the risk factors of sudden death. Regular exercise may lead to improved lung capacity and respiratory muscle tone. Over the long term, participation in physical activity may help the asthmatic to maintain lung function.

near-fatal asthma Asthma symptoms that cause severe breathing difficulties that do not result in death.

Epidemiology

In 2009, asthma was thought to affect approximately 22 million people in the United States alone, with nearly 6 million of all affected persons being children.[1] Worldwide, asthma appears to affect approximately 300 million individuals, with prevalences ranging from 1% to 18% of the population in different countries.[2,11] North America and western European countries have lower incidences of asthma in the 3- to 14-year-old populations, whereas Africa, Latin America, and sections of Asia have higher rates of asthma symptoms in these groups. Individuals having allergies, eczema, or a genetic predisposition appear to be at higher risk for developing the disease.[2] Boys tend to have higher incidences than girls; however, in the adult population, women appear to have a higher rate of asthma compared with males.[2] The annual death toll from asthma worldwide has been hypothesized to be 250,000 from all causes, although the specific link for death is not known.[11]

Sudden death asthma varies by geographic location and population characteristics. In Spain, mortality ranges from 800 to 1000 each year.[12] The trends for asthma death appear to be decreasing in the United States and other countries. In the United States, the mortality rate from 1994 to 1996 was 2.1 per 100,000; during the years from 1997 to 1998, the rate dropped to 2.0 per 100,000.[13] In 2002, the rate declined to 1.4 per 100,000, suggesting the existence of better asthma control or better intervention methods when life-threatening exacerbations occurred.[13] The number of sudden deaths of children and adolescents is lower than in other age populations, most likely due to the lower frequency of children participating in organized sports.[14]

Asthma is a leading cause of atraumatic sudden death in athletes, after all other cardiac causes of sudden death.[15] Although the mortality rate for individuals participating in athletics is low, deaths do occur **(Table 11.1)**. In one study examining asthma mortality rates from 1993 to 2000 before and after athletic competition, 61 deaths met the criteria for death from asthma-related complications, with more deaths in whites versus African Americans by a 2 to 1 ratio, which is in contrast to most other published reports.[16] Eighteen athletes died during competition and 14 during a practice event. Of these, 57% were competitive athletes and 43% were recreational athletes. For sporting activities, basketball and track appeared to have the highest rate of asthma deaths.[16] Early fall, followed by the summer and spring, appeared to be the season in which the most asthma deaths occurred.[16] In a review of asthma deaths in U.S. schools from 1990 to 2003, 42% of asthma deaths were attributed to children participating in some form of physical activity prior to death.[17]

Pathophysiology

Asthma is associated with both chronic and acute effects. Exposure to the appropriate stimuli will result in inflammation and airway constriction. Acutely, this can lead to respiratory distress, decreased oxygen absorption, hypoxia, and, in the extreme case, asphyxia. Long-term effects of persistent airway inflammation can also lead to airway remodeling, which can lead to a long-term decline in lung function.

Airway inflammation is almost always persistent in patients with asthma, regardless of whether an asthmatic is having symptoms.[2] The airway inflammation is produced by an increase of mast cell production and activation and an increased number of eosinophils and other inflammatory cells, such as T lymphocytes, macrophages, and neutrophils and cellular mediators (chemokines, cytokines, histamine, prostaglandin D_2, and nitric oxide).[18–25] Mast cell degranulation, which causes mucous secretion and inflammation, has been shown to correlate with the history of asthma severity and the duration of fatal asthma attacks.[26–28] Whereas these cellular and mediator events cause inflammation, structural changes result in narrowing of the airways.

Remodeling of the airways is also a result of altered extracellular matrix changes, with depositions of fibronectin, tenascin, collagens, and proteogylcans.[29–32] These changes cause thickening of the walls (large and small airways), representing the chronic inflammation associated with asthma, and appear to be pronounced in the small airways and alveolar parenchyma.[33,34] Individuals with fatal asthma showed signs of increased protein content in the inner and outer sections of the small airways in the lungs, with increased fibronectin and matrix metalloproteinases found in the outer areas of the small airways and peribronchiolar parenchyma.[35]

TABLE 11.1	Sporting Activities and Characteristics Associated with Asthma Mortality	
Event/Characteristic	Number	Percentage*
Sport Participation		
Organized	35	57
Recreational	26	43
Season of Asthma Fatality		
Spring	13	22
Summer	19	31
Fall	24	39
Winter	5	8
Type of Sport		
Basketball	13	21
Track/running	7	12
Football	5	8
Baseball	3	5
Soccer	3	5
Swimming	2	3
Cheerleading	2	3
Other	16	26

Note: Based upon 61 athletes identified who suffered asthma fatality.
Source: Becker JM, Rogers J, Rossini G, Mirchandani H, D'Alonzo GE. Asthma deaths during sports: report of a 7-year experience. *J Allergy Clin Immunol.* 2004;113:264–267. Reprinted with permission.

The causes of fatal asthma are linked to airway restriction. In postmortem studies, bronchial epithelial damage has been found, along with blockage of the **airway lumen** with mucus, and airway smooth muscle hypertrophy and hyperplasia, suggesting that death was due to chronic and persistent airway inflammation.[36–39] Jerath et al.[40] reported 21 cases of deaths attributed to airway mucus plugging, and 19 cases that showed smooth muscle hypertrophy.

airway lumen The inner lining of the bronchial airways.

Prevention and Predisposing Factors

The severity of asthma and sudden death asthma is variable, depending on the cause or risk factors of the breathing difficulty. The risk factors for fatal asthma appear to be similar across all individuals in multiple countries and include physiologic and psychological attributes.[4,41–43] When asthma deaths do occur, the symptoms and fatality occur rapidly, with or without triggers.[3,44,45] In one study, 10 asthma deaths were attributed to severe exacerbations that required hospitalization within 1.3 hours after onset of symptoms; other reports showed that 50% of asthma deaths were attributed to individuals with a history of "severe" asthma.[6,46] Early recognition and aggressive treatment are likely to result in better long-term outcomes, but identification of risk factors is still paramount and is discussed in this section.

Intrinsic Risk Factors

Family History

Although the link between genetics and asthma death is unclear, past studies have indicated that a family link may be involved in asthmatic death.[47,48] Using the Utah Population Database for genealogy, asthma mortality was examined from 1904 until 2006.[49] Of the 1553 asthma deaths, a significantly higher risk of death was found when first-degree relatives rather than second- or third-degree relatives were affected, thus supporting the hypothesis that a genetic link may predispose a person to sudden death from asthma.

Ethnicity

Racial or ethnic differences may also contribute to higher risk for asthma and asthma exacerbations, which may be correlated with socioeconomic factors,[2] but their correlation with sudden asthma death is still uncertain. In a study of football players in Philadelphia, asthma prevalence was higher in African American athletes compared with white athletes. Not only was the prevalence among African Americans higher, but also the ratio of African American athletes with asthma was higher compared with white athletes.[50] The specific genetic markers studied by various investigators vary but include pathogenesis associated with allergens (IgE antibodies), hyperresponsiveness, inflammation, and immune responses.[51–53] Individuals who had sudden-onset asthma exacerbations, compared with individuals who had slower-onset asthma exacerbations, had almost identical characteristics with respect to their overall age, gender, ethnicity, and socioeconomic status.[43]

Athleticism

Asthma and asthma symptoms have been found in endurance, cold-weather, and summer-sport athletes and participation in athletic events could predispose these athletes to exacerbations that may lead to death. Compared with nonasthmatic individuals, cross-country skiers have a higher risk for asthma, and physician-diagnosed asthma was found to be higher in track and field athletes versus control subjects.[46,54] These rates of occurrence appear to be due to the training periods and prolonged hyperventilation associated with their respective sport, as well as exposure to environmental conditions and pollens or allergens.[55] Asthma and asthma symptoms were found in 14% of elite summer athletes, with **atopy** found in 48% of all athletes. The odds ratios for occurrence of atopy were found to be 5.49 in speed and power athletes, 2.88 for long distance runners, and 10.8 for swimmers compared with controls.[55] These results appear to suggest that elite summer athletes have an increased occurrence of asthma and asthma symptoms that is strongly associated with atopy.

atopy A predisposition to developing a hypersensitivity reaction to a common environmental antigen.

Past History of Severe Exacerbations, Poor Asthma Control, and Other Factors

A past history of asthma hospitalizations and poor asthma control are related to an increased risk of fatal asthma.[56,57] Other findings that increase the risk of asthma deaths include quickly deteriorating symptoms, usually within 3 hours of the first asthma exacerbation or attack, and nonadherence to prescribed inhaled corticosteroids 2 weeks prior to the attack.[58,59]

Extrinsic Risk Factors

Environmental Factors

Multiple environmental risk factors, such as allergens, infections, smoke, and pollution, can cause an asthma exacerbation or even death.[60] Allergens such as dust mites, dander, and mold are inherent risk factors for causing asthma and asthma exacerbations.[61–63] Exposure to tobacco smoke early in life is associated with a higher incidence of asthma and asthmatic symptoms during infancy.[2,64] Pollution (indoor and outdoor) remains inconclusive as a factor in the development of asthmatic symptoms or exacerbations but has been shown to decrease lung function in people exposed to polluted areas.[65,66] There have been reported cases of children with asthma who died from anaphylaxis that was not recognized.[67] **Respiratory syncytial virus (RSV)** and parainfluenza virus contracted in childhood may lead to asthma symptoms later in life.[68,69] This may be due to permanent damage to lung tissue.

respiratory syncytial virus (RSV) A virus that causes an infection in the lungs, leading to respiratory distress.

Asthma Medications

Many over-the-counter (OTC) and prescription asthma medications can cause severe exacerbations or even death. OTC nonsteroidal anti-inflammatory drugs (NSAIDs) were found to be associated with a rapid onset of asthma exacerbations in a review of cases of asthma fatality.[70] Although the death rate is relatively low, athletes with asthma need to be monitored closely when taking NSAIDs. Beta blockers may also predispose an individual to severe asthma exacerbations. However, their effect on the airways is that of bronchoconstriction. Thus, these medications may either block the effects of β-agonists used to treat asthma or directly cause airway constriction.

Illicit Drug Use

Illicit use of drugs and alcohol has been found to be a risk factor in asthma death. From 1994 to 1999, 44 deaths from asthma were recorded in Cook County, Illinois.[40] At the time of death, 17% of these patients had used inhaled corticosteroids, and 8 patients were using systemic corticosteroids, with 22 patients using a β-adrenergic agonist. Toxicologic reports found that 12 patients had consumed alcohol and 3 cocaine. Other reports imply that use of illicit drugs, such as heroin and cocaine, along with alcohol increases the risk of severe asthma exacerbations.[71] However, overdose-related inability to protect the airway most likely contributed to these deaths.

Early Identification

Symptoms of Severe Asthma

Exacerbations include difficulty speaking in complete sentences, chest pain, wheezing, shortness of breath, drowsiness, confusion, use of accessory muscles for breathing, and sweating.[72,73] As respiratory complications worsen, individuals may become drowsy or experience mental status changes or loss of consciousness. These symptoms may be brought on by or made worse with exercise. Individuals who have near-fatal asthma may show other signs of respiratory distress, such as inability to lie supine, talk coherently, or sit upright and may be agitated.[58] In asthmatics, exercise is a common trigger. Athletes with exercise-induced bronchospasm may experience these same symptoms after several minutes of exercise. Symptoms of exercise-induced bronchospasm can be as subtle as coughing or wheezing after exercise.

Physical Examination

In many cases, symptoms may be subtle, and past history may not identify all individuals with asthma. The sensitivity and specificity of the standard history questions are not known,[74] but the preparticipation physical examination and health history questionnaire is recommended as a tool to determine risk for or identify asthma in athletes.[75] Auscultation of the lungs may reveal wheezing and a prolonged expiratory phase of respiration. Impending respiratory failure may be indicated by decreased breath sounds on auscultation or absence of wheezing associated with decreased air movement. However, in the absence of an acute asthma attack, the physical findings may be minimal.

At the time of a severe asthma attack and pending respiratory failure, the athlete may present with mental status changes due to hypoxia. Vital signs will reflect hypotension and bradycardia, similar to shock.[72,73] The skin, especially of the mouth, fingers, and feet, may appear blue or cyanotic. As respiratory distress progresses, the work of breathing will lead to poor air movement and fatigue. The accessory muscles of breathing will be required. As these muscles fatigue, confusion from hypoxemia will result. As respiratory complications worsen, individuals may become drowsy or experience mental status changes such as agitation or loss of consciousness. Impending respiratory failure will lead to decreased breath sounds on auscultation or absence of wheezing associated with decreased air movement. All of these findings are ominous and should be identified as indications to initiate cardiopulmonary resuscitation, recovery breathing, and notification of emergency medical services.

A respiratory rate greater than 30 breaths per minute and heart rate greater than 120 beats per minute are signs of respiratory distress.[58] The athlete may increase sweating. These physical findings of respiratory distress are nonspecific to asthma and may be seen in athletes with other causes of respiratory failure, such as anaphylaxis.

Pulmonary Tests

If early identification and signs and symptoms suggest that an athlete has asthma, several special tests can be implemented to help confirm the diagnosis. Personal-best **peak expiratory flow rate (PEFR)** can be measured by the athlete on a daily basis to direct management of asthma. Predicted peak flow rate can be determined based on age, sex, and size. Peak flow that improves by more than 20% approximately 10 minutes after administration of a quick-acting bronchodilator can help diagnose asthma. Limitations of PEFR include the following:

peak expiratory flow rate (PEFR) The maximal rate that a person can exhale during a short maximal expiratory effort after a full inspiration.

- Mild airflow obstruction may be present.
- Reduced peak flow occurs in both obstructive and restrictive diseases.
- Peak flow measurements are not sufficient to distinguish upper airway obstruction.
- The accuracy of this test depends entirely upon patient effort and technique. Therefore, the athlete should be coached to ensure a maximal effort.
- **Peak flow meters** cannot be routinely calibrated, so only relative changes should be monitored.

peak flow meter A hand-held device that is used to measure peak expiratory flow rate.

Office **spirometry** can be calibrated and used to distinguish normal from abnormal lung function. Abnormalities of obstructive or restrictive patterns can be characterized by spirometry. **Forced expiratory volume in the first second of expiration** (FEV_1) is one measure used to monitor airway obstruction. Airflow obstruction based on spirometry is graded as mild, moderate, severe, and very severe according to the FEV_1:

spirometry A pulmonary function test that measures the volume of air as a function of time.

- Mild obstruction: FEV_1 of 70% to 99%
- Moderate obstruction: FEV_1 of 50% to 69%
- Severe obstruction: FEV_1 of 35% to 49%
- Very severe obstruction: FEV_1 of less than 35%

forced expiratory volume in the first second of expiration (FEV_1) The volume of air that is forced out of the lungs in 1 second.

This grading system correlates with other tests using the criteria of FEV_1 less than 40%, low oxygen saturation, partial pressures of oxygen less than 90%, or carbon dioxide concentrations greater than 45 mm Hg.[72,73] The reversibility of the obstructive abnormality can be assessed after administration of a bronchodilator. An increase in FEV_1 of 12% or greater following bronchodilator administration is diagnostic of asthma. Some patients with asthma have irreversible airway obstruction due to chronic airway inflammation or scarring (airway remodeling).

pulse oximeter A device that indirectly monitors the oxygen saturation in the blood, usually via the fingertip.

An arterial blood oxygen concentration less than 8 kPa even after breathing supplemental oxygen and an arterial carbon dioxide concentration greater than 6 kPa are objective laboratory test results indicating impending respiratory failure.[76] Blood oxygen concentration can be measured using a hand-held **pulse oximeter** and blood concentrations below 90% typically reflect hypoxemia. These measurements can be taken in the field and on the sidelines. The pulse oximeter should not be used to diagnosis asthma or monitor long-term asthma control.

Exercise Tests

Athletes should be screened for asthma prior to participation in all forms of exercise, because exercise may be a causative factor for developing severe asthma exacerbations that can lead to death. Although exercise appears to be a trigger for near-fatal or fatal asthma, the method by which this occurs remains speculative. With abrupt cessation of exercise, the FEV_1 can drop by up to 50% within a 10- to 20-minute period; however, this change in FEV_1 has not been shown to be a causative factor for sudden-onset asthma exacerbations.[43,77]

Other Tests

A majority of athletes with asthma can be diagnosed based on history, physical examination, and pulmonary testing. In rare cases, the diagnosis may not be clear and may require further testing. Methacholine is known to evoke a bronchoconstriction response. Individuals with asthma tend to respond to lower concentrations of this drug. Methacholine testing is generally considered the gold standard in diagnosing asthma. The eucapnic hyperventilation test is an alternative test for exercise-related bronchospasm. This test requires the individual to hyperventilate while breathing in controlled concentrations of carbon dioxide. This allows the tested individual to safely, voluntarily increase ventilatory rate as might be expected in response to exercise. The increase in ventilation will lead to bronchoconstriction in individuals with exercise-induced asthma. This technique is accepted by the International Olympic Committee as proof of exercise-induced asthma.

Differential Diagnosis

Anaphylaxis

Anaphylaxis symptoms can mimic asthma exacerbations, so a proper medical history is warranted to potentially identify risk factors for athletes to develop anaphylaxis. A slow or absent response to asthma medications given to alleviate respiratory distress may help differentiate asthma attacks from an anaphylactic response.[67]

Other Medical Conditions

Other respiratory conditions can appear similar to asthma. **Vocal cord dysfunction** can cause wheezing.[78] The rapid respiratory rate associated with hyperventilation syndrome or panic attacks can be difficult to differentiate from the rapid respiratory rate often seen in asthma. Although these conditions are relatively benign, they can occur alone or along with asthma, further complicating the diagnosis of asthma. Vocal cord dysfunction and hyperventilation often respond to relaxation and breathing techniques, indicating there may be significant psychological factors involved.

vocal cord dysfunction
Abnormal closure of the vocal cords that causes airflow obstruction, usually during the inspiratory phase of the breathing cycle.

Spontaneous pneumothorax is an abnormal collection of air between the pleural lining and lung tissue that can produce chest pain and shortness of breath similar to asthma. Weakening in the alveoli can lead to blebs, which rupture and release air into this space. Although the exact cause of these blebs is unknown, the increased respiratory rate and airway resistance associated with asthma could also lead to this condition.

Management of Acute Respiratory Distress

Acute respiratory distress in the athlete should be handled emergently whether the athlete has known asthma or not. In their review of asthma death in children, Rainbow and Browne[67] suggest that asthma exacerbations should be managed closely to ensure that the athlete is suffering from asthma symptoms, not anaphylaxis. Symptoms of anaphylaxis mimic asthma exacerbations, but may also include other signs, such as gastrointestinal upset, urticaria, wheezing, hypotension, and slow or no response to asthma medications to alleviate symptoms due to inability to inhale sufficiently.[67] In these cases, the clinician should suspect anaphylaxis and treat accordingly. Epinephrine is the first-line treatment for asthma exacerbations associated with anaphylaxis and is a second-line drug for other acute asthma exacerbations. Epinephrine produces both α-agonist effects to decrease edema and β-agonist effects to assist with bronchodilation, with minimal side effects for patients with severe asthma. The medical professional should have an epi-pen on hand for either anaphylaxis or severe asthma exacerbation.

Supplemental Oxygen

The athlete in respiratory distress should be treated immediately **(Figure 11.1; Table 11.2)**. Provide oxygen to help maintain oxygen saturation of the blood above 92% (as measured by pulse oximetry) and improve symptoms.[79]

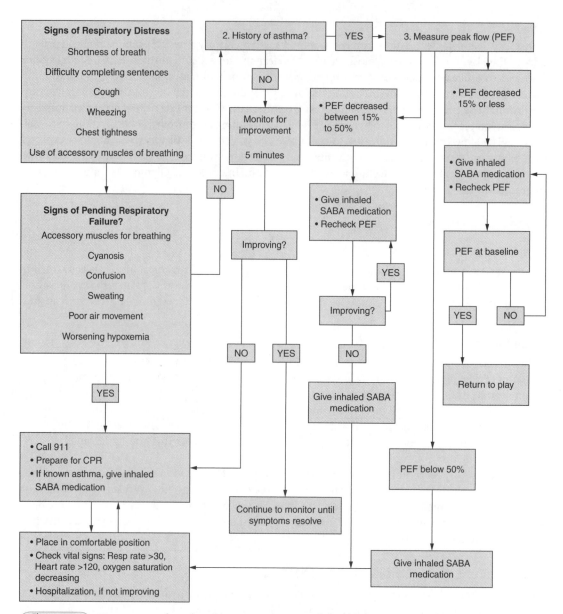

Signs of Respiratory Distress

Shortness of breath

Difficulty completing sentences

Cough

Wheezing

Chest tightness

Use of accessory muscles of breathing

Signs of Pending Respiratory Failure?

Accessory muscles for breathing

Cyanosis

Confusion

Sweating

Poor air movement

Worsening hypoxemia

YES

• Call 911
• Prepare for CPR
• If known asthma, give inhaled SABA medication

• Place in comfortable position
• Check vital signs: Resp rate >30, Heart rate >120, oxygen saturation decreasing
• Hospitalization, if not improving

2. History of asthma? — YES — 3. Measure peak flow (PEF)

NO

Monitor for improvement

5 minutes

NO

Improving?

NO   YES

• PEF decreased between 15% to 50%

• Give inhaled SABA medication
• Recheck PEF

YES

Improving?

NO

Give inhaled SABA medication

Continue to monitor until symptoms resolve

• PEF decreased 15% or less

• Give inhaled SABA medication
• Recheck PEF

PEF at baseline

YES   NO

Return to play

PEF below 50%

Give inhaled SABA medication

Figure 11.1 Management flow chart for acute asthma attack in athletes. Given signs of respiratory distress, the athlete should be monitored for signs of impending respiratory failure first (step 1). If these signs are not present, the athlete may be managed differently based on the presence of known asthma (step 2). Athletes with asthma should be checked for peak expiratory flow (step 3). CPR indicates cardiopulmonary resuscitation; PEF, peak expiratory flow; SABA, short-acting β-agonist.
Source: From Becker JM, Rogers J, Rossini G, Mirchandani H, D'Alonzo GE. Asthma deaths during sports: report of a 7-year experience. *J Allergy Clin Immunol.* 2004;113:264–267. Copyright © (2004), Reprinted with permission from Elsevier.

Medications

Short-Acting β-Agonists

Short-acting β-agonists are the first-line treatment for an acute asthma exacerbation. Athletes with known asthma should have a short-acting β-agonist readily available. Onset of action is 5 to 15 minutes.

TABLE 11.2	Equipment List for Management of Acute Exacerbation of Asthma

Necessary

1. Short-acting β-agonist inhaler with spacer
2. Spacer: may be improvised with a tape roll
3. Peak flow meter: to monitor lung function
4. Stethoscope: auscultation of lungs for wheezing and air movement
5. Oxygen
6. Communication device: cell phone to call 911 if indicated

Recommended

1. Nebulizer
2. Steroids (oral or IV)
3. Ipratropium bromide (metered dose inhaler with spacer or nebulizer solution)
4. Epinephrine (EpiPen for anaphylaxis or solution for IV use): if allergic reaction or anaphylaxis is considered
5. Combitube: for blind intubation and ventilatory support (if trained)
6. Bag and valve with mask: for manual respiratory support
7. First-generation antihistamine (diphenhydramine): for allergen-triggered attacks or anaphylaxis

Inhaled β-agonists can be repeated as often as every 1 to 2 hours if need.[79] Nebulized $β_2$-agonists are often used for severe asthma exacerbations, although a **metered dose inhaler** with a spacer is as effective as a **nebulizer**.[79–83] Continuous nebulization of short-acting β-agonist medication may improve lung function over the course of intermittent treatment during acute exacerbations.

> **metered dose inhaler**
> A pressurized hand-held device that uses propellants to deliver medication to the lungs.

Inhaled Atropine or Ipratropium Bromide

Inhaled ipratropium bromide may be used as a second-line drug. Ipratropium bromide, an anticholinergic medication, is used to inhibit muscarinic receptors in airway smooth muscle to increase bronchodilation and appears to be effective when added to $β_2$-agonist administration, with little or limited adverse effects.[72,84,85] Ipratropium bromide showed promising results when administered early and frequently to treat acute asthma exacerbations.[86,87]

> **nebulizer** A device used for delivering medication into the lungs during inhalation.

Magnesium Sulfate

Magnesium sulfate has been postulated to be an effective medical therapy for acute asthma exacerbations due to its inhibition of airway smooth muscle constriction.[72] Magnesium sulfate acts on cholinergic terminals and mast cells, inhibiting acetylcholine and histamine release; it also inhibits calcium ion intake in the airway bronchial smooth muscle in acute asthma exacerbations.[88] When used in combination with other asthma therapies, magnesium sulfate has been effective in improving lung function in patients who have severe asthma.[89,90] The side effects of magnesium sulfate are relatively minimal, but toxicity can occur with high doses and should be monitored.[72]

Hospitalization

Athletes who require $β_2$-agonist therapy more often than every 2 to 3 hours, have not improved after administration of systemic glucocorticoids, or require supplemental oxygen need to be admitted to the hospital. Other factors that may necessitate hospitalization include a history of rapid progression of severity in past exacerbations, poor adherence to an outpatient medication regimen, inadequate access to medical care, or a poor social support system at home. If respiratory failure occurs, ventilatory support can be provided via an artificial airway.

Management of Chronic Asthma

Long-Acting Inhaled β-Agonists

The long-acting inhaled β-agonist medications are best used as controller medications, often in conjunction with an inhaled steroid. Long-acting β-agonist medications may accumulate in the body and result in tachycardia. Tachyphylaxis or decreased effectiveness of this type of medication can occur. The Food and Drug Administration warns that these medications should only be used in conjunction with steroids and for the shortest amount of time necessary.[91,92] Other studies show that long-acting β_2-agonists, particularly salmeterol, may increase the risk of severe adverse effects and death.[93] The exact mechanism is unknown. Some suggest that inappropriate use of this type of medication as a rescue medication is to blame. Although the use of long-acting β_2-agonists has increased since the early 1990s, asthma death rates, particularly in European and South American countries, actually decreased, suggesting that other factors may influence asthma mortality.[94,95]

Mast Cell Stabilizers

Inhaled mast cell stabilizers remain an option for exercise-induced asthma, but should never be used for rescue. These medications will only prevent the release of inflammatory mediators in the airway in response to stimuli. They do not directly treat inflammation or lead to bronchodilation. This type of medication needs to be used regularly prior to exposure or exercise.

Steroids

Long-term relief may require either oral or inhaled steroids. The national guidelines for the treatment and prevention of asthma recommend a stepwise treatment plan for asthma based on severity of asthma. For mild to moderate asthma, the addition of inhaled steroids is recommended. For severe exacerbations of asthma, systemic steroids are recommended. Oral steroids are as effective as intravenous (IV) steroids and may be used for control of asthma symptoms to prevent worsening of exacerbations as part of a stepwise treatment plan based on symptoms and peak flow meter monitoring.[72,88]

Other Medications

Leukotriene inhibitors may be beneficial as third-line medications to block the products of inflammation. Theophylline is a third-line medication whose exact effect and benefit for asthmatics is unknown. This medication seems to increase respiratory drive and may have some bronchodilating effect.[76]

Prevention Through Education

Education plays a vital role in controlling and recognizing an asthma attack. In one study, 31% of cases resulting in asthma deaths in school-aged children had delays of treatment medication, with 17% of all treating respondents stating they had no knowledge that the asthmatic child had asthma or that quick relief medications were available.[17] Other studies show that adherence rates for taking prescribed asthma medications range from 30% to 70% with children, and are frequently lower than 50%.[96,97] These figures represent a need for better educational practices for asthmatic patients as well as those who care for them.

Compliance with prescribed medication is needed in order to lessen the severity and frequency of asthma exacerbations in athletes. The rationale for medication noncompliance is speculative, but includes forgetfulness, lack of understanding about how to use the asthma medication as prescribed by physicians, intentional factors of taking the medication differently than prescribed (e.g., decreased dosage or frequency), or even lack of understanding of the need to take medication.[98–100] One of the most common causes for treatment failure with inhaled medications is poor inhaler technique when using a metered dose inhaler. The challenge of poor technique can often be overcome by adding a spacer to the inhaler. Newer dry powder medications do not present the same challenges with administration technique.

Health care providers should use a pharmacologic and psychological approach to education that stresses common procedures along with avoidance of triggers that may predispose an athlete to asthma exacerbations.[98] Education should include the rationale for the need to take asthma medications, address the individual's concerns over the adverse affects of prescribed medications, and address any barriers that preclude individuals from using their medications, such as difficulties with medication delivery methods. In addition, if feasible, athletes should avoid known triggers for asthma attacks and be educated on how to prevent attacks by using sanitary procedures in the home such as cleaning clothes and bed sheets, using filters, and controlling bug populations that are known to cause asthma.

Return-to-Play Considerations

There are no specific guidelines regarding return to play following an asthma attack in the *NCAA Sports Medicine Handbook* or other published literature. Initial treatment with inhaled β-agonist medication should relieve symptoms as well as return lung function to baseline. If asthma exacerbation symptoms are not resolved after three repeated uses of a short-acting β-agonist inhaler (with spacer), the athlete should be referred to an appropriate health care facility.[101] Lung function may be monitored on the sidelines with a peak flow meter. It is important that the asthmatic athlete be familiar with this type of device in order to perform this monitoring appropriately and obtain reliable information. It is best to have a baseline reading and a stepwise treatment plan based on peak flow readings for the specific athlete; however, predicted norms can be calculated (or located in a table) based on height, gender, and age. However, it is important to consider that ethnicity may affect lung function as well.[101] These general management strategies are also published in the National Athletic Trainers' Association Asthma Position for control of asthma exacerbations and can be used by clinicians to determine if/when an athlete could return to play.[102]

Once the athlete's symptoms have resolved and lung function has returned to baseline, the athlete could potentially return to play. Some thought should be given to the circumstances that might have led to the exacerbation. These may include external stimuli that can be avoided, a change in environmental conditions, or infections.[103] In the latter case, further evaluation of the athlete may be necessary prior to return.

There are likewise no specific guidelines for return to play after hospitalization for asthma. An appropriate work-up looking for common inciting factors should be performed. Should pneumonia be the underlying cause, 2 to 6 weeks of convalescence may be necessary. Activity should begin on a low aerobic level and be increased slowly, while monitoring the athlete for recurrent symptoms. The athlete's lung function should be at baseline prior to any activity. The athlete may need to repeat the use of a rescue inhaler during or following activity if symptoms return. If this occurs on a regular basis, the athlete should decrease or stop the inciting activities altogether until a physician fully evaluates the athlete. Physicians should consider referring difficult-to-control asthma patients to a pulmonologist.

Conclusion

If controlled properly, asthma should not limit athletes' participation in sports or, worse, lead to life-threatening breathing exacerbations. Most asthma management procedures are preventive, including educating the athlete about asthma and identifying environmental factors and potential triggers through medical testing and history. When a life-threatening breathing exacerbation does occur, multiple management steps can be implemented to resolve the breathing difficulties, including administration of medications, use of supplemental oxygen, and hospitalization. The guidelines and information presented in this chapter should act as a resource for practicing clinicians to implement for all levels and types of athletes to properly control and manage asthma.

Clinical Case Scenario

1. Tara, a freshman on the collegiate cross-country team, has been having breathing difficulties during her afternoon runs. Approximately 10 minutes after beginning her run, she coughs and has difficulty catching her breath. The difficult breathing episodes decrease after cessation of exercise. She seeks assistance from the athletic trainer about her condition. Tara is 5′4″ tall and weighs 100 pounds. She states that she has been having difficulty breathing on many occasions during the past year but attributed this to being out of shape. She did not seek medical assistance in the past, and there is no family history of lung abnormalities.
   1. What screening tools or methods could assist with identifying Tara's symptoms?
   2. What environmental conditions or factors could be contributing to her breathing difficulties?
   3. What is the best course of treatment for Tara?

Key Terms

airway lumen

anaphylaxis

atopy

bronchoconstriction

exacerbation

forced expiratory volume in the first second of expiration (FEV_1)

metered dose inhaler

near-fatal asthma

nebulizer

peak expiratory flow rate (PEFR)

peak flow meter

respiratory syncytial virus (RSV)

spirometry

vocal cord dysfunction

References

1. National Heart Lung and Blood Institute. What is asthma? Available at: http://www.nhlbi.nih.gov/health/dci/Diseases/Asthma/Asthma_WhatIs.html. Accessed February 22, 2010.
2. Global Initiative for Asthma (GINA). Global strategy for asthma management and prevention 2009 (update). Available at: http://www.ginasthma.com/Guidelineitem.asp??l1=2&l2=1&intId=1561. Accessed March 11, 2010.
3. Sur S, Crotty TB, Kephart GM, et al. Sudden-onset fatal asthma. A distinct entity with few eosinophils and relatively more neutrophils in the airway submucosa? *Am Rev Resp Dis*. 1993;148:713–719.
4. Rea HH, Scragg R, Jackson R, et al. A case-control study of deaths from asthma. *Thorax*. 1986;41(11):833–839.
5. Sears MR, Rea HH. Patients at risk for dying of asthma: New Zealand experience. *J Allergy Clin Immunol*. 1987;80:477–481.
6. Wasserfallen JB, Schaller MD, Feihl F, Perret CH. Sudden asphyxic asthma: a distinct entity? *Am Rev Respir Dis*. 1990;142:108–111.
7. Ferrer A, Torre A, Roca J, et al. Characteristics of patients with soybean dust induced acute severe asthma requiring mechanical ventilation. *Am Rev Respir Dis*. 1990;142:429–433.
8. Kallenbach JM, Frankel AH, Lapinsky SE, et al. Determinants of near fatality in acute severe asthma. *Am J Med*. 1993;95:265–272.
9. Woodruff PG, Emond SD, Singh AK, Camargo CA Jr. Sudden-onset severe acute asthma: clinical features and response to therapy. *Acad Emerg Med*. 1998;5:695–701.
10. Martinez FD. Sudden death from respiratory disease in sports [in Spanish]. *Arch Bronconeumol*. 2008;44(7):343–345.
11. Masoli M, Fabian D, Holt S, Beasley R. The global burden of asthma: executive summary of the GINA Dissemination Committee report. *Allergy*. 2004;59(5):469–478.

12. Soler M, Chatenoud L, Negri E, La Vecchia C. Trends in asthma mortality in Italy and Spain, 1980–1996. *Eur J Epidemiol.* 2001;17:545–549.

13. Sly RM. Decreases in asthma mortality in the United States. *Ann Allergy Asthma Immunol.* 2000;85(2):121–127.

14. Byard RW, James RA, Gilbert JD. Childhood sporting deaths. *Am J Forensic Med Pathol.* 2002;23:364–367.

15. Maron BJ. Sudden death in young athletes. *N Engl J Med.* 2003;349:1064–1075.

16. Becker JM, Rogers J, Rossini G, Mirchandani H, D'Alonzo GE. Asthma deaths during sports: report of a 7-year experience. *J Allergy Clin Immunol.* 2004;113:264–267.

17. Greiling AK, Boss LP, Wheeler LS. A preliminary investigation of asthma mortality in schools. *J School Health.* 2005;75(8): 286–290.

18. Akbari O, Faul JL, Hoyte EG, et al. CD4+ invariant T-cell–receptor+ natural killer T cells in bronchial asthma. *N Engl J Med.* 2006;354(11):1117–1129.

19. Galli SJ, Kalesnikoff J, Grimbaldeston MA, et al. Mast cells as "tunable" effector and immunoregulatory cells: recent advances. *Annu Rev Immunol.* 2005;23:749–786.

20. Kay AB, Phipps S, Robinson DS. A role for eosinophils in airway remodeling in asthma. *Trends Immunol.* 2004;25(9): 477–482.

21. Peters-Golden M. The alveolar macrophage: the forgotten cell in asthma. *Am J Respir Cell Mol Biol.* 2004;31(1):3–7.

22. Wenzel S. Mechanisms of severe asthma. *Clin Exp Allergy.* 2003;33(12):1622–1628.

23. Barnes PJ. Cytokine modulators as novel therapies for asthma. *Annu Rev Pharmacol Toxicol.* 2002;42:81–98.

24. Miller AL, Lukacs NW. Chemokine receptors: understanding their role in asthmatic disease. *Immunol Allergy Clin North Am.* 2004;24(4):667–683.

25. Ricciardolo FL, Sterk PJ, Gaston B, Folkerts G. Nitric oxide in health and disease of the respiratory system. *Physiol Rev.* 2004;84(3):731–765.

26. Carroll NG, Mutavdzic S, James AL. Distribution and degranulation of airway mast cells in normal and asthmatic subjects. *Eur Respir J.* 2002;19:879–885.

27. Carroll NG, Mutavdzic S, James AL. Increased mast cells and neutrophils in submucosal mucous glands and mucus plugging in patients with asthma. *Thorax.* 2002;57:677–682.

28. Elliott JG, Abramson MJ, Drummer OH, Walters EH, James AL. Time to death and mast cell degranulation in fatal asthma. *Respirology.* 2009;14:808–813.

29. Chakir J, Shannon J, Molet S, et al. Airway remodeling-associated mediators in moderate to severe asthma: effect of steroids on TGF-beta, IL-11, IL-17, and type I and type III collagen expression. *J Allergy Clin Immunol.* 2003;111:1293–1298.

30. de Medeiros Matsushita M, da Silva LF, dos Santos MA, et al. Airway proteoglycans are differentially altered in fatal asthma. *J Pathol.* 2005;207:102–110.

31. Laitinen A, Altraja A, Kampe M, et al. Tenascin is increased in airway basement membrane of asthmatics and decreased by an inhaled steroid. *Am J Respir Crit Care Med.* 1997;156:951–958.

32. Roche WR, Williams JH, Beasley R, Holgate ST. Subepithelial fibrosis in bronchi of asthmatics. *Lancet.* 1989;1:520–524.

33. de Magalhaes Simoes S, dos Santos MA, da Silva Oliveria M, et al. Inflammatory cell mapping of the respiratory tract in fatal asthma. *Clin Exp Allergy.* 2005;35:602–611.

34. Hamid Q, Song Y, Kotsimbos TC, et al. Inflammation of small airways in asthma. *J Allergy Clin Immunol.* 1997;100:44–51.

35. Dolhnikoff M, da Silva LFF, de Araujo BB, et al. The outer wall of small airways is a major site of remodeling in fatal asthma. *J Allergy Clin Immunol.* 2009;123:1090–1097.

36. Carroll N, Carello S, Cooke C, James A. Airway structure and inflammatory cells in fatal attacks of asthma. *Eur Respir J.* 1996;9:709–715.

37. Dunnill MS. The pathology of asthma with special reference to changes in the bronchial mucosa. *J Clin Pathol.* 1960;13:27–33.

38. Heard BE, Hossain S. Hyperplasia of bronchial muscle in asthma. *J Pathol.* 1971;110:319–331.

39. Saetta M, Di Stefano AD, Rosina C, Thiene G, Fabbri LM. Quantitative structural analysis of peripheral airways and arteries in sudden fatal asthma. *Am Rev Respir Dis.* 1991;143:138–143.

40. Jerath Tatum AM, Greenberger PA, Mileusnic D, Donoghue ER, Lifschultz BD. Clinical, pathologic, and toxicologic findings in asthma deaths in Cook County, Illinois. *Allergy Asthma Proc.* 2001;22:285–291.

41. Boulet LP, Deschesnes F, Turcotte H, Gignac F. Near-fatal asthma: clinical and physiologic features, perception of broncho-constriction, and psychologic profile. *J Allergy Clin Immunol.* 1991;88:838–846.

42. Lang DM. Asthma deaths and the athlete. *Clin Rev Allergy Immunol.* 2005;29:125–129.

43. Barr RG, Woodruff PG, Clark S, Camargo CA Jr. Sudden-onset asthma exacerbations: clinical features, response to therapy, and 2-week follow-up. *Eur Respir J.* 2000;15:266–271.

44. Campbell S, Hood I, Ryan D, Biedrzycki L, Mirchandani H. Death as a result of asthma in Wayne County Medical Examiner cases, 1975–1987. *J Forensic Sci.* 1990;35(2):356–364.

45. Robertson CF, Rubinfeld AR, Bowes G. Deaths from asthma in Victoria: a 12-month survey. *Med J Aust.* 1990;152(10): 511–517.

46. Hessel PA, Mitchell I, Tough S, et al. Risk factors for death from asthma. *Ann Allergy Asthma Immunol.* 1999;83:362–368.

47. Burke W, Fesinmeyer M, Reed K, Hampson L. Family history as a predictor of asthma risk. *Am J Prev Med.* 2003;24:160–169.

48. Hao K, Chen C, Wang B, et al. Familial aggregation of airway responsiveness: a community-based study. *Ann Epidemiol.* 2005;15:737–743.

49. Teerlink CC, Hegewald MJ, Cannon-Albright LA. A genealogical assessment of heritable predisposition to asthma mortality. *Am J Respir Crit Care Med.* 2007;176:865–870.

50. Kukufka DS, Lang DM, Porter S, et al. Exercise-induced bronchospasm in high school athletes via a free running test: incidence and epidemiology. *Chest.* 1998;116:1613–1622.

51. Holloway JW, Beghe B, Holgate ST. The genetic basis of atopic asthma. *Clin Exp Allergy.* 1999;29(8):1023–1032.

52. Strachan DP. Hay fever, hygiene, and household size. *BMJ.* 1989;299(6710):1259–1260.

53. Wiesch DG, Meyers DA, Bleecker ER. Genetics of asthma. *J Allergy Clin Immunol.* 1999;104(5):895–901.

54. Larsson K, Ohlsen P, Larrson L, et al. High prevalence of asthma in cross-country skiers. *Br Med J.* 1993;307:1326–1329.

55. Helenius IJ, Tikkanen HO, Sarna S, Haahtela T. Respiratory pathophysiologic responses. *J Allergy Clin Immunol.* 1998;101:646–652.

56. Chiung-Zuei C, Cheng-Hung L, Yung-Chi C, et al. Clinical features of fatal asthma. *Kaohsiung J Med Sci.* 2006;22:211–216.

57. Gelb AF, Schein A, Nussbaum E, et al. Risk factors for near-fatal asthma. *Chest.* 2004;126:1138–1146.

58. Restrepo RD, Peters J. Near-fatal asthma: recognition and management. *Curr Opin Pulm Med.* 2008;14:13–23.

59. Rothwell RPG, Rea HH, Sears MR, et al. Lessons from the national asthma mortality study: deaths in hospital. *N Z Med J.* 1987;100:199–202.

60. Busse WW, Lemanske RF Jr. Asthma. *N Engl J Med.* 2001;344(5):350–362.

61. Hogaboam CM, Carpenter KJ, Schuh JM, Buckland KF. Aspergillus and asthma—any link? *Med Mycol.* 2005;43(suppl 1):S197–S202.

62. Sporik R, Holgate ST, Platts-Mills TA, Cogswell JJ. Exposure to house dust mite allergen (Der p l) and the development of asthma in childhood. A prospective study. *N Engl J Med.* 1990;323(8):502–507.

63. Wahn U, Lau S, Bergmann R, et al. Indoor allergen exposure is a risk factor for sensitization during the first three years of life. *J Allergy Clin Immunol.* 1997;99(6):763–769.

64. Dezateux C, Stocks J, Dundas I, Fletcher ME. Impaired airway function and wheezing in infancy; the influence of maternal smoking and genetic predisposition to asthma. *Am J Respir Crit Care Med.* 1999;159(2):403–410.

65. American Thoracic Society. What constitutes an adverse health effect of air pollution? Official statement of the American Thoracic Society. *Am J Respir Crit Care Med.* 2000;161(2 pt 1):665–673.

66. Gauderman WJ, Avol E, Gilliland F, et al. The effect of air pollution on lung development from 10 to 18 years of age. *N Engl J Med.* 2004;351(11):1057–1067.

67. Rainbow J, Browne GJ. Fatal asthma or anaphylaxis. *Emerg Med J.* 2002;19:415–417.

68. Gern JE, Busse WW. Relationships of viral infections to wheezing illnesses and asthma. *Nat Rev Immunol.* 2002;2(2):132–138.

69. Sigurs N, Bjarnason R, Sigurbergsson F, Kjellman B. Respiratory syncytial virus bronchiolitis in infancy is an important risk factor for asthma and allergy at age 7. *Am J Respir Crit Care Med.* 2000;161(5):1501–1507.

70. Plaza V, Serrano J, Picado C, Sanchis J. Frequency and clinical characteristics of rapid-onset fatal and near-fatal asthma. *Eur Respir J.* 2002;19:846–852.

71. Levenson T, Greenberger PA, Donoghue ER, et al. Asthma deaths confounded by substance abuse: an assessment of fatal asthma. *Chest.* 1996;110:604–610.

72. Holley AD, Boots RJ. Review article: management of acute severe and near-fatal asthma. *Emerg Med Aus.* 2009;21:259–268.

73. Rodrigo GJ, Rodriquez Verde M, Peregalli V, Rodrigo C. Effects of short-term 28% and 100% oxygen on $PaCO_2$ and peak expiratory flow rate in acute asthma: a randomized trial. *Chest.* 2003;124:1312–1317.

74. Bernhardt DT, Roberts WO. *Preparticipation Physical Evaluation.* 4th ed. Elk Grove Village, IL: American Academy of Pediatrics; 2010.

75. Hammerman SI, Becker JM, Rogers J, et al. Asthma screening of high school athletes: identifying the undiagnosed and poorly controlled. *Ann Allergy Asthma Immunol.* 2002;88:380–384.

76. Finnish Medical Society Duodecim. Treatment of acute exacerbation of asthma. In: *EBM Guidelines. Evidence-Based Medicine* [Online]. Helsinki, Finland: John Wiley & Sons; 2007. Accessed June 2010.

77. Randolph C. Exercise-induced asthma: update on pathophysiology, clinical diagnosis, and treatment. *Curr Probl Pediatr.* 1997;27:53–77.

78. Eichner RE. Asthma in athletes: scope, risks, mimics, trends. *Curr Sports Med Rep.* 2008;7(3):118–119.

79. Dennis RJ, Solarte I, FitzGerald M. Asthma in adults. In: Young C, et al., eds. *BMJ Clinical Evidence Handbook.* London: BMJ Publishing Group; 2008:502–503.

80. Rodrigo GJ, Rodrigo C. Continuous vs. intermittent β agonists in the treatment of acute adult asthma. A systematic review with meta-analysis. *Chest.* 2002;122:160–165.

81. Lin RY, Sauter D, Newman T, et al. Continuous versus intermittent albuterol nebulization in the treatment of acute asthma. *Ann Emerg Med.* 1993;22:1847–1853.

82. Papo MC, Frank J, Thompson AE. A prospective, randomized study of continuous versus intermittent nebulized albuterol for severe status asthmaticus in children. *Crit Care Med.* 1993;21:1479–1486.

83. Woolcock AJ. Inhaler technology: new concepts for the millennium. A special report. *Postgrad Med.* 1999;106(7 suppl):18–21.

84. Silverman R. Treatment of acute asthma. A new look at the old and at the new. *Clin Chest Med*. 2000;21:361–379.

85. Stoodley RG, Aaron SD, Dales RE. The role of ipratropium bromide in the emergency management of acute asthma exacerbation: a metaanalysis of randomized clinical trials. *Ann Emerg Med*. 1999;34:8–18.

86. Plotnick LH, Ducharme FM. Acute asthma in children and adolescents: should inhaled anticholinergics be added to beta(2)-agonists? *Am J Respir Med*. 2003;2:109–115.

87. Rodrigo GJ, Castro-Rodriguez JA. Anticholinergics in the treatment of children and adults with acute asthma: a systematic review with meta-analysis. *Thorax*. 2005;60:740–746.

88. Dominguez LJ, Barbagallo M, Di Lorenzo G, et al. Bronchial reactivity and intracellular magnesium: a possible mechanism for the bronchodilating effects of magnesium in asthma. *Clin Sci (London)*. 1998;95:137–142.

89. Rowe BH, Bretzlaff JA, Bourdon C, Bota GW, Camargo CA Jr. Intravenous magnesium sulfate treatment for acute asthma in the emergency department: a systematic review of the literature. *Ann Emerg Med*. 2000;36:181–190.

90. Silverman RA, Osborn H, Runge J, et al. IV magnesium sulfate in the treatment of acute severe asthma: a multicenter randomized controlled trial. *Chest*. 2002;122:489–497.

91. Butland BK, Anderson HR, Cates CJ. The association between recent asthma medication and asthma death in a British case-control study. *Thorax*. 2009;64(suppl IV):A28.

92. Suissa S, Ernst P. Current reviews of allergy and clinical immunology. *J Allergy Clin Immunol*. 2001;107:937–944.

93. Castle W, Fuller R, Hall J, Palmer J. Serevent nationwide surveillance study: comparison of salmeterol with salbutamol in asthmatic patients who require regular bronchodilator treatment. *BMJ*. 1993;306:1034–1037.

94. Chatenoud L, Malvezzi M, Pitrelli A, La Vecchia C, Bamfi F. Asthma mortality and long-acting beta$_2$-agonists in five major European countries, 1994–2004. *J Asthma*. 2009;46:546–551.

95. Neffen H, Baena-Cagnani C, Passalacqua G, Canonica GW, Rocco D. Asthma mortality, inhaled steroids, and changing asthma therapy in Argentina (1990–1999). *Resp Med*. 2006;100:1431–1435.

96. Bender B, Milgrom H, Rand C. Nonadherence in asthmatic patients: is there a solution to the problem? *Ann Allergy Asthma Immunol*. 1997;79:177–185.

97. Milgrom H, Bender D, Ackerson L, et al. Noncompliance and treatment failures in children with asthma. *J Allergy Clin Immunol*. 1996;98:1051–1057.

98. Horne R. Compliance, adherence, and concordance: implications for asthma treatment. *Chest*. 2006;130:65S–72S.

99. Cochrane GM, Horne R, Chanez P. Compliance in asthma. *Respir Med*. 1999;93:763–769.

100. Horne R, Weinman J. Self-regulation and self-management in asthma: exploring the role of illness perceptions and treatment beliefs in explaining non-adherence to preventer medication. *Psychol Health*. 2002;17:17–32.

101. Allen TW. Sideline management of asthma. *Curr Sports Med Rep*. 2005;4:301–304.

102. Miller MG, Weiler JM, Baker R, Collins J, D'Alonzo G. National Athletic Trainers' Association position statement: management of asthma in athletes. *J Athl Train*. 2005; 40(3):224–245.

103. Weiler JM, Layon T, Hunt M. Asthma in United States Olympic athletes who participated in the 1996 Summer Games. *J Allergy Clin Immunol*. 1998;102:722–726.

Exertional Hyponatremia

Lawrence E. Armstrong, PhD, FACSM

Brendon P. McDermott, PhD, ATC

Definition of Condition

Physiologic hyponatremia is a state that involves a **serum sodium** or **plasma sodium** (Na^+) concentration below the adult normal range of 135 to 145 $mEq \cdot L^{-1}$. In sport, industrial, and military settings, the clinical condition known as **symptomatic exertional hyponatremia (EH$_s$)** involves a serum or plasma Na^+ concentration of less than 130 $mEq \cdot L^{-1}$ because that is the approximate threshold for the appearance of clinical signs and symptoms **(Table 12.1)**. Sodium concentrations below 125 $mEq \cdot L^{-1}$ in the presence of symptoms require immediate medical treatment. The approximate threshold for coma is 120 $mEq \cdot L^{-1}$. In nonexercising adults who consume a high volume of water chronically, these thresholds may be lower.[1]

Etiology

EH$_s$ is among the few noncongenital, nontraumatic conditions that result in sudden death, pulmonary or cerebral edema, and coma. Among athletes, EH$_s$ typically results from consumption of a large volume of **hypotonic** fluid that greatly exceeds renal excretory capacity. Thus, it is important to distinguish the physiologic state of hyponatremia (which involves a definition based on the serum sodium concentration, and may or may not result in distinct signs and symptoms) from EH$_s$ (which involves distinct signs and symptoms, heralds a potentially life-threatening illness, but involves a serum Na^+ level below 130 $mEq \cdot L^{-1}$).

Although few authors doubt that **fluid overload** is involved in EH$_s$,[2–4] published evidence demonstrates that retention of excess water is not always present. As shown in **Figure 12.1**, some athletes experience hyponatremia when dehydrated. This figure illustrates the relationship between plasma Na^+ concentration and percent body mass change after an Ironman triathlon; the gray rectangle represents the normal range (135–145 $mEq \cdot L^{-1}$). Blood was sampled from 330 competitors at the finish line; 11 were hyponatremic with a weight gain (lower right), 47

physiologic hyponatremia
Sodium deficiency in which plasma sodium concentration is at least less than 135 $mEq \cdot L^{-1}$ and may or may not be accompanied by symptoms of hyponatremia.

serum sodium Concentration of sodium found in the clear, pale-yellow liquid that separates from a clot during coagulation of blood.

plasma sodium Concentration of sodium within the fluid portion of blood.

symptomatic exertional hyponatremia (EH$_s$) Sodium deficiency that involves a plasma sodium concentration of less than 130 $mEq \cdot L^{-1}$ accompanied by typical symptoms (headache, nausea, vomiting, extreme weakness, etc.). This is the result of the replacement of sodium losses with hypotonic fluids, the loss of total body sodium, or both.

TABLE 12.1	Categories of Acute Exertional Hyponatremia and the Onset of Symptoms During Exercise		
Category	Plasma Na+ Concentration Range (mEq·L−1)	Approximate Amount of Excess Fluid (L) Required[a]	
Mild hyponatremia	130–135[b]	0.0–0.9	
Moderate EH_s	125–129[b]	1.2–2.4	
Severe EH_s	<125[b]	>2.4	
Approximate threshold for the onset of EH_s symptoms[c]	125–130[a]	0.9–2.4	

[a] Fluid excess = (Fluid intake, L) – (Sweat loss, L) – (Urine volume, L); from Speedy DB, Noakes TD, Rogers IR, et al. Hyponatremia in ultradistance events. *Med Sci Sports Exerc.* 1999;31:809–815; and Armstrong LE. Exertional hyponatremia. In: *Exertional Heat Illnesses.* Champaign, IL: Human Kinetics; 2003:103–135.

[b] Compiled from references 14, 15, 24, 25, 26 in Chapter 6 of Armstrong LE. *Exertional Heat Illnesses.* Champaign, IL: Human Kinetics; 2003.

[c] The presence or absence of symptoms depends on body size, total body water, beverage composition, total fluid volume, rate (L/h) of fluid intake, sweat rate, and sweat sodium concentration.

Abbreviations: EH_s, symptomatic exertional hyponatremia; L, liters; Na+, sodium.

Source: Reprinted from Speedy DB. Hyponatremia in ultradistance triathletes. *Medicine & Science in Sports & Exercise.* 31(6):809–815, 1999.

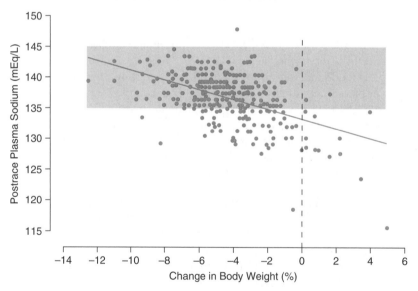

Figure 12.1   The relationship between change of body weight (%) and postrace plasma sodium concentration (mEq·L−1). Each point represents one of 330 Ironman triathletes who completed a 3.8-km swim, 180-km bicycle ride, and 42.4-km run. The lower left and lower right quadrants illustrate different types of hyponatremia (see text). Compare with Figure 12.2.
Source: Speedy DB. Hyponatremia in ultradistance triathletes. *Med Sci Sports Exerc.* 1999;31(6):809–815. Reprinted with permission.

were hyponatremic with a loss of body weight (lower left), and the vast majority of triathletes (272 or 87%) were not hyponatremic.[5] Generally, finishers with the lowest plasma Na$^+$ concentrations (and therefore the greatest risk of serious medical complications) either gained weight or had the smallest weight losses. Such a weight gain (interpreted as fluid retention) supports excessive water consumption as a primary component of the etiology of EH$_s$. Further, a weight gain during an Ironman triathlon is noteworthy considering that these endurance athletes likely lost 0.8 to 1.0 L of sweat per hour, or about 9 to 12 L total (average duration of 12.4 hours).[3]

The meaning of Figure 12.1 becomes clearer if one mentally superimposes **Figure 12.2** over it. The latter figure depicts the array of possible changes in normal water and sodium balance that might occur. The lower quadrants in Figure 12.2 represent the two types of hyponatremia. In terms of the extracellular fluid volume (which includes blood), athletes who *gained* weight represent **hypervolemic hyponatremia** (lower right quadrant) and those who *lost* weight represent **hypovolemic hyponatremia** (lower left quadrant). Further, those who lost weight likely did so because their sweat sodium loss was large and the extracellular fluid contracted; normal sodium and chloride levels are essential to maintain normal volume in the extracellular fluid compartment. Other characteristics that distinguish hypovolemic hyponatremia (i.e., weight loss) from hypervolemic hyponatremia (i.e., weight gain) appear in **Table 12.2**. Determination of relative hypovolemia due to sodium loss, versus hypervolemia due to fluid overload, should guide the clinical management of EH$_s$.

hypotonic Having an osmotic concentration less than that of normal blood.

fluid overload An excess of total body fluid volume (hypervolemia).

hypervolemic hyponatremia An excess of total body water (fluid overload) with an expanded extracellular fluid volume and increased whole-body sodium. A common sign of this condition is extremity edema (puffiness).

hypovolemic hyponatremia A reduced extracellular volume with deficits of total body sodium and water.

Retention of Excess Fluid

As shown in **Table 12.3**, Montain and colleagues[7] calculated the volume of *excess fluid* (i.e., fluid intake that exceeds sweat volume) required to dilute plasma Na$^+$ to 120 mEq·L^{-1} in three hypothetical ultramarathon runners with body masses of 50, 70, and 90 kg. All began with the same initial plasma Na$^+$ concentration (140 mEq·L^{-1}) and ran at a pace of 10 km·h^{-1} for 9 hours. The volume of fluid that would induce serious EH$_s$ (120 mEq·L^{-1}) was different, primarily due to differences of total body water and sweat Na$^+$ concentration. The reader should note that this critical volume (bottom row of Table 12.3) is only 2.2 L for the 50-kg athlete who has "salty sweat" (60 mEq·L^{-1}). Similar to the case report discussed earlier, this volume is relatively small; it represents only 200 mL of excess fluid per hour when consumed during a 9-hour event.

In a case report, a healthy 21-year-old man consumed a total of 10.3 L, but his fluid loss (urine plus sweat) of 7.5 L was greater than the mean of nine other study participants who served as a comparison

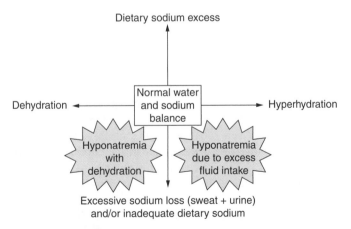

Figure 12.2 Interactions of sodium and water turnover (i.e., gain versus loss). The lower left and lower right quadrants illustrate different etiologies. Compare with Figure 12.1.

TABLE 12.2	Fluid-Electrolyte Characteristics and Etiologies of Two Types of Symptomatic Exertional Hyponatremia	
	Hypovolemic Hyponatremia	**Hypervolemic Hyponatremia**
Water balance	Water deficit	Water excess
Primary mechanism of hypotonic hyponatremia[a]	Sodium loss with intake of hypotonic fluid	Fluid overload
Whole-body dehydration	Present	Absent
Extracellular fluid volume	Contracted, due to sodium loss	Expanded, due to water excess
Clinical edema	Absent	Present
Etiology	Primary sodium deficiency occurs via sweat and renal losses, diarrhea, or vomiting that is replaced with water	Water excess occurs by oral ingestion or renal impairment; hypothetically, drugs (e.g., NSAIDs) or excessive AVP secretion may inhibit renal water excretion in some cases

[a] Compiled from references 27, 47, and 57 in Chapter 6 of Armstrong LE. *Exertional Heat Illnesses.* Champaign, IL: Human Kinetics; 2003.

Abbreviations: AVP, arginine vasopressin; NSAID, nonsteroidal anti-inflammatory drug.

group.[6] His total urine volume of 2.3 L demonstrated that renal function was not impaired, once he ceased exercising and drinking. Thus, he retained 2.8 L in 7 hours; this represented the excess fluid consumed (i.e., intake minus fluid lost in urine and sweat) and demonstrates a key etiologic factor. The 2.8 L was a small part (5%) of his **total body water** (estimated as 64% of body mass or 52.1 L), but retaining this much excess fluid was enough to alter the concentration of extracellular Na^+ to the point that physiologic hyponatremia became symptomatic. Further, his sweat rate (range, 0.54–0.84 $L \cdot h^{-1}$) and his urinary excretion rate (range, 0.28–0.63 $L \cdot h^{-1}$) were normal during 7 hours in the heat. This demonstrates that little excess fluid (2.8 L in 7 hours = 400 $mL \cdot h^{-1}$) can induce symptoms.

total body water The water content of the human body, in both intracellular and extracellular fluid compartments.

Epidemiology

The incidence of EH_s in competitive athletics is not well documented, with the exception of mass-participation distance events. However, there has been a widespread increase in public awareness regarding EH_s in recent years. Siegel et al.[2] assessed blood Na^+ levels in collapsed runners following the Boston marathon and found 4.8% had experienced EH_s. Interestingly, this represents fewer than 1% of participants at this race between 2001 and 2008 and only includes collapsed runners. The prevalence of **asymptomatic hyponatremia** was 12.5% in the London marathon in 2003;[8] in other observational studies, EH_s incidence ranged from 0%[9] to 29%[10] of participants. Clearly, the prevalence of asymptomatic hyponatremia (<135 $mEq \cdot L^{-1}$) is greater than that of EH_s (<130 $mEq \cdot L^{-1}$).[3,6]

Thus far, incidence rates of EH_s are unreported in sports such as American football. This condition is typically an afterthought for the medical staff covering the sidelines of such sports, but may occur more often than reported. Presumably, an athlete may overestimate the need to hydrate prior to and during activity, leading to EH_s. Any symptoms athletes exhibit are

asymptomatic hyponatremia Sodium deficiency in which plasma sodium is below normal levels (typically 130–135 $mEq \cdot L^{-1}$), but the patient experiences no symptoms.

TABLE
12.3

Calculated Water Excess Required to Dilute Plasma Na⁺ to 120 mEq·L⁻¹ in Ultramarathon Runners with Different Body Masses

	Runner A			Runner B			Runner C		
Body mass (kg)	50			70			90		
Body mass (lb)	111			155			199		
Total body water (L)	31.5			44.0			56.6		
Initial plasma Na⁺ concentration (mEq·L⁻¹)	140.0			140.0			140.0		
Initial extracellular fluid volume (L)	12.5			17.5			22.5		
Initial extracellular Na⁺ content (total mEq)	1750			2450			3151		
Volume of pure water consumed (L·9h⁻¹)	6.1			8.6			11.1		
Sweat loss (L·9h⁻¹) ^{a}	6.1			8.6			11.1		
Three Sweat Na⁺ Concentrations (mEq·L⁻¹)^b	20	40	60	20	40	60	20	40	60
Resultant Na⁺ loss (total mEq)	122	244	366	172	344	516	222	444	666
Resultant plasma Na⁺ concentration (mEq·L⁻¹)	136	132	128	136	132	128	136	132	128
Fluid excess that dilutes plasma Na⁺ to 120 mEq·L⁻¹ ^{c,d} (L)	4.2	3.2	2.2	5.9	4.5	3.0	7.6	5.8	3.9
(L·h⁻¹)	0.5	0.4	0.2	0.7	0.5	0.3	0.8	0.6	0.4

Pure water intake equals sweat loss.

^{a} Running at 10 km·h⁻¹ for 9 hours.

^{b} Sweat sodium (Na⁺) concentration decreases with physical training, heat acclimatization, and low-sodium diets.

^{c} (Initial TBW volume) × [(Na⁺ concentration after exercise)/(120 mEq·L⁻¹)] = Final TBW volume.

^{d} Fluid excess = (Final TBW volume) − (Initial TBW volume).

Abbreviations: L, liters; L·h⁻¹, liters per hour; mEq, milliequivalents; Na⁺, sodium; TBW, total body water.

Source: Adapted from Montain SJ, Cheuvront SN, Sawka MN. Exercise associated hyponatremia: quantitative analysis to understand the aetiology. *Br J Sports Med.* 2006;40:98–106.

assumed to be a result of exertion and heat exposure, and resolve with the consumption of meals following workouts. It is important to note, however, that this has not been documented. Further, EH$_s$ is most commonly reported in events or contests lasting in excess of 4 hours.[10,11] A much more common condition resulting from team sport activities lasting 2 to 3 hours is exercise dehydration,[12] the signs and symptoms of which often mimic those of mild EH$_s$ (light-headedness, fatigue, dizziness, etc.). It is difficult to pinpoint the prevalence of either condition in team sports because both are rapidly corrected when athletes consume meals (including Na⁺) and fluids following exercise (provided fluids are not consumed in excess). Given the overwhelming percentage of athletes who lose weight during activity,[12] the incidence of exercise dehydration clearly exceeds that of EH$_s$. Future research should identify the prevalence of both conditions following team sport activities.

Pathophysiology

Sodium and chloride are extracellular ions; potassium is an intracellular ion. The regulation of sodium and potassium concentration, on both sides of a cell membrane, is critical for proper nerve conduction, muscle contraction, movement of fluids and solutes throughout the body, and optimal health. This explains the skeletal muscular twitching and cramps, muscular weakness, and physical exhaustion that are part of the clinical picture of advanced EH$_s$.[13,14] A delayed onset of symptoms, sometimes reported long after exercise ends, likely occurs because osmotic equilibration between the brain and plasma requires more than 2 hours to achieve.[15]

When a large volume of hypotonic fluid is consumed, the extracellular fluid becomes dilute because the fluid moves from the intestine directly into blood. As extracellular tonicity falls, water flows into cells and they swell.[16] This explains the pulmonary edema that occurs in severe cases of EH$_s$, as well as the neurologic symptoms of nausea, vomiting, grand mal seizure, and coma.[13,17] If the hyponatremia is not corrected, edema often leads to pulmonary arrest.

Brain edema usually accompanies severe EH$_s$. If the brain does not adapt osmotically, the pressure of the swollen brain on the skull can lead to reduced cerebral blood flow, cerebral hypoxia, and pressure necrosis.[18] Autopsies have revealed obliteration, flattening, and herniation of brain structures.[17,19,20] Postmortem examinations also have identified edema and congestion of the heart, liver, kidneys, and intestine as well as pink, frothy fluid in the trachea and bronchi.[17]

Predisposing Factors and Prevention

After reviewing the clinical and scientific literature, we have identified nine factors that predispose athletes to EH$_s$. The following list summarizes the factors and provides a simple way to prevent or counteract each threat to health.

1. A large volume of hypotonic fluid (relative to blood plasma) is consumed within a few hours.[6] When compared with fluid lost during exercise (e.g., in sweat or urine), the excess volume is small (see previous discussion in this chapter and Table 12.3).

    Prevention: Consume fluids during exercise so as not to exceed weight loss of 2% of body mass, because this compromises performance. Contrarily, weight gain should not occur during activity. Simple body weight measurements can be used to determine individual sweat rate **(Table 12.4)**.[21]

2. Sodium (Na$^+$) or sodium chloride (NaCl, table salt) losses in sweat and urine are not replaced adequately by dietary food or fluids.

    Prevention: Consume ample dietary Na$^+$ when training in a hot environment and as a part of daily meals. Easy ways to ensure an adequate intake are to use the salt shaker more liberally with meals, or to eat canned soups, potato chips, or pretzels on a daily basis. *Note:* Sport drinks are relatively dilute and vary in electrolyte concentration; they do little to retard the development of physiologic hyponatremia or symptomatic EH$_s$.[22]

3. The absence of heat acclimatization predisposes active individuals to EH$_s$ because of relatively large Na$^+$ losses in sweat and urine. A decreased sweat Na$^+$ concentration is one of several physiologic adaptations that occur during heat acclimatization.[23] Opposing this, sweat rate increases during a 2-week heat acclimatization period, increasing the likelihood that a sodium deficit will occur.

    Prevention: Undertake 8 to 14 days of training in the heat, gradually increasing the exercise duration and intensity.

4. Exercise duration is a primary predisposing factor. Reports of EH$_s$ occur most often in distance running events that are 42.2 kilometers or longer,[3–5,8,10,11,24,25] triathlons that last 7 to 17 hours,[26] repeated days of military training,[27] and long hikes.[28] Slower runners may be at greater risk of EH$_s$ because they linger at aid stations or do not pass aid stations without drinking. Further, Davis and colleagues[24] observed a significant inverse relationship ($p < 0.0002$) between postrace serum sodium level in marathoners and the time elapsed before presentation at a hospital emergency department. None of the marathon runners who experienced EH$_s$ completed the race in less than 4 hours.

<table>
<tr><td>**TABLE 12.4**</td><td>**Self-Testing Program for Optimal Hydration**</td></tr>
</table>

1. Make sure you are properly hydrated BEFORE the workout—your urine should be clear.
2. Do a warm-up run to the point where perspiration is generated, then stop. Urinate if necessary.
3. Weigh yourself naked on an accurate scale.
4. Run for 1 hour at an intensity similar to your targeted race.
5. Drink a measured amount of a beverage of your choice during the run if and when you are thirsty. It is important that you keep track of exactly how much fluid you take in during the run.
6. Do not urinate during the run.
7. Weigh yourself naked again on the same scale you used in step 3.
8. You may now urinate and drink more fluids as needed. Calculate your fluid needs using the following formula:
    A. Enter your body weight from step 3 in kilograms _____
       (To convert from pounds to kilograms, divide pounds by 2.2)
    B. Enter your body weight from step 7 in kilograms − _____
       (To convert from pounds to kilograms, divide pounds by 2.2)
    C. Subtract B from A = _____
    D. Convert your total in C to grams by multiplying by 1000 × 1000
       = _____
    E. Enter the amount of fluid you consumed during the run in milliliters + _____
       (To convert from ounces to milliliters, multiply ounces by 30)
    F. Add E to D = _____

This final figure is the number of milliliters (mL) that you need to consume per hour to remain well hydrated. If you want to convert milliliters back to ounces, simply divide by 30.

Source: Casa DJ. Proper hydration for distance running: Identifying individual fluid needs. *Track Coach*. 2004;167: 5321–5328. Reprinted with permission.

Prevention: Consume salty foods or salt capsules with water during long-duration events. Do not consume fluids at every water station, and avoid overconsumption by using a personalized hydration plan that is based on sweat rate (Table 12.4). Sport drinks contain low levels of sodium and thus do little to maintain normal whole-body sodium balance. Instead, during postexercise meals, consume foods that are high in sodium (e.g., canned soups, pretzels).

5. Published evidence suggests that environmental heat stress (see below) interacts with the mind-sets or personality characteristics of some individuals to increase the desire to consume a large amount of hypotonic fluid. Considerable evidence indicates that EH_s often occurs in those who premeditate drinking a large volume of water[6,29,30] or believe that consuming excess water will prevent heat illness.[31] This behavior is aggravated by that noted in item 6.

   Prevention: Educate athletes about the risk of EH_s due to fluid overload; train them to drink adequately but not excessively, according to individual needs. Athletes will be less likely to overconsume fluids if they understand their personal body water losses (Table 12.4) through exercise.

6. Although no systematic study has verified this hypothesis, some authorities[30] believe that the instructions of race organizers and medical directors to "drink as much water as possible" resulted in overdrinking and EH_s at numerous road races during the 1980s and 1990s. As a result of educational efforts and recent position statements of professional sports medicine organizations,[32,33] this disturbing trend has changed considerably.

   Prevention: Explain the risk of EH_s due to fluid overload; encourage competitors to drink adequately but not excessively, according to individual needs.

7. A genetic tendency for high sweat Na^+ concentration (e.g., 80–100 mEq·L^{-1}) increases the risk of a whole-body sodium deficit, as found in individuals who carry the trait for cystic fibrosis but do not express it phenotypically.[34] Virjens and Rehrer[35] reported one case of EH_s that occurred after 2.5 hours of cycling. Their calculations indicated that the cyclist's sweat contained a sodium concentration of at least 100 mEq·L^{-1}. Athletes should check for white salt deposits on a uniform, jersey, or shorts after a strenuous bout of exercise in a hot environment. This indicates that he/she has a high sweat Na^+ concentration.

    Prevention: At meals, consume foods that are high in sodium (e.g., canned soup).

8. At least four previous studies have indicated that female hikers and marathon runners were more likely than males (19 women versus 4 men) to develop serious symptomatic EH_s (see Armstrong et al.[6] for a summary of these cases). This may occur because the average woman has less total body water than the average man, and therefore requires a smaller volume of water to dilute extracellular sodium (see Table 12.3).

    Prevention: Drink no more fluid than the volume that one loses in sweat; do not *gain* weight during a workout or race, because this represents a fluid excess. Additionally, we have observed that women are generally more ardent about following advice and instruction and thus may err on the side of excess with respect to hydration, or at least fail to adjust volume for their size. Thus, the notion of hydration recommendations for the masses has less value and perhaps some danger. Rather, individuals should ascertain their own needs (Table 12.4).[36]

9. Annual seasons influence development of EH_s. Because exercise in a hot environment and the resulting internal hyperthermia stimulate considerably greater water turnover (i.e., sweat loss with hypotonic fluid intake) than comparable exercise in a cool environment, most cases of EH_s occur during summer months.

    Prevention: During summer months, heed the recommendations in items 1 through 8 of this list.

arginine vasopressin (AVP) Pituitary hormone that limits production of urine by stimulating water reabsorption in the kidneys (also known as antidiuretic hormone or ADH).

Two potential predisposing factors require further research before their validity can be established. The first involves abnormal secretion of the hormone **arginine vasopressin (AVP)**, which regulates water excretion at the kidneys. One case report[6] involved an abnormal AVP response (+460% despite a fluid intake of 10.3 L) in a young, healthy male. In contrast, another publication reported that 14 runners with symptomatic EH_s all had normal blood AVP concentrations.[37] The second potential predisposing factor involves the use of nonsteroidal anti-inflammatory drugs (NSAIDs). These medications are known to potentiate the effect of AVP on the renal collecting ducts, with the result of impaired diuresis. One report of EH_s in three marathon runners observed that all three used NSAIDs during the race; unfortunately, investigators did not measure the volume of water consumed.[29]

Recognition

We believe that there are two periods in which athletic trainers and health care professionals can recognize this condition. First, an athlete may sense symptoms during or shortly after exercise. Second, EH_s symptoms may occur hours after an event, when the athlete is likely to perceive initial symptoms to be a result of exercise and may not be aware of EH_s.

Early Recognition

Early recognition involves the prompt identification of signs and symptoms as related to EH_s during, or even before, exercise. Prior to exercise, an athlete may overhydrate with the goal of avoiding dehydration-related decrements in exercise performance. Although slight hyperhydration prior to an event may be recommended,[32,33] extreme overhydration should be discouraged. Signs and symptoms may include dizziness, light-headedness, and puffiness.[3] A preparticipation body weight can help identify pre-exercise hyponatremia, if body weight is greater than a valid baseline measure. Athletes exhibiting signs or symptoms prior to exercise should not participate until a normonatremic state is verified. As a general rule, it is a good idea to assess body weight just prior to competition so that a postexercise weight can be used to quantify weight gain or loss.

Athletes may recognize symptoms during exercise, including headache, dizziness, muscular twitching, extremity tingling or swelling, and physical exhaustion (Table 12.5). The most common symptoms reported by patients include (in order of incidence) nausea, vomiting, dizziness, light-headedness, headache, and puffiness.[38] Because many of these symptoms are also symptoms of intense exercise, low blood glucose level, dehydration, head in-

TABLE 12.5	Signs and Symptoms of Acute Exertional Hyponatremia	
Change of mental status	Encephalopathy
Nausea	Disorientation, confusion
Vomiting	Incoordination
Headache	Combative behavior
Dizziness	Physical exhaustion
Muscular twitching	Muscular weakness
Grand mal seizures	Cardiac arrest
Coma	Respiratory arrest
Somnolence	Pulmonary edema
Tingling	Cerebral edema

jury, or heat illness, these disorders are difficult to distinguish from EH_s. Athletes experiencing these symptoms during exercise should pay close attention to their fluid consumption and take steps to correct what may be the cause. During workouts, athletes should not gain weight. Medical professionals should include EH_s in the differential diagnosis and take a complete history in which other conditions are ruled out. The most efficient method of diagnosing EH_s on site is the use of a hand-held analyzer, which can measure serum Na^+ concentration within 2 minutes.[39–43]

Recognition Following Exercise or Collapse

After an exercise bout or competition, symptoms of exertional hyponatremia may appear acutely or with a gradual progression over several hours. A collapsed, semiconscious, or unconscious athlete should be evaluated for all of the potential causes of sudden death in sport. Because vital treatment for these conditions varies widely (from on-site whole-body cooling for exertional heat stroke to prompt IV hypertonic saline for EH_s, whether on site or during transport), an efficient assessment is necessary.[39–44] The key differential with EH_s is blood Na^+ assessment, which should be measured in collapsed athletes in the medical tent. If the medical staff does not have access to a portable sodium analyzer, it is then necessary to rule out other conditions (e.g., exertional heat stroke, ruled out with a rectal temperature < 40°C [104°F]) prior to emergency transport. Clinical symptoms matched with a blood Na^+ concentration below 125 $mEq \cdot L^{-1}$ warrant a diagnosis of EH_s and initiation of treatment. This is a medical emergency.

When athletes complain of mild symptoms following an exercise bout, a complete history should be taken that includes questions regarding fluid volume consumed, use of NSAIDs, and food consumption. Vital signs should be assessed, which are typically normal with mild to moderate EH_s, at least initially. If the history suggests EH_s, blood Na^+ levels should be measured. Some athletes in this state may worsen over time. Athletes should be educated to recognize the symptoms of EH_s that may occur immediately after an event.

Athletes also may experience symptoms of EH_s hours after the event. Emergency department personnel should include EH_s in differential diagnoses, and blood Na^+ concentration should be assessed prior to treatment.

Treatment

The overall goal of EH_s treatment is to reduce intracellular fluid volume to a normal level; treatment is guided by a patient's signs and symptoms. A secondary goal is to avoid producing complications, such as central pontine myelinolysis, due to rapid correction of EH_s (see "Complications of Correcting

Hyponatremia" later in this chapter). Three main factors determine emergency room or mass medical tent therapeutic interventions for EH$_s$: (1) the presence of central nervous system dysfunction, (2) the onset of symptoms (acute or chronic), and (3) volume status.[42] On the sidelines or in a medical tent, the important factors are central nervous system dysfunction and serum Na$^+$ levels **(Figure 12.3)**. Athletes typically demonstrate an acute onset during an event or training session. **Table 12.6** lists recommended equipment to have in preparation for treating potential EH$_s$ cases.

Athletes with mild symptoms, normal total body water volume, and a mildly altered blood Na$^+$ level (130–135 mEq·L^{-1}) should restrict fluid and consume salty foods or a small volume of oral hypertonic solution (e.g., three to five bouillon cubes dissolved in 240 mL of hot water). This can be continued until spontaneous diuresis and correction of blood Na$^+$ concentration occur; this management may require

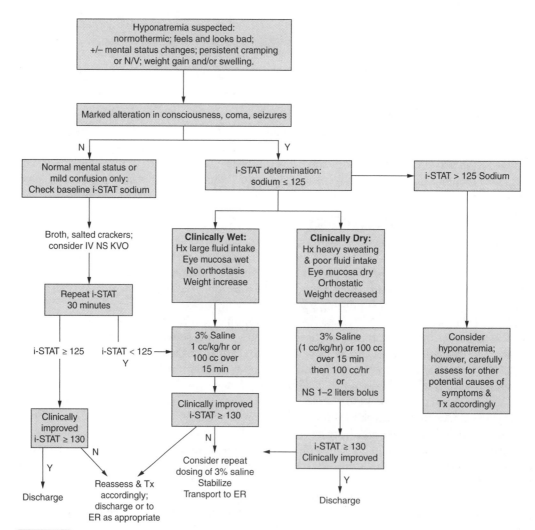

Figure 12.3 Symptomatic hyponatremia treatment algorithm. ER indicates emergency room; Hx, history; i-STAT, the i-STAT System hand-held blood sodium analyzer from Abbott Laboratories (Abbott Park, IL); IV, intravenous; KVO, keep vein open; NS, normal saline; N/V, nausea/vomiting; Tx, treatment.
Source: O'Connor FG, Pyne S, Adams WB, Brennan FH, Howard T. *Managing Emergencies in Mass Participation Events: Medical Triage and Algorithms.* Betnesda, MD: USUHS Consortium for Health and Military Performance; 2009:3. Reprinted with permission.

hours (or can take less than an hour), but is successful in stable patients.[43] Normal (0.9% NaCl) saline therapy is contraindicated with EH$_s$ because of the risk of exacerbating fluid overload.

If an athlete's status deteriorates, or if he or she initially presents with severe symptoms, hypertonic saline (3–5%) via IV infusion is indicated. The use of IV hypertonic saline rapidly corrects symptoms of EH$_s$ and decreases intracellular fluid volume.[3,25] Serial measures of blood sodium concentration should be monitored throughout treatment (about every 100 mL of IV fluid). To avoid complications, hypertonic saline administration should be discontinued when blood sodium concentration reaches 128 to 130 mEq·L^{-1}. IV fluids should not be provided to patients without blood Na$^+$ assessment. If severe EH$_s$ symptoms due to fluid overload do not resolve within 30 minutes of IV administration, a loop diuretic (e.g., furosemide) may be considered.[41] This is only an option after a laboratory assessment of osmolality verifies euvolemic or hypervolemic EH$_s$, because diuretic use may be hazardous when hypovolemic EH$_s$ exists (i.e., reduced extracellular volume; see Table 12.2).[45]

TABLE 12.6	Suggested Equipment and Supplies for Treatment of Exertional Hyponatremia

Hypertonic saline, catheters, stopcock connections, needles

Tourniquets

Portable blood Na$^+$ analyzer

Bouillon cubes

Salty foods (e.g., potato chips)

Potable water

Rectal thermometer (which reads to 43°C [109.4°F]) to rule out exertional heat stroke

Styrofoam cups

Microwave oven

Emergency cot, bench, or treatment table

Equipment to measure vital signs

Stretchers or cots

OSHA-compliant nonlatex gloves

Sharps and biohazard disposal containers

Alcohol wipes, gauze, and tape

Tables for supply access and organization

Stretchers and wheelchairs

Digital scale

Cell phone to call for transport or to ED to alert for incoming hyponatremia

Abbreviations: ED, emergency department; Na$^+$, sodium; OSHA, Occupational Safety and Health Administration.

A delay in treatment results in poor outcomes and increased morbidity. Prompt recognition and treatment are associated with minimal morbidity.[40,41] Also, numerous case reports suggest that the rapid correction of blood Na$^+$ concentration with IV hypertonic saline as opposed to IV normal saline results in decreased morbidity with an absence of sequelae.[39–43]

The athlete with severe EH$_s$ should be transported to a medical facility following or during treatment. Once a patient arrives at the emergency department, an assessment of plasma osmolality should be used to indicate hypo- or hypervolemia. Patients with persistent hypovolemia despite normal serum Na$^+$ values should then be treated with IV normal saline. The progress of symptoms and blood Na$^+$ levels will guide the decision for follow-up care.

Complications of Correcting Hyponatremia

In the past, as a result of a focus on dehydration management following large events, intravenous normal saline administration was aggressively administered. However, athletes with EH$_s$ either did not recover quickly or their symptoms progressed to the point that some died. Normal saline administration does not correct fluid overload and is contraindicated for EH$_s$.

Central nervous system manifestations (e.g., confusion, convulsions, coma) require treatment. **Central pontine myelinolysis (CPM)** is a potential complication of very rapid correction of blood Na^+ levels, or a rapid serum change to more than 130 mEq $Na^+ \cdot L^{-1}$. CPM involves the destruction of the myelin sheath in brain cells. This then leads to a rapid decline in neurologic function and acute paralysis. In the treatment of acute EH_s, CPM has not been documented with the use of 3% hypertonic saline in otherwise healthy individuals.[41] CPM most often occurs when a gradual onset leads to EH_s and a rapid correction takes place.[41] If a chronic onset (>48 hours) is confirmed, a slower rate of correction of blood Na^+ concentration is warranted, but this is rare among athletes. Although some authorities recommend a blood Na^+ correction rate of 1 mEq$\cdot$h^{-1} until the patient becomes asymptomatic,[45] others state that 1 to 3.4 mEq$\cdot$h^{-1} is appropriate for most cases of EH_s.[24] Serial measures of blood Na^+ levels to monitor progress are important, and correction rates more rapid than 5 mEq$\cdot$h^{-1} are not advised. The overall management of EH_s should not be compromised due to concern about CPM in any acute case of EH_s. The risks of severe EH_s outweigh the potential of CPM in otherwise healthy athletes, and the potential for CPM is greater in chronic cases.[41,46]

Recovery

When treated appropriately with IV hypertonic saline, EH_s spontaneously resolves without complications. Chronic morbidity is rare.[39,41] Although the expected time course of recovery following EH_s is not well documented, it appears to be largely dependent on the severity of the condition (i.e., the severity and duration of brain swelling determine the resultant morbidity or mortality).[3] Rapid recognition and appropriate treatment reduce the risk of encephalopathy or central nerve damage.[3,39-41]

We recommend that EH_s patients follow up with a primary care physician within 3 to 7 days after their episode, to ensure absence of lasting sequelae. The physician will ensure normal fluid turnover, kidney function, diet, neuropsychological processing, and daily function. A plan for future prevention should be developed with a knowledgeable athletic trainer, exercise physiologist, or sports medicine–trained physician. An appropriate course of return to activity should be discussed upon patient discharge.

Return-to-Play Considerations

To our knowledge, few complications exist following mild or moderate EH_s when treatment is prompt and appropriate. In such cases, return to activity should be guided by a plan to avoid future episodes of EH_s, specifically, an individualized hydration plan.[32] This plan should incorporate individual exercise intensity and duration, environmental conditions, sweat rate, and sweat Na^+ concentration. This plan also should be informed by the history and factors that contributed to the initial EH_s episode.

It is true that EH_s can be avoided if athletes do not consume fluids during exercise. However, severe dehydration (i.e., >7% body mass loss) compromises health. Further, exercise performance and cardiovascular, thermoregulatory, and cognitive function are all compromised by dehydration of more than 2% of body mass and should be avoided.[32,33] Therefore, athletes should strive to maintain hydration within a relatively narrow range by considering both dehydration and EH_s when developing a personalized hydration plan.

Current Return-to-Play Recommendations

Specific civilian and military recommendations do not exist for return to activity following EH_s. The National Athletic Trainers' Association position statement regarding exertional heat illnesses recommends a gradual increase in activity following physician clearance, but this recommendation lacks scientific or case report confirmation.[47] Recent expert panels have avoided this aspect of EH_s management and have focused on acute treatment.[39] If prompt recognition and treatment occur, the athlete should be encouraged to return to activity. Competitor education should be designed to prevent a subsequent episode. With a hydration and nutrition plan in place, most athletes should be able to return within 48 to 72 hours.

In our opinion, athletic trainers and sport dietitians can act in the following ways to raise athlete awareness about EH_s:

- Send out electronic information sheets to describe EH_s and ways to avoid it.
- Provide accurate digital floor scales during prolonged endurance events.
- Encourage athletes to heed thirst sensations during training and competition. Athletes should drink when thirsty and stop drinking when they feel full.
- Teach athletes how to measure sweat rate, with a goal of replacing lost fluid (i.e., in sweat or urine) so that body weight loss does not exceed 2%.
- Teach athletes what 4-, 6-, and 8-ounce containers look like, so they know how much fluid to replace.

Event directors should seek consults with athletic trainers and sport dietitians so that EH_s educational information can be disseminated in race packets, at race trade shows and expositions, at exhibits, and to medical staffs.

Summary

Exertional hyponatremia is one of a few illnesses that are potentially fatal to otherwise healthy athletes, laborers, and military personnel. This illness involves a serum Na^+ concentration between 130 and 135 mEq·L^{-1}. Symptomatic exertional hyponatremia involves signs and symptoms such as disorientation, depression, nausea, vomiting, muscular twitching, and grand mal seizure. Severe cases (serum Na^+ level < 125 mEq·L^{-1}) may involve coma, pulmonary or cerebral edema, and respiratory arrest. Despite these facts, few athletes realize that excessive fluid consumption may cause illness, hospitalization, or occupational disability.

Reports of EH_s most often arise from military training, long hikes, distance running events (≥42.2 km) and triathlons (7–17 hours). Many individuals who experience EH_s are motivated to drink "as much fluid as possible" during or after exercise. Body size, total body water, beverage composition, sweat rate, and sweat Na^+ concentration are important etiologic factors. The simplest way to reduce the risk of EH_s is to ensure that fluid is consumed at a rate that equals, or is slightly less than, sweat rate. After exercise, consumption of sodium-rich beverages and foods (e.g., low-fat soup, dissolved bouillon, or stew with crackers) also reduces morbidity due to EH_s.

Clinical Case Scenario

1. To our knowledge, one case report[6] represents the only published data that continuously tracked EH_s as it developed. A 21-year old, healthy man (K.G.) was participating in a research investigation in which dietary sodium was controlled for 7 days prior to the onset of symptoms. In a hot environment (41°C [106°F]), hyponatremia was verified as a plasma Na^+ concentration of 126 mEq·L^{-1} after only 4 hours of exercise. Prior to the blood sample, this man had consumed breakfast and a snack containing 17 and 6 mEq·L^{-1} Na^+, respectively.

   Four etiologic factors caused his plasma Na^+ to fall to 122 mEq·L^{-1} (plasma osmolality of 253 mOsm·kg^{-1}) by hour 7: (1) K.G. entered the day with a "low normal" plasma Na^+ (134 mEq·L^{-1}) because he had hyperhydrated during the previous night; (2) K.G. consumed 10.3 L of fluid in 7 hours; (3) his blood sample indicated an inappropriately large release of arginine vasopressin (i.e., antidiuretic hormone), which coincided with a decrease of urine volume to 0 mL·h^{-1}; and (4) his personal goal was to consume as much water as possible during exercise, because he believed that this would help him avoid heat illness. This constellation of four factors resulted in fatigue and nausea (hour 4).

   Later that evening, despite no eating or drinking, he complained of increasing nausea and malaise, which prompted the attending physician to transfer him to a nearby hospital. Upon admission, his serum Na^+ level was still 122 mEq·L^{-1}. Treatment consisted of administration of hypertonic IV saline solution (5% NaCl) and overnight fluid restriction. The patient was released at 11:00 AM the next morning in an asymptomatic state.

1. Upon admittance of this patient to the hospital, what would your differential diagnosis be?

2. What are the main factors contributing to this case of hyponatremia?

3. What could this athlete have done to help prevent this incident from occurring?

4. What take-home instructions would you give this man upon his release from the hospital?

Key Terms

arginine vasopressin (AVP)

asymptomatic hyponatremia

central pontine myelinolysis (CPM)

fluid overload

hypervolemic hyponatremia

hypotonic

hypovolemic hyponatremia

physiologic hyponatremia

plasma sodium

serum sodium

symptomatic exertional hyponatremia (EH_s)

total body water

References

1. Farrell DJ, Bower L. Fatal water intoxication. *J Clin Pathol.* 2003;56:803–804.
2. Siegel AJ, d'Hemecourt P, Adner MM, et al. Exertional dysnatremia in collapsed marathon runners. *Am J Clin Pathol.* 2009;132:336–340.
3. Armstrong LE. Exertional hyponatremia. In: *Exertional Heat Illnesses.* Champaign, IL: Human Kinetics; 2003:103–135.
4. Noakes TD, Norman RJ, Buck RH, et al. The incidence of hyponatremia during prolonged ultradistance exercise. *Med Sci Sports Exerc.* 1990;22:165–170.
5. Speedy DB, Noakes TD, Rogers IR, et al. Hyponatremia in ultradistance events. *Med Sci Sports Exerc.* 1999;31:809–815.
6. Armstrong LE, Curtis WC, Hubbard RW, et al. Symptomatic hyponatremia during prolonged exercise in heat. *Med Sci Sports Exerc.* 1993;25(5):543–549.
7. Montain SJ, Cheuvront SN, Sawka MN. Exercise associated hyponatremia: quantitative analysis to understand the aetiology. *Br J Sports Med.* 2006;40:98–106.
8. Kipps C, Sharma S, Pedoe DT. The incidence of exercise-associated hyponatremia in the London Marathon. *Br J Sports Med.* doi:10.1136/bjsm.2009.05935.
9. Schenk K, Gatterer H, Ferrari M, et al. Bike Transalp 2008: liquid intake and its effect on the body's fluid homeostasis in the course of a multistage, cross-country, MTB marathon race in the central Alps. *Clin J Sport Med.* 2010;20:147–152.
10. Hiller WDB, O'Toole ML, Massimino F, Hiller RE, Laird RH. Plasma electrolyte and glucose changes during the Hawaiian Ironman Triathlon. *Med Sci Sports Exerc.* 1985;17:S219.
11. Almond CSD, Shin AY, Fortescue EB, et al. Hyponatremia among runners in the Boston Marathon. *NEJM.* 2005;352:1550–1556.
12. Mueller F, Colgate B. *Annual Survey of Football Injury Research, 1931–2009.* Chapel Hill, NC: National Center for Catastrophic Injury Research; 2009. Available at: http://www.unc.edu/depts/nccsi/. Accessed July 2, 2010.
13. Arieff A. Central nervous system manifestations of disordered sodium metabolism. *Clin Endocrin Metab.* 1984;13:269–294.
14. Ayus JC, Achinger SG, Arieff A. Brain cell volume regulation in hyponatremia: role of sex, age, vasopressin, and, hypoxia. *Am J Physiol Renal Physiol.* 2008;295:F619–F624.
15. Pollock AS, Arieff AI. Abnormalities of cell volume regulation and their functional consequences. *Am J Physiol.* 1980;239:F195–F205.
16. Goldberger E. *A Primer of Water, Electrolyte, and Acid-Base Syndromes.* 6th ed. Philadelphia: Lea and Febiger; 1980:58–120.
17. Chen X, Huang G. Autopsy case report of a rare acute iatrogenic water intoxication with a review of the literature. *Forensic Sci Int.* 1995;76:27–34.

18. Arieff AI. Management of hyponatremia. *BMJ*. 1993;307:305–308.
19. Helwig FC, Schultz CB, Curry DE. Water intoxication: report of a fatal case with clinical, pathological, and experimental studies. *JAMA*. 1935;104:1569–1574.
20. Rashkind M. Psychosis, polydipsia, and water intoxication: report of a fatal case. *Arch Gen Psych*. 1974;30:112–116.
21. Casa DJ. For distance running—identifying individual fluid needs. *Track Coach*. 2004;167:5321–5328.
22. Weschler LB. Exercise-associated hyponatremia. A mathematical review. *Sports Med*. 2005;35(10):899–922.
23. Armstrong LE, Maresh CM. The induction and decay of heat acclimatization in trained athletes. *Sports Med (New Zealand)*. 1991;12(5):302–312.
24. Davis D, Marino A, Vilke G, Dunford J, Videen J. Hyponatremia in marathon runners: experience with the inaugural Rock'n'Roll Marathon. *Ann Emerg Med*. 1999;34:540–541.
25. Speedy DB, Noakes TD, Rogers IR, et al. Hyponatremia in ultradistance triathletes. *Med Sci Sports Exerc*. 1999;22:165–170.
26. Noakes TD, Norman RJ, Buck RH, et al. The incidence of hyponatremia during prolonged ultradistance exercise. *Med Sci Sports Exerc*. 1990;22:165–170.
27. U.S. Army Center for Health Promotion and Preventive Medicine. Hyponatremia hospitalizations, U.S. Army 1989–1996. *Med Surv Monthly Rep*. 2000;6:9–11.
28. Garigan T, Ristedt DE. Death from hyponatremia as a result of acute water intoxication in the Army basic trainee. *Mil Med*. 1999;3:234–238.
29. Romero JC, Stameloni RJ, Dafu ML, et al. Changes in fluid compartments, renal hemodynamics, plasma renin, and aldosterone secretion induced by low sodium intake. *Metabolism*. 1968;37:10–19.
30. Speedy DB, Noakes TD, Boswell T, et al. Response to a fluid load in athletes with a history of exercise induced hyponatremia. *Med Sci Sports Exerc*. 2001;33:1434–1442.
31. Noakes TD, Goodwin N, Rayner BL, Branken T, Taylor RKN. Water intoxication: a possible complication during endurance exercise. *Med Sci Sports Exer*. 1985;17:370–375.
32. Sawka MN, Burke LM, Eichner ER, et al. American College of Sports Medicine position stand. Exercise and fluid replacement. *Med Sci Sports Exerc*. 2007;39:377–390.
33. Casa DJ, Armstrong LE, Hillman SK, et al. National Athletic Trainers' Association position statement: fluid replacement for athletes. *J Athl Train*. 2000;35:212–224.
34. Smith HR, Dhatt GS, Melia WMA, Dickinson JG. Cystic fibrosis presenting as hyponatraemic heat exhaustion. *BMJ*. 1995;310:579–580.
35. Vrijens DM, Rehrer NJ. Sodium-free fluid ingestion decreases plasma sodium during exercise in the heat. *J Appl Physiol*. 1999;86(6):1847–1851.
36. Chorley J, Cianca J, Divine J. Risk factors for exercise-associated hyponatremia in non-elite marathon runners. *Clin J Sport Med*. 2007;17(6):471–477.
37. Speedy DB, Rogers IR, Noakes TD, et al. Exercise-induced hyponatremia in ultradistance triathletes is caused by inappropriate fluid retention. *Clin J Sport Med*. 2000;10:272–278.
38. Hew TD, Chorley JN, Cianca JC, Divine JG. The incidence, risk factors, and clinical manifestations of hyponatremia in marathon runners. *Clin J Sport Med*. 2003;13:41–47.
39. Hew-Butler T, Ayus JC, Kipps C, et al. Statement of the Second International Exercise-Associated Hyponatremia Consensus Development Conference, New Zealand, 2007. *Clin J Sport Med*. 2008;18:111–121.
40. Hew-Butler T, Anley C, Schwartz P, Noakes T. The treatment of symptomatic hyponatremia with hypertonic saline in an Ironman triathlete. *Clin J Sport Med*. 2007;17:68–69.
41. Speedy DB, Noakes TD, Schneider C. Exercise-associated hyponatremia: a review. *Emerg Med*. 2001;13:17–27.
42. Lien YH, Shapiro JI. Hyponatremia: clinical diagnosis and management. *Am J Med*. 2007;120:653–658.
43. Hiller WD, O'Toole ML, Fortess EE, et al. Medical and physiological considerations in triathlons. *Am J Sports Med*. 1987;15: 164–167.
44. Casa DJ, Armstrong LE, Ganio MS, Yeargin SW. Exertional heat stroke in competitive athletes. *Curr Sports Med Rep*. 2005;4: 309–317.
45. Clark JM, Gennari FJ. Encephalopathy due to severe hyponatremia in an ultramarathon runner. *Western J Med*. 1993;159: 188–189.
46. Ayus JC, Krothapalli RK, Arieff AI. Treatment of symptomatic hyponatremia and its relation to brain damage: a prospective study. *N Engl J Med*. 1987;317:1190–1195.
47. Binkley HM, Beckett J, Casa DJ, Kleiner DM, Plummer PE. National Athletic Trainers' Association position statement: exertional heat illnesses. *J Athl Train*. 2002;37:329–343.

Anaphylactic Shock, Hypothermia, Diabetes, and Wilderness Medicine

Susan W. Yeargin, PhD, ATC

Brad E. Yeargin, MEd, ATC, CES

Jeffrey M. Anderson, MD, FACSM

Anaphylaxis

Anaphylaxis is an acute, potentially life-threatening systemic reaction that can occur to anyone, anywhere, at any time. Athletic populations are continuously exposed to allergens that may induce anaphylaxis. Because of the rapid onset of symptoms, early recognition and appropriate treatment is imperative to lower potential morbidity and mortality.

> **anaphylaxis** A serious allergic reaction that is rapid in onset and may cause death.

Definition

In April 2004, a multidisciplinary symposium on the definition and management of anaphylaxis proposed the following definition: "Anaphylaxis is a serious allergic reaction that is rapid in onset and may cause death."[1] The multidisciplinary group agreed that anaphylactic reactions progress as part of a clinical continuum. An exposure may initially cause relatively minor symptoms, but can rapidly progress to life-threatening cardiovascular and respiratory compromise. Pumphrey[2] reports that in a 10-year retrospective study of 202 fatal anaphylaxis cases, the time interval from reception of stimulus to death for food induced anaphylaxis was between 25 and 35 minutes. The interval found for an insect sting was 10 to 15 minutes, whereas fatal drug-induced anaphylaxis occurred at 10 to 20 minutes. Therefore, any delay in recognition and appropriate treatment can increase incidence of death.[2]

Epidemiology

Anaphylaxis is a relatively common problem, affecting up to 2% of the population.[3] Recent epidemiologic studies have shown an increase in the number of anaphylaxis cases presenting in emergency departments of hospitals worldwide.[4] It has been reported that up to 1500 deaths per year result from anaphylaxis in the United States.[5] Health care professionals working with athletic populations must be able to recognize signs and symptoms manifesting with the condition as well as be able to provide appropriate acute care.

Pathophysiology

An allergic reaction begins only when a **trigger** introduces an allergen and it crosses an epithelial or endothelial barrier or both. The manifestation of signs and symptoms of anaphylaxis is caused by the release of mediators from mast cells and basophils. Organs with greater concentrations of basophils and mast cells will predictably exhibit greater signs and symptoms of anaphylaxis. These organs include the skin (90% of cases), respiratory tract (70%), gastrointestinal tract (30% to 45%), cardiovascular system (10% to 45%), and the central nervous system (10% to 15%).[6]

trigger Anything that introduces an allergen that can cause a potential anaphylactic reaction.

Mediators released from the stimulation of mast cells and basophils include histamines, leukotrienes, and prostaglandins as well as other chemokines and chemotactic factors. Histamine is one of the most important mediators due to its influence on multiple organ systems. Histamine release is directly responsible for vasodilation, increased vascular permeability, hypersecretion of mucus, and spasm of smooth muscle. As a result, victims experience a decrease in vascular resistance that can lead to cardiovascular shock. Histamine levels present in the blood serum of anaphylaxis victims directly correlate with the severity of an anaphylactic reaction.[7]

Triggers

The potential triggers that can cause an anaphylactic reaction are infinite.[8] Triggers are classified as immunologic and nonimmunologic. Anaphylactic reactions associated with foods, medications, latex products, and insect stings fall into the immunologic classification, whereas nonimmunologic triggers include exercise and cold. Foods, medications, and insect stings are among the most common provoking factors for anaphylaxis, but anaphylaxis can be induced by any agent capable of producing a sudden degranulation of mast cells or basophils.[7]

Food-associated anaphylaxis is the most common cause of anaphylaxis treated in emergency departments across the United States in younger populations.[9] Most food cases are not fatal and have a gradual onset of signs and symptoms. The most common food culprits are tree nuts, peanuts, cow's milk, eggs, soy, wheat, shellfish, and fish. However, any food may be implicated.[9]

Exercise-induced anaphylaxis (EIA) is most commonly associated with food ingestion. Food-dependent exercise-induced anaphylaxis (FDEIA) tends to occur when food ingestion is followed by exercise within 2 to 4 hours. Athletes may not experience a reaction from ingestion of the food or exercise alone but only in conjunction.[9] EIA may be triggered by other cofactors or can occur with exercise alone. Additional cofactors include alcohol, temperature, drugs, humidity, seasonal changes, and hormonal changes.

The onset of anaphylaxis following an insect sting (order Hymenoptera) is generally rapid following envenomation. Fatal reactions begin within 30 minutes of the sting, emphasizing the importance of prompt recognition and appropriate treatment. Most fatal reactions are not preventable because the reaction commonly occurs on the first sting or subsequent stings with no prior history of anaphylactic shock.[1]

Predisposing Factors

Anaphylaxis does not discriminate on the basis of age, race, sex, or socioeconomic status. The condition can strike any person, at any time, in any venue. Some populations with diseases that impede prompt recognition of a known trigger or the manifestation of signs and symptoms are at greater risk of a severe, life-threatening, or fatal reaction. Such diseases include atopy, vision or auditory impairment, and neurologic and psychiatric disorders.[10]

Certain concomitant factors have been reported to increase the risk of a fatal episode of anaphylaxis. Factors that increase risk include exercise, exposure to extreme temperature or humidity, general illness, use of certain medications (e.g., nonsteroidal anti-inflammatory drugs [NSAIDs]), acute infection, increased emotional stress, and menses. Additionally, individuals with concomitant respiratory or cardiovascular diseases such as asthma are at greater risk.[8]

Recognition

Anaphylaxis cases are commonly underrecognized by health care professionals and therefore are undertreated.[3,11,12] Simons[8] reported that life-saving epinephrine may not be administered promptly due to lack of recognition of signs and symptoms, a perception that the episode is mild, or a delay in diagnosis. In 2006 the National Institute of Allergy and Infectious Diseases and the Food Allergy and Anaphylaxis Network developed criteria for recognition of anaphylaxis.[13] These criteria are reported to capture 95% of anaphylaxis cases.[1] If a victim presents with one of the three criteria, he or she is likely to have anaphylaxis **(Figure 13.1)**. These criteria may prove to be invaluable to health care professionals for the initial recognition and early appropriate treatment of anaphylaxis.

Anaphylaxis cases have an initial acute onset (<60 min) of signs and symptoms that may be followed by secondary reaction.[14–16] This second reaction is termed a **biphasic** or **protracted reaction** and may occur from 1 to 24 hours after the initial reaction. The secondary reaction usually affects the same organ systems as the original reaction and may present in up to 20% of anaphylaxis cases.[17] There is no clear consensus regarding factors that may predispose a victim to a secondary reaction. Lieberman[18] notes from reviewing various studies that reaction severity, time to onset of symptoms after stimulus introduction, and history of a secondary reaction have been mentioned as risk factors. Additionally, from an emergency treatment perspective, secondary reactions tend to be associated with a delay in epinephrine administration as well as inadequate dosage amounts.[18]

biphasic reaction   The recurrence of symptoms of anaphylaxis within 72 hours of an initial attack with no further exposure to the allergen.

protracted reaction   An anaphylactic reaction that lasts for hours to days without clear resolution of signs and symptoms.

Table 13.1 lists signs and symptoms associated with anaphylaxis. The most common manifestations of an anaphylactic reaction are urticaria (hives) and angioedema (welts).[8] Cutaneous signs may not always be present in rapidly progressing reactions; therefore, the health care professional should not rule out anaphylaxis due to a lack of skin involvement. Respiratory distress is also commonly seen with reactions. Exacerbation of allergy-type symptoms will manifest, followed by complaints of "tightness" in the throat and chest. As anaphylaxis progresses, the victim will experience coughing, wheezing, and dyspnea and may become cyanotic. Tachycardia is an early reliable sign of cardiovascular involvement. Cardiovascular collapse will progress as mass vasodilation occurs. Most fatal cases of anaphylaxis result from respiratory compromise and cardiovascular collapse.[19]

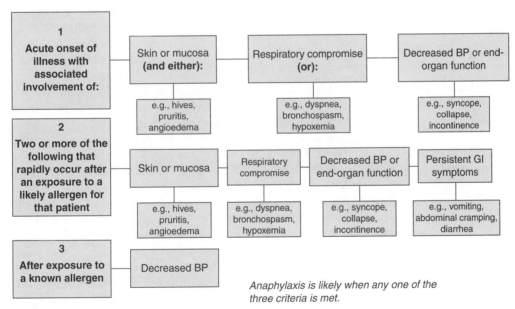

Anaphylaxis is likely when any one of the three criteria is met.

Figure 13.1   Visual representation of the anaphylaxis criteria of the National Institute of Allergy and Infectious Diseases and the Food Allergy and Anaphylaxis Network.
Source: Adapted from Manivannan V, Decker WW, Stead LG, Li JT, Campbell RL. Visual representation of National Institute of Allergy and Infectious Disease and Food Allergy and Anaphylaxis Network criteria for anaphylaxis. *Int J Emerg Med.* 2009;2(1):3–5.

<table>
<tr><td>

TABLE 13.1 — Signs and Symptoms of Anaphylaxis

Cutaneous, Subcutaneous, and Mucosal Tissues

Flushing, pruritus (itch), urticaria (hives), angioedema, rash, pilar erection

Periorbital and conjunctival: Pruritus, erythema, and swelling

Lips, tongue, and palate: Pruritus and swelling

Pruritus of external auditory canals, genitalia, palms and soles

Respiratory

Nasal: Pruritus, congestion, rhinorrhea, sneezing

Larynx: Pruritus and tightness in throat, dysphonia and hoarseness, dry cough, stridor, dysphagia

Lungs: Apnea, chest tightness, deep cough, wheezing

Cyanosis

Gastrointestinal

Nausea, cramping, abdominal pain, vomiting, diarrhea

Cardiovascular

Chest pain, palpitations, tachycardia, bradycardia or other dysrhythmia

Altered mental status, hypotension, shock, cardiac arrest

Central Nervous System

Aura of impending doom, anxiety, irritability, throbbing headache, disorientation

Other

Metallic taste in mouth

Uterine contractions in postpubertal females

</td></tr>
</table>

Rapidly developing signs and symptoms indicate an increased risk of a severe and potentially life-threatening anaphylactic reaction.[3] Initially mild cutaneous signs should not be overlooked, because they may be indicative of the potential onset of a severe anaphylactic reaction. Progression of signs and symptoms should be monitored closely and appropriate treatment rendered if indicated. Symptoms that are not immediately life threatening can progress rapidly unless treated promptly and appropriately.

Acute Treatment

Early recognition is the first life-saving measure in the acute treatment of anaphylaxis. Emergency treatment is dependent on the training of available medical personnel on the scene and on availabl e equipment. All victims of anaphylaxis should be transported to the hospital for advanced medical care and observation of potential biphasic or protracted reactions.

The most important drug in the treatment of anaphylaxis is epinephrine (adrenaline). The World Health Organization states that epinephrine should be the drug of choice for the treatment of acute anaphylaxis.[19] Anecdotal evidence and international consensus opinion agree that the drug should be administered when the initial signs and symptoms present, regardless of their severity. Epinephrine injected intramuscularly eases respiratory distress and restores adequate cardiac output. The drug reverses peripheral vasodilation and reduces edema. Additionally, it dilates bronchial airways, increases myocardial force contraction, and suppresses histamine release. Anaphylaxis-related fatalities usually result from delayed administration of epinephrine.[19] There is no absolute contraindication to the use of epinephrine in a patient with anaphylaxis.[8] Athletes with a history of reactions should be prescribed and carry an **epinephrine autoinjector**. Health care professionals trained to administer an autoinjector should immediately utilize the drug at the first sign of anaphylaxis.

epinephrine autoinjector
Intramuscular drug delivery system preloaded with a specific dosage of epinephrine for use during an emergency anaphylactic reaction.

In some cases victims may not respond to initial dose of epinephrine, necessitating a second dose. Anecdotal evidence suggests that the drug can be administered every 5 to 20 minutes depending on the response of the victim. Retrospective studies suggest that 18% to 35% of victims may require a second dose.[20,21]

Once anaphylaxis is recognized in an individual, emergency medical services (EMS) should be immediately activated. Airway, breathing, and circulation should be continuously monitored and epinephrine administered. The athlete should be placed in a comfortable position until advanced medical personnel arrive. If respiratory distress is evident, supplemental oxygen and maintaining the athlete in a seated position will ease breathing difficulties. As cardiovascular signs and symptoms (e.g., hypotension) begin to manifest, laying the individual in a supine position with feet elevated will assist with circulatory problems, decreasing the risk of cardiovascular shock. An automated external defibrillator (AED) should be readily available. Victims should be encouraged to remain still, minimizing movement, until advanced medical personnel arrive on scene.

A trigger causing a reaction may be difficult to discern. If a stinger from a bee is present, the first responder should remove it as quickly as possible. The method of removal is not as important as early removal.[22] Vomiting should not be induced in victims of food or drug allergies. Airway, breathing, and circulation should be continuously monitored and cardiopulmonary resuscitation begun if necessary. **Figure 13.2** lists key steps of treatment of acute anaphylaxis.

Return to Participation

An athlete who experiences an anaphylactic reaction must follow up with his or her primary care physician (PCP) prior to returning to activity. If warranted, the PCP may refer the patient to an allergist/immunologist. In most cases of anaphylaxis, the trigger can be determined and avoidance measures developed. The physician may use a number of strategies to assist the athlete in returning to safe participation. Strategies include pharmacologic prophylaxis, short-term challenge and desensitization, and long-term desensitization. The athlete should be educated on avoidance measures, signs and symptoms of recurrence, and appropriate use of a prescribed epinephrine autoinjector.[19] A detailed anaphylaxis emergency action plan can be developed with the athlete. Comorbidities such as asthma should be managed. These strategies will help reduce the risk of recurrence and provide life-saving skills for the athlete if the condition returns.

Return to participation is individualized and gradual, with close monitoring of the athlete. Health care providers working with athletes with a history of anaphylaxis should be aware of the condition prior to the start of conditioning sessions, practices, or competition. They should be able to recognize the signs

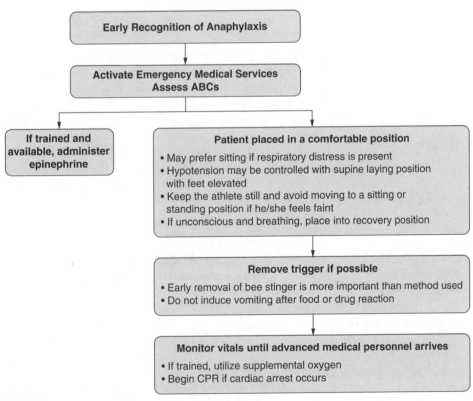

Figure 13.2 Emergency treatment of acute anaphylaxis.

and symptoms and provide prompt appropriate treatment. Individualized anaphylaxis emergency plans should be provided and reviewed with coaches and health care providers working with the athlete.

Prevention

The most successful treatment for anaphylaxis is the prevention of a reaction from occurring. A thorough history is invaluable to a clinician prior to assessing and treating a potential reaction, developing diet plans, and dispensing or prescribing medications. Implementation of prevention strategies is imperative for athletes with a history of anaphylaxis. Avoidance of known triggers is the basis of all long-term risk reduction for recurrence of anaphylaxis. Additional strategies include development of an anaphylaxis emergency action plan, wearing a medical identification tag, and education of patients, first responders, and health care professionals concerning the recognition and acute treatment of anaphylaxis.[8] Individuals with a history of anaphylactic reactions should not exercise alone.

Despite aggressive avoidance measures and immunomodulation, anaphylaxis may recur. Mullins[23] reports that 1 in 12 anaphylaxis victims will have a recurrence that will require emergency administration of epinephrine or hospitalization in any given year. When this situation occurs, emergency preparedness is essential. Those at risk for recurrence of anaphylaxis should carry one or more epinephrine autoinjectors and have an anaphylaxis emergency action plan. First responders and clinicians must be aware of the history of the patient, whether through previous documentation or a medical alert tag. The rate at which the reaction will progress and how the patient will respond to treatment is impossible to predict; therefore, early recognition, administration of epinephrine, and activation of EMS is imperative.[8]

Prevention is not an option in the case of an initial acute anaphylactic reaction. This type of reaction is unpredictable and may be a result of any type of allergen. The most important step in providing prompt appropriate treatment for an athlete suffering from anaphylaxis is recognition of the condition.[8] Whenever possible, athletic trainers and physicians covering athletic events should carry an epinephrine autoinjector for emergency use.

Hypothermia

One condition that is of concern with participation in sports or physical activity because of the possibility of long-term morbidity or of death is **hypothermia**. This potentially deadly condition is possible in organized sport and the physically active. Common scenarios include a winter sport athlete who is working out alone, an organized sport event in which check-in stations are far apart, accidental water immersion while exercising, or a sudden unexpected change in environmental conditions **(Table 13.2)**. Even though hypothermia is commonly associated with cold weather conditions, it has been recorded in environments as warm as 10°C to 15.6°C (50–60°F).[24] According to the most recent CDC report, a total of 4607 hypothermia deaths occurred during the period 1999 to 2002.[25] The incidence rates of hypothermia in athletes have yet to be reported. Death from hypothermia can be prevented through prompt diagnosis in combination with fast treatment and immediate transport.

hypothermia Clinically defined as being when core body temperature drops below 35°C (95°F) as a result of the human body losing more heat than it can produce. Central nervous system dysfunction is also present in this condition.

Definition

Hypothermia is clinically defined as occurring when core body temperature drops below 35°C (95°F) as a result of the human body losing more heat than it can produce. Hypothermia is classified into different degrees of severity **(Table 13.3)**.[26–29] It can be progressive if the person is left untreated.

Hypothermia encountered by health care providers in a natural setting is commonly termed **accidental hypothermia**. This is an important differentiation, because there are cases in which hypothermia is purposefully induced. Core body temperature may be purposefully lowered in a controlled hospital setting to decrease the morbidity and mortality of victims of spinal cord injury and cardiac-related surgical procedures, as well as numerous other circumstances. Hyperthermic (heat stroke) victims have been noted to have "hypothermic freefall." This occurs when the victim's temperature overshoots into hyperthermic ranges during the attempt to quickly decrease core body temperature.

accidental hypothermia Hypothermia that occurs in natural settings.

TABLE 13.2 Examples of Sports and Physical Activity in Which Hypothermia Is Possible

Sport or Activity	Example
Snow sports	Cross-country skiing
	Snowshoeing
	Biathlon
	Outdoor hockey
	Skating
	Snowboarding
	Snowmobiling
Physical activity commonly done in wet and/or cold conditions	Jogging
	Marathons, ultramarathons, triathlons
Adventure	Adventure racing
	Open-water swimming
	Mountaineering
	Rock or ice climbing
	Exploring
Occupational	Military branches, special operations
	Cold water fisherman
	Postal delivery
	Winter emergency response personnel

For the purposes of this chapter, the term *hypothermia* will refer to accidental hypothermia. This occurs in an outdoor setting in which the person did not purposefully engage in inducing hypothermia but instead found himself or herself in a situation in which hypothermia happened unintentionally.

Hypothermia may be labeled as acute, subacute, or chronic. The divisions refer to the length of time the cooling mechanism is experienced by the individual. Hypothermia seen in organized sport or physical activity is typically acute hypothermia. Victims are exposed to cold ambient conditions or cold water for a short period of time, resulting in hypothermia. An example is falling through the ice while cross-country skiing. Subacute hypothermia occurs when an individual is slowly cooled over time due to exposure. An example is an individual who is not dressed appropriately for the cold weather while competing in a long-term outdoor event. Chronic hypothermia also involves prolonged exposure and occurs in combination with substance abuse or a chronic medical condition.[29]

TABLE 13.3 Classification of Hypothermia

Classification	Core Body Temperature
Mild hypothermia	32–35°C (89.6–95°F)
Moderate hypothermia	28–32°C (82.4–89.6°F)
Severe hypothermia	<28°C (<82.4°F)

Epidemiology

Reported mortality rates due to hypothermia range greatly, depending on the source. One survey reported an overall mortality rate of 17%; in this survey, 84% of the victims had a core body temperature assessed as below 32°C (89.6°F), indicating moderate to severe hypothermia.[30]

Some populations of particular interest related to hypothermia are the elderly, individuals with chronic medical conditions, and individuals who have no accountability. Older individuals (60 years of age and older) may have physiologic differences that possibly predispose them to hypothermia (as discussed later in this chapter). Individuals with chronic medical conditions such as cardiac conditions and diabetes are also more susceptible to hypothermia. Individuals without significant family or friends are at risk due to lack of accountability. Examples are nonmarried individuals, homeless, and the elderly. Without accountability, individuals may be missing without others realizing the need to look for them.[26,29]

Pathophysiology

Heat Loss and Cold Stressors

Heat is lost from the body via convection, conduction, radiation, and evaporation (see Chapter 5). Heat can also be gained through convection, conduction, and radiation, as well as being produced metabolically.

cold stressor Any intrinsic or extrinsic factor that encourages heat loss from the body.

Several **cold stressors** can lead heat loss to overwhelm heat gain. When the ambient conditions are colder than the skin, convection and conduction are used as primary pathways for heat loss. With the temperature gradient in favor of the environment, the only source for heat gain is through metabolic production. Wind conditions increase heat loss through convection and evaporation. If clothing is wetted through rain, snow, or water immersion, heat is lost faster through conduction or evaporation. Water immersion can increase heat loss 20-fold. Athletes exercising in the cold may have an additional cold stress in the form of dry air. The lack of humidity causes irritation of smooth muscle within and surrounding the lungs, leading to bronchospasm.[28,29,31] Even though heat loss is occurring at the skin in each of these cases, blood at this level is cooled and circulated through the core, resulting in a decrease in core body temperature.

Metabolic

shivering A thermogenic response initiated by the autonomic nervous system in order to produce heat to combat cold stressors.

The creation of heat (thermogenesis) through **shivering** depends on the contraction of skeletal muscle. This is an involuntary process initiated by the hypothalamus and the sympathetic nervous system. Shivering starts in the trunk musculature and progresses to the extremities as hypothermia progresses.[26,28,32] The intensity of shivering increases as the cold stress or length of exposure increases. As more muscles are used for shivering, the need for oxygen increases.

It is theorized that adult humans may have nonshivering thermogenesis capabilities, but the evidence is sparse. Research supports the release of hormones such as epinephrine, norepinephrine, cortisol, and corticosterone to activate mobilization of metabolic fuels into the blood. Fats, lipids, and carbohydrates can be used for energy in voluntary and involuntary muscle contractions.[26,28] Thermogenesis through voluntary skeletal muscle contraction can easily be accomplished through physical activity if the victim still has coordination. Moving in place, walking, and jogging are all good examples of voluntary thermogenesis.

Cardiovascular

As core body temperature decreases, progressive vasoconstriction is activated in an attempt to keep warmed blood centrally in the body. This will limit the amount of heat being transferred from the skin to the environment. The response is mediated by the hypothalamus in an effort to retain heat in the most critical areas of the body, the visceral organs. This vital vasoconstriction occurs starting at 34°C to 35°C (93.2–95°F) and peaks at 31°C (87.8°F). Warmed blood is shunted centrally to protect vital organs.[27–29] As a result, skin and extremity temperatures decrease and oxygen levels to these areas decrease. At first, heart rate, cardiac output, and mean arterial pressure increase to compensate for the shift in blood flow.[33] As hypothermia progresses, nerve conduction slows within the heart and the cardiac cycle increases, slowing the heart rate. This can potentially lead to ventricular fibrillation.[28] A hypothermic victim may initially present with tachycardia, which over time will become bradycardia.[26]

Respiratory

The respiratory system initially responds to hypothermia through increased respiration rate (hyperventilation) to meet the demands of oxygen for voluntary and involuntary thermogenesis. Similar to the reaction of the heart, respiration slows as hypothermia progresses. Over time, carbon dioxide retention increases, resulting in respiratory acidosis and possible pulmonary edema. Sporadic breathing patterns and cessation of breathing are possible at very low body temperatures.[26,28]

Renal

Skin vasoconstriction causes a cascade of nervous system and hormonal responses leading to an increased urine volume production by the kidneys. This "cold diuresis" leads to an initial loss of body fluids through urine.[28] If the athlete begins competition in a hydrated state, this urine loss may not be clinically significant. However, because most athletes begin exercising in a hypohydrated state, this obligatory loss may have practical implications on performance and future physiologic responses. As hypothermia continues, the kidneys begin to conserve fluids and electrolytes to aid in heat conservation.[28]

Cellular

As core body temperature decreases, cell metabolism decreases, ultimately leading to cell death. Additionally, cooling dehydrates the cell until enzyme and electrolyte concentrations are toxic. The water in extracellular fluid freezes into crystals, concentrating the cell even further. Intracellular water freezes as well, permanently damaging the cell.[29]

Predisposing Factors

Numerous extrinsic and intrinsic factors predispose a person to hypothermia. The majority of these factors have been identified through case studies[27] and a few through controlled cold water immersion studies.[29]

Extrinsic Factors

- *Environmental:* Ambient temperatures below skin and core temperatures encourage heat loss over heat gain. Air movement and wind accelerate heat loss by convection and evaporation. Wind chill (a combination of low ambient temperature and wind) accelerates heat loss by convection and evaporation.
- *Cold water immersion:* Water convectively transfers heat loss 70 times greater than air. Therefore, individuals in conditions of rain, melting snow, or cold water immersion are at risk for hypothermia no matter whether they are in mild or extreme cold conditions. The water temperature, amount of immersed body surface, and number of body parts involved with exercise can all encourage heat loss leading to the development of hypothermia.[27,28] Whole or partial water immersion is a common factor in mortalities from hypothermia.[25] An example of an athlete at risk is an open-water swimmer because this sport involves cold water continuously flowing by the skin while both arms and legs exercise, resulting in significant heat loss through convection.[34]
- *Wet clothing:* Unexpected wetting of clothing can double heat loss in cold weather conditions as compared with dry clothing[27] and is a common factor found in hypothermia mortality cases.[30] This particular predisposing factor is significantly relevant not only in cold environmental conditions but also in mild conditions.
- *Body type:* Individuals who have less body fat are susceptible to greater amounts of heat loss.[27] When vasoconstriction is peaking during hypothermia, skin and fat are responsible for insulating the body to retain heat. There is an inverse relationship between heat loss and subcutaneous fat. Therefore, the less fat a person contains, the more heat loss is possible.[28] This relationship is a significant predisposing factor, particularly in athletes, who stereotypically have lower fat percentages. Individuals with less body fat have demonstrated less toleration of cold water and begin shivering earlier.[35,36] Another body type at a disadvantage in combating cold conditions are those individuals who do not have significant muscle mass in order to generate sufficient heat.[28] Examples include children, the elderly, and women.

- *Age and gender:* Individuals who are older than 60 years may be predisposed to hypothermia. A reduced vasoconstriction response and heat retention compared with younger counterparts has been reported in controlled studies.[37,38] The metabolic rate of these individuals may also be significantly decreased, affecting heat production.[39] Additionally, older individuals may not be as sensitive to cold sensation or perceptions, which could possibly affect behavioral thermoregulation.[27] Research has also indicated that older individuals have a faster decrease in core body temperature as compared with younger individuals when holding fitness level constant.[37] Many also assume that the elderly have a lower physical fitness level, which is a predisposing factor in itself (explored later in the chapter). Even though this population may be more at risk, an epidemiologic study reported no differences in presenting temperatures or mortality no matter the age of the individuals who arrived at hospitals with hypothermia.[30]

  Children may be predisposed to hypothermia because of their body type, which has a higher body surface area to mass ratio and lower amounts of fat. However, their physiologic responses are still appropriate and can adjust to handle cold the same as adults, possibly just differently.

  There is no overwhelming evidence that there are gender differences in terms of hypothermia risk.[27] There were no significant differences in core body temperature when hypothermic males and females were compared. However, with a higher incidence of hypothermic males found outdoors and already injured, it may be safe to assume that males engage in riskier behavior that possibly can predispose them to the condition.[30,40]
- *Illness and injury:* Those with a chronic condition, illness, or a systemic infection may be more at risk for hypothermia. Those who have been injured and therefore cannot remove themselves from the exposure situation are also at risk.[30]

Intrinsic Factors

- *Substance abuse:* Alcohol stimulates vasodilation, which increases heat loss; inhibits shivering, decreasing heat production; and decreases the amount of glucose available, which affects shivering capabilities. Alcohol increases urine production, resulting in mild hypohydration. An intoxicated individual's sensations are decreased; therefore, cold and pain are not fully felt or comprehended by the individual, which may affect appropriate behavioral thermoregulation. Additionally, alcohol increases risky behavior, often resulting in an immobilizing injury while in cold conditions and increased length of exposure outside.[28,41]

  The rate of oxygen released from hemoglobin decreases during hypothermia. In smokers this rate declines even further, decreasing oxygen and increasing carbon dioxide in their blood. Thus, smokers develop hypothermia faster and their cells reach necrosis earlier.[29]
- *Exercise intensity:* When an individual is exercising in cold or wet conditions but at moderate to high intensities, core body temperature can be maintained. However, if the exercise intensity is low (such as walking or slow jogging), core body temperature can actually decrease. Exercise in rainy conditions or exercising prior to getting wet in cold conditions leads to a greater decline in core body temperature as compared with not exercising. Exercising in water or rain significantly increases the risk for hypothermia.[27,28,42]
- *Physical fitness:* A physically fit person may be able to exercise and shiver for longer during hypothermic risk situations, allowing for heat generation to maintain core body temperature. Physically fit individuals have greater metabolic heat production and vasoconstriction responses during cold exposure, which aid significantly in greater heat production and reductions in heat loss as compared with sedentary individuals.[28,43,44] Individuals with low physical fitness will fatigue earlier, leading to an earlier decrease in body temperature. Exertional fatigue has been demonstrated to be a predisposing factor to hypothermia in research studies.[45]
- *Hypoglycemia:* Because shivering is dependent on mobilized energy sources within the body, an individual who has not been eating appropriately to prepare for the needs of exercising in the cold may be predisposed to hypothermia.[27] Shivering may actually be impaired due to the

resulting hypoglycemia. It has been demonstrated that carbohydrates (glucose) are a fuel of preference during shivering in cold air exposure.[46] If an individual does not have significant carbohydrate stores to mobilize as a result of underfeeding, this becomes a significant predisposing factor. Additionally, the continuation of exercise and ultimately heat production may be in jeopardy without available carbohydrate stores. Food restriction for 48 hours in itself, even without hypoglycemia, has been shown to decrease shivering.[47] Low caloric intake (less than 1200 kcal/day) or hypoglycemia can decrease metabolic heat production. Because shivering and exercise are the only means of heat production through metabolism, blunting or impairing these mechanisms places the individual at a higher risk for hypothermia.[48] Dehydration does not affect vasoconstriction or shivering, so therefore may not play a role in predisposing someone to hypothermia.[26,49]

- *Time and place:* The majority of accidental hypothermia cases within Northern America occur between October and March, the coldest and wettest months of the year, respectively. Weekends have the highest incidence, probably due to alcohol consumption and lack of accountability for longer time periods. There is no specific geographic demographic in hypothermia; cases have been documented in all 50 U.S. states.

Recognition

The key diagnostic criterion for hypothermia is a temperature of less than 35°C (95°F).[27–29] Only a temperature assessed rectally, esophageally, or with a telemetric temperature sensor can be trusted to obtain an accurate measurement in individuals who have been active.[32,50] However, in an emergency situation in the field, rectal assessment is the only option for the first and transitional responder.[50]

Signs and symptoms can differ among individuals, the earliest being a sensation of coldness, shivering, apathy, and personality changes. As hypothermia progresses, other signs and symptoms usually include uncontrollable shivering, grayish pale skin color, palpable cold skin, immobile extremities progressing from distal (fingers, toes) to proximal (elbows, knees), inability to move after rest, decreased pulse, decreased blood pressure, delayed pupil responses, decreased respiration rate, and central nervous system dysfunction.

Central nervous system dysfunction can manifest in many ways **(Table 13.4)**. An easy way to remember important key signs is "the umbles" **(Table 13.5)**. Certain signs and symptoms only manifest at critical core body temperature thresholds, which can help the clinician determine the severity of hypothermia **(Figure 13.3)**.[27–29] It may be relevant to assess central nervous system dysfunction through the use of standard concussion assessments. These tools cover orientation questions, word recall, and saying numbers and months backwards. These tools also assess balance function. All are relevant if one is trying to confirm a case of mild hypothermia but probably are not needed to recognize moderate to severe hypothermia.

Hypothermic individuals can lack behavioral thermoregulation mechanisms because of the condition's effect on the central nervous system. Examples include not adding clothing for warmth, not looking for shelter, and not drinking or eating. As central nervous system dysfunction worsens, hypothermic individuals have actually been found to start taking off all their clothing.[28] This particular factor of recognition is amongst several that are different and similar than hyperthermia victims **(Table 13.6)**.

Treatment

Once an individual with hypothermia is found, treatment can be given externally or internally or both. The first responder and the transitional responder are mainly limited to external treatments. Internal treatments can only be initiated in an advanced hospital setting. It should be noted that because of the significant decrease in vital signs as hypothermia progresses and the possibility of the absence of vital signs at the peripheries, actions and treatments should always be initiated even if no vital signs are found.[27] Great care should be taken not to jostle or move the victim a great deal while providing initial care and transporting. Increased movement or jostling may cause ventricular fibrillation.[26,33,51] Keeping the victim as horizontal as possible is recommended.

TABLE 13.4 Manifestations of Central Nervous System Dysfunction by Categories

Category	Progressive Signs or Symptoms
Personality	Apathetic
	Withdrawn
	Belligerent
	Combative behavior
	Irritability
	Any exaggerated emotional responses
Behavior	Lethargy
	Drowsiness
	Removing clothing
	Lack of behavioral thermoregulation
	Vague communication
	Marked memory disturbances and lapses
Coordination	Slow and slurred speech
	Lack of dexterity
	Staggering
	Collapse
	Decreased to absent reflexes
Consciousness	Complete exhaustion
	Responds verbally but not oriented
	Responds to only painful stimuli
	Coma

TABLE 13.5 Common Signs Associated with Hypothermia: The "Umbles"

"Umbles"	Sign or Symptom
Grumbles	Irritability, personality change
Mumbles	Slurring of speech, difficulty articulating speech
Stumbles	Coordination issues, ataxia
Fumbles	Dexterity issues

There is no recommendation of differing treatment type depending on the mechanism of hypothermia. Therefore, no matter the circumstances, actions and treatment in general should be initiated. Initial actions to take include the following:[28–30]

- Place the individual in a warm, dry, environmentally protected, safe shelter while waiting for transitional care to arrive.
- Place the individual in a comfortable position while minimally jostling him or her.
- Obtain and monitor vital signs such as pulse, respiration rate, blood pressure, pupil response, and consciousness level.
- If possible, attempt to gain a history of the length and circumstances of exposure.
- If the victim is shivering, allow shivering to continue and do not limit or discourage it. Spontaneous rewarming can occur with successful productive shivering.
- Remove wet clothing (preferably by cutting, in order to minimize movement).
- Administer cardiopulmonary resuscitation (CPR) if indicated by a primary survey.

Rewarming falls into the following three categories: passive external, active external, and active internal. Passive external rewarming aims to remove sources of heat loss and use the body's own thermogenesis (shivering or physical activity) to rewarm the individual. Shivering can increase heat production fivefold above baseline, allowing for spontaneous self rewarming.[52] It is thought that loss of shivering may slow rewarming strategies by 37%.[47] This provides insight into why victims of moderate to severe hypothermia warm slower.

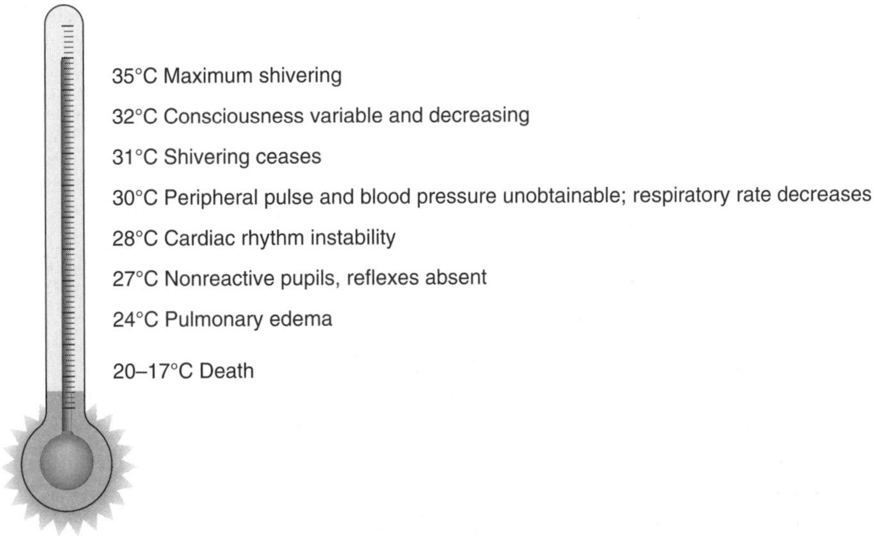

35°C Maximum shivering

32°C Consciousness variable and decreasing

31°C Shivering ceases

30°C Peripheral pulse and blood pressure unobtainable; respiratory rate decreases

28°C Cardiac rhythm instability

27°C Nonreactive pupils, reflexes absent

24°C Pulmonary edema

20–17°C Death

Figure 13.3 Signs and symptoms of hypothermia at critical temperature points that can be assessed in the field.

Active rewarming uses forced air and other convective warming products and water immersion. Forced air (convective) rewarming has been supported as more effective compared with passive rewarming in a few foundational studies.[53–55] It has been suggested that the trunk should be targeted in rewarming efforts,[23,33] because warming the extremities may cause cold blood to be circulated within the core and potentially cause cardiac arrhythmias. Use of warm water has been recommended, but there is no overwhelming evidence for this particular treatment method as compared with hyperthermia. Its use

TABLE 13.6 Hyperthermia and Hypothermia: Similarities and Differences

		Differences	
	Similarities	Hyperthermia (Heat Stroke)	Hypothermia
Etiology	Core body temperature (CBT) change affecting all anatomic organ systems	CBT is high (>40°C [104°F])	CBT is low (<32°C [89.6°F])
Diagnosis	Commonly misdiagnosed and not listed on death certificates, leading to underestimated incidence rates	Only one clinical diagnosis of heat stroke	Three levels of clinical diagnosis of hypothermia
Recognition	Central nervous system dysfunction	May initiate personal behavioral protective measures	May not initiate personal behavioral protective measures
Treatment	Initiated as soon as possible	Cooling is aggressively fast	Warming is slow
Return to play	It is possible to return to play from both conditions	Guidelines have been established	No guidelines have been established

depends on the situation and means of the responders. Water immersion is more supported in advanced care settings.[56]

The external treatment options that are possible in the field are as follows:

- Warm forced-air circulation around the body (commercial products)
- Layering traditional or heating blankets
- Warm water immersion (it is suggested the water be no hotter than 42°C [107.6°F])
- Hot water bottles placed on major arteries
- Another person's body heat
- Warm drinks that contain carbohydrates if the victim is conscious and can tolerate them
- Natural inhalation of warm air (not forced)

The goal of the first responder should be to initiate the actions and treatments just discussed as soon as possible in all hypothermia cases. An individual with hypothermia should be warmed slowly (1–2°C/h), especially in the care of first responders. Little research has been published on this topic, however, and it is considered a controversial subject among advanced care providers in areas in which hypothermia is common.[33]

First responders should be aware of the potential for "rewarming shock," which can manifest as syncope and cardiac instability. It is theorized that with warming, blood pressure decreases, the heart is not supplied with enough blood, and myocardial ischemia results, leading to an infarction.[33]

A controversial treatment issue is whether CPR should be initiated in the field. One hospital survey indicated that individuals with hypothermia have a higher survival rate if CPR is initiated in the field as compared with in the emergency department.[30] Another researcher has suggested starting with ventilations only if a pulse cannot be detected and hypothermia is suspected. Once rescue breathing has been provided, a pulse should be reassessed in hopes that oxygen may have aided in cardiac function, resulting in a palpable pulse. If a pulse can still not be found, CPR should be initiated.[33]

Active internal warming methods always occur in a hospital setting because they involve numerous surgical techniques. Internal treatments include warm saline lavage of the peritoneal cavity, thoracic cavity, and pericardium and warm water inserted into the stomach, bladder, and colon, hemodialysis, and cardiopulmonary bypass.[28,29] The only internal treatments that a first or transitional responder may initiate if the responder is appropriately trained is administration of warm intravenous fluid.

Recovery and Return-to-Play Issues

A sparse amount of research on the recovery of hypothermic individuals has been done, and none on athletes who have experienced hypothermia. One study followed up with survivors of severe hypothermia and found no difference in quality of life after the incident.[57] After release from the hospital, subjects indicated an ability to return to normal lifestyles. The subjects in this study were young and healthy. Outcomes in older populations are unknown.

No studies have been done on return to activity for athletes who have experienced hypothermia. The guidelines given in **Figure 13.4** are believed by the authors to be the first attempt at providing guidelines for return to play. Return-to-play guidelines for exertional heat stroke were used to develop this initial set of guidelines.[58]

Prevention

Table 13.7 addresses each predisposing factor listed earlier with simple preventive measures. Additional discussion follows.

Organized Sport and Event Planning

Have athletes who plan to exercise in cold environments complete a physical focused on predisposing factors to cold illnesses. Using the factors discussed earlier in this chapter can help clinicians create an appropriate questionnaire. For cold-weather sporting events, have medical personnel and check-in stations in place in order to appropriately monitor participants **(Table 13.8)**. Emergency action plans should

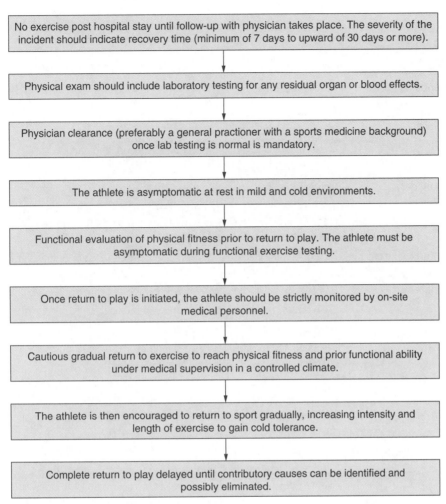

No exercise post hospital stay until follow-up with physician takes place. The severity of the incident should indicate recovery time (minimum of 7 days to upward of 30 days or more).

Physical exam should include laboratory testing for any residual organ or blood effects.

Physician clearance (preferably a general practitioner with a sports medicine background) once lab testing is normal is mandatory.

The athlete is asymptomatic at rest in mild and cold environments.

Functional evaluation of physical fitness prior to return to play. The athlete must be asymptomatic during functional exercise testing.

Once return to play is initiated, the athlete should be strictly monitored by on-site medical personnel.

Cautious gradual return to exercise to reach physical fitness and prior functional ability under medical supervision in a controlled climate.

The athlete is then encouraged to return to sport gradually, increasing intensity and length of exercise to gain cold tolerance.

Complete return to play delayed until contributory causes can be identified and possibly eliminated.

Figure 13.4   Return-to-play guidelines for hypothermia.

be written, posted, and reviewed regularly. A risk management algorithm for hypothermia similar to **Figure 13.5** should be used in developing cold-weather policies at institutions or events in which cold-weather exercising is common. Evaluating the environmental conditions and then comparing them to predeveloped tables and charts is suggested. (The National Athletic Trainers' Association position statement on cold weather injuries contains such charts.[26]) Following wind chill risk charts is recommended to assess risk, develop plausible time frames in which to exercise if it is necessary, or make participation or event decisions. As environmental conditions change, risk management strategies should be updated. Limiting the duration of cold exposure during a practice or an event is an easily implemented preventive measure.[26–28]

Clothing

Appropriate clothing is the best preventive measure against hypothermia. An inner, middle, and outer layer should be used. The inner layer lies against the skin and wicks away sweat and moisture. The purpose of the middle layer is to provide warmth and insulation. The outer layer should allow moisture to evaporate and defend against air, wind, and rain.[26,27] It should be noted that individuals have different

TABLE 13.7 Prevention of Hypothermia

Predisposing Factor	Preventive Measure
Environmental conditions	Layer warm clothing.
	Wear appropriate underwear.
	Wear mittens and a hat to cover fingers, head, and ears.
	Limit length of time outside.
Breathing dry air	Lightly cover the mouth and nose with outerwear.
Extended length of exposure outside alone	Tell one to two people your estimated start and end time and the exact place one is exercising, and agree upon a plan should you not contact them at the estimated end time.
Thin or unseen ice	Ensure that the path that is taken is either free of water or that all ice is safe to cross before moving forward.
Wet clothing	Bring additional clothing to change into if the current weather becomes wet.
	Wear shoes that will keep snow and water out.
	Wear wicking and breathable material.
Body type	Be aware and increase vigilance during events or situations with athletes of low body fat and/or low muscle mass.
Age	Be aware and increase vigilance during events or situations with athletes older than 60.
Substance abuse	Avoid drinking any type of alcohol within 24 hours of exercising or traveling in the cold.
	Stop smoking.
Exercise intensity	Keep a moderate to high intensity of exercise when risks of hypothermia are greater.
	Avoid getting wet while exercising at low intensities.
Physical fitness	Be aware and increase vigilance during events or situations in which normally sedentary people are participating.
Hypoglycemia	Ensure appropriate carbohydrate feeding prior to exercising in the cold.
Time and place	Be aware and increase vigilance during events or situations that occur between October and March.
	Ensure accountability.
Illness and injury	Consider participation or length constraints on individuals who are injured.
	All athletes with a chronic medical condition should be cleared by a physician prior to participation.

clothing needs and that a strict standard may not be useful in events in which multiple people are exercising. Technology in clothing is ever changing. Research is varying, and there is no "perfect" choice of clothing fabric materials. However, clothing that won't hold moisture, that dries easily, is breathable, and is loose fitting is best.[26–28,59] Additional tips include wearing outerwear on the head to prevent significant heat loss through this area of the body and wearing appropriately fitted socks, shoes, and gloves to allow adequate blood flow.

TABLE 13.8	List of Recommended Prevention Measures for Cold-Weather Events

1. Send educational materials to athletes, coaches, and/or parents prior to the event regarding the recognition and prevention of cold-weather injuries and illnesses.
2. Have an appropriate number of medical personnel for the number of participants and length of event.
3. Provide fluids at the start and finish of the race as well as at numerous stations along the event. Fluids at the start and finish can be a mix of cool and warm fluids. Fluids should contain carbohydrates and electrolytes.
4. Set up numerous medical stations throughout the event. If stations are far apart, have personnel responsible for sweeping the course in between. Communication should be coordinated so that all stations are involved.
5. The main medical station and key course stations should be equipped with warming products (i.e., blankets, forced-air heaters).
6. Additional equipment at key medical stations should include the following: rectal probes, pen lights, sphygmometer, stethoscope, and a watch with a second hand, in addition to a well-stocked typical medical kit.
7. Ensure that local hospitals are aware of the event in order to be prepared.

Nutrition

Good diet and hydration habits may help prevent hypothermia. Exercising in the cold requires more energy, dictating higher caloric needs to meet the metabolic demand. Good hydration is a basic habit of good health, even though research indicates that dehydration does not affect physiologic function in the cold.[27]

Cold Acclimatization

Cold acclimatization can be defined as a set of beneficial adaptations by the body to handle repetitive cold exposure. Various research studies have examined cold acclimatization, with varying results. The type and intensity of cold exposure affects the adaptations made. It is commonly accepted that individuals experience cold acclimatization adaptations within four categories: metabolic, insulative, hypothermic, or a combination of these. However, no consistent adaptations have been found across research studies and models. Some examples of adaptations include enhanced shivering, possibly enhanced nonshivering thermogenesis, a lower shivering threshold, improved muscle blood flow, and maximized cutaneous vasoconstriction. Scientists examining this phenomenon may be far away from a universal explanation of cold acclimatization. This response by the body, however, can be accepted as a beneficial response, no matter the type of acclimatization adopted by the body as a preventive measure.[28,60]

cold acclimatization A complex series of beneficial adaptations made over 14 days that enhances heat production and minimizes heat loss while exposed to cold conditions.

hypoglycemia A low serum glucose level that affects physiologic function.

type 1 diabetes An autoimmune illness that causes the pancreas to not produce adequate amounts of insulin.

Diabetes

Diabetes is not a common cause of sudden death in young athletes. However, in addition to the long-term risks of the disease, diabetes and its treatment can be a source of short-term risk. With intensive treatment of diabetes, the risk of **hypoglycemia** increases. It is this resultant hypoglycemia that carries the greatest degree of risk to the young athlete.

In discussing diabetes, it is important to understand the difference between type 1 and type 2 diabetes. **Type 1 diabetes** is an autoimmune illness involving the destruction of the pancreatic islet cells, which produce **insulin**. Individuals with type 1 diabetes do not produce adequate amounts of their own insulin and require the administration of exogenous insulin

insulin A hormone produced by the pancreas that helps glucose into cells for use.

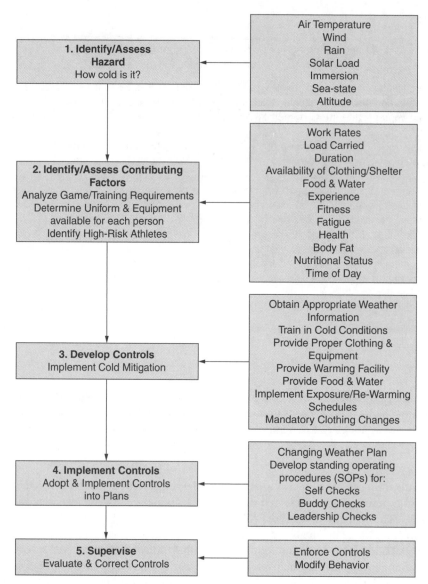

Figure 13.5   Risk management process for evaluating cold stress and strain.
Source: Castellani JW, Young AJ, Ducharme MB, et al. American College of Sports Medicine position stand: prevention of cold injuries during exercise. *Med Sci Sports Exerc.* 2006;38(11):2012–2029. Reproduced with permission from Wolters Kluwer Health.

type 2 diabetes A disease in which the pancreas produces large amounts of insulin; however, cells become less sensitive and resistant to it.

to survive. **Type 2 diabetes** is a disease of insulin resistance. Individuals with type 2 diabetes produce copious amounts of their own insulin, but over time become less sensitive to it. Type 2 diabetes is associated with hyperinsulinemic states, particularly obesity. It is largely a disease of lifestyle. The type 2 diabetic patient is optimally managed via promotion of physical activity and dietary interventions, rather than with exogenous insulin, although the administration of exogenous insulin may become necessary as type 2 diabetes progresses. Type 2 diabetes has traditionally been associated with older individuals, but with the increase in obesity in the United States, it is becoming more common in younger individuals. However, it remains very uncommon in young athletes, largely due to their active lifestyle. Therefore, for the remainder of this section the focus is on the young athlete with type 1 diabetes.

Acute Risks

As noted earlier, the risk of sudden death associated with diabetes in the young athlete is very low. The primary risks faced by the diabetic athlete are the extremes of glycemic control, both hypoglycemia and hyperglycemia. Unless the diabetes is severe and uncompensated, the risks of hyperglycemia are predominantly long term. Hypoglycemia, however, can progress rapidly, leading to dangerously low serum glucose levels. Hypoglycemia is defined as a serum glucose level below the lower limits of normal. Normal glucose levels are typically between 72 and 100 mg/dL.[61]

Signs and symptoms associated with hypoglycemia can be divided into two categories: adrenergic symptoms and neuroglycopenic symptoms. The adrenergic symptoms include tachycardia, sweating, palpitations, hunger, anxiety, and tremor. As the name implies, these symptoms are triggered by the release of the counterregulatory hormone epinephrine. In the setting of hypoglycemia, the counterregulatory hormones **glucagon** and epinephrine are secreted from the pancreatic islet cells and adrenal medulla, respectively, in an attempt to raise serum glucose levels. Both of these counterregulatory hormones stimulate glycogenolysis and gluconeogenesis. Epinephrine also serves to block glucose uptake by skeletal muscle and causes the adrenergic symptoms of hypoglycemia noted earlier. The release of glucagon and epinephrine usually occurs as serum glucose levels fall below 70 mg/dL, although this response can become blunted with ongoing recurrences of hypoglycemia, longstanding diabetes, or with the development of autonomic neuropathy.[61] As glucose levels fall further, additional counterregulatory hormones, namely cortisol and growth hormone, also increase in an effort to stabilize serum glucose levels.

glucagon A hormone produced by the pancreas that helps serum glucose by stimulating glycogen release.

The neuroglycopenic symptoms of hypoglycemia are triggered by the direct effect of diminished glucose supply to the brain. Glucose is the primary fuel for the brain, so its depletion has dramatic effects on cerebral function. Central nervous system symptoms of hypoglycemia include drowsiness, confusion, stupor, weakness, slurred speech, vertigo, and paresthesias. Severe neuroglycopenia can lead to seizures and loss of consciousness.[61] It is important to note that the diabetic athlete who is sleeping or has a blunted adrenergic response to hypoglycemia is at particular risk of neuroglycopenic symptoms because of his or her inability to detect the adrenergic warning symptoms.

There also exists a somewhat poorly understood phenomenon known as the "dead in bed" syndrome. First described by Tattersall and Gill in 1991,[62] this syndrome involves a young diabetic person who retires to bed at night in otherwise excellent health, only to be found dead the next morning. The lack of disruption of the bedding of these individuals indicates a rather sudden event leading to their demise. The precise incidence of "dead in bed" syndrome is unclear, but studies suggest that it accounts for 4.7% to 27.3% of all unexplained sudden deaths in type 1 diabetics.[63] The exact nature of this event also remains unknown, but evidence exists that suggests involvement of both autonomic neuropathy and overnight hypoglycemia.[64] Both autonomic neuropathy and hypoglycemia affect cardiac repolarization and can lengthen the QT interval, which can lead to fatal ventricular arrhythmia. A case report was published in 2010 in which retrospective glucose monitoring documented severe hypoglycemia in a 23-year-old type 1 diabetic individual at the time that he died overnight in his bed.[65]

On the other end of the glycemic control spectrum lies the risk associated with uncontrolled hyperglycemia. With hyperglycemia, the elevated serum glucose levels result in spillage of glucose into the urine. This glycosuric effect exerts an osmotic influence on the urine while in the renal tubules, drawing more fluid into the tubules and increasing urine output. The increased urine output leads to progressive dehydration and further hyperglycemia, which then leads to added glycosuria. With the increased flow of urine through the distal tubules of the kidney, potassium secretion into the urine increases, leading to profound hypokalemia.

Despite the high serum glucose levels, the lack of insulin diminishes the cells' capability to utilize glucose as an energy source. The hypoinsulinemic state in combination with elevated catecholamine levels results in lipolysis, and triglycerides are broken down to free fatty acids and glycerol. The free fatty acids provide the substrate for the formation of ketone bodies. These ketoacids lower serum pH, creating a metabolic acidosis. As a result of this metabolic cascade, the diabetic patient develops marked dehydration, dramatic hyperglycemia, acidosis, and electrolyte imbalances. This is the process known as diabetic ketoacidosis (DKA). DKA accounts for 8% to 29% of all hospital admissions for patients with a primary diagnosis of diabetes.[66] Its mortality rate in some populations has been estimated at around 4%, but mortality rates are higher in older patients.[67] This would imply a lower mortality rate in younger, healthier athletes.

Glycemic Control with Exercise

Glycemic control during exercise in the normal individual is intricately controlled by a variety of complementary hormonal interactions. The precise hormonal responses to exercise vary with type of exercise (moderate vs. intense, aerobic vs. resistance), duration of exercise (short, intermediate, or long), and environmental conditions. The most commonly discussed mode of exercise is intermediate to prolonged moderate activity, such as with distance running. In this scenario, the body functions in the optimal manner to provide an adequate supply of glucose to exercising muscle and subsequently adapts to diminishing glycogen stores. Glucose is obviously required as fuel for the exercising muscle, so there must be a stimulus for glycogenolysis and gluconeogenesis to meet this demand. As mentioned previously, a twofold to fourfold rise in catecholamines helps to meet this need. Additionally, epinephrine works on the pancreatic islet cells to diminish insulin production. Although this action would seem to be counterproductive in that insulin serves to augment glucose uptake into the exercising muscle cells, it is important to note that exercise itself serves to assist with glucose uptake into the muscle by causing the translocation of GLUT-4 receptors to the cell surface.[68] In fact, it has been previously established that muscle can take up glucose in the absence of insulin.[69] In the normal individual with functional insulin secretion, there is constant counterregulatory management of serum glucose levels to keep them in the normal range. This fine control is lost in athletes with type 1 diabetes because their insulin level is determined not by the body's innate response, but by their exogenous insulin dosing.

Intense exercise elicits a somewhat different response. The tremendous need for glucose in the setting of intense exercise necessitates a dramatic rise in plasma catecholamines, reaching levels of 14 to 18 times normal.[70] This adrenergic surge helps provide the necessary glucose via the mechanisms described previously, but when the intense exercise ceases, it takes a short while for catecholamine levels to decline, creating a state of temporary hyperglycemia. In the individual with normal insulin secretion, this relative hyperglycemia is met by a surge of insulin that maintains glucose homeostasis.[71] However, the type 1 diabetic individual lacks this inherent response. It is even possible for people with well-controlled type 1 diabetes to experience significant hyperglycemia secondary to intense exercise.[72,73]

To complicate matters further, many sports are not purely moderate or purely high intensity. Rather, they involve a baseline of moderate activity with overlying bouts of intense energy demand. Sports such as soccer, basketball, field hockey, and football are typical of this scenario. In this setting, the normal hormonal milieu of the athlete is constantly adjusting to maintain glucose homeostasis. However, maintaining this homeostasis is a substantial challenge to the individual without endogenous insulin production.

Finally, the body's response to falling glucose levels can also be altered by previous episodes of hypoglycemia. An episode of hypoglycemia has been shown to blunt the body's hormonal response to a subsequent episode of hypoglycemia for the next 12 to 24 hours.[74] Because of this blunting of the protective counterregulatory response, the athlete with type 1 diabetes must practice added caution with exercise that occurs within this window of time after a hypoglycemic episode.

Insulin Delivery

Intensive treatment of diabetes is the current standard of care, with evidence that tight control of serum glucose values alter the risk of long-term complications.[75] However, with this intensive control, the risk of hypoglycemia increases twofold to threefold, especially in perturbing activities such as exercise.[75,76] Intensive treatment of diabetes requires subcutaneous insulin infusion either via multiple daily injections or, optimally, the use of an insulin pump.

The use of multiple daily injections involves the baseline injection of a long-acting insulin, such as insulin glargine (Lantus) or insulin detemir (Levemir). These injections can be performed once or twice a day to provide a baseline level of insulin for the athlete with type 1 diabetes. Then, prior to meals, the athlete uses a bolus injection of a rapid-acting insulin, such as insulin lispro (Humalog), aspart (Novo-Log), or glulisine (Apidra). These rapid-acting insulins have an onset of effect within the first 15 minutes of injection, a peak effect on serum glucose in 45 to 75 minutes, and a lasting effect of 3 to 5 hours. Therefore, the athlete can expect the peak effect of a bolus dose approximately 1 hour after injection.[76] The drawbacks to the use of multiple daily injections are the number of daily injections the athlete must perform (three to four) and, more important, the lack of flexibility this offers in insulin dosing. When a fixed basal dose of insulin has been injected, there is little room for flexibility if exercise plans change, which is common in team sports.

The insulin pump has greatly assisted athletes in the control of their serum glucose levels. It works by providing a steady baseline infusion of insulin that can be adjusted by the athlete depending on the demands of a particular time of day. In addition to this baseline infusion, the athlete can also trigger bolus injections of insulin to cover carbohydrate intake. The optimal insulin to use in an insulin pump is a rapid-acting insulin. The insulin pump is connected via tubing to a cannula that is inserted subcutaneously in sterile fashion. The cannula can typically stay in place for 2 to 3 days, but then needs to be moved to prevent infection. The connection between the cannula and the pump is an interlocking connector that allows the pump to be disconnected from the cannula for short periods of time. This can come in handy with collision sports. As noted earlier, exercise itself facilitates glucose uptake into muscle cells, and insulin requirements during exercise are lowered. Therefore, the pump can be removed, if needed, during athletic participation as long as the athlete monitors his or her serum glucose level.

It is difficult to make absolute insulin dosing recommendations that apply to all situations. Several variables need to be taken into account in formulating recommendations. Insulin absorption will vary with the site of injection or infusion. Rapid-acting insulin absorption from an exercising limb, such as the leg of a runner, will be enhanced. This causes a more rapid and more pronounced effect than when an injection site such as the abdomen is used.[77] The abdomen is also preferred over the arm because the increased fat layer diminishes the possibility of intramuscular injection. Intramuscular injection causes a striking increase in insulin absorption and a dramatic drop in serum glucose values.[78] Additionally, ambient conditions will have an effect on insulin absorption, with hot and humid conditions potentially enhancing absorption.[79]

The optimal prevention of acute diabetic complications comes from education of the athlete. Athletes need to be educated regarding the proper nutritional intake for exercise, the basics of insulin dosing and administration during exercise, the importance of assessing serum glucose content, the guidelines for proper serum glucose levels for exercise, and the proper response to abnormal glucose levels.

Prevention of Acute Complications

In the setting of athletic participation, the type 1 diabetic must be very vigilant of serum glucose levels in order to control them. The normal adrenergic response to exercise still persists with these individuals, but they lack the endogenous counterbalancing response of insulin. Although the benefits of exercise are as substantial for the diabetic athlete as they are for the nondiabetic athlete, the type 1 diabetic faces the risk of hypoglycemia, which can occur during exercise and up to 12 to 24 hours afterward.[80,81] The type 1 diabetic also faces the risks of hyperglycemia due to the catecholamine surge of intense exercise, as noted previously.[82,83] Managing the dosing of insulin is imperative to diminish this risk.

Maintenance of Euglycemia

Athletes who use multiple daily injections of insulin for glycemic control will need to alter both their insulin doses and nutritional intake depending on their glycemic status, exercise demand, and timing of their exercise sessions. It has been shown that the use of rapid-acting analogues prior to a meal leads to a greater likelihood of hypoglycemia during postprandial exercise than does the use of regular human insulin.[80] Also, diminishing the dose of preprandial rapid-acting insulin can decrease the likelihood of hypoglycemia during and after postprandial exercise.[81] Therefore, it is recommended that athletes who plan on exercising after eating alter their bolus injection to account for both the duration and type of exercise planned. Some athletes train prior to eating in the morning, which makes alteration of their insulin dosing more difficult. In this situation, it is best that they decrease their evening long-acting insulin dose the night before. Once again, the magnitude of this decrease should be determined by both the intensity and duration of the planned exercise the next morning.

It is difficult to determine exactly how much to decrease doses because of all of the variables associated with insulin's response to exercise noted previously. Athletes with type 1 diabetes need to be vigilant, checking their serum glucose level regularly and noting how they respond to different alterations. It has been suggested that a 20% to 50% decrease in the evening's long-acting insulin dose is appropriate,[82] but the proper adjustment needs to be determined by the individual athlete. Because of the somewhat unpredictable response of serum glucose level to these alterations, it is essential that the athlete always have a source of rapidly absorbed carbohydrate available to him or her.

The use of the insulin pump gives an athlete greater control and flexibility regarding insulin dosing. With pump users, it has been shown that diminishing the basal rate of insulin infusion by 50% prior to exercise will help prevent hypoglycemia.[83–85] Because insulin can remain active for approximately 30 minutes once it has bound to its receptor, it can be helpful to initiate this insulin reduction 30 minutes prior to exercise.[83] As mentioned earlier, the insulin pump may need to be removed for certain types of exercise such as collision or water sports. It is recommended that the pump be removed approximately 30 minutes prior to exercise because of the aforementioned insulin receptor binding effects. For prolonged exercise of an hour or more, additional boluses of insulin should be administered at a dose of approximately 50% of the normal insulin dose for that hour in order to prevent a hypoinsulinemic state.[83]

Obviously, the dosage recommendations just noted should be altered depending on other variables. As noted earlier, a previous episode of hypoglycemia can increase the risk of hypoglycemia with subsequent exercise in the next 12 to 24 hours.[74] Also, fluctuations in ambient temperature can affect insulin sensitivity. Insulin sensitivity is also increased as an athlete becomes more fit. Therefore, the insulin regimen may need to change as an athlete becomes better conditioned. If an athlete is sick, the levels of stress hormones, particularly cortisol and catecholamines, are elevated. These hormonal fluctuations will also alter glycemic control, raising serum glucose levels. The same effect can be seen in the setting of injury.[76] Regardless of the alterations made to insulin dosing, athletes must pay close attention to the responses of their serum glucose level to various situations. They face numerous alterations to their training and practice schedules, as well as to their eating schedules. Athletes should always be equipped with an ingestible source of carbohydrate supplementation should their serum glucose level dip too low.

Assessment and Response

Athletes with type 1 diabetes should know their serum glucose level going into exercise. Beginning exercise with a serum glucose level that is either too low or too high will predispose to hypoglycemia or hyperglycemia, so alterations need to be made to address these issues before exercise is started. The American Diabetes Association recommends that type 1 diabetics avoid exercise if their glucose levels are above 250 mg/dL and there is evidence of ketosis. The group also recommends caution if glucose levels are above 300 mg/dL without ketosis. If glucose levels are below 100 mg/dL, it recommends ingesting additional carbohydrate prior to exercise.[86]

The National Athletic Trainers' Association (NATA) recommends measuring serum glucose levels two to three times at 30-minute intervals prior to exercise to determine the trajectory of glucose movement. During exercise, its recommendation is to measure blood glucose every 30 minutes if possible. After exercise, NATA recommends that athletes who experience delayed postexercise hypoglycemia check their blood glucose every 2 hours for up to 4 hours following exercise.[76]

Once an athlete with type 1 diabetes develops a stable schedule of insulin, diet, and exercise, it may not be necessary to check his or her serum glucose level as regularly during exercise. However, if there is perturbation to an athlete's food intake, exercise schedule and intensity, insulin dosing, or physiologic milieu (as a result of illness, injury, or environment), the athlete should be diligent about checking his or her serum glucose level periodically during exercise. Exhaustive exercise and hypoglycemia share many common symptoms, so it may be important to check serum glucose levels in these situations to ensure that hypoglycemia is addressed early, if it develops. Also, if the athlete has experienced a recent episode of hypoglycemia, added vigilance is necessary because of the increased risk of recurrent hypoglycemia. The athlete also needs to know not to use insulin to treat transient hyperglycemia during intense exercise.[71] As noted earlier, the hormonal response of intense exercise will elevate serum glucose levels, so if athletes chase these levels with additional insulin boluses, they place themselves at greater risk of postexercise hypoglycemia.

Prevention of Late Hypoglycemia

After exercise, muscle and liver glycogen stores are replenished using circulating plasma glucose. Exercise also increases muscle sensitivity to insulin. These combined factors can lead to a delayed hypoglycemic response to exercise, which can occur 6 to 24 hours after exercise.[87] It most commonly occurs at times when activity levels change, such as progression to a new level of competition or with two-a-day practices in the preseason. Late hypoglycemia often occurs overnight. In addition to the acute risks of hypoglycemia, this nocturnal hypoglycemia can disturb sleep patterns, impair recovery, and contribute to subjective feelings of fatigue and diminution of a sense of well-being.[79]

Prevention of late hypoglycemia can require as little intervention as the addition of a late-night snack before bed. Also, insulin doses can be reduced, either as part of a multiple daily injection or an insulin pump regimen. Bussau et al.[88] have reported that a 10-second maximal sprint before moderate-intensity exercise can attenuate the hypoglycemic response in the 45 minutes after exercise. The same group has also used a postexercise 10-second maximal sprint to boost counterregulatory hormones and attenuate the hypoglycemic response in the 120 minutes after moderate-intensity exercise.[89] It is unknown whether these interventions have any effect on hypoglycemia occurring 6 to 24 hours after exercise.

Management of Hypoglycemia

Hypoglycemia is generally defined as a blood glucose level less than 70 mg/dL. If the athlete is conscious, coherent, and able to follow directions, the hypoglycemia is considered mild. If the athlete is unconscious, combative, disoriented, or unable to follow directions, the hypoglycemia is considered severe. Obviously, management of mild and severe hypoglycemic episodes differs.

Mild Hypoglycemia

The management of mild hypoglycemia centers on oral carbohydrate replacement. In this setting, the athlete should be removed from exercise and given 15 to 20 g of fast-acting carbohydrate. This can be attained with 4 to 6 glucose tablets, 2 tablespoons of honey, 4 to 6 ounces of fruit juice or sweetened carbonated beverage, or 8 ounces of low-fat milk.[61,71,76] Fatty foods slow gastric emptying, delaying the absorption of carbohydrate, so higher-fat foods such as candy bars should be avoided. Also, sports beverages contain lower amounts of carbohydrate, so larger volumes are required to achieve 15 to 20 g of carbohydrate. For instance, an equal volume of Gatorade has just less than one half of the carbohydrate of apple or grape juice.[61] This makes sports drinks suboptimal sources of carbohydrate to treat hypoglycemia, and the other alternatives noted previously should be made available. After ingestion of the carbohydrate, the serum glucose level should be reassessed every 15 minutes. If there is no response in symptoms or serum glucose level after 15 minutes, the initial carbohydrate dose can be repeated. If there is still no response after a second dose, NATA recommends activating the emergency medical system.[76] It is important to keep in mind that hypoglycemia triggers the counterregulatory hormone response, so proper dosing of the carbohydrate is important. Blindly giving an amount of carbohydrate that is too large is likely to stimulate a hyperglycemic rebound.

If the athlete responds properly to the oral carbohydrate dose, he or she may be returned to exercise once symptoms resolve and the serum glucose level is above 80 mg/dL. In returning an athlete to exercise, it is prudent to have him or her also ingest some low-glycemic-index carbohydrate, such as a bagel or bread, to prevent a recurrence of the hypoglycemia.

Severe Hypoglycemia

Severe hypoglycemia obviously requires more emergent intervention. The emergency medical system should be activated, and measures should immediately be taken on site to raise serum glucose levels.

Glucagon should be administered intramuscularly to the athlete. Injectable glucagon comes in kits with a syringe, powdered glucagon, and fluid with which to mix it. Once the glucagon is solubilized, it can be injected into the deltoid, quadriceps, or gluteal musculature. Parents and athletic trainers should be trained in how to mix and administer the glucagon. In a situation in which an athlete is traveling without an athletic trainer or parent, the coach should be able to administer the glucagon.

It is important to realize that glucagon has its primary effect by stimulating hepatic release of glycogen. In a situation in which hepatic glycogen has been depleted, the glucagon may not have an adequate effect. In the setting of severe hypoglycemia, emergency medical personnel can administer intravenous dextrose in the form of 50% dextrose in water ($D_{50}W$). It should be obvious that there is no role for the use of oral carbohydrate in the unresponsive athlete. Attempts to force oral consumption of carbohydrate can lead to choking and aspiration.

Wilderness Considerations

In the traditional sport or physical activity setting, certain services exist when sudden-death situations arise. For instance, cell phone service, ambulance responses of less than 30 minutes, supplies and equipment, and numerous trained and nontrained helpers are probably available. In the wilderness, such amenities may not exist. Therefore, in possible sudden-death situations, protocols may need to be altered. **Table 13.9** addresses each topic covered in this book and how the wilderness medicine protocol or treatment may be different from the traditional setting.

Wilderness settings can range from a simple 1-hour hike in front country to a 30-day hike in back country. *Front country* usually refers to wilderness that is within 1 day of hiking. Examples include local parks or hiking trails that only require a day's worth of sun to hike. *Back country* refers to anything past front country, usually wilderness that takes more than 1 day to reach. Which part of the wilderness you are in during a sudden-death situation has the potential to change the treatment protocol.

Providing care in an unconventional setting calls for thinking outside the box. Conventional medicine applied in the wilderness can sometimes increase risk to the victim instead of decrease it. For example, traditional spine boarding techniques used on a sport field could be detrimental to the rock climber who needs to be carried off a mountain over a period of 2 hours.

The health care professional who responds in the wilderness needs many characteristics. "An experienced rescuer will have learned not to expect a predictable and comfortable work environment. Flexibility, innovation, and a certain amount of courage are required to cope with the varied and constantly evolving nature of medical care in the wild or remote setting."[90] However, the skill needed most of all is analyzing the risk/benefit ratio. Responders must not allow emotional attachment or the excitement of the situation to cloud their judgment. The benefit must clearly outweigh the risk when treating victims in the wilderness. "Every treatment (or decision not to treat) and every emergency evacuation (or decision to stay in the field) involves risk that the medical problems will become worse because of what we've done."[90]

The responder is challenged to develop a plan that makes the most sense for the environment and situation surrounding the victim. It is imperative to strive for the ideal treatment for a victim, but the clinician must be at peace with not being able to provide that if supplies or equipment are missing. Instead, resourcefulness and compromise are needed.

The first steps in providing care in a wilderness setting are similar to a primary survey in the traditional setting. However, a few differences do exist. Ensuring scene safety may take longer and involve more complications. Environmental conditions such as lightning may be possible, as well as natural dangers such as moving rock. The health care provider's safety comes before that of the victims. Also, the likelihood that more than one victim is involved is higher as compared with the traditional setting.

During the secondary survey, a more detailed history may be needed because situations may be multifaceted and predisposing factors may be relevant for several days leading up to the event. It has been suggested to use the mnemonic SAMPLE: *s*ymptoms, *a*llergies, *m*edications, *p*ertinent history, *l*ast

TABLE 13.9	Differences in Wilderness Protocols from Those Used in Traditional Settings		
Condition	**Injury or Illness**	**Assessment**	**Treatment**
Head injuries	Traumatic brain injury or concussion	Consider mechanism of injury; may rule out spinal injury (spinal cord injury); observation	Emergency evacuation necessary for persistent disorientation, inability to retain new memory, history of recent previous concussion, skull fracture, high-velocity impact, or signs or symptoms of increased ICP.
Spinal cord injuries		Spine may be cleared if: • Patient is reliable; no tenderness to firm spine palpation; intact distal motor and sensory exam • Finger abduction, wrist extension • Plantar flexion and dorsiflexion • Sharp/dull discrimination	Spine-injured patient may need to walk to safety. Utilize rigid equipment, including back pack, trekking, and tent poles, to stabilize the patient. All gaps should be filled with significant padding to minimize movement with transportation. Apply a cervical collar as soon as this can be done safely.
Asthma			Evacuation necessary if not improving with albuterol inhaler. Epinephrine 0.3 mg should be administered if available and if personnel have been trained.
Exertional heat stroke		Assessment based on altered CNS, environmental factors, and exercise intensity	Treatment includes removing clothing and utilizing any cooling method available, including streams and ponds.
Traumatic injury	Dislocations	Note obvious deformity	Attempt reduction if: • Shoulder, patella, digits • Mechanism of indirect force Apply traction and splint as unstable if: • Other joints • Neurovascular compromise
	Fractures	Severe deformity with NVS compromise should be realigned, then splinted	Splint with any material available.
	Impaled objects		Remove unless impaled in the globe of eye or removal would increase bleeding.
Lightning			If patient is in full cardiac arrest consider ceasing CPR after 30 minutes.
Anaphylaxis			Administer epinephrine 0.3 mg in 5- to 20-minute intervals if signs and symptoms do not resolve. May need additional dose if biphasic reaction occurs.
Hypothermia		Assessment based on CNS dysfunction and mechanism of cold exposure	Rewarming the victim accomplished through removal of wet clothing, utilization of sleeping bags, and other individuals' body heat.

CNS, central nervous system; CPR, cardiopulmonary resuscitation; ICP, intracranial pressure; NVS, neurovascular status.

ins (food) and outs (urine and bowel), and *e*vents leading up to the accident. Some additional acronyms that can easily be remembered in the field or in the wilderness during sudden-death situations are AVPU and STOPEATS. AVPU is useful for assessing any of the sudden-death topics covered in this book. The responder is looking for the victim to be either *a*lert, responsive to *v*erbal stimuli, responsive to *p*ainful stimuli, or *u*nresponsive.[91] This can give the health care provider an idea of consciousness level and is easier to remember than the Glasgow Coma Scale. STOPEATS provides insights into the many different factors that can cause central nervous system dysfunction. The letters represent *s*ugar (hypoglycemia), *t*emperature (hyperthermia or hypothermia), *o*xygen (hypoxia), *p*ressure (intracranial bleeding or swelling), *e*lectricity (lightning), *a*ltitude, *t*oxins (venom, allergic reagents), and *s*alts (electrolytes). This will allow the health care provider to develop a differential diagnosis.

high-altitude pulmonary edema (HAPE) A condition that only manifests in high-altitude outdoor settings in which low oxygen levels trigger swelling of lung tissue, filling them with fluid.

high-altitude cerebral edema (HACE) A condition that only manifests in high-altitude outdoor settings in which low oxygen levels trigger swelling of brain tissue.

In addition to the topics covered within this book, two additional illnesses associated with the wilderness can result in sudden-death situations: **high-altitude pulmonary edema (HAPE)** and **high-altitude cerebral edema (HACE)**. These illnesses could possibly be seen in sports situations but are more commonly encountered in the mountain setting. HAPE and HACE are both caused by a reduction in oxygen saturation (usually below 90%). The tissues most susceptible to a decrease in oxygen are the lungs and brain. HACE is caused by an increase in vasodilation and blood flow to the brain. HAPE is caused by pulmonary artery vasoconstriction that results in pulmonary hypertension. In both cases, capillaries dilate and leak, resulting in edema of the tissues. HACE tends to develop over 24 hours, whereas HAPE tends to develop over several days. Predisposing factors for both conditions include a past history of altitude illness, rapid ascent, a "low-lander" (a person who lives below 1000 m), exertion, and cold air. Prevention of HACE and HAPE includes a gradual ascent, frequent rests, frequent descents intermixed with ascents, avoidance of depressants, and staying well hydrated and fed.[90,92–95]

HACE's early signs and symptoms include headache, loss of appetite, and nausea. As swelling increases intracranial pressure, these symptoms progress in severity. Central nervous system dysfunction arises and is similar to the signs and symptoms of concussion. Mental status, consciousness, orientation, and coordination are all affected. Vomiting might also be present and persistent at a progressed stage. Treatment is simply to descend as fast as possible to transitional care. If descent is not possible, rest, pain medications, and hydration should be provided. Once transitional care can be obtained, supplemental oxygen should be given.[90,94,95]

HAPE's early signs and symptoms include shortness of breath and a dry cough. A low-grade fever may be present. Individuals with an existing or recent respiratory illness are at greater risk for HAPE. As HAPE progresses, "crackly" breathing can be heard in the chest with or without a stethoscope. Difficulty in breathing and cough worsen. Descent should be immediate, and supplemental oxygen given if possible. If descent means strenuous exercise, it is possible that staying at the location and resting might be the better treatment because exertion will worsen the edema. Without treatment, however, respiratory failure and death are possible.[90,92–94]

Clinical Case Scenarios

1. John, a 22-year-old white NCAA Division I cross-country athlete, was reported by his teammates to athletic training personnel to have been stung by a hornet and not feeling well. The incident occurred at the beginning of the workout in August on running trails a half mile away from campus (starting point). Environmental conditions that day included a dry bulb temperature of 26.7°C (80.1°F) and a relative humidity of 76%. The athlete continued to run after the sting for approximately 1 mile (approximately 7 minutes) in order to arrive at the water break point, where athletic training personnel were stationed. He initially complained of itching on his palms and feet, his face was red and hot, and he was sweating profusely. Hives were slightly recognizable on his body at this time. During the conversation, hives started to progressively form on his body. No previous history of an anaphylactic reaction existed prior to this incident. EMS was activated when the athlete's throat

started swelling and he began having difficulty breathing. The athlete was kept in a supine position and made as comfortable as possible. His vital signs were monitored. The athlete was turned to a recovery position as he started to vomit. An ambulance arrived at the site approximately 17 minutes after the sting. John received an epinephrine shot, a Benadryl shot, and IV fluids on the ambulance. At the hospital, he received an additional liter of IV fluids. A second shot of epinephrine and Benadryl was administered approximately 45 minutes after the first injections.

1. What triggers played a role in this reaction?
2. What factors mediated the severity of the response?
3. What precautions will the medical staff need to have in place before John practices again?

2. Hailey is a 5′4″, 110-pound cross-country skier in Vermont. She is a freshman on the college's intercollegiate team. She had been "initiated" onto the team Friday night. It was late October, but early in the training season. The team was hosting its first meet the following week. Hailey and her roommate went for an additional workout on the cross-country trails Saturday morning in order to better prepare for the meet. Hailey's ski caught on a rock, making her fall onto a thin sheet of ice on the small creek they were skiing next to. As she scrambled to get up, she fell through the ice and ended up sitting in waist-high cold water. Her friend helped her out of the creek, and they continued their workout for another hour. The environmental conditions were a temperature of 1.6°C (35°F) with 10% humidity. By the time they returned to the ski shack, Hailey was complaining, grumpy, and cold. As soon as they stopped to remove their skis and outwear, Hailey began to shiver violently. The athletic trainer took her pulse and blood pressure, which were 160 and 150/90, respectively. The athletic trainer had Hailey remove all her wet clothing, put dry clothing on from her team locker with the help of her friend, and wrap herself in blankets. Hailey was placed in front of a heat blower while being asked to sip hot chocolate and eat granola bars. Within 30 minutes, Hailey felt better and her vital signs had returned to normal.

1. What were the major predisposing factors to Hailey developing hypothermia? Which factors were within Hailey's control? Which ones were not?
2. Why did the athletic trainer choose these particular treatments? What precautions should be taken with these treatments?

3. Brayden had been training for his first triathlon all summer. Race day came on September 30 in Colorado, with beautiful fall conditions: 15.6°C (60°F) and 20% humidity. As he dove into the mountain lake, it was shockingly cold compared with the pool in which he had been training. He completed the half-mile swim, dried off, and changed into his new biking and running clothes. As he neared the finish of the bike portion, the sky turned cloudy, the air cooled, and it started to drizzle. Brayden was already shivering when he began running the 10 miles. His clothes and socks were wet after 2 miles of running. Brayden became increasingly frustrated as he kept tripping on rocks and cracks in the road. At the finish line Brayden refused to wave at his parents as they cheered for him. He was unable to remove the time chip from his shoe and became upset with the volunteer helping him. Brayden ignored the offer of mylar blankets, food, and hot fluids by the volunteers.

1. What predisposing factors of hypothermia are at play in this scenario but are not provided in the text?
2. What signs, symptoms, and behavior is Brayden exhibiting at the end of the scenario?
3. How might this situation progress further?
4. What should medical volunteers do to help Brayden?

4. Dan and Jen were hiking in the Sierra Nevada with four other friends. They hiked 10 miles on the first day, set up camp, ate a full dinner, and had 7 hours of sleep. On the beginning of the second day of hiking, Jen became hungry and tried a handful of berries she found next to the trail. As the group continued to hike, Jen told Dan that she was not feeling well and needed to stop. Dan turned to Jen and noticed hives on her arms, neck, and chest. Dan stopped the rest of the group. A trained provider in the group found Jen's pulse to be 130, and her respiratory rate was increased. As the group member began to take a history, Jen started to have significant difficulty with breathing. The

group member gave Jen 0.3 mg of epinephrine through intramuscular injection, made her comfortable, and monitored her vital signs while calming her.

1. What will need to be done once Jen starts to recover?
2. What will need to be done if Jen's signs and symptoms continue or get worse?
3. How would this situation differ if it were to occur at a soccer field?

Key Terms

accidental hypothermia

anaphylaxis

biphasic reaction

cold acclimatization

cold stressor

epinephrine autoinjector

glucagon

high-altitude cerebral edema (HACE)

high-altitude pulmonary edema (HAPE)

hypoglycemia

hypothermia

insulin

protracted reaction

shivering

trigger

type 1 diabetes

type 2 diabetes

References

1. Sampson HA, Munoz-Furlong A, Bock SA, et al. Symposium on the definition and management of anaphylaxis: summary report. *J Allergy Clin Immunol.* 2005;115(3):584–591.
2. Pumphrey R. Anaphylaxis: can we tell who is at risk of a fatal reaction? *Curr Opin Allergy Clin Immunol.* 2004;4(4):285–290.
3. Lieberman P, Camargo CA Jr, Bohlke K, et al. Epidemiology of anaphylaxis: findings of the American College of Allergy, Asthma and Immunology Epidemiology of Anaphylaxis Working Group. *Ann Allergy Asthma Immunol.* 2006;97(5):596–602.
4. Poulos LM, Waters AM, Correll PK, Loblay RH, Marks GB. Trends in hospitalizations for anaphylaxis, angioedema, and urticaria in Australia, 1993–1994 to 2004–2005. *J Allergy Clin Immunol.* 2007;120(4):878–884.
5. Neugut AI, Ghatak AT, Miller RL. Anaphylaxis in the United States: an investigation into its epidemiology. *Arch Intern Med.* 2001;161(1):15–21.
6. Simons FE. Anaphylaxis. *J Allergy Clin Immunol.* 2010;125(2 suppl 2):S161–S181.
7. Kemp SF, Lockey RF. Anaphylaxis: a review of causes and mechanisms. *J Allergy Clin Immunol* 2002;110(3):341–348.
8. Simons FE. Anaphylaxis: recent advances in assessment and treatment. *J Allergy Clin Immunol.* 2009;124(4):625–636; quiz 637–638.
9. Sampson HA. Anaphylaxis and emergency treatment. *Pediatrics.* 2003;111(6 pt 3):1601–1608.
10. Lieberman P. Anaphylaxis. *Med Clin North Am.* 2006;90(1):77–95.
11. Campbell RL, Luke A, Weaver AL, et al. Prescriptions for self-injectable epinephrine and follow-up referral in emergency department patients presenting with anaphylaxis. *Ann Allergy Asthma Immunol.* 2008;101(6):631–636.
12. Klein JS, Yocum MW. Underreporting of anaphylaxis in a community emergency room. *J Allergy Clin Immunol.* 1995;95(2):637–638.
13. Sampson HA, Muñoz-Furlong A, Campbell RL, et al. Second symposium on the definition and management of anaphylaxis: summary report—Second National Institute of Allergy and Infectious Disease/Food Allergy and Anaphylaxis Network symposium. *J Allergy Clin Immunol.* 2006;117(2):391–397.

14. Brazil E, MacNamara AF. "Not so immediate" hypersensitivity—the danger of biphasic anaphylactic reactions. *J Accid Emerg Med.* 1998;15(4):252–253.

15. Douglas DM, Sukenick E, Andrade WP, Brown JS. Biphasic systemic anaphylaxis: an inpatient and outpatient study. *J Allergy Clin Immunol.* 1994;93(6):977–985.

16. Stark BJ, Sullivan TJ. Biphasic and protracted anaphylaxis. *J Allergy Clin Immunol.* 1986;78(1 pt 1):76–83.

17. Lee JM, Greenes DS. Biphasic anaphylactic reactions in pediatrics. *Pediatrics.* 2000;106(4):762–766.

18. Lieberman P. Biphasic anaphylactic reactions. *Ann Allergy Asthma Immunol.* 2005;95(3):217–226.

19. Kemp SF, Lockey RF, Simons FE. Epinephrine: the drug of choice for anaphylaxis. A statement of the World Allergy Organization. *Allergy.* 2008;63(8):1061–1070.

20. Korenblat P, Lundie MJ, Dankner RE, Day JH. A retrospective study of epinephrine administration for anaphylaxis: how many doses are needed? *Allergy Asthma Proc.* 1999;20(6):383–386.

21. Uguz A, Lack G, Pumphrey R, et al. Allergic reactions in the community: a questionnaire survey of members of the anaphylaxis campaign. *Clin Exp Allergy.* 2005;35(6):746–750.

22. Visscher PK, Vetter RS, Camazine S. Removing bee stings. *Lancet.* 1996;348(9023):301–302.

23. Mullins RJ. Anaphylaxis: risk factors for recurrence. *Clin Exp Allergy.* 2003;33(8):1033–1040.

24. Reynolds K, Williams J, Miller C, Mathis A, Dettori J. Injuries and risk factors in an 18-day Marine winter mountain training exercise. *Mil Med.* 2000;165(12):905–910.

25. Murphy T, Zumwalt R, Fallico F, et al. Hypothermia-related deaths—United States, 1999–2002 and 2005. *MMWR.* 2006;55(10):282–284.

26. Cappaert TA, Stone JA, Castellani JW, et al. National Athletic Trainers' Association position statement: environmental cold injuries. *J Athl Train.* 2008;43(6):640–658.

27. Castellani JW, Young AJ, Ducharme MB, et al. American College of Sports Medicine position stand: prevention of cold injuries during exercise. *Med Sci Sports Exerc.* 2006;38(11):2012–2029.

28. Armstrong LE. *Performing in Extreme Environments.* Champaign, IL: Human Kinetics; 2000.

29. Martyn JW. Diagnosing and treating hypothermia. *Can Med Assoc J.* 1981;125(10):1089–1096.

30. Danzl DF, Pozos RS, Auerbach PS, et al. Multicenter hypothermia survey. *Ann Emerg Med.* 1987;16(9):1042–1055.

31. Regnard J. Cold and the airways. *Int J Sports Med.* 1992;13(suppl 1):S182–S184.

32. Tikuisis P, Bell DG, Jacobs I. Shivering onset, metabolic response, and convective heat transfer during cold air exposure. *J Appl Physiol.* 1991;70(5):1996–2002.

33. Giesbrecht GG. Emergency treatment of hypothermia. *Emerg Med (Fremantle).* 2001;13(1):9–16.

34. Castro RR, Mendes FS, Nobrega AC. Risk of hypothermia in a new Olympic event: the 10-km marathon swim. *Clinics (Sao Paulo).* 2009;64(4):351–356.

35. Smith RM, Hanna JM. Skinfolds and resting heat loss in cold air and water: temperature equivalence. *J Appl Physiol.* 1975;39(1):93–102.

36. Glickman-Weiss EL, Nelson AG, Hearon CM, et al. Effects of body morphology and mass on thermal responses to cold water: revisited. *Eur J Appl Physiol Occup Physiol.* 1993;66(4):299–303.

37. Budd GM, Brotherhood JR, Hendrie AL, Jeffery SE. Effects of fitness, fatness, and age on men's responses to whole body cooling in air. *J Appl Physiol.* 1991;71(6):2387–2393.

38. Falk B, Bar-Or O, Smolander J, Frost G. Response to rest and exercise in the cold: effects of age and aerobic fitness. *J Appl Physiol.* 1994;76(1):72–78.

39. Wagner JA, Robinson S, Marino RP. Age and temperature regulation of humans in neutral and cold environments. *J Appl Physiol.* 1974;37(4):562–565.

40. Graham TE. Thermal, metabolic, and cardiovascular changes in men and women during cold stress. *Med Sci Sports Exerc.* 1988;20(5 suppl):S185–S192.

41. Fox GR, Hayward JS, Hobson GN. Effect of alcohol on thermal balance of man in cold water. *Can J Physiol Pharmacol.* 1979;57(8):860–865.

42. Patton JF, Vogel JA. Effects of acute cold exposure on submaximal endurance performance. *Med Sci Sports Exerc.* 1984;16(5):494–497.

43. Bittel JH, Nonotte-Varly C, Livecchi-Gonnot GH, Savourey GL, Hanniquet AM. Physical fitness and thermoregulatory reactions in a cold environment in men. *J Appl Physiol.* 1988;65(5):1984–1989.

44. Sugahara M, Taimura A. Relationship between thermoregulation and cold induced vasodilation during cold exposure with regard to maximal oxygen uptake. *Jpn J Physiol Fitness Sports Med.* 1996;46(1):101–110.

45. Young AJ, Castellani JW, O'Brien C, et al. Exertional fatigue, sleep loss, and negative energy balance increase susceptibility to hypothermia. *J Appl Physiol.* 1998;85(4):1210–1217.

46. Vallerand AL, Jacobs I. Energy metabolism during cold exposure. *Int J Sports Med.* 1992;13(suppl 1):S191–S193.

47. Giesbrecht GG, Goheen MS, Johnston CE, et al. Inhibition of shivering increases core temperature afterdrop and attenuates rewarming in hypothermic humans. *J Appl Physiol.* 1997;83(5):1630–1634.

48. Askew EW. Environmental and physical stress and nutrient requirements. *Am J Clin Nutr.* 1995;61(3 suppl):631S–637S.

49. O'Brien C, Young AJ, Sawka MN. Hypohydration and thermoregulation in cold air. *J Appl Physiol.* 1998;84(1):185–189.

50. Bagley JR, Judelson DA, Spiering BA, et al. *Validity of Field Expedient Measurement Devices to Assess Core Body Temperature During Rest and Exercise in the Cold.* Fullerton, CA: California State University, Fullerton; 2010.

51. Rogers I. Which rewarming therapy in hypothermia? A review of the randomized trials. *Emerg Med.* 1997;9:213–220.

52. Kempainen RR, Brunette DD. The evaluation and management of accidental hypothermia. *Respir Care.* 2004;49(2): 192–205.

53. Goheen MS, Ducharme MB, Kenny GP, et al. Efficacy of forced-air and inhalation rewarming by using a human model for severe hypothermia. *J Appl Physiol.* 1997;83(5):1635–1640.

54. Steele MT, Nelson MJ, Sessler DI, et al. Forced air speeds rewarming in accidental hypothermia. *Ann Emerg Med.* 1996;27(4): 479–484.

55. Ittner KP, Bachfischer M, Zimmermann M, Taeger K. Convective air warming is more effective than resistive heating in an experimental model with a water dummy. *Eur J Emerg Med.* 2004;11(3):151–153.

56. Zachary L, Kucan JO, Robson MC, Frank DH. Accidental hypothermia treated with rapid rewarming by immersion. *Ann Plast Surg.* 1982;9(3):238–241.

57. Walpoth BH, Walpoth-Aslan BN, Mattle HP, et al. Outcome of survivors of accidental deep hypothermia and circulatory arrest treated with extracorporeal blood warming. *N Engl J Med.* 1997;337(21):1500–1505.

58. McDermott BP, Casa DJ, Yeargin SW, et al. Recovery and return to activity following exertional heat stroke: considerations for the sports medicine staff. *J Sport Rehabil.* 2007;16(3):163–181.

59. Rissanen S, Rintamaki H. Thermal responses and physiological strain in men wearing impermeable and semipermeable protective clothing in the cold. *Ergonomics.* 1997;40(2):141–150.

60. Young AJ. *Homeostatic Responses to Prolonged Cold Exposure: Human Cold Acclimatization.* New York: Oxford University Press; 1996.

61. Kirk SE. Hypoglycemia in athletes with diabetes. *Clin Sports Med.* 2009;28(3):455–468.

62. Tattersall RB, Gill GV. Unexplained deaths of type 1 diabetic patients. *Diabet Med.* 1991;8(1):49–58.

63. O'Reilly M, O'Sullivan EP, Davenport C, Smith D. "Dead in bed": a tragic complication of type 1 diabetes mellitus. *Ir J Med Sci.* 2010;179(4):585–587.

64. Tu E, Twigg SM, Semsarian C. Sudden death in type 1 diabetes: the mystery of the 'dead in bed' syndrome. *Int J Cardiol.* 2010;138(1):91–93.

65. Tanenberg RJ, Newton CA, Drake AJ. Confirmation of hypoglycemia in the "dead-in-bed" syndrome, as captured by a retrospective continuous glucose monitoring system. *Endocr Pract.* 2010;16(2):244–248.

66. Kitabchi AE, Nyenwe EA. Hyperglycemic crises in diabetes mellitus: diabetic ketoacidosis and hyperglycemic hyperosmolar state. *Endocrinol Metab Clin North Am.* 2006;35(4):725–751.

67. Henriksen OM, Roder ME, Prahl JB, Svendsen OL. Diabetic ketoacidosis in Denmark: incidence and mortality estimated from public health registries. *Diabetes Res Clin Pract.* 2007;76(1):51–56.

68. Thorell A, Hirshman MF, Nygren J, et al. Exercise and insulin cause GLUT-4 translocation in human skeletal muscle. *Am J Physiol.* 1999;277(4 pt 1):E733–E741.

69. Richter EA, Ploug T, Galbo H. Increased muscle glucose uptake after exercise. No need for insulin during exercise. *Diabetes.* 1985;34(10):1041–1048.

70. Sigal RJ, Fisher S, Halter JB, Vranic M, Marliss EB. The roles of catecholamines in glucoregulation in intense exercise as defined by the islet cell clamp technique. *Diabetes.* 1996;45(2):148–156.

71. MacKnight JM, Mistry DJ, Pastors JG, Holmes V, Rynders CA. The daily management of athletes with diabetes. *Clin Sports Med.* 2009;28(3):479–495.

72. Berger M, Berchtold P, Cuppers HJ, et al. Metabolic and hormonal effects of muscular exercise in juvenile type diabetics. *Diabetologia.* 1977;13(4):355–365.

73. Mitchell TH, Abraham G, Schiffrin A, Leiter LA, Marliss EB. Hyperglycemia after intense exercise in IDDM subjects during continuous subcutaneous insulin infusion. *Diabetes Care.* 1988;11(4):311–317.

74. Davis SN, Galassetti P, Wasserman DH, Tate D. Effects of antecedent hypoglycemia on subsequent counterregulatory responses to exercise. *Diabetes.* 2000;49(1):73–81.

75. The effect of intensive treatment of diabetes on the development and progression of long-term complications in insulin-dependent diabetes mellitus. The Diabetes Control and Complications Trial Research Group. *N Engl J Med.* 1993;329(14): 977–986.

76. Jimenez CC, Corcoran MH, Crawley JT, et al. National Athletic Trainers' Association position statement: management of the athlete with type 1 diabetes mellitus. *J Athl Train.* 2007;42(4):536–545.

77. Koivisto VA, Felig P. Effects of leg exercise on insulin absorption in diabetic patients. *N Engl J Med.* 1978;298(2):79–83.

78. Frid A, Ostman J, Linde B. Hypoglycemia risk during exercise after intramuscular injection of insulin in thigh in IDDM. *Diabetes Care.* 1990;13(5):473–477.

79. Peirce NS. Diabetes and exercise. *Br J Sports Med.* 1999;33(3):161–172; quiz 172–173, 222.

80. Tuominen JA, Karonen SL, Melamies L, Bolli G, Koivisto VA. Exercise-induced hypoglycaemia in IDDM patients treated with a short-acting insulin analogue. *Diabetologia.* 1995;38(1):106–111.

81. Rabasa-Lhoret R, Bourque J, Ducros F, Chiasson JL. Guidelines for premeal insulin dose reduction for postprandial exercise of different intensities and durations in type 1 diabetic subjects treated intensively with a basal-bolus insulin regimen (ultralente-lispro). *Diabetes Care.* 2001;24(4):625–630.

82. Ruegemer JJ, Squires RW, Marsh HM, et al. Differences between prebreakfast and late afternoon glycemic responses to exercise in IDDM patients. *Diabetes Care.* 1990;13(2):104–110.

83. Schiffrin A, Parikh S. Accommodating planned exercise in type I diabetic patients on intensive treatment. *Diabetes Care.* 1985;8(4):337–342.

84. Edelmann E, Staudner V, Bachmann W, et al Exercise-induced hypoglycaemia and subcutaneous insulin infusion. *Diabet Med.* 1986;3(6):526–531.

85. Sonnenberg GE, Kemmer FW, Berger M. Exercise in type 1 (insulin-dependent) diabetic patients treated with continuous subcutaneous insulin infusion. Prevention of exercise induced hypoglycaemia. *Diabetologia.* 1990;33(11):696–703.

86. Zinman B, Ruderman N, Campaigne BN, Devlin JT, Schneider SH. Physical activity/exercise and diabetes mellitus. *Diabetes Care.* 2003;26(suppl 1):S73–S77.

87. Lisle DK, Trojian TH. Managing the athlete with type 1 diabetes. *Curr Sports Med Rep.* 2006;5(2):93–98.

88. Bussau VA, Ferreira LD, Jones TW, Fournier PA. A 10-s sprint performed prior to moderate-intensity exercise prevents early post-exercise fall in glycaemia in individuals with type 1 diabetes. *Diabetologia.* 2007;50(9):1815–1818.

89. Bussau VA, Ferreira LD, Jones TW, Fournier PA. The 10-s maximal sprint: a novel approach to counter an exercise-mediated fall in glycemia in individuals with type 1 diabetes. *Diabetes Care.* 2006;29(3):601–606.

90. Isaac JE, Johnson DE. *Wilderness and Rescue Medicine: A Practical Guide for the Basic and Advanced Practitioner.* 3rd ed. Portland, ME: Wilderness Medical Associates; 2007.

91. Teasdale G, Jennett B. Assessment of coma and impaired consciousness. A practical scale. *Lancet.* 1974;2(7872):81–84.

92. Stream JO, Grissom CK. Update on high-altitude pulmonary edema: pathogenesis, prevention, and treatment. *Wilderness Environ Med.* 2008;19(4):293–303.

93. Bartsch P, Mairbaurl H, Maggiorini M, Swenson ER. Physiological aspects of high-altitude pulmonary edema. *J Appl Physiol.* 2005;98(3):1101–1110.

94. Hackett PH, Roach RC. High-altitude illness. *N Engl J Med.* 2001;345(2):107–114.

95. Hackett PH. The cerebral etiology of high-altitude cerebral edema and acute mountain sickness. *Wilderness Environ Med.* 1999;10(2):97–109.

Emergency Action Plans

Ron Courson, ATC, PT, NREMT-I, CSCS

Although most injuries in athletics are relatively minor, life-threatening injuries are unpredictable and can occur without warning. Because of the relatively low incidence rate of catastrophic injuries, heath care providers may develop a false sense of security. However, **catastrophic injuries or illnesses** can occur during any physical activity and at any level of participation. The most common causes of sudden death in athletics are cardiac events, head and spinal cord injuries, exertional heat illness, asthma, and sickle cell crisis (exertional sickling). There is often a heightened public awareness associated with the nature and management of these events. Medicolegal interests may lead to questions regarding the qualifications of the personnel involved, the preparedness of the organization, and the actions taken.

catastrophic injury or illness A sudden death or disability in which there is life-altering physical or mental impairment, or both.

Proper management of emergencies in athletics is critical **(Figure 14.1)**. Emergencies should be handled by trained medical and allied health personnel. Preparation should include education and training, maintenance of emergency equipment and supplies, appropriate use of personnel, and formation and implementation of an **emergency action plan** (EAP).[1–6]

emergency action plan (EAP) A written document that defines the standard of care for the management of emergencies in athletics.

The Need for an Emergency Action Plan

Emergencies are rarely predictable, and they call for a rapid, controlled response. An EAP should include all necessary contingencies, even the worst-case scenario. Health care providers should take lessons from past emergencies: experience is a great teacher. The National Athletic Trainers' Association (NATA) position statement "Emergency Planning in Athletics" provides guidelines for the development and implementation of an EAP (see "Resources").[2]

Athletic health care providers may be responsible for the care of others in addition to athletes, such as coaches, officials, and spectators. All personnel involved with the organization or sponsorship of athletic activities share a professional and legal responsibility to provide for the emergency care of an

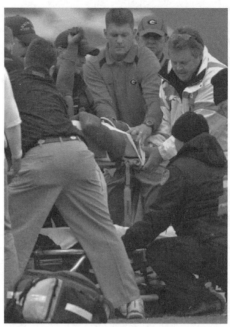

Figure 14.1 Proper management of emergencies in athletics is critical.

standard of care The manner in which an individual must act based on his or her training and education.

injured person and a legal duty to develop, implement, and evaluate an emergency plan for all sponsored athletic activities. A written EAP document defines the **standard of care**. The absence of an EAP frequently is a basis for claims and suits based on negligence. Thus, each institution or organization that sponsors athletic activities should have a written emergency plan. The EAP should be comprehensive and practical and flexible enough to adapt to any emergency situation. The EAP should be developed in consultation with local emergency medical services (EMS) personnel, and the written document should be approved and signed by the medical director for the athletic organization. The EAP should be distributed to attending physicians, athletic trainers and athletic training students, institutional and organizational safety personnel and administrators, coaches, and strength and conditioning staff.

Legal Basis for an Emergency Plan

The existence of an emergency plan for athletics is an accepted standard of care. Sports medicine providers have a duty to provide reasonable and prudent care in a timely manner. Sports medicine providers additionally have a duty to foresee the possibility of emergency situations in athletics and to develop a plan to address such situations. Court cases in recent years have addressed or alluded to emergency care and the emergency plan. In a landmark legal case in 1993 regarding emergency action planning, *Kleinknecht v. Gettysburg College*, the parents of a college lacrosse player who suffered sudden cardiac arrest during lacrosse practice brought a negligence action against the college. The Court of Appeals held that the college owed the player a duty of care as well as a duty to take reasonable precautions against the risk of reasonably foreseeable life-threatening injuries during participation in athletic events.[7] Adequate planning includes expediting emergency vehicles to the site of an accident and ensuring the availability of medical personnel qualified to care for the injured athlete.

Case Study of an Emergency Action Plan

A 53-year-old white male football official for the Southeastern Conference (SEC) collapsed with sudden cardiac arrest shortly after completing a 1.5-mile run as a part of the official's physical performance assessment. Prior to this episode, the official had completed a physical examination, including baseline lab tests and a graded exercise treadmill stress test, and had been cleared by his physician to officiate.

After completing the run, which was performed in the early morning to avoid any heat problems, the official walked off the track to begin cooling down. After drinking a cup of electrolyte drink, he sat down on a bleacher to watch the next group of officials run. Shortly after sitting down, he collapsed. Two athletic trainers quickly assessed the downed official, who was not breathing and had no pulse. Cardiopulmonary resuscitation (CPR) was initiated within seconds of his collapse, and the paramedic crew on stand-by trackside was notified. The official was in ventricular fibrillation and was defibrillated by paramedics less than 3 minutes after collapsing. Defibrillation converted his heart to a stable rhythm, and he was administered oxygen and intravenous fluids. The official was transported by helicopter to a hospital emergency department, where he was further evaluated and subsequently underwent a heart catheterization. The official made a full recovery and returned the following year to once again officiate SEC football games.

This case study demonstrates the effectiveness of an emergency plan. The official's physical performance assessment was conducted by the SEC Sports Medicine Committee, consisting of certified athletic trainers and physicians from Southeastern Conference schools. The athletic trainers organize and administrate the conditioning test. The test that year was conducted in Birmingham, Alabama, the site of the SEC office. Because there is no SEC school in Birmingham, arrangements were made to conduct the test on the track at a local university. The athletic trainers made an advance visit to the site to familiarize themselves with the venue. Arrangements were made in advance to have gates open with access to the track and to have an ambulance and paramedic crew on site. The athletic trainers met prior to the test and made assignments. The ambulance was positioned at the end of the track, and athletic trainers were assigned stations on the track in the event of an injury or illness. A cellular phone was present for emergency communication from the track, as well as the radio in the ambulance.

When the incident occurred, the emergency plan worked as planned and an excellent outcome was achieved. Given this particular situation, time was especially important, because rapid defibrillation is a critical factor in survival of sudden cardiac arrest. For each minute delay from the time of onset to the time of defibrillation, studies indicate a 10% decrease in survivability rate. Without prior arrangements for a defibrillator and trained personnel on site to operate it, the official would most likely not have survived.

The Sports Medicine Team Concept

The goal of the sports medicine team is the delivery of the highest possible quality health care to the athlete. An athletic emergency situation may involve certified and student athletic trainers, emergency medical technicians, physicians, and coaches working together. Just as with an athletic team, the sports medicine team must work together as an efficient unit in order to accomplish its goals. In an emergency situation, the team concept becomes even more critical, because seconds may mean the difference between life or death or permanent disability. The sharing of information, training, and skills among the various emergency medical providers helps to reach the goal of the delivery of the highest-quality emergency health care to the athlete.

Components of the Emergency Plan

The EAP should be specific to each individual athletic venue and encompass the following subjects:

1. Emergency personnel
2. Emergency communication
3. Emergency equipment
4. Medical emergency transportation
5. Venue directions with map

Box 14.1 provides a sample venue-specific emergency action plan for football practice.

Box 14.1

Example Venue-Specific Emergency Action Plan

FOOTBALL PRACTICE EAP: Butts-Mehre Hall: Woodruff Practice Fields
July 2010

<u>Address</u>: 1 Selig Circle

<u>Venue Directions</u>:
<u>Butts-Mehre Hall</u> is located on Pinecrest Street (cross street Lumpkin). Two entrances provide access to building:

1. Main Entrance: front of building on Pinecrest Street (directly across from Barrow Elementary School)
2. Locker Room Entrance: rear of building, access from driveway off of Smith Street

<u>Football Practice Fields</u> are located with two fields adjacent to Smith Street. Two gates located on Smith Street provide access to artificial turf practice fields and access road. Be aware that construction may modify EAP: plan accordingly each day prior to practice!

<u>GPS Coordinates</u> (in event of the need for a medical helicopter transport): 33 56.54 / 83 22.83 (practice field 2)

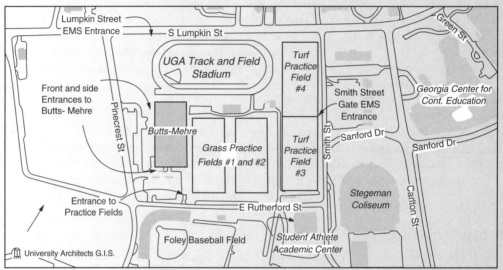

Football: Butts-Mehre Hall, Woodruff Practice Field

<u>Emergency Personnel:</u>
<u>Butts-Mehre Hall:</u> certified athletic trainers, student athletic trainers, and physician (limited basis) on site in athletic training trailer, located on grass practice field 2 during construction
<u>Football Practice Fields:</u> certified athletic trainers and student athletic trainers on site for practice & workouts

<u>Emergency Communication:</u>
<u>Butts-Mehre Hall:</u> fixed telephone lines in athletic training trailer adjacent to practice fields:
(000-000-0000) or (000-000-0000)

<u>Football Practice Fields:</u> certified athletic trainers carry cellular telephones
Ron Courson 000-000-0000; Emily Miller 000-000-0000; Philip Young 000-000-0000;
Anish Patel 000-000-0000; Ryan McGovern 000-000-0000
Fixed telephone line under practice shed   000-000-0000

<u>Emergency Equipment:</u>
<u>Butts-Mehre Hall:</u> emergency equipment (AED, trauma kit, splint kit, spine board, Welch Allen vital signs monitor, Philips MRx 12 Lead EKG/defibrillator) located within athletic training trailer
<u>Football Practice Fields:</u> emergency equipment (AED, trauma kit, splint kit, spine board) maintained on motorized medical cart parked adjacent to practice shed during practice; additional supplies maintained under practice shed; additional emergency equipment accessible from athletic training trailer adjacent to practice fields

Emergency Personnel

For athletic practices and competitions, the **first responder** to an emergency situation is typically a member of the sports medicine staff—most commonly a certified athletic trainer—or EMS personnel. A team physician may not always be present at every organized practice or competition. The type and degree of sports medicine coverage for an athletic event may vary widely, based on such factors as the sport or activity, the setting, and the type of training or competition. The first responder in some instances may be a coach, strength and conditioning staff, or other institutional personnel. Certification in CPR and **first aid**, knowledge concerning the prevention of disease transmission, and review of the existing EAP should be required for all athletic personnel associated with practices, competitions, skills instruction, and strength and conditioning; copies of training certificates or cards should be maintained.

first responder The first person present at the scene of a sudden illness or injury.

first aid Emergency treatment administered to an injured or sick person before professional medical care is available.

The development of an EAP cannot be complete without the formation of an emergency team. The emergency team may consist of a number of health care providers, including physicians, emergency medical technicians, certified athletic trainers, athletic training students, coaches, equipment managers, and, possibly, bystanders. For example, game officials may play a critical role in the emergency plan by keeping the field clear of others when an emergency arises, allowing the health care providers room to work. The roles of these individuals within the emergency team may vary depending on various factors such as the number of members of the team, the athletic venue itself, or the preference of the head athletic trainer.

There are four basic roles within the emergency team. The first and most important role is establishing the safety of the scene and providing immediate care of the athlete. Acute care in an emergency situation should be provided by the most qualified individual on the scene. Individuals with lesser qualification should yield to those with more appropriate training. The second role, EMS activation, may be necessary in situations in which emergency transportation is not already present at the sporting event. This should be done as soon as the situation is deemed an emergency or a life-threatening event. Time is the most critical factor under emergency conditions. Activating the EMS system may be done by anyone on the team. However, the person chosen for this duty should be someone who is calm under pressure and who communicates well over the telephone. This person should also be familiar with the specific location and address of the sporting event.

The third role, equipment retrieval, may be done by anyone on the emergency team who is familiar with the types and location of the specific equipment needed. Athletic training students, equipment managers, and coaches are good choices for this role. The fourth role of the emergency team is that of directing EMS personnel to the scene. One member of the team should be responsible for meeting emergency medical personnel as they arrive at the site of the emergency. Depending on ease of access, this person should have keys to any locked gates or doors that may slow the arrival of medical personnel. An athletic training student, equipment manager, or coach may be appropriate for this role.

When forming the emergency team, it is important to adapt the team to each situation or sport. It may also be advantageous to have more than one individual assigned to each role. This allows the emergency team to function even though certain members may not always be present. Preparation is the key to emergency response. The health care team should regularly review the EAP and rehearse emergency simulations to work effectively as a team.

Sports medicine staff may pursue specialized in-service training in required skill areas or advanced training such as CPR/first aid instructor, emergency medical technician (EMT) or paramedic, prehospital trauma life support (PHTLS), or advanced cardiac life support (ACLS). Sports medicine staff may additionally develop standardized emergency protocols in areas such as automated external defibrillators (AEDs), oxygen/airway adjuncts, head and cervical spine management, and so forth. **Appendix 14.1** is an example of an emergency protocol for the use of an AED.

Emergency Communication

Communication is the key to quick emergency response. Athletic trainers and emergency medical personnel must work together to provide the best emergency response capability and should have contact information, such as a telephone tree, established as a part of preplanning for emergency situations. Communication prior to the event is a good way to establish boundaries and to build rapport between both groups of professionals. If emergency medical transportation is not available on site during a particular sporting event, then direct communication with the emergency medical system at the time of injury or illness is necessary.

Access to a working telephone or other telecommunications device, whether fixed or mobile, should be ensured. The communication system should be checked prior to each practice or competition to ensure it is in proper working order. A back-up communication plan should be in effect should there be a failure of the primary communication system. At any athletic venue, whether home or away, it is important to know the location of a functioning telephone. Prearranged access to the phone should be established if it is not easily accessible.

Other considerations include:

- What number do you call?
- Is 911 universal?
- Do you have to dial a prefix number (such as "9") to get off campus?
- Are 911 calls screened by the campus or venue operator before they go out?
- Do security personnel/police/sheriff have radio contact with "public service access points" or dispatch centers to get EMS activated?

A copy of the EAP should be posted by the telephone **(Figure 14.2)**. When activating EMS, the following information should be provided:

- Name and telephone number of the caller and the address to which to respond
- Number of athletes affected
- Condition of athlete(s)
- First aid treatment initiated
- Specific directions
- Other information as requested by the dispatcher

Emergency Equipment

All necessary emergency equipment should be at the site and quickly accessible. Personnel should be familiar with the function and operation of each type of emergency equipment. Equipment should be in good operating condition, and personnel must be trained in advance to use it properly. Emergency equipment should be checked on a regular basis and its use rehearsed by emergency personnel. The emergency equipment available should be appropriate for the level of training of the emergency medical providers.

The creation of an equipment inspection log book for continued inspection is strongly recommended. A few members of the emergency team should be trained and responsible for the care of the equipment. It is also important to know the proper way to care for and store the equipment. Equipment should be

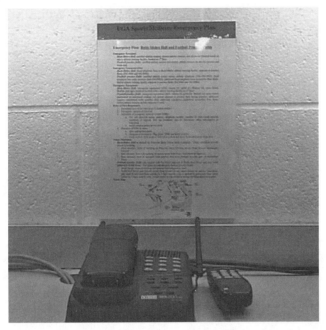

Figure 14.2 A copy of the emergency action plan should be posted by the telephone.

stored in a clean and environmentally controlled area. It should be readily available when emergency situations arise.

The equipment available should be based on the type of event being covered and the possible emergency scenarios anticipated. For example, when covering an outdoor event with the possibility of exertional heat illness, such as a distance road race, health care providers should have ready in advance an ice-water immersion tub, a rectal thermometer, IV fluids, and other necessary equipment. Health care providers covering an event in which sickle cell trait athletes are participating should have oxygen and IV fluids available. **Table 14.1** provides a sample trauma bag checklist detailing basic emergency equipment for athletics, and **Table 14.2** lists recommended emergency equipment for athletic venues.

Medical Emergency Transportation

Emphasis should be placed on having an ambulance on site at high-risk sporting events. EMS response time should be factored in when determining whether on-site ambulance coverage is warranted **(Box 14.2)**. Consideration should be given to the capabilities of the transportation service available (i.e., basic life support or advanced life support) and the equipment and level of trained personnel on board the ambulance. In the event that an ambulance is on site, it should be in a designated location with rapid access to the site and a cleared route for entering and exiting the venue.

In the medical emergency evaluation, the primary survey assists the emergency care provider in identifying emergencies requiring critical intervention and in determining transport decisions. In an emergency situation, the athlete should be transported by ambulance, where the necessary staff and equipment are available to deliver appropriate care. Emergency care providers should refrain from transporting unstable athletes in inappropriate vehicles. Care must be taken to ensure that the activity areas are supervised should the emergency care provider leave the site to transport the athlete. Any emergency situations in which there is impairment in level of consciousness or in airway, breathing, or circulation (ABCs) or there is neurovascular compromise should be considered a "load and go" situation, and emphasis should be placed on rapid evaluation, treatment, and transportation.

TABLE 14.1 University of Georgia Trauma Bag Checklist

AIRWAY

- Emergency Airway Kit
  OPA – 6 sizes
  NPA – 6 sizes
  King LT – sizes 4 & 5 and/or
  Combitube and syringe
- Bite blocker
- V-Vac suction with extra canister

BREATHING

- Pocket mask
- Bag-valve-mask
- Nonrebreather mask
- *Oxygen tank w/ regulator*
- Oxygen tubing
- *Pulse oximeter*
- *Albuterol inhaler/spacer*

CIRCULATION

- *AED w/ extra pads*
- Wound Dressing Kit
- Tourniquet

GENERAL SUPPLIES

- Adult BP cuff
- Large Adult BP cuff
- Stethoscope
- *EpiPen (youth)*
- *EpiPen (adult)*
- *Aspirin*
- *Glucagon kit *
- *Insta-Glucose tube *
- *Blood glucose kit *
- *Penlight*
- Paramedic shears
- Scissors
- Gloves
- PPE Kit
- Protective glasses
- Thermal blanket
- Cervical collar
- Sterile saline
- Betadine solution
- Emergency mgmt. guidelines notepad
- Pen

* As needed
Check regularly
Check expiration date
Abbreviations: AED, automated external defibrillator; BP, blood pressure; NPA, nasopharyngeal airway; OPA, oropharyngeal airway; PPE, personal protective equipment.

Venue Directions with Map

The EAP should include specific directions to the venue, including the exact street address, cross streets, and any landmarks that may make the site easier for EMS to locate. Ideally, prior to the start of the athletic season, a meeting should be held at the athletic venue site with sports medicine staff members and EMS personnel to familiarize everyone with the exact location and discuss emergency management issues. Plans should be made for ambulance ingress and egress to the site in terms of gates, stadium portals, and so forth. If helicopter transport is a viable option, a landing site should be designated and its GPS coordinates included in the EAP. Host providers should orient visiting health care providers to the venue and discuss emergency procedures prior to the competition. Visiting health care providers should explore the issue of emergency care prior to arrival.

Emergency Care Facilities

In designing the EAP, incorporate the emergency care facilities to which injured individuals will be taken. It is helpful, if possible, to notify emergency receiving facilities in advance of scheduled events and contests. Factors to consider in the selection of the appropriate emergency care facilities include location with respect to venue and level of capabilities. Reviewing the plan with facility staff is helpful. Additionally, in-service training of emergency department physicians and nurses may be beneficial. For example, reviewing emergency football equipment removal on an annual basis prior to the start of football season may help to facilitate proper removal of helmet and shoulder pads in the management of a head or cervical spine injury in the emergency department.

EAP Pocket Emergency Card

Sports medicine health care professionals should consider preparing pocket emergency cards. This index card–sized item can be laminated and carried on person in the event of an emergency. The EAP cards should include the emergency action plan with written directions and highlighted map on one side and the pertinent medical information of participating athletes, such as medical conditions, allergies, and medications, on the other side. **Table 14.3** provides an example of pertinent medical information that can be printed on a pocket emergency card.

TABLE
14.2

Recommended Emergency Equipment for Athletic Venues

Automated external defibrillator (AED)

Airway management supplies (oropharyngeal and nasopharyngeal airways)

Oxygen delivery system and pulse oximeter

Suction device (manual, battery, or oxygen powered)

Body substance isolation equipment (per OSHA guidelines)

Wound care supplies

Vital signs assessment: blood pressure cuff, stethoscope, penlight

Emergency shears

CPR pocket mask

Bag-valve-mask

Rigid cervical collar

Long spine board, strapping system, cervical/head immobilization device

Extremity splints

Face mask removal tools if the sport involves use of a helmet with face mask

CPR, cardiopulmonary resuscitation; OSHA, Occupational Safety and Health Administration.

Box 14.2

Emergency Action Plan Tip: EMS Response Time

It is beneficial to know the average EMS response time for your region. This information is available through your local EMS agency. The length of your region's EMS response time may factor into your emergency plan. For example, a metropolitan high school with a local fire/rescue station two blocks away will generally have a quicker response time than a rural high school with the closest station 15 miles away. If a longer response time is anticipated, it may be prudent for care providers to have the necessary equipment to provide extended emergency care until EMS arrives. When reviewing EMS response, factor in both horizontal and vertical response times. Horizontal response time is measured from the time the EMS call goes out until the dispatched unit arrives on scene. Once the unit arrives, time is required to remove emergency equipment from the unit and travel to the site of the patient. Vertical response time is measured from the time the dispatched unit arrives on scene until patient treatment begins.

Emergency Documentation

A written emergency plan should be reviewed and approved by the team members and institutions involved. If multiple facilities or sites are used, each will require a separate plan. Documentation should encompass the following:

- Who is responsible for documenting the events of the emergency situation
- Follow-up documentation on evaluation of the response to the emergency situation, such as time of injury, treatment start, EMS call, arrival, treatment provided, and departure
- Documentation of periodic rehearsal of the emergency plan
- Documentation of institutional personnel training

When an athletic emergency occurs, postepisode documentation is an important component and should not be neglected. Reasons for documentation include the medicolegal record, continuity of care,

TABLE 14.3	Sports Medicine–Pertinent Medical Conditions
Athlete A	hx concussion
Athlete B	sickle cell trait
Athlete C	allergic to Septra (sulfa drugs), yellow jackets
Athlete D	hx asthma, hx concussion
Athlete E	hx concussion with LOC, amnesia
Athlete F	hx concussion, catheter ablation, PSVT
Athlete G	heart murmur, concussion
Athlete H	hx concussion, hx heat cramps
Athlete I	hx heat cramps, exertional headaches
Athlete J	allergic to PCN, hx severe heat cramps, hx concussion, endocarditis prophylaxis, heat syncope
Athlete K	sickle cell trait
Athlete L	hx concussion, hx HTN
Athlete M	hx concussion
Athlete N	hx concussion, EIB, endocarditis prophylaxis, hx stingers
Athlete O	hx asthma
Athlete P	hx concussion
Athlete Q	hx asthma
Athlete R	hx concussion
Athlete S	hx heat cramps
Athlete T	allergic to PCN
Athlete U	family hx cardiomyopathy
Athlete V	craniotomy age 10 (blood clot)
Athlete W	exercise-induced headaches, hx heat illness
Athlete X	allergic to sulfa and Ceclor, hx concussion
Athlete Y	hx of heat syncope, hx of concussion, exertional headaches
Athlete Z	hx hypertension, allergic to penicillin, hx concussion, Norvasc, lisinopril

EIB, exercise-induced bronchoconstriction; HTN, hypertension; hx, history; LOC, loss of consciousness; PCN, penicillin; PSVT, paroxysmal supraventricular tachycardia.

quality assurance, organization of thought processes, and research and statistical review. Written documentation of all actions taken during treatment and transport can be very useful in situations in which liability is an issue. It should also be noted that consent is implied during most athletic emergencies.

Catastrophic Incident Guidelines

Catastrophic incident guidelines should be developed in the event of a sudden death or of an injury that results in disability or an alteration of quality of life of a student-athlete, coach, or staff member. A catastrophic incident management team should be developed, along with a checklist of chain of command responsibilities. Although there are many types of catastrophic incidents, not all will require activation of the emergency plan. However, a catastrophic injury/incident plan can be considered a companion document to the emergency plan. This written plan should include both direct and indirect catastrophic athletic injuries and incidents.

Either direct or indirect catastrophic incidents can affect a sports program. Direct or sport-related fatalities include heat stroke, brain injury, and commotio cordis; indirect fatalities can be from natural causes (e.g., heart attack, stroke), crime-related (e.g., homicide or assault), or accidental (e.g., fall, car crash). Disabling or life-altering catastrophic incidents can also be divided into direct or indirect causes. Direct incidents include catastrophic events occurring during organization-sponsored sport participation or travel, including spinal cord injury, coma, loss of paired organs or use of an extremity or extremities, and severe brain injury. Indirect incidents could include any of these injuries occurring to a member of the sports organization, but outside of a sport-related activity.

Depending on the sport sponsor, sport venue, and nature of the emergency, certain notifications may need to be made; these should be described in the emergency plan. Obviously, in the high school setting, a minor athlete's parents will need to be notified. Depending on the school or system size, the athletic coordinator, principal, and possibly the district superintendent may also need to be notified of the incident.

Notifications at the collegiate level might include the athletic director, one or more deans or vice-presidents, and, in the event of a catastrophic event, possibly the president or CEO of the college or university. The parents, spouse, or other family members of the injured student-athlete may also need to be notified. Travel plans for the parents or spouse of the injured athlete should be considered if distance is a factor. Counseling may need to be made available for students, team members, and the sports medicine team. When there is considerable media interest, the sports information director or other institutional media relations personnel should be included to handle media inquiries. The institutional insurance carrier, risk management office, legal counsel, or a combination of these should also be notified.

The catastrophic injury plan should include the formation of a catastrophic injury team. Obvious members of this team would include the organization's athletic director or coordinator, the head athletic trainer, sports information or media relations personnel, senior administrators, the team physician, and organizational legal counsel. This team will direct all aspects of crisis management, including providing appropriate counseling (athlete, family, and team), releasing information to the media, and documenting the incident. **Figure 14.3** provides an example of a catastrophic incidence guideline card and emergency contact information card.

Conclusion

It is critically important to properly prepare for athletic emergencies. An athlete's survival may hinge on how well trained and prepared athletic health care providers are. Organizations sponsoring athletic activities invest "ownership" in an EAP by involving athletic administration personnel, sport coaches, and sports medicine personnel. It is important to review the EAP yearly with all athletic personnel, including CPR and first aid refresher training. Through development and implementation of an emergency action plan, health care providers help to ensure that athletes will have the best care provided when an emergency situation does arise.

Clinical Case Scenario

1. A 19-year-old black male student-athlete collapsed during intercollegiate basketball practice. He had no previous symptoms of palpitations, dizziness, or syncope and no family history of sudden death or cardiac abnormalities. Evaluated on court by the certified athletic trainer, he was found to be in cardiac arrest. An AED was applied, with the analysis (delivered in less than 2 minutes) finding the athlete to be in ventricular fibrillation. One shock was delivered, and he was converted to a perfusing rhythm. Two rescue breaths were administered following the shock, and the athlete began breathing. Oxygen

Emergency Contact Information Card

Emer. Contact	Department/Area	Office	Home	Cell/Pager
Michael Adams	University President			
Steve Bryant	Assoc. Athletic Trainer			
Eric Baumgartner	NCAA Compliance			
Ron Courson	Assoc. Athletic Director			
Frank Crumley	Interim Dir. of Athletics			
Claude Felton	Assoc. AD/SID			
Greg McGarity	Director of Athletics			
Kevin Hynes	Chaplain			
Tom Jackson	University Spokesperson			
Arthur Johnson	Assoc. Athletic Director			
Barbara Boyd	UGAA Travel Coordinator			
Robert Miles	Asst. Ath. Dir.: Life Skills			
Fred Reifsteck	Head Team Physician			
Joe Scalise	Counselor			
Tricia Searels	Counselor			
Steve Shewmaker	University Legal Affairs			
Ed Tolley	UGAA Legal Counsel			
Jeanne Vaughn	UGAA Insurance Coord.			
Craig White	Assoc. Athletic Director			
Peggy Whitfield	Human Resources			
Carla Williams	Assoc. Athletic Director			
Jimmy Williamson	Chief of Police			

A

CRISIS MANAGEMENT GUIDELINES

Contact Ron Courson/Steve Bryant; Fred Reifsteck, MD
* work with medical specialists assisting athlete

Contact UGAA/UGA administration
* Greg McGarity notifies Michael Adams, notifies legal counsel
* Claude Felton notifies Tom Jackson
* Contact Frank Crumley/Carla Williams

Designate athletic administrator point person

Contact/update sport staff if not yet familiar with situation

Contact family by appropriate individual (assist as needed):
* Eric Baumgartner: compliance
* Barbara Boyd: travel   000-000-0000
* Air Med International

Assign athletic staff member to be with family at all times upon Arrival; assist family as needed; protect from outside persons

Involve appropriate counseling/ministerial support

Coordinated media plan
* No contact with media/comments from athletic training staff, hospital staff or med. personnel except through SID

Meeting with athletes to discuss situation
* No outside discussion of meeting with media

Contact catastrophic/malpractice insurance providers
* Borden Perlman: 000-000-0000
* NCAA: American Specialty: 000-000-0000
* Seabury & Smith (malpractice):   000-000-0000
* HPSO (malpractice):   000-000-0000

Complete documentation of events from everyone involved in incident

Collect and secure all equipment/materials involved

Construct detailed time line of events related to the incident

Catastrophic incident stress management as necessary for individuals involved in incident

B

Figure 14.3   Emergency contact information card **(A)** and crisis management guidelines **(B)**.

was administered with a nonrebreather mask, and the athlete was transported to a nearby hospital for further evaluation. An angiogram revealed normal coronary arteries, and an echocardiogram revealed hypertrophic cardiomyopathy. An implantable cardioverter defibrillator was implanted 2 days following the episode of sudden cardiac arrest. The athlete was medically disqualified from further intercollegiate athletic activity; however, he remains in good health.

1. What were critical components in the athlete's life being saved in this scenario?
2. Knowledge of the steps required for this EAP was critical in saving this athlete's life. Who should be instructed and knowledgeable of the school's EAP?
3. What other monthly or yearly maintenance or planning had to occur to allow all of the steps within this EAP to work as planned?

Key Terms

catastrophic injury or illness

emergency action plan (EAP)

first aid

first responder

standard of care

Resources

1. National Athletic Trainers' Association position statement: emergency planning in athletics. Available at: http://www.nata.org/statements/position/emergencyplanning.pdf.
2. Inter-Association Task Force recommendations on emergency preparedness and management of sudden cardiac arrest in high school and college athletic programs: a consensus statement. Available at: http://www.nata.org/statements/consensus/SCA_statement.pdf.

References

1. Courson RW. Preventing sudden death on the athletic field: the emergency action plan. *Curr Sports Med Rep.* 2007;6:93–100.
2. Andersen J, Courson RW, Kleiner DM, McLoda TA. National Athletic Trainers' Association position statement: emergency planning in athletics. *J Athl Train.* 2002;37(1):99–104.
3. Guideline 1c: emergency care and coverage. In: Klossner D, ed. *2010–11 NCAA Sports Medicine Handbook.* Indianapolis, IN: National Collegiate Athletic Association; 2010. Available at: http://www.ncaapublications.com/productdownloads/MD11.pdf. Accessed November 8, 2010.
4. Sideline preparedness for the team physician: consensus statement. *Med Sci Sports Exerc.* 2001;33(5):846–849.
5. Drezner JA, Courson RW, Roberts WO, et al. Inter-Association Task Force recommendations on emergency preparedness and management of sudden cardiac arrest in high school and college athletic programs: a consensus statement. *J Athl Train.* 2007;42(1):143–158.
6. Hazinski MF, Markenson D, Neish S, et al. Response to cardiac arrest and selected life-threatening medical emergencies: the medical emergency response plan for schools. A statement for healthcare providers, policymakers, school administrators, and community leaders. *Circulation.* 2004;109(2):278–291.
7. *Kleinknecht v. Gettysburg College*, 989 F2d 1360 (3rd Cir 1993).

University of Georgia Sports Medicine Automated External Defibrillator Policies and Procedure, November 2010

Introduction

Sudden cardiac arrest (SCA) affects over 400,000 people annually in the United States, and is the leading cause of death in young athletes. Athletes are considered the healthiest members of our society, and an unexpected death during training or competition is a tragic event with wide-spread implications. Healthy-appearing competitive athletes may harbor unsuspected cardiovascular disease with the potential to cause sudden death. Cardiopulmonary resuscitation (CPR) is critical to maintaining the supply of oxygen to vital organs; nevertheless, the single most effective treatment for cardiac arrest is defibrillation. Access to early defibrillation and an automated external defibrillator (AED) should be part of standard emergency planning for coverage of athletic activities.

The American Heart Association uses four (4) links in a chain (the "Chain of Survival") to illustrate the important time-sensitive actions for victims of SCA.

- Early recognition of the emergency and activation of the emergency medical services (EMS) or local emergency response system: "phone 911."
- Early bystander CPR: immediate CPR can double or triple the victim's chance of survival from VF (ventricular fibrillation) SCA.
- Early delivery of a shock with a defibrillator: CPR plus defibrillation within 3 to 5 minutes of collapse can produce survival rates as high as 49% to 75%.
- Early advanced life support followed by post resuscitation care delivered by healthcare providers.

Recognition of SCA

Recognition of SCA in athletes may be difficult due to the relatively low overall occurrence. High suspicion of SCA should be maintained for any collapsed and unresponsive athlete. Barriers to recognizing SCA in athletes may include inaccurate assessment of pulse or respirations, misinterpretation of agonal gasping as adequate respiration, and confusion of myoclonic or seizure-like activity with purposeful movement.

Management of SCA

CPR

Victims of cardiac arrest from VF can benefit from CPR if immediate defibrillation is not present. CPR provides a small but critical amount of blood flow to the heart (and brain) and may extend the timeframe for successful termination of ventricular fibrillation (VF) with electric shock. CPR is especially important if a shock is not delivered for 4 or more minutes after collapse.

Defibrillation does not "restart" the heart; defibrillation "stuns" the heart, briefly stopping VF and other cardiac electrical activity. If the heart is still viable, its normal pacemakers may then resume firing and produce an effective ECG rhythm that may ultimately produce adequate blood flow.

"Effective" chest compressions are essential for providing blood flow during CPR. To give "effective" chest compressions, "push hard and push fast." Compress the adult chest at a rate of 100 compressions per minute (in time with the song "Stayin' Alive" by the BeeGees), with a compression depth of 1½ to 2 inches (approximately 4 to 5 cm). Allow the chest to recoil completely after each compression, and allow approximately equal compression and relaxation times. Minimize interruptions in chest compressions.

Rescuer fatigue may lead to inadequate compression rates or depth. Significant fatigue and shallow compressions are seen after 1 minute of CPR, although rescuers may deny that fatigue is present for ≥5 minutes. When 2 or more rescuers are available, it is reasonable to switch the compressor about every 2 minutes (or after 5 cycles of compressions and ventilations at a ratio of 30:2). Every effort should be made to accomplish this switch in <5 seconds. If the 2 rescuers are positioned on either side of the patient, one rescuer will be ready and waiting to relieve the "working compressor" every 2 minutes.

AED

An AED should be applied as soon as possible and turned on for rhythm analysis in any collapsed and unresponsive athlete. CPR should be implemented while waiting for an AED. Any interruptions in chest compressions should be minimal, stopping only for rhythm analysis and shock.

The rescuer providing chest compressions should be prepared to resume CPR, beginning with chest compressions, as soon as a shock is delivered. When 2 rescuers are present, the rescuer operating the AED should be prepared to deliver a shock as soon as the compressor removes his or her hands from the victim's chest and all rescuers are "clear" of contact with the victim. The lone rescuer should practice coordination of CPR with efficient AED operation.

Healthcare providers must practice efficient coordination between CPR and defibrillation. Analyses of VF waveform characteristics predictive of shock success have documented that the shorter the time between a chest compression and delivery of a shock, the more likely the shock will be successful. Reduction in the interval from compression to shock delivery by even a few seconds can increase the probability of shock success. When VF is present for more than a few minutes, the myocardium is depleted of oxygen and metabolic substrates. A brief period of chest compressions can deliver oxygen and energy substrates, increasing the likelihood that a perfusing rhythm will return after defibrillation (elimination of VF).

Shock First Versus CPR First

When any rescuer witnesses SCA and an AED is immediately available on-site, the rescuer should use the AED as soon as possible. When the SCA is not witnessed and/or the time interval from collapse to first shock is greater than 5 minutes, two minutes of CPR should be performed prior to defibrillation.

Advanced Airway

Once an advanced airway (endotracheal tube or Combi-Tube) is in place, 2 rescuers no longer deliver cycles of CPR (ie, compressions interrupted by pauses for ventilation). Instead, the compressing rescuer should give continuous chest compressions at a rate of 100 per minute without pauses for ventilation.

The rescuer delivering ventilation provides 8 to 10 breaths per minute. The 2 rescuers should change compressor and ventilator roles approximately every 2 minutes to prevent compressor fatigue and deterioration in quality and rate of chest compressions. When multiple rescuers are present, they should rotate the compressor role about every 2 minutes.

Provisions to Coordinate with Local EMS

In the event of a cardiopulmonary emergency, the 911 emergency system should be activated as quickly as possible. The first responders should provide initial care as appropriate to the situation and coordinate with other emergency medical service providers upon their arrival in the provision of CPR, defibrillation, basic life support, and advanced life support.

Operator Considerations

The University of Georgia Sports Medicine program utilizes the Philips FR2 AED unit. These AEDs are semi-automatic defibrillators that use an algorithm that analyzes the patient's electrocardiographic (ECG) rhythm and indicates whether or not it detects a shockable rhythm **(Figure 1)**. They require operator interaction in order to defibrillate the patient. AEDs are for use by trained personnel (first responders, certified athletic trainers, athletic training students, and team physicians) who are authorized by a physician/medical director and have, at a minimum, American Heart Association (or comparable) CPR and AED training.

Procedures for Training and Testing in the Use of AED

Personnel using the AED must complete a training session each year to include instruction in:

- The proper use, maintenance, and periodic inspection of the AED
- Defibrillator safety precautions to enable the user to administer a shock without jeopardizing the safety of the patient, the user, or other individuals
- Assessment of an unconscious person to determine if cardiac arrest has occurred and the appropriateness of applying an AED
- Recognizing that an electrical shock has been delivered to the patient and that the defibrillator is no longer charged
- Rapid, accurate assessment of the patient's post-shock status to determine if further activation of the AED is necessary
- The operations of the local emergency medical services system, including methods of access to the emergency response system, and interaction with emergency medical services personnel
- The role of the user and coordination with other emergency medical service providers in the provision of CPR, defibrillation, basic life support, and advanced life support
- The responsibility of the user to continue care until the arrival of medically qualified personnel

Procedures to Ensure the Continued Competency Required for AED Use

Sports medicine personnel using the AED should complete a review session every ninety days (90) using the AED training device and/or the AED computer simulation software to ensure continued competency in the use of the device. A record will be maintained documenting medical staff competency training on the AED.

Medical Control Reporting and Incident Review

The AED digitally records patient data, including ECG rhythm and delivered shocks. A digital audio recording of scene activity is available. Recorded data may be transferred by direct connection to a printer

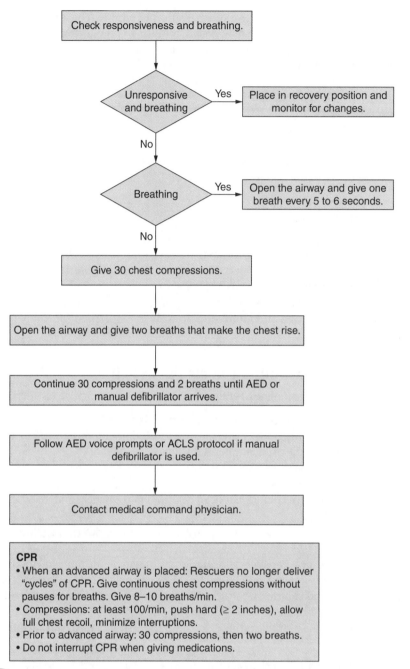

Check responsiveness and breathing.

Unresponsive and breathing → Yes → Place in recovery position and monitor for changes.

No

Breathing → Yes → Open the airway and give one breath every 5 to 6 seconds.

No

Give 30 chest compressions.

Open the airway and give two breaths that make the chest rise.

Continue 30 compressions and 2 breaths until AED or manual defibrillator arrives.

Follow AED voice prompts or ACLS protocol if manual defibrillator is used.

Contact medical command physician.

CPR
• When an advanced airway is placed: Rescuers no longer deliver "cycles" of CPR. Give continuous chest compressions without pauses for breaths. Give 8–10 breaths/min.
• Compressions: at least 100/min, push hard ($\geq$ 2 inches), allow full chest recoil, minimize interruptions.
• Prior to advanced airway: 30 compressions, then two breaths.
• Do not interrupt CPR when giving medications.

Figure 1   Basic Life Support Treatment Algorithm.

or computer or by modem to a remote computer. Following an incident of application, the data will be downloaded from the AED and reviewed by both the medical director and the attending physician(s) at the emergency facility where emergency care was provided. In addition, a report detailing the emergency scene and treatment will be documented in writing.

Location of and Maintenance Required for AEDs

The University of Georgia Sports Medicine program has fifteen (15) Philips FRx AED units. They are located at:

1–2. Butts-Mehre Hall (football)
3. Foley Field (baseball)
4. Tennis Complex satellite athletic training room
5. Women's Athletic Complex (soccer)
6. Women's Athletic Complex (softball)
7. Ramsey Center (volleyball)
8. Ramsey Center (swimming/diving)
9. Equestrian Arena
10. E. B. Smith Golf Center
11–13. Stegeman Coliseum
14. Coliseum Training Facility (gymnastics)
15. Coliseum Training Facility (basketball)

There are two (2) Philips MRx manual/automated defibrillators with 12-lead EKG capability located in the physician examination rooms in Butts-Mehre Hall and Stegeman Coliseum. Based upon coverage issues, these units may either be maintained in the athletic training facility or carried on-site to the athletic venue. There are additionally two (2) Philips FRx AED units located in the strength & conditioning facilities in Butts-Mehre Hall and Stegeman Coliseum and three (3) Philips FRx AED units located in Butts-Mehre Hall in the first floor loading dock area and in public access areas on the second and third floors.

The AEDs perform an automatic self-test every 24 hours. If service is required, the AED activates an alarm. The non-rechargeable lithium batteries have a five-year life. If batteries require replacement, the AED activates an alarm. Personnel using the AED on a regular basis and after each time the AED is used should inspect and clean the AED and check to make sure that all necessary supplies and accessories are readily available.

Approved by _____ **Date:**_____

Fred Reifsteck, M.D.

References

1. Andersen J, Courson RW, Kleiner DM, McLoda TA. National Athletic Trainers' Association position statement: emergency planning in athletics. *J Athl Train.* 2002;37(1):99–104.
2. Hazinski MF, Markenson D, Neish S, et al. Response to cardiac arrest and selected life-threatening medical emergencies: the medical emergency response plan for schools: a statement for healthcare providers, policymakers, school administrators, and community leaders. *Circulation.* 2004;109(2):278–291.
3. 2005 American Heart Association guidelines for cardiopulmonary resuscitation and emergency cardiovascular care. *Circulation.* 2005;112(24 suppl):IV1–IV203. Part 4: adult basic life support. *Circulation.* 2005;112(24 suppl):IV19–IV34. Part 5: electrical therapies: automated external defibrillators, defibrillation, cardioversion, and pacing. *Circulation.* 2005;112(24 suppl):IV35–IV46.

Strategies to Reduce the Risk of Sudden Death in Mass Participation Sporting Events

Kevin R. Ronneberg, MD

William O. Roberts, MD, MS, FACSM

Reducing the risk of death and providing medical coverage for a mass participation event requires a combination of **primary** and **secondary intervention strategies** that include cancellation parameters, education, equipment allocation, and field care protocols. Preplanning is essential to coordinate the many resources, including local emergency medical services (EMS), police, communications personnel, volunteer medical staff, and local hospital emergency departments, that must come together to form the event's medical team. The primary goal of the medical team and the event administration should be safety of participants, volunteers, staff, and community members.

The role of the medical director is to develop a plan for educating event participants and medical staff prior to an event, for allocating and placing resources in appropriate locations on the day of the event, and for integrating medical protocols for on-site care and EMS transfer of care. Understanding the types and incidence of medical encounters and providing timely response to participants in need are essential aspects of the event safety net. This chapter discusses the steps involved in preparing for and implementing a well-designed medical plan to decrease the burden placed on the community EMS system, prevent unnecessary risk to participants and event staff, reduce the risk of event-associated death, and provide timely response for those who need care.

Safety is the number one goal of any mass participation event; this includes the safety of the participants, the volunteers, the event staff, and the community at large. Mass participation events are planned and can be considered a scheduled disaster with the possibility of developing into a **mass casualty incident (MCI)**, which is defined as any event that overtaxes the community medical system's assets. Adequate preparation will contribute to the safety of the participants and community by preventing an increased burden on EMS and local emergency rooms and hospitals.

primary intervention strategy A rule or action designed to reduce an adverse or unwanted outcome that does not leave those at risk a choice (e.g., not starting a race on a hot day).

secondary intervention strategy A recommendation designed to reduce an adverse or unwanted outcome that leaves the decision in the hands of the participant (e.g., recommending that participants not start a race on a hot day).

mass casualty incident (MCI) Any event with casualties that overtax the community medical system's assets.

Emergency Action Plan

The medical director, event staff, and public safety officials should develop a coordinated, written **emergency action plan (EAP)** that outlines event-day policy well in advance of the event to reduce debates about critical decisions during the event.[1] An **incident command center** and **incident command coordinator** should be located at a key event site to facilitate the response to an adverse event, and their role should be embedded in the EAP.[2] These entities should work with EMS to determine who will be the incident commander and include that person, along with representatives from the race medical team and the race administration, in development of the document. The document needs to be reviewed annually, rehearsed regularly, and communicated to all who are involved so there is a clear understanding of the expectations, roles, and responsibilities in any emergencies that occur. Include phone numbers, emergency response protocols, and event cancellation protocols in the EAP.

Emergency Contact Information

A comprehensive EAP includes telephone contact information for local utilities, local media (for weather or other pertinent public announcements), direct access to the police and fire departments and the Federal Bureau of Investigations (FBI), the event director, the medical director, and other emergency contacts. The state Department of Public Health and the state emergency management agency are groups that can assist with the public safety aspect of the program and should be considered for inclusion in an EAP. Establish an emergency phone number for the race director and medical director to be used for emergency communication on race day. Use of ham radio and hand-held radio communication, in addition to cell phones, creates redundancy should one system fail in an emergency. Coordination is necessary when using multiple communication systems (see "Communications on the Course," later in this chapter).

Response to Emergency or Perceived Threat

Provide instruction to all volunteers and event staff on the emergency incident response protocol and physical threat protocol. Establish protocols that maximize the safety of participants, volunteers, and spectators; notify the appropriate EMS, police, or fire team; and alert the event staff chain of command. Create an incident report form for the event to be completed as soon as possible by all personnel involved once the situation is under control. Instruct event staff to refer all media, insurance, family member, or other inquiries to the appropriate event official.

Examples of incidents to address in an EAP include identification of a suspicious package; a significant injury, illness, or death during the event; significant property damage; protests along the course of the event; gas leaks; and any perceived threat, such as vehicles on the course or individuals with weapons at the event. For perceived threats, an evacuation protocol should identify key individuals to lead the participants, volunteers, and spectators to predetermined shelter areas. These areas are usually specified in site safety plans for a given venue and are available through the venue's public safety officers.

Event Cancellation or Delay

Each event needs to identify a specific procedure in the EAP to address adverse conditions that may lead to delay or cancellation, including the key individual or group decision makers and the specific cancellation parameters. Weather is a primary consideration for cancellation or delay and should be anticipated in the EAP. Specific conditions may include heat, cold, ice, snow, rain, lightning, wind, and air quality. Event-specific guiding principles for delay or cancellation need to be in place for each condition identified.

An example of a condition to consider is heat and humidity. The American College of Sports Medicine recommends cancellation at 82°F (27.8°C) **wet bulb globe temperature (WBGT)** for well-conditioned and acclimatized athletes.[3] This recommendation may not be useful for the average participant in an endurance event, especially if the participant is not

Example of a Weather-Related Event Delay or Cancellation Protocol

The specific criteria used to delay or postpone the race shall be:

- *Lightning*—If you can hear it, clear it. Resume in 30 minutes after the last thunder or lightning.
- *Heat*—The race will be cancelled if the wet bulb globe temperature at the start of the marathon is >69°F.*
- *Cold*—The race will be cancelled if the ambient temperature at the start of the race is <−15°F.
- *Ice*—The race will be cancelled if the roads are icy, traction is deemed unsafe, and the necessary precautions to mitigate the conditions cannot be undertaken.

Additional information used to decide shall include, but not be limited to:

- How acclimated to the conditions are the participants?
- What time did the weather report come in?
- What areas are affected?
- How long will these areas be affected?
- Is there a risk of potential danger to event participants, spectators, or volunteers?

*Wet bulb globe temperature considers effects of temperature, humidity, and radiant heat. A single index is computed using a weighted mathematical formula. The flag system used by Twin Cities in Motion for the marathon and ten mile for WBGT is: White Flag = Hypothermia Risk, <50°F; Green Flag = Low Risk, 50°F–58°F; Yellow Flag = Caution, 59°F–63°F; Red Flag = Extreme Caution, 64°F–68°F; and Black Flag = Extreme Risk, >69°F ("Event Cancellation Threshold" = 69°F).

acclimatized to the conditions or the conditions are unexpectedly or unseasonably hot.[4] Event recommendations will vary based on geographic location and season (**Box 15.1**). The Twin Cities Marathon developed outcome-based start WBGT criteria to predict the likely incidence of casualties and the likelihood of a mass casualty incident to help guide decisions regarding starting the race (**Figure 15.1**).[4]

Other considerations for delay or cancellation include public utilities emergencies, traffic accidents, and crime scenes. These are less predictable and require a systematic approach to communicate changes to the course, time of start, or cancellation to all participants and event staff.

Develop a communication plan that includes public safety officials, EMS, participants, and event volunteers for delay or cancellation. Consider how this communication will occur for those already on the course if the event is under way or if volunteers are on the course waiting for the event to begin. It is critical to have an evacuation plan for severe weather or other threats that require moving people to shelter or out of a specific area. Identify shelter near the start and finish of your event, procure access to the space for race day, and have a plan to direct or lead people to the safety of the shelter should the need arise.

Providing On-Site Care for Participants

For mass participation events, it is necessary to understand the incidence and likely locations of medical encounters. Each event may have different types and rates of injury that will require differing allocation of medical assets. Factors that affect medical casualty rates include weather, acclimatization of participants, length of the event, course layout, and number of participants. For example, in a marathon point-to-point road race, the field of play that must be covered by the medical staff is 26.2 miles (42 km). The distance alone creates challenges in the effective distribution of assets; provision of medical care; communication; and transportation of athletes, volunteers, and supplies. Other events, such as bike or cross-country ski races, may have longer courses and introduce equipment and speeds that may contribute to trauma injury, which expands the list of life-threatening encounters. Rural or back-country course locations may have limited course accessibility for ambulances, complicating race rescue operations. Open-water swims and triathlon events require protocols for open-water safety and rescue.

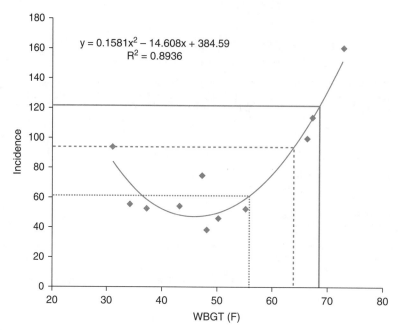

Figure 15.1   Risk levels based on mass casualty incident (MCI) risk. The figure represents the experience at Twin Cities Marathon and demonstrates a correlation of start time temperatures and number of medical casualties thereby helping to predict when an MCI may occur based on start temperatures. The cancel level (represented by the solid line) lies at 20.5°C (69°F). The high-risk level (dashed line) is placed just below the cancel level, and the caution level (dotted line) below that.

MCI is any event with casualties that overtaxes the community medical system assets. This number will be different for each event depending on resources, date, and geographical location of race. The symbols that fall between the dashed and solid lines are races where there was an MCI at the finish area for the race (not affecting the entire 26.2-mile course or community resources on non-finish areas of the event). The one symbol above the solid line represents a race day where there was an MCI for the community resources along the entire course including the finish area. This figure demonstrates a correlation of start time temperatures and number of medical casualties thereby helping to predict when an MCI may occur based on start temperatures. The Do Not Start wet bulb globe temperature (WBGT) is calculated using an incidence of 130 unsuccessful starters per 1,000 finishers that intersects the curve at a WBGT of 20.5°C (69°F) on the temperature axis.

Source: Reproduced with permission from Wolters Kluwer Health. Roberts WO. Determining a "Do not start" temperature for a marathon on the basis of adverse outcomes. *Med Sci Sports Exerc*. 2010;42(20):226–232.

Encounter Rates

Medical encounters for Twin Cities Marathon participants average 24 per 1000 finishers,[5] but vary from 8 to 40 per 1000 for cooler (24–50°F [⁻4.4–10°C]) to warmer (72°F [22.2°C]) WBGT conditions (unpublished data, W. O. Roberts). These encounter rates will differ for other races at different times of the year, with different topography, and at different altitudes. In general, as the temperature and humidity increase, the number of dropouts along the course also increases, race times slow, and overall medical encounters increase.

Differential Diagnosis for the Event

To prepare an effective medical plan, anticipate the most common medical needs that will be encountered on race day. The differential diagnosis for collapse of a participant defines the education, staffing, supply, and equipment needs for the event. In endurance events, there are relatively few life-threatening or serious problems to consider as the cause of collapse. A standardized approach to evaluation and treatment guides the medical team to an efficient care system and helps differentiate the life-threatening from the self-limited causes.

At first sight of some participants who collapse in the finish area, the severity of the problem is not always clear and is often benign despite a "shocklike" appearance. Collapse before the finish often heralds a life-threatening event. The differential diagnosis for marathon collapse includes sudden cardiac arrest, exertional heat stroke, hypothermia, exercise-associated hyponatremia, hypoglycemia or insulin shock, respiratory arrest (including asthma or anaphylaxis), and exercise-associated collapse.[6–15] These conditions are central to developing a medical plan to reduce adverse outcomes during the event.

Staffing Model and Equipment Needs

Recruiting medical staff for the event can be done through local organizations based on the staffing model for the event type and course layout. The medical committee should include representatives from participating organizations such as local EMS, the American Red Cross, the National Ski Patrol, the National Mountain Bike Patrol, the state Athletic Trainers Association, and local physicians and emergency room staff. Boston uses Federal Disaster Management Assistance Teams (DMAT) on the course of the Boston Marathon. Units are supported by the Department of Health and Human Services and can be looking for training opportunities. Organizers may also check with a state's Medical Reserve Corp for volunteer support and event administration.

Each group involved must understand the requirements for medical care provided on race day to best use their resources and expertise to achieve the goals of ensuring participant safety, decreasing the burden on community safety and medical services, and responding to life-threatening situations. The number and qualifications of medical volunteers will vary based on the number of entrants, race distance and type, anticipated worst-case weather conditions, and availability of human resources.[16]

The Event Course

Providing medical coverage for a large geographic area such as a race course for an endurance event presents challenges in delivering uniform emergency response along every portion of the course and requires a combination of fixed and mobile assets. A line-of-sight reporting system using volunteers as spotters takes advantage of the network of course marshals placed within sight of each other along the course **(Figure 15.2)**. These nonmedical volunteers, equipped with mobile phones and a medical emergency phone number, can activate an emergency response and provide relevant information to the medical team and race staff in the event of a medical crisis.

Placement of medical aid stations immediately following each fluid stop along the course helps participants know where to predictably seek aid or notify medical personnel of another participant in need of assistance. Medical personnel available at fixed aid stations will not be effective in responding to a collapsed participant in other areas of the course, so mobile teams are needed for rapid response. If resources allow, dedicated advanced life support (ALS) ambulances positioned along the course to respond to downed participants will have less impact on community medical services during the event. Ambulances stationed at fixed aid stations can provide a controlled environment for assessment and treatment of casualties during inclement weather. These ambulances can be activated for transport or emergency response in the case of a mass casualty incident.

If there are areas of the course that are known to be difficult for emergency vehicles to access, consider stationing medical personnel trained in advanced cardiac life support (ACLS) in those areas on medically outfitted all-terrain vehicles to allow for rapid response, early initiation of treatment, and means of transporting the participant to a location more accessible to a standard ambulance. Medical personnel from the local EMS department or National Bike Patrol teams on bicycles equipped with automated external defibrillators (AEDs) and basic first aid kits can be spaced at 1- to 2-mile intervals and travel with the flow of participants to respond quickly to a collapsed participant in between medical aid stations. They will be able to initiate treatment while the EMS system is activated. Likewise, the National Ski Patrol can provide the same service during cross-country ski or other winter outdoor events.

A   B

Figure 15.2   **A:** Spotter platforms allow medical volunteers to look down to observe for participants having difficulty. **B:** Numbering light posts and landmarks allows response teams to locate collapsed participants more easily. The locations are placed on the course map.

Communications on the Course

The key to an effective medical team is good communication between each of the groups providing care along the course and in the finish area. Ham radio operators can provide communication throughout the whole of the course, and medical team members can be outfitted with radios along the course and finish area. Route all communications through a central command or dispatch, which serves to coordinate responses from the course medical staff. Always have a backup form of communication. Using a combination of ham radio, two-way radios, and cell phones provides the necessary redundancy to ensure that the communication plan will not fail at a critical time. Unless the local EMS service supports a different protocol, the first call for any collapsed runner is 911, followed by initiating the event medical emergency protocol to activate on-course personnel. Confidential exchanges should be done by mobile phone, because radio communications can be monitored by anyone with access to a radio.

Dropouts Along the Course

There will be participants who, for various reasons, choose to not continue competing in the event and drop out along the course. Provide means to transport these individuals to the finish area to prevent worsening of an overuse injury or prolonged exposure to hot, cold, or wet conditions that can facilitate progression of existing medical conditions.

The Finish Area

Coordination of the finish area medical team includes coverage of the final few hundred meters of the race, the finish chute, and the finish area grounds where participants congregate with family, friends, and fellow competitors following completion of the race. During multisport events such as a triathlon, this includes coverage of the transition areas.

The vast majority of medical casualties will occur immediately following the finish line. Have trained personnel who can identify and differentiate ill participants from those who temporarily look ill located throughout the first 100 meters after the finish line. Use physicians, athletic trainers, or other medical personnel trained in identification of medical casualties to triage and initiate medical care in this area. When a collapsed participant needs assessment and treatment, the triage medical staff can transport him or her to the medical tent or on-site facility, which should be in close proximity to the finish line. Some participants are able to walk with assistance; for others, have wheelchairs, stretchers, or gurneys available for transport within the finish area. Security fencing or barricades in place along the final stretches of the course and following the finish line may impede access to a downed participant. Determine how an emergency team will access collapsed participants in these locations and move them to the on-site medical facility or ambulance so as to avoid a delay in treatment.

At the finish line, establish cardiac arrest teams staffed by emergency personnel who are trained in ACLS and have the skills to intubate and use the most recent technologies for effective resuscitation of a downed and unconscious event participant. Locate the arrest teams in strategic areas to respond to a collapse on either side of the finish line; anticipate any potential impedance to accessing a collapsed participant for resuscitation and transport. Place a second cardiac arrest team inside the on-site medical facility or treatment area to respond to participants who arrest after the initial triage and require stabilization prior to transport. Use standard language such as "Code Blue" to alert and mobilize the teams.

Once participants have moved through the finish chute and congregate within the finish area grounds, it is more difficult to identify participants in need of medical attention. Plan to have medical staff spaced throughout the finish grounds and a means of communicating with them to coordinate care. Divide the finish area grounds into a grid to help locate downed participants. Use visible identifiers to label the locations, such as numbers on light posts or landmarks. Elevated stations such as lifeguard stands or scissor lifts with medical team volunteers on them will help with spotting collapsed participants and guiding the responding medical team. Teams can carry flags to help responding personnel find the site more readily. Assign trained medical staff (e.g., from the American Red Cross) armed with radios, AEDs, and, if appropriate, golf carts with medical cots (for transport of collapsed participants to the on-site medical facility) to each of the grid sections. If you have a system to bring participants who have dropped out of the event to the finish area, locate medical staff at the drop-off location in case there is a need for medical evaluation and intervention.

The On-Site Medical Facility

Locate a site within the finish area to set up your medical care facility that has convenient and timely access to the finish line chute and also allows for ambulance egress. If there is not a climate-controlled area, such as an arena or convention center, that allows space, consider a large tent that can be heated or cooled as conditions warrant. Tents can also have temporary floors placed in them if you are unable to set up over a blacktop surface to allow for wheelchair access.

Inside your medical care area, create an entrance and exit that facilitate easy movement of ill participants, wheelchairs, and ambulance gurneys. Identify each participant who enters the tent and log patients out at discharge to know who is currently being treated or who has been treated by the medical team and to enable families and friends to track participants. For many events that use computerized chip timing, the chip may be scanned with a hand-held detection device to improve the speed and accuracy of the registration process in lieu of visual identification of a race number.

Assign medical teams, including a physician and nurse, responsibility for attending to participants brought to specific beds or cots in the care area. Resident physicians; medical, physical therapy, or nursing students; emergency medical technicians (EMTs); and nonmedical volunteers can assist with support tasks for the medical team and gain experience and exposure to event care. Use physicians with the most mass participation medical care experience to supervise the tent processes. Some of the roles to consider for a supervising physician include help with decisions regarding initiating intravenous fluids, administering medications or hypertonic sodium chloride, moving a poorly responding patient to a higher level of care, and assisting with discharge and disposition decisions for participants who presented with more severe problems. Use the records of the previous year's medical encounters at the event, if available, to guide the appropriate number of medical personnel required.

Define space in the medical tent that may be used for a code team to perform resuscitation or for cooling of participants, because these procedures may have unique privacy and space requirements. Confirm that electricity or lighting is available and sufficient for the medical care you are providing. The following section discusses the preparation and resources that should be available in the medical tent and finish area to address the conditions that potentially lead to death.

Evaluation of Collapsed Athletes

The primary goal of each event is participant safety. In providing on-site care for mass participation events, know your capabilities and appropriately use your resources to facilitate timely recognition and treatment of potentially lethal conditions. For example, knowing that the highest volume of casualties in a marathon occurs from 3.5 to 5 hours after the start and that the number of encounters in the 4- to 6-hour range has increased as the average finish time has increased to over 4 hours will affect how the medical team is assigned. Determine triage guidelines for medical staff who will be encountering participants in need of medical care. Consider any participant presenting to the medical team with chest pain, major trauma, shortness of breath, seizure, or unconsciousness a candidate to go directly into a standby ambulance to start evaluation, treatment, and transfer to the emergency facility without delay. This eliminates unnecessary delay during evaluation in the medical tent for potentially life-threatening problems.

For the remaining participants who have presented with collapse near the finish area, locate triage physicians or other appropriately trained personnel at the entrance to the medical tent or treatment area to help direct participants to the appropriate level of care within the on-site medical facility. In most cases, full emergency intervention is not needed for participants presenting for postrace care. Most who collapse at the end of an event experience a physiologic condition termed **exercise-associated collapse** (EAC). The task of the medical team is to differentiate these participants from those with conditions that may lead to death or morbidity. A systematic approach to the collapsed athlete will help to identify those who have life-threatening conditions.

exercise-associated collapse (EAC) A physiologic condition that occurs after an endurance event. The pathophysiology of EAC is postural hypotension that results when the loss of muscle pumping action caused by the cessation of exercise is combined with cutaneous vasodilation.

A collapsed and breathing athlete brought to the on-site medical facility should be placed on a cot with the legs elevated to aid in venous return of blood that pools in the lower extremities following exertion. Poolside chaise loungers work well to raise the legs by placing the athlete's feet at the head of the lounger and using the adjustable back on the lounger to elevate the legs. Initiate a medical record; obtain vital signs, including pulse and blood pressure; and, if the athlete is awake and conversant, record a history of symptoms. If a prerace medical history had been submitted and approved for use by the race-day medical team by the participant, this is accessed as well (**Box 15.2**). If the athlete is able to take oral hydration, offer water, a carbohydrate-electrolyte sports drink, or bouillon broth.

Athletes who are experiencing EAC will begin to improve within minutes, with decreased subjective symptoms and normalization of blood pressure and pulse. For those who continue to have symptoms after several minutes of conservative treatment, obtain a rectal temperature measurement to rule out hyperthermia or hypothermia. Rectal temperature is the only accurate and precise core measurement available in the field, and other methods should not be used.[17–21] Consider an intravenous (IV) line

Use of Personal Health Records for On-Site Endurance Event Medical Care

Access to a collapsed athlete's medical history is a challenge for mass participation events. Pre-participation screening is not logistically feasible in most cases and thus we have for years depended on participants writing their medical history on the back of the race bib with poor participation. This process also does not provide any ability to collect aggregate data on athletes' medical histories to help in research efforts around participant health and safety. Over the last several years event medical directors have begun to explore the use of personal health records to capture medication, allergy, past medical history, family history, [and] race day contact information among other data points that could be beneficial to the medical team on race day. Participation rates have been in the 5–15% rate as this has been voluntary and there has not been a compelling argument for most participants to use such a record.

The American Road Race Medical Society is supportive of work to develop a common questionnaire to collect participant information that will be portable from one event to another and provide similar data points that can be collected to further research in endurance event medicine.

Opportunities for electronic systems include point of care documentation of presenting symptoms, assessment and treatment that is provided along the course or in the finish area, as well as participant access electronically to their personal event day medical discharge instructions and medical treatment documentation. Pre-event screening of participants for use of medications, disease processes, and history of medical encounters at races will allow for proactive messaging of educational material that can be personalized.

placement for those who are unable to take fluids orally and consider including a sodium measurement to rule out exercise-associated hyponatremia prior to any fluid flush.[22]

Intravenous Fluid Use

Many finishers of endurance events look very ill with or without having collapsed, but appear similar to very sick individuals who show up in emergency rooms, where IV placement and initiation of fluid infusion would be automatic. Given that most collapsed athletes are healthy and will recover when provided appropriate support and recovery time, IV fluids are rarely necessary in participants after an endurance event and can be avoided without compromising safety (**Box 15.3**). If IV hydration is deemed appropriate, the preferred IV fluid is dextrose 5% in normal saline solution (D_5NS) for the first liter to help address the caloric substrate depletion that occurs with endurance events. Each subsequent liter is normal saline unless there is a need for glucose. As soon as an athlete is tolerating oral intake, that becomes the preferred method of rehydrating and obtaining nutrition.[23]

Twin Cities Marathon IV Protocol

Use the following criteria to determine the need for starting IV fluids:

- continued symptoms after laying supine with leg elevation for 10–30 minutes
- systolic blood pressure <100 with continued symptoms
- orthostatic blood pressure drops with change of position
- heart rate persists >100 bpm
- rectal temperature is >104°F or <95°F and not responding to temperature correction protocols
- severe muscle spasms
- anorexia or nausea that is not improving
- hypoglycemia <60 mg/dL
- confused
- or just "not doing well" based on clinical assessment

This protocol requires point of care blood analysis (iStat™ or similar analyzer) for Na, K, BUN, and glucose prior to administering IV fluids.

Sudden Cardiac Arrest

Cardiac arrest occurs in 1 in 50,000 to 100,000 finishers, with a slight majority of cases occurring at or near the finish area; the remainder are spread out across the entire course **(Figure 15.3)**.[24–26] Survival rate is dependent on rapid access to defibrillation and timely initiation of cardiopulmonary resuscitation (CPR). The time to defibrillation has been improved by the availability of AEDs.[25]

In the finish area, designate code teams to respond to any suspected cardiac arrest. These teams should be made up of physicians, nurses, paramedics, or others with experience in running ACLS codes. Have available equipment needed to manage arrests on site: oxygen, defibrillators (AED or manual), intubation kits including induction medication, IV fluids, catheters and tubing, and current ACLS medications.

On the course, make sure to have aspirin and sublingual nitroglycerin tablets available for use by athletes with suspected cardiac chest symptoms on a medical doctor's advice. Have AEDs readily available along the course at medical aid stations and with mobile medical staff. AED availability should be integrated into the plan for areas of the course that are difficult to access.

Participants with cardiac arrest will present as either already collapsed and unconscious or collapsed with complaints of chest pain. Following cardiac arrest, brief seizure-like activity may occur and should not be confused with seizure disorder. Seizure-type activity should prompt an assessment of airway, breathing, and pulse and the placement of an AED to assess for cardiac dysrhythmia. Also consider hyperthermia and hyponatremia as causes of seizure-type activity and pursue these potential diagnoses if there is effective cardiac output.

Exertional Heat Stroke

Exertional heat stroke often occurs in participants of endurance events.[3,27,28] The incidence rate is site dependent and increases with ambient temperature, relative humidity, and level of radiant sun exposure. Other factors that contribute to the risk of exertional heat stroke include lack of acclimatization, dehydration, intensity of exercise, illness, medications, and supplements. It is a common misconception that exertional heat stroke only occurs during warm-weather events.[29] The incidence rate at the Twin Cities Marathon (TCM) varies based on weather conditions, ranging from 0 to 1 cases per 10,000 participants in cool weather (WBGT < 55°F [12.8°C]) to 10 to 15 cases per 10,000 participants in warm-weather races (72–78°F WBGT [22.2–24.4°C]) (unpublished data, W. O. Roberts). TCM participants have had rectal temperatures as high as 108°F (42.2°C) during cool-weather events.

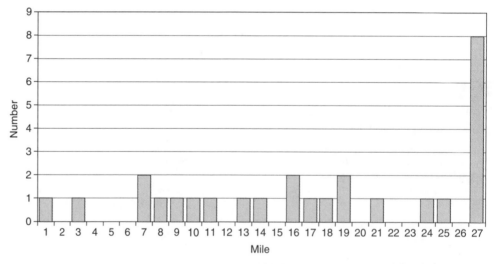

Figure 15.3   Locations of sudden cardiac arrests during three different marathons—the Twin Cities Marathon (TCM), Marine Corps Marathon (MCM), and London Marathon (LM)—across the last three decades. The arrests can occur at any point along the course, although the most frequent site is in the finish area (the 26-mile mark through the post finish line area).

Participants with exertional heat stroke will present with symptoms of confusion, lethargy, poor coordination, slurred speech, or collapse.[28] On the race course, heat-affected participants may, in addition to collapsing to the ground, exhibit unsteady or wobbly gait, inability to maintain an upright athletic posture, or failure to make straight-line progress on the course.[28] All volunteers on the course must be trained to identify these symptoms and notify medical personnel.

Diagnosing exertional heat stroke requires assessment of core temperature by rectal thermometer.[17–21] Oral, aural canal, or temporal artery scan measurements are not accurate and can be misleading, causing delays in critical care for heat-related injury **(Figure 15.4)**.[17–21] Obtaining a rectal temperature measurement requires a rectal thermometer, lubricant, and medical personnel who are willing to perform the procedure. Sheets or other barriers can provide privacy for the collapsed athlete. If a rectal thermometer is not available and there is concern regarding exertional heat stroke, it is acceptable to treat empirically until a normal temperature can be documented. It is critical to lower the temperature of an athlete with exertional heat stroke quickly to avoid end-organ damage and possibly death. This diagnosis is one for which initiation of treatment in the field can prevent morbidity and mortality, whereas transport in an ambulance to an emergency department that is not prepared to treat heat injury can be fatal. Treat first and do not delay treatment for transport if at all possible.

There are many ways to cool victims with exertional heat stroke.[30–37] The necessary equipment should be part of the medical supplies. The most efficient means of heat transfer is circulating ice water in cooling tubs that allow the trunk and limbs to be submerged.[28,30–32,34] Use of this method requires a large area and caution because the walking surface will get wet and slippery. A reasonable alternative, though not as effective, for events with an expected low incidence of extertional heat stroke is the use of rotating ice-water towels.[28] Towels are soaked in ice water, wrung out, and then draped over the athlete from head to toe, replacing them continuously. This requires less space but does not solve the concerns regarding wet surfaces. The chosen protocol and equipment should be familiar to the medical team so that rapid cooling can be initiated when the problem is identified.

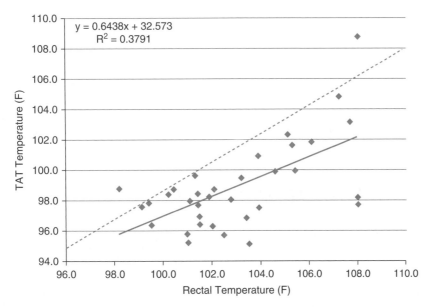

Figure 15.4   There is very poor correlation between temporal artery thermometer (TAT) temperatures and rectal temperatures after a marathon. Note the dashed "line of identity" and the discrepancy in measure at very high body temperatures.

Source: Reproduced with permission from Wolters Kluwer Health. Ronneberg K, Roberts WO, McBean AD, et al. Temporal artery temperature measurements do not detect hyperthermic marathon runners. *Med Sci Sports Exerc.* 2008;40(8):1373–1375.

Exercise-Associated Hyponatremia

Symptomatic exercise-associated hyponatremia (EH$_s$) is relatively uncommon in mass participation events, but can be fatal if not identified and treated appropriately.[22,38–42] Medical volunteers should be familiar with the increase in hyponatremia risk for finishers after the 4-hour mark and the symptoms of light-headedness, headache, nausea, vomiting, weight gain, puffiness, muscle cramps, mental status change, or prolonged seizure.[22,38,43] These athletes are often indistinguishable from those with exertional heat stroke except for the former's normal rectal temperature and normal blood pressure and heart rate.

A participant who has any of the symptoms just described, does not respond to laying supine with legs elevated, and has a normal rectal temperature should be tested for hyponatremia with a point-of-care device or transferred to an emergency facility for a sodium level assessment if there is no on-site capability. These athletes require IV access for administration of hypertonic saline.

Development of exertional hyponatremia occurs over a few hours and should be treated quickly to correct the intracellular fluid shifts that occur with prolonged hyponatremia. If encephalopathy is present, hypertonic saline can be given intravenously on site as soon as the diagnosis is known and continued during transport to the emergency department. Adult emergency department personnel are not accustomed to caring for patients with EH$_s$ and generally use chronic or subacute hyponatremia protocols that require slow correction to avoid rapid fluid shifts and cell death. Prior to the event, education for the race-day emergency department staff in rapid EH$_s$ correction protocols will improve outcomes. Emergency departments should either stock hypertonic saline or have quick access to it on race day. Have a written protocol to follow in the case of hyponatremia **(Box 15.4)**.

Anaphylaxis, Respiratory Distress, and Hypoglycemia or Insulin Shock

In addition to previously mentioned medical supplies, include epinephrine and diphenhydramine or other antihistamines for use by the medical team to address airway constriction or anaphylactic reactions. For insulin shock, provide glucometers, lancets, and test strips, along with some form of easily absorbed sugar and 50% dextrose in water (D$_{50}$W) for IV administration.

Conclusion

A collaborative effort among event officials, local EMS, and medical volunteers that addresses primary and secondary prevention strategies will improve event and community safety. Each event will have to tailor its prevention strategies according to the type of event, number of participants, environmental conditions, and resources available. With a focus on participant safety and implementing a well-designed medical plan, the risk of death from weather-related conditions, sudden cardiac arrest, heat stroke, hyponatremia, and other problems can be reduced.

Box 15.4

Twin Cities Marathon Protocol for Treatment of Exercise-Associated Hyponatremia

Sodium <135 meq/L and asymptomatic

- Observe for diuresis
- 4 bouillon cubes dissolved in 4 ounces water and drink over 5–15 minutes

Sodium <135 meq/L and encephalopathy

- Give 100 mL 3% saline over 10 minutes (may repeat every 10 minutes until improving)
- Drip 50–70 mL/hr using an infusion pump to control rate
- Transfer to emergency department

Clinical Case Scenarios

1. A young woman (early 20s) is transported by Gator into the medical area after collapsing just after the marathon finish line. The race started with a temperature in the mid-60s (°F) and low humidity, and the temperature is now 80°F (26.7°C). She is confused and lethargic; pale, sweaty, and warm to touch; and requires total assistance to transfer. She is placed directly into a tub of ice water and immersed to her neck. After 10 minutes she is starting to make some logical statements, recalls her name and family details, and is able to remember she finished the race. At that point, she is removed from the tub and a rectal temperature of 106°F (41.1°C) is obtained. An IV is started, and her serum sodium level is measured at 145 mmol/L. Cooling is continued with rapidly rotating ice towels, and at 28 minutes she has a rectal temperature of 100°F (37.8°C). At 45 minutes her rectal temperature is 98.6°F (37°C), but she has had 20 minutes of vomiting. She is transferred to the local emergency facility.
    1. Are there weaknesses in this protocol?
    2. What, if anything, would you do differently?
    3. How would you set up the standard operating procedures for your tent?
2. A 42-year-old woman presents to the medical tent transported in a wheelchair by the finish line triage personnel at 6 hours after the start time. She is unable to walk, but answers questions. The current temperature is 60°F (15.6°C) and there is a dark cloud cover. She is assumed to be dehydrated by the attending team, and IV D_5NS is started to run as fast as possible. The IV starter gets a blood sample for sodium analysis. While waiting for the Na^+ result, the athlete becomes more confused and less responsive. She has a normal blood pressure and her pulse is in the 80s.
    1. What do you do at this point?
    2. Her rectal temperature is 99°F (37.2°C). The sodium level comes back to the care team and she continues to worsen. The Na^+ level is 122 mmol/L. What do you do next?
    3. What, if anything, would you change in your policy and procedure manual?
3. The forecast is for 70° to 75°F (21.1–23.9°C) with a relative humidity of 95% at sunrise for the marathon race—an unexpectedly hot day. The forecast five days earlier had been for a start temperature of around 50°F (10°C) and a high temperature of 65°F (18.3°C) during the race. The race has never been run in these conditions, and the two previous races that started in the mid-60s with high humidity put the three hospitals in the vicinity of the finish area onto divert status for 2 to 3 hours. Your race has no written policy. The race committee asks your opinion on race morning.
    1. What do you do?
    2. Who is at risk?
    3. What can you do for the future?

Key Terms

emergency action plan (EAP)

exercise-associated collapse (EAC)

incident command center

incident command coordinator

mass casualty incident (MCI)

primary intervention strategy

secondary intervention strategy

wet bulb globe temperature (WBGT)

References

1. Drezner JA, Courson RW, Roberts WO, et al. Inter Association Task Force recommendations on emergency preparedness and management of sudden cardiac arrest in high school and college athletic programs: a consensus statement. *Prehosp Emerg Care.* 2007;11(3):253–271.

2. Chiampas G. Enhancing community disaster resilience through mass sporting events. *J Disaster Med Pub Health Preparedness.* 2011; in press.

3. Armstrong LE, Casa DJ, Millard-Stafford M, et al. ACSM position stand: exertional heat illness during training and competition. *Med Sci Sports Exerc.* 2007;30(3):556–572.

4. Roberts WO. Determining a "Do not start" temperature for a marathon on the basis of adverse outcomes. *Med Sci Sports Exerc.* 2010;42(20):226–232.

5. Roberts WO. A twelve year profile of medical injury and illness for the Twin Cities Marathon. *Med Sci Sports Exerc.* 2000;32(9):1549–1555.

6. Brennan FH, O'Connor FG. Emergency triage of collapsed endurance athletes: a stepwise approach to on-site treatment. *Phys Sportsmed.* 2005;33:3.

7. Ewert GD. Marathon race medical administration. *Sports Med.* 2007;37(4–5):428–430.

8. Holtzhausen LM, Noakes TD. Collapsed ultraendurance athlete: proposed mechanisms and an approach to management. *Clin J Sport Med.* 1997;7(4):247–251.

9. Nicholl J, Williams B. Medical problems before and after a popular marathon. *Br Med J.* 1982;285:1465–1466.

10. Nicholl J, Williams B. Popular marathons: forecasting casualties. *Br Med J.* 1982;285:1464–1465.

11. O'Connor FG, Pyne S, Brennan FH. Exercise associated collapse: an algorithmic approach to race day management. *Am J Med Sports.* 2003;5:212–217, 229.

12. Roberts WO. Medical management and administration manual for long distance road racing. In: Brown C, Gudjonsson B, eds. *International Association of Athletics Federations Competition Medical Handbook for Track and Field and Road Racing. A Practical Guide.* 3rd ed. Monaco: Imprimerie Multiprint; 2006:45–81.

13. Roberts WO. Exercise-associated collapse care matrix in the marathon. *Sports Med.* 2007;37(4–5):431–433.

14. Roberts WO. Exercise-associated collapse in endurance events: a classification system. *Phys Sportsmed.* 1989;17(5):49–55.

15. Roberts WO. Heat and cold: what does the environment do to marathon injury? *Sports Med.* 2007;37(4–5):400–403.

16. Sanchez LD, Corwell B, Berkoff D. Medical problems of marathon runners. *Am J Emerg Med.* 2006;24(5):608–615.

17. Armstrong LE, Maresh CM, Crago AE, et al. Interpretation of aural temperatures during exercise, hyperthermia, and cooling therapy. *Med Exerc Nutr Health.* 1994;3(1):9–16.

18. Casa DJ, Becker SM, Ganio MS, et al. Validity of devices that assess body temperature during outdoor exercise in the heat. *J Athl Train.* 2007;42(3):333–342.

19. Deschamps A, Levy RD, Cosio MG, et al. Tympanic temperature should not be used to assess exercise induced hyperthermia. *Clin J Sports Med.* 1992;2(1):27–32.

20. Roberts WO. Assessing core temperature in collapsed athletes. *Phys Sportsmed.* 1994;22(8):49–55.

21. Ronneberg K, Roberts WO, McBean AD, et al. Temporal artery and rectal temperature measurements in collapsed marathon runners. *Med Sci Sports Exerc.* 2008;40(8):1373–1375.

22. Hew-Butler T, Ayus JC, Kipps C, et al. Consensus statement of the Second International Exercise-Associated Hyponatremia Consensus Development Conference, New Zealand, 2007. *Clin J Sport Med.* 2008;18:111–121.

23. Sawka MN, Burke LM, Eichner ER, et al. ACSM position stand: exercise and fluid replacement. *Med Sci Sports Exerc.* 2007;39(2):377–390.

24. Maron B, Poliac LC, Roberts WO. Risk for sudden death associated with marathon running. *J Am Coll Cardiol.* 1996;28:428–431.

25. Roberts WO, Maron BJ. Evidence for decreasing occurrence of sudden cardiac death associated with the marathon. *J Am Coll Cardiol.* 2005;46(7):1373–1374.

26. Tunstall Pedoe DS. Marathon cardiac deaths: the London experience. *Sports Med.* 2007;37(4-5):448–450.

27. Kenefick RW, Cheuvront SN, Sawka MN. Thermoregulatory function during the marathon. *Sports Med.* 2007;37(4–5):312–315.

28. Roberts WO. Exertional heat stroke in the marathon. *Sports Med.* 2007;37(4–5):440–443.

29. Roberts WO. Exertional heat stroke during a cool weather marathon: a case study. *Med Sci Sports Exerc.* 2006;38(7):1197–1203.

30. Armstrong LE, Crago AE, Adams R, et al. Whole-body cooling of hyperthermic runners: comparison of two field therapies. *Am J Emerg Med.* 1996;14(4):355–358.

31. Brodeur VB, Dennett SR, Griffin LS. Exertional hyperthermia, ice baths, and emergency care at the Falmouth Road Race. *J Emerg Nursing.* 1989;15(4):304–312.

32. Casa DJ, McDermott BP, Lee EC, et al. Cold water immersion: the gold standard for exertional heat stroke treatment. *Exerc Sport Sci Rev.* 2007;35(5):141–149.

33. Casa, DJ, Anderson JM, Armstrong LE, et al. Survival strategy: acute treatment of exertional heat stroke. *J Strength Cond Res.* 2006;20:462.

34. Costrini AM. Emergency treatment of exertional heat stroke and comparison of whole body cooling techniques. *Med Sci Sports Exerc.* 1990;22(1):15–18.

35. Proulx CI, Ducharme MB, Kenny GP. Safe cooling limits from exercise induced hyperthermia. *Eur J Appl Physiol.* 2006;96(4): 434–445.

36. Roberts WO. Managing heatstroke: on-site cooling. *Phys Sportsmed.* 1992;20(5):17–28.

37. Sinclair W, Rudzki S, Leicht A, et al. Efficacy of field treatment to reduce body core temperature in hyperthermic subjects. *Med Sci Sports Exerc.* 2009;41(11):1984–1990.

38. Almond CS, Shin AY, Fortescue EB, et al. Hyponatremia among runners in the Boston Marathon. *N Engl J Med.* 2005;352: 1550–1556.

39. Ayrus JC, Varon J, Areiff AI, et al. Hyponatremia, cerebral edema, and noncardiogenic pulmonary edema in marathon runners. *Ann Intern Med.* 2000;132(9):711–714.

40. Davis DP, Videen JS, Marino A, et al. Exercise-associated hyponatremia in marathon runners: a two year experience. *J Emerg Med.* 2001;21(1):47–57.

41. Speedy DB, Rogers IR, Noakes TD, et al. Diagnosis and prevention of hyponatremia in an ultradistance triathlon. *Clin J Sports Med.* 2000;10:52–58.

42. Speedy DB, Noakes TD, Rogers IR, et al. Hyponatremia in ultradistance triathletes. *Med Sci Sports Exerc.* 1999;31(6): 809–815.

43. Chorley J, Cianca J, Divine J. Risk factors for exercise-associated hyponatremia in non-elite marathon runners. *Clin J Sport Med.* 2007;17(6):471–477.

Educational Considerations for the Prevention of Sudden Death in Sport and Physical Activity

Stephanie M. Mazerolle, PhD, ATC

Rebecca M. Lopez, PhD, ATC, CSCS

Tutita M. Casa, PhD

> *It's not knowing what to do, it's doing what you know.*
> —Anthony Robbins

The purpose of this book is to provide an evidence-based approach to the prevention of sudden death in sport and physical activity. Unfortunately, even when health care and medical professionals are knowledgeable about the best evidence-based practice, it is not uncommon for this knowledge to not always be carried out on the field.[1,2] It is essential that medical personnel are provided with the knowledge needed to prevent sudden death and also educated in a fashion that allows them to prevent, recognize, and treat such occurrences when they occur in real life.

This chapter addresses three important areas that educators should consider when teaching adults to help ensure that evidence-based practices are properly used in the clinical setting: (1) the learner, (2) the learning process, and (3) the context in which the learning takes place.[3] The diversity among the adult learners involved (e.g., physicians, athletic trainers, and emergency medical services [EMS] personnel), including their level of experience (e.g., a student versus a certified professional) and the various settings in which the teaching and learning will take place, must be considered in order to plan an effective instructional session regarding sudden death in sport. For instance, education on the prevention, recognition, and treatment of hyponatremia would not involve the same teaching strategies during a 1-hour medical meeting before a marathon as it would in a semester-long emergency procedures course. The backgrounds and skills of the learners likely would differ significantly between both groups, the teaching strategies should vary considerably across the two settings for a multitude of reasons, and the contexts would provide different opportunities and challenges.

Although the learners and contexts will differ significantly, this chapter attempts to clarify the ways in which educators can support processes that would allow learners to prevent cases of sudden death. Specifically, this chapter does the following:

1. Draws from the field of adult education to understand the ideal setting in which to educate personnel
2. Presents educational considerations within the sports realm that may affect this ideal
3. Offers tips on how to overcome some constraints
4. Identifies learning goals across most common causes of sudden death in sport
5. Shares general teaching strategies to address different learning goals
6. Provides samples of these teaching strategies that address the most common causes of sudden death in sport

Understanding Your Learners Using Adult Education Principles

It is important to understand the needs of adult learners in order to teach them in a manner that will more likely result in them applying their knowledge to novel situations so as to prevent sudden death. As Merriam[3] summarizes, several generalizations describe adult learners. First, they tend to have an independent self-concept and can direct their own learning. For instance, although continuing education experiences are required in medical fields to maintain licensure or certification, keep the provider current and accountable, and promote advanced clinical practice, having practitioners select which sessions to attend may be more beneficial than assigning them to certain ones.

Second, adult learners have accumulated personal and professional experiences that can serve as a fertile learning resource. For example, an athletic trainer who was a high-level athlete and suffered major injury would use this experience to relate to causes of sudden death. Third, their learning needs are closely related to their social roles. Consider that an accomplished orthopedist volunteering her services at an ultramarathon medical tent would play a different role than she would in the operating room.

Fourth, adult learners are problem centered and desire to immediately apply their knowledge. It would not be surprising, for instance, that an athletic training student participating in a football rotation would seek out information about concussions after witnessing one for the first time. Finally, adult learners are more internally than externally motivated. For example, although the authors in this book would advocate that all medical personnel fully understand the causes of sudden death in sport, a team physician for the track and field and swimming teams may not see the need to know as much about concussions as compared to one in charge of football.

It also is important for educators to consider the different types of learning that may occur. The setting that is familiar to many educators is the one in which formal learning takes place. By definition, formal learning is highly structured and tends to be based in the classroom and institutionally sponsored.[4] Much of adult learning, however, can take place in more informal settings. Marsick and Watkins[4] note that whereas informal learning is typically intentional, it is not highly structured, is not bound to the classroom, and may or may not be encouraged by an institution. Informal learning also includes incidental learning, which is learning that occurs as a consequence of another activity, such as the completion of a task or an interpersonal interaction. Many health care professionals, including athletic trainers and nurses, engage in informal learning activities more often than formalized continuing education activities, particularly because these activities are viewed as a means to enhance clinical skills and abilities.[5] Although formal activities are necessary and effective, particularly to maintain certification or licensure as well as to advance the knowledge of the health care professional, informal learning activities appear to stimulate the interest of and promote learning for the health care and medical professional more so than formal activities.[5]

Consequently, the instructional methods discussed in this chapter were selected based not only on the content to be addressed but also on what the authors feel are appropriate for the types of learners found across the medical and sports professions. Evidence demonstrates that adult learners learn best when the instructional methods are learner centered, allowing them to draw upon their previous experiences and perceived needs.[6–9] Adult learners often seek out new information that directly relates to their current needs, position, and career goals.[10] They also are goal-oriented, practical, often critical of new information being presented, and self-motivated. Educators should keep these characteristics in mind as they motivate, connect, and engage the learner through established objectives, present realistic and appropriate examples, provide feedback and reinforcement, and allow them the opportunity to transfer knowledge gained to novel situations.

Considerations for Planning Continuing Education

Characteristics of different settings may affect the manner in which important information on sudden death is presented, because the learners and context can vary. For instance, depending on the venue, there may be different medical personnel (e.g., ATCs, MDs, PTs, RNs, EMTs) involved in the care of athletes, as well as nonmedical personnel who play differing roles (e.g., coaches, parents). Time, availability and accessibility of equipment, and the background knowledge of participants all help dictate the manner in which one should educate different constituents about the prevention of sudden death in sport. This chapter discusses four common venues—some that support more formal learning and others that allow for more informal learning opportunities—where these previously mentioned factors play different roles (Table 16.1). Each venue and issues specific to a given event (e.g., a professional track meet versus a high school football tournament) provide different advantages and disadvantages for carrying out one's educational goals.

Traditional Educational Setting

College courses in an athletic training education program (ATEP), sports medicine fellowships, or a physician-type home learning curriculum are traditional educational settings that can last a few weeks or months. They may follow regulated educational competencies, use traditional educational materials such as textbooks and journal articles, and may include a hands-on laboratory portion. One of the advantages of this setting is the ability of the educator to develop a strong rapport with the audience, which can aid in the delivery of material, retention of material for the learner, and, in some cases, allow learners to feel more comfortable and more engaged in the learning activities. In the classroom setting, the educator is able to capitalize on a variety of teaching strategies that would not only best suit learners and meet the educational objectives of the material being presented but also assist in their retention of the objectives (see Table 16.1). The traditional educational setting also allows the material presented to be covered in depth so that learning outcomes can include mastery of particular subject areas. Time, however, can become a disadvantage in this setting if a program has a large number of regulated competencies to cover in the course of a semester. In this case, the learning outcome may shift to exposure to a broad range of topics rather than mastery of a few. Overall, however, this educational setting has many advantages, including availability of equipment, accessibility of resources, and the time to adequately cover all the necessary information.

Professional Development

Staff training (e.g., review of emergency action plans [EAPs]), workshops, mini-courses, symposiums, and any sessions used as continuing education may last a few hours or several days. One of the advantages of the professional development setting is that the educational goals can be very specific; therefore, a topic can be thoroughly addressed. In staff training, this setting could be effective in implementing new treatment strategies or making revisions to EAPs. One disadvantage of this educational setting is that if this training is performed annually, some employees may view it as another job requirement and may not use it as an opportunity for professional development and growth. Another potential disadvantage of this setting is the level of competency of the personnel; some may be at different levels given their previous educational and professional preparation regarding certain causes of sudden death. Related to this, another challenge is the existence of different priorities among personnel regarding selecting the section of the session topic.

TABLE 16.1 Differences Across Common Educational Venues for Sports Medicine

Venue	Approximate Time	Audience's Background	Availability and Accessibility of Materials/Equipment	Group Size	Optimal Teaching Strategies	Some Advantages	Some Disadvantages
Acute, singular athletic event	15 min to 2 hours	Varied	Emergency equipment for basic first aid and advanced life support	Ranges from small groups to hundreds	Background connection Algorithms	Information disseminated to large number of health care professionals	Limited amount of time to cover many topics
Professional development	Several hours to several days	Medical professionals	Usually uses the equipment regularly available to them (spine board, AED, etc.) to review EAP	Small to moderate	Experiential learning Strategic questioning	Provides an opportunity for continuing education	Not targeted to individual participant's needs
Clinical setting, rotations, practicums (part of 3 to 8 weeks)	20 to 50 hours per week for a semester (varies)	Student	Depends on site of clinical rotation (e.g., a high school may not have some essential equipment, such as an immersion tub or AED)	Ranges from 1 to 15 students	Capitalize on teachable moments Dialogic discussion Experiential learning Strategic questioning	Allows hands-on, real-life experiences	Exposure to incidence of injury may be low depending on setting; may have disconnect between classroom and clinical experiences
Traditional educational setting—credentials, courses for both athletic training and medical students	Semester	Student	Depends on classroom or laboratory equipment available	Approximately 1 to 15 students	Lecture Experiential learning Dialogic discussion	Ability for in-depth focus on particular conditions	May rely on hypothetical situations and therefore lack a sense of realism

AED, automated external defibrillator.

Clinical Rotation

Clinical rotations comprise real-life, field-setting opportunities for students, such as internships and practicums, and can take place at various settings, including professional, intercollegiate, or high school athletic events, physical therapy clinics, and physicians' offices. They can last a few weeks, a semester, or longer. A definite advantage of this educational setting is the potential for real-life hands-on experiences followed by direct feedback from a clinical instructor for enhanced performance. However, a disadvantage of this setting is that because of the decreased incidence of catastrophic injuries in athletic settings, learners may have a limited exposure (if any) to a potentially life-threatening injury. Another disadvantage is the possibility of a disconnect between what is taught in the classroom and the experiences learners undergo in their clinical assignments. The ability of the clinical supervisor or instructor to identify and use a teachable moment is the key to a positive learning experience and can serve as the catalyst for bridging the gap between classroom knowledge and clinical application.

Acute Athletic Event

Mass medical tent meetings take place in large-scale athletic events (e.g., marathons, triathlons) where a large number of medical professionals (including MDs, ATCs, EMTs, and/or RNs) come together to care for injured individuals. These meetings may last anywhere from 15 minutes to a couple of hours prior to the start of the event. These educational settings have advantages, particularly when the medical director is very familiar with the event, the course, the volunteers, and so forth. In this situation, the medical director can use the allotted time (however brief) to effectively disseminate the most valuable information to a large number of medical professionals. Some disadvantages may occur when the medical director does not know the audience or their expertise well or when a variety of medical professionals with diverse educational backgrounds come together to deliver health care with differing plans of action. For example, some medical professionals may believe that tympanic temperature should be used to rule out exertional heat stroke during a road race whereas others believe that only a rectal temperature measure should be used. These differences are significant and can greatly affect the course of action when providing care. Therefore, it is essential that the medical director ensure that everyone is on the same page.

Overall, each venue for sport medicine–related education has its distinct advantages and disadvantages. Knowing the audience and their level of expertise, the goals and specific needs of the athletes and medical providers in each of these settings, and the strengths of each of these settings will enhance the learning process to aid in the prevention of sudden death in sport.

Tips on Overcoming Constraints

Educating others on the prevention of sudden death in the athletic setting does not always occur free of obstacles. Educators may face a number of constraints pertaining to the time available, the audience's background or relationship with the educator, the availability or accessibility, or both, of equipment necessary in the treatment of an emergency situation, and group size. Regardless, educators should try to mitigate these circumstances to the best of their abilities to achieve their learning objectives. This section offers some suggestions.

Time

Although one may not encounter a life-threatening condition in the athletic setting as often as other conditions (e.g., ankle sprains, anterior cruciate ligament [ACL] tears), it is still imperative to allocate time to cover the prevention, recognition, and treatment of medical emergencies. In a mass medical tent, it is not uncommon for there to be a 30-minute to 1-hour meeting prior to the start of the event during which emergency protocols need to be quickly explained to medical staff who have volunteered to provide medical coverage for the event. The medical director must choose which topics to cover in more depth than others. The decision on which topics to cover may depend on previous experiences, environmental conditions on the day of the event, or the experience and knowledge of the medical volunteers. In this example of a mass medical event, it would behoove the medical director to spend time in the days leading to the event offering a pretraining type of workshop with a group of medical professionals of varying credentials who will serve as leaders during the event and ensure that the proper protocols are being followed. These meetings can include Web-based learning programs and the review of EAPs and other specific documents that should be discussed prior to the event.

Other educational forums may encounter time constraints in juggling many topics in little time. Sometimes having to cover many competencies in the classroom results in a superficial pass at many topics rather than focusing on fewer content areas. The technique of learning over time can be used, for instance, in a classroom setting or in a clinical rotation, when a topic is introduced. Essential learning objectives, such as those that would be included in the prevention, recognition, and management of an emergency situation, can be included in various courses across a curriculum to ensure that students are being exposed to the information several times, across several months or years, and are also able to apply it in a clinical setting.

Audience's Background and Instructor's Relationship with the Audience

One of the most important factors to consider when educating others on the prevention of sudden death in sport is your audience. In traditional educational settings, such as a classroom or clinical rotation, the educator usually has time to get to know the students and earn their trust. However, in other settings, such as continuing education seminars or mass medical events, the group leader or medical director may have limited knowledge of the audience's background. This obstacle can be overcome by having attendees complete a basic survey prior to the session (e.g., position, years in the field, self-analysis of knowledge of each condition). To enhance learning and prevent personnel from feeling intimidated, the meeting or workshop can be set up so that personnel can sit or work with anyone they already know. Eliciting feedback from the audience at the beginning to capture their general background can help the educator to adapt the session to the learners' needs. Questions regarding past experiences with a particular condition may also assist in capturing the audience and helping them identify with the person leading the meeting or seminar.

If the instructor knows the audience well, the goal is to make a personal connection with them. For example, an athletic trainer with high school experience speaking to a group of other high school athletic trainers can easily grasp their attention and make a connection by simply starting off with examples of issues in that setting. If an instructor is speaking to individuals with different educational backgrounds, such as a physician speaking to athletic trainers, it is important to display both an understanding and an appreciation of their role in the sports medicine team and how this teamwork is essential in an emergency situation.

Availability and Accessibility of Materials or Equipment

The availability and accessibility of equipment can sometimes be a constraint in the learning process. Working with others in the profession to combine resources is a great way to have enough equipment to go around. This teamwork approach also results in the formation of a support system. For example, an athletic training education program can join forces with the athletic training staff of the same university to train both the staff and the students on various aspects of the EAP (e.g., spine boarding protocol, exertional heat stroke [EHS] protocol with rectal thermometry and cold water immersion, dealing with cardiac emergencies). The training also can be set up to have different stations so that members of the audience can rotate between stations and interact with one another.

Group Size

Group size can impede the learning process if not addressed adequately. Combining efforts with colleagues at other organizations or schools and ensuring there are sufficient educators for the number of attendees present can alleviate the disconnect that may occur with larger groups. When dealing with larger group sizes, such as in a mass medical tent or large symposium, address lower-level learning goals as a whole group and then use small groups to address higher-level learning goals.

When working in small groups, assign a specific role to each individual in a group. For example, if reviewing two-person cardiopulmonary resuscitation and automated external defibrillator (CPR/AED) skills with four people, assign one person to be the first responder leader who will do respirations, another to do compressions, the third rescuer to be in charge of the AED, and a fourth to facilitate the scenario, call 911, and so on. Supply various scenarios and have the individuals rotate through the different roles so that everyone has had a chance to experience the different responsibilities and gain confidence with each of the roles.

Learning Goals for Causes of Sudden Death in Sport

Prior to teaching various causes of sudden death in sport, it is imperative to know the amount of time allotted, the venue, the event, and inherent risks in the sport, as well as the audience and the level of knowledge expected. Depending on the amount of time allotted, medical directors may have to pick and choose the conditions for which participants are at a greater risk on that particular day. For instance, in cold environmental conditions, medical staff may be inclined to spend more time on the treatment of hypothermia in the medical tent. As depicted in Table 16.1, the coverage of topics related to sudden death may vary depending on the various settings and the amount of time dedicated to the session. Regardless of these situational differences, it is imperative to ensure that the take-home message is the same. **Table 16.2** lists learning goals across all causes of sudden death in sport covered in this text. Each condition should be properly defined so that the audience is clear on the topic being discussed, particularly if there are various points of view on a particular condition. Regardless of the format of delivery, the goal is that at the conclusion of the session the audience leaves with a clear understanding of the key points for the prevention, recognition, and treatment of these conditions.

Table 16.2 provides an overview of the learning goals for the most pertinent causes of sudden death that should be addressed with all personnel across all venues. The table begins with the preventive measures for each condition. Based on the Strength of Recommendation Taxonomy (SORT), the grades A, B, or C can be given to a particular preventive strategy to indicate the level of evidence in the literature supporting that strategy.[11] For instance, a grade of A indicates that a recommendation is based on consistent and high-quality experimental data. A grade of B signifies that a particular recommendation is based on limited or inconsistent good-quality data, whereas a grade of C reflects a recommendation based on case studies, opinion, or usual practice. The table then addresses the learning goals necessary in the recognition and treatment of each cause of sudden death. The "Recognition" column lists the most significant indicators. This information is followed by both immediate and long-term treatment options that should be taken.

Finally, because even the most diligent care can result in a fatality, the table indicates the level of evidence that supports the likelihood of an ability to prevent a fatality for each cause of sudden death. It is important to note that a strength of recommendation of C in this column is not indicative of improper treatment or less likelihood of survival. Because of the potential for death in these conditions, it may be difficult or near impossible to conduct consistent-quality research on various treatment options with human subjects. For instance, because it is known that using an AED within minutes for a patient in cardiac arrest increases the chance of survival, it would be unethical to conduct an experiment in which individuals in an experimental group would receive the treatment and others in the control group would not. Therefore, when using Table 16.2, it is imperative to be aware that a grade of C only signifies that the recommendation is based on case studies, consensus, usual practice, and so forth, rather than consistent evidence from randomized controlled trials.

Despite the inability to always prevent one of the dangerous conditions listed in Table 16.2 from occurring (i.e., a cardiac emergency may not always be preventable), fatalities from these conditions can often be prevented. Preventing a fatality may require proper education regarding the prevention of the condition (e.g., proper tackling techniques to prevent cervical injury), proper recognition of a condition (e.g., signs and symptoms, such as low blood sodium levels in the diagnosis of hyponatremia), and proper emergency management of a condition (e.g., cold water immersion for exertional heat stroke). It is essential for medical professionals to comprehend the most recent, evidence-based clinical practices when it comes to sudden-death conditions in sport; the key points discussed in each chapter in this book as well as those outlined in Table 16.2 help provide this knowledge.

Ensuring that medical professionals have the equipment to properly treat athletes in an emergency situation is also paramount. For example, although an athletic trainer may have the knowledge of how to

TABLE 16.2 Learning Goals Across Causes of Sudden Death

Cause of Sudden Death	Learning Goals					
	Prevention	Ability to Prevent Condition	Recognition	Treatment		Ability to Prevent Fatality
				Immediate	Long-Term	
Head injury	1. Proper use of equipment (helmet, pads, etc.).	C	1. CNS dysfunction (headache, dizziness, postural instability, altered LOC, blurred vision, loss of alertness, confusion, etc.).	1. Thorough on-field assessment of injury (primary survey, secondary survey, general observation, etc.) to determine initial severity.	1. Computerized neuropsychological tests, ideally used in comparison with baseline scores to determine cognitive recovery over time (BESS and GSC can be used in accordance).	B
	2. Adaptation; respect for rules.	C	2. Educational intervention.	2. Cranial nerve testing, BESS, SAC, or SCAT2.	2. Continued observation of symptoms.	B
	3. Increased cervical muscle strength.	B	3. Retrograde/anterograde amnesia.	3. Use of Graded Symptom Checklist (GSC).	3. Although important to manage on a case-by-case basis, a stepwise return-to-play process may begin once athlete is asymptomatic.	C

	Prevention		Recognition	Treatment	Return to play	
Exertional sickling	1. SCT athletes should be allowed to set their own pace.	B	1. Weakness > pain. 2. Slumps to ground. 3. Can talk at first. 4. Muscles "normal." 5. Temp < 39.4°C (103°F). 6. Can occur early in the workout.	Practice EAP. Check vital signs. Supplemental oxygen. Cool the athlete if needed. Failing immediate improvement, call 911, attach an AED, and start an IV.	Individualize.	B
	2. SCT athletes should build up slowly in training, with longer breathers, and extreme performance tests should be avoided.	B				
	3. At onset of struggling, SCT athletes should stop and get help.	B				
	4. Predisposing factors should be controlled.	B				
Exertional heat stroke	1. Adjust practice times, sessions, and equipment according to environmental conditions and fitness level.	B	1. CNS dysfunction (mental status change, dizziness, collapse, irritability, irrational behavior, confusion). 2. Core body temperature > 40°C (104°F), measured via rectal probe immediately following collapse.	1. Cold water immersion until core body temperature is at or below 38.9°C (102°F). 2. Monitor vitals. 3. After body temperature is below 38.9°C (102°F), transport to the hospital and monitor blood work for elevated enzyme levels.	Return to play should involve a gradual introduction and consequent combinations of exercise, heat, and protective equipment under the supervision of a medical professional.	B
	2. Ensure fluids are available and easily accessible before, during, and after practice. Encourage rehydration.	B				
	3. Allow athletes to acclimatize to the heat over the course of the first 10 to 14 days by gradually increasing intensity and duration of exercise.	B				

(continued)

TABLE 16.2 Learning Goals Across Causes of Sudden Death (*Continued*)

Cause of Sudden Death	Prevention	Ability to Prevent Condition	Recognition	Immediate	Long-Term	Ability to Prevent Fatality
			Learning Goals			
				Treatment		
Cardiac	1. Cardiovascular screening in athletes inclusive of ECG can reliably detect conditions predisposing to SCA.	B	1. High suspicion of SCA should be maintained in any collapsed and unresponsive athlete.	1. Early activation of the EMS system and call for additional rescuer assistance.	1. Induced hypothermia for resuscitated SCA victims with VF arrest can improve survival and decrease neurologic complications.	A
	2. Emergency response planning for SCA should ensure access to early defibrillation.	B	2. Myoclonic activity is common after SCA in young athletes and should not be mistaken for a seizure.	2. Early CPR.	2. The majority of athletes with a history of malignant ventricular arrhythmias, SCA, or conditions predisposing to SCA should be restricted from participation in moderate-intensity and high-intensity sports.	B
	3. The presence of trained rescuers to initiate CPR and access to AEDs can greatly improve survival after SCA.	A		3. Immediate retrieval of the AED.		
				4. An AED should be applied as soon as possible in any collapsed and unresponsive athlete for rhythm analysis and defibrillation if indicated.		

Anaphylaxis and hypothermia	1. Athletes with a history of anaphylaxis should have an anaphylaxis emergency action plan, carry injectable epinephrine, and practice avoidance of known triggers.	1. Because of the unpredictable nature of an acute anaphylactic reaction, recognition of the signs and symptoms is key to low morbidity and mortality rates.	1. Early recognition of anaphylaxis should immediately be followed by activation of EMS. Assess vital signs; place victim in a comfortable position that minimizes movement; administer epinephrine if trained, remove trigger if possible; administer supplemental oxygen. Begin CPR if respiratory distress is present.	C
	2. Older (>60), low-fitness, and low-body-fat athletes are more at risk for hypothermia and should be carefully monitored when participating in cold-weather sports and physical activity.	2. Anaphylaxis is likely when one of the following three criteria is met: (a) acute onset with involvement of skin or mucosa with either respiratory compromise or decreased BP; (b) rapid involvement of two or more of the following after an exposure: skin or mucosa, respiratory compromise, decreased BP and/or persistent GI symptoms; (c) decreased BP after exposure to a known allergen.	2. Epinephrine (adrenaline) is the gold standard in the treatment of acute anaphylaxis. The drug should be administered at the presentation of initial signs and symptoms of anaphylaxis.	C
	3. Avoidance of alcohol, use of higher-calorie diets, layered clothing, and weather watching should be followed by athletes prior to and during exercise in cold weather.	3. Hypothermia, across severity levels, includes a rectal temperature below 35°C (95°F); intense shivering; cold, pale skin; depressed vital signs; and CNS dysfunction.	3. Hypothermic treatments should be initiated by moving the person to a safe environment while minimizing movement of the victim. If vital signs cannot be found after extensive assessment, CPR should begin.	C

(continued)

TABLE 16.2 Learning Goals Across Causes of Sudden Death (*Continued*)

Cause of Sudden Death	Prevention	Ability to Prevent Condition	Recognition	Immediate	Long-Term	Ability to Prevent Fatality
				Learning Goals		
					Treatment	
Anaphylaxis and hypothermia (*Continued*)				4. Rewarming the trunk, hips to shoulders (and head), through blankets and forced-air commercial products should begin as soon as possible. Rewarming should be a slow process in order to avoid activating cardiac complications.		
Asthma	1. Control asthma symptoms in athletes with known asthma.	B	1. Establish the diagnosis of asthma or exercise-induced bronchospasm.	1. Identify vital signs associated with respiratory failure.	Return to play when asthma is under control. May need to add long-acting medications.	C
	2. Avoid other triggers in athletes with asthma and extrinsic allergens.	B	2. Identify ominous symptoms of respiratory distress.	2. Use short-acting inhaled β-agonist medications and monitor response.		
	3. Encourage the maintenance of good conditioning in the preseason.	C	3. Know the role of peak flow measurements in managing asthma chronically.	3. Other supportive care if available: oxygen, steroids, nebulizer, other inhaled medications.		
	4. Educate about recognition and control of asthma.	C				

Condition	Prevention	Grade	Recognition	Treatment	Treatment Goals	Grade
Spinal cord injuries	1. Ensure safe equipment and facilities.	C	1. Bilateral neurologic findings or complaint.	1. Apply manual in-line cervical stabilization.	1. Support vital signs.	A
	2. Medical personnel should be present at high-risk activities.	B	2. Significant cervical spine pain with or without palpation.	2. Expose airway and maintain breathing.	2. Control inflammation, edema, and secondary injury.	B
	3. Teach and adhere to safety rules.	B	3. Obvious spinal column deformity.	3. Monitor vital signs.	3. Minimize duration of spinal cord compression.	B
	4. Avoid behaviors known to carry risk, such as head-down contact.	B	4. Unconsciousness or altered LOC.	4. Transfer to full-body immobilization device.	4. Restore cervical stabilization.	A
	5. Use properly fitted and maintained protective equipment.	C		5. Transport to Trauma I emergency department.		
	6. Use spotters.	C				
	7. Have and rehearse an EAP.	C				
	8. Use proper training and physical conditioning that match activity requirements.	B				
	9. Perform preparticipation medical evaluations.					
Exertional hyponatremia	1. Athletes should begin exercise euhydrated and after eating normally. A hydration plan should be in place to avoid both hyperhydration and dehydration during exercise.	B	1. Blood Na^+ level < 130 $mEq \cdot L^{-1}$.	1. Administer hypertonic saline (3–5% NaCl).	Return to play/duty should involve a hydration/nutrition plan to avoid recurrence. Also, a monitored and gradual return to activity is warranted.	C
	2. If specific and individual sweat rate and sweat Na^+ concentrations are known, a personalized nutrition and hydration plan can be implemented.	B	2. CNS dysfunction (mental status change, dizziness, collapse, irritability, irrational behavior, confusion, etc.).	2. Monitor vital signs.		
				3. After blood sodium levels are returned to above 130 $mEq \cdot L^{-1}$, if there is an absence of CNS dysfunction, transport to emergency room for blood work and follow-up.		

Abbreviations: AED, automated external defibrillator; BESS, Balance Error Scoring System; BP, blood pressure; CNS, central nervous system; CPR, cardiopulmonary resuscitation; EAP, emergency action plan; ECG, electrocardiogram; EMS, emergency medical services; GI, gastrointestinal; LOC, level of consciousness; SAC, Standardized Assessment of Concussion; SCA, sudden cardiac arrest; SCAT2, Sport Concussion Assessment Tool 2; SCT, sickle cell trait; VF, ventricular fibrillation.
Note: Grades A, B, and C are provided based on SORT.

treat a cardiac emergency, proper treatment may not be possible if an AED is not immediately accessible. As mentioned in Chapter 14 on emergency action planning, having set protocols in place for the treatment of life-threatening conditions will greatly affect whether athletic training staff members, medical tent personnel, or medical professionals in any other setting are prepared to save someone's life. Depending on the venue, the amount of time allotted to discuss the EAP as well as to practice the EAP with hands-on instruction and experience may vary. Knowledge of the proper long-term treatment of various conditions is also imperative in the prevention of sudden death in sport in order to prevent sequelae and ensure an athlete's safe return to participation.

General Teaching Strategies for Different Learning Goals

There are numerous considerations in deciding which teaching method may be most appropriate to use across the various venues. Although several techniques can prove to be effective—including ones that are not highlighted in this chapter—this section offers some guidance on how to make these decisions. The learner and learning context need to be considered first before deciding which learning style the teaching strategies would best support.

Begin by considering your audience and who they are as learners. Ask yourself:

1. What is my relationship with the audience?
2. What is their background knowledge of the given topic?
3. What do they need to learn next?

An audience that trusts you and feels comfortable engaging in the given activities is important in any session. Obviously, the better you know your audience, the easier it will be for you to determine their level of understanding of the topic. For instance, your medical students may know a lot about exertional heat stroke and understand the importance of measuring a patient's rectal temperature but have yet to have the opportunity to do so. Considering your audience is a critical step because you may have an informative session planned, but it could be much too simplistic or complicated for any given group. Go the extra mile to get to know your audience, or even just a few members, prior to the event.

Components related to the learning context of formats that encourage more formal learning and that need your consideration include the time available to teach, the group's size, and the amount of and access to any necessary equipment **(Table 16.3 and Table 16.4)**. We provide some information to help you make the best possible decisions for how to teach, time being the factor that has the greatest impact. The venues tend to dictate the amount of time, but this can certainly vary. We have grouped time spans accordingly:

- Up to about 30 minutes, such as during a briefing at a mass medical team meeting prior to a marathon or during a professional presentation at a symposium
- About 1 hour, such as during a clinical staff meeting or guest lecture in a class
- Several hours, such as during a workshop training session or clinical supervision of a student (e.g., medical rounds, athletic training students in clinical rotations)
- Several days, such as during a course or a professional development session, including staff training for the EAP (e.g., spine boarding, CPR/AED recertification, concussion protocol)

You also will likely teach different group sizes. We consider groups of up to about 25 participants, which could include a class or your staff, and groups with more than 25 people, such as may be present during a workshop at a conference or at a mass medical team meeting. Finally, in some cases you may have sufficient equipment for your audience that is readily available, whereas in other cases its availability may be limited. The accessibility of this equipment will also vary, such as the feasibility of filling a tub with ice and water for the treatment of EHS.

The teaching methods recommended in this chapter have been provided to address different levels and types of learning objectives as well as a variety of various learning environments (e.g., a traditional classroom versus an acute, singular event). These methods, summarized in **Table 16.5**, include background

TABLE 16.3 Considerations for Discussion-Based Teaching Methods as They Relate to Time and Group Size

Time Available	Use of Lecture as It Relates to Time[a]	Group Size[c]	Use of Dialogic Discussions and Strategic Questioning[b]
Up to 30 minutes	Lecture	Up to 25	Not recommended
		Greater than 25	
~1 hour	Limited lecture	Up to 25	Problem-based discussion and strategic questioning
		Greater than 25	Strategic questioning
Several hours	Limited lecture	Up to 25	Problem-based discussion and strategic questioning
		Greater than 25	Strategic questioning
Several days	Limited lecture	Up to 25	Problem-based discussion and strategic questioning

[a] Although lecture can be used effectively over any time period to address lower-level objectives, it should be used sporadically and in conjunction with other teaching methods that allow learners to interact with higher levels of thinking given more time.
[b] Dialogic discussion is more effective with smaller groups. However, you can break down a slightly larger group and have about four to five people interact before moving the discussion back to the whole audience.
[c] The numbers given for group size are approximate.

TABLE 16.4 Considerations for Use of Equipment Related to Time

Time Available	Use of Equipment
Up to 30 minutes	Use equipment to model.
~1 hour	*Very limited amount and accessibility of equipment:* Use equipment to model, then rotate through small groups.
Several hours	*Equipment available and accessible to about ten participants at a given time:* Have groups of about four to five perform the given skill as a second group observes and provides feedback. Have the groups switch roles.
Several days	*Equipment available and accessible to about five participants at a given time:* Have small groups perform the given skill simultaneously.

connection, dialogic discussion, experiential learning, directed instruction, lectures, teachable moments, and strategic questioning. The teaching strategies are grouped according to whether they present more formal or informal learning opportunities. Both skill- and cognitive-based objectives are addressed. The following section discusses each method and its applicability to preventing sudden death in sport. **Table 16.6** highlights factors that should be considered to effectively implement the suggested teaching methods, and **Table 16.7** lists do's and don'ts for the various methods.

		TABLE 16.5	Summary of Teaching Methods and Implementation		

Teaching Strategy	Description	Targeted Learning Goals	Advantages	Disadvantages	Application to Various Venues
Background connection	Connection made between experience and knowledge	Development of professional practice beliefs	Learn by doing and experience	Time	All
Dialogic discussion	Development of own opinions and meanings regarding information	Demonstrate higher-order thinking	Ownership over learning Development of critical-thinking skills	Time consuming Use only with small groups	All
Directed instruction	Modeling with constructive feedback on performance	Hands-on acquisition of skills	Active learning by student Promote psychometric skill mastery	Basic skills only Time for instructor to model and provide feedback	Traditional setting Clinical setting
Experiential learning	Application to realistic situation in simulated fashion	Demonstrate knowledge and skill application	Development of skill competence	Time	Traditional setting Clinical setting
Lecture	Transmission of knowledge from instructor to student	Understanding of concepts and theory	Convey important concepts and facts Direct	Limits skill-based implementation or use of critical-thinking skills	All
Teachable moment and strategic questioning	Real-life application of knowledge and skills (not fabricated)	Real-life and real-time application of skills and knowledge	Real-time development of skills and confidence Development of higher-order thinking	Recognition of the situation Timing Responsibilities of the instructor	Clinical setting Acute, singular event

This chapter draws from adult education principles and presents a simple strategy to be used regardless of the instructional method selected to help guide the session. The mnemonic *backwards ABCs* refers to *c*apture, *b*uild, and *a*pply—a strategy that attempts to tap into learners' life experiences, speak to their given social roles, and address a problem on which they immediately can apply the knowledge being imparted. Prior to the delivery of information, the adult learner must be engaged, ready to learn, and prepared for the material to be discussed and must understand the purpose of the learning session;

TABLE 16.6 Factors to Consider for Teaching Methods

Teaching Method	Minimum Level of Connection to Audience	Time	Maximum Group Size	Types of Objectives	Equipment Availability and Accessibility
Directed instruction	Any level of connection	A minimum of 1 hour	Up to 25	Lower-level skills	Need availability and accessibility
Experiential learning	Any level of connection	A minimum of 1 hour	Up to 25	Lower-level skills	Need availability and accessibility
Lecture	Any level of connection	With sessions of up to 30 minutes; kept brief during other sessions	No maximum	Lower-level skills	Dependent on situation to model
Problem-based discussions	High; participants need to feel safe to debate	A minimum of 1 hour	Up to 25	High-level skills	Dependent on situation
Strategic questioning	Medium	A minimum of 30 minutes	Up to 25	Various	Dependent on situation

TABLE 16.7 Do's and Don'ts of Teaching Methods and Venues

Teaching Method	Do	Don't
Experiential learning	• Use personal experiences to help create authenticity for the activity • Establish clear objectives for the experience or activity • Allow for reflection, sharing, and application	• Rush or limit time for self-reflection and analysis • Downplay the personal experiences and thoughts of the learner
Directed instruction	• Provide clear, detailed instructions • Provide enough time for application and feedback • Encourage continual application of the skill • Monitor progress and provide positive, but constructive, feedback on performance	• Use ambiguous statements • Try to incorporate more than one skill at a time • Move on before a skill has been mastered

(continued)

| TABLE 16.7 | Do's and Don'ts of Teaching Methods and Venues (*Continued*) |

Teaching Method	Do	Don't
Lecture	• Use when you have a limited amount of time • Reflect on delivery, because it is important • Capture the audience • Involve the audience in multiple ways, such as through structured questions • Use sparingly with other teaching methods if you have more than an hour with your audience	• Be aware of time (more than 20 minutes will lose attention) • Rely on a lecture if you have an hour with your audience
Teachable moment	• Recognize opportunities across all settings • Use with any learner • Incorporate multiple teaching methods	• Allow barriers to hinder its use • Think there is not enough time to utilize • Underestimate its impact on learners
Problem-based discussions	• Use with higher-level objectives • Allow learners to grapple with the topic • Encourage multiple perspectives • Allow your audience to talk more than you do • Encourage participants to consider one another's ideas	• Take on the role as the sole authority • Evaluate too many of the learners' contributions • Avoid conflicting views
Strategic questioning	• Be purposeful with questioning • Ask open-ended questions • Encourage exploration • Take into consideration the learners' knowledge level and prior experiences when developing questions	• Ask close-ended questions • Be quick to provide an answer

capture helps achieve this goal. One way to help the audience to be engaged and captured is to provide relevant background reading or literature. Once the audience has an understanding of the purpose of the education and is engaged, the educator can *build* and expand upon the learner's existing knowledge. This is the nucleus of the session and is grounded in the objectives. Finally, the learner must be provided opportunities to *apply* the newfound knowledge.

Specific Instructional Strategies

background connection Activities that support both formal and informal learning opportunities by encouraging learners to connect their previous experiences and knowledge with sudden-death conditions.

Background connection activities support both formal and informal learning opportunities by encouraging learners to connect their previous experiences and knowledge with sudden-death conditions. These activities are founded on the perspective that adults learn within a social context and therefore must have opportunities to construct their knowledge of the topic at hand by being engaged within a similar context.[12] Dialogue is often the most important element for this approach to teaching, because it engages both the learner and the instructor.[13]

Using exertional heat stroke as an example, first have the learners write and discuss their trepidations regarding the use of rectal thermometers prior to learning how to accurately measure and record a core body temperature. Encourage them to reflect upon how their clinical instructors, mentors, and athletes might feel as well, and use the reflections as a way to dispel the myths or trepidations associated with the technique. Consider sharing a previous experience with the use of rectal temperature assessment and your personal trepidations; this personal story may help learners relate to your experiences and help them feel more comfortable and interested in the material to be covered. Moreover, provide statistics that demonstrate that they are not alone in discomfort with use of the technique, as research shows that only 18% of athletic trainers use rectal thermometers when diagnosing EHS.[2] Once this background has been established, provide them with the necessary information regarding the practicality of use, the validity of the rectal thermometer (or lack of validity in other devices), and the accessibility of the supplies necessary for implementation of the technique. Finally, allow them to apply the new information learned by presenting them with case studies or scenarios.

Formal Learning Opportunities

Several teaching strategies support more formal learning opportunities and address both skills and cognitive aspects of understanding sudden death in sport. This section begins with lectures, a teaching format that may be the most familiar to readers, then presents directed instruction and experiential learning, which allow learners to immediately apply their skill-based knowledge. Finally, dialogic discussions engage learners in higher-level cognitive objectives, allowing learners to have more authority regarding the direction of the conversation compared with a more instructor-directed lecture.

Lectures can be effective in conveying basic information in a brief amount of time but can be ineffective in stimulating higher-level thinking and gauging student learning. Lectures would be appropriate to use for presenting, for example, the pathophysiology of conditions, the signs and symptoms associated with a particular condition, and the policies and procedures related to the diagnosis or treatment of a condition, as well as for reviewing protocols. It is important to realize that the use of lecture is often the foundation of most of the teaching methods discussed in this chapter, as the learner needs a certain amount of background prior to learning; however, varied instruction is important to help with the learner's retention and application of material.

lectures An instructional method that is teacher centered and takes place in a formal setting.

The use of the backwards ABCs is beneficial when planning a lecture. Before imparting the background information to learners, the instructor must find a way to grab their attention. Using emergency planning as an example, one might share the story of the college football referee whose life was saved due to effective implementation of their EAP by the Syracuse sports medicine staff. Because the actual footage is accessible, consider playing the tape prior to the start of the presentation. Upon completion of the presentation, allow the audience to ask questions but also provide an opportunity for them to apply the information shared. This can be accomplished by asking simple questions such as, "If you were in the same situation, would you have been prepared?" Using the backwards ABCs, the following is a sample outline for a lecture.

Sample Lecture: Emergency Planning and Cardiac Issues

1. Capture
   a. Review a video clip of an EAP being implemented (e.g., college referee and Syracuse medical staff).
   b. Present a case involving the failure to implement emergency planning, or discuss the successful outcomes of planning.
2. Build background
   a. Review the following statements on emergency planning/preparedness, cardiac issues, and AEDs:
      i. National Athletic Trainers' Association (NATA) position statement: Emergency Planning in Athletics[14]

      ii. American Medical Society for Sports Medicine (AMSSM) consensus statement: Sideline Preparedness for the Team Physician[15]

     iii. NATA official statement: Automated External Defibrillators[16]

     iv. NATA official statement: Commotio Cordis[17]

      v. NATA[18]/AMSSM[19] consensus statement: Recommendations on Emergency Preparedness and Management of Sudden Cardiac Arrest in High School and College Athletic Programs

3. Apply learning

  a. Solicit audience involvement by asking questions such as, "What would you do in this position?" or "What obstacles have you faced when planning?"

  b. Have the audience reflect on their current EAPs, and determine whether they are fully prepared for an emergency.

directed instruction A method that uses a combination of modeling, performance, and constructive feedback for skill instruction and mastery. This teaching method is most effective for communicating psychomotor skill development, not complex theoretical concepts. Directed instruction provides learners with the opportunity to apply new knowledge and associated skills in a controlled environment with immediate feedback on performance.

Directed instruction, like lecture, is an instructional method that is teacher centered and takes place in a more formal setting. However, it is a method that uses a combination of modeling, performance, and constructive feedback for skill instruction and mastery. The teaching method is most effective for communicating psychomotor skill development, not complex theoretical concepts.[20] At the core, directed instruction provides the learner with the opportunity to apply new knowledge and associated skills in a controlled environment with immediate feedback on performance. There is constant interaction between the learner and the instructor. The learner must be actively engaged in the task(s) and be willing to accept feedback, whereas the instructor clearly defines the objectives, provides step-by-step instructions (modeling can be a part of this), and provides feedback during application.

There are many examples for which directed instruction can be used regarding sudden death in sport, including rectal temperature assessment, EpiPen training, and AED administration. Spine boarding an athlete with a suspected cervical neck injury is an ideal example for the use of directed instruction. Prior to the start of the lesson, capture the learners by providing a situation in which you have spine boarded an injured athlete or show a video demonstrating the correct technique. The video provides a good foundation for discussion prior to demonstration of the skill as well as models the correct implementation of the skill set. The following outline provides more suggestions regarding the use of directed instruction to teach proper spine boarding techniques.

Sample Directed Instruction: Spine Boarding

1. Capture

  a. Share a personal experience with spine boarding an athlete.

  b. Have the students share, drawing upon their clinical experiences, a situation in which they were involved in spine boarding an athlete.

2. Build background

  a. Cover NATA's position statement on the acute management of the cervical spine injured athlete.[21]

  b. Provide only the most crucial information regarding proper spine boarding techniques, as set forth in the position statement.

experiential learning A method that allows for firsthand application of skills and knowledge, resulting in a realistic application of a learner's knowledge. Experiential learning requires learners to reflect upon their experiences to promote understanding and skill development and is often implemented in real time.

3. Apply learning

  a. Make sure all learners practice applying manual stabilization of the head.

  b. Simulate real-life conditions.

  c. Videotape the experience, then review it with the group to provide feedback on performance.

Experiential learning is a method that allows for firsthand application of skills and knowledge, resulting in a realistic application of a learner's knowledge. Experiential learning, like directed instruction, is activity centered, but differs in its facilitation and main objective. Ultimately, experiential learning requires learners to reflect on their experiences to promote understanding and skill development and is often implemented in real time (e.g., clinical rotation experience, residency). This instructional method is ideal for concepts related to preventing sudden death in sport for many reasons; most important, however, is the need for the learner to have authentic experiences in order to retain and master necessary skills.[22] Successful implementation of experiential learning requires the learner to be actively engaged in the process, have the opportunity to reflect upon the experience, and possess the knowledge and ability to critically analyze the situation. Experiential learning is not only a great teaching tool for the athletic training or medical student but also an effective tool for the adult learner partaking in continuing education units.

With any given situation, incorporate experiential learning by providing time for exploration ("doing it"), sharing ("What happened?"), processing ("What is important?" or "What needs to be changed?"), generalizing ("So what?"), and application ("Now what?"). An example of implementing experiential learning is to have the learner use cold water immersion to treat an exertional heat stroke in a laboratory setting or to have a student in a clinical rotation run baseline testing sessions for a group of athletes with the Balance Error Scoring System (BESS) as a preventive measure for concussion management.

Sample Experiential Learning: Cold Water Immersion for Treatment of Exertional Heat Stroke

1. Capture
   a. Dispel myths about using cold water immersion (e.g., budgetary constraints or the thought that rapid cooling will initiate seizures).
2. Build background
   a. Refer to Chapter 5 on EHS and the following position statements:
      i. NATA position statement: Exertional Heat Illnesses[23]
      ii. American College of Sports Medicine (ACSM) position stand: Exertional Heat Illness During Training and Competition[24]
   b. Include information regarding set-up, monitoring of core body temperature, and removal from the tub.
3. Apply learning
   a. Encourage all learners to experience cold water immersion (both being immersed and performing the skill).
   b. Provide medical coverage at an event at which this modality would be commonly used (e.g., Falmouth Road Race, Marine Corp Marathon, among others).

Dialogic discussions, which are rooted in the premise that learning is a social process, encourage higher-level thinking by promoting problem solving and learning through open-ended activities that challenge students to make decisions and critically apply their knowledge.[12,13,25] Unlike lectures, the educator is not disseminating knowledge, but rather is facilitating learning by challenging students to reflect on their perspectives and beliefs when making decisions. Meaningful dialogic discussions are meant to encourage disagreements among the group, which they then should work out based on evidence. This approach can encourage and promote teamwork and capitalizes on a learner's previous experiences and knowledge.

dialogic discussion A method of encouraging higher-level thinking by promoting problem solving and learning through open-ended activities, which challenge students to make decisions and critically apply their knowledge. Dialogic discussion facilitates learning by challenging students to reflect upon their perspectives and beliefs when making decisions.

Unlike strategic questions (discussed later), dialogic discussion challenges learners to recall their cognitive knowledge and appraise their experiences and beliefs to respond to a particular question or problem. Like strategic questioning, the main aim dialogic discourse: is to stimulate higher-level functioning. For example, when referencing cervical spine injuries in an emergency procedures course or annual staff meeting, raise the question "How would you handle a situation in which an EMT attempts to supersede your authority as the individual applying manual stabilization to a suspected cervical neck injury?" Ask others whether or not they agree with this approach and to provide support for their positions, which may include some alternatives. Disagreements between learners will occur and should be anticipated.

Sample Dialogic Discussion: Spine Boarding and Cervical Spine Care

1. Capture
   a. Describe a situation in which optimal care was not provided to an athlete or patient with a suspected spinal column injury.
   b. Ask: "What would you want to be done differently if you were that athlete? Why would you want that to change?" Follow up with others to have them weigh in on the proposals offered.
2. Build background
   a. Refer to Chapter 7 on cervical spine injuries.
   b. Review the following NATA position statements:
      i. Acute Management of the Cervical Spine-Injured Athlete[21]
      ii. Head-Down Contact and Spearing in Tackle Football[26]
3. Apply learning
   a. Ask: "How would you handle a situation in which an EMT attempts to supersede your authority as the individual applying manual stabilization?"
   b. Follow up with: "What steps would you take to prevent this situation from happening?"

Informal Learning Opportunities

Although they are not always aware of their learning, adults also learn from less formal situations,[4] so it is important for instructors to realize that they can serve as facilitators in this process. Informal learning opportunities are usually not considered as meeting the continuing education requirement, but rather as a means to promote and advance clinical practice and patient care.[5] Strategic questioning and teachable moments are instructional methods often used to help promote learning and critical thinking for health care and medical providers.[27–29] Additionally, the two methods can be highly effective when combined.

strategic questioning A type of questioning that requires the educator or clinical instructor to ask purposeful questions that challenge learners to analyze the situation and solve the problem. Strategic questioning is helpful in developing critical-thinking skills but requires some planning and anticipation on the instructor's part.

Strategic questioning is meant to evaluate learners' comprehension level and their understanding of the relevance and importance of information, as well as their opinions and beliefs. Strategic questions are important in helping learners develop critical thinking skills, a fundamental skill for the medical care professional.[30] This type of questioning requires the educator or clinical instructor to ask purposeful questions that challenge the learner to analyze the situation and solve the problem. Moreover, questions are often used to funnel the learner's level of understanding and often follow a pattern: "What?" "So what?" and "Now what?"[28,29] For example, a clinical instructor who is going to start using ImPACT computerized testing for concussion management may pose this question to his or her learners: "What are some barriers you may encounter while implementing baseline testing for concussion prevention?" Follow-up questions would include "How could you overcome those barriers?" and "What issue is most critical to address for a successful outcome?" The questions are not designed as a means of memory recall, but rather for application and evaluation of a situation.

With strategic questioning, learners are able to demonstrate a skill while receiving feedback on performance and to develop confidence, competence, and critical thinking skills simultaneously. Similar to teachable moments (discussed next), strategic questioning is helpful in developing critical thinking skills but requires some planning and anticipation on the instructor's part.[28,29] Recognizing an appropriate situation and when to implement the questioning style is a greater part of the planning process compared with the other teaching methods discussed so far.

When using strategic questioning, remember the importance of making a connection with the learner. For example, after allowing learners to perform the concussion evaluations, have them reflect on the experience. Use this opportunity to impart more information regarding the evaluation while asking purposeful questions. These questions allow learners to draw their own conclusions and reflect on what they learned during the real-life learning experience.

Sample Strategic Questioning: Concussion Management

1. Capture
   a. Present the signs and symptoms of concussions.
   b. Discuss the long-term repercussions of concussions, return to play following a concussion, or the myths commonly associated with concussions.
2. Build background
   a. Review the following position statements:
      i. AMSSM consensus statement: Concussion (Mild Traumatic Brain Injury) and the Team Physician[31]
      ii. NATA position statement: Management of Sport-Related Concussions[32]
      iii. NATA consensus statement on concussion in sport[33]
3. Apply learning
   a. Have learners evaluate their own performance before providing a critique.
   b. Once the evaluation is complete, ask "What is the next step?" or "How will you proceed given the clinical findings?"
   c. Have learners continue with the care and handling of the situation (talk to parents, coaches, etc.).

A **teachable moment** is an important method of instruction, particularly in clinical settings, that helps create authenticity, critical thinking, and the application of knowledge and skills. These concepts are very applicable to medical care as they help the learner transition from the student to the practitioner. The previously mentioned teaching methods require planning; however, teachable moments cannot truly be planned. Rather, needs can be anticipated and recognized. Teachable moments use real-life events to help modify or encourage behavior, and, although hard to capture, they are highly effective tools in promoting learning for the medical or health care student.[27,34] Teachable moments, particularly in the athletic training setting, can provide an authentic experience for the student by allowing for skill development and professional discussion during real-time patient care.[27] Examples include the evaluation of a concussion on the sideline of a football game, a reflection through professional discourse following an injury evaluation, or the implementation of an emergency action plan.

> **teachable moment** An important method of instruction, particularly in the clinical setting, that helps create authenticity, critical thinking, and the application of knowledge and skills. Teachable moments capture real-life events to help modify or encourage behavior, and, although hard to capture, they are highly effective tools in promoting learning for the medical or health care student.

Barriers to the use of this teaching method include time, appropriateness, oversight (a teachable moment not being recognized), and lack of initiative or interest of the parties involved.[27] Despite these barriers, it is important to realize that although it may not be appropriate to immediately discuss or allow for application by the learner, professional discourse following the teachable moment can be just as effective for learning. This ultimately becomes a mentoring and modeling of professional behaviors, which is also important for learning.

Conclusion

This chapter has outlined four specific educational venues in which health care and medical care professionals may have the opportunity to disseminate and discuss information regarding the prevention of sudden death in sport. For additional resources, please see the selected references.[35–38] Each venue presents various advantages and disadvantages; however, when the learner is considered along with the given context of learning (the venue), decisions about how to support the learning process become clearer. It is important to remember that health care and medical professionals will use knowledge and skills with which they feel comfortable and medically trained; therefore, we must continue to provide educational opportunities to facilitate the implementation of best practices, especially when it comes to the prevention of sudden death in sport.

Key Terms

background connection

dialogic discussion

directed instruction

experiential learning

lectures

strategic questioning

teachable moment

References

1. Dombek PM, Casa DJ, Yeargin SW, et al. Athletic trainers' knowledge and behavior regarding the prevention, recognition and treatment of exertional heat stroke at the high school level [abstract]. *J Athl Train*. 2006;41(suppl 2):S47.
2. Mazerolle SM, Scruggs IC, Casa DJ, et al. Current knowledge, attitudes, and practices of certified athletic trainers regarding recognition and treatment of exertional heat stroke. *J Athl Train*. 2010;45(2).
3. Merriam SB. Andragogy and self-directed learning: pillars of adult learning theory. In: Merriam SB, ed. *The New Update on Adult Learning Theory*. San Francisco: Jossey-Bass;2001:3–13.
4. Marsick VJ, Watkins KE. Informal and incidental learning. In: Merriam SB, ed. *The New Update on Adult Learning Theory*. San Francisco: Jossey-Bass; 2001:25–34.
5. Armstrong KJ, Weidner TM. Formal and informal continuing education activities and athletic training professional practice. *J Athl Train*. 2010;45(3):279–286.
6. Zemke R, Zemke S. 30 things we know for sure about adult learners. *Innovation Abstracts*. 1984:8.
7. O'Brien G. Principles of adult learning. Southern Health Organization, Melbourne, Australia. Available at: http://www.southernhealth.org.au/cpme/articles/adult_learning.htm. Accessed December 2, 2005.
8. Zemke R, Zemke S. Adult learning—what do we know for sure? Training. June 1995. Available at: http://www.msstate.edu/dept/ais/8523/Zemke1995.pdf. Accessed July 11, 2010.
9. Donovan MS, Branford JD, Pellegrino JW. *How People Learn: Bridging Research and Practice*. Washington, DC: National Academies Press; 2000.·
10. Brookfield SD. *Understanding and Facilitating Adult Learning*. San Francisco: Jossey-Bass; 1986.
11. Ebell MH, Siwek J, Weiss BD, et al. Strength of Recommendation Taxonomy (SORT): a patient-centered approach to grading evidence in the medical literature. *J Am Board Fam Pract*. 2004;17:59–67.
12. Adams P. Exploring social constructivism: theories and practicalities. *Education 3-13*. 2006;34(3):243–257.
13. Hanson JM, Sinclair KE. Social constructivist teaching methods in Australian universities—reported uptake and perceived learning effects: a survey of lecturers. *High Educ Res Develop*. 2008;27(3):169–186.
14. Andersen JC, Courson RW, Kleiner DM, McLoad TA. National Athletic Trainers' Association position statement: emergency planning in athletics. *J Athl Train*. 2002;37(1):99–104.
15. Sideline preparedness for the team physician. *Med Sci Sports Exerc*. 2001;33(5):846–849.
16. National Athletic Trainers' Association. Official statement—automated external defibrillators. 2003. Available at: http://www.nata.org/sites/default/files/AutomatedExternalDefibrillators.pdf.
17. National Athletic Trainers' Association. NATA official statement on commotio cordis. October 2007. Available at: http://www.nata.org/sites/default/files/CommotioCordis.pdf.
18. Drezner JA, Courson RW, Roberts WO, et al. Inter-Association Task Force recommendations on emergency preparedness and management of sudden cardiac arrest in high school and college athletic programs: a consensus statement. *J Athl Train*. 2007;42(1):143–158.
19. Drezner JA, Courson RW, Roberts WO, et al. Inter-Association Task Force Recommendations on emergency preparedness and management of sudden cardiac arrest in high school and college athletic programs: a consensus statement. *Clin J Sport Med*. 2007;17(2):87–103.
20. Rosenshine B. Unsolved issues in teaching content: a critique of a lesson on Federalist Paper no 10. *Teach Teach Educ*. 1986;2(4):301–308.
21. Swartz EE, Boden BP, Courson RW, et al. National Athletic Trainers' Association position statement: acute management of the cervical spine-injured athlete. *J Athl Train*. 2000;44(3):306–331.
22. Mensch JM, Ennis CD. Pedagogic strategies perceived to enhance student learning in athletic training. *J Athl Train*. 2002;37(4):S199–S207.
23. Binkley HM, Beckett J, Casa DJ, Kleiner DM, Plummer PE. National Athletic Trainers' Association position statement: exertional heat illnesses. *J Athl Train*. 2002;37(3):329–343.
24. Armstrong LE, Casa DJ, Millard-Stafford M, et al. American College of Sports Medicine position stand: exertional heat illnesses during training and competition. *Med Sci Sports Exerc*. 2007;556–571.

25. Casa TM, Casa DJ. Dialogic discourse: higher-level learning through class discussions. *Athl Ther Today.* 2007;12(2):25–29.

26. Heck JF, Clarke KS, Peterson TR, et al. National Athletic Trainers' Association position statement: head-down contact and spearing in tackle football. 2004;39(1):101–111.

27. Rich VJ. Clinical instructors' and athletic training students' perceptions of teachable moments in an athletic training clinical education setting. *J Athl Train.* 2009;44(3):294–303.

28. Barnum MG. Questioning skills demonstrated by approved clinical instructors during clinical field experiences. *J Athl Train.* 2008;43(3):284–292.

29. Barnum MG, Guyer MS, Levy LS, et al. Questioning and feedback in athletic training clinical education. *Athl Train Educ J.* 2009;4(1):23–27.

30. Walker SE. Active learning strategies to promote critical thinking. *J Athl Train.* 2003;38(3):263–276.

31. Concussion (mild traumatic brain injury) and the team physician: a consensus statement. *Med Sci Sports Exerc.* 2006;38(2):395–399.

32. Guskiewicz KM, Bruce SL, Cantu RC, et al. National Athletic Trainers' Association position statement: management of sport-related concussions. *J Athl Train.* 2004;39(3):280–297.

33. McCrory P, Meeuwisse W, Johnston K, et al. Consensus statement on concussion in sport: the 3rd international conference on concussion in sport held in Zurich, November 2008. *J Athl Train.* 2009;44(4):434–448.

34. Buyck D, Lang F. Teaching medical communication skills: a call for greater uniformity. *Fam Med.* 2002;34(5):337–343.

35. Mazerolle SM, Casa TM, Casa DJ. Heat and hydration curriculum issues: part 1 of 4—hydration and exercise. *Athl Ther Today.* 2009;14(2):39–44.

36. Mazerolle SM, Casa TM, Casa DJ. Heat and hydration curriculum issues: part 2 of 4—exercising in the heat. *Athl Ther Today.* 2009;14(3):42–47.

37. Mazerolle SM, Yeargin SW, Casa TM, Casa DJ. Heat and hydration curriculum issues: part 3 of 4—rectal thermometry. *Athl Ther Today.* 2009;14(4):25–31.

38. Mazerolle SM, Lopez RM, Casa TM, Casa DJ. Heat and hydration curriculum issues: part 4 of 4—cold water immersion. *Athl Ther Today.* 2009;14(5):12–17.

Managing Emergencies in Mass Participation Events: Medical Triage and Algorithms

From O'Connor FG, Pyne S, Adams WB, Brennan FH, Howard T. *Managing Emergencies in Mass Participation Events: Medical Triage and Algorithms.* Bethesda, MD: USU Consortium for Health and Military Performance, 2009:3. Reprinted with permission.

Presented at the 2010 Marine Corps Marathon Symposium

Francis G. O'Connor, MD, MPH
Medical Director, Consortium for Health and Military Performance (CHAMP)
Associate Professor of Military and Emergency Medicine
Uniformed Services University of the Health Sciences

Scott Pyne, MD
Former Medical Director, Marine Corps Marathon
Consultant, Sports Medicine
US Navy Medical Department

W. Bruce Adams, MD
Medical Director, Marine Corps Marathon
Senior Medical Officer
USMC Reserve Medical Entitlements Determinations
Wounded Warrior Regiment
Quantico, VA

Fred H. Brennan, Jr., DO
Director, Seacoast Center for Athletes
Team Physician, University of New Hampshire
Somersworth, NH

Thomas Howard, MD
Director, Sports Medicine Fellowship Program
Fairfax Family Practice
Fairfax, VA

Chris G. Pappas, MD, FAAFP
Director, Primary Care Sports Medicine
Womack Family Medicine Residency Program
Fort Bragg, NC

I. MCM Collapsed Athlete Algorithm

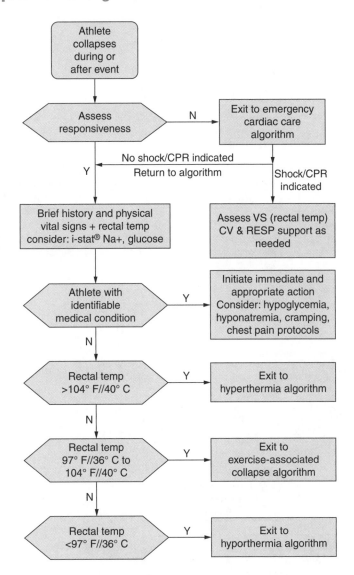

II. MCM Emergency Cardiac Care Algorithm (BLS Setting with AED)

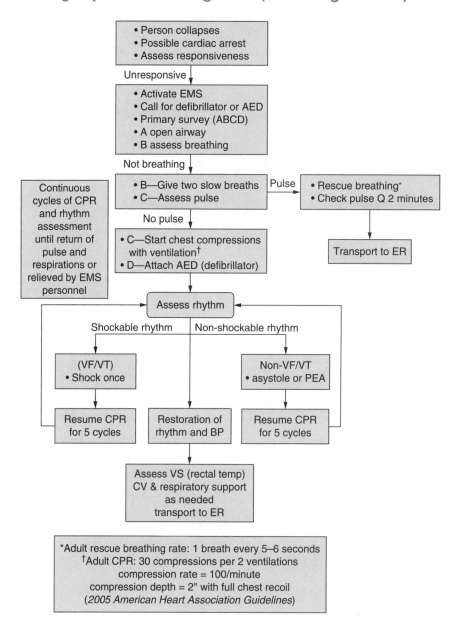

- Person collapses
- Possible cardiac arrest
- Assess responsiveness

Unresponsive

- Activate EMS
- Call for defibrillator or AED
- Primary survey (ABCD)
- A open airway
- B assess breathing

Not breathing

- B—Give two slow breaths
- C—Assess pulse

Pulse

- Rescue breathing*
- Check pulse Q 2 minutes

Transport to ER

No pulse

- C—Start chest compressions with ventilation†
- D—Attach AED (defibrillator)

Continuous cycles of CPR and rhythm assessment until return of pulse and respirations or relieved by EMS personnel

Assess rhythm

Shockable rhythm

(VF/VT)
- Shock once

Resume CPR for 5 cycles

Non-shockable rhythm

Non-VF/VT
- asystole or PEA

Resume CPR for 5 cycles

Restoration of rhythm and BP

Assess VS (rectal temp)
CV & respiratory support as needed
transport to ER

*Adult rescue breathing rate: 1 breath every 5–6 seconds
†Adult CPR: 30 compressions per 2 ventilations
compression rate = 100/minute
compression depth = 2" with full chest recoil
(*2005 American Heart Association Guidelines*)

III. MCM Exercise-Associated Collapse Algorithm

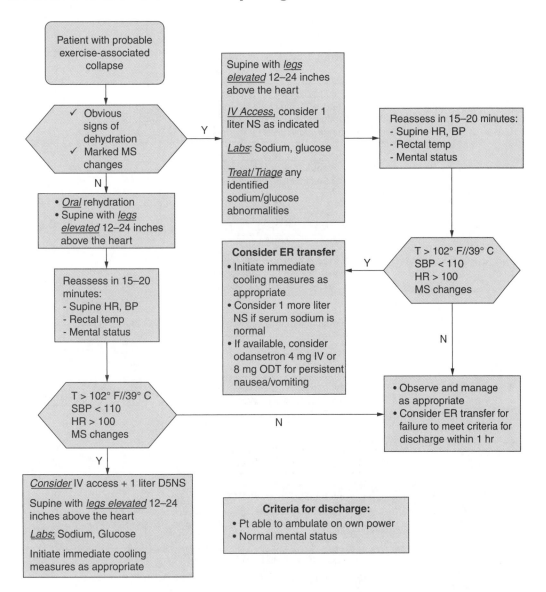

Patient with probable exercise-associated collapse

- ✓ Obvious signs of dehydration
- ✓ Marked MS changes

Y →

Supine with _legs elevated_ 12–24 inches above the heart

IV Access, consider 1 liter NS as indicated

Labs: Sodium, glucose

Treat/Triage any identified sodium/glucose abnormalities

→

Reassess in 15–20 minutes:
- Supine HR, BP
- Rectal temp
- Mental status

N ↓

- _Oral_ rehydration
- Supine with _legs elevated_ 12–24 inches above the heart

↓

Reassess in 15–20 minutes:
- Supine HR, BP
- Rectal temp
- Mental status

Consider ER transfer
- Initiate immediate cooling measures as appropriate
- Consider 1 more liter NS if serum sodium is normal
- If available, consider odansetron 4 mg IV or 8 mg ODT for persistent nausea/vomiting

← Y

T > 102° F//39° C
SBP < 110
HR > 100
MS changes

N ↓

↓

T > 102° F//39° C
SBP < 110
HR > 100
MS changes

——— N ———→

- Observe and manage as appropriate
- Consider ER transfer for failure to meet criteria for discharge within 1 hr

Y ↓

Consider IV access + 1 liter D5NS

Supine with _legs elevated_ 12–24 inches above the heart

Labs: Sodium, Glucose

Initiate immediate cooling measures as appropriate

Criteria for discharge:
- Pt able to ambulate on own power
- Normal mental status

IV. MCM Hyperthermia Algorithm

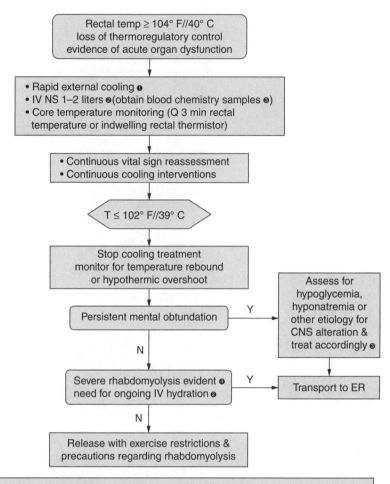

Rectal temp ≥ 104° F//40° C
loss of thermoregulatory control
evidence of acute organ dysfunction

↓

• Rapid external cooling ❶
• IV NS 1–2 liters ❷(obtain blood chemistry samples ❸)
• Core temperature monitoring (Q 3 min rectal temperature or indwelling rectal thermistor)

↓

• Continuous vital sign reassessment
• Continuous cooling interventions

↓

T ≤ 102° F//39° C

↓

Stop cooling treatment
monitor for temperature rebound
or hypothermic overshoot

↓

Persistent mental obtundation ── Y ──→ Assess for hypoglycemia, hyponatremia or other etiology for CNS alteration & treat accordingly ❸

↓ N

Severe rhabdomyolysis evident ❹ need for ongoing IV hydration ❷ ── Y ──→ Transport to ER

↓ N

Release with exercise restrictions & precautions regarding rhabdomyolysis

---

All temperatures are rectal!

❶ Rapid cooling options: Ice bath immersion, whole body ice massage, continuous dousing with ice water &/or ice water-soaked sheets. Fans if available. Consider cooled IV fluids. Stop cooling when temperature drops below 101–102.

❷ IVF: NS 2L bolus unless signs of overhydration or CHF (then NS @ KVO rate); reassess ongoing IVF needs from clinical response, urine output, and labs. Cooled fluids for heat casualty.

❸ Immediate Na, Gluc, K +/− Cr, BUN, Cl & Hct (e.g. i-Stat®); Treat hypoglycemia and hyponatremia per protocols.

❹ If rhabdomyolysis suspected, need CPK, BMP, AST, ALT, LDH, uric acid & UA w/Micro if available. Add Ca^{++}, PO_4 & Mg for severe RHABDO.

V. MCM Hypothermia Algorithm

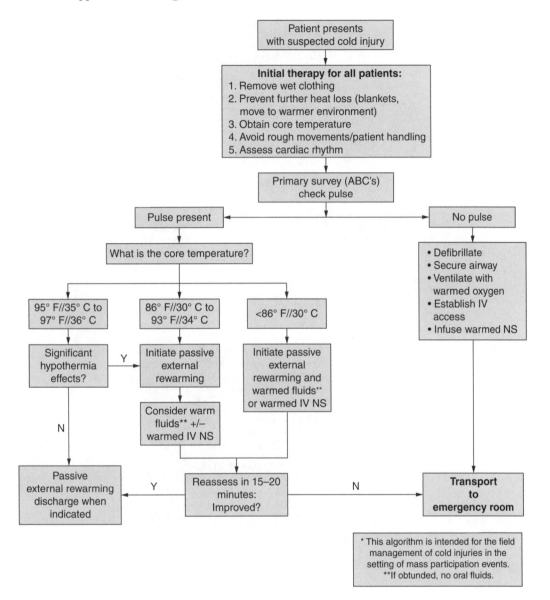

Patient presents with suspected cold injury

Initial therapy for all patients:
1. Remove wet clothing
2. Prevent further heat loss (blankets, move to warmer environment)
3. Obtain core temperature
4. Avoid rough movements/patient handling
5. Assess cardiac rhythm

Primary survey (ABC's) check pulse

Pulse present

No pulse

What is the core temperature?

No pulse
- Defibrillate
- Secure airway
- Ventilate with warmed oxygen
- Establish IV access
- Infuse warmed NS

95° F//35° C to 97° F//36° C

86° F//30° C to 93° F//34° C

<86° F//30° C

Significant hypothermia effects?

Y → Initiate passive external rewarming

Initiate passive external rewarming and warmed fluids** or warmed IV NS

Consider warm fluids** +/− warmed IV NS

N

Passive external rewarming discharge when indicated

Y ← Reassess in 15–20 minutes: Improved?

N → **Transport to emergency room**

* This algorithm is intended for the field management of cold injuries in the setting of mass participation events.
**If obtunded, no oral fluids.

VI. MCM Exercise-Associated Muscle Cramps Algorithm

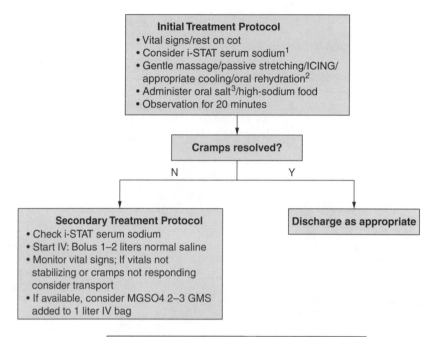

Initial Treatment Protocol
- Vital signs/rest on cot
- Consider i-STAT serum sodium[1]
- Gentle massage/passive stretching/ICING/ appropriate cooling/oral rehydration[2]
- Administer oral salt[3]/high-sodium food
- Observation for 20 minutes

Cramps resolved?

N　　　　　　　　Y

Secondary Treatment Protocol
- Check i-STAT serum sodium
- Start IV: Bolus 1–2 liters normal saline
- Monitor vital signs; If vitals not stabilizing or cramps not responding consider transport
- If available, consider MGSO4 2–3 GMS added to 1 liter IV bag

Discharge as appropriate

[1]An i-STAT serum sodium should be considered for patients with severe systemic cramping, or cramping associated with neurologic complaints such as persistent numbness or tingling. These symptoms may be clues to hyponatremia.

[2]Oral rehydration fluid should be a fluid of choice; however, an electrolyte solution such as gatorade, or a salty broth, should be encouraged.

[3]Oral salt ingestion if no contraindications. May empty small packet or ½ TSP salt on tongue then chase with water/sports drink (repeat PRN). Try salted chips, pretzels, crackers. May try electrolyte tabs (often have low sodium content).

VII. MCM Chest Pain Algorithm

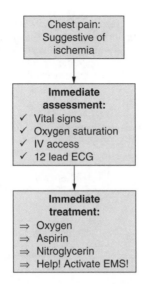

Chest pain:
Suggestive of
ischemia

**Immediate
assessment:**
✓ Vital signs
✓ Oxygen saturation
✓ IV access
✓ 12 lead ECG

**Immediate
treatment:**
⇒ Oxygen
⇒ Aspirin
⇒ Nitroglycerin
⇒ Help! Activate EMS!

Immediate General Treatment

• Activate EMS
• Oxygen: 4 L/min by mask or cannula
• Aspirin: 325 MG tablet should be administered (chewed)
• Nitroglycerin: One sublingual tablet (0.03 to 0.04 mg)
  should be administered and may be repeated twice at 5-minute
  intervals. Systolic BP should be greater than 90–100 mm Hg.

VIII. MCM Hyponatremia Algorithm

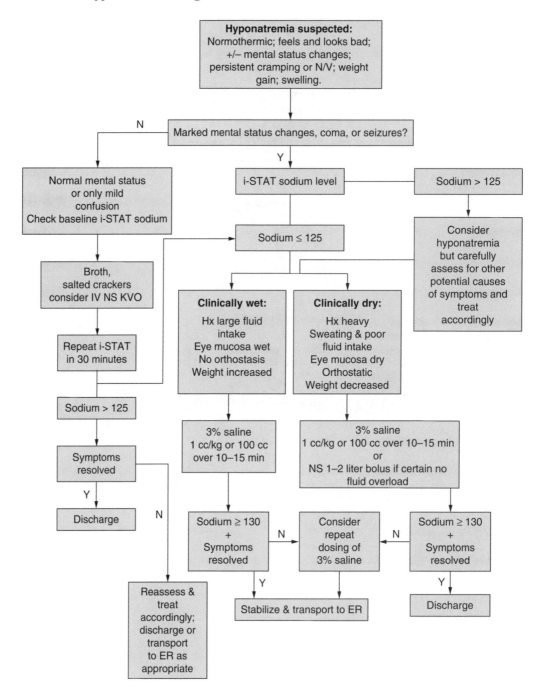

IX. MCM Hypoglycemia Algorithm

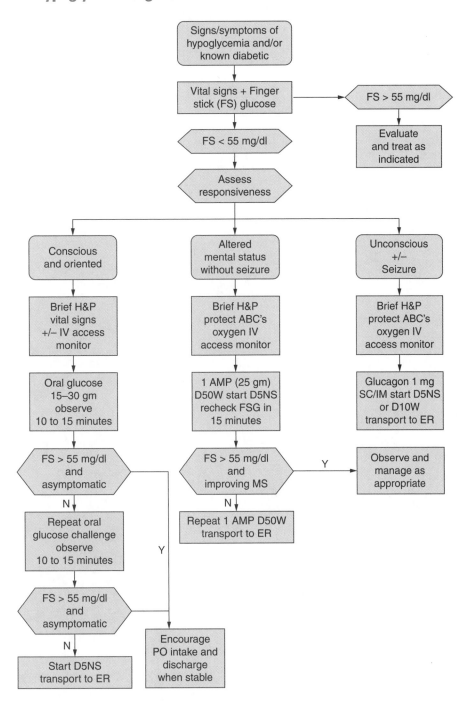

Handouts, Postings, and Review Summary Sheets

Compiled by Julie DeMartini, MA, ATC
Written by the following:
Kristin Applegate, MA, ATC
Douglas J. Casa, PhD, ATC, FACSM, FNATA
Julie DeMartini, MA, ATC
Holly Emmanuel, MA, ATC

Kerri Gavin, MA, ATC
Katherine Jensen, MA, ATC
Rachel Karslo, MA, ATC
Jessica Martschinske, MA, ATC
Lindsey McDowell, MA, ATC

Kelly Pagnotta, MA, ATC, PES
Danielle Pinkus, MA, ATC
Roberto Ruiz, MA, ATC
Rebecca (Becca) Stearns, MA, ATC
Megan VanSumeren, MA, ATC

Commotio Cordis

Definition: Commotio cordis is caused by a blunt, nonpenetrating blow to the chest that causes ventricular fibrillation. The blow must occur directly over the left ventricle during a 15- to 30-millisecond window in the cardiac cycle, which represents 1% of the cardiac cycle. Commotio cordis is also referred to as a cardiac concussion and is usually unassociated with any structural damage to the ribs, sternum, or heart.[1-7]

Incidence: A commotio cordis event is unexpected and hard to prevent. It is most common in young males (about 15 years old) with pliable chest walls. Common sports in which commotio cordis occurs are baseball, softball, ice hockey, football, lacrosse, and karate, as well as during collisions or horseplay. Commotio cordis accounts for 3% of cases of sudden death in athletes.[1-7]

Prevention[8,9]

Setting Specific

1. Educate coaches, parents, officials, and players in the recognition, signs, and symptoms of commotio cordis.
2. Train coaches and officials in CPR and automated external defibrillator (AED) use as well as basic first aid.
3. Ensure that AEDs will be available immediately in the event of an emergency.
4. Make sure coaches and administrators know where AEDs are located.
5. Make sure AEDs are accessible at all times.
6. Have an emergency action plan (EAP) at all venues and involve proper personnel in the implementation of the EAP as well as during rehearsals.
7. Make sure officials are enforcing safety rules and taking proper safety precautions.

Athlete Specific

1. Use proper chest protection for the sport.
2. Use age- and level-appropriate safety balls.
3. Make sure safety equipment is used as directed and meets all standards of governing bodies.
4. Teach proper techniques to avoid being hit.
5. Turn away from the ball correctly (i.e., baseball).
6. Use common sense to avoid size, strength, and skill disparities among participants.

Predisposing Factors[8,10]

1. Young age
2. Male
3. Pliable chest wall
4. Object
   a. Size (about the size of a baseball)
   b. Speed (30–40 mph)
   c. Force of impact
   d. Site of impact (over left ventricle)

Recognition[8]

Differential Diagnosis

1. Cardiovascular disease
2. Hypertrophic cardiomyopathy (HCM)
3. Coronary artery abnormalities
4. Myocarditis
5. Arrhythmogenic right ventricular cardiomyopathy
6. Ion channelopathies
7. Blunt trauma injury
8. Illicit drug use
9. Pulmonary conditions

Signs and Symptoms[10]

1. Look for the athlete that is hit in the chest by either an object or someone else and then collapses.
2. The precipitating impact is usually an innocent blow, not uncommon for the sport.
3. Brief periods of consciousness are followed by collapse and ventricular fibrillation.

Treatment

Immediate Care[8,9]

1. Defibrillate as soon as possible.
   a. Survival declines 7% to 10% every minute defibrillation is delayed.
   b. Survival rate is only about 15%.
2. Guidelines recommend that one attempted defibrillation be followed by immediate CPR, beginning with chest compressions.

Extended Care

1. Survivors should undergo a thorough cardiac evaluation, including at least 12-lead electrocardiogram, ambulatory Holter monitoring, and echocardiogram.[8,9]

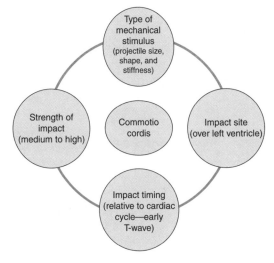

Figure 1　Variables contributing to commotio cordis.

Return to Play

Because of lack of data regarding susceptibility for recurrent events, eligibility for return to play is left to individual clinical judgment.

References

1. Abrunzo TJ. Commotio cordis. The single most common cause of traumatic death in youth baseball. *Am J Dis Child.* 1991;145(11):1279–1282.
2. Cooper PJ, Epstein A, MacLeod IA, et al. Soft Tissue Impact Characterisation Kit (STICK) for ex situ investigation of heart rhythm response to acute mechanical stimulation. *Prog Biophys Mol Biol.* 2006;90:444–468.
3. Geddes LA, Roeder RA. Evolution of our knowledge of sudden death due to commotio cordis. *Am J Emerg Med.* 2005;23:67–75.
4. Kohl P, Nesbitt AD, Cooper PJ, Lei M. Sudden cardiac death by commotio cordis: role of mechano-electric feedback. *Cardiovasc Res.* 2001;50:280–289.
5. Link MS, Maron BJ, Wang PJ, et al. Reduced risk of sudden death from chest wall blows (commotio cordis) with safety baseballs. *Pediatrics.* 2002;109:873–877.
6. Link MS, Wang PJ, VanderBrink BA, et al. Selective activation of the K+ ATP channel is a mechanism by which sudden death is produced by low-energy chest-wall impact (commotio cordis). *Circulation.* 1999;100:413–418.
7. Maron BJ, Doerer JJ, Haas TS, Tierney DM, Mueller FO. Sudden deaths in young competitive athletes: analysis of 1866 deaths in the United States, 1980–2006. *Circulation.* 2009;119:1085–1092.
8. Maron BJ, Estes NAM III, Link MS. Task Force 11: commotio cordis. *J Am Coll Cardiol.* 2005;45:1371–1373.
9. Salib EA, Cyran SE, Cilley RE, Maron BJ, Thomas NJ. Efficacy of bystander cardiopulmonary resuscitation and out-of-hospital automated external defibrillation as life-saving therapy in commotio cordis. *J Pediatrics.* 2005;147:863–866.
10. Maron BJ, Link MS, Wang PJ, Estes NAM III. Clinical profile of commotio cordis: an underappreciated cause of sudden death in the young during sports and other activities. *J Cardiovasc Electrophysiol.* 1999;10:114–120.

Cardiac: Congenital Conditions

Definition: Heart conditions (e.g., hypertrophic cardiomyopathy [HCM], mitral valve prolapse, anomalous coronary arteries, myocarditis, Marfan syndrome) with predisposing or mutating genetic factors that can lead to sudden cardiac death (SCD) in sports.[6] These genetic conditions present with a structural cardiac abnormality.[3,11] Sudden cardiac arrest (SCA) is the leading cause of unexpected death in exercising young athletes, most commonly those younger than 30 years.[3,6,11]

Incidence: HCM is the most common form of SCA, and it is present in 1 in 500 of the general population.[6,11] It is important to note that all genetic heart conditions are different, and they present with varying signs and symptoms. However, in an emergency situation all are handled in the same manner regarding SCD.

Prevention

Setting Specific

1. Implementation of emergency action plan (EAP)
   a. EAP should be reviewed and practiced by all potential first responders[3]
   b. Establish catastrophic incident guidelines[3,4]
2. Automated external defibrillator (AED) on site and publicly accessible[3,4,11]
3. Coaches and athletic staff trained and certified in cardiopulmonary resuscitation (CPR) and AED use[3,4]
4. Education of coaches and staff regarding signs and symptoms of SCD[3,4]
5. Preparticipation exam (PPE) for all athletes, including cardiovascular questions and exam (**Table 1**)

Athlete Specific

1. PPE: Detailed family and personal history, physical exam (**Table 1**)
   a. PPE may recommend or lead to electrocardiogram (ECG), echocardiogram, ultrasound, among other tests[8–10]
2. Appropriate physical fitness level
3. Competition level: recreational versus competitive
4. Environmental acclimation

Predisposing Factors

Intrinsic [2,3,5,6,10,12]

1. Genetic predisposition
2. History of SCD in family member
3. Arrhythmias/palpitations
4. Heart murmurs
5. Unexplained syncope
6. Unexplained or exertional fatigue
7. Exertional dyspnea
8. Systemic hypertension
9. Increased or irregular pulse rate
10. Bradycardia/tachycardia
11. Unexplained weakness or dizziness
12. Chest pain

Extrinsic

1. Intensity
   a. Static vs. dynamic components
   b. Multiple/repeated all-out exercise (sprints)
2. Specific sport
3. Poor physical fitness or conditioning level
4. Environmental conditions

TABLE 1	Recommendations for Preparticipation Screening[2,5,7,9,13]

Family History

Premature sudden cardiac death

Heart disease in surviving relatives younger than 50 years

History of cardiomyopathy, coronary artery disease, Marfan syndrome, long QT syndrome, severe arrhythmias, or other disabling cardiovascular disease

Personal History

Heart murmur

Systemic hypertension

Fatigue

Syncope or near syncope

Excessive or unexplained exertional dyspnea

Exertional chest pain or discomfort

Physical Examination

Heart murmur (supine/standing)

Femoral arterial pulses (to exclude coarctation of aorta)

Stigmata of Marfan syndrome

Brachial blood pressure measurement (sitting)

Further Testing and Imaging That May Be Warranted by History and Examination

Exercise electrocardiogram (ECG)

12-lead ECG

Echocardiogram

Cardiac magnetic resonance imaging (MRI)

Multidetector computed tomography (CT)

Recognition

Differential Diagnosis

1. Heart attack
2. HCM
3. Marfan syndrome
4. Myocarditis
5. Commotio cordis
6. Athlete's heart
7. Coronary anomalies
8. Valvular disease
9. Heat illness
10. Exertional sickling
11. Stroke

Signs and Symptoms

1. Hypertrophic cardiomyopathy
   - Left ventricle wall thickness > 13 mm[6,11]
2. Marfan syndrome
   - Arm span-to-height ratio greater than 1.05, tall figure, long and thin limbs, hyperextensibility and ligamentous laxity, scoliosis, chest wall deformity, lens dislocations, and near-sightedness[6]
3. Anomalous coronary artery
   - Syncope during exercise[6]
4. Mitral valve prolapse
   - Can present with midsystolic click and murmur of mitral regurgitation[6]
5. Myocarditis and pericarditis
   - Inflammatory condition that can develop with flu or cold; can be resolved with treatment[6]

Treatment[1-3,11,13]

Immediate Care

1. Call 911 and activate the EAP.
2. Initiate CPR.
3. Retrieve emergency equipment (AED).
   Note: Defibrillation should occur within 3 to 5 minutes of time of collapse.
4. Continue CPR and AED use until emergency medical services (EMS) and advanced life support equipment arrives.

Extended Care[1-3,11,13]

1. Transport athlete via EMS to an emergency care facility.
2. Perform diagnostic imaging (echocardiogram, ECG, cardiac magnetic resonance imaging).
3. Athlete should follow up with primary physician or cardiologist.
4. Implement catastrophic incident plan, if necessary.

Return to Play[6,7,10]

1. Decisions can only be made by a medical doctor (primary physician or cardiologist) and will vary with each disease or genetic condition.
2. Decisions should be based on the 36th Bethesda Conference materials, the National Athletic Trainers' Association consensus statement on SCA, and the American Heart Association guidelines.
   a. Different recommendations exist for each disease or disorder.
   b. Classification of sports (**Figure 1**) compares static and dynamic components of sports to advise safe participation for athletes with genetic heart conditions.

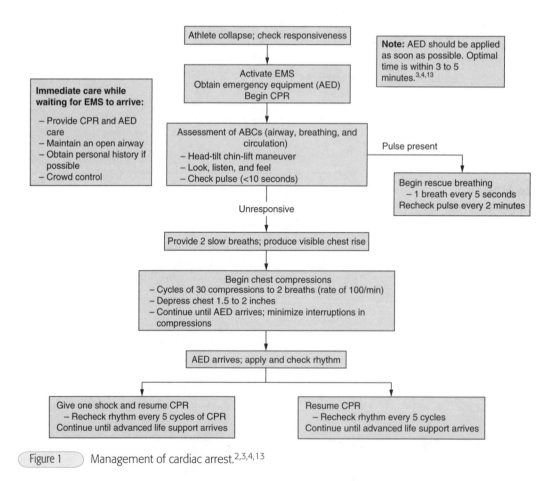

Figure 1 Management of cardiac arrest.[2,3,4,13]

References

1. ECC Committee, Subcommittees and Task Forces of the American Heart Association. 2005 American Heart Association guidelines for cardiopulmonary resuscitation and emergency cardiovascular care, part 5: electrical therapies. Automated external defibrillators, defibrillation, cardioversion, and pacing. *Circulation.* 2005;112(suppl 24):IV35–46.

2. ECC Committee, Subcommittees and Task Forces of the American Heart Association. 2005 American Heart Association guidelines for cardiopulmonary resuscitation and emergency cardiovascular care, part 7.2: management of cardiac arrest. *Circulation.* 2005;112(suppl 24):IV58–66.

3. Drezner JA, Courson RW, Roberts WO, et al. Interassociation Task Force recommendations on emergency preparedness and management of sudden cardiac arrest in high school and college athletic programs: a consensus statement. *J Athl Train.* 2007;42:143–158.

4. Andersen J, Courson RW, Kleiner DM, McLoda TA. National Athletic Trainers' Association position statement: emergency planning in athletics. *J Athl Train.* 2002;37:99–104.

5. Maron BJ, Douglas PS, Graham TP, Nishimura RA, Thompson PD. 36th Bethesda Conference: Task Force 1—preparticipation screening and diagnosis of cardiovascular disease in athletes. *J Am Coll Cardiol.* 2005;45:1322–1326.

6. Maron BJ, Ackerman MJ, Nishimura RA, et al. 36th Bethesda Conference: Task Force 4—HCM and other cardiomyopathies, mitral valve prolapsed, myocarditis, and Marfan syndrome. *J Am Coll Cardiol.* 2005;45:1340–1345.

7. Mitchell JH, Haskell W, Snell P, VanCamp SP. 36th Bethesda Conference: Task Force 8—classification of sports. *J Am Coll Cardiol.* 2005;45:1364–1367.

8. The periodic health evaluation of elite athletes: a consensus statement from the International Olympic Committee. *J Athl Training.* 2009;44(5):538–557.

9. Panhuyzen-Goedkoop NM. Preparticipation cardiovascular screening in young athletes. *Br J Sports Med.* 2009;43(9):629–630.

10. Maron BJ. Distinguishing hypertrophic cardiomyopathy from athlete's heart physiological remodeling: clinical significance, diagnostic strategies and implications for preparticipation screening. *Br J Sports Med.* 2009;43(9):649–656.

11. Link MS. Prevention of sudden cardiac death: return to sport considerations in athletes with identified cardiovascular abnormalities. *Br J Sports Med.* 2009;43(9):685–689.

12. Maron BJ, Pelliccia A, Spirito P. Cardiac disease in young trained athletes. Insights into methods for distinguishing athlete's heart from structural heart disease, with particular emphasis on hypertrophic cardiomyopathy. *Circulation.* 1995;91:1596–1601.

13. O'Connor FG, Pyne S, Adams WB, Brennan FH, Howard T. *Managing Emergencies in Mass Participation Events: Medical Triage and Algorithms.* Bethesda, MD: USUHS Consortium for Health and Military Performance; 2009.

Coronary Artery Disease

Definition: Coronary artery disease (CAD) is established in the presence of any of the following: (1) a history of myocardial infarction confirmed by conventional diagnostic criteria, (2) a history suggestive of angina pectoris with objective evidence of inducible ischemia, and (3) coronary atherosclerosis of any degree demonstrated by coronary imaging studies.[1]

Prevention[3,4,10,14]
Setting Specific

1. An emergency action plan (EAP) needs to be in place and practiced.
2. Automated external defibrillators (AEDs) should be available on site and with public access, in order to provide a response time of less than 5 minutes.
3. Ensure proper first aid, cardiopulmonary resuscitation (CPR) and AED training for officials involved at events with older athletes (e.g., athletic trainers, physicians, coaches, referees, supervisors at athletic facilities overseeing events).
4. The EAP should be rehearsed to familiarize those involved with the proper procedures.

Athlete Specific

1. Preparticipation exam (PPE); see **Table 1**.
2. Maintaining an appropriate diet and physical fitness level.

Elements of an Emergency Action Plan for Sudden Cardiac Arrest

1. Develop a written emergency action plan.
2. Establish an effective communication system and post the EAP at each venue, usually near a telephone.
3. Designate a coordinator for the EAP and train likely responders in CPR, first aid, and AED use.
4. Have access to on-site or centrally located AEDs and the items listed in the "Equipment" section.
5. Know the proper entrance and exit for emergency transportation.
6. Practice and review the EAP annually with potential first responders.

Predisposing Factors[1,8,12]
Risk of exercise-related events increases with the presence of the following factors.

Intrinsic

1. Coronary atherosclerosis
2. Extent of disease
3. Left ventricular dysfunction
4. Inducible ischemia
5. Electrical instability
6. Intensity of the competitive sport and intensity of participant's effort

Extrinsic

1. Intensity of the competitive sport
2. Intensity of participant's effort
3. Unhealthy, unbalanced diet (high in fat, sugar, salt, etc.)
4. No regular physical activity
5. Smoking history
6. Age
7. Gender
8. Cholesterol levels

Equipment

1. AED kit
   - Razor
   - Towel
   - Scissors
   - Antiperspirant
   - Extra pads
2. Stethoscope
3. BP cuff
4. Cell phone
5. CPR mask
6. Supplemental O_2

TABLE
1

Recommendations for Preparticipation Screening[2,5,7,9,13]

Family History

Premature sudden cardiac death

Heart disease in surviving relatives less than 50 years old

History of cardiomyopathy, coronary artery disease, Marfan syndrome, long QT syndrome, severe arrhythmias, or other disabling cardiovascular disease

Personal History

Heart murmur

Systemic hypertension

Fatigue

Syncope or near syncope

Excessive or unexplained exertional dyspnea

Exertional chest pain or discomfort

Physical Examination

Heart murmur (supine/standing)

Femoral arterial pulses (to exclude coarctation of aorta)

Stigmata of Marfan syndrome

Brachial blood pressure measurement (sitting)

Further Testing and Imaging That May Be Warranted by History and Examination

Exercise electrocardiogram (ECG)

12-lead ECG

Echocardiogram

Cardiac magnetic resonance imaging (MRI)

Multidetector computed tomography (CT)

Recognition

Differential Diagnosis[1]

1. Congenital heart disease
2. Valvular heart disease
3. Hypertrophic cardiomyopathy
4. Mitral valve prolapse
5. Myocarditis
6. Seizure

Other Salient Findings

1. CAD is most common in masters athletes (adults older than 35 years)
2. An acute cardiac event may happen in 6.5 people per 100,000 per year. Events are more common in men than women.[11]
3. Exercise increases the risk for heart attack, yet not exercising increases the risk for heart attack during daily activity.[12]
4. Prior cardiovascular disease, smoking, and recent episodes of fatigue or flulike symptoms may greatly increase risk of acute cardiac events.[8]

5. Athletes with diagnosed CAD should have their left ventricular function assessed. These athletes should undergo maximal exercise testing to assess their exercise capacity and the presence or absence of provocable myocardial ischemia.[1]

6. In those 35 years and older, coronary heart disease accounts for 80% of all sudden cardiac deaths.[14]

Treatment

Immediate Treatment (Acute)

1. Check responsiveness.
2. Activate EMS (dial 911).
3. Retrieve AED and begin CPR.
4. Continue CPR until advanced life support providers arrive and take over.
5. See **Figure 1**.

Extended Care[1,3]

1. Transport to hospital for emergency care.
2. Diagnostic imaging.
3. Surgery or stent placement (depending on severity).
4. Follow up with primary care physician or cardiologist.

Return to Play[1]

1. Any patient who has had a heart attack or has been diagnosed with any form of heart disease cannot return to play without clearance of his or her personal physician or cardiologist.

2. Physical training and competition should cease after recent myocardial infarction or myocardial revascularization until recovery is deemed complete by a physician.

3. In general, patients after stent placement for stable CAD symptoms should avoid vigorous exercise training for approximately 4 weeks.

4. Following coronary bypass surgery, patients should avoid vigorous activity until their incisions can tolerate vigorous activity.

5. All athletes with atherosclerotic CAD should have their atherosclerotic risk factors aggressively treated, which may reduce the risk of exercise-related events.

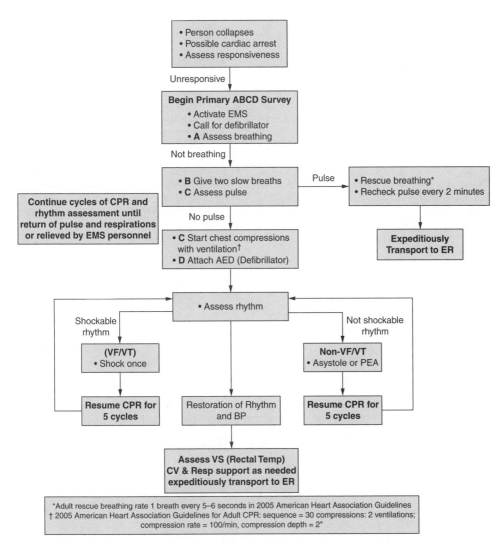

- Person collapses
- Possible cardiac arrest
- Assess responsiveness

Unresponsive

Begin Primary ABCD Survey
- Activate EMS
- Call for defibrillator
- **A** Assess breathing

Not breathing

- **B** Give two slow breaths
- **C** Assess pulse

Pulse

- Rescue breathing*
- Recheck pulse every 2 minutes

Expeditiously Transport to ER

No pulse

Continue cycles of CPR and rhythm assessment until return of pulse and respirations or relieved by EMS personnel

- **C** Start chest compressions with ventilation†
- **D** Attach AED (Defibrillator)

- Assess rhythm

Shockable rhythm

Not shockable rhythm

(VF/VT)
- Shock once

Non-VF/VT
- Asystole or PEA

Resume CPR for 5 cycles

Restoration of Rhythm and BP

Resume CPR for 5 cycles

Assess VS (Rectal Temp) CV & Resp support as needed expeditiously transport to ER

*Adult rescue breathing rate 1 breath every 5–6 seconds in 2005 American Heart Association Guidelines
† 2005 American Heart Association Guidelines for Adult CPR: sequence = 30 compressions: 2 ventilations; compression rate = 100/min, compression depth = 2"

Figure 1   Flowchart for emergency cardiac care. AED indicates automated external defibrillator; CPR, cardiopulmonary resuscitation; CV, cardiovascular; EMS, emergency medical services; ER, emergency room; PEA, pulseless electrical activity; VF/VT, ventricular fibrillation/ventricular tachycardia; VS, vital signs. From O'Connor FG, Pyne S, Adams WB, Brennan FH, Howard T. *Managing Emergencies in Mass Participation Events: Medical Triage and Algorithms.* Bethesda, MD: USUHS Consortium for Health and Military Performance, 2009:3. Reprinted with permission.

References

1. Thompson PD, Balady GJ, Chaitman BR, Clark LT, Levine BD, Myerburg RJ. 36th Bethesda Conference: Task Force 6—coronary artery disease. *J Am Coll Cardiol.* 2005;45(8):1348–1353.

2. Maron BJ, Douglas PS, Graham TP, Nishimura RA, Thompson PD. 36th Bethesda Conference: Task Force 1—preparticipation screening and diagnosis of cardiovascular disease in athletes. *J Am Coll Cardiol.* 2005;45(8):1322–1326.

3. Andersen J, Courson RW, Kleiner DM, McLoda TA. National Athletic Trainers' Association position statement: emergency planning in athletics. *J Athl Training.* 2002;37:99–104.

4. Drezner JA, Courson RW, Roberts WO, et al. Inter-association Task Force recommendations on emergency preparedness and management of sudden cardiac arrest in high school and college athletic programs: a consensus statement. *J Athl Train.* 2007;42:143–158.

5. The periodic health evaluation of elite athletes: a consensus statement from the International Olympic Committee. *J Athl Training.* 2009;44(5):538–557.

6. O'Connor FG, Pyne S, Adams WB, Brennan FH, Howard T. *Managing Emergencies in Mass Participation Events: Medical Triage and Algorithms.* Bethesda, MD: USUHS Consortium for Health and Military Performance; 2009.

7. Freeman J, Froelicher V, Ashley E. The ageing athlete: screening prior to vigorous exertion in asymptomatic adults without known cardiovascular disease. *Br J Sports Med.* 2009;43:696–701.

8. Van Teeffelen WM, de Beus MF, Mosterd A, et al. Risk factors for exercise-related acute cardiac events: a case-control study. *Br J Sports Med.* 2009;43:722–725.

9. Prakken NH, Velthuis BK, Cramer MJ, Mosterd A. Advances in cardiac imaging: the role of magnetic resonance imaging and computed tomography in identifying athletes at risk. *Br J Sports Med.* 2009;43:677–684.

10. Drezner JA. Preparing for sudden cardiac arrest—the essential role of automated external defibrillators in athletic medicine: a critical review. *Br J Sports Med.* 2009;43:702–707.

11. Chevalier L, Hajjar M, Douard H, et al. Sports-related acute cardiovascular events in a general population: a French prospective study. *Eur J Cardiovasc Prevent Rehabil.* 2009;16:365–370.

12. Thompson PD, Franklin BA, Balady GJ, et al. Exercise and acute cardiovascular events: placing the risks into perspective. *Circulation.* 2007;115:2358–2368.

13. Maron BJ, Araujo CGS, Thompson PD, et al. Recommendations for preparticipation screening and the assessment of cardiovascular disease in masters athletes. *Circulation.* 2001;103:327–334.

14. Myerburg RJ, Estes NAM III, Fontaine JM, Link MS, Zipes DP. 36th Bethesda Conference: Task Force 10—automated external defibrillators. *J Am Coll Cardiol.* 2005;45(8): 1369–1371.

Exertional Heat Stroke

Definition: Exertional heat stroke (EHS) occurs when core body temperature is elevated to a dangerous level (usually ≥ 40.5°C [105°F]) with concomitant signs of organ system failure due to hyperthermia.[1,2] This occurs when the thermoregulatory system is overwhelmed due to excessive heat production or inhibited heat loss and can progress to thermoregulatory system failure. The first marker of exertional heat stroke is often central nervous system dysfunction or changes; if not treated immediately and effectively, it can lead to death.[1,2]

Incidence: Heat stroke is the second leading cause of sudden death in athletes and can rise to the number one cause of sudden death in athletes during the summer months. The incidence of fatal EHS in American football players was about 1 in 350,000 participants from 1995 to 2002. Popular road races have reported as many as 1 to 2 EHS cases per 1,000 entrants.[3]

Prevention[1,2,4,5]

Setting Specific

1. Employ on-site medical care (e.g., athletic trainers or sports medicine physicians) that has authority to restrict the athlete from participating due to any associated risk factors (medical, environmental, or otherwise).
2. Ensure appropriate equipment is available and ready for use in the event that an athlete has EHS (e.g., immersion tub, accurate temperature measurement, water/ice).
3. Adjust starting times and practice times to avoid the hottest part of the day.
4. Implement heat acclimatization guidelines.

Athlete Specific

1. Educate athletes and coaches regarding the prevention, recognition, and treatment of heat illnesses and the risks associated with exercising in hot, humid environmental conditions.
2. Ensure the preparticipation physical exam includes medical history questions specific to heat illnesses.
3. Ensure athletes have access to water and are allowed water breaks throughout practice.
4. Monitor body weight changes during multiple-practice days or at the end of practice to ensure proper rehydration.
5. On hot days, limit the use of protective equipment and athletic equipment that act as barriers to evaporation.
6. Ensure that athletes have proper fitness leading into preseason or practice and get proper sleep every night.

Predisposing Factors[4]

Intrinsic

1. High intensity of exercise/poor physical conditioning
2. Sleep loss
3. Dehydration/inadequate water intake
4. Use of diuretics/certain medications (e.g., antihistamines)
5. Overzealousness/reluctance to report problems, issues, illness
6. Inadequate heat acclimation
7. High muscle mass/body fat
8. Presence of a fever
9. Skin disorder (e.g., miliaria rubra or sunburn)

Extrinsic

1. High ambient temperature, solar radiation, and humidity
2. Athletic gear or uniforms
3. Peer/organizational pressure
4. Inappropriate work-to-rest ratios based on intensity, wet bulb globe temperature, clothing, equipment, fitness, and athlete's medical condition
5. Predisposing medical conditions (e.g., malignant hyperthermia, cystic fibrosis)
6. Lack of education and awareness of heat illnesses among coaches, athletes, and medical staff
7. No emergency plan to identify and treat exertional heat illnesses
8. Minimal access to fluids before and during practice and rest breaks
9. Delay in recognition of early warning signs

Recognition	Signs and Symptoms[1-4]
Differential Diagnosis	1. Collapse of athlete
1. Heat exhaustion	2. Core body temperature of $\geq 40.5°C$ (105°F) taken via a rectal thermometer soon after collapse
2. Exertional hyponatremia	3. CNS dysfunction (disorientation, confusion, dizziness, irrational or unusual behavior, inappropriate comments, irritability, headache, inability to walk, loss of balance/muscle function, vomiting, diarrhea, loss of consciousness)
3. Exertional sickling	4. Athlete may have lucid interval prior to rapidly deteriorating symptoms
4. Diabetic emergency	
5. Concussion	
6. Heat syncope	

Treatment

Immediate Treatment (Acute, <1 hr)[3,6]

1. Immediately remove protective equipment, uniform, and any other clothing with the exception of undergarments.
2. Immerse the athlete up to the shoulders in ice water while continuously monitoring temperature if possible. If not, check temperature every 10 minutes. The athlete's symptoms may worsen during initial 10 minutes if cooling was immediately initiated. Despite this, cooling should continue until a safe temperature is reached. Cooling is most efficient if water temperature is close to $2°C$ (35.6°F).[10] If a rectal thermometer is unavailable, cool the athlete for 15 to 20 minutes or until athlete begins to shiver.
3. If ice-water immersion is not available, the athlete should be doused with cold water, fanned, and have ice placed over or massaged over his or her body. Cold, wet ice towels may be used if ice immersion is not available.
4. Remove from immersion tub when temperature reaches $39°C$.[12] Depending on starting temperature, cooling even in ice water usually takes 15–20 minutes, but may take 30 minutes.
5. The athlete should *not* be transported to the hospital if on-site medical care and appropriate cooling is available. Only when the athlete's core temperature has been cooled to 102.5°F or below should he or she then be transported.

Extended Care (>1 hr)[3,6]

1. After the athlete is removed from cooling tub, monitor athlete (approximately 30 to 60 minutes for large-scale medical events or approximately 15 minutes for a college or high school location and transport immediately to medical facility after cooling is complete if in another setting).
2. Refer the athlete to the hospital for follow-up care and analysis.
3. The hospital staff should maintain proper body temperature and monitor cardiovascular, renal, hepatic, musculoskeletal, and blood values.

Return to Play[7]

1. Must be cleared by team physician before any attempt to return to play begins.
2. Follow a gradual return to activity monitored by on-site medical personnel.
3. Exercise should progress from easy to moderate and occur in a climate-controlled facility over the course of several days. Once this has been accomplished with no complications, exercise can progress to strenuous. Gradually introduce athlete to warmer environments until heat acclimatization is reached. Eventually the athlete may begin to exercise with equipment. Each stage should occur over the course of weeks. The athlete should successfully accomplish each stage on multiple successive days before progressing.
4. If possible, a heat tolerance test should be conducted to evaluate thermoregulatory function.
5. The athlete may return to full participation once heat acclimatization and fitness is restored and he or she is cleared by a physician.

Common Misconceptions[2]

1. Athlete will no longer be sweating when he or she collapses.
2. Rectal temperature must be greater than 40.5°C (105°F).
3. Athlete must be severely dehydrated.
4. Athlete can only succumb from EHS after a lengthy exercise session.
5. EHS can only occur in hot and humid environments.
6. All athletes with EHS will become unconscious.
7. Cold water immersion will cause vasoconstriction and shivering and therefore further increase core body temperature.
8. Oral, aural, forehead sticker, and tympanic temperatures are an accurate representation of core body temperature in athletes exercising in the heat.[2,9,11]

Preparticipation Exam Questions

1. Have you ever been diagnosed with heat stroke? If so, how long ago? Have you had any complications since then? How long did it take you to return to full participation? Did you have any complications upon your return to play?
2. Have you ever been diagnosed with heat exhaustion? If so, when? How many times?
3. Have you ever had trouble or complications from exercising in the heat (e.g., feeling sick, throwing up, dizzy, lack of energy, decreased performance, muscle cramps)?
4. How much training have you been doing recently (in the past 2 weeks)? Has this been performed in warm or humid weather?
5. Have you been training the last two months or so? Would you say you are in poor, good, or excellent condition?
6. Describe your drinking habits. (Are you conscious of how much you consume? Is your urine consistently dark?)
7. Would you consider yourself a heavy or a salty sweater?
8. How many hours of sleep do you get per night? Do you sleep in an air-conditioned room?
9. Do you take any supplements or ergogenic aids?

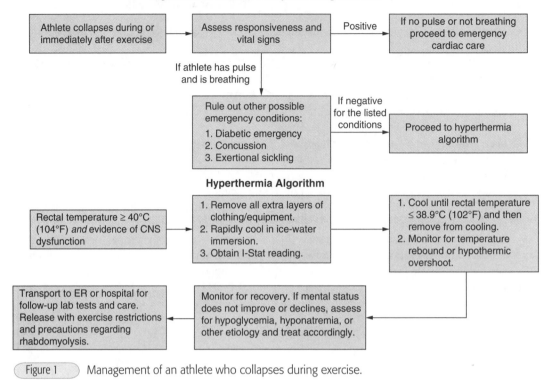

Algorithm for Athlete Collapse During Exercise

| Athlete collapses during or immediately after exercise | → | Assess responsiveness and vital signs | Positive → | If no pulse or not breathing proceed to emergency cardiac care |

If athlete has pulse and is breathing

Rule out other possible emergency conditions:
1. Diabetic emergency
2. Concussion
3. Exertional sickling

If negative for the listed conditions →

Proceed to hyperthermia algorithm

Hyperthermia Algorithm

Rectal temperature ≥ 40°C (104°F) *and* evidence of CNS dysfunction →

1. Remove all extra layers of clothing/equipment.
2. Rapidly cool in ice-water immersion.
3. Obtain I-Stat reading.

→

1. Cool until rectal temperature ≤ 38.9°C (102°F) and then remove from cooling.
2. Monitor for temperature rebound or hypothermic overshoot.

Transport to ER or hospital for follow-up lab tests and care. Release with exercise restrictions and precautions regarding rhabdomyolysis. ←

Monitor for recovery. If mental status does not improve or declines, assess for hypoglycemia, hyponatremia, or other etiology and treat accordingly. ←

Figure 1 Management of an athlete who collapses during exercise.

References

1. Binkley HM, Beckett J, Casa DJ, Kleiner DM, Plummer PE. National Athletic Trainers' Position Statement: exertional heat illnesses. *J Athl Train.* 2002;37:329–343.
2. Casa DJ, Armstrong LE. Exertional heatstroke: a medical emergency. In: Armstrong LE, ed. *Exertional Heat Illnesses.* Champaign, IL: Human Kinetics; 2003:29–56.
3. Armstrong LE, Casa DJ, Millard-Stafford D, et al. Exertional heat illnesses during training and competition. *Med Sci Sports Exerc.* 2007;39(3):556–572.
4. Casa DJ, Almquist J, Anderson S, et al. Inter-association Task Force on Exertional Heat Illnesses consensus statement. *NATA News.* June 2003:24–29.
5. Rav-Acha M, Hadad E, Epstein Y, Heled Y, Moran DS. Fatal exertional heat stroke: a case series. *Am J Med Sci.* 2004;328:84–87.
6. Casa DJ, Anderson JM, Armstrong LE, Maresh CM. Survival strategy: acute treatment of exertional heat stroke. *J Strength Cond.* 2006;20(3):462.
7. McDermott BP, Casa DJ, Yeargin SW, et al. Recovery and return to activity following exertional heat stroke: considerations for the sports medicine staff. *J Sport Rehab.* 2007;16:163–181.
8. Casa DJ, Armstrong LE, Ganio MS, Yeargin SW. Exertional heat stroke in competitive athletes. *Curr Sports Med Rep.* 2005;4:309–317.
9. Ganio MS, Brown CM, Casa DJ, et al. Validity and reliability of devices that assess body temperature during indoor exercise in the heat. *J Athl Training.* 2009;44:124–135.
10. Proulx CI, Ducharme MB, Kenny GP. Effect of water temperature on cooling efficiency during hyperthermia in humans. *J Appl Physiol.* 2003;94:1317–1323.
11. Moran DS, Mendal L. Core temperature measurement methods and current insights. *Sports Med.* 2002;32:879–885.
12. Proulx CI, Ducharme MB, Kenny GP. Safe cooling limits from exercise-induced hyperthermia. *Eur J Appl Physiol.* 2006;96:434–445.

Head Injuries

Definition: Concussion is "a complex pathophysiological process affecting the brain, induced by traumatic biomechanical forces."[1] Concussion may be caused either by a direct blow to the head or by impulsive forces transmitted to the head by direct impacts elsewhere on the body. Concussion typically results in the rapid onset of a short-lived impairment of neurologic function that resolves spontaneously. It may result in neuropathologic changes, but the acute clinical symptoms largely reflect a functional disturbance rather than a structural injury. Concussion results in a graded set of clinical symptoms that may or may not involve loss of consciousness. Resolution of the clinical and cognitive symptoms typically follows a sequential course; however, it is important to note that, in a small percentage of cases, postconcussive symptoms may be prolonged. No abnormality is seen on standard structural neuroimaging studies in concussion.[1]

Prevention

Setting Specific

1. Ensure a safe playing field or area for all athletes. Remove all possible hazards.
2. Ensure proper implementation of the emergency action plan (EAP) and an understanding of standing orders, including policies regarding return to play following previous head injuries.
3. Policies should include baseline measurements of balance, neuropsychologic testing, and use of the graded symptom checklist.
4. Ensure the reconditioning and maintenance of all safety equipment, including helmets.

Athlete Specific

1. Properly fit all safety equipment, including helmets and mouth guards.
2. Educate athletes regarding proper sport-specific techniques (e.g., tackling, checking).
3. Educate athletes and coaches/staff regarding concussion signs and symptoms as well as about risks associated with playing with head injuries.
4. Although certain equipment is advocated for use, there is no conclusive evidence showing the efficacy of neck-strengthening equipment, mouth guards, or headbands (in soccer).

Predisposing Factors

Intrinsic

1. Previous head injury

Extrinsic

1. Sport played (e.g., football, hockey, wrestling)
2. Position on the team (e.g., defensive backs in football)
3. Referees not making appropriate calls (i.e., allowing poor technique)
4. Poor technique

Recognition[1,2]

See **Figure 1** and **Figure 2**.

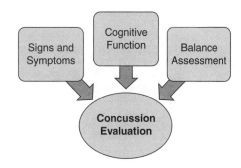

Figure 1   Evaluation of concussion.

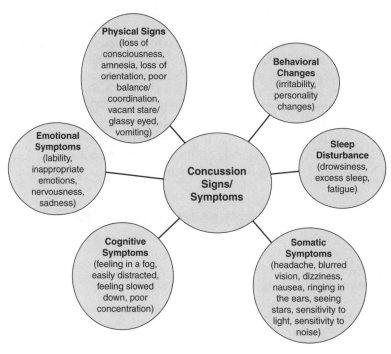

(Figure 2)   Signs and symptoms of concussion.

Balance Error Scoring System (BESS) for Balance Assessment[3]

1. All tests are performed barefoot without ankles taped.
2. Each test is performed for 20 seconds.
3. One point is given for each error committed during each 20-second trial (see **Table 1**).
4. The three stances are as follows: double leg (tests A and D), single leg (performed on nondominant leg; tests B and E), and tandem (nondominant leg in front; tests C and F).
5. Tests A through C are done on a firm surface such as the floor.
6. Tests D through F are done on an uneven surface such as foam.

TABLE 1

Balance Error Scoring System Errors
Hands lifted off iliac crests
Opening eyes
Step, stumble, or fall
Moving hip into more than 30 degrees of flexion or abduction
Lifting forefoot or heel
Remaining out of position for more than 5 seconds
The BESS score is calculated by adding one error point for each error or any combination of errors occurring during a movement.

Treatment

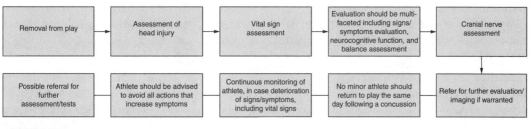

Figure 3 Algorithm for head injury assessment and treatment.

Return to Play[2,4]

- No athlete considered a minor should return to play the same day.
- The athlete should be symptom free at rest and exertion.
- Neurocognitive and balance testing should return to baseline (or normative values) at rest and following exertion.

Postconcussion Syndrome	Second Impact Syndrome
Postconcussion syndrome (PCS) is a condition in which the signs and symptoms of head injury last for a long period (i.e., weeks, months, or years). PCS can lead to learning disabilities and permanent cognitive challenges, including difficulty concentrating and memory loss. PCS has been associated with an earlier onset of Alzheimer's, depression, and Parkinson disease.	Second impact syndrome (SIS) is a medical emergency that occurs when the athlete suffers another concussion before the first one has fully healed, usually resulting in death or permanent neurologic damage. The exact mechanism of SIS is not understood; however, it does appear that adolescents are more at risk than adults.

References

1. McCrory P, Meeuwisse W, Johnston K. Consensus statement on concussion in sport. 3rd International Conference on Concussion in Sport held in Zurich, November 2008. *Clin J Sport Med* 2009;19:185–200.
2. Guskiewicz KM, Bruce SL, Cantu RC, et al. National Athletic Trainers' Association position statement: management of sport-related concussion. *J Athl Train.* 2004;39(3):280–297.
3. Guskiewicz KM, Ross SE, Marshall SW. Postural stability and neuropsychological deficits after concussion in collegiate athletes. *J Athl Train.* 2001;36(3):263–273.
4. Oliaro S, Anderson S, Hooker D. Management of cerebral concussion in sports: the athletic trainers' perspective. *J Athl Train.* 2001;36:257–262.
5. Sterr A, Herron KA, Haywood C, Montaldi D. Are mild head injuries as mild as we think? Neurobehavior concomitants of chronic post-concussion syndrome. *BMC Neurology.* 2006;6:7.
6. Notebaert AJ, Guskiewicz KM. Current trends in athletic training practices for concussion assessment and management. *J Athl Train.* 2005;40:320–325.
7. Almquist J, Broshek D, Erlanger D. Assessment of mild head injuries. *Athl Ther Today.* 2001;6:13–17.

Cervical Spine Injuries

Definition: A catastrophic cervical spine injury can be defined as "structural distortion of the cervical spinal column associated with actual or potential damage to the spinal cord." Serious spinal cord injuries can potentially cause devastating sequelae such as permanent neurologic impairment and premature mortality.[1]

Incidence: The estimated incidence of cervical spine injuries with spinal cord damage in the United States is 11,000 cases. Athletics is the fourth most common cause of cervical spine injuries; it the second most common in people younger than 30 years.[1] Cervical spine injuries are likely to occur in high-contact sports such as football, ice hockey, rugby, and lacrosse as well as in sports in which falling from a high elevation is possible, such as skiing, gymnastics, swimming and diving, track and field, and cheerleading.

Prevention

Setting Specific

1. Teaching of proper tackling technique in American football.
2. Strict enforcement of head-down contact rules by officials.[2]
3. Establishment and rehearsal of an emergency action plan that includes the skills needed to properly manage a cervical spine injury.
4. Athletic trainers working with gymnastics, ice sports, or water sports require expertise in the special extrication considerations associated with spine boarding an athlete from gymnastic pits, on ice, and in water.
5. Establish rapport with local emergency medical services (EMS).

Athlete Specific

1. Proper sizing and maintenance of the integrity of protective equipment.
2. Only use helmets that meet National Operating Committee for Standards on Athletic Equipment (NOCSAE) standards.
3. Use proper tackling techniques.

Predisposing Factors

Intrinsic

1. Poor bracing techniques
2. Improper tackling techniques
3. Stenosis of the spinal canal
4. Slow reaction time

Extrinsic

1. Poorly fitted or maintained protective equipment
2. Nature of sport and position played

Equipment List

1. Spine boards
2. Straps
3. Cervical collars
4. Head blocks
5. Stretcher
6. Portable electric screwdriver
7. Trauma sheers
8. Backup cutting tools (e.g., FM Extractor, Trainer's Angel, Schutt removal tool)

Recognition

Differential Diagnosis

1. Head injuries/concussions
2. Neck sprains/strains
3. Whiplash
4. Brachial plexus injuries (i.e., burners/stingers)
5. Cervical disc injuries

Signs and Symptoms

1. Axial loading is the primary mechanism for catastrophic cervical spine injury in athletics.[1,2]
2. Key signs and symptoms often include neck pain with palpation, bilateral neurologic symptoms in upper or lower extremities, inability to move extremities (paresthesia/paresis), and/or unconsciousness.

Treatment

Immediate Care

1. Ensure that cervical spine is in a neutral position and immediately apply manual stabilization.
2. Face mask should be removed within 1 minute once decision to immobilize and transport has been made, regardless of current respiratory status.[1,3,4,5]
3. A powered screwdriver is generally the fastest way to remove a face mask and produces the least head movement.[4]
4. Removal of helmet and shoulder pads should be deferred until the athlete has been transported to an emergency medical facility, except under specifically appropriate circumstances.[4]
5. Independent removal of the helmet or shoulder pads in American football and ice hockey is not recommended.[4]
6. A jaw-thrust maneuver should be used to open airway if needed.
7. Whenever possible, manual stabilization should be maintained.
8. Athletic trainers should purchase proper backboards for typical athlete size in the sport (e.g., football, basketball, volleyball).

Extended Care

1. The athletic trainer or team physician should accompany the athlete to the hospital.
2. Computed tomography (CT) should be used as the primary diagnostic test; radiographs and magnetic resonance imaging (MRI) are not recommended.

Rehearsal and Education Considerations

1. Mock scenarios should be timed.
2. Mock patients should wear equipment.
3. The person holding cervical spine stabilization should direct all movement with a count.
4. Groups should debrief after all practice sessions.
5. Special extrication considerations associated with spine boarding an athlete from gymnastic pits, on ice, and from water may require extra practice.

Return to Play[6,7]

1. There is no current consensus on specific return-to-play (RTP) guidelines.
2. RTP decisions should be based on the mechanism of injury, degree of anatomic damage, and the athlete's age and response to recovery.
3. Athlete must be symptom free, and have full range of motion (ROM) and strength.
4. Experts agree that odontoid abnormalities, atlanto-occipital fusion, and Klippel-Feil fusions above C3 are absolute contraindications to contact or collision sports.
5. Athletes must be cleared by a physician on a case-by-case basis.

Common Misconceptions

1. Protective equipment should be removed prior to immobilization.
2. Rescuers should always keep cervical spine in position found.
3. The head-tilt chin-lift maneuver can be used to open the airway in an athlete with a suspected cervical spine injury.
4. Screwdrivers or cutting tools alone are a reliable way to remove a face mask.

References

1. Swartz EE, Boden BP, Courson RW, et al. National Athletic Trainers' Association position statement: acute management of the cervical spine injured athlete. *J Athl Train.* 2009;44(3):306–331.

2. Heck JF, Clarke KS, Peterson TR, Torg JS, Weis MP. National Athletic Trainers' Association position statement: head-down contact and spearing in tackle football. *J Athl Train.* 2004;39(1):101–111.

3. Kleiner DM, Almquist JL, Bailes J, et al. *Prehospital Care of the Spine-Injured Athlete: A Document from the Inter-Association Task Force for Appropriate Care of the Spine-Injured Athlete.* Dallas, TX: National Athletic Trainers' Association; 2001.

4. Swartz EE. Efficient football helmet face mask removal. *Athl Ther Today.* 2007;24;21–24.

5. Torg JS, Guille JT, Jaffe S. Current concepts review: injuries to the cervical spine in American football. *J Bone Joint Surg.* 2002;84(1):112–122.

6. Vaccaro AR, Klein AR, Circcoti M, et al. Return to play criteria for the athlete with cervical spine injuries resulting in stinger and transient quadriplegia/paresis. *Spine J.* 2002;2(5):351–356.

7. Eddy D, Congini J, Loud K. Review of spine injuries and return to play. *Clin J Sport Med.* 2005;15(6):453–458.

Exertional Sickling

Definition: Exertional sickling is a condition of genetic predisposition in which risk of sudden death in sport in a sickle trait–positive athlete is 30 times higher than in non–sickle trait athletes.[1,2] Exertional sickling is a medical emergency involving ischemia of blood to the skeletal muscles due to a "log jamming" of red blood cells within the vessels. This will quickly cause cell death. These athletes must be transported immediately to a hospital.

Incidence: Athletes who are sickle trait positive number approximately 1 in 12 of those of African descent, about 1 in 100 of those of Hispanic descent, and 1 in 2,000 to 10,000 of those not of African descent.[4] Sickle cell trait is predominantly seen in people from backgrounds that have a high risk of malaria.[2] In the past decade, sickling-related death in sport has accounted for about 5% of all sudden death in sports; most of these deaths have been in preseason conditioning workouts.[1,4,5]

Prevention[1,4,5,7]

Setting Specific: Think SAME

1. Screen all athletes. If you know who to monitor, you know who to look after.
2. Acclimatization. Build up intensity of exercise slowly when conditioning or lifting. Do not perform workouts while febrile.
3. Modify drills. Avoid timed sprints or miles. No repeat sprints beyond 500 m without a rest break. No all-out exertion of any kind over 2 to 3 minutes without a rest break. Adjust work-to-rest cycles for heat accordingly.
4. Educate. Sports medicine staff, coaches, and athletes all need to be educated on the signs, symptoms, and immediate treatment of exertional sickling.

Athlete Specific: Think PUSH

1. Participation. Encourage the athlete to participate in preseason strength and conditioning programs to enhance preparedness.
2. Unique personal history. Sickle trait–positive athletes need to be addressed individually to monitor their specific triggers.
3. Set the tone. Sickle trait–positive athlete should feel comfortable reporting unusual symptoms immediately.
4. Hydration. Dehydration fosters sickling.[6] Urine color charts are useful for self-monitoring.

Predisposing Factors[1,2,4-6]

Intrinsic

1. Sickle trait positive
2. Illness
3. Dehydration
4. Asthma

Extrinsic

1. High ambient temperature
2. High altitude
3. Unacclimatized
4. Timed or repeat sprints
5. Few or no rest periods

Equipment List[1,2,4-6]

1. Emergency action plan (EAP) for sickling episode
2. Cell phone
3. Supplemental O_2
4. Rectal thermometer
5. Blood pressure cuff and stethoscope
6. Wrist watch

Recognition[1,2,4,5]

Differential Diagnosis[1,3–6]	Signs and Symptoms
1. Exertional heat illness 2. Dehydration 3. Heat syncope 4. Asthma attack 5. Cardiac conditions	1. Central nervous system dysfunction 2. Muscle "cramping," usually in lower back and legs 3. Ischemic pain 4. Swelling 5. Weakness 6. Tenderness 7. Inability to catch breath 8. Fatigue 9. Rhabdomyolysis

Treatment[1,2,4,5]

Immediate Treatment (Acute, <1 hr)

1. Cease activity.
2. Check vital signs.
3. Activate emergency medical services (EMS).
4. Administer high-flow oxygen (varies per state).
5. Cool athlete, if necessary (based on body temperature).
6. Call ahead to hospital and tell staff to expect explosive rhabdomyolysis.

Extended Treatment (>1 hr)

1. Immediate transport is recommended to minimize the effects of a sickling episode.
2. Extended care will need to address any lasting effects, such as kidney failure or liver failure, if present.

Return to Play[1,2,4,5]

1. Return to play (RTP) requires physician clearance.
2. RTP needs to be individualized based on level and severity of symptoms.

References

1. National Athletic Trainers' Association. Consensus statement: sickle cell trait and the athlete. Paper presented at: Annual Meeting of the National Athletic Trainers' Association; June 27, 2007; Anaheim, CA.
2. National Collegiate Athletic Association. Section 3c: the student-athlete with sickle cell trait. In: *2009–2010 NCAA Sports Medicine Handbook*. Indianapolis, IN: NCAA; 2009:86–88.
3. National Human Genome Research Institute. Learning about sickle cell disease. February 2007. Available at: http://www.genome.gov/10001219.
4. Eichner ER. Sickle cell trait. *J Sport Rehab*. 2007;16:197–203.
5. Eichner ER. Sickle cell trait and the athlete. *Gatorade Sports Sci Institute Sports Sci Exchange*. 2006;19:1–6.
6. Bergeron MF, Cannon JG, Hall EL, Kutlar A. Erythrocyte sickling during exercise and thermal stress. *Clin J Sport Med*. 2004;14:354–356.
7. Listed as Probable: Thoughts on Medicine in Sports. NCAA makes recommendation for sickle trait testing as part of lawsuit settlement. July 10, 2009. Available at: http://www.listedasprobable.typepad.com /blog/2009/07/as-part-of-the-ncaas-team-physician-listserve-i-recently-received-a-news-release-with-the-following-announcementthe-ncaa-is.html.

Lightning

Definition: A cloud-to-ground lightning flash is the product of the buildup and discharge of static electric energy between the charged regions of the cloud and the earth.[7] The thunder heard is caused by the rapid heating of the air surrounding the lightning strike. The range at which thunder is audible is approximately 16.09 km (10 miles).[1,5,7]

Incidence: Lightning kills approximately 100 people each year in the United States.[6]

- 92% of casualties occur between May and September, with the most during July.[6,7]
- 45% of the deaths and 80% of the casualties occur between 10:00 AM and 7:00 PM.[6,7]
- All fatalities had this in common: they were near the highest object or were the tallest object in the immediate area.[7]

Prevention

Setting Specific[1,7]

1. Monitor local weather forecasts.
2. Actively watch the weather, looking for high winds, darkening clouds, and so forth.
3. Define and locate safe buildings to evacuate to at each venue.
4. Use the 30-30 rule.

Athlete Specific[1,7]

1. Be aware of your hair standing on end.
2. Be aware of the sound of sizzling.
3. Crouch in a lightning-safe position: feet together, weight on the balls of your feet, head lowered, and ears covered.[4]

The 30-30 Rule[7]

Criteria for suspension of activities	By the time the flash-to-bang count approaches 30 seconds, all individuals should already be inside a safe shelter.
Criteria for resumption of activities	Wait at least 30 minutes after the last sound (thunder) or observation of lightning before leaving the safe shelter to resume activities.

Responsibilities of the Sports Medicine Team[8]

1. Establish authority and a policy on when to end the game.
2. Remove individuals from activity and/or stands when appropriate. Make sure you understand your crowd size, because this may change your evacuation methods.[8]
3. Know of a place suitable for habitation prior to a lightning storm.
4. Watch and monitor local weather forecasts and warnings.[1,7]

Recognition[1,2]

Signs and Symptoms	
Minor injury	Usually are conscious or have had a temporary loss of consciousness Possible temporary blindness or deafness Confusion or amnesia lasting hours to days Vitals are stable, but may present mild hypertension Possible tympanic membrane rupture Possible parasthesias, muscle pain, or headaches lasting days to months
Moderate injury	May be disoriented, combative, or comatose Possible temporary paralysis of upper/lower extremities Those affected extremities can appear blue, mottled, pale, pulseless If true hypovolemic shock exists, look for blunt abdominal injury or fracture First- and second-degree burns usually occur a few hours after injury Probable tympanic membrane injury Temporary cardiopulmonary standstill
Severe injury	Cardiac arrest with ventricular standstill or fibrillation Possible direct brain damage from the lightning strike, or hypoxia secondary to cardiac arrest Blunt trauma such as skull fractures and intracranial injuries

Treatment

Immediate Treatment

1. You may encounter anywhere from one victim to a triage situation.
   - The victims who are breathing and have a pulse, regardless of the state of consciousness, are generally going to do well.
   - The victims without a pulse and respiration are the ones on whom the rescuer can have the most impact.[2]
2. Treatment goes to the apparent dead first.[4,7,8]

Extended Treatment

1. All lightning strike victims should be transported to a hospital to be assessed and monitored.
2. Possible referral to specialists will depend on the severity of injuries.[3]

Immediate Treatment Kit List

1. Automated external defibrillator (AED) with appropriate kit inclusions
2. Cellular phone
3. Blankets
4. Splints
5. Burn treatment kit

Return to Play[3]

Given the variability of injury and the possibility of a multitude of sequelae, no return-to-play guidelines have been established. Depending on the severity of lighting injury, those who have received minor injuries have the greater chance of return to play, whereas those with severe injuries have a variable prognosis. The most important aspect of return to play is clearance from a physician.[3]

Minor injury recovery	Gradual recovery May suffer permanent neurologic damage or posttraumatic stress disorder Hospitalized with possible referral depending on severity of injury
Moderate injury recovery	Highly likely to survive Hospitalization for a few days with monitoring Possible temporary or permanent sequelae, including sleep disorders, parasthesias, generalized weakness, personality changes, and difficulty with fine motor functions and some mental functions
Severe injury recovery	Recovery is poor unless treated rapidly with resuscitation Prognosis is variable

References

1. Cooper MA, Andrews CJ, Holle RL. Lightning injuries. In: Auerbach PS, ed. *Wilderness Medicine*. 5th ed. St. Louis, MO: Mosby/Elsevier; 2007.
2. Cooper MA, Parkes R, Mayer M, et al. Treatment of lightning injury. In: Andrews CJ, Cooper MA, Darveniza M, Mackerras D, eds. *Lightning Injury: Electrical, Medical, and Legal Aspects*. Boca Raton, FL: CRC Press; 1995.
3. Cooper MA. Lightning injuries: follow-up and prognosis. In: Andrews CJ, Cooper MA, Darveniza M, Mackerras D, eds. *Lightning Injury: Electrical, Medical, and Legal Aspects*. Boca Raton, FL: CRC Press; 1995.
4. Kithil R. Lightning safety for campers and hikers. National Lightning Safety Institute. 1998. http://www.lightning-safety.com/index.html.
5. National Weather Service. Lightning, the underrated killer. Available at: http://www.lightningsafety.noaa.gov.
6. Roeder WP, Cooper MA, Holle R, et al. Lightning safety awareness. *Bull Am Meteorol Soc*. 2003;84(2):260–261.
7. Walsh KM, Bennett B, Cooper MA, et al. National Athletic Trainers' Association position statement: lightning safety for athletics and recreation. *J Athl Train*. 200;35(4):471–477.
8. Zimmermann C, Cooper MA, Holle RL. Lightning safety guidelines. *Ann Emerg Med*. 2002;39(6):660–664.

Asthma

Definition: Asthma is a chronic inflammatory disorder of the airways characterized by variable airway obstruction and bronchial hyperresponsiveness. Airway obstruction can lead to recurrent episodes of wheezing, breathlessness, chest tightness, and coughing.[2]

Incidence: Asthma currently affects over 300 million individuals worldwide[2] and 20 million Americans, with 5 million being under the age of 18 years.[5] Asthma is the cause of 4200 to 5000 American deaths per year.[1]

Prevention

Setting Specific

1. Prepare an emergency action plan (EAP).
2. Perform a preparticipation exam (PPE) for all athletes that includes asthma-related questions, lung auscultations, and peak flow meter (PFM) testing.
3. Prepare an asthma action plan.[1,2,8]
4. An automated external defibrillator (AED) should be available on site.
5. Athletic trainers should carry a PFM at practices and games.
6. Inhalers should be carried at all practices and games by student athletes or athletic trainers.
7. Supplemental oxygen should be available (if state regulations allow).

Athlete Specific

1. Carry a fast-acting inhaler at all times.
2. Know personal triggers of asthma attacks.
3. Perform a proper warm-up before exercise.[7]
4. Include detailed history on PPE (see **Table 1**).

Predisposing Factors

Intrinsic

1. Genetic factors
2. Obesity
3. Gender (male)
4. Diet
5. Respiratory infections
6. Strong emotional expressions

Extrinsic

1. Exposure to allergens (e.g., dust mites, animal fur, mold, pollen)
2. Tobacco smoke
3. Chemical irritants
4. Air pollution
5. Occupational sensitizers (asthma caused by exposure to an agent encountered in the work environment[1])

Equipment List

1. Athlete's inhaler
2. AED
3. Peak flow meter
4. Supplemental oxygen
5. CPR mask
6. Pulse oximeter
7. Emergency card (asthma action plan)

TABLE 1 — Questions Regarding Asthma to Include in a Preparticipation Examination

1. Do you have a family history of asthma?
2. Do you have any known allergens?
3. What is your level of exercise activity?
4. Have you experienced any of the following symptoms: chest tightness, coughing (at night or during exercise), shortness of breath, difficulty sleeping, wheezing, or use of accessory muscles to breathe?
5. Are these symptoms improved by asthma medication?
6. If asthma is known, how often is a rescue inhaler used? (Three or more times a week is considered uncontrolled asthma.[1])

Recognition

Differential Diagnosis

1. Cardiac condition: pulse rate low (or absent); PFM should not be affected
2. Vocal cord dysfunction: requires visualization of paradoxic vocal cord motion[1]
3. Pollution irritation: will resolve when taken out of environment
4. General sickness (bronchitis): no fever; should also not exercise
5. Anaphylactic shock
6. Cystic fibrosis
7. Choking: no breathing; look for foreign object and universal choking sign; perform Heimlich maneuver
8. Panic disorder
9. Decreased fitness level

Signs and Symptoms

1. PFM < 80% of best or normal value[1]
2. Presence/significant increase in wheezing, chest tightness
3. Respiratory rate > 25 breaths per minute[1]
4. Pulse > 120 beats per minute[2]
5. Weak breath sounds[2]
6. Unconsciousness

Treatment

Immediate

1. Inhalation of fast-acting medication (rapid-acting β_2 agonist).[1]
2. Calm athlete down.
3. Activate emergency medical services (EMS) if athlete is breathless.[2]
4. Activate EMS if no response to medication within 3 hours, or if there is further deterioration.[1]
5. Instruct athlete in proper breathing techniques.
6. Measure PFM.[1,2]
7. Administer supplemental oxygen if available.

Extended Care

1. Refer to pulmonologist (for pulmonary function testing[3] and spirometry[6]).
2. Include sport-specific testing.
3. Regular use of daily medication (controller).
4. Review of current medication.[3]

Return to Play

1. After acute asthma attack and inhalation of fast-acting medication, reassess athlete after each hour.[2]
2. Continue to monitor throughout rest of activity.[2]
3. If hospitalization is necessary, the athlete must be cleared by a medical doctor.[2]

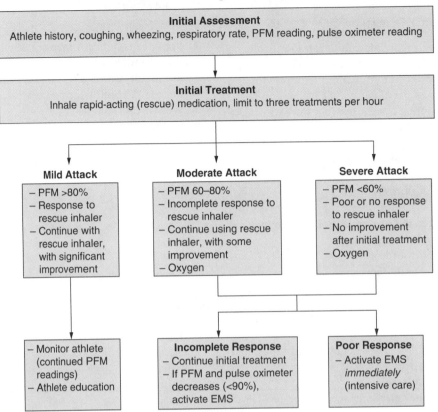

Acute Clinical Management of Asthma

Initial Assessment
Athlete history, coughing, wheezing, respiratory rate, PFM reading, pulse oximeter reading

Initial Treatment
Inhale rapid-acting (rescue) medication, limit to three treatments per hour

Mild Attack
– PFM >80%
– Response to rescue inhaler
– Continue with rescue inhaler, with significant improvement

Moderate Attack
– PFM 60–80%
– Incomplete response to rescue inhaler
– Continue using rescue inhaler, with some improvement
– Oxygen

Severe Attack
– PFM <60%
– Poor or no response to rescue inhaler
– No improvement after initial treatment
– Oxygen

– Monitor athlete (continued PFM readings)
– Athlete education

Incomplete Response
– Continue initial treatment
– If PFM and pulse oximeter decreases (<90%), activate EMS

Poor Response
– Activate EMS *immediately* (intensive care)

Figure 1 Acute clinical management of asthma. Information from Global Initiative for Asthma (GINA). *Global Strategy for Asthma Management and Prevention.* 2008. Available at: http://www.ginasthma.org; and National Athletic Trainers' Association Position Statement: Management of Asthma in Athletes. *J Athl Train.* 2005;40(3):224–245.

References

1. Global Initiative for Asthma (GINA). *Global Strategy for Asthma Management and Prevention.* 2008. Available at: http://www.ginasthma.org.
2. National Athletic Trainers' Association Position Statement: Management of Asthma in Athletes. *J Athl Train.* 2005;40(3):224–245.
3. National Asthma Education and Prevention Program. *Expert Panel Report II: Guidelines for the Diagnosis and Management of Asthma.* Publication 97-4051. Bethesda, MD: National Institutes of Health; 1997:12–18.
4. Centers for Disease Control and Prevention, National Asthma Control Program. *America Breathing Easier.* 2007. Available at: http://www.cdc.gov/ASTHMA/aag/2007/index.html.
5. Asthma and Allergy Foundation of America. Asthma facts and figures. Available at: http://www.aafa.org/display.cfm?id=8&sub=42#prev.
6. Rundell KW, Im J, Mayers LB, et al. Self-reported symptoms and exercise-induced asthma in the elite athlete. *Med Sci Sports Exerc.* 2001;33:208–213.
7. Weiler JM. Exercise-induced asthma: a practical guide to definitions, diagnosis, prevalence, and treatment. *Allergy Asthma Proc.* 1996;17:315–325.
8. Partridge MR. Delivering optimal care to the person with asthma: what are the key components and what do we mean by patient education? *Eur Respir J.* 1995;8:298–305.

Exertional Hyponatremia

Definition: Exertional hyponatremia is defined as serum sodium levels lower than 130 mmol/L resulting from overconsumption of water (or other low-solute beverages) or from the inadequate replacement of sweat sodium losses.[1]

Incidence: The overall incidence of exertional hyponatremia is relatively low; however, it may greatly differ depending on the specific event (e.g., ultra-endurance events vs. anaerobic events). Its incidence in ultra-endurance events has been reported to range between 0 and 79.4 in 1000 participants.[1]

Prevention[1–4,6]

Setting Specific

1. Availability of on-site medical care (by certified athletic trainers, sports medicine physicians, etc.)
2. Education of medical care providers on proper recognition and treatment of exertional hyponatremia (and differential diagnoses)
3. Availability of proper emergency equipment (core temperature monitoring device, IV equipment, i-STAT System hand-held blood analyzer, sodium supplementation, automated external defibrillator, etc.)

Athlete Specific

1. Risk education
2. Modification of normal dietary intake (i.e., increase sodium, moderate hypotonic fluids)
3. Education regarding sweat rate: match fluid intake with sweat/urine loss, with no more than 150% replacement of body weight loss
4. Rehydration with fluids containing sufficient sodium (e.g., sports drinks)

Predisposing Factors[1–4]

Intrinsic

1. High sodium concentration in sweat ("salty sweaters")
2. Decreased renal function
3. Hormonal insufficiencies
4. Females
5. Older individuals
6. High sweat rates

Extrinsic

1. Long distance events (>4 hours)
2. Slow-paced endurance events or athletes
3. Use of nonsteroidal anti-inflammatory drugs (NSAIDs)
4. Overconsumption of water (exceeding sweat/urine loss)
5. Low dietary sodium

Equipment List for Diagnosis and Treatment of Hyponatremia

1. Hand-held blood analyzer (Abbott Laboratories)
2. Rectal thermometer
3. Plasma sodium analyzer
4. Automated external defibrillator (AED)
5. Intravenous (IV) equipment
6. Normal/hypertonic saline
7. Sodium supplementation

Recognition

Differential Diagnosis[1,5]

1. Heat exhaustion
2. Heat stroke
3. Rhabdomyolysis
4. Dehydration
5. Heat cramps
6. Heat syncope
7. Cardiac condition

Signs and Symptoms[1,4,5]

1. Altered mental status: disorientation, lethargy, combative, syncope, coma
2. Muscular disturbances: twitching, cramping, weakness, incoordination
3. Headache
4. Nausea/vomiting
5. Physical exhaustion
6. Swelling of extremities
7. Pulmonary or cerebral edema
8. Seizures
9. Respiratory arrest
10. Core temperature typically lower than 40°C
11. Plasma sodium levels less than 135 mmol/L

Treatment[1,4,5]

Immediate Treatment (Acute, Based on Severity)

1. Call 911
2. Retrieve AED in case of respiratory arrest
3. Obtain plasma sodium levels
4. Oral hydration with salty fluids (e.g., bouillon)
5. Consumption of salty foods (e.g., potato chips) if hyponatremia is minor
6. Normal saline/hypertonic saline IV

Extended Care

1. Transfer to emergency medical facility (EMS)
2. Continue to administer IV saline
3. Monitor plasma sodium levels
4. Monitor plasma osmolality levels

Return to Play

1. Cleared by physician
2. Gradual and monitored activities
3. Education or reeducation on proper hydration and dietary considerations (to reduce risk of subsequent incidents)

TABLE 1 Categories of Exertional Hyponatremia (EH)[1]

Category	Plasma Na+ Concentration Range (mEq·L⁻¹)	Approximate Amount of Excess Fluid (L)
Mild EH	130–135	0.0–0.9
Moderate EH	125–129	1.2–2.4
Severe EH	<125	>2.4
Threshold for Onset of EH	125–130	0.9–2.4

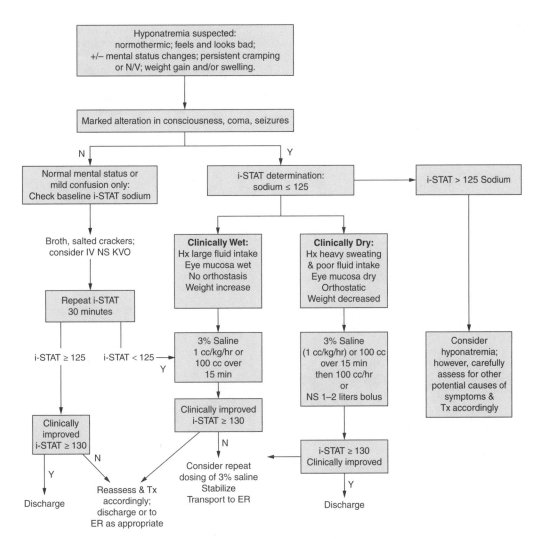

Figure 1 Algorithm for recognition and treatment of exertional hyponatremia. ER indicates emergency room; Hx, history; i-STAT, the i-STAT System hand-held blood analyzer from Abbott Laboratories (Abbott Park, IL); IV, intravenous; KVO, keep vein open; NS, normal saline; N/V, nausea/vomiting; Tx, treatment. From O'Connor FG, Pyne S, Adams WB, Brennan RJ, Howard T. *Managing Emergencies in Mass Participation Events: Medical Triage and Algorithms*. Bethesda, MD: USUHS Consortium for Health and Military Performance; 2009:3. Reprinted with permission.

References

1. Armstrong LE. *Exertional Heat Illnesses.* Champaign, IL: Human Kinetics; 2003.
2. Sawka MN, Burke LM, Eichner ER, et al. American College of Sports Medicine position stand: exercise and fluid replacement. *Med Sci Sports Exerc.* 2007;39(2):377–390.
3. Hew-Butler T, Verbalis JG, Noakes TD. Updated fluid recommendation: position statement from the International Marathon Medical Directors Association (IMMDA). *Clin J Sport Med.* 2006;16:283–292.
4. Armstrong LE, Casa DJ, Watson G. Exertional hyponatremia. *Curr Sports Med Rep.* 2006;5:221–222.
5. Binkley HM, Beckett J, Casa DJ, et al. National Athletic Trainers' Association position statement: exertional heat illnesses. *J Athl Train.* 2002;37(3):329–343.
6. Casa DJ, Armstrong LE, Hillman SK, et al. National Athletic Trainers' Association position statement: fluid replacement for athletes. *J Athl Train.* 2000;35(2):212–224.

Hypothermia

Definition: A decrease in core body temperature below 35°C (95°F). Described as a general cooling of the body, hypothermia can occur in temperatures above freezing if exposure is prolonged or occurs in wet, windy environments.[1,2]

Prevention[2–4]

Setting Specific

1. Emergency action plan
2. Automated external defibrillator (AED)
3. Education and training (CPR, first aid, AED use)
4. Implementing windchill guidelines for practices and competitions
5. Ample supplies on the field (warm fluids, heat packs, additional dry clothing, external heaters, rectal thermometer, telephone/radio, warm tub for immersion)

Athlete Specific

1. Proper clothing and equipment
2. Proper diet and fluid intake
3. Preparticipation examinations

Equipment List

1. AED
2. Blankets
3. Rectal thermometer (low-reading)
4. Blood pressure cuff
5. Warm liquid
6. Cell phone
7. Transportation
8. Warm shelter nearby

Predisposing Factors[2,3]

Intrinsic

1. Previous cold injuries or medical conditions (e.g., exercise-induced bronchospasm, Raynaud syndrome, anorexia nervosa, cold urticaria, cardiovascular disease)
2. Low caloric intake, dehydration and fatigue
3. Ethnicity
4. Nicotine, alcohol, and drug use
5. Body size and composition
6. Aerobic fitness level and training
7. Sex
8. Age

Extrinsic

1. Clothing
2. Environmental factors
   - Low air temperature
   - Humidity, rain, or immersion
   - Air movement
   - Little thermal radiation
   - Windchill index (see **Figure 1**)

Recognition

Differential Diagnosis[2,3]	Signs and Symptoms

1. Frostbite/frostnip
2. Cold urticaria
3. Rapid onset of itching, redness, and swelling of the skin after cold exposure
4. Exercise-induced bronchospasm
5. Nonfreezing cold injuries
  • Chilblains (pernio): inflammatory response to cold exposure
  • Trench foot: prolonged exposure (12 hours to 4 days) in cold/wet environments causing a swollen and edematous foot with aches, pains, and increased sensitivity.
	1. Mild hypothermia: 35–37°C (95–98.6°F); shivering, increased blood pressure, amnesia, dysarthria, poor judgment, behavior change, ataxia, apathy
	2. Moderate hypothermia: 32–34°C (90–94°F); all previous symptoms *plus* stupor, shivering ceases, pupils dilate, cardiac arrhythmias, decreased cardiac output, unconsciousness
	3. Severe hypothermia: below 32°C (90°F); all previous symptoms *plus* ventricular fibrillation, hypoventilation, loss of reflexes and voluntary motion, acid-based disturbances, no response to pain, reduced cerebral blood flow, hypotension, bradycardia, pulmonary edema, no corneal reflexes, areflexia, electroencephalographic silence, asystole
	  • Patients may appear to be dead, clinically, but due to cooled cerebral cells they can survive 45 to 60 minutes.[5]

Treatments[2,3]

General Hypothermia

1. Obtain rectal temperature.
2. Remove wet or damp clothing.
3. Use blankets to rewarm and move athlete to a warm environment.[6]
4. Apply heat only to trunk and other areas of the axilla, chest, and groin.[6]
5. Provide warm fluids, preferably with 6% to 8% carbohydrate.[6]

Specific Hypothermia

1. Avoid friction massage.
2. Observe for signs of cardiac arrhythmia.
3. Determine necessity of CPR.
4. Determine necessity of transport/contact emergency medical services (EMS).
5. Monitor vital signs.
6. Aggressive rewarming strategies (inhalation rewarming, heated intravenous solutions, peritoneal lavage, blood rewarming, use of antiarrhythmia drugs) when and if possible.

Frostbite

1. Superficial: Slow rewarming with water below 37°C (98°F).
2. Deep: Slow rewarming with water between 37°C and 40°C (98°F and 104°F). Thawing is complete when tissue is pliable and color and sensation have returned.
3. Avoid friction massage.

4. Avoid rewarming when the possibility of refreezing is present; protect from additional damage until transport to a medical facility is possible.
5. Avoid dry heat/steam.

Chilblains

1. Remove wet and constrictive clothing.
2. Wash and dry the area gently; then elevate the area and cover with warm, loose, and dry clothing or blankets.
3. Do not disturb blisters.
4. Do not apply friction massage, creams, or lotions.
5. Do not use high levels of heat or allow weight-bearing on the affected area.

Trench Foot

1. Thoroughly clean and dry the feet.
2. Apply warm packs or soak in warm water.

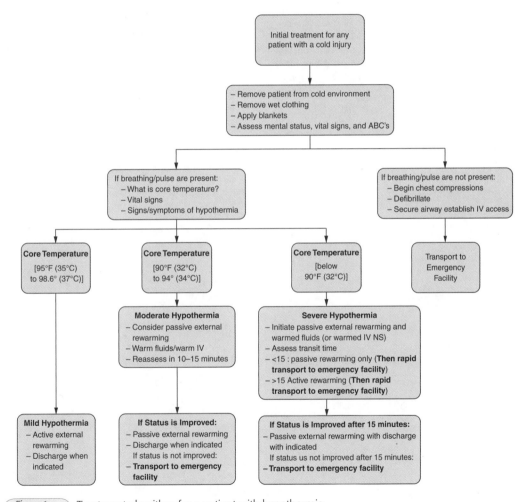

Figure 1 Treatment algorithm for a patient with hypothermia.
Source: From O'Connor FG, Pyne S, Adams WB, Brennan FH, Howard T. *Managing Emergencies in Mass Participation Events: Medical Triage and Algorithms*. Bethesda, MD: USUHS Consortium for Health and Military Performance, 2009:3. Reprinted with permission.

Return to Play

Hypothermia

1. Core temperature above 37°C (98°F)
2. All signs and symptoms extinct
3. Physician clearance

Frostbite

1. Tissues thawed
2. Sensations intact
3. Full recovery from surgery
4. Physician clearance

Chilblains

1. Blisters healed
2. Symptoms gone
3. Physician clearance

Trench Foot

1. No infections present
2. Healed and functioning feet
3. Physician clearance

References

1. Rehberg RS. *Sports Emergency Care: A Team Approach.* Thorofare, NJ: Slack; 2007.
2. Cappaert TA, Stone JA, Castellani JW, et al. National Athletic Trainer's Association position statement: environmental cold injuries. *J Athl Train.* 2008;43(6):640–658.
3. Catellani JW, Young AJ, Ducharme, MB, et al. American College of Sports Medicine Position stand: prevention of cold injuries during exercise. *Med Sci Sports Exerc.* 2006;38(11):2012–2029.
4. Biem J, Koehncke N, Classen D, Dosman J. Out of the cold: management of hypothermia and frostbite. *Can Med Assoc J.* 2000;168(3):305–311.
5. Martyn J. Diagnosing and treating hypothermia. *Can Med Assoc J.* 1981;125(10):1089–1096.
6. Kempainen RR, Brunette DD. The evaluation and management of accidental hypothermia. *Respir Care J.* 2004;49(2):192–205.
7. O'Connor FG, Pyne S, Adams WB, et al. *Managing Emergencies in Mass Participation Events: Medical Triage and Algorithms.* USUHS Consortium for Health and Military Performance; 2009.

Anaphylaxis

Definition: There currently is not a universally agreed-upon definition of anaphylaxis. The National Institute of Allergy and Infectious Disease and the Food Allergy and Anaphylaxis Network have agreed that "anaphylaxis is a serious allergic reaction that is rapid in onset and may cause death." The European Academy of Allergology and Clinical Immunology Nomenclature Committee proposed the following: "Anaphylaxis is a severe, life-threatening, generalized or hypersensitivity reaction that is characterized by rapidly developing life-threatening airway and/or breathing and/or circulation problems usually associated with skin and mucosal changes."[1]

Prevention

Setting Specific

1. Establishment and rehearsal of an emergency action plan that clearly describes the steps that must to be taken in the event of an anaphylactic reaction. The anaphylaxis action plan should be shared with all caregivers and school staff.
2. Certified athletic trainers are knowledgeable in the use of epinephrine autoinjectors, such as Epi-pens and can provide life-saving acts in the case of severe reactions.
3. Knowledge of athletes who have allergic reactions, who needs Epi-pens, and what they're allergic to.
4. Inform coaches and other staff of those with allergies and their triggers.

Athlete Specific

1. Avoid known triggers such as foods, medications, insects, latex, and so on. For exercise-induced anaphylaxis, avoid cold air or cold water exposure.
2. Epi-pens should be carried at all times by those who have life-threatening allergies. It is recommended that certified athletic trainers also be prescribed autoinjectors.
3. It is recommended that those who have had an anaphylactic reaction be referred to an allergist or immunologist to reinforce information and provide additional information, testing, and therapy to the patient.[1–3]
4. Those at risk for anaphylaxis should wear or hold medical identification.[1]

Predisposing Factors

Intrinsic[2]

1. Age.
2. Diseases such as concomitant allergic rhinitis and eczema, asthma, chronic obstructive pulmonary disease, other respiratory diseases, cardiovascular diseases, mastocytosis, and clonal mast cell disorders.
3. Other conditions can impede prompt recognition of symptoms, such as vision or hearing impairment, neurologic disorders, psychiatric disorders, autism spectrum disorder, and developmental delay.

Extrinsic

1. The use of medications such as any that act on the central nervous system (CNS) (e.g., diphenhydramine, chlorpheniramine, and other first-generation H_1-antihistamines, or any CNS-active chemical such as ethanol) or recreational drugs can interfere with the recognition of anaphylaxis. Beta-blockers and angiotensin-converting enzyme inhibitors used to manage cardiovascular disease can make anaphylaxis more difficult to treat.[1]
2. Exercise, exposure to extreme temperatures or humidity, disrupted routine, feeling unwell, acute infection, emotional stress, menses, ingestion of nonsteroidal anti-inflammatory drugs.[4]

Recognition

Differential Diagnosis[5]	Signs and Symptoms
1. Asthma attack (life threatening) 2. Low blood pressure with a purpuric rash can be a sign of septic shock (life threatening) 3. Faint 4. Panic attack 5. Idiopathic urticaria	1. Sudden and rapid onset of symptoms 2. Airway problems: airway swelling (throat and tongue swelling), difficulty breathing and swallowing with a feeling that the throat is closing, hoarse voice, stridor 3. Breathing problems: shortness of breath, wheezing, cyanosis, feeling tired, confusion due to hypoxia 4. Circulation problems: signs of shock (pale, cool, clammy skin), increased pulse, low blood pressure, feeling faint, dizziness, cardiac arrest 5. Skin changes: erythema, urticaria, angioedema (most commonly in the lips, eyelids, mouth, and throat)[1,6]

Treatment

See **Figure 1**.

Equipment List

1. Epi-pen
2. Cellular phone
3. Benadryl
4. Ice
5. Blood pressure cuff and stethoscope
6. Wrist watch to take pulse
7. CPR mask
8. Automated external defibrillator (AED)
9. Emergency contact cards

Most Common Triggers

1. Food: peanuts, tree nuts, shellfish, fish, milk, eggs
2. Drugs: muscle relaxants, antibiotics, non-steroidal anti-inflammatory drugs, and aspirin
3. Insects: venom from stinging insect or saliva from a biting insect
4. Other: latex, animal dander, grass, pollen,
5. Nonimmunologic: exercise, cold air/water, heat, radiation, ethanol

Key Preparticipation Exam Questions

1. Any known allergies?
2. Is the allergy life threatening?
3. What symptoms are experienced during an allergic reaction?
4. What treatment is used?
5. Any side effects to medication?

References

1. Soar J, Pumphrey R, Cant A, et al. Emergency treatment of anaphylactic reactions: guidelines for healthcare providers. *Resuscitation*. 2008;77(2):157–169.
2. Sampson HA, Munoz-Furlong A, Campbell RL. Second symposium on the definition and management of anaphylaxis: summary report—Second National Institute of Allergy and Infectious Disease/Food Allergy and Anaphylaxis Network Symposium. *Ann Emerg Medicine*. 2006;47(4):373–380.
3. Liberman DB, Teach SJ. Management of anaphylaxis in children. *Pediatr Emerg Care*. 2008;24(12):861–869.
4. Simons FE. Anaphylaxis: recent advances in assessment and treatment. *J Allergy Clin Immunol*. 2009;124(4):625–636.
5. Soar J. Emergency treatment of anaphylaxis in adults: concise guidance. *Clin Med*. 2009;9(2):181–185.
6. Tse Y, Rylance G. Emergency management of anaphylaxis in children and young people: new guidance from the Resuscitation Council (UK). *Arch Dis Child*. 2009;94(4):97–101.
7. Borchers AT, Naguwa SM, et al. The diagnosis and management of anaphylaxis. *Compr Ther*. 2004;30(2):111–120.
8. Lieberman P. The diagnosis and management of anaphylaxis: an updated practice parameter. *J Allergy Clin Immunol*. 2005;115(3):S483–S523.

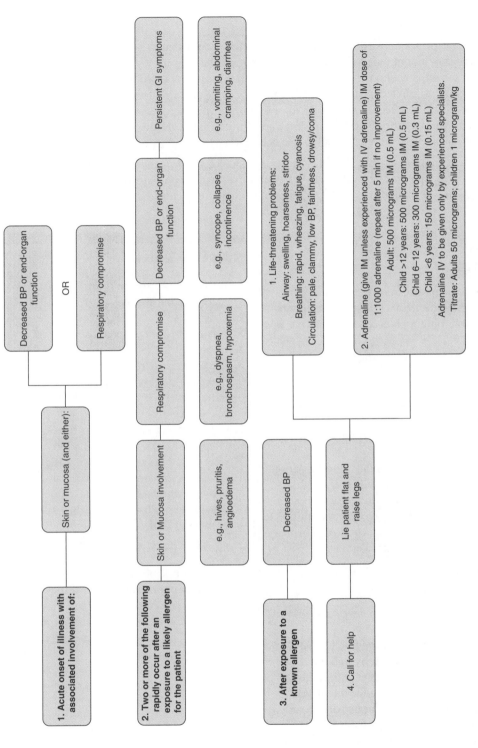

Figure 1 Visual representation of the anaphylaxis criteria (likely when any one of the first three criteria, marked in bold, is met) and treatment of the condition.

Source: Adapted from Manivannan V, Decker WW, Stead LG, Li JT, Campbell RL. Visual representation of National Institute of Allergy and Infectious Disease and Food Allergy and Anaphylaxis Network criteria for anaphylaxis. *Int J Emerg Med.* 2009;2(1):3–5; and Tse Y, Rylance G. Emergency management of anaphylaxis in children and young people: new guidance from the Resuscitation Council (UK). *Arch Dis Child Educ Pract Ed.* 2009;94:97–100.

Diabetes

Definition: Diabetes mellitus is a disorder of carbohydrate metabolism that is caused by inadequate production or utilization of insulin and inefficient use of blood sugar.[1] Diabetes mellitus is classified into two types. Type 1 is also known as insulin-dependent diabetes, in which the pancreas produces little or no insulin. In type 2 diabetes (non-insulin dependent diabetes), the pancreas either produces an insufficient amount of insulin, or the cells do not effectively respond to the insulin. Diabetic emergencies include hypoglycemia and hyperglycemia. Normal fasting blood glucose levels are 60 to 100 mg/dL. Hypoglycemia occurs when blood glucose levels fall below 70 mg/dL; hyperglycemia occurs when blood glucose levels exceed 180 mg/dL.

Incidence: According to statistics from the Centers for Disease Control and Prevention, it is estimated that 23.6 million people are affected by diabetes. Among this group, approximately 185,000 are younger than 20 years, and 7.8 million are aged 20 to 39 years. This age group constitutes the majority of athletes, which is of concern in the athletic environment.[2]

Prevention

Setting Specific[1–4]

1. Perform a preparticipation examination (PPE) to determine the presence of a preexisting condition and obtain glucose levels to serve as baseline.
2. Develop an emergency action plan (EAP) focusing on hypoglycemic and hyperglycemic emergencies to prevent condition from worsening.
3. Educate athletes, parents, athletic trainers, and primary care doctors in the recognition and initial treatment of hypoglycemia and hyperglycemia.
4. Develop a diabetes care plan: blood glucose monitoring guidelines, insulin therapy guidelines, list of other medications, guidelines for hypoglycemia and hyperglycemia recognition and treatment, emergency contact information, and athlete's medical alert tag.

Athlete Specific[1,3,4]

1. Education in exercise nutrition.
2. Ensure preexercise glucose levels are within normal limits.
3. Monitor glucose levels throughout play.
4. Be sure to maintain proper hydration.
5. Review practice and/or weight lifting and conditioning plans and make adjustments daily.
6. Create a diabetes care kit to be with the athlete at all times, including a diabetes care plan, blood glucose monitoring equipment and supplies (blood glucose meter and test strips), supplies to treat hypoglycemia that include sugary foods (e.g., glucose tablets, sugar packets) or sugary fluids (e.g., orange juice, nondiet soda), and a glucagon injection kit, supplies for urine or blood ketone testing, a "sharps" container for proper disposal of syringes and lancets, and spare batteries for the blood glucose meter and/or insulin pump.

Predisposing Factors[5]

1. Impaired glucose tolerance and/or impaired fasting glucose
2. Over age 45
3. A family history of diabetes
4. Overweight
5. Do not exercise regularly
6. Low high-density lipoprotein (HDL) cholesterol level or high triglyceride levels, high blood pressure
7. Certain racial and ethnic groups: non-Hispanic blacks, Hispanic/Latino Americans, Asian Americans, Pacific Islanders, American Indians, and Alaska Natives
8. Women who had gestational diabetes, or who have had a baby that weighed 9 pounds or more at birth

Recognition

Differential Diagnosis

1. Hypoglycemia
2. Hyperglycemia
3. Anaphylaxis
4. Exertional sickling
5. Heart attack
6. Genetic heart condition
7. Head injury
8. Heat illness
9. Stroke

Signs and Symptoms: Hypoglycemia

1. Sudden onset
2. Pale, cool, clammy skin
3. Mood changes, disorientation, confusion, stupor
4. Unresponsiveness (late stages)

Signs and Symptoms: Hyperglycemia

1. Gradual onset
2. Flushed, warm, dry skin
3. Frequent urination
4. Irregular breathing
5. Fruity or sweet odor on breath
6. Nausea, feeling and looking ill
7. Drowsiness, disorientation
8. Unresponsiveness (late stages)

Emergency Equipment Checklist[1-2,4,6]

1. Diabetes care plan
2. Medical alert tag
3. Glucometer
4. Test strips
5. Sugary foods (glucose tablets)
6. Sugary fluids (orange juice)
7. Glucagon injection kit
8. Insulin syringes
9. Insulin
10. Alcohol swabs
11. Urine testing supplies
12. Ketone testing supplies (ketone strips)
13. Sharps container
14. Spare batteries
15. Pump tubes
16. Nickel (to open pump)

Treatment

Immediate Treatment[1]

1. Check for life-threatening conditions (ABCs).
2. If athlete's medical history is unknown, look for a medic alert tag, or ask bystanders whether they know if the athlete has diabetes.
3. If athlete is conscious, give him or her some form of sugar (e.g., glucose paste, cake icing, table sugar, candy, fruit juice, nondiet soda) to help restore a normal balance. *Note:* Do not give food or drink if athlete is experiencing an altered state of consciousness. A glucagon injection may serve as an alternate method of restoring a normal blood glucose level.
4. If it is unclear whether the diabetic emergency is due to hypoglycemia or hyperglycemia, give a form of sugar—if sugar levels are low, recovery will be rapid; if they are high, additional sugar will not harm the athlete.
5. If the athlete is not feeling better within 5 minutes, activate the emergency medical services (EMS).

6. If the athlete is unconscious, activate EMS immediately, retrieve emergency equipment, and do not give anything orally.
7. Monitor and document vital signs until EMS arrives.

Extended Care[1,4]

1. Continue to monitor blood glucose levels to ensure normal levels.
2. Once blood glucose levels are within normal range in a hypoglycemic athlete, the athlete may consume a snack (e.g. sandwich, bagel).
3. Transport to emergency department if necessary.
4. Follow up with primary care physician, team physician, dietician, and nutritionist.

Questions and Actions Regarding Diabetes That Should Be Included in the Preparticipation Physical Examination in Athletics

Family History

1. Does anyone in your family have diabetes (type 1 or type 2)?
2. Has anyone in your family experienced a diabetic emergency (hypoglycemia, hyperglycemia, diabetic coma)?

Personal History

1. Have you been diagnosed with diabetes (type 1 or type 2)? If so, are you able to regulate your blood glucose levels?
2. Do you use insulin shots?
3. Do you use an insulin pump?
4. Do you take any medications to control your diabetes?
5. Have you ever experienced a diabetic emergency (hypoglycemia or hyperglycemia)?

Physical Examination

1. Obtain resting blood glucose levels.
2. Obtain fasting blood glucose levels.
3. Obtain exercising blood glucose levels.

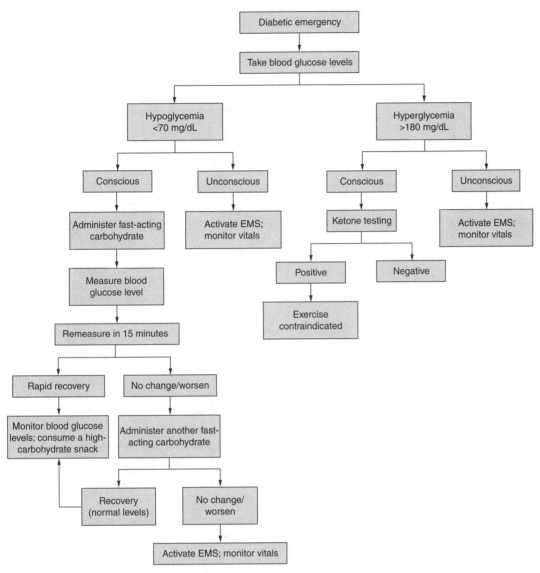

Figure 1   Management of a diabetic emergency.[6–9]

References

1. Rehberg, Robb S. *Sports Emergency Care: A Team Approach.* Thorofare, NJ: Slack; 2007.
2. Chansky, Michael E, Jillian G, et al. Hyperglycemic emergencies in athletes. *Clin Sports Med.* 2009;28:469–478.
3. Jimenez CC. Diabetes and exercise: the role of the athletic trainer. *J Athl Train.* 1997;32:339–343.
4. Jimenez, Carolyn C, et al. National Athletic Trainers' Association position statement: management of the athlete with type 1 diabetes mellitus. *J Athl Train.* 2007;42(4): 536–545.
5. American Diabetes Association. Risk factors. Available at: http://www.diabetes.org/diabetes-basics/prevention/risk-factors/.
6. American Diabetes Association. Preventing and treating severe hypoglycemia. Available at: http://www.diabetes.org/preventing.jsp.
7. American Diabetes Association. Hypoglycemia. Available at: http://www.diabetes.org/type-1-diabetes/hypoglyce-mia.jsp.
8. Sigal RJ, Kenny GP, Wasserman DH, et al. Physical activity/exercise and type 2 diabetes: a consensus statement from the American Diabetes Association. *Diabetes Care.* 2006;29: 1433–1438.
9. Zinman B, Ruderman N, Campaigne BN, et al. Physical activity/exercise and diabetes. *Diabetes Care.* 2004;27: S58–S62.

GLOSSARY

accidental hypothermia Hypothermia that occurs in natural settings.

acclimation Adaptive changes that occur in response to experimentally induced changes in particular climatic factors. Used most often in research studies to refer to the artificial process of acclimatization that is induced via climate-controlled chambers.

acclimatization A complex series of adaptive responses that demonstrate improved homeostatic balance in multiple organs; usually requires 10 to 14 days for responses to develop adequately. The body can acclimatize (to varying degrees) to hot, cold, high altitude, underwater, and air-polluted environments.

Adson test A test for thoracic outlet syndrome; the humerus is abducted to 90° and is externally rotated, the elbow flexed to 90°, and the head turned to the side being tested.

airway access Ability to expose and maintain breathing through an injured patient's airway.

airway lumen The inner lining of the bronchial airways.

anaphylaxis A life-threatening allergic reaction with symptoms that develop rapidly.

anterograde amnesia Sometimes referred to as posttraumatic amnesia, it is characterized by difficulty remembering events immediately following the injury.

apoptosis Process of programmed cell death.

arginine vasopressin (AVP) Pituitary hormone that limits production of urine by stimulating water reabsorption in the kidneys (also known as antidiuretic hormone or ADH).

arrhythmogenic right ventricular cardiomyopathy Progressive fibro-fatty replacement of the right ventricular myocardium, causing wall thinning and right ventricular dilatation.

arterial pressure index (API) A measure of arterial flow determined by dividing the systolic pressure of the lower extremity (cuff just above the ankle) by the systolic pressure of the upper extremity (brachial artery); acceptable level is greater than 0.90.

asymptomatic hyponatremia Sodium deficiency in which plasma sodium is below normal levels (typically 130–135 mEq·L^{-1}), but the patient experiences no symptoms.

atopy A predisposition to developing a hypersensitivity reaction to a common environmental antigen.

automated external defibrillator (AED) Computerized device that analyzes the heart rhythm, determines whether a shock is needed for a ventricular arrhythmia, charges to an appropriate shock dose, and uses audio and visual instructions to guide the rescuer.

axial load A situation in which the head and neck is flexed between 20° and 30° and the head serves as a point of contact.

background connection Activities that support both formal and informal learning opportunities by encouraging learners to connect their previous experiences and knowledge with sudden-death conditions.

Balance Error Scoring System (BESS) A clinical sideline measure of postural stability.

biphasic reaction The recurrence of symptoms of anaphylaxis within 72 hours of an initial attack with no further exposure to the allergen.

blunt injury   A mechanism of lightning injury by which the lightning strike causes a repercussive force creating blunt injuries such as ruptured tympanic membranes or violent muscular contractions that cause dislocations or fractures.

bronchoconstriction   Constriction of the airways.

catastrophic cervical spinal cord injury   An injury in which a structural distortion of the cervical spinal column has occurred and is associated with actual or potential damage to the spinal cord.

catastrophic injury or illness   A sudden death or disability in which there is life-altering physical or mental impairment, or both.

central pontine myelinolysis (CPM)   Brain dysfunction caused by destruction of the myelin sheath of nerve cells within the brainstem. This occurs most often when low blood sodium levels are corrected too quickly via hypertonic intravenous saline.

cerebral concussion   A complex pathophysiologic process affecting the brain, induced by traumatic biomechanical forces that results in a rapid but transient onset of neurologic dysfunction; typically does not result in any structural brain injury that can be identified using traditional imaging techniques, including computed tomography scans and magnetic resonance imaging.

cold acclimatization   A complex series of beneficial adaptations made over 14 days that enhances heat production and minimizes heat loss while exposed to cold conditions.

cold stressor   Any intrinsic or extrinsic factor that encourages heat loss from the body.

cold water immersion (CWI)   Cooling via immersion in a tub of water with temperatures ranging from approximately 2° to 13°C (35°–55°F), with faster cooling occurring at lower temperatures and when the water is circulated. Often referred to as *ice-water immersion*.

commotio cordis   Nonpenetrating, blunt trauma to the chest, usually from a firm projectile such as a baseball, lacrosse ball, or hockey puck, that induces ventricular fibrillation and sudden cardiac arrest.

contact injury   A mechanism of lightning injury by which the lightning strikes an object to which the victim is connected.

core body temperature   Temperature of the internal organs or thermal core as measured by a valid device (i.e., rectal thermometer, gastrointestinal thermistor).

coronary artery disease (CAD)   Condition in which plaque builds up inside the coronary arteries.

deep vein thrombosis (DVT)   A blood clot that forms in a vein deep in the body, most typically in the lower extremity but also possible in the upper extremity.

dehydration   The process of water loss leading to hypohydration. Usually measured by body mass loss, urine color, urine osmolality, urine specific gravity, or plasma osmolality (the gold standard).

dialogic discussion   A method of encouraging higher-level thinking by promoting problem solving and learning through open-ended activities, which challenge students to make decisions and critically apply their knowledge. Dialogic discussion facilitates learning by challenging students to reflect upon their perspectives and beliefs when making decisions.

diffuse brain injury   Brain injuries that result in widespread or global disruption of neurologic function and are not usually associated with macroscopically visible brain lesions except in the most severe cases. Structural diffuse brain injury (diffuse axonal injury) is the most severe type of diffuse injury because when axonal disruption occurs, it often results in disturbance of cognitive functions, such as concentration and memory.

direct fatality   A fatality resulting directly from participation in the fundamental skills of a sport.

direct injury   An injury resulting from participation in the skills of a sport.

direct injury   A mechanism of lightning injury by which the lightning strikes the person or object directly.

directed instruction   A method that uses a combination of modeling, performance, and constructive feedback for skill instruction and mastery. This teaching method is most effective for communicating psychomotor skill development, not complex theoretical concepts. Directed instruction provides learners with the opportunity to apply new knowledge and associated skills in a controlled environment with immediate feedback on performance.

ejection fraction   Fraction of total volume of blood pumped by the heart during each cardiac cycle; normal is greater than 50%.

emergency action plan (EAP)   (1) A written document that defines the standard of care for the management of emergencies in athletics. (2) For a mass participation event, a written document that outlines event-day policy well in advance of the event to reduce debates about critical decisions during the event and to establish protocols for emergency situations.

emergency management   Treatment of an acute injury or condition that poses a risk of sudden death.

epidural hematoma   A brain injury characterized by pooling of blood between the dura mater (outermost meningeal layer) and the skull.

epinephrine autoinjector   Intramuscular drug delivery system preloaded with a specific dosage of epinephrine for use during an emergency anaphylactic reaction.

equipment intensive   Sports or activities that require the user to wear protective equipment such as helmets and shoulder pads.

equipment removal   Skills executed in an emergency injury situation to remove protective equipment that interferes with the ability to effectively treat or immobilize a victim.

exacerbation   Worsening of a disease or condition.

exercise-associated collapse (EAC)   A physiologic condition that occurs after an endurance event. The pathophysiology of EAC is postural hypotension that results when the loss of muscle pumping action caused by the cessation of exercise is combined with cutaneous vasodilation.

exertional heat stroke (EHS)   a medical emergency involving life-threatening hyperthermia (rectal temperature > 40.0–40.5°C [104–105°F]) with concomitant central nervous system dysfunction; treatment involves cooling the body.

exertional sickling   Medical emergency occurring when an athlete with sickle cell trait experiences the sickling of red blood cells.

experiential learning   A method that allows for firsthand application of skills and knowledge, resulting in a realistic application of a learner's knowledge. Experiential learning requires learners to reflect upon their experiences to promote understanding and skill development and is often implemented in real time.

explosive rhabdomyolysis   Potentially fatal condition involving the breakdown of skeletal muscle fibers, resulting in the release of muscle fiber contents into circulation.

first aid   Emergency treatment administered to an injured or sick person before professional medical care is available.

first responder   The first person present at the scene of a sudden illness or injury.

fluid overload   An excess of total body fluid volume (hypervolemia).

forced expiratory volume in the first second of expiration (FEV₁) The volume of air that is forced out of the lungs in 1 second.

fulminant ischemic rhabdomyolysis Rapid breakdown of muscle tissue due to decreased blood flow.

Graded Symptom Checklist Sometimes referred to as a Postconcussion Symptom Scale, it is a Likert symptom inventory scale used to evaluate both the number and severity of symptoms commonly associated with cerebral concussion and other forms of traumatic brain injury.

glucagon A hormone produced by the pancreas that helps increase serum glucose level by stimulating glycogen release.

ground current See *step voltage.*

heat balance equation Describes the net rate at which a person generates and exchanges heat with his or her environment. It is composed of body heat content (S), metabolic rate (M), work rate (W), evaporative heat transfer (E), convective heat transfer (C), conductive heat transfer (K), and radiant heat exchange (R): $S = M - (\pm W) - E \pm R \pm C \pm K$.

high-altitude cerebral edema (HACE) A condition that only manifests in high-altitude outdoor settings in which low oxygen levels trigger swelling of brain tissue.

high-altitude pulmonary edema (HAPE) A condition that only manifests in high-altitude outdoor settings in which low oxygen levels trigger swelling of lung tissue, filling them with fluid.

hypertrophic cardiomyopathy Pathologic hypertrophy (thickening) of the ventricular wall muscle, usually asymmetric and involving the ventricular septum. Echocardiogram demonstrates a left ventricular wall thickness greater than 16 mm (normal, <12 mm; borderline, 13–15 mm), left ventricular end-diastolic diameter less than 45 mm, and impaired diastolic filling. Histopathologic examination shows disorganized cellular architecture and myocardial disarray.

hypervolemic hyponatremia An excess of total body water (fluid overload) with an expanded extracellular fluid volume and increased whole-body sodium. A common sign of this condition is extremity edema (puffiness).

hypoglycemia A low serum glucose level that affects physiologic function.

hypothermia Clinically defined as being when core body temperature drops below 35°C (95°F) as a result of the human body losing more heat than it can produce. Central nervous system dysfunction is also present in this condition.

hypotonic Having an osmotic concentration less than that of normal blood.

hypovolemic hyponatremia A reduced extracellular volume with deficits of total body sodium and water.

immobilization The use of external stabilization devices such as extrication collars and a spine board with straps to secure an injured patient's body so that it will not move during transport or emergency treatment.

impact injury A brain injury resulting from a direct blow to the head.

impulse injury A brain injury resulting from an acceleration or deceleration force, setting the head—and therefore the brain—in motion, without directly contacting the head (e.g., whiplash injuries).

incident command center The location of the administrative group specifically placed at a key event site to facilitate the response to an adverse event.

incident command coordinator The person in charge of the incident command center.

indirect fatality   A fatality caused by systemic failure as a result of exertion while participating in a sport activity or by a complication that was secondary to a nonfatal injury; examples include cardiac failure and an asthma attack.

insulin   A hormone produced by the pancreas that helps glucose into cells for use.

ion channel disorder   A primary electrical disease of the heart predisposing to lethal ventricular arrhythmias and characterized by mutations in ion channel proteins that lead to dysfunctional sodium, potassium, calcium, and other ion transport across cell membranes.

keraunoparalysis   A transient paralysis, extreme vasoconstriction, and sensory disturbance caused by a lightning strike.

lectures   An instructional method that is teacher centered and takes place in a formal setting.

lift and slide   A transfer technique to a spine board for a potential spine-injured victim who is lying supine.

Marfan syndrome   Inherited disorder of connective tissue that affects multiple organ systems, causing a progressive dilatation and weakness (cystic medial necrosis) of the proximal aorta that can lead to rupture and sudden death.

mass casualty incident (MCI)   Any event with casualties that overtax the community medical system's assets.

mechanoelectric coupling   Physical stimulation of the heart with the production of electrical consequences. This phenomenon has been attributed to the presence of stretch-sensitive ion channels within cardiac myocytes and has been implicated as a factor in cases of commotio cordis.

metabolic equivalent (MET)   Ratio comparing a person's metabolic rate while seated and resting to his or her metabolic rate while performing some task.

metered dose inhaler   A pressurized hand-held device that uses propellants to deliver medication to the lungs.

near-fatal asthma   Asthma symptoms that cause severe breathing difficulties that do not result in death.

nebulizer   A device used for delivering medication into the lungs during inhalation.

neutral alignment   A situation in which the head and neck rest in an aligned position, as in the anatomic position. The cervical spine will present in a slight lordotic curve and the space around the cord will be maximized.

Paget-Schroetter syndrome (PSS)   Axillosubclavian deep vein thrombosis without secondary cause (trauma).

peak expiratory flow rate (PEFR)   The maximal rate that a person can exhale during a short maximal expiratory effort after a full inspiration.

peak flow meter   A hand-held device that is used to measure peak expiratory flow rate.

physiologic hyponatremia   Sodium deficiency in which plasma sodium concentration is at least less than 135 mEq·L^{-1} and may or may not be accompanied by symptoms of hyponatremia.

plasma sodium   Concentration of sodium within the fluid portion of blood.

pneumothorax (PTX)   Air that has leaked into the pleural space, either spontaneously or as a result of traumatic tears in the pleura following chest injury or iatrogenic/surgical procedures.

primary intervention strategy   A rule or action designed to reduce an adverse or unwanted outcome that does not leave those at risk a choice (e.g., not starting a race on a hot day).

prodrome   An early indication or symptom of impending disease or illness.

protracted reaction   An anaphylactic reaction that lasts for hours to days without clear resolution of signs and symptoms.

pulmonary embolism (PE)   Complication of a venous thromboembolism; a clot (embolus) breaks off and travels through the blood to the lung, impeding blood flow.

pulse oximeter   A device that indirectly monitors the oxygen saturation in the blood, usually via the fingertip.

rectal temperature   Body temperature taken rectally. In most medical situations this involves a rectal probe inserted 10 cm past the anal sphincter. This has been validated as an accurate tool for temperature assessment in exercising individuals and is the most common form used in heat stroke cases.

respiratory syncytial virus (RSV)   A virus that causes an infection in the lungs, leading to respiratory distress.

retrograde amnesia   Difficulty remembering events immediately preceding (or leading up to) the injury.

second impact syndrome   A brain injury that occurs when an athlete sustains a second injury to the brain before the symptoms associated with an initial brain injury have fully cleared; may cause delayed catastrophic deterioration resulting in the death or persistent vegetative state after a brain injury, caused by transtentorial brainstem herniation.

secondary intervention strategy   A recommendation designed to reduce an adverse or unwanted outcome that does not leaves the decision in the hands of the participant (e.g., recommending that participants not start a race on a hot day).

serum sodium   Concentration of sodium found in the clear, pale-yellow liquid that separates from a clot during coagulation of blood.

shivering   A thermogenic response initiated by the autonomic nervous system in order to produce heat to combat cold stressors.

sickle cell trait (SCT)   A condition resulting from inheriting one gene for normal hemoglobin (A) and one gene for sickle hemoglobin (S). Strenuous exertion in SCT can cause red blood cells to sickle when they release their oxygen. This may then cause these cells to "logjam" in small blood vessels, which, as the athlete tries to continue exercising, may result in fulminant rhabdomyolysis.

side flash   A mechanism of lightning injury by which the lightning strikes a nearby object, then a portion of the strike side-steps to a nearby person.

space available for the cord (SAC)   The natural space surrounding the spinal cord, where cerebral spinal fluid will freely circulate.

spirometry   A pulmonary function test that measures the volume of air as a function of time.

Sport Concussion Assessment Tool 2 (SCAT2)   A clinical evaluation tool that combines measures of orientation, mental status, postural stability, and symptoms.

standard of care   The manner in which an individual must act based on his or her training and education.

Standardized Assessment of Concussion (SAC)   A clinical measure of mental status commonly used in the management of concussion.

step voltage   A mechanism of lightning injury by which the lightning strikes the ground and radiates outward from the strike to affect those within the radiating current. Also known as *ground current*.

strategic questioning   A type of questioning that requires the educator or clinical instructor to ask purposeful questions that challenge learners to analyze the situation and solve the problem. Strategic questioning is helpful in developing critical-thinking skills but requires some planning and anticipation on the instructor's part.

subdural hematoma   A brain injury characterized by accumulation of blood between the outermost (dura mater) and middle (arachnoid mater) meningeal layers.

sudden cardiac death (SCD)   The sudden death of an individual during or within 1 hour after exercise due to a cardiovascular disorder.

symptomatic exertional hyponatremia (EH_s)   Sodium deficiency that involves a plasma sodium concentration of less than 130 mEq·L^{-1} accompanied by typical symptoms (headache, nausea, vomiting, extreme weakness, etc.). This is the result of the replacement of sodium losses with hypotonic fluids, the loss of total body sodium, or both.

teachable moment   An important method of instruction, particularly in the clinical setting, that helps create authenticity, critical thinking, and the application of knowledge and skills. Teachable moments capture real-life events to help modify or encourage behavior, and, although hard to capture, they are highly effective tools in promoting learning for the medical or health care student.

tetraplegia   Paralysis caused by illness or injury to a human that results in the partial or total loss of use of all of the individual's limbs and torso.

total body water   The water content of the human body, in both intracellular and extracellular fluid compartments.

trigger   Anything that introduces an allergen that can cause a potential anaphylactic reaction.

type 1 diabetes   An autoimmune illness that causes the pancreas to not produce adequate amounts of insulin.

type 2 diabetes   A disease in which the pancreas produces large amounts of insulin; however, cells become less sensitive and resistant to it.

upward leader   A mechanism of lightning injury by which the victim becomes a weak, incomplete part of the lightning channel ascending to complete the lightning channel to earth.

ventricular fibrillation (VF)   A lethal ventricular arrhythmia characterized by rapid ventricular depolarization leading to disorganized and asynchronous contraction of the ventricular muscle and inability to pump blood effectively.

vocal cord dysfunction   Abnormal closure of the vocal cords that causes airflow obstruction, usually during the inspiratory phase of the breathing cycle.

wet bulb globe temperature (WBGT)   The most widely used heat stress index in industry and sports; may be used to assess the severity of hot environments. It is derived from a formula that incorporates the dry bulb, wet bulb, and black globe temperature. A measure of heat stress that incorporates air temperature, the water content of the air, and radiant heat from the sun.

INDEX